Strategy, Policy, and Central Management

8th EDITION

WILLIAM H. NEWMAN
Bronfman Management Scholar
and
Director of the Strategy Research Center
Graduate School of Business
Columbia University

JAMES P. LOGAN
Professor of Management
College of Business and Public Administration
University of Arizona

Published by

G49 **SOUTH-WESTERN PUBLISHING CO.**

CINCINNATI   WEST CHICAGO, ILL.   DALLAS   PELHAM MANOR, N Y.   PALO ALTO, CALIF.

To the memory of

SAMUEL BRONFMAN

and his belief in

the creative capacity

of independent

business enterprise

PREFACE

Strategy has moved to center stage. A select tool for large corporations only a few years ago, strategy is now widely used as a prime integrating device by all kinds of enterprises.

More than fashion and cliche are involved. In a turbulent world, a company—even a not-for-profit enterprise—needs a clear vision of just what their mission is. A forward-looking, proactive attitude is necessary just to keep abreast of changes. Moreover, social pressures require sharper thinking about interfaces with many special-interest groups. Alliances, boycotts, and government aid have become part of the game. In this stormy sea, strategy is the concept now widely used by central managers to synthesize a workable course of action for the enterprise to follow.

Accompanying this spread of strategy as a key management concept is a demand to "make it work." Central managers are increasingly concerned with integrating strategy with policy, organization, programming, and control. Lofty objectives unconnected to actual operations are no longer acceptable. This means that strategy itself has to be more operational. Thus, the ties between strategy and shorter-run action must be spelled out.

This new edition of *Strategy, Policy, and Central Management* includes these recent developments. It separates the main strategic issues of small and large corporations. It puts strategy into an action mode. It repeatedly links strategy formulation to other phases of management. And it casts the entire managerial process in terms of socially responsible behavior.

The major changes in this new edition—from a teaching viewpoint—deserve special mention.

Separate Strategy Analysis of Business-units and Diversified Corporations

Strategy/policy problems can be understood much more easily by focusing first on strategic business-units. These single-line "companies" are the basic resource converters. They adapt to customer needs, assemble resources, compete, innovate, succeed or fail in providing economic services. That is where the primary social action takes place. And because such business-units are the centers of integrated action, they receive primary attention in this book.

Diversified corporations can be viewed as collections or combinations of business-units. Each corporation guides and assists its several businesses, in a non-operating role. The chief *strategic* problem facing a diversified corporation is allocating its resources among its subunits, and perhaps acquiring new ones or divesting misfits. This we call the "portfolio" strategy. The design of a good portfolio is crucial because cash flows and profits must be balanced and synergies obtained.

Separation of these two levels of strategy assists students and managers alike in grasping central management problems. Each level is treated in a separate Part of this book.

International Dimension

An international dimension is woven throughout this book. In keeping with guidelines from the American Assembly of Collegiate Schools of Business (AACSB), professors are given an option to introduce international issues as an integral part of their course. Three aids are provided:

1. At the end of each chapter, at least one of the questions for class discussion raises an international question.
2. In the sets of integrating cases at the close of each Part, half of the cases have a foreign setting. In addition, four chapter cases and one comprehensive case also involve international strategy or policy issues.
3. A summary chapter shows how the entire framework of the book applies to the management of multinational companies.

By using these questions and cases and the multinational management chapter, U.S. business can be seen in a world context.

A Model That Ties Strategy to Action

Strategy formulation is the glamorous part of the work of senior executives. Recently strategy has also won attention from a wide range of academics. However, strategy alone is impotent. It must be translated into more specific action guides, a suitable organization developed, and a whole series of implementation steps taken. Unless strategy is seen as only a vital part of the total central management task, it will be ineffective.

This book is built around a model, or framework, for (a) sorting out major pieces of the total picture, and (b) relating these pieces to each other. The strategy → policy → organization → programs → activating → control sequence is, of course, a convenient simplification. Nevertheless, it has proved to be a powerful conceptualization. Derived from James O. McKinsey's management consulting approach, it has aided innumerable companies.

Moreover, the model helps students integrate their more specialized courses in terms of managing a total business.

Several mechanisms that improve the linkages between strategy and action are introduced in this edition of the book. For instance, "strategic thrusts," an element of strategy, and "target results," an expression of agreed upon objectives, move the concepts of strategy into an action mode. "Key actor analysis," likewise, is mainly concerned with achieving results. The separation of corporate portfolio issues from business-unit strategy clarifies the way corporate choices actually get reflected in short-run actions. In each of the policy chapters (Part 2) the interrelations between strategy and policy are sharpened.

We do give primary attention to strategy and to policies that reinforce a selected strategy. Accordingly, the exploration of organizing and activating in Parts 4 and 5 enables students and managers to comprehend the total cycle.

New Cases—Small and Large Companies in Diverse Settings

Over half the cases are new, and six others are so updated and revised that they will be virtually new for teaching purposes. The situations presented range from small new business ventures to large mature corporations. Service, retail, and raw material companies as well as manufacturing concerns are included. International settings include Japan, Australia, Sri Lanka, Nigeria, South Africa, Brazil, Paraguay, England, and Finland. So, while cases are being used to test concepts, students will concurrently acquire a rich background in business problems.

The three-tier arrangement of cases, so successful in previous editions, has been continued. This provides:

(a) End-of-chapter cases,
(b) integrating cases for groups of chapters, and
(c) comprehensive cases covering the entire range of the book.

This scheme gives instructors wide flexibility in blending the cases and the text to fit their particular needs.

Acknowledgements

No comprehensive book such as this is possible without the help of numerous other people. The model is a lineal descendant of a diagnostic approach to company-wide problems used by James O. McKinsey, founder of the preeminent consulting firm. Recent modifications reflect studies being made at the Strategy Research Center, Graduate School of Business, Columbia University. The cases come directly or indirectly from a large number of business executives who are willing to share their knowledge and experience with tomorrow's prospective leaders. And many educators have contributed ideas both to the development of the model and to cases.

We want to specifically acknowledge permission from the Executive Programs of the Graduate School of Business, Columbia University, to reproduce cases first written for their use. Colleagues at Columbia kindly contributed four cases: R.S. Alexander, The Hancock Company; M. Anshen, Reed Shoe Company; and E.K. Warren, Scott-Davis Corporation (R) and Southeast Textiles. Camilla Koch has again served as the indefatigable maestro of the many steps between us and the publisher. For all this help we are grateful.

William H. Newman
James P. Logan

CONTENTS

LIST OF CASES
End of Chapter
Integrating Comprehensive

International and foreign-based cases marked with *

SOCIAL RESPONSIBILITY AND CENTRAL MANAGEMENT

Vital Role of Enterprises

Western nations, and especially the United States, rely on thousands of independent enterprises to convert resources into desired goods and services. Moreover, these enterprises provide most of the initiative for improving and adapting this flow of goods and services to new wants. Consequently, successful management of these enterprises is vital to many people, and in fact to the survival of our pluralistic society.

This book examines the way a single enterprise can select and pursue its particular role in the complex overall process of converting resources. We will be concerned with devising favorable relationships between the enterprise and its many outside contributors, and also with designing an internal system for effectively utilizing the resources received.

The external relationships and the internal system are interdependent because the terms necessary to attract resources place restraints on the internal system, and the output of the internal system restrains the rewards that the enterprise can offer to outsiders for their cooperation.

This interdependence requires the managers of an enterprise to think in terms of a total, interacting set of forces. The central managers[1] of each enterprise must fit a whole array of activities together into an integrated whole. It is this need for both external and internal integration that makes central management unique and challenging.

Although we shall deal mostly with private, profit-seeking companies, the same approach and many of the same factors apply to not-for-profit ventures. The key tasks of central managers in both types of enterprises are alike. Management problems are affected more by the kind of services

---

[1] Central managers (or central management) include all the senior executives who concentrate on running the enterprise as an integrated whole. We prefer the term "central management" rather than "top management" because it is more descriptive and also because it carries less connotation of social status and use of power.

1

provided and by the size of operations—as we shall frequently note through-out the book—than by the form of ownership. The critical task for each firm is to find a unique niche where it can render distinctive service.

Conceptual Framework

To set the stage, this first chapter explains three related viewpoints that we shall use throughout the book:

1. Socially responsible action for a business enterprise, we shall argue, is that course which enables the enterprise to function as a dynamic resource converter on a continuing basis.
2. Central management is the group within each enterprise that designs a particular course which enables the firm to perform in such a socially responsible fashion.
3. To assist central management to fulfill this role, an analytical framework is presented. This framework—which also forms the structure of our book —aids in sorting numerous influences and issues into a related sequence of thought and in building a coherent view of total company activities. In other words, the framework assists central management to act in a socially responsible manner.

Each of these viewpoints needs elaboration because their application is much more complex than this simple, abstract statement suggests.

ACTING IN A SOCIALLY RESPONSIBLE MANNER

A business firm, like any other social institution, can endure only if it continues to contribute to the needs of society. And in our current topsy-turvy world all facets of "the establishment" are being challenged. It is important, then, that present—and aspiring—business managers understand how the companies they direct help meet social needs.

The concept of social responsibility is far from clear. Some idealists would like to include every reform that is socially desirable. But business executives have neither the competence nor the means to undertake improvements in prisons, churches, classrooms, and other areas remote from their normal activity. So, to give practical meaning to the idea, we need an approach to social responsibility for business managers that relates to actions and outcomes directly affected by executive decisions.

A useful approach is to think of a manager as a *resource converter*. From the viewpoint of society, an enterprise justifies its existence by converting resources into desired outputs. (a) Resource inputs of labor, materials, ideas, government support, capital, and the like are converted by a firm into (b) outputs of goods, services, employment, stimulating experiences, markets, and other things desired by those who provide the inputs. The job of central managers is to design and maintain a converting mechanism that will generate continuing flows of these inputs and outputs.

An auto garage, for instance, converts labor, parts, machinery, and capital into auto repair services, jobs, rent, etc. Likewise, a poultry farmer converts chicks, feed, labor, equipment, and other resources into outputs of eggs, meat, jobs, a market for grain, and a profit on capital. Civilized society depends on a continuing flow of such conversions. And when we talk of the social responsibility of business managers, we are mainly concerned about the effectiveness and the side effects of resource conversions.

This concept of central managers dealing primarily with resource conversion puts the emphasis on constructive action. Three basic elements are involved: (1) building continuing exchange flows with resource suppliers, (2) designing an internal conversion technology, and (3) integrating and balancing the external and internal flows.

Building Continuing Exchange Flows with Resource Suppliers

The relationship with each resource supplier always involves an exchange. The diagram below shows these flows for five typical outside groups. For a specific company there will be a wider variety of subgroups, but the underlying concept is the same. Each group of contributors provides a needed resource and receives in exchange part of the output flow of the enterprise.

Much more than money is involved. Typically, an array of conditions provides the basis for continuing cooperation. Employees, for instance, are concerned about meaningful work, stability of employment, reasonable supervision, future opportunities, and a whole array of fringe benefits in addition to their paychecks. Suppliers of materials want a continuing market, sure and prompt payment, convenient delivery times, quality standards suited to their facilities, minimum returns, and the like. Investors are concerned about uncertainty of repayment, security, negotiability of their claims, veto of major changes, and perhaps some share in the management. For each resource contributor, mutual agreement about the conditions under which the exchange will continue is subject to evolution and periodic renegotiation.

Because a steady flow of resources is necessary, wise central managers will:

1. *Predict changes* in conditions under which each resource group will be willing and able to continue its cooperation.
2. Conceive and promote *revised exchange* of inputs and outputs that will (1) be attractive to the resource group and (2) be viable for the enterprise.
3. Start discussions of changes *early* to allow time for psychological as well as technical adjustments.
4. Assist and work with *other agencies* concerned with the change.

Central managers devote a substantial part of their efforts to negotiating —or guiding their subordinates in negotiating—these agreements covering the bases of cooperation. It is a never-ending process because in our dynamic world the needs of resource suppliers shift, their power to insist on fulfilling

ENTERPRISE = RESOURCE CONVERTER

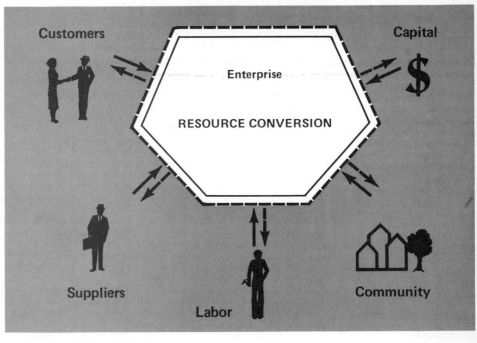

→ Resource inputs

←- - - Need satisfaction outputs

their needs changes, and the value of their contributions to the enterprise varies. In fact, most of the widely discussed "social responsibility" issues deal with some modification of previous conditions of cooperation, such as:

Input Group	Reason Prompting a Change
Labor	"Equal opportunity" for women and minorities.
Investors	Inflation protection; public disclosure of information.
Community	Environmental protection; uninterrupted supply of energy.
Suppliers of materials	Predictable, long-run markets.
Customers	"Consumerism" pressures for quality guarantees, informative labeling.

The real core of social responsibility of a business executive is the maintenance of resource flows on mutually acceptable terms. And this is a very difficult assignment in times of rapidly changing values and expectations— as the succession of crude oil crises illustrates. But note that social responsibility, at least in our view, is not something new, tacked onto an executive's job. Rather, it is reflected in the recognition of shifting social needs and the approach an executive takes in adapting to them. Thus, when we examine adjustments to environmental changes, in Parts 1 and 2, we shall repeatedly deal with socially responsible action.

Designing an Internal Conversion Technology

Each enterprise, large or small, must maintain a balance between the outputs it generates and the satisfaction it has agreed to provide its suppliers of resources. For instance, promises of stable employment must be compatible with protection promised to suppliers of capital. Such ability to make ends meet depends, partly, on the skill of executives in devising a *conversion technology* suited to their particular company. The way the resources are converted strongly affects the outputs available. So, in addition to negotiating agreements assuring the continuing availability of resources, central managers must design internal systems to effectively utilize the resources.

Every enterprise has its technology for converting resources into outputs. For example, a school has its teaching technology, an insurance company has its technology for policy risks, and a beauty shop has its technology for shaping unruly hair.

This internal conversion technology involves much more than mechanical efficiency. The desired outputs, as we have already noted, include interesting jobs, low capital risks, minimum pollution of the environment, improved job opportunities for women and minorities, and a host of other features. Consequently, devising a good internal conversion technology is a very complex task.[2] This selection of an internal conversion technology is one of the key elements in each company's strategy—as will be illustrated in Chapter 5.

Integrating and Balancing the External and Internal Flows

Important as attracting resources and designing conversion technologies may be, it is the *combination* of (a) responding to new "needs" of resource contributors and (b) restricting total responses to what total output permits that poses the final challenge to central management. Socially responsible executives must respond quickly enough to the ever-

---

[2]In abstract symbols, the technology should meet the following conditions: With each resource contributor designated by subscripts 1, i, e, s, c, . . . n and

S   = satisfactions required by a resource contributor
C   = contributions by a resource contributor
CT = conversion technology
O   = total output of satisfactions
then:

$$O = (S_1 + S_i + S_e + S_s + S_c \cdot \ldots S_n)$$
$$O = fCT (C_1 + C_i + C_e + C_s + C_c \cdot \ldots C_n)$$

And as viewed by each resource contributor:

$$S_x = > C_x$$

changing desires of resource contributors to maintain a continuing flow of needed resources, and at the same time, they must keep their enterprise alive by generating the right quantity and mix of outputs to fulfill commitments. If they do not, some key resource will be withdrawn and the enterprise will collapse.

Throughout this book we shall be exploring ways in which companies can effectively cope with a dynamic environment—partly by adjusting the exchanges of inputs and outputs with resource groups, and partly by reshaping their conversion technology to generate desired outputs. A recurring theme will be anticipating pressures for change. By adjusting promptly to new conditions, a company usually increases its "output" and thereby makes a greater social contribution.

Considering a company as a resource converter uses a broad social viewpoint. We suggest that this is a better way to conceive of "the purpose of a company" than the more common cliche "to make a profit." Every successful resource converter must indeed make a profit in order to continue to attract capital. But this is a narrow oversimplification. To survive, a company must also provide attractive employment, be a good customer, earn continuing support of governments and the community, and serve customers well. The task for central management is to find a way to do all these things simultaneously while keeping abreast of changes in each field.

An approach to this complex task is outlined at the close of this chapter and is then elaborated throughout the book.

BUSINESS-UNITS VERSUS DIVERSIFIED CORPORATIONS

The best way to understand the strategic problems involved in business is to think first in terms of a company making a single line of products which are sold to a similar set of customers. Such an enterprise faces the full array of transactions—with employees, suppliers, customers, governments. It must wisely allocate resources, assume risks, make trade-offs between alternative courses of action—all with an eye to future service, balance, and survival—as indicated in the preceding pages.

A diversified corporation, of course, has several different lines of business. Nevertheless, we can consider the strategy and policy problems related to each product line as though that segment of the corporation were a separate enterprise. Each such division has its own competitors, its own opportunities and threats, and its own strategy. It may draw on corporate resources, but the survival of that part of the total business depends upon how well it adapts to its particular environment. For convenience in this book we shall call such a product division a "company" (or occasionally "firm," "business-unit," or "enterprise"), regardless of its actual legal status. This usage emphasizes the importance of managing a product division of a large corporation with the same vigor and adaptability as a truly independent single-line company.

The senior executives of a diversified corporation do face an additional set of strategic issues which are distinct from those of their "companies." They must decide which companies to expand and which to contract; perhaps they will launch or acquire new firms; and they must devise ways to help their companies operate successfully. This overriding level we call "corporate management."

Because companies are on the firing-line—where products and services must stand up to competition and where the ability to attract resources is really tested—the primary emphasis in this entire book is on managing these basic businesses. We will consider corporate management in Part 3 and again in Part 4, but only after planning and organizing for the underlying companies have been explored. Contrary to occasional popular criticism of a large corporation, socially responsible actions of business originate largely at the operating level.

CENTRAL MANAGEMENT VIEWPOINT

Integrated, Timely Action

Central management is concerned with the total enterprise—the "whole business." As already noted, an array of interactions with external groups must be negotiated, and internal systems that utilize available resources to best advantage must be designed. When dealing with such matters, central management takes its own unique perspective. Other executives will be confronted with the same problems, but with a more specialized viewpoint.

Central managers give particular attention to interdependence. Commitments to customers must be reconciled with vacation schedules for employees; automated production must not generate air pollution; high-risk research and price competition may cause an unbearable cash squeeze—these examples only suggest the many *interrelationships* between different aspects of a company's operations. Somehow, someone must develop an *integrated* course of action.

Specialized attention to segments of a firm's activities is also necessary, of course. With the knowledge explosion, specialists are essential. But as specialists deal with ever-narrower scopes, the task of integration becomes more difficult and more vital. A major distinctive characteristic of the central management viewpoint is this relating of parts to the whole, integrating them into a *balanced, workable* plan.

A second distinctive concern of central management is setting *priorities* for the enterprise. A robust firm in our volatile environment has many different options, yet only a few can be pursued. People in marketing, finance, research, and other functional fields naturally differ in their recommendation of the best path to follow. Also, some persons are more sensitive to social needs than others, and eagerness to take risks will vary. So, to achieve concerted, unified action, one or two objectives must be singled out and plans for achieving these goals must be specified. This process clarifies the *mission* to be sought. Optimum results are obtained only when such guidance is clearly accepted throughout the organization.

Central management, then, focuses on missions and priorities on the one hand, and on interrelationships, functional integration, and a balanced plan of action on the other.

But being aware of central management's point of view still leaves us with a practical question: How can we (and central managers) proceed to "analyze" such intricately involved situations?

Need for Analytical Framework

Even the preceding terse description indicates that the task of central management is complex. And, as with any complex situation, a tested approach that divides the complicated mass into simpler elements can be very helpful. The approach outlined in this book is basically a framework for thinking about central management issues. It expedites analysis, and it assists in forming a synthesis of action to be taken.

Of course, any single approach must be adapted and amplified to fit the peculiarities of a specific company. In a small importing firm, for instance, organization may be relatively unimportant, whereas political outlook is crucial. On the other hand, the senior executives in a young electronics company may be predominantly concerned about technology and additional sources of capital.

Most useful is an approach that draws attention to a limited (comprehensible) number of basic issues in a systematic arrangement, and at the same time, is reasonably complete in the potential opportunities for improvement it flags or suggests. Such a way of thinking about central management problems is more important than an exhaustive listing of all possible difficulties.

FUTURE-ORIENTED APPROACH

To maintain a forward-looking view of the central management job, the following approach is very useful:

1. Design company *strategy* on the basis of continuous matching of (a) anticipated opportunities and problems in the industry with (b) distinctive company strengths—and limitations.
2. Amplify and clarify this strategy in *policy*, which serves as a more specific guide to executives in the various functional divisions of the company.
3. When a diversified corporation is involved, plan for a *balanced portfolio strategy* covering the several business-units (companies), and modify the strategies and policies of the business-units to fit into this consolidated plan.
4. Set up an *organization* to carry out the strategy and policy. This involves making clear who does what, and also developing key personnel who can push forward in the direction singled out in the strategy.

5. Guide the *execution* of the strategy and policy through the organization. This calls for programming, activating, and controlling the operations.

Since this division of tasks of central management will be used throughout the book, the nature of each section should be recognized from the start. So let us take a closer look at what is involved.

Analyzing the Outlook for the Company

Many factors impinge on the future development of any enterprise. Some cities grow; others decay. New ways to control insect pests may obsolete chemical plants; new social mores may obsolete college dormitories. Inflation distorts cost structures; international travel upsets foreign exchange rates; war in the Middle East creates new shortages of petroleum supply— this list of opportunities and problems could go on and on.

A practical way to bring some kind of order out of this array of environmental changes is to concentrate on an industry. This industry may be one the company is already in or one that it is thinking about entering. The aim of these industry analyses is to predict growth, profitability, and especially the key factors for future success.

Turning to the specific company, its strengths and limitations relative to its competitors should be carefully assessed. Then, by matching the company strengths with key factors for success in the industry, the outlook for the company can be predicted. For even sharper analysis, the way key actors in the environment are likely to respond to company moves can be predicted. This sequence of analysis is elaborated in Chapters 2, 3, and 4.

Of course, the company need not stand still. It can take steps to alter its strengths, and by its actions it may modify the services or the prices of the entire industry. Similarly, an industry occasionally makes a dent on the environment. For instance, business representatives participate in debates on national priorities and help shape guidelines for protection of our natural environment. On balance, however, each company must adapt to its environment. And corporate management must compare a variety of such environments.

Designing Company Strategy

Armed with the forecast of the world in which the company will operate, central management shifts to active, positive thinking: "What are we going to do about it?" "What should be the mission of our unique enterprise, and what steps do we have to take to fulfill that goal?"

Picking the right mission obviously is crucial. It is also difficult. To be most useful, the master strategy should (a) identify the particular services—that is, the product-market *domain*—which the company will promote; (b) select a basic resource conversion technology by which these services will be created—a technology that hopefully will give the company some *differential advantage* as a supplier; (c) with this concept of its economic and social mission, determine the major *thrusts* necessary to move the company from its present course to the desired one; and finally, (d) establish the *criteria* and the standards that will be used to measure achievement. No strategy is complete without all four of these dimensions being clarified.

A critical judgment in designing strategy is what to accept as unchangeable. Every company possesses (or can attract) only limited resources, and it has to be careful that the goals it sets are doable. In addition to sensing a future opportunity, central management must realistically assess the cost of grasping the opportunity in terms of people, outside help, money, and other resources. It must then decide whether "that is something we can do." This issue, along with other aspects of strategy formulation, is explored in Chapter 5.

Establishing Policy

Strategy concentrates on basic directions, major thrusts, and overriding priorities. The full implication of the strategy, however, is clarified by thinking through the more detailed policy that guides execution of the strategy. Central managers of each company must actively participate in shaping policy (a) partly because working through the policy implications is an excellent way to check the practicality of a basic concept and (b) especially to make sure that the intent of strategy is correctly interpreted into the work of the various departments of the company.

Almost all companies need policy guidance on product lines, customers, pricing, and sales promotion. Likewise, the implication of strategy on research and development, production, and procurement should be expressed in policy. In the personnel area, policy on selection, compensation, and industrial relations helps build the desired manpower resources; and financial policy regarding allocation and sources of capital shape money resources. Each of these fields is examined in Part 2. A significant role of policy is to indicate the direction and degree of emphasis these and other sensitive fields should receive in order to effectively project company strategy.

Most attention in this book is directed toward change—adapting to new opportunities and pressures. Nevertheless, during the time any given strategy is in effect, consistent integrated action is highly important. Policy is a major tool of central management for securing such consistent behavior. Policy permeates the numerous daily activities of a firm and helps establish a normal, predictable pattern of behavior.

Strategy for Diversified Corporations

A company, as we are using that term, focuses on a particular type of business, say life insurance or video cassette recorders. Each of such businesses has its own markets, technology, competitors, and other distinctive features. Therefore, strategy and policy must be fitted to that business—as just outlined.

A diversified corporation, however, faces a different set of issues. It has a family of business-units. It must decide which of these businesses to expand and which to contract. Capital and other scarce resources must be allocated to the various businesses. Perhaps ways can be found for one of its business-units to help another. Mergers or divestments may be arranged. These issues which are connected with diversification will be explored in Part 3.

Note that the "company" or business-unit continues to be the primary building block for managerial planning. The strength of any diversified corporation rests predominantly on its separate businesses. They are the sources of growth, earnings, stability, etc. And each of these business-units gains strength through its own strategy and policy. For this reason, it is wise first to develop a strategy and policy for each business-unit which will enable that business to adapt best to its opportunities and threats. Then a combined corporate strategy and policy for all the businesses can be devised as a superstructure.

Building an Organization

Strategy and policy, at both the business-unit and corporate levels, are carried out by an organization. Unless this organization is well designed for its tasks, the plans, however sound, may lead to mediocre results. In fact, if the strategy relies on, say, pioneering in a new field, an ineffective organization that failed in such leadership could bring disaster.

The way in which activities are combined into sections and departments will affect the choice of problems to receive first attention, the speed of coordination, and the cost of performing the service. Decentralization is well suited to a strategy stressing local service, but it encounters difficulty with computerized production scheduling. A strategic decision to expand internationally alters the optimum power and location of staff units. Product diversification usually modifies the range of decisions that can be made wisely in the senior corporate office. As these examples indicate, central management must appraise the company organization in terms of where tasks critical to the success of its strategy can be performed most effectively.

Also vital are executives with qualities and experience that fit the organization design. These and related organization issues are examined in Part 4.

Guiding Execution

With strategy, policy, and organization decided, the stage is set. Actual achievement, however, awaits the action. Central management necessarily relies heavily on junior executives for immediate supervision of operations. But senior executives can never fully divest themselves of leadership in the execution phase of purposeful endeavor. As explained in Part 5, this phase includes specific programming of nonrepetitive work, communicating and motivating, and exercising control over the rate and the quality of performance.

Substantial amounts of time are necessary for this make-happen effort. Many people, inside the company and out, have to be contacted personally, and unexpected difficulties inevitably call for on-the-spot adjustments. But during the process the executives are accumulating both information and a subjective feel for the actual performance of company services that are immensely valuable in planning the following cycles of activity.

Interaction and Evolution

The chart below depicts the broad division of central management tasks that we have briefly described—analyzing company outlook, designing strategy, establishing policy, setting up organization, and guiding execution.

Three qualifications to the simple sequence shown in the chart should be made explicit. First, in a going concern each phase influences all the others

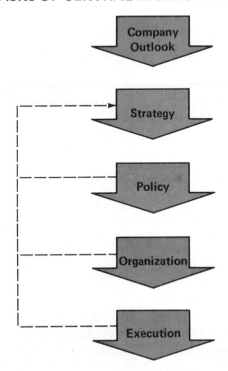

TASKS OF CENTRAL MANAGEMENT

to some degree. Firmly established policy or organization, for instance, may make a proposed strategy easy (or difficult) to put into action; in that case, policy or organization influences the choice of strategy. Such a "reverse flow" is suggested by the light line on the side of the chart. Nevertheless, while some of this "reverse flow" is always present, the primary sequence for a dynamic service enterprise is the one emphasized on the chart and used as the structure of this book.

Second, for diversified corporations a separate analysis of outlook, strategy, and policy will be necessary for each business-unit. And in the process of combining these business-unit plans into a balanced corporate plan, some constraints and modifications of the strategy or policy of a business-unit may arise.

Third, a neatly integrated package of strategy, policy, organization, and execution does not stay neat. The environment changes. Even the company's own success creates the need for revision. Consequently, the broad process described must be repeated and repeated again. Minor adjustments and refinements will be occurring most of the time. Major reshuffling, however, is expensive in both financial and human terms; so, like tooling-up for a new automobile model, a particular design should be followed long enough to learn how to use it well and to recoup the investment. But, it is recognized that sooner or later retooling will be necessary.

These qualifications—the interaction between parts and the need for successive revisions—do not diminish the usefulness of the basic model proposed. Quite the opposite, these added complexities make an analytical framework even more valuable as an aid to orderly thinking.

The versatility of the model is further developed in Chapter 24 where it aids in the examination of managing multinational enterprises. Coming at the end of the book, Chapter 24 also serves as a review of the step-by-step breakdown in Parts 1 through 5.

QUESTIONS FOR CLASS DISCUSSION

1. "Where were you *last* year?" the K-Mart buyer said to the Plasto Company president who was offering lamps for the Christmas rush at bargain prices. The buyer already knew the answer, that Plasto had been busy with Sears, Roebuck & Co.'s business, and turned the president away empty-handed. During the previous year Sears had abandoned a price-cutting campaign designed to attract customers in an effort to improve profit margins. Sales dropped and Sears

cut orders to its suppliers sharply. Plasto went from feast to famine as its sales were cut in half. Efforts by Plasto to find new customers have not been successful. Other lamp manufacturers appear to have cut their own prices by at least 20 percent.

Have Sears' actions been socially responsible? K-Mart's? Plasto's? Other lamp manufacturers'?

2. (a) What is the social responsibility of an electric utility company? Consider air and water pollution, uninterrupted consumer service, conservation of energy resources, stable employment, prices charged for services, effect of transmission lines on the landscape, adequate profits to attract investment for expansion, aiding rural and community development, and support of good government. (b) What do you consider to be the chief task of central management of an electric utility?

3. To help finance its steady growth over the past decade (20% per year), Electronic Parts, Inc. has borrowed regularly from the major commercial bank in its medium-sized city (the other two local banks are quite small) at an interest rate two- to two-and-one-half percentage points above the prime rate charged by major New York banks. Now the firm's increasing need for capital has led to a loan size which is larger than the legal loan limits of the bank. Banks in Phoenix and Los Angeles, seeing an opportunity, have offered loans at less than two percentage points above the prime rate—a savings to Electronic Parts, Inc. of about $50,000 each year. The local bank's response has been to form a coalition with banks from several small cities nearby. The coalition will lend funds needed by Electronic Parts, Inc. in the foreseeable future and will continue to provide advice about many financial matters for an interest charge equal to the past rates. If Electronic Parts, Inc. switches to the large-city banks, will its action be socially responsible?

4. (a) Foreign corporations own all or substantial blocks of the stock of several U.S. businesses. Examples include Lever Brothers, Shell Oil, A&P, Ciba-Geigy Pharmaceuticals, BIC Pens. Do you believe that such U.S. businesses are less responsive to U.S. social problems (unemployment, inflation, consumer protection, and the like) than are locally owned companies? (b) Do you believe that businesses in Europe or developing countries which are owned by U.S. corporations are responsive to the social problems in the countries in which they are located? (c) What is your general conclusion about socially responsible behavior of multinational corporations?

5. Apply the concept of an enterprise being a resource converter to (a) a hospital and (b) a university. From a social viewpoint, is alertness to social and technological changes by hospital and university managers as significant as such alertness by soap and soup manufacturers? What means are available to encourage changes by hospital and university managers?

6. Explain *your* understanding of the phrase, "social responsibility."

7. (a) Is a company acting in a socially responsible manner if it spends a million dollars to eliminate discharge of sulphur fumes from its plant (as suggested by the State Environmental Protection Agency), and then passes this additional expense on to its customers in the form of higher price? (b) In the same vein, how about increasing wages above levels prevailing in the community, and passing on these costs to customers?

8. (a) Automobile manufacturers in the United States pay their unskilled and semi-skilled employees (according to their union contracts) at wage rates well

above those of the average of other U.S. manufacturers. One result has been that General Motors had to pay employees in its Frigidaire Division wage rates one to two dollars per hour above the rates paid by other makers of major household appliances. As a result, General Motors reported losses from the Frigidaire Division for a number of years. Was this socially responsible action? (b) Eventually G.M. sold its well-known trademark and closed a Dayton, Ohio, plant which had been used to build the appliances. Local governments lost a considerable amount of tax income and the employees searched for jobs elsewhere, some in General Motors' Delco Division which is also located in Dayton. Was this socially responsible action?

9. Social standards change. We praised pioneers for clearing land and draining swamps, but now similar action is illegal. Likewise, legislation and company practice protecting women workers was hailed as a social advance fifty years ago; now such practice is unfair discrimination. And so forth. (a) Is it the responsibility of company central managements to decide what social standards should be in their own organizations? (b) Since a new standard often affects previous jobs, markets, financial returns, and other prevailing resource conversion patterns, should central management work to accept some standards, such as equal employment opportunity in hiring; keep others from the past, such as seniority in firing; and reject others, such as long, flowing hair for men working in sales?

CASE 1
Snowbird Snowmobiles

You are sizing up a potential job as assistant to the president of Snowbird Snowmobiles, Inc. and have gathered the following information from key persons.*

Marketing V.P. "Snowmobiling has become a major winter sport. It offers healthy, family-oriented winter activity, easily obtained by millions of non-urban Americans. Few other outdoor activities are available in the winter that do not require exceptional physical fitness. . . . There are already about four million snowmobiles in the U.S. and Canada. With three active users per machine, that means around twelve million people are enjoying the thrill of skimming over the snow going places they could never reach before.

"In some ways, snowmobiling is a cross between skiing and motorcycling, except that it is easier and safer than either of these sports. There is nothing like it for speed, and power, and fun. And it fills a niche for a winter sport everyone can enjoy. Snowmobiling has had a phenomenal growth in about fifteen years. Already,

---

*A modern snowmobile has two skis in front and two belts with cleats in the rear. A gasoline motor drives the belts as fast as you dare go. The rider(s) sits astride a padded bench, protected only in the front with a streamlined hood and large windshield. Spring suspension, shock absorbers, self-starter ease the ride. So just flip the switch and zip across the snow.

according to the National Sporting Goods Association, people are spending over half as much for snowmobiling equipment as skiing equipment. There are lots of local clubs with visiting back and forth.

Retail Sales of Sporting Equipment		
Summer		
Camping appliances	$463	million
Fishing tackle	608	"
Golf clubs, balls, bags	704	"
Tennis rackets, ball, strings	799	"
Water skis	114	"
Winter		
Bowling balls	116	"
Ice skates & hockey equipment	92	"
Skis, boots, bindings	505	"
Snowmobiles	267	"

"Currently we are still recovering from too rapid, undisciplined growth. Ask the E.P.A. rep; she can give you that story. Five years ago there were forty-eight companies selling snowmobiles. They flooded the market and couldn't maintain service. Then the bubble burst. Within two years over a third of the companies folded. But then competition got really rough. Last year there were only eleven in business, and now we are seven! Unfortunately, the bankrupt companies left a lot of unsold inventory in dealers' hands. So price competition has been fierce. Maybe one or two more companies will withdraw, but most of us believe the shakeout is over. With the underlying growth in snowmobiling, five or six companies could have very satisfactory volume.

Year	New Products Sold (number)		
	Industry	*Snowbirds*	*Share*
Near-term future*	(250,000–300,000)	(65,000)	(25)%
This year	200,000	48,000	24
Last year	250,000	45,000	18
Two years ago	300,000	45,000	15
Peak—five years ago	500,000	60,000	12

*Company estimate.

"Product improvement has been substantial. The noise level is now a mere fraction of what it was in the early days. Machines are more rugged with an average life of seven years, up from three. Safety is improved. We have been leaders in this, but all surviving companies have made vast improvements. Of course, this has contributed to increasing the retail price of a good snowmobile to over $2,000."

Representative of U.S. Environmental Protection Agency. "A few years ago snowmobiles were a major headache—noisier than an airplane and dashing all over the place. Protests came from all directions, and the hot-rod snowmobilers were just as vociferous. But there has been improvement and we are getting fewer complaints.

"The noise now is like a garden tractor, thanks to an industry association standard. We have a regulation calling for an even lower standard, but have temporarily postponed its effective date to see how the public reacts to present machines.

"Damage to the natural terrain is still being debated. Originally we included snowmobiles along with other off-the-road vehicles (such as dune-buggies which are tearing up fragile desert ecology) in exclusion from national parks and other public lands. Two considerations lead to postponing that regulation also. As the industry association claims, we do not yet have hard evidence that snowmobiles have any lasting effect on the ground or vegetation. Apparently, when the snow melts their tracks go with it. More important, a whole network of snowmobile tracks have been established—75,000 miles; and most snowmobilers stick to the tracks. We are continuing to keep an eye on what happens because there are a lot of people who think we should outlaw snowmobiles except in remote areas and for commercial purposes. Safety is outside our jurisdiction, but I understand it also is improving. Fatalities last year were down to 121. Partly that reflects better equipment. Mostly it is safety training by local clubs. When people skim a few inches over a slick surface at fifty miles an hour in a light-weight vehicle (about 300 pounds), the driver better know how to dodge a tree or rock."

Production V.P. "Some things we can act on—like engineering in better quality—but in the plant we have to take what volume comes. We have capacity to produce at least 50% more machines than we did last year, which means our overhead is high. That particularly hurts because we also have seasonal valleys. To limit investment in inventory, our policy is to work short shifts or shut down entirely. I personally think this uncertainty about when there will be work is why we have a union. Here in St. Cloud [Minnesota] the workers have few opportunities to find other work during layoffs.

"We also watch our parts inventory which can get out of hand because we buy our engines from Japan and all the machined parts and accessories from some distance. To most of our suppliers we're a small customer. But, by concentrating all purchases of a particular item with a single supplier we can get quick deliveries when we need them.

"Actually our competitors are in the same fix. The largest company, Bombardier, is located in a small town in Canada and I guess they have more delivery problems than we do. But their labor rates are lower than ours.

"Our three models—Stag, Stallion, Silver Fox—are similar in construction and in many of their parts so that does not complicate production very much. I came up through production and know the operations. We did bring in several engineers to work on new designs and quality; they are very important in our picture."

Finance V.P. "Here's our income statement and balance sheet in condensed form. A couple of items may not be clear.

"In addition to snowmobiles, we sell a fine line of snowmobile clothing including gloves and helmets. We subcontract the manufacture of this clothing but perform all other functions ourselves. As you see, the income from all the supplementary items adds significantly to snowmobile sales, and we would like to see this grow.

Balance Sheet (in 1,000,000's)

Cash	$ 2	Accounts payable	$ 7
Accounts receivable	4	Bank loan	5
Inventory	29	Accrued items	3
Current assets	35	Current liabilities	15
Plant & equipment,		Mortgage loan	4
net	12	Paid in capital	20
		Retained earnings	8
	$47		$47

Income Statement
(financial data in 1,000,000's)

	Last year actual	1–3 year projection	3–5 year projection
Assumptions:			
Industry volume (1,000 units)	200	250	300
Companies in industry	7	6	6
Snowbird share of market	24%	26%	30%
Inflation rise (total from last year)	—	20%	40%
Gross profit margin	21%	23%	24%
Financial results:			
Snowmobile sales	$64	$103	$168
Sales of parts, accessories & clothing	18	29	47
Total sales	82	132	215
Cost of goods sold	65	102	163
Gross profit	17	30	52
Marketing expense	7	11	18
General & administrative expense	7	10	15
Interest expense	1	2	4
Total expenses	15	23	37
Operating profit	2	7	15
Income taxes	1	4	8
Net profit	$ 1	$ 3	$ 7

"Due to industry conditions, profit margins are unsatisfactory. When the industry moves beyond the liquidation of weak companies and demand picks up, the profit ratio should change dramatically. The two projections on the income statement show what should happen with even conservative assumptions.

"Our inventory is high. Part of the explanation is that we continue to own all the inventory held by our distributors. In this respect, they are like manufacturers' agents and we sell directly to many small dealers. This arrangement helps us get wide distribution without operating our own regional offices. Even so, the inventory is too high. If we could cut it five million we could pay off the bank loan.

"Nevertheless, we are in a strong financial position. A public stock issue back in the boom days gives us all the equity capital we need—at least so long as we stick to the snowmobile business."

President. "You've talked with our top people, except for the person we brought in to manage our clothing line. It's a lean organization, and that is part of the reason we are talking to you. There is just no slack to devote to unusual problems; we don't have time to think about what we might do differently.

"We have come through a very stormy period, and are now Number 2 in the industry. It is time for the tide to turn, and when it does we want to take full advantage of the position we have worked hard to achieve."

Questions

(1) As part of the process of evaluating you, the president of Snowbird asks you to submit any recommendations you have for improving future prospects for the company.

(2) If you were offered the job, at a reasonable salary, would you take it? Why?

Part 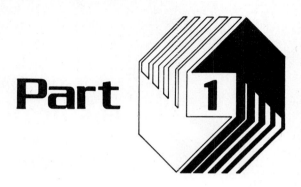 1

DETERMINING BUSINESS-UNIT STRATEGY

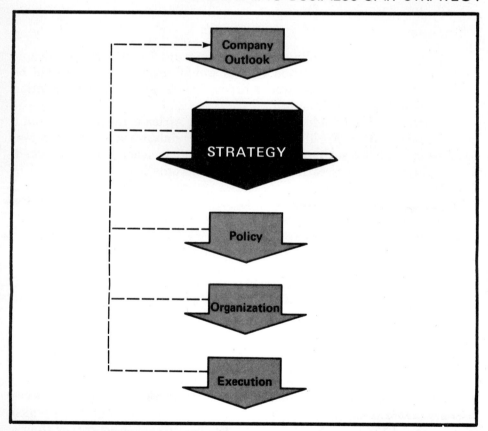

PREDICTING THE DYNAMIC ENVIRONMENT

Change

A sharp cutback in gasoline supplies would upset our economy. People could not get to work, vacation resorts would close, railroads would be rejuvenated, social relations would become more provincial—to mention only a few of the ramifications.

Similarly, the rise of independent nations in Africa is much more than a local political matter. World sources of raw materials are jeopardized; potential new markets for such items as radios and pharmaceuticals are created; fair-employment practices in, say, Detroit, become even more crucial in foreign diplomacy; added strain is placed on satellite communication.

These examples of change illustrate a major problem for modern executives: adapting the direction and the operation of their enterprises to shifts in the technological, social, political, and economic environment of the United States and the world. Change is the one thing business managers know will occur.

This chapter highlights the nature of changes that are taking place and the manager's task in forecasting them. As pointed out in Chapter 1, anticipating environmental shifts is crucial to formulating strategy and setting wise policy.

DYNAMIC SETTING OF BUSINESS

For the central manager, predicting *both* (a) a major change and (b) its impact on operations is necessary. Note in the following examples—which convey only an impression of the changes affecting business rather than a full description—how this dual purpose of analysis recurs.

Technological Changes

Electronic computers. The dramatic development of computers has become the classic example of a new generation of technology. Computer capabilities have been increasing tenfold every three or four years. Meanwhile the minimum size has dropped from that of a freight car to a wristwatch. Clearly, the physical capabilities have outrun our knowledge of how to use this electronic wonder.

Most commercial (as contrasted with scientific) computers today merely perform clerical operations that can be done more slowly on other machines. On balance, they have increased rather than decreased employment because they are turning out vast quantities of data that previously had not been compiled. But the outpouring of numbers is hardly a revolution.

The new uses that will have the most influence on business strategy still lie in the future. Banks, for example, may maintain a whole set of books for depositors, pay their bills, and provide subtotals for use on annual income tax returns. And these changes may contribute to a rearrangement of our financial institutions. Medical diagnosis, traffic control, libraries, and chemical analysis are among the many other possibilities. Eventually the postal clerk sorting mail may be as obsolete as a telegraph operator. Computers will be common in the automobile of tomorrow, controlling fuel intake and firing of engines, brake pressure, and perhaps steering.

In the management field, computers are already performing "programmed" tasks such as reordering inventory. If it wishes, management can be informed daily whether Joe Jones is meeting his sales quota; but with all the talk about a computer being able to learn, it will be a long time before the machine decides when to fire Joe. More helpful is the computer's ability to simulate parts of a complex business decision; here again, the bottleneck is program design and useful input data rather than machine capacity.

Manipulative biology. Potentially more upsetting than electronics are the technological advances in biology. By tinkering with the DNA structure of a reproductive cell, new living forms can be created. One hopeful prospect is transferring genetic information among species of plants, thereby designing hardy plants which contain high protein. Such plants could substantially improve the world food supply, especially for countries where the present diet is deficient in protein.

A related technique is cloning—producing identical copies. Thus, a prize-winning bull or cow might be duplicated over and over again. This process coupled with the use of surrogate mothers could quickly change animal husbandry throughout the world.

One disturbing aspect of manipulative biology is the possibility of applying such techniques to human beings. Even the idea of being able to predetermine the sex of a new baby has caused intense debate. So as often happens, technological developments become entwined with social and political pressures.

Energy and resources. The difficulty of maintaining a balance between the accelerating use and the supply of natural resources is illustrated by basic energy. Our insatiable appetite for electrical energy may outstrip the supply that can be economically produced. For Europe and Japan especially, the uncertain supply of oil from the Middle East has stepped up construction of nuclear power plants. In the United States, we can postpone heavy reliance on nuclear plants by turning back to coal. But the required investment in any shift away from oil is tremendous. As a result, manufacture of products requiring high energy inputs is moving out of our traditional industrial centers.

Perhaps the supply of fresh pure water, rather than energy, will become the bottleneck expansion. Most large metropolitan areas in the country face serious water shortages, and the decline in water tables suggests that the problem may be more than lack of adequate facilities. Clearly, we are going to need new technologies to help us use water more effectively.

At the same time, control of water pollution is essential. Both communities and plants will have to use new techniques to hold down contamination.

One of our greatest potential resources is the ocean. It contains vast mineral resources and has a capacity to support both animal and plant life that is virtually untapped.

New processes. From time to time some great scientist predicts that the rate of discovery and invention will decline. Up to date, these predictions have been very wrong, and the talent being devoted to scientific research suggests that just the opposite will occur. Consider the laser beam, a recently discovered high-frequency ray that has vastly greater potential than the x-ray. In military usage, laser scanning systems promise much greater accuracy than radar. The possible civilian applications are numerous. For example, a highly focused laser beam can produce temperatures above 10,000° C., and a machine using such a beam might greatly expedite drilling tunnels for highways, water, or similar uses. Other applications lie in sending laser beams through glass "wires," a development that is speeding up conversion of telephone lines into TV cables (and reducing the demand for copper wire). The laser beam is basically a single discovery that opens up a whole array of possibilities.

In the field of medicine almost daily announcements are made of advances in diagnostic techniques, control, or treatment for virus infections, mental disease, abnormal weight, and many other aspects of health.

We do not know just where dramatic changes in technology will occur. The very small sample of possibilities briefly mentioned above suggests that substantial changes are already in the making.

Social and Political Changes

Like technology, the social-political environment of a company presents both opportunities and obstacles. Also like technology, part of the changes can be foreseen—the forces that will generate them are already known. The nature, magnitude, and timing of other social changes are shrouded in uncertainty.

Population. The United States now has over 220 million people, an increase of over 70 million since the end of World War II. Population growth, looked at in total, means more consumers and more workers—more people who buy and more people who can turn out goods and services needed.

A few years ago estimates of population growth to 300 million by the turn of the century were common. These estimates were based on a high birth rate in the 1950's and early 1960's. Recently, attitudes toward family formation, birth control, and responsibility of rearing children have contributed to a sharp drop in the birth rate. Now the century-end population is often predicted at 260 million, with a stable population shortly thereafter. Clearly, the population pressure for economic growth is dropping.

Our population is highly mobile. We move from farm to city and from city to suburb. During the current century, the proportion of people living in rural territory (places of 2,500 or less) has dropped from 60% to 30%. No longer can we assume that our labor force will have attitudes toward work and self-reliance engendered by a farm background.

More striking in recent years has been the move from downtown areas to the suburbs. In fact, in the largest population centers (those with over 2 million people) the population of the central cities actually decreased in the period 1950–1980. Only Houston has continued to grow. Declines occurred in Boston, Chicago, New York, Philadelphia, Detroit, San Francisco, and Washington. At the same time, the suburbs of most of these cities grew 50%–90%.

This move to the outskirts has not only helped boom housing and the construction industry, it has also revolutionized retail selling. Concurrently, it has created mass need for urban renewal. The older areas in the central cities typically house our lowest income group; this leads to overcrowding and poor maintenance. And such conditions foster social deterioration—frustration, indifference, drug addiction, crime. Slums are not new. Those of the 19th century were far worse physically, but usually they had more social resilience.

Compounding the urgency for urban renewal is the fact that a high proportion of recent migrants from the farm to the city centers are black. The whole array of issues connected with racial injustice is intermingled with the consequences of urban decay. Here then is a part of the total business environment calling for a type of imagination and skill quite different from that needed in a laboratory generating new technology.

Workforce. Women are the most dynamic element in our workforce. Not only are they over 40% of all entries into the workplace, but also they are moving into many jobs previously held only by men—from bank tellers to corporate directors. Only a generation ago "progressive" labor laws sought to protect women (and children); now *any* differentiation is illegal. This shift in social and legal values greatly enlarges the supply of able people for key posts.

More people are spending more time in school. By 1990 over 40 percent of the labor force will have attended one or more years of college. This educational change affects business in several ways. A better educated population means better skills available in the work force. Many of these skills are needed for modern sophisticated operations; but people with college educations can no longer be regarded as exceptional individuals, and problems arise in matching skills and aspirations to the work available. The corollary is that workers for dirty, boring, backbreaking jobs will become more difficult to find and more restive about their assigned tasks.

Managers must also learn to deal with a number of potentially productive employees whose lifestyles and values sharply curtail the importance they attach to their jobs. Employment of such men and women will never be satisfactory to either the individual or the company until some concurrence on worthwhile goals is achieved.

The role of unions is also changing. Originally a blue-collar institution, union action has extended to teachers and numerous other government groups, salespeople, engineers, and supervisors. Our labor laws foster monopoly power of various classifications of workers, and society has not yet learned how to cope with the pressures they can exert. For the business manager, collective pressure in a bargaining atmosphere calls for a basic change in the process by which a large number of policy decisions are made.

Government policy. Government action impinges on business in a variety of ways. Most obvious is an increasing array of direct regulation—dealing with such issues as antitrust, fair trade (advertising, pricing, and the like), sale of securities, labor relations, minimum wages, or air pollution. Taxes take a larger bite of gross revenues than do profits, and the way they are levied sharply influences company behavior.

On the other hand, nearly every kind of business benefits, at least indirectly, from import restrictions, subsidies, research grants, financial aids, or other forms of assistance. Moreover, government is a tremendous customer; all levels of government combine to buy 21% of the total goods and services produced (more in wartime). For some industries, such as aerospace, the federal government is virtually the only customer. Of course, the level of these supports and purchases responds to a variety of political forces.

Overriding partisan politics is war. Apart from the question of sheer survival, a major war drastically alters allocation of resources and the activities companies are permitted to perform. Consequently, one of the elements in every company strategy is what provision, if any, should be made for the possibility of war.

International development. The birth of a new nation or a new government in power occurs almost monthly. Especially in Africa, we are witnessing the formation of many new states, and throughout the world feelings of nationalism are strong. At the same time, radio, movies, magazines, and travel have greatly expanded the aspirations of "have not" nations. This inherently unstable situation is complicated by the "have" nations in their jockeying for influence and for economic or military advantage.

In this milieu the businessperson faces contradictory factors. Great human need and perhaps incentive for local investment are countered by occasional confiscation of mines and oilwells, import quotas, and similar acts. The result is widely fluctuating risk in dealing with developing countries.

Inflation and unemployment. Permeating and confusing all these changes is inflation. Annual price and wage increases of 5% to 10% have become almost normal. In many countries 10% to 15% is considered modest. To reduce the injustices created by such changes, indexing of obligations (automatic adjustment upward on the basis of a stipulated price index) is increasingly common. But indexing gives only partial relief because it rarely matches cost increase precisely and typically there is a lag in the adjustment. Business managers, especially, find that inflation brings baffling uncertainty.

Government efforts to restrain inflation clash with very strong pressures to increase, rather than decrease, expenditures. Most stubborn is high unemployment. Few governments, of any political persuasion, are prepared to take firm anti-inflationary action if it means increasing the demoralizing burden of unemployment. In addition, military budgets are sacrosanct and social security payments irreversible. Politically acceptable cutbacks are indeed very hard to find.

One of the main ways to check inflation is to increase productivity—i.e., generate more output with a given input of resources. And it is enterprise managers—the resource converters we described in Chapter 1—who carry the initiative in improving productivity! No single company can sweep back the tide, but each technological advance helps.

Economic changes

Total output. The preceding discussions concern business executives because technology and social and political forces are examples of changes in the methods executives might use and the environment in which they operate. But what of the overall results, the total flow of goods and services?

U.S. business has had its ups and downs, and some industries have grown much faster than others. Nevertheless, the total output is impressive. Industrial production, according to the Federal Reserve Board Index, by 1980 more than doubled its 1962 average. And the 1962 level was three times the production in 1929, the year of the Big Crash and the peak of prosperity up to that time. This achievement in the production of goods is more impressive when we realize that during the past twenty years most of the increases in work-hours have gone into services and government. In fact, at present more people work in services and government than in the production of goods (farming, manufacturing, and mining). This means that future increases in productivity will have to be found more in the office than in the plant.

Total income. The market side of the same picture is the overall capacity of people to buy the output. In 1929, the first year for which the Department of Commerce statistics are available, disposable personal income amounted to $83 billion. This looks small indeed from the lofty heights of 1980 when people had over $1,700 billion available to spend or to save. With all effects of price changes removed, and on a per capita basis so that population increases are washed out, the additions to income still look impressive. Using the 1958 dollar as a standard, compare the per capita disposable personal income in the following years: 1929, $1,236; 1950, $1,646; 1980, $3,075.

Income distribution. An outstanding economic fact and a major factor in keeping the economy in high gear is the redistribution of income, especially to the lower income classes. In 1950, only 14% of American families had incomes of over $6,000 per year; some 40% had incomes of less than $3,000. Today, over 90% have incomes of more than $6,000, and only 4% have less than $3,000 to spend. With more women working, now over half the families have two or more wage earners; the median family income now is about $20,000.

The "middle-class" has grown enormously. This is the group that now has "discretionary" spending power and it has been using its discretion to create a continuing demand for goods and services which make ordinary living easier and leisure more varied. This is the group that upgrades luxuries into necessities and buys huge quantities of consumer durables—color TV sets, microwave ovens, air-conditioners, and second family cars.

Income distribution still provides its problems. The average for nonwhite families is only three-fifths of that for white families. Nevertheless, as the accompanying table shows, some progress is being made; over the 25-year period, nonwhite family income increased at a faster rate than that of white families.

Median Family Income
(Current dollars)

	Total	White		Nonwhite	
			Index		Index
1947	$ 3,031	$ 3,157	(100)	$1,614	(100)
1972	11,116	11,149	(366)	7,106	(440)

Stress and Strain

Change, the theme of this chapter so far, produces stress in any individual or organization that goes through it. Pouring new wine into old bottles builds pressure that must be planned for beforehand or mopped up after the explosion.

The turret lathe operator who must develop new skills when electronic controls are added to the machine, the company that must change its organization structure when new products are added or when sales growth makes the old relationship among executives inefficient, the downtown hotel that finds its survival threatened by motels, and the stock-brokerage firm that loses clients to banks and mutual funds—all must plan for some adaptation in their way of operating.

These stresses do not come only from changes initiated within the company itself. The uncertainties from the international political scene and from changes in government policy often bring a feeling of uneasy tension combined with frustration—a feeling that unmanageable forces might be taking one toward some impending disaster and that there is nothing to be done about it. Psychiatrists occasionally call this an Age of Anxiety.

Management has the never-ending task of providing enough stability and continuity of action to permit efficient performance, and at the same time, of adjusting company operations to the array of changes suggested in the preceding pages. The socially responsible response to a dynamic, imperfect world is to identify tasks that need doing and then to do them well.

SCANNING AND FORECASTING COMPANY ENVIRONMENT

The following chart depicts the dynamic environment in which a company operates and the changes—technological, social, political, and economic—that have an impact on it.

If management can forecast important changes in company environment, it clearly is in a better position to deal with the opportunities and the problems that these changes will create. But, three practical hurdles have to be surmounted to capture such benefits:

1. The critical aspects of the environment must be identified.
2. Techniques for forecasting each of these factors must be selected and predictions must be made.
3. The forecast must be incorporated into the decision-making process.

Selecting Critical Features of the Environment

The task of predicting even a dozen major variables is substantial. Consequently, central management must be selective in what it pays attention to. Boeing will obviously be more concerned with aerospace exploration than will the Coca-Cola Company.

COMPANY ENVIRONMENT

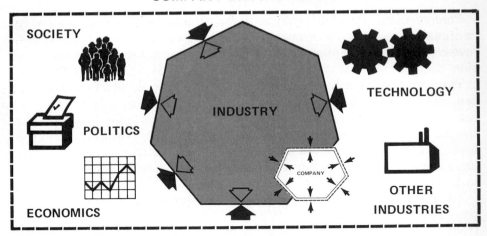

A first set of variables to be forecast can be derived from the industry in which a company is currently operating. Industry analysis, explored in the next chapter, helps spot those environmental factors most likely to force sharp expansion or decline in total volume. For the furniture industry, new home construction is significant; whereas for computers, new technology is crucial. *Each industry* must be analyzed to ascertain where to center forecasting effort that will be most relevant to it.

These easily recognized variables are not enough. Some *general* scanning of the future environment is also desirable (a) to identify possible changes that previously had been considered so unlikely or so minor in impact that they were omitted from regular examination, and (b) to pick up ideas for new directions the company might take outside its industry as currently conceived. The rise in importance of air pollution to the automobile industry illustrates (a), and new opportunities in the publishing field created by remote electronic typesetting is an example of (b). Although a company (and certainly a person) can undertake systematic forecasting of only a very select part of its total environment, the list of factors watched should be open-ended.

Forecasting Techniques

Probably each of the key environmental items will require its own forecasting method. Interest rates, price movements, oil discoveries, tax exemptions, lower tariffs, cost-cutting inventions, social mobility rates, substitute products, use of leisure time, political stability in Africa, reduction of the sonic boom, low-cost water desalination, labor union power—these merely illustrate the kinds of factors that may be crucial to one industry or another. Unfortunately, no universal forecasting model exists. Two common techniques—economic forecasting and technical forecasting—will be discussed to indicate what is involved.

Economic Forecasting

Gross national product (GNP). A widely used technique to predict economic conditions is in terms of the gross national product, which systematically summarizes many diverse influences in the national economy. In the
words of the Department of Commerce, "The gross national product estimates the market value of the nation's output of goods and services."

Two views: total costs and total sales. There are two different ways of
measuring total output. Since they are essentially two aspects of the same
thing, they will have to add up to the same amount. First, gross national
product is the sum of costs incurred in producing all the goods and services
made during the year. Let's look at the following table.

National Income and Product Accounts
1st Quarter, 1980
(Annual rate, in billions of current dollars)

Costs of Output		Sales (or Uses) of Output	
Compensation of employees	$1,552	Personal consumption expen-	
Rentals paid to persons.	27	ditures.	$1,634
Net interest	147	Government purchases of goods	
Business taxes and depreciation. .	488	and services	518
Corporate profits.	175	Private investment in U.S.	389
Income of unincorporated firms. .	13	Net exports	-21
Gross national product	2,520	Gross national product	2,520

On the left-hand side we find amounts paid to those who contributed
toward making the gross national product. These are the costs of output.
Included here are the wages of workers, net rents and royalties, net interest
on capital loans and securities, business taxes and depreciation, corporate
profits, and income of unincorporated enterprises and farms.

In the example given in the table, the total costs incurred in producing
final goods in the economy was measured at an annual rate of $2,520 billion.
In passing we may note that all these costs, except business taxes and
depreciation charges, reflect a flow of earned income. This income was available for personal expenditures, income tax, or investment.

Second, the right-hand side of the table shows the uses made of the total
output of goods and services. For direct and immediate consumption, people
were buying at the rate of $1,634 billion, or 65% of the total. Government
bodies—federal, state, and local—used 20% of the total. Investment in private houses, plant and equipment, inventories, and the like used 15%.

One important thing to note about the gross national product is that it is
a *measure* expressed in dollars. Having such a measure, subject to statistical
manipulations, is a great advantage in trying to estimate the significance of
changes in economic, political, and social affairs, since it enables us to avoid

the confusion of merely saying "more" or "less." With gross national product statistics, we can answer the question, "How much?" We can also chart the movements of a country from depression to prosperity or its steady long-term rate of economic development.

Use of GNP in long-run forecasting. Often business strategy must be established on the basis of forecasted conditions five, ten, or twenty years hence. The impact, for instance, of adding a new product line or leasing branch plants is likely to be greatest at least ten years after the original decision is made. Clearly, many of the dynamic factors discussed in the first part of this chapter will have a bearing on that future business environment. Can the gross national product concept be helpful in forming a sharper picture of the future and thereby aid in the design of strategy?

An example from a forecast of 2000 will show how the gross national product idea may be used for this purpose. Among the changes discussed earlier in this chapter were rising population, shorter hours of work, increasing output per worker-hour, and inflation. These facts can be used to estimate GNP for 2000:

> Since the people who will be in the 2000 workforce are already living, we can come pretty close in estimating the number of workers at that time. Assuming that the increase in the proportion of homemakers and older people working will offset an increase in the number of adults in school, we can be reasonably sure that the work force in 2000 will be about 122 million.
>
> The output per worker-hour has shown an annual increase during the past half-century of 2.5%. However, the rate of increase has been slowing down in the last few years, so that a projected increase of 2% per annum is more conservative.
>
> Applying the 2% annual increase to the gross national product per worker in 1975 ($16,440), we arrive at a 2000 output per worker of $27,000.
>
> Now, the forecast of gross national product in 2000 is easy. Multiplying the output per worker by the number in the labor force, the impressive result is $3,294 billion in 1975 dollars. Finally, allowing for, say, 7% inflation per year the estimate in current dollars for 2000 jumps to about $18,000 billion.

The important point in this example is not the specific figures but the way knowledge about several diverse factors can be combined to give us a prediction of the total volume of business that is likely to be done several years hence. Of course, as new facts become available, they must be weighed, and revisions of the forecast must be made if necessary. Yet the gross national product framework can serve as a summation device, much as a profit and loss statement summarizes the results of a wide variety of activities within a company.

Technological Forecasting

Hazardous though economic forecasting may be, it is well understood compared with predicting changes in technology. A cure for cancer, an economic way of desalinating water (which would open up vast areas of the world to agriculture), and a practical electric motor for automobiles are just three of the myriads of discoveries that might alter the lives of millions of people—and companies. We know that massive research effort is devoted to such challenges, yet our ability to forecast them is limited. Even when the underlying technology is known, our ability to say *when* and *at what cost* a process or product will hit the market is unimpressive. Witness the use of atomic energy to generate electricity; in the mid-1960's utility companies bet on nuclear plants to meet rising demands, but by 1980 nuclear plants provided only 5% of our electrical energy. Environmental issues slowed construction, and costs were far above expectations. Brownouts, higher prices, and profit declines resulted. Clearly, the forecasts had been wrong.

One method of predicting technological achievement is by analogy: "Salk discovered polio vaccine, therefore someone will discover a way to prevent cancer." Or, "Costs of generating electricity have been falling by X percent a year, therefore they will continue to drop at X percent." As with any reasoning by analogy, the reliability is greatly improved by checking the similarity of the situations. Also, if we can develop some theory of how the discovery-development process works, then we can select our analogies with even better precision. With these refinements, forecasting by analogy gives results that are somewhat better than flipping a coin!

The "Delphi" technique—named for the ancient oracle—uses the combined judgment of a group of experts. Various procedures for consulting the experts may be followed, such as independent conclusions, comparison of reasons supporting the conclusions, statistical analysis and feedback to the experts, unstructured discussion among the experts, and revised conclusions. This technique does result in a highly informed guess, and as a by-product it gives a list of conditioning events that can be monitored to update the forecast. The chief drawback of the Delphi technique is the expense of identifying and securing the cooperation of a panel of experts qualified to deal with the change being forecast.

Note that the Delphi technique not only merges the judgment of the panel; it also permits each expert to use theory, analogy, trends, intuition, or whatever forecasting method is preferred. Incidentally, the method may be adapted to forecasting political and social changes.

Making Use of Forecasts

Forecasts have no value to a company until they enter into its decision-making process. Basically, this practical use occurs when the prediction is accepted as a *planning premise,* that is, when the prediction becomes a part of the assumed environment used in formulating strategy and other future plans. The concept of a planning premise does not require a single, unalterable assumption. The premise may be stated as a range (for example, copper prices up 25% to 40%) or as a probability (20% chance of a strike at the Baltimore plant); and explicit provision may be made for revising the premise as new information is obtained.

Many of the environmental forecasts first become premises for industry analysis, to be discussed in the next chapter. For example, the 2000 forecast of gross national product quoted previously can be related to the total U.S. demand for new plant and equipment by estimating how much of the increase will be goods (rather than services) and then projecting the new plant that will be needed to produce this additional output. Allowance must also be made for replacing and modernizing existing capacity. One prediction based on this approach is that business expenditures for plant and equipment in 2000 will be running around $280 billion (1975 prices).

Some forecasts may be tied directly to company strategy, bypassing the industry analysis stage. A chemical company, for instance, predicted that social and governmental restraints on the use of insecticides would become increasingly severe during the 1980's, with biological insect control taking their place. This forecast led to a shift in research effort and also to abandoning the construction of a California plant.

Forecasting requires hard work, and operating executives often lack the patience and the objectivity needed for good long-range predictions. Consequently, a recurring problem, which we will explore in Part 4 is how to use experts for reliable forecasts and then get operating executives to accept these projections. Formal approval by central management of particular planning premises helps; but unless executives have personal confidence in these premises, they are likely to introduce hidden safety factors into the plans. So, when forecasting is assigned to individuals, the forecasters not only have to be right most of the time, they also have to convince a lot of executives that they are right.

SUMMARY

An essential part of company strategy is a plan for adapting company action to its environment. This is no simple matter because the environment is continuously changing. New technology, social shifts, political realignments and pressures, as well as the more commonly recognized economic changes, all create problems and opportunities. The many examples of exciting new developments noted in this chapter indicate how dynamic the setting of business is. To adjust most effectively, central management should try to predict important changes before they occur. And these predictions should not only identify the new factors, they also should anticipate how such shifts in the dynamic environment will affect the company.

In practice, no company can systematically monitor every part of its environment that might change. The task is too great. So the process involves (a) identifying crucial aspects of the dynamic environment, (b) selecting a forecasting method and making frequent forecasts for each of these aspects, and (c) taking steps to insure that the forecasts are actually used by company executives in formulating plans. Since the ability to make good long-range forecasts is limited, especially in the technical-social-political areas, management needs arrangements for frequent measurement. Built-in flexibility in the planning mechanisms is also needed. In other words, the total managing process that this book examines is no one-time affair; it is a recycling, never-ending—and challenging—undertaking.

A very helpful way to relate shifts in the dynamic environment to current operations of a company is to move first from the general environment to an industry analysis, and then to assess how the particular company stands in that industry. This narrowing-down process is described in the next chapter.

 QUESTIONS FOR CLASS DISCUSSION

1. "The growing mood of conservatism in American society is probably related to the maturation of the population and the waning of the youth culture," said Jeffrey Evans of the National Institute of Child Health and Human Development as quoted in *Business Week*. Do you agree that the American population is maturing? (The median age in 1970 was 28 years; in 1980, 30 years; and, in 2000, is predicted to be 35 years). What "youth culture" could be waning? Will the mood of conservatism then grow? How might this affect dress designs? Shoe designs? The sale of surfboards? Travel by train? Pension funds?

2. The age mix of our population is shifting. Comparing 1970 and 1985, the 5- to 17-year-olds drop from 53 million to 43 million, while the 25- to 44-year-olds increase from 49 million to 70 million; the over-65 group rises from 20 million to 28 million. What types of business are significantly affected by these changes? Do you think the changes will affect politics? Social attitudes?

3. Says one experienced management consultant, "In the years 1985 to 1990, managers in the 45- to 65-year age group, a group that has traditionally held 60% to 70% of senior management jobs, will number only between 11% and 18% of the total population segment in management. Or, to put it another way, business employment will contain 88% more 20- to 34-year-olds than 45- to 59-year-olds, an inexperienced-to-experienced ratio of almost 2 to 1." (a) Does this indicate that there will be too few senior managers who have the experience to guide the newcomers? (b) How might your career as a new or young executive be affected? (c) Many personnel executives, surveyed in 1980, said, "We've simply not given much thought to the subject." Any ideas as to why not?

4. (a) Assume that the president of a mobile home manufacturing company asks you, "What are the half dozen key factors in the environment that I should watch in order to anticipate the growth or decline in our industry?" Give your answer. (b) Do the same for eggs.

5. U.S. consumers spend about $5 billion annually in beauty salons and barber shops. This total has been increasing somewhat faster than the gross national product, and the trend is expected to continue. (a) Does this information have significance for your campus barber shop? (b) What other trends should the manager of that shop predict, if any? Why?

6. In the past, international agreements to restrict the world supply of a basic product such as rubber, coffee, or copper have fallen apart within a few years. Either discord among the supplying countries and/or new sources of supply have led to renewed competition. (a) Do you think such agreements will be more stable in the future? Use crude oil as an example—or bauxite (aluminum ore). (b) After answering (a), appraise the method you used to make your forecast. What are the strengths and the weaknesses of that forecasting method?

7. One of the most pervasive changes confronting a central manager is inflation. Should the manager of a small enterprise, say, a dry-cleaning firm with six retail outlets, try to forecast the amount of future inflation? If so, for how long a period? How would such forecasts help the manager run the business?

8. (a) "From 1980 until 1985, '86, or '87, major problems are likely to arise from the labor surplus that will be caused by the enormous size of the 25- to 44-year group as it bulges through the economic arteries." So state many demographers. What will happen to the competition for jobs? Will blacks, other minorities, women, and older people face continuing difficulties in the marketplace? Will those who have jobs try to protect them by tightening seniority and by shortening the hours of work?

   (b) "In the 1990's, the problems will begin to shift. As the much smaller age group born in the 1960's and 1970's moves up the job ladder, labor shortages will develop." Will you have difficulty finding a job?

   (c) "Then, after the turn of the century, as the baby-boom generation retires, the ratio of dependents to active workers will increase, straining the ability of the economy to support nonworkers." What will this mean for company pension plans? For jobs for those older than 65? For the design of jobs and tasks in business?

9. Each year new forecasts of the gross national product and its components are made by professional forecasters. Explain how a company in each of the following industries could use such forecasts to its advantage: (a) air-conditioner manufacturing, (b) real estate development, (c) ski resort business. In each situation, do you recommend that the forecasts be given to operating executives in their original form, or should the basic forecasts be translated into some "intervening" variables? In the latter case, what variables?

10. "Several years ago, the American Council of Life Insurance noticed an intriguing change: More people than in the past were bequeathing their bodies to medical schools, and a few schools actually had to reject surplus cadavers. At the same time, debate was growing about giving terminal patients the 'right to die' without futile artificial life maintenance systems." (*Wall Street Journal.*)

   (a) The Council reasoned that people who were willing to discuss death and corpses might be more willing to buy life insurance without the hard-sell of a face-to-face salesperson. Do you agree? Should this lead to greater use by insurance companies of advertising and direct-mail selling?

(b) The Council suggests that those companies struggling to anticipate outside change and affected more than ever by pressure groups, advancing technology, governmental decisions, and other outside forces use their own permanent employees to think systematically about change rather than hiring outside consultants or buying research. How might regular employees be utilized to do this? What would you need to be able to do such systematic thinking and forecasting?

CASE 2
Consumers, Inc.

C.D. Elson feels lucky to have landed a job in corporate planning at Consumers, Inc. directly out of business school. Good jobs are scarce, and this one provides an early opportunity to show analytical skill and judgment. Elson's present assignment, however, can't be resolved on a computer.

Consumers, Inc. is a diversified corporation with divisions specializing in proprietary drugs, cosmetics, small electrical appliances such as hair driers, specialty mail-order and contest administration, luggage, outdoor furniture, and other lines which are directly related to final consumers. As part of its strategy, the company wants to establish a strong position in new growth areas. The Director of Corporate Planning outlined Elson's assignment as follows.

"The fastest growing segment of the U.S. population is no longer youth; just the opposite—it's the over-65's. We never have thought through where we want to be in that market. We should have a forecast of where the major opportunities lie so that we can establish ourselves to meet the growing demand as our other markets mature. Your task is to study the social and economic impact of the increasing numbers of over-65's in the U.S., and then single out two or three activities that can be best served by private enterprise."

Elson has scanned published materials and interviewed an array of experts. She finds that opinions vary sharply on what is likely to happen. The following excerpts from her notes reflect these differences.

Size and Nature of the Need

The elderly (65 years and older) part of the U.S. population increased 24% between 1970 and 1980, and is expected to increase another 20% during the following decade to 1990. These growth rates compare with 8.5% and about 9.5% for the total population. Older people are replacing children. The number of children, 5 to 19 years, actually decreased over 9% in the 1970's and may drop another 3.5% in the 1980's.

Of course, the age distributions within the total population will continue to be affected by the post-World War II baby boom, and then the sharply declining birth rates reflecting changes in attitudes about marriage, careers for women, use of the pill, etc. The big difference in over-65's, however, is longer life spans. Only two-fifths of people born in 1910 were expected to reach 65. Today, that proportion is three-fourths—almost double.

Not only do more people reach age 65. They are living much longer after 65. One current estimate for the 25 million now 65 is that life expectancy for men is 13.9 years and for women 18.3 years.

But these estimates are subject to change. Most things that *might* happen would extend life. For example, researchers are working on drugs that will slow down the aging process. It is not expected that a person will be able to remain perpetually at, say, 30 or 40; more likely one's active, working life would be extended twenty or more years. This would drastically change family formation, work patterns, leisure, social structure, etc. A possibility for *reducing* life expectancy is a shift to social approval of suicide by the elderly.

All of these changes in life expectancy could substantially alter the size of the market if Consumers, Inc. starts selling hearing aids.

The expansion of the over-65's creates a social burden, especially in terms of government outlays. The public costs of caring for the old are about three times the costs of caring for the young. The federal government alone now spends about 25% of its budget for the elderly (social security, Medicare, federal retirement, welfare), or 5% of the GNP. This is double the share a decade ago, and the proportion is likely to continue to grow.

A political hassle is brewing. The elderly are becoming a larger block of voters, and if they unite in pressing for services (as, say, the war veterans do), legislators will hesitate to say no. On the other hand, the working population may revolt. The number of active workers per retiree has dropped from about 9 to 1 in 1940 to 6 to 1 today, and if present trends continue it could be 4 to 1 by the year 2000. Maybe the young will try to call a halt. And Elson comments that the way this conflict is resolved will affect the size of the over-65 market and who will say where the money should be spent.

A further important variable affecting the size of the elderly market that Consumers, Inc. might wish to tap is the age at which people retire from employment. Will people be spending their own money or will government be the source of funds? As recently as 1949 about half of the men over 65 worked, including nearly one-third of those over 70. Now, only about one-fifth work (15% over 70). Many elect "early retirement" before reaching 65.

Three factors may contribute to reversing the trend toward early retirement: (1) Inflation is seriously eroding savings for old age and the value of private pensions. So, many men and women may have to work to maintain even a reduced standard of living. (2) Monetary pressures to restrict government spending, coupled with a youth revolt noted above, may trim back government subsidies for our elder citizens. (3) Work opportunities may be more plentiful for those who elect to continue working. Already federal law prohibits most compulsory retirement at age 65 and includes discrimination on the basis of age along with race, sex, religion, etc. The irony of this effort to extend the working life of present employees is that it will slow down promotion opportunities for younger people. How do we get Old Bill out of the way?

Elson wrote down a quote from an economist: "Sure, there will be a lot of people out there with a lot of wants. But consider carefully who is going to have money to pay for what."

Health Care

The type of expenditure for which the elderly group differs most from the rest of the population is health care. On the average, a person in the 19 to 64 age bracket spends only 38% as much as one 65 or over, and expenditures for each person under 19 is 14%. In total in 1980 the personal health care bill for the 25 million elderly was about $50 billion. Elson notes, "There should be something in there which Consumers, Inc. can do."

Health care is delivered in different ways. In addition to visits to doctors' offices, a person may:

1. go to a hospital for "acute" care;
2. move into an "extended care" facility—nursing home, convalescent home, rehabilitation center (all called nursing homes in this case);
3. become an "outpatient"—visiting the hospital or clinic periodically for treatment;
4. have a visiting nurse or paramedic administer necessary treatment at the patient's home.

The expense per day diminishes sharply as one moves down the list. Because of the very high cost of care at a hospital, there is much discussion about restructuring the way health care is provided, but change in this industry has been very slow.

An official of the American Medical Association told Elson, "My advice to Consumers, Inc. is to stay away from performing health care services. In spite of the efforts of our Association, the drift toward government regulation if not operation of facilities seems irresistible. Even in those areas where proprietary (for profit) companies are encouraged to enter the squeeze is rough. You may try to provide excellent services, but find that you have to do unwise things to meet federal and state requirements—and that third-party payers (Blue Cross, Medicare, and the like) will not reimburse the resulting costs. I realize that the federal government is already paying two-thirds of the health care expenditures of the elderly—but subsidies always lag behind actual outlays and Consumers, Inc. can't turn to some tax-supported agency to pay off your deficits. The politicians are into public health, and the voters won't let them back out."

This viewpoint was by no means unanimous. The one service area where private business still predominates is nursing homes—75% are proprietary (for profit). And this is relevant to Elson because 90% of the residents in nursing homes are 65 or over.

The modern era of nursing homes was born when Medicare and Medicaid started covering payments in extended care facilities.[1] Help in financing construction is also

---

[1] Medicare is a federal government health insurance program for persons 65 or over who are eligible for social security. Uncle Sam pays about two-thirds of the insurance cost. Medicaid covers almost all the medical expenses of financially indigent persons, many of whom are elderly.

often available. Expansion was very rapid, and many poorly qualified entrepreneurs entered the industry in the early 1970's. As a result, there have been low profits, some failures, and many complaints about quality of service.

A few companies have acquired a whole chain of nursing homes, and are applying business management methods to the operations. Basically their concept is to have expert central staff develop standards for operation, and then through training and close supervision run each home according to these standards. The standards typically include quality of nursing care, quality of food, design and maintenance of facilities, sales promotion and community relations to assure that the home is fully utilized, budgets and frequent cost and cash flow reports, and financial incentives for administrators.

Under favorable circumstances, this business-like approach has enabled homes to earn a satisfactory—though not exceptional—return on investment. Supporters of the approach believe that, like a motel chain, as they build a reputation for reliable service they will attract a "preferred clientele" and that as the entire organization gains experience real costs will go down. The primary problems to date have been with recruiting, training, and retaining personnel. Dealing with people who are ill, often elderly with little to look forward to and perhaps somewhat senile, takes special skills and emotional attitudes. Not everyone has these qualities.

The most widely advocated new kind of organization in the health field is an HMO (Health Maintenance Organization). Unlike the usual fee-for-service practice, an HMO provides its members whatever services they may need for a fixed pre-paid fee. Each HMO has its own staff of doctors and clinics; in addition, it may operate its own hospital(s) or nursing home or it may contract for such services by existing facilities. Thus, the HMO is both a financier and a provider of care. Because these two functions are combined, there is an emphasis on preventive medicine and, in fact, HMO members spend less time in hospitals than do comparable people served by the usual disconnected enterprises.

The leading HMO's are the Kaiser group which enrolls over 20% of the population in northern California, and operates elsewhere ($1 billion income per year). This group is non-profit, but an HMO can be proprietary. To date, most HMO enrollments are tied to employment in cooperating companies or agencies, and the basic concept has not yet been adapted to the elderly.

Housing

The elderly also have distinctive housing needs—much less space than families with children, one floor, minimum outside maintenance, close to shopping centers or public transportation, and low real estate taxes. The time-honored practice of old folks living with children or their relatives is fast disappearing, in spite of its many economic and social advantages.

To meet the need, "retirement communities" are springing up all over the country, especially in warmer climates. Leisure Village, Holiday City, Fun City, Seaside Condominiums are examples. They range in accommodations from plush to modest. Almost all have a clubhouse for joint social activities, a swimming pool and other physical recreation, including access to nearby golf courses, perhaps hobby clubs, and the like.

Many retirement communities are little more than real estate developments, whereas others give much more attention to continuing social structure and services. Individual property ownership rather than rentals is the predominant pattern.

Urban planners usually advocate mixed communities with various ages, occupations, races, and income levels all represented. And Fair Housing laws support this concept even though retirement communities (at least the large ones which create economies) often buck this trend.

"Life-time care communities" are more complex. They combine the features of a retirement community, HMO, nursing home, and a communal dining service. In such a setting, personal relationships and social structure become very important. Thus skillful, sensitive administration is vital.

Services for the Young-Olds

A professor of gerontology told Elson, "It's a mistake to focus on health alone. A large majority of the over-65's are vigorous people with more freedom to do what they please than most of us. The challenge is to keep them active. Think in terms of the young-olds and the old-olds. The distinction is more a matter of energy and physical condition than it is of age. Today, many people are not seriously restricted in their activities at age 75."

These young-olds can be important consumers. In addition to the usual food and clothing, they may be attracted to products or services which take a relatively high amount of their own time. Among the commonly recognized items that may appeal to the young-olds are:

Travel—by auto or airplane, often in tours, in the U.S. or abroad.

Recreation and hobbies—already mentioned in connection with retirement communities but by no means restricted to such settings.

Continuing education—related to cultural interests, hobbies, or perhaps new careers.

Counseling—aid on investments, employment, retraining and the like to other elderly persons or to younger people.

Most of such fields also appeal to other adults. So market segmentation may be appropriate; i.e., design the service or product so that it appeals especially to the young-olds. The total group of elderly is larger than the entire population of Canada, so segmentation is a feasible approach. There is danger, of course, that inflation will wipe out much of the purchasing power of retirees.

Question

Assume you are C.D. Elson. What two or three activities would you recommend to the Director of Corporate Planning? In preparing your answer, treat the material in the case merely as background; make your own forecasts and seek other alternatives to consider.

ASSESSING THE COMPANY'S FUTURE STRENGTHS

Analysis of Industry and Company

The dynamic environment, discussed in Chapter 2, does create opportunities and problems. For a specific company to respond constructively to this setting, however, it must sharpen its focus. It must (a) analyze prospects and requirements for success in specific industries, and then (b) carefully assess its strengths and weaknesses relative to competitors in those industries.

For example, the manager of Office Communications, Inc. may foresee rapid growth of electronic "word-processors" which greatly speed up editing and reproduction of personalized letters and internal memos. But industry analysis indicates that such word processors will be supplied by large companies with major R&D strength; and the relative strength of Office Communications lies in combining standard equipment with inter-office communications systems. Clearly, this firm is not well suited to compete in the manufacture of word-processors. Instead, it should focus on ways to incorporate word-processors into tailor-made total office systems.

Such analyses of particular industries and companies provide essential insights for wise strategy formulation, considered in Chapter 5; they also contribute important background for policy designed to execute the strategy. (Policy issues are explored in Part 2.)

Framework for Analysis

This chapter explains an outline that will help to analyze industries and to position a company in each industry; it gives a way to sift and classify ideas, determine their relationships, and weigh their importance. The key topics are given in the outline which follows.

The nature of each of these topics will be examined in the following pages. All subheadings may not be significant for a particular company, but the list as a whole suggests a range of factors that should be considered.

Of course, a company may be involved in two or more industries and may be considering many others; if so, separate analyses should be made for each industry. Moreover, since the environment, industry, and company all change overe time, the thinking must be updated. Having a framework of analysis makes such extensions and revisions easier to do.

I. Outlook for Industry

A. Demand for Products or Services of the Industry
   1. Long-run growth or decline
   2. Stability of demand for products
   3. Stage in product life cycle

B. Supply of Products or Services
   1. Capacity of the industry
   2. Availability of needed resources
   3. Volatility of technology
   4. Social constraints
   5. Inflation vulnerability

C. Competitive Conditions in the Industry
   1. Structure of the industry
   2. Government support and regulation

D. Conclusions
   1. Prospects for volume and profits
   2. Key factors for success in industry

II. Position of the Company in Industry

A. Market Position of the Company
   1. Relation of company sales to total industry and to leading competitors
   2. Relative appeal of company products
   3. Strength of the company in major markets

B. Supply Position of the Company
   1. Comparative access to resources
   2. Unique productivity advantages
   3. R&D strength

C. Special Competitive Considerations
   1. Relative financial strength
   2. Community and government relations
   3. Ability and values of company managers

D. Conclusions
   Comparative strengths and weaknesses of the company in terms of key success factors identified in I.

DEMAND FOR PRODUCTS OR SERVICES OF THE INDUSTRY

Long-run Growth or Decline

The end uses of an industry's products provide a key to future demand. For instance, if the familiar flashlight battery were used only for flashlights, the demand would be stable and mature. Actually, small dry cells are used in portable radios, cassettes, action toys, emergency lights, and a variety of gadgets. The popularity of the portable entertainment devices, especially, has contributed to a high growth rate.

Dry cells illustrate two other aspects of demand that may be significant. First, dry batteries have a *derived demand*. They are used only in association with some other product, and it is the popularity of these other products that leads to the demand for dry batteries. Many other items have a similar dependency on a different product for their sale. Manufacturers can do little to influence total industry sales; instead, their sales efforts focus on increasing their share of the market.

Second, the *focus of research and development effort* is not on new devices that will increase the demand for batteries. Of course, the manufacturers are glad to provide data to the designers of toys and radios, but these end products involve such different considerations that the battery manufacturers feel they have little to contribute. Instead, research by battery manufacturers is directed toward reduction of cost and improvement of quality.

After the possible uses of a product or a service of an industry have been explored, it is often desirable to classify potential customers by type and area. Thus the customers for automobile insurance may be grouped as private and commercial, and they may be further divided between states and regions. This information will be useful in determining the probable demand in the future; it will also provide a basis for sound sales policy.

Stability of Demand for Products

Demand for a product or a service may be steady and predictable or it may be volatile and uncertain. The following factors give insight regarding stability.

Substitutes. The desire for the utility or satisfaction rendered by a product may be reasonably stable, yet the demand for the product itself may be quite unstable because of increased or decreased use of substitutes that render this same satisfaction. Fresh oranges, a leading item in most grocery stores not so long ago, are becoming less abundant because frozen juice is an effective substitute. Ballpoint and felt-tip pens have reduced the demands for pencils. In each case the problem has been not so much a decline in the demand for the service as the substitution of one product for another.

**Fluctuations in Demand for Different
Kinds of Products
(Index numbers of physical volume, 1948 = 100)**

	U.S. Shoes	Automatic Dishwashers	Railroad Freight cars	Electricity (kilowatt hours)
1948 (postwar recovery) ..	100	100	100	100
1954 (recession)	109	96	32	162
1965 (prosperity).........	124	573	69	344
1969 (recession)	109	941	61	461
1972 (prosperity).........	98	1422	42	550
1975 (recession)	77	1166	64	594

Durability of products. Durable products have wide fluctuations in demand. Houses, airports, and washing machines once constructed render services over a period of time, and consequently the demand for such products is more active during *periods of original construction* than during periods when existing facilities are merely being replaced. Also, the replacement of durable goods can often be postponed for a substantial period of time. For these reasons the demand for durable products tends to fluctuate over wider ranges than does the demand for such things as food, clothing, travel, and entertainment, which must be replenished to render additional services. Speculation may play a part in fluctuations of demand for almost any product; however, the more durable the product, the more lasting the maladjustment that may result from the unwarranted speculation.

Necessity versus luxury. Necessities, such as food and medical care and other products that people have come to regard as essential to their well being, will enjoy a more stable demand than products such as swimming pools and foreign travel that are purchased only at times when people have funds over and above what is necessary for the first class of goods. Sometimes a product or a service—for example, air-conditioning or long-distance telephoning—is a necessity in one of its uses or for one group of customers, whereas it is regarded as a luxury by another group of customers.

The federal government is a large buyer of some products. These purchases go primarily to the armed services; but from time to time, purchases for space exploration, stockpiling, atomic research, and the like assume large proportions. Here again the demand is likely to change sharply, and it is difficult to predict because it depends on national and international politics fully as much as on economic factors.

Stage in Product Life Cycle

Many products pass through a life cycle, as shown in the chart which follows. Although the phases vary widely in length, experience with an array of products—from penicillin to automatic pinsetters in bowling alleys —does show that the concept is a useful analytical tool. Clearly, when electric refrigerators are already in 90% of the homes, growth prospects are much lower than for microwave ovens, which are in less than 1% of the homes; refrigerators have reached the maturity phase. A shift from maturity to decline typically occurs when a substitute product or service appears on the scene—witness what happened to the small-town newspaper.

CLASSICAL PRODUCT LIFE CYCLE

In addition to a way of analyzing demand, the life-cycle concept bears directly on key factors for success. In the growth phase a company can take risks with overcapacity and even with quality in an effort to establish a market position; profit margins will permit production inefficiencies. By contrast, in the maturity phase efficient use of plant and close attention to production costs become much more important.

As already noted, separate demand analysis is necessary for industries with multiproducts or those serving several distinct markets. The several product-markets may be in different phases of the life cycles; one may be a necessity whereas another is a semiluxury; and each will have its own vulnerability to substitution.

SUPPLY OF PRODUCTS OR SERVICES

The outlook for profitable operations in an industry depends not only on the demand, but also on the available supply and cost of bringing such products to the market.

Capacity of the Industry

In a dynamic business system, some industries are likely to have excess capacity while others have inadequate capacity. At one stage, sulfa was the wonder antibiotic drug and pharmaceutical producers expanded greatly to meet the urgent demand. Then penicillin and aureomycin came along, and the sulfa producers found themselves with a large capacity that could not be used. In the finance field, stockbrokers have been plagued with excess capacity when interest in stock speculation declines. In addition to such drops in demand, excess capacity may result from overexpansion. Sometimes a field of business looks so attractive that too many firms enter it. Thus there may be an excess of resort hotels or office buildings in a given locality because promoters expanded their facilities too fast.

Undercapacity is common in any expanding industry. If a new service like retirement villages meets with wide public acceptance, the original facilities will probably not be able to fill the demand. Or a rapid increase in demand for, say, the Chinese language may make the number of qualified teachers quite inadequate.

Significance of undercapacity. When capacity of an industry is scarcely adequate to meet demand, most companies will enjoy profitable operations. Products will find a ready market, prices will be firm, and a high level of operation will permit spreading overhead costs over many units.

The significance of undercapacity also depends on the *ease of entering* the industry. If a new concern can be established with comparatively small capital and within a reasonably short period of time, undercapacity will probably be a temporary matter. The production of plastic toys, for example, requires little more than a few molding machines and assembly space; consequently, the capacity of a plant making this type of product can be easily expanded to meet demand. Similarly, the advertising agency industry is characterized by ease of entry. In contrast, virgin copper production requires an expensive plant and access to satisfactory ore deposits, with the result that few firms enter the business.

The possibility of expansion or contraction of *imports* from foreign countries must be taken into account for some commodities. The importation of sugar from the Philippines has long been a crucial factor in the outlook for the domestic sugar industry. The extent of imports is, of course, strongly influenced by tariffs and foreign exchange, which may allow only certain types of goods to enter local markets at competitive prices.

Effect of excess capacity. Excess capacity will have a depressing influence on the outlook for an industry, for it may lead to low prices, low rates of operation, and a high proportion of sales expense.

The seriousness of excess capacity depends, in part, upon how large depreciation, interest, and other expenses connected with the facilities are in relation to total costs. If, as in the chemical fertilizer industry, these overhead charges are a high percent of total expenses, the individual companies may cut prices to low levels in an attempt to secure volume and at least some contribution above out-of-pocket expenses toward the fixed burden. On the other hand, if the bulk of expense goes for materials and labor, the excess capacity will have much less effect on supply and price because the relation between out-of-pocket costs and prices will be the controlling influence— whether the plant is busy or not.

Durability of the excess capacity is also important. In the textile business, for instance, excess looms and other equipment were available for many years. The failure of a particular company did not *remove* this *capacity,* for the equipment was merely sold—usually at a low price—to another firm and again placed in operation. As a result, profitable operations were very difficult. Scrapping of existing facilities must sometimes be considered when overcapacity exists, although the usual pattern is the development of more efficient methods and machinery that make operation of the old facilities impossible at competing prices.

Availability of Needed Resources

The sheer existence of an adequate supply of raw materials may be a factor in the outlook of a few industries, notably those depending upon a natural resource such as timber, crude oil, iron ore, or other minerals. In most cases, however, the problem is the price at which the materials can be obtained.

Changes in raw material prices have varying effects on different industries. For example, public utilities have relatively stable rates, and firms selling through catalogs have fixed prices for at least a season. For such companies, a fall in raw material prices increases the gross margin, and rising prices decrease the profit margin. In other industries, such as textiles or containers, the selling price is comparatively flexible and may be adjusted as material prices go up or down.

The number of suppliers is also important. When there are only a few, they are much more likely to exact high prices and stipulate terms of delivery. And if those few form an alliance, as OPEC countries did with respect to crude oil, their bargaining position is further enhanced.

The supply of labor may be critical. In doing farming and truck-farming, for instance, laborers willing to work the long hours simply may not be available. Likewise, when skills that take a long time to develop are necessary—as in surgery—the rate of industry expansion may be constrained.

Occasionally labor unions have a negative effect on the outlook for an industry. Restrictions on productivity, as on the railroads, may hamper operations and increase costs to an extent that substitute services or products become established. Especially in mature industries where innovations are needed to reduce costs or cater to different customers, an unprogressive stance can be harmful. But unions differ in their conservatism and in their strength. So here again specific analysis is necessary.

While materials and labor are most likely to call for serious attention, the availability of each needed resource should be assessed—as the resource converter model discussed at the beginning of Chapter 1 implies.

Volatility of Technology

Industries vary in the frequency with which new products are introduced and the frequency of changes in processing technology. For example, technology jumps quickly in the pharmaceutical, space, and urban-renewal industries.

When confronted with such volatile technology, managers must give close attention to research and development (R&D). They must be prepared to move promptly when either their own efforts or competitors' create important innovations. The frequency of change means that market positions are insecure; consequently, caution in making capital investments is required. Success depends, in part, on being agile.

Social Constraints

Companies must act in a socially acceptable manner or face all sorts of delays and harassment. Having the facilities, resources, and technology to supply a desired service or product is not enough. In addition, all the activities of a company are expected to meet various social norms.

The catch is that these norms are not clearly defined. They keep changing, and various segments of society have quite different views on what is acceptable. Moreover, some industries are under more pressures than others.

Vague though the standards may be, the outlook for an industry should weigh the constraints within which that industry is expected to operate. For example, the norms may relate to:

Pollution of the air, water, ground, etc.

Environmental protection—e.g., strip mining

Equal opportunity in employment, steady jobs

Dealing with people who are unpopular with strong pressure groups—communists, South Africans, Israelis, R.O.T.C., the Mafia, those involved in abortion clinics, etc.

Integrity, honesty, "questionable payments," and the like

The potential seriousness of social constraints is indicated by the prolonged delay they imposed on a positive energy program for the country.

Inflation Vulnerability

Inflation may hurt an industry in several ways. Most common is costs rising faster than selling prices. This squeeze is likely to occur when prices are regulated by a public commission, as for utilities, and upward adjustments lag behind increases in costs. Occasionally, long-term selling commitments are made with inadequate provision for raising the selling price to absorb rising costs.

Inflation may cause dislocation of sales volume. The demand for some products, especially non-durable luxuries, is "price elastic" and consumers simply do not buy when they feel the price is high. In contrast, real estate and other durable products may have a speculative boom—and a later collapse.

Still another likely impact, which is less obvious at first, is inability to generate replacement capital. Sales may be made at what appears to be an attractive profit margin above the actual costs; but when the inventory and equipment have to be replaced the money taken in is insufficient to cover the new prevailing costs. The longer the production cycle and the more capital-intensive the technology, the more likely is such a capital shortage to arise.

Summarizing: demand for an industry's services or products is only part of the picture. The ability to effectively meet that demand depends upon how well the industry can cope with problems of resource availability, volatility of technology, social constraints, and vulnerability to inflation.

COMPETITIVE CONDITIONS IN THE INDUSTRY

The outline thus far has suggested that the outlook for an industry will be determined by the balance of the various forces bearing on demand and supply. Competitive conditions within the industry will often affect the manner and the rapidity with which these forces work themselves out.

Structure of the Industry

Some industries are dominated by a few *large companies,* the actions of which are of major importance to the future profitability of the entire industry. For example, the Federal Trade Commission has alleged that profits in the farm machinery industry have been abnormally high, partially due to the fact that the industry was dominated by two or three large companies. In contrast, other industries are characterized by *atomistic competition,* in which each small firm seeks to adjust the current condition as rapidly as possible. The weaving of dress goods and numerous other branches of the textile industry typify this type of competition.

Companies in an industry also vary as to *stability* and *financial strength.* For instance, the women's ready-to-wear industry is characterized by many unstable and financially weak firms. Here firms are organized, operate for a limited period of time, and then pass out of the picture so rapidly that widespread goodwill among customers or reputation for dependability is difficult to establish. Competitive conditions tend to be chaotic and unpredictable.

The *attitude* of the management of companies in an industry may also affect the outlook. The typical managements in some industries are likely to engage in activities that may give them an immediate benefit irrespective of the future repercussions of their actions. In contrast, the typical managements in other industries tend to adhere strictly to an accepted code of business ethics and are inclined to take a long-run industry viewpoint in their actions.

Organized cooperative effort has a significant effect upon the outlook for some industries. There are literally hundreds of *trade associations,* which are the central agencies for such voluntary action. Many of these associations do little more than sponsor an annual convention and perhaps a trade paper. Others, like insurance associations, engage in research and compilation of information of interest to its members, lobby in national or state legislatures, conduct a public relations campaign, and promote fair trade practices. While the scope of government-industry cooperation is in a state of flux, it is likely that the trade association will assume increasing importance in this regard.

In general, beware of the industry where size, strength, and leadership of companies are so weak that competition is chaotic. At the other extreme, be cautious about tackling large, financially strong, well-managed, aggressive companies—unless prospects for rapid industry growth are high.

Government Support and Regulation

Even the most ardent advocates of "American individualism" will admit that the forces of supply and demand should not be given free sway in the contemporary business world. There are, however, wide differences of opinion regarding the extent to which government should seek to restrict and regulate these forces. During recent years government regulation has been extended on many fronts, and it appears likely that this tendency will continue.

Federal and state governments have for some time regulated in considerable detail the activities of utilities and life insurance companies. There is much discussion as to the desirability of extending this concept to other industries such as aerospace or even to all industries vital to public welfare. If for a given industry any action in this direction seems likely, it is highly important to study the nature and the effects of the regulations that might be imposed.

The government often provides *special advantages* to particular industries. Our merchant marine is heavily subsidized; many other industries are protected from foreign competition by tariffs; agricultural products have been granted large subsidies. In order to qualify for such special advantages, it is often necessary for the industry to conform to stipulations and regulations of the government. This is particularly true in the agricultural industries where the whole program of subsidies is associated with a plan for controlled production and marketing.

Government bodies exercise influence over general *trade practices*. The Federal Trade Commission Act has been strengthened so that the commission may more effectively regulate what it considers unfair methods of competition; at the same time special powers were granted over advertising of foods, drugs, health devices, and cosmetics. It is quite probable that additional statutes regulating trade practices will be enacted from time to time.

Such government action is frankly and deliberately designed to modify the underlying forces of demand and supply. It is part of the composite picture of the outlook for any industry.

Emerging Synthesis

Industry analysis along the lines outlined should lead to two vital conclusions:

1. Outlook for volume and profits in the industry.
2. Key factors necessary for company success in the industry.

These conclusions will be essential input in the designing of an effective company strategy.

Perhaps the total picture will have to be broken down into several different industries or subindustries to highlight the opportunities and to identify what is required to achieve them. On the other hand, the conclusions need not be burdened with all the detail checked during the analysis; it is the dominant emerging factors that should be sifted out.

MARKET POSITION OF THE COMPANY

Success comes from matching opportunity with capability. The industry analyses, just discussed, should flag an array of opportunities, so we next examine the particular strengths and weaknesses of a company to grasp these opportunities.

Can the company get its share of new markets? Is it fortified against impending hazards? Does it enjoy a favorable or unfavorable cost position as compared with its competitors? Will its management make it a leader in the industry? Such factors as these will determine whether a specific enterprise will get along better or worse than the industry as a whole. Answers to these questions will also point to the particular problems that become the core of company strategy.

Relation of Company Sales to Total Industry and to Leading Competitors

The ups and downs of a total industry often obscure how well a specific company is being managed. A revealing way to screen out such external influences is to watch company sales as a percentage of its total industry and to watch its major competitors.

A dramatic example of loss of industry position is Univac—the computer subsidiary of Sperry Rand Corporation. Although its forebearer was the leading pioneer in digital computers, Univac failed to capture the lion's share of the market. Here was a company very technically oriented. It was good at product development, but slow in exploiting commercially sound products. Its competitors, notably IBM, were more sensitive to customer needs and had stronger marketing organizations. As soon as the key to success embraced the market as well as the laboratory, Univac slipped.

A company's share of its target market typically is closely related to its profitability. The Strategic Planning Institute has found that for a wide range of businesses, higher market share is linked to higher profits (see accompanying chart). This relationship probably reflects economies based on greater experience, economies of scale, and relative bargaining power. Clearly, the "little guy" must find a distinctive niche in order to prosper.

Hospitals, banks, and even churches or professional athletic teams can use the market share concept. Measurement may be more difficult and profit may not be the goal, but the tie to viability is much the same.

Relative Appeal of Company Products

The market position of a company is strongly influenced by the quality and the distinctiveness of its products. The TV set that has unique engineering features, the motel that serves good food, the hospital equipment that has dependability and durability, or the airline with a good on-time record is the product that will improve its position in the market. The important characteristics from the *user's point of view* should be determined and the company's products appraised in terms of these characteristics. In this process it is necessary to distinguish between various price ranges, because the controlling characteristics may not be the same for, say, low-priced shoes and high-priced shoes.

RELATION OF MARKET SHARE TO PROFITABILITY

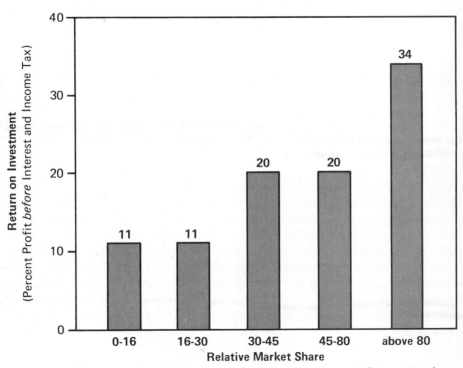

Relative Market Share
(Percentage of Company Sales to its Three Largest Competitors)

Source: Strategic Planning Institute.
This chart and later ones are based on confidential data covering the experience of over 1000 highly diversified business-units. In its PIMS Program the Institute makes very sophisticated statistical analyses of over 50 variables affecting profits and cash flow. Only a few of the simple relationships are shown on these charts, but the inferences are consistent with the more elaborate findings.

Sometimes the past success of a company is attributable to a single product, whereas future success in the industry must be built upon an *ability to develop new products*. For example, the Mead Johnson Company has enjoyed very large sales of its prepared baby cereal "Pablum," but possible substitutes or changes in ideas regarding child feeding made this single product an inadequate base for maintenance of a leading position in the industry. This company, fully recognizing the danger, developed a wide line of baby foods and then hit upon another winner—Metrecal.

The importance of a full line of products depends on both customer buying habits and the appeal the company elects to stress. When buying men's shirts—or skis—the customer expects to find a full range of sizes and would like an array of colors in each size. In contrast, the manager of a mutual fund or theatre production may focus on providing the best single product which appeals to a particular segment of the market. In the medical field there is debate about whether doctors, and clinics, should be generalists or specialists.

Strength of the Company in Major Markets

A company's position in its industry is also affected by its reputation in major markets. For instance, some motels cater to commercial travelers and business conferences, while competitors carefully nurture the tourist trade. Supplementary services and sales promotion then, help to focus on their target market.

Often the reputation of a firm varies by area as well as by type of customer. This is illustrated by different brands of coffee. Many local brands exist that are known in only one metropolitan area or perhaps one region; even the nationally advertised brands experience substantial differences in consumer acceptance in different sections of the country. In the same way, a particular manufacturer of farm machinery may have a strong *dealer organization* in the corn-belt states but have weak dealers and acceptance in the cotton states.

Reputation is an intangible thing including, in addition to being known, a prominence for giving service, for offering a good buy in terms of product and price, and for fair dealings. Many companies, as already indicated, have a niche in the industry where they are outstanding. For purposes of forecasting, the problem is to identify those areas or types of trade from which a company will obtain its business and then consider the prospects for such groups on the basis of the outlook for the general industry.

A small firm may deliberately cater to a particular segment of the market or concentrate on a narrower line of products than do the large firms, which are obligated to offer a complete line. Crown Cork & Seal Company, for instance, grew by focusing on aerosol and beverage cans; for these products its engineering and delivery service is outstanding. But it does not try to compete with the big American Can and Continental Can companies for the large-volume food business.

SUPPLY POSITION OF THE COMPANY

The position of a firm in its industry depends upon its ability to deal with supply factors as well as with demand or market factors. Its relative supply position influences the extent and the direction of company expansion and may be the key to survival itself.

Comparative Access to Resources

Ready and inexpensive access to raw materials is a major asset for companies using bulky products. The newsprint mills of Canada, for instance, now have a controlling advantage over their former competitors in Wisconsin, Michigan, or the New England states because the virgin timber in the latter areas has been cut off and logs—or pulp—must be transported long distances to the mills. In fact, most of the remaining mills in these areas have turned to specialty paper products to counteract the disadvantage of their location.

Location with respect to labor is sometimes a definite advantage or disadvantage to a company. Minimum-wage legislation and union activity have greatly reduced geographic differentials in wage rates within the United States, so "cheap labor" is now obtainable only in foreign countries. Occasionally a company located in a rural area is at a disadvantage if expansion requires that skilled workers must be induced to move from the cities.

In some industries, location close to markets is crucial. This is obvious for retail stores for which buyer traffic may mean the difference between success or failure. Printing firms that wish to serve advertising agencies must locate nearby so as to provide the necessary speed in service. For heavy products like cement, shipping expense becomes a significant factor.

Industry analysis, already discussed, should have indicated the significance—or the insignificance—of a favorable location with respect to raw materials, labor, or markets.

Favorable access to resources and customers may arise from ownership of contractual ties as well as from physical location. A primary advantage sought in vertical integration of ore mines and steel plants, of oil wells, refineries and filling stations, is assured supply. In times of inflation favorable costs also arise from vertical ties. Of course, in dynamic industries vertical ties can become an oppressive burden. So, when analyzing the supply position of a company, its long-term commitments both upstream and downstream should be compared with those of major competitors.

Unique Productivity Advantages

"Experience is a great teacher." The second time we perform a task it is easier than the first, the third time easier than the second, and so on. In fact, experience is so important for complex activities that cost estimates and output schedules in the aircraft and space industries are adjusted for the number of times a particular product has been produced, and The Boston Consulting Group has developed a whole theory of competitive behavior on the concept.

According to the experience curve theory, the company with the most cumulated experience (a result of high market position) should have the lowest production costs. Personal learning plus opportunities to specialize and automate should lead to higher productivity. In practice, newcomers may catch up. Nevertheless, the theory does signal the possibility of significant differences in productivity among companies.

An offsetting consideration is that a company's facilities may become outmoded. A prime consideration is whether the plant can make products suited to the trends in demand. To take an example from a service industry, high-ceiling hotel rooms without air-conditioning no longer serve the lodging market satisfactorily. Bowling alleys as a form of entertainment are in a similar fix.

Often such outmoded facilities are doubly disadvantageous because other companies are also likely to have excess equipment for the declining products; therefore, profit margins tend to be narrow, especially in contrast to margins on the expanding products that may be in short supply.

Flexibility of equipment is often a factor in operating costs. For example, large jet planes such as the Boeing 747 are efficient for transatlantic and cross-continental flights, but they are expensive and hard to handle on short runs where traffic is lighter. Smaller, flexible planes cost more to operate per passenger mile than a 747 when the latter is fully loaded on a long flight, but they have decided advantages in filling varying needs. Again, the crucial point is having equipment suited to the market the company wants to serve.

R&D Strength

If the industry analysis indicates that research and development is a key success factor, then any company staking its future in that domain must have access to current technology. The need is well recognized in pharmaceuticals and electronics, but also is vital in some divisions of agriculture, communications, energy, office equipment, space—to name just a few examples.

Small companies cannot afford broad-ranging, basic research. However, even a tiny technically oriented firm may be a pioneer in a very specific application. Also, licensing is common practice in some industries, in which case an ability to qualify as a licensee is crucial.

For R&D strength, like access to resources and productivity, a company must assess its strengths relative to competitors as a basis for its strategy.

SPECIAL COMPETITIVE CONSIDERATIONS

Three further considerations, in addition to market and supply factors, influence the ability of an enterprise to grasp new opportunities; namely, financial strength, community and government relations, and ability and values of company executives.

Relative Financial Strength

Adequate capital provides one of the necessary means to put plans of the business administrator into action. A company may enjoy a distinctive product, an unusually low cost, or some other advantage over its competitors; but virtually every type of expansion requires additional capital for inventory and accounts receivable if not also for fixed assets. Moreover, if a firm is to maintain its position, it must have sufficient financial strength to withstand depressions and aggressive drives by competitors for choice markets. Competition may force a company to expand the variety of products offered for sale, to establish district warehouses and local sales organizations, or to buy new equipment, and this requires capital.

The simplest way for a company to meet these capital requirements is from its own cash balances, which may be larger than necessary for day-to-day operations. Most concerns, however, do not carry large amounts of idle cash (or nonoperating assets readily convertible into cash such as government securities), in which case financial strength is primarily a question of ability to borrow new capital or to secure it from stockholders. Ability to raise new capital will reflect not only past and probable future earnings, but also the existing debt structure and fixed charges of the company. So, the entire financial structure of the company should be examined, particularly if there are likely to be major readjustments in industry operations.

Community and Government Relations

Governments are required to treat everyone alike formally. Nevertheless, over time one company may have antagonized governmental officials while another firm carefully developed good rapport. Also important, representatives of a company may have learned governmental procedures and the particular issues which are sensitive. Friendships help, but even more significant is identification with a cause that is cherished by a block of voters (along lines considered in the next chapter). The overall effect is that companies do differ in their ability to work with governments.

Community relations are even more intangible. For a variety of reasons a company may (or may not) be regarded as a "good citizen." Then when special police protection, a zoning variance, or perhaps prompt resolution of a complaint is needed, opposition does not automatically arise. Most of the time, for most companies good community and government relations lead simply to a permissive situation, but at times of crises the right to continue operating may be at stake.

Ability and Values of Company Managers

The most important single factor influencing the position of a company in its industry is the ability of its executives. The executives of a business turn potential sales into actual sales, keep costs in line, and face the endless stream of new and unanticipated problems.

The qualities desired for executives are numerous and vary to some extent for different types of companies; for example, the manager of a specialty shop needs a style sense, whereas the head of a hospital must have ability to supervise a diverse collection of professional employees. Outstanding research capability may be a key to success, or a willingness to take risks.

No single executive should be expected to have all the talents required, but within the management group there should be vision, creativeness, supervisory ability, human understanding, diligence, and other qualities essential to the planning, direction, and control of the enterprise. In fact, partly due to age and to the personal motivations of people in central management posts, the capacity of company managements differs sharply.

In predicting the future of a business, it is also necessary to consider the extent to which success is dependent on a few individuals and the provision that has been made for a succession of capable leadership. This is crucial in the outlook for a small "one-man company."

Matching Company Strengths with Keys to Success in Industry

Each company has its particular strengths—and weaknesses. These can be assessed in terms of successful firms in the company's present industry. Much more significant for strategic planning, however, is to think in terms of *future* requirements in growth areas. As already noted, a vital conclusion from industry analyses is the identification of key factors for future success. Now, the revealing question is how does the company match up to these *key success factors?*

Rarely will the match between company strengths and key success factors be perfect. Where a mismatch appears and where weaknesses might bar success, attention can then be directed to the feasibility and the cost of overcoming the handicap.

SUMMARY

The base from which a company strategy is developed is an insightful recognition of (a) dynamic conditions in the environment where the company operates, (b) the prospects for its industry generally, and (c) its position in that industry. A systematic analysis of each of these aspects should be made frequently by the top executives of the company. A continuing review is desirable of the demand for the products of the industry, the factors affecting supply, and the competitive conditions. Similarly, analysis of company position calls for appraisal of the relative standing of the company in markets and in supply, and also review of its competitive strength.

Clearly a great many facts and forecasts bear on a company outlook. Some device is needed to put these data into a systematic relationship. The outlines in Chapters 2 and 3 provide a method of putting the array of data into meaningful order.

Such an analysis is far from a mechanical or routine matter, however. Keen judgment is especially vital in attaching *relative importance* to the numerous factors. A general outline, such as the one discussed in the last two chapters, suggests possibilities but strategic planners must decide which are the key factors for the specific business.

 ## QUESTIONS FOR CLASS DISCUSSION

1. The simple hamburger stand has grown into what is now called the "fast-food industry"—replete with expensive outlets and TV advertising. Some analysts believe that fast-food chains such as McDonald's are now at the mature stage, perhaps entering decline, in their product-life-cycle. Use the outline of this chapter (a) to prepare an industry outlook, and (b) to assess McDonald's position in the industry.

2. Coca-Cola Co., Atlanta, the well-known manufacturer of syrups for soft drinks, recently entered the U.S. wine market by purchasing Taylor Wine Co. (a producer and bottler of New York State wines) and several small California wineries. (a) Based on what you know of changes in the sizes of various age groups in the U.S., of tastes of the old and the young for various drinks, and of changes in discretionary income now and in the future, do you think that this entry into the wine market was a sound idea? (b) Coca-Cola is using the Taylor brand name for both its New York and California wines and is sharply reducing the varieties of wines sold to standardize the products and make the taste of the few varieties sold uniform and consistent from year to year and place to place.

What do you think of this idea which appears to be a transfer from the soft-drinks industry? Will standardization and uniformity help Coca-Cola compete with the many other wine producers? (The ten largest wineries sell about 70 percent of the total volume shipped in the U.S. Gallo has about 30 percent and United Vintners, a Heublein corporation subsidiary which uses the Colony brand name, about 15 percent of the total.)

3. (a) Compare what you consider to be the key success factors in the following industries: aerospace, auto repair, cigarettes, coal mining, cosmetics, electric utilities, ski resorts, women's dresses. (b) In which industry would you prefer to build your career?

4. Several years ago bowling became a very popular pastime. New large bowling alleys were constructed in all parts of the country, and companies making bowling alley equipment prospered. Many people still bowl, but the rapid growth has stopped; both equipment manufacturers and alleys are in financial difficulties. (a) What characteristics of demand are illustrated in the experience of the bowling industry? (b) To what extent do you think skiing will have a similar experience? Explain the similarities and dissimilarities present.

5. How does the "ease of entry" of new firms into the restaurant industry as compared to the difficulty of entry into the basic aluminum industry affect: (a) the nature of competition in each industry, and (b) the crucial factors for success in each industry?

6. Company analysis outlined in this chapter focused on profit enterprises. To test the applicability of the same approach to nonprofit enterprises, use the outline to analyze the outlook for your university or college. Use both the industry section and the company position section.

7. Lowering of tariff barriers, improvements in transportation, and greater similarities in consumer tastes due to more travel and better communications —all tend to increase international trade. How does this trend affect the outlook of an English manufacturer of men's suits? a U.S. manufacturer of children's dresses?

8. Assume that you have decided to open a new carwash establishment in the city in which you now live. Your alternatives on production methods range from a hand operation with only hoses, brushes, and rags as equipment to a fully automatic tunnel that can be run by a single individual who collects money as the cars enter. (a) Would you invest in the capital intensive process or the labor intensive process? (b) Does your answer to (a) imply a general view that new operations in your city in any line of business should be as capital intensive (or labor intensive) as technology will permit? (c) What other competitive strengths do you believe will be crucial to your success in your new venture?

9. What future do you see in the construction industry for Ericson Company which has been building 3- and 4-bedroom, single-family houses in Southern California for the last thirty years? Ericson builds houses that sell for the median price in its location ($100,000 in 1980 dollars), uses union labor entirely and buys materials (lumber, plywood, fasteners, etc.) from local wholesalers. Until 1979, but not since, the increase in prices of the finished product outstripped increases in labor and materials costs.

10. What effect does the "indexing" of wage rates and salaries in union-organized companies and of Social Security payments to the changes in the Consumers Price Index published by the U.S. Department of Labor have on the incomes

of the recipient, on the costs of the companies, and on the general price inflation?

CASE 3
Fact Oil Company (R)

The board of directors of the FACT Oil Company has before it a recommendation from the firm's executive group for the expenditure of about $2,200 million on new capital investment over the next eleven years. Approval will mean a marked departure from previous company strategy and a chance to be an early entrant in a new and developing source of energy.

The company's situation. FACT Oil, unlike the integrated major oil companies such as Texaco, Gulf, Shell, and Exxon, has been primarily a transportation, refining, and wholesale distributing company. It purchases crude oil in Venezuela and from producers in the United States, refines the oil in the U.S., and sells refinery products through its own distribution network to independent retailers east of the Rocky Mountains. This way of operating has been reasonably successful in the past, but company executives, looking forward to 1990 and beyond, do not believe that it will be as successful in the future.

Since they see no way to follow the strategy of the integrated majors (worldwide exploration and production, refining outside the United States, and worldwide marketing), they propose something else—becoming a raw material supplier to energy consumers in the United States as well as continuing current operations on the same physical scale. "We believe energy requirements will increase by 50% by the year 2000 and we want to increase our share of that growing market. Since U.S. demand is above the indigenous supply capability and while the majors in the industry meet the deficiency by oil and gas imports, we have an alternate strategy—to develop 'frontier' indigenous sources and search for attractive niches on this 'frontier.'"

Table 1 and Chart 1 represent the proposal.

Table 1—Summary*

	1980	1995 Stand Pat	1995 Proposed
Sales (millions)	$2,600	$3,900	$5,100
Net income (millions)	159	90	440
% on sales	6.1	2.3	8.6
Assets (millions)	$3,100	3,100	5,300

*Estimates included predicted rises in energy prices and costs above the general price level. Changes in general price level not included.

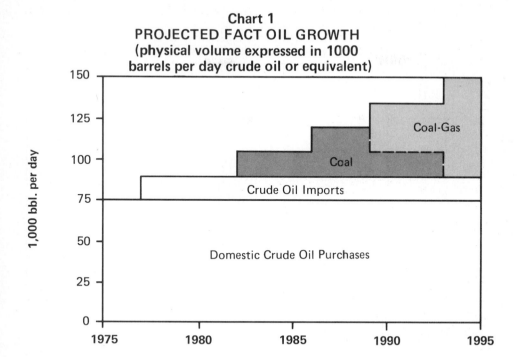

Chart 1
PROJECTED FACT OIL GROWTH
(physical volume expressed in 1000
barrels per day crude oil or equivalent)

Approval is requested for (a) the proposed coal-based concept and (b) expenditures of $400 million this year to begin mine development.

An array of facts and predictions bears on the wisdom of the proposed shift in strategy. The primary data that company management has available are summarized below.

Energy demand and supply. The United States is the world's largest user of energy. Its consumption in 1980 was 50% more than all of Western Europe, whose combined population was much larger (75%) than the U.S. total. This demand for energy comes from many sources: generation of electricity, 27%; transportation, 25%; industry (excluding electricity), 24%; residential and commercial (excluding electricity), 18%; and other, 6%. Despite many uncertainties, America's appetite for energy may perhaps double by the year 2000.

Chart 2 reflects a projected annual growth rate in U.S. use of energy of 1.8%. This rate is well below the 1900–1975 average of 3.4%. It is also less than various predictions of the rate of growth of U.S. Gross National Product. The forecast is that the U.S. economy can grow at a higher rate than the use of energy. Conservation factors in the use of gasoline by automobiles, in the use of oil and gas for house-heating and in generating and using electricity for power are expected to slow down the rate of the growth of energy.

The Office of Emergency Preparedness of the United States has independently developed an energy demand projection based on maximum efforts in conservation in the United States. *See Demand with Conservation chart, page 65.*

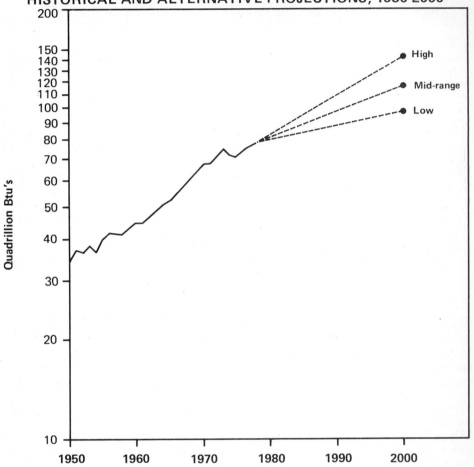

Chart 2
U.S. ENERGY CONSUMPTION
HISTORICAL AND ALTERNATIVE PROJECTIONS, 1950-2000

Source: S. H. Schurr, *Energy in America's Future, Resources for the Future* (Baltimore: Johns Hopkins Press, 1979), page 194.

Conservation efforts required to achieve the above forecast would be to: improve home insulation; upgrade commercial construction standards; shift 10% of freight from trucks to rail; set up freight consolidation centers; provide more mass transit (produce smaller, more efficient autos); design more efficient air-conditioners; recycle waste heat and scrap metal; and replace inefficient industrial processes.

The uncertainty regarding the effectiveness of conservation measures and about other influences and demand is indicated in the range shown on Chart 2.

Demand with Conservation

Year	All Energy	Oil Consumed
1985	92 quadrillion Btu's*	17.5 million bbls. daily
1990	106 " "	19.5 " " "

*One quadrillion British Thermal Units (Btu's) equals the amount of energy produced by 172 million barrels of oil, 1 trillion cubic feet of natural gas, or 41.6 million tons of coal.

The future sources of energy for the U.S. are also uncertain. New discoveries of domestic oil and gas are barely keeping pace with withdrawals, so added imports seem inevitable (and expensive). Nuclear energy, once regarded as a great way to conserve natural resources, is subject to so many political constraints that its future contribution to supply is very unclear. Few major sites remain for water power. Solar and geothermal energy will remain highly localized under known technology. Coal is abundant, but as explained in later discussion, mining and conversion problems must be overcome. The following table indicates the typical range of informed estimates of U.S. energy sources in 2000. Of course, with the projected total rising more than 50%, even a constant share of the total implies strong growth.

Estimates of Sources of U.S. Energy

	1975	2000
Oil	46%	39% to 42%
Natural Gas	29	30 to 32
Coal	19	18 to 21
Nuclear	2	2 to 6
Hydro, Solar and Geothermal	4	3 to 6
	100%	

Coal. In all of the energy projections given on the preceding pages, coal plays an important role.

How much coal does the United States have? There is no single answer, and expert estimates differ. The U.S. Geological Survey has identified 1.5 trillion tons—theoretically enough to last for 2,500 years at a mining rate of 600 million tons a year. But most of this cannot be recovered with existing technology at the prices current in the 1980's. The best estimate of readily recoverable reserves is 450 billion tons, enough to last the U.S. for 200 years beyond 1995 at a then-projected mining rate of 2 billion tons per year. And this assumes no advances in technology or in real prices from 1975 to 1995. One hundred and twenty-five million tons are low sulfur (1% S or less), and 75% of this is in the Western area that runs south from Montana and North Dakota through Wyoming, Utah, and Colorado to the Four Corners area of northern Arizona and New Mexico. Most of the western coal can be strip-mined at a cost (in 1980) of $12 to $16 per ton, compared to deep-mining costs of $20 to $25. These are costs at the minemouth, and they pertain to utility-grade coal—not the low-sulfur, low-ash, high Btu content, strong coal sold for metallurgical purposes.

U.S. Production of Bituminous Coal
(millions of net tons)

Year	Amount	Year	Amount
1920	569	1970	603
1940	461	1975	650
1960	416	1980	760

Predictions made in the 1970's of greatly expanded demand for coal have been borne out by rapidly rising prices rather than major increases in output. Restrictions on output have not been arbitrary but have been the natural consequence of: the time required to develop and open a new mine (2 to 5 years); delayed investment in new mines while company managements waited for clarification of federal legislation on strip mining (land restoration adds $2 to $6 a ton to costs and is impossible where rainfall is less than 10 inches per year); a 28% decline in productivity as mine-safety legislation began to be obeyed by the coal owners and enforced somewhat by the Interior Department; and shortages of skilled miners.

Despite their long experience, the managements of existing coal companies were not able to increase output substantially in an environment with new constraints to which they had to adjust.

Coal prices paid by utility companies increased, on the average, from $8 per ton in 1973 to $21 per ton in 1980.

Coal gasification and liquefaction. The technology to convert bituminous coal or lignite into a gas with 900 to 1,000 Btu's per cubic foot (natural gas averages 1,032 Btu's) is a combination of the Lurgi technology developed in Germany during the 1930's to turn coal into a medium-Btu gas and a newer "methanation" process to bring the heating value up to 950 Btu's per cubic foot. Two pilot plants have been in operation since 1974.

On a commercial scale, El Paso Natural Gas and Western Gasification Company broke ground in 1975 for coal mines and gasification plants that they planned to have in operation in northwestern New Mexico in 1978. El Paso's project was announced in 1971. Four years later it had received approvals from the state and federal governments and the Navajo tribe to invest $180 million in a coal mine and about $700 million in the total project (the original estimate of the investment cost was 40% less). Governmental approval and the ground-breaking turned out not to mean that the coal gasification plants would be built, however. After further litigation and the skyrocketing of construction costs, El Paso Natural Gas abandoned the project and turned to buying liquified natural gas from Algeria.

American Natural Resources Co. then took up the idea of building a commercial-scale gasification plant in North Dakota. It announced plans to spend $1.2 billion for one plant to produce 125 million cubic feet a day of pipeline quality gas from coal. This proposal—strongly favored by officials of the Energy Department—has been both rejected and approved by various commissions and legislative bodies as the company sought to have its investment and a 13% rate of return guaranteed by, first, the Federal Government, and then by several gas pipeline companies (which are regulated by the Federal Power Commission). One more project was announced in 1980 by E.G. & G. Inc. A subsidiary, E.G. & G. Syn Fuels, Inc., bought 3,800 acres in Massachusetts and planned to have a plant operating in 1986—if environmental regulations could be met and if the Federal Government would, eventually, guarantee its loans.

Four processes for producing liquid fuel from coal are under study in various places around the world. Only South Africa is in actual production with plants reported to be highly subsidized. The other three processes are expected to still be in the laboratory stage beyond 1981. One pilot plant processing 20 tons per day was opened in 1969 and abandoned five years later. Hydrogenation, the process with the most promise, was predicted in 1974 to require 10 to 20 years for development at a "prudent rate."

The Energy Department, and its predecessors in Washington, have often announced that "the top priority now is developing a synthetic-fuels industry that could make a petroleum-like liquid and a synthetic form of natural gas from coal." Priorities have become plans but, as yet, plans have not become plants.

A few years ago the Interior Department received "only three" industry proposals to participate with the federal government in building a coal-to-oil demonstration plant—far fewer than were expected. The demonstration plant was estimated to cost from $100 million to $400 million and would produce a coal liquid suitable for use as boiler fuel. An executive of one nonbidding company said that the firm decided to refrain from bidding "because of tight money and because Washington is still weighing what steps, if any, it will take to assure the ability of synthetic fuels to compete with crude oil."

Management's proposal. The presentation by the executive group to a special meeting of the board of directors of FACT Oil Company opened with a review of alternate possibilities that had been considered as a means for the company to maintain its share of the energy market.

(1)Enter into a large program of crude oil exploration and production. The risks are large (1 successful exploratory well in 10 drilled) and new operations of drilling on the continental shelf of the United States require an advanced technology that FACT Oil Company does not have, since to date it has primarily purchased crude oil. Exploring abroad means high political risks, with ownership of any oil pools found remaining with the host government. Expansion based on foreign crude oil also contributes to the U.S. balance of payments problems and would require the company to double or treble the size of its transportation system.

(2) Expand the company's refineries in the United States and increase marketing efforts with a company brand and company-leased retail stations. Refining capacity in the U.S. is low and products are imported from abroad because refineries have had low profit margins on the average for the past decade. Prospects depend on competition from foreign refineries and on the stringency of environmental regulations such as those of the state of Delaware. Other oil companies are not attempting

to increase market share in the U.S. by adding retail stations but are pushing marketing elsewhere in the world. There are more than sufficient retail outlets in existence to meet U.S. demand.

*(3) **Produce synthetic crude from either oil shale in Colorado or the Athabaskan tar sands.*** The technology of getting oil from shale has been stuck at the pilot plant stage since 1958 when Union Oil finally abandoned the first major attempt. Three consortiums are still working in the Piceance Basin with little chance for success until at least 1990. Use of Athabaskan tar sands, in northern Canada, has encountered much higher investment and operating costs than anticipated. One 50,000 barrel-per-day refinery has had a loss for eight years. Closing down a much larger project during construction was forestalled only by a capital injection of a billion dollars by the Canadian government.

*(4) **Coal gasification and liquefaction.*** Executives of the firm believe this path holds the best promise. Political risks of expropriation are nil. Natural gas has been in short supply in the United States for over two years and all reliable forecasts expect a continued shortage for the next 10 years. New gas wells are being drilled only in unusual circumstances when the probability of finding gas is above 0.6.

While two natural gas transmission line companies have already begun projects to turn coal into pipeline quality gas, FACT executives see this as an opportunity not really explored by the major oil and gas producers. They believe it to be a niche into which they can move and establish a solid position. Until the gasification plants are ready, coal can be mined and sold on the market—especially low-sulfur coal, for which demand appears to be increasing rapidly. The company has obtained options on low-sulfur coal leases in Montana, near the Yellowstone River, and in West Virginia. The Montana coal could be strip-mined; the Eastern coal would be mined underground.

*(5) **Recommendation.*** "That the directors approve our plan to purchase, develop, and implement the coal-based program. The project economics are illustrated in Chart 3. The predicted return on coal mining of 12% on the investment has minimal risk. Coal is a proven commodity with an assured market. The 17% predicted return on the gasification plant has some risk, but we can hold off entering the market until the price is right (about $9.00 per 10^6 Btu or per 1,000 cubic feet). We can sell the gas to utilities. Will they buy? Yes, the French have contracted for liquefied natural gas from Algeria at $6.00 per 1,000 cubic feet, and both Mexico and Canada are moving toward this price from $5.00 in 1981. Alternatively, we can sell the gas to industrial users such as steel companies for furnace gas or to electric utilities if the nuclear-power programs continue to be delayed for cost and safety reasons and if the first experimental U.S. fast-breeder reactor does not come on-stream in 1985.

"Therefore, we request approval of: (1) the coal-based concept so that intensive and specific planning can be undertaken, and (2) immediate approval to exercise our options to buy coal leases and purchase one existing mine at a cost of $400 million."

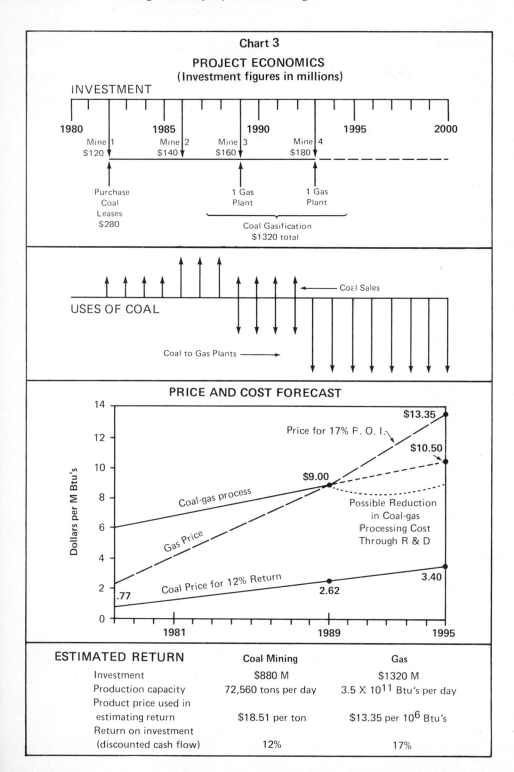

Chart 3

PROJECT ECONOMICS
(Investment figures in millions)

INVESTMENT

1980   1985   1990   1995   2000

Mine 1   Mine 2   Mine 3   Mine 4
$120 $140 $160 $180

Purchase   1 Gas   1 Gas
Coal   Plant   Plant
Leases
$280   Coal Gasification
                            $1320 total

USES OF COAL

← Coal Sales

Coal to Gas Plants ⟶

PRICE AND COST FORECAST

Dollars per M Btu's

$13.35

Price for 17% P. O. I.

$10.50

$9.00

Coal-gas process

Possible Reduction
in Coal-gas
Processing Cost
Through R & D

Gas Price

Coal Price for 12% Return   3.40

.77   2.62

1981   1989   1995

ESTIMATED RETURN	Coal Mining	Gas
Investment	$880 M	$1320 M
Production capacity	72,560 tons per day	3.5×10^{11} Btu's per day
Product price used in estimating return	$18.51 per ton	$13.35 per 10^6 Btu's
Return on investment (discounted cash flow)	12%	17%

Questions

(1) What outlook do you see for coal gasification as a source of energy in the United States? For coal?

(2) What is your appraisal of the strategy of the integrated major energy companies?

(3) As a director, how would you vote on the recommendations by the FACT Oil Company executives?

PREDICTING RESPONSES OF KEY ACTORS

In the preceding two chapters we treated the external dynamics as irrepressible forces to which a firm should adjust, and the relative strengths and weaknesses of the firm as a given inheritance. The present chapter digs deeper into that setting. It looks at the way key people are likely to respond to fresh actions which we or other persons initiate. To at least a limited degree, each of us tries to reshape our world. So we need to predict responses and counter-responses to initiatives we or our peers thrust into the system. The wisdom of any strategic move depends in part on the resistance and retaliation, or the cooperation, which that move is likely to evoke.

After distinguishing between passive and hostile environments, this chapter deals with two issues: How are key actors likely to respond to our thrusts? In light of that predicted response, what kind of alignments among actors should we try to establish?

HOSTILE VERSUS PASSIVE ENVIRONMENT

Passive Environment

Our pioneer heritage creates a bias about strategy. In the traditional Western scenario, the physical obstacles were great, but customers liked the new services provided, employees welcomed new and better jobs, and supporting organizations such as railroads cooperated. Despite a few hostile Indians in the background and occasional feuds between the cattlemen and settlers, the environment was basically friendly and benevolent. Our task in that setting would have been to provide the vision, mobilize resources, and share in the hard systematic work of turning opportunity into achievement.

Note that in this view a series of well-planned moves would have overcome the obstacles, and that the response of people affected was pre-set. Occasionally such a relatively simple situation exists, but most strategy today runs into other people's strategy and must deal with their countermoves.

Hostile Environment

In a "hostile" environment several key groups will resist the moves called for in our strategy. In fact, they probably will be aggressively pursuing their own objectives which may include our fitting into *their* plans. How much direct conflict arises will depend, of course, on the strategy we elect. Perhaps some arrangement can be found which will be at least acceptable to two or more groups. But negotiations will be necessary, and in that process our strategy may have to be modified. Everyone is pushing; our aim in this game is to position ourselves so that we are not pushed way off course—or, if we are lucky and smart, occasionally get pulled along toward our goal by their efforts (like riding the surf).

The scramble for production of wide-body, medium-range jet airplanes—at the end of the 1970's—illustrates this kind of process. Airbus Industries, a joint French-German venture, was several years ahead in the market with its 240-seat model. Boeing countered with a proposed new line of planes (B767, B777) focused on a similar market segment. The physical characteristics of both Airbus and Boeing lines were sharply competitive: lower fuel consumption, less noise, wide-body, medium-range, around 200-passenger size. But much more than plane design was involved in making sales in the important international market. Foreign airlines need the financial backing of their local governments, and that backing could be secured only by recognizing other concerns of the respective governments. To help deal with local employment and nationalism, Boeing negotiated subcontracts for components in Italy and Japan, and for Rolls-Royce engines in England. Airbus, via the French government, courted Spain with support for entry into the Common Market, and India with broad trade benefits. Clearly the groups vitally concerned extended beyond the plane producers and airline customers, and an array of interlocking strategies on issues far removed from plane production were involved.

Lease financing of computers is a simpler example of a hostile environment—as we are using the term. For several years financial firms thought lease financing was a splendid investment. The firm with capital to invest located a company that had just made a large purchase of computers. The financial firm bought the computers from the user and leased them back again. In this arrangement the user in effect borrowed capital at favorable terms and usually obtained tax benefits; the lessor found an attractive investment. Soon, however, more people became involved. Smaller manufacturers of computers and peripheral equipment relied on (and often had formal agreements with) leasing firms to help make sales. But these manufacturers also relied on local service companies to maintain their equipment, and this service was vital to keep the equipment running—and the lease viable. Then, users occasionally went bankrupt or their needs changed, so part of the equipment had to be resold; and this often brought in a fifth party. The business was complicated by rapid technological change, and by a practice of manufacturers such as Digital Equipment Corporation to lower prices on older models.

Consequently, to be successful in lease financing of computers, a financial firm has to develop formal or informal understandings with equipment manufacturers, service companies, technical consultants, and resale agents in addition to its direct "customers," the equipment users. Each of these "actors" has a particular environment and a particular strategy, and the terms on which cooperation will be continued have to be negotiated.

In both of these examples, wide-bodied jets and computer leasing, strategy goes beyond selecting an attractive domain. Key parts of the environment are busily pushing their own objectives, and our strategy must be linked to theirs. Directly or indirectly we try to manipulate this environment. In the process our strategy may be modified, especially because the various actions and reactions of other actors are hard to predict.

In a "hostile" environment, strategy must be adroit and adaptive. Relationships with key actors vary widely. We may elect to fight with a competitor head-on, as Avis does with Hertz. Or the competition may be mixed with cooperation, even to the point where competition is publicly denied, as is the usual relation among universities and among hospitals.

Sometimes a desired result is so expensive or so risky that no one firm wants to seek it alone. So a joint venture focused on a particular outcome is created. The pipeline bringing crude oil from the north slope of Alaska is such a venture. Several pilot plants experimenting with gasification of coal also are jointly sponsored by companies which compete on most other fronts.

In many other relationships mutual dependence is pervasive and continuing. Professional football and the TV networks, for instance, have a durable marriage; clearly the football teams could not operate in their present manner without the broadcast income. Automobile manufacturers and their dealer organizations are likewise dependent on each other.

Coalitions and alliances may be multifaceted. For example, a company in the specialized business of insuring real estate titles is valuable to— and also dependent on the goodwill of—mortgage lenders, surveyors, real estate brokers, and in some areas local lawyers who make the title search. In this arena, exchange of favors and mutual trust is vital to success. Similarly, in the growing field of solid-waste disposal, strategy must recognize the interaction between equipment manufacturers (and their maintenance organizations), trash collectors, environmental control agencies, bond underwriters, and users of the output such as steam for utility generators.

Society is increasingly complex and interdependent, in terms of technology, trade, regulation, and geographic scope. External alignments must fit these trends, and change with them. And as just illustrated, there are a variety of choices in the way the relationships will be structured.

ANALYSIS OF KEY ACTORS

Success and, indeed, survival of every business depends upon either obtaining the support or neutralizing the attacks of key actors in its environment. We live in a highly interdependent world. And to steer a course through this ever-changing structure, we need a keen insight into the behavior of those actors who affect our fate.

Who Must Be Considered?

Resource suppliers and customers interact directly with the business. As suggested in the discussion of the *resource converter model* in Chapter 1, included here are employees, material suppliers, bankers, stockholders, governmental agencies, other community groups, and the like. Because all these contributors are more or less dependent on our company, they are often called "stakeholders." Typically, an exchange relationship exists—a trading of inducements for inputs; so for actors in these groups we are concerned with both what we give up and what we get in return.

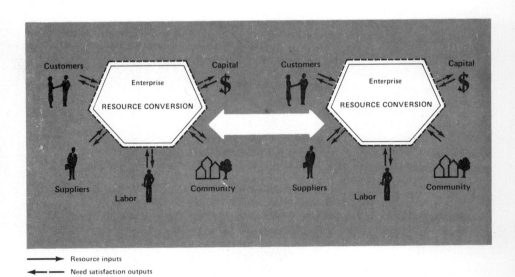

→ Resource inputs
←--- Need satisfaction outputs

Competitors are also important—competitors for *resources* and competitors for *customers*. Unless we are careful, the actions of these people can upset our best laid plans. The analysis can be extended to a third level—to the resource suppliers, customers, and competitors of our competitors—but this extension is necessary only in special cases.

As a practical matter, only *key* actors in the above groups warrant close analysis. A "key" actor is a stakeholder or competitor who in relation to us has a lot of *power*. A customer who buys over twenty-five percent of our output, the only available supplier of fuel for our plant, a competitor who has the capability of hiring away our engineering staff, a regulatory agency that approves the quality of our new products—are examples of key actors.

What Are the Motivations of Key Actors?

Because we want to predict what key actors are likely to do if left alone, how they will respond to our initiatives, and often how we can modify their behavior, it behooves us to know what makes them tick. How do they normally behave, and what might cause them to change?

A key actor, like any of us, operates in a specific social/economic system, and has a going enterprise with its particular resources and established relationships with external groups. (We should know what these are.) Inevitably there will be *patterns of behavior*—normal responses to normal pressures. This established flow gives us a base line for predicting future behavior. To understand it we should do our best to look at the world as the key actor sees it.

Just as we appraise our own relative strengths and weaknesses in estimating our own outlook—see the second half of the preceding chapter—so too should we size up the strengths and weaknesses of each key actor. Such a "capability profile" of our competitors is especially valuable. This assessment will tell us what is *possible* for the key actor to do and where her or his limitations lie.

Next, we take an empathetic look at the future. For these actors, what *new pressures and opportunities* are likely to arise (shifts in their markets, cost changes, new technology, etc.), and how are they likely to react? In particular, what will be absorbing most of their attention? what internal or external resource limitations will they confront? what commitments which restrict their options are they likely to make? what are their chief risks? what could upset their plans?

Experience indicates that a surprising amount of information about any organization operating in the public sphere can be assembled by systematic observation. Speeches, press releases, published data, announced plans, positions taken on controversial issues—when regularly pulled together and analyzed—give a broad picture. And many kinds of alignments with key actors provide personal contacts which are an additional source of data. More subtle is assessing the personalities of important executives, and the values they cherish. But even here, insights can be picked up directly and indirectly.

Such a key actor assessment serves several purposes: (1) The predicted behavior indicates what the actor is likely to try to impose on other actors—including us. (2) From the assessment, events or actions which will appeal to the actor can be surmised, and also weaknesses and vulnerabilities. These conclusions can be very useful in negotiating a desired alignment with that actor. (3) More specifically, the likely reaction of the actor to particular strategic moves that we might initiate can be predicted.

What Is the Relative Power of Key Actors?

Power, in the present context, is the ability of key actors to modify the conduct of others, and on the other hand, their ability to prevent someone else modifying their conduct. Obviously, relative power will affect which actor can pursue a strategy with the least concession to others.

In relationships between business organizations, power is based largely on an *ability to restrict the flow of desired inputs on attractive terms*. Thus, if OPEC can withhold needed crude oil it has a lot of power over petroleum refineries, or if a bank can withdraw necessary loans it has power over the borrower. To simplify the discussion, we will consider a large customer withholding an order, or a governmental agency withholding approval, as other examples of restriction of a desired input.

When we start analyzing power relationships, we soon see that there are degrees of power, costs of exercising power, and all sorts of countervailing power. For example, the degree of power I have over you depends on the number of good *alternative* sources you can turn to for the input I am providing. The fewer and less attractive the alternatives you have, the greater is my power. So one consideration in designing strategy is its effect on the number of alternatives which will remain open to you and to me. For instance, you may be a large and prestigious customer but I will hesitate to sell you a third of my output if there are few ways to replace this volume in the event you threaten to withdraw.

Of course, the other side of the coin is that I have power over you *if* you lack alternative sources of supply. Or, if through the help of my friends, the teamsters, I can delay your use of alternative sources, the impact is similar. Coalitions gain strength when, directly or indirectly, their membership can narrow the number of options various actors have.

The kind of power we are discussing is *potential;* only rarely is it actually exercised. In fact, most people are reluctant to use their power—for several reasons. The person being pressured may call up countervailing power and will start to develop new alternatives (coal, solar energy, etc. as alternatives for crude oil); future friendship and trust will be lost; a reputation for harsh dealings may spoil relationships with other suppliers. On the other hand, total reluctance to use power can undercut the influence of a person who will soon be regarded as a "paper tiger." Consequently, in assessing power we have to consider willingness to use it as well as capability.

In summary, the analytical approach just outlined gives a basis for setting up external alignments. First, key actors are identified—the external organizations or groups whose continuing cooperation is vital to our strategic moves. Second, for each key actor an assessment is made of his or her motivations, strengths and weaknesses, probable future behavior, and likely response to our actions. Third, the relative power of each key actor to pursue a particular course is estimated. This analysis provides insights about present and probable future behavior of the human forces in our environment; these are the dynamic elements from which a realistic interaction strategy must be forged.

CHOICE OF ALIGNMENTS

As when a nation designs its international strategy, a look first at the simpler one-to-one relationships shows the varying colored pieces that then must be fitted into the overall mosaic.

One-to-One Relationships

A business-unit's relations with its diverse resource suppliers, customers, and competitors are sure to take different forms. They range from close cooperation to sharp conflict. The matrix on the next page suggests a way to deal with this array.

When cooperation is likely to pay off. On one axis of the matrix we show the benefits to us of cooperating with a specific key actor. Our interests may be highly interdependent, as between Pratt & Whitney and Boeing in designing engines for the new wide-bodied jets; or, at the other extreme, the interest may be as contrary as NBC and CBS—what one wins in the number of viewers, the other loses. (Even in this latter example cooperation in dealing with other media or regulatory agencies may be beneficial.)

The other axis reflects relative power—our ability to impose our will on the other actor compared with the actor's capacity to make us conform to his or her will. Availability of alternatives and back-up resources are the usual sources of such power. Sears Roebuck and a small South Carolina manufacturer of dungarees are a classical example of the range on this scale.

The words in the quadrants merely suggest the kind of relationship with a key supplier or customer that we can readily achieve under the different conditions. Of course, each actor will view the situation from a unique perspective, and may prefer a course of action different from ours. So some negotiation and testing of power may be necessary.

The matrix has to be modified if it is applied to relations with *competitors*. As already noted, cooperation with a competitor can have a *negative* impact for us, and consequently behavior in the first and third quadrant may be direct conflict rather than cooperation.

AN APPROACH TO ONE-TO-ONE RELATIONSHIPS
(with a key supplier or customer)

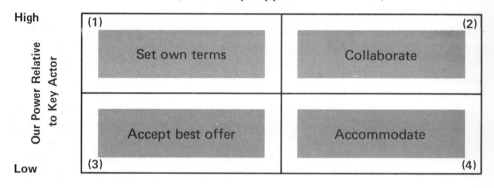

Note:
If the key actor is a *competitor* instead of a supplier, the horizontal scale ranges from high to *negative* on the left end, and the suggestive terms change to "Fight aggressively" in quadrant 1 and "Defend" in quadrant 3.

Open warfare, the Avis versus Hertz syndrome, is implied for competitors finding themselves on the left side of the matrix. Rarely, in fact, is a fight to the death selected as a strategy. Besides being illegal if done deliberately in restraint of trade, competition is usually tempered by common interests which call for joint action on some fronts while competing on others. And clearly the business-unit whose relative power is weak will try to stall and look for new alternatives (e.g., a special market niche) where the big competitor will not follow. So the strategy choices for firms finding themselves in this kind of environment focuses more on selecting the basis (or bases) on which to compete, and determining the extent of joint action which will be acceptable on other dimensions.

Where the benefits of working together predominate (the righthand side of the matrix), cooperative alignments are called for. The more dynamic and uncertain the environment, the more attractive will be joint efforts with financiers, equipment suppliers, customers, regulatory agencies, etc. The electronics and computer industries grew rapidly partly because collaboration has been the prevailing relationship between suppliers and users. In contrast, the energy program in the late 1970's moved at a snail's pace in part because collaboration between interested parties proved very hard to sustain. (Governmental and public concern dealt more with who-would-get-what than with pooling resources to confront the monumental task.)

Relative power obviously affects the kind of joint action it is wise to seek. Two comparatively strong actors—for instance, Texas Instruments and General Motors approaching computerization of automobiles—can work as roughly equal partners. However, if one firm is weak relative to the other, it will probably have to "accommodate"; i.e., fit into the changing situation as best it can, accepting the dictates of the stronger actor as constraints while trying to develop some capabilities which will be attractive to the dominant partner.

While these two considerations, relative power and potential benefits of cooperation, provide insight into desirable one-to-one alignments, other factors deserve careful attention. Are the stakes high or low? If low, perhaps a modification of the traditional relationship does not warrant the expense. Legislation may prohibit certain kinds of joint effort. Past experience with either fighting or collaborating sets the stage for future alignments. Because all such factors are likely to vary from actor to actor, the optimum path to pursue in each relationship calls for particular attention.

Use of supplier analysis. A specific case will illustrate how the type of analysis just outlined clearly shaped the strategy of one company, Ethicon Sutures, at a critical stage in its development. Ethicon manufactures surgical sutures for stitching-up operations ranging from delicate eye repair to leg amputations. For years, surgeons threaded sutures through the eye of the needle used. (The needles, of course, vary greatly in size and shape.) Then a new kind of needle was invented that could be crimped at the factory onto the end of a piece of suture. This arrangement saved the trouble of threading the needle, but much more important, it reduced the hole that was pierced to draw the suture through the tissue.

Ethicon adopted a strategy of featuring the new needle-suture combination, each encased in a sterile container. But it ran into difficulty obtaining needles. Its primary needle supplier dealt chiefly in textile needles; surgical needles were a sideline. So when Ethicon asked this supplier to devise a technology to make the new type of needle, the supplier expressed reluctance and insisted on large volumes of each size and shape. Moreover, to increase volume the supplier reserved the right to sell needles to other suture companies. A second supplier, also focusing on textile needles, was even less interested; and a third, much smaller manufacturer lacked capital to tool up for the full line and also lacked quality control so important for the surgical market.

In terms of the matrix, the primary supplier had substantial power over Ethicon but did not see much benefit in close collaboration, so its relations with Ethicon fell in the first quadrant. Ethicon was in a weak bargaining position, yet the outcome of negotiations was vital to its new strategy. Further analysis of the R&D activity of the primary supplier indicated that this company intended to move away from the needle business. So Ethicon predicted that long-run prospects were poor for getting the relationship into quadrant 4, let alone quadrant 2.

Consequently, Ethicon decided it could not risk staying so dependent on an uninterested supplier. It first explored a joint venture with the smaller company to make one or two sizes of the new needle, but soon worked out an arrangement to acquire a stockholder position in the company. That enabled Ethicon to establish a collaborative relation with the company—quadrant 2. Several years were needed to develop the capability of this company to make the various kinds of needles with the necessary quality. And, as Ethicon cut back on purchases of traditional needles, its old suppliers became even less interested in maintaining prompt delivery and quality. All this slowed Ethicon's growth and delayed pushing its new product across the total market. But in the end Ethicon escaped from its dependent and therefore weak position.

Degrees of Collaboration

Economic theory and much of the business literature is preoccupied with competition. We are conditioned to think in terms of zero-sum games. A broader view of society, however, highlights the mechanisms by which people cooperate. The miracle of modern civilization is the way specialized outputs are combined, traded, and combined again to generate sophisticated services and goods. So when we talk of collaboration as one form of external alignment, we are dealing with a fundamental phenomenon.

Collaboration between key actors varies in degree.

1. *Informal mutual aid* is the most common. You help me as a neighborly act; later I probably return the favor. Sociologist Peter Blau observes that this sort of cooperation permeates social relations; it differs from economic exchanges in the unspecified nature of the return help, and requires a high amount of trust that mutually supportive actions will be continued.[1] This is the foundation of "good-will" with employees, suppliers, customers, bankers, and a host of other points in the environment.
2. *Formal agreements* covering the scope and nature of cooperation become necessary when advance commitments are large and when many individuals must have a consistent understanding about the relationship.
3. *Joint ventures* break out a particular area for intense collaborative activity and provide for a pooling of knowledge and resources related to that activity. The joint venture may be a temporary consortium for a large project such as the construction of a dam, or it may be a corporation with indefinite life.

---

[1]See Peter M. Blau, *Exchange and Power in Social Life* (New York: John Wiley & Sons, 1964).

4. *Mergers* carry collaboration to the extreme where separate identity is sacrificed for the benefits of central direction of the combined activities.[2]

Many other variations are possible. Nevertheless, these four degrees of collaboration clearly indicate the profound impact that external alignments can have on the process of strategy formulation.

Collaboration implies some sharing of decision-making. When American Motors undertakes selling Renault automobiles in the U.S. and probably using some Renault parts in its own production, clearly American Motors' strategy in the U.S. will include Renault inputs and vice versa. And under "accommodation" the adjustment of our initial plans is likely to be even greater. In other words, strategic planning involves dynamic give-and-take in which more than our own interests must be considered.

Of course, managers of a business-unit may choose to limit the extent of collaboration. Crown Cork & Seal, for instance, as a point of strategy, rarely installs can-making equipment in customers' plants—as do its leading competitors—because it wishes to retain greater flexibility. This successful company builds strong informal ties to its suppliers and customers but minimizes formal agreements.

The alignment with each key actor is a separate, unique relationship. The approach to shaping these relations outlined thus far stresses a one-to-one analysis because each key actor is important to us and each presents a distinct set of factors and opportunities. Nevertheless, a *collective view* of all of a company's external alignments is also desirable.

A company develops a reputation for aggressiveness, for fair dealings, for consistency, and the like, so the way one actor is treated raises expectations in other dealings. For example, in its early history Sears, Roebuck & Co. had a reputation for squeezing its suppliers once they became highly dependent on Sears' purchase orders. Later, Sears adopted a strategy of assuring its efficient suppliers that they could earn reasonable profits; and to carry out this strategy, close collaboration in product design and production scheduling is often undertaken. Not every one of Sears' thousands of suppliers agrees with the application, but the policy is clear: it does not use its power for short-run benefits, but rather for building a reputation as an attractive customer.

It is entirely possible to be ruthless in some spheres and cooperative in others—say, purchasing and labor relations—but some public rationalization of such behavior is desirable in order to create an aura of reliability, even integrity.

---

[2]An economist, Oliver E. Williamson, has recently argued in *Markets and Hierarchies*, (New York: The Free Press, 1975), that merged operations are more effective than competitive markets for handling exchange when mutual trust is vital. Mutual trust is necessary, he says, when uncertainty is high and key actors are few (two features of a hostile environment we listed at the opening of this chapter).

The combined set of alignments must also be weighed in terms of the total demands on resources. Few business-units have the personnel and capital to support several aggressive fights at the same time. In fact, even simultaneously maintaining close collaboration in several different areas may create severe problems of internal coordination. So, while the very essence of strategy deals with change, it is often advisable to ration or stagger the volatility.

Coalitions

The careful analysis of each key actor recommended early in this chapter provides the underlying data base upon which the various relationships are built. That same bank of data may suggest desirable alliances or coalitions. A coalition is an agreement among at least three actors on joint action; often some of the actors have only indirect relationships with each other.

Circumstances leading to coalitions. Often a business-unit discovers that by itself it cannot bring about the changes it desires. It lacks the necessary power. To reach its objectives it rallies allies. In practice this use of allies in coalitions is much more common than generally realized.

Quite diverse organizations may form a coalition around a common cause. For example, the "gun lobby" which opposes restrictions on private ownership and use of guns is supported by strange bedfellows: hunters, people who want guns to protect their homes, criminals, and firms with a commercial interest in the sale of guns and ammunition. Acting separately they would have limited impact on Congress, but their united strength has been remarkably potent.

In the gun lobby example, each participant has a direct concern about the outcome. A variation is found in the support of tariff barriers. Here, trading of support is common—I'll support your protection if you'll support mine. Such mutual helping of friends is found in all sorts of business situations from the sale of consulting services to "professional courtesy" among doctors. We are not suggesting that participants in such coalitions are cavalier about giving their support, although some may be; considerable effort may be devoted to deserving the support. Rather, the point is that coalitions are necessary to achieve the desired impact.

As already noted, the allies may embrace people who are only indirectly involved. Thus, in the finance company example cited at the beginning of this chapter, equipment manufacturers, service agencies, and resale brokers are all included in the coalition. All are required to make the purchase and lease-back practice a viable business, and each actor has to adopt a strategy regarding the coalitions to be joined.

Basically, when coalitions are formed, one or more business-units recognize that they cannot passively wait until the people with whom they have direct dealings are all set to act. Instead, they actively sponsor a whole chain of events by several different agencies. Consider a grain dealer wishing to sell feed to catfish raisers. Taking a cue from the way frying chickens are now raised and marketed by the millions, the grain dealer has to interest farmers in mass production of catfish in artificial lakes. This is appealing because catfish are very efficient converters of grain feed into meat. But to market the output, local "factories" are necessary to clean, cut, package, and freeze the meat. Refrigerated trucks must take the frozen fish to wholesale distribution points. And a marketing company has to sell the product either to "fish and chips" and other restaurants or to a slowly emerging retail-store market. These are the main actors, although cooperation of zoologists, government inspectors, and others is also essential.

The way such a new "industry" is developed and the successful entrepreneurs establish themselves is through a coalition. Perhaps one enterprise will undertake two or more steps, but complete vertical integration is unlikely. So someone has to appreciate what conditions are necessary to attract collaborators into each step, and then induce related actors to adjust their activities in a way that will create these conditions. The leading and profitable firms in this new business will be those who have mastered the art of forming and guiding coalitions.

Coalition in the health field. Coalitions may be vital in all sorts of settings. For example, an old hospital located in the downtown section of a typical city faced a dismal outlook. Its leading doctors and full-paying patients were moving to the suburbs; a proud history carried with it outmoded facilities; Medicaid patients could not provide or attract resources for rebuilding. The bold new strategy was to become a teaching hospital focusing on specialities; this would attract a high-quality staff, and full-paying patients would be sent for special treatment on referral from suburban hospitals. However, a wide array of allies were needed. The state medical authorities had to bow to local political pressure for a teaching hospital in that part of the state. The Veterans Administration had to locate one of its new health centers on an adjacent site, providing an additional volume of use of the specialty capabilities. The city had to clear land for new buildings and help finance a closed (safe) parking garage. The trustees had to raise additional funds for upgrading the plant. And this hospital complex had to be a significant part of a broad plan for revitalizing the downtown section of the city.

Throughout several years of planning and development, the critical job of the hospital administrators was to keep all the contributing elements in back of the plan. This proved to be predominantly a political task. Alternative suggestions kept appearing, usually with sponsorship from competing locations. To meet these challenges some modifications in the original strategy were negotiated. A continuing promotional effort has been necessary to sustain commitment to the venture at national, state, and local levels. Withdrawal of support at any one of these levels would probably kill the plan.

Coalitions may be necessary for survival, as the above examples indicate. We suggest that they be approached as elaborations of the simpler direct alignments every enterprise must cultivate. A coalition network is indeed more complicated since more actors are involved and inducements to cooperate may come from third parties, but the analysis of motivations and options of each key actor is still the starting point.

CONCLUSION

Predicting the behavior of key actors is an important supplement to judgment about the industry and company outlook recommended in the previous chapters. The broader forecasts about the setting in which company action will take place are indeed essential; but those forecasts pass over the more specific help or hindrance which can be expected from other people who are also active in that same setting. A forecast of likely moves of at least the key actors should be added to our total assessment.

Especially useful is a prediction of the responses and counter-responses of key actors to our own initiatives. The business environment is not inert and passive. Instead, many firms are each pushing their own programs, and these firms may welcome or oppose what we try to do. The ensuing negotiations may then modify previous drives. A whole array of alignments with stakeholders and competitors will be developed. Obviously, we should try to anticipate how this dynamic give-and-take process will work out.

Such a careful analysis of our competitors, our major suppliers, and our major customers will provide valuable input into the decision-making of central management. It probably will influence the design of strategy and the choice of policy.

An approach for predicting the responses of key actors has been outlined in this chapter. First comes careful analysis—leading to capability profiles —of key actors: *who* must be considered, *what* motivates each one, what is the *relative power* of each. Then with this background, the likely alignments are predicted. Among the possible arrangements which should be considered are (1) simple one-to-one relationships, (2) varying degrees of collaboration where joint action appears feasible, and (3) coalitions.

The next chapter will discuss how these forecasts, along with those from Chapters 2 and 3, are used to design a strategy for a business-unit.

We should note, again, that strategy formulation does not follow a simple sequence. Instead, it is iterative. Forecasts suggest possible strategies; analysis of these strategies calls for further forecasts; these new forecasts point to other alternatives; and so on. This recycling is especially true of key actor analysis because we are specifically concerned with the way competitors and stakeholders are likely to respond to various strategic moves that we are contemplating. The recommended approach continues to be useful throughout. But the first application rarely will provide all the estimates which will eventually be needed.

QUESTIONS FOR CLASS DISCUSSION

1. Boeing invested $3 billion in developing its new series of wide-bodied planes—the 767, and 777 briefly discussed in the opening of this chapter. This sum was twice the net worth of the company. Make a list of the dozen most important key actors Boeing should have analyzed prior to embarking on such a large program. (If you don't know company names, at least identify them by function.) Explain why you selected these actors.

2. Select a "competitor" of the college or university you are now attending, and prepare a "key actor" analysis along the lines outlined on pages 74 and 75 (patterns of behavior, capability profile, new pressures and opportunities). How might this information be useful to your college in its planning?

3. (a) Where would you place each of the following on the matrix appearing in this chapter? Assume that you are the first actor named in each pair: (1) a Chevrolet dealer in relation to the Chevrolet Division of General Motors; (2) your school cafeteria in relation to you; (3) the Springfield Hospital in relation to the union which is the certified bargaining agent for nurses in the hospital; (4) Exxon and the prime contractor building a supertanker for you.

   (b) Do the descriptive words in the quadrant selected in each situation suggest what you think the relationship would be?

4. In the Ethicon example described in the chapter, the company needed specially designed sterile containers as well as special needles. The containers were to be molded plastic tubes, which could be produced by quite a few firms. What degree of collaboration should Ethicon seek in obtaining these containers?

5. If you were president of a shoe manufacturing company, under what circumstances might you collaborate (a) with a competitor for customers, (b) with a competitor for labor, and (c) with a competitor for leather?

6. MacMillan observes, "Coalition members do not join the coalition without bringing with them their demands, and the support of these members could easily be given to alternative coalitions . . . Each member will, therefore, make a set of demands on the coalition to commit itself to certain goals. . . . However, it is often impossible for the coalition to satisfy *all* the demands of *all* its members. . . . A potential member will join only if he feels that the policy commitments of the coalition will promote his own goals, and he will stay only as long as he expects the coalition to be successful."[3] Use the hospital example appearing near the end of this chapter to illustrate MacMillan's points.

7. Assume that you are an executive in the public utility company serving your home area. Also assume that careful studies made by your company show that

---

[3]Ian MacMillan, *Strategy Formulation: Political Concepts* (St. Paul: West Publishing Company, 1978).

a new nuclear generating plant (with a full complement of safety devices) is clearly the most economical way to meet the growing demand for power in that area. Consequently, the management committee of your company has tentatively decided to seek approval to build the nuclear plant. The belief of the management committee, however, is that a *coalition* supporting the project must be formed if government approval is granted over the anticipated opposition of environmental groups. What membership do you suggest for such a coalition? Why do you think these people will support the project? What power do they have over whom? What kind and how powerful a coalition might the opposition muster?

8. The resource converter model was used in Chapter 1 to explain social responsibilities of business. In this chapter the stakeholders identified in that model are singled out as potential "key actors." This clearly implies a connection. But (a) by definition actors have power over us, whereas (b) social responsibility usually refers to situations where we have power over other persons. Do you agree with the limitation placed on social responsibility in (b) above? Are coalitions and one-to-one collaborations outside the scope of social responsibilities?

CASE 4
Essex Creek Disposal Co.

Essex Creek Disposal Co. faces difficult questions about who should take the initiative and who should bear the cost of "environmental protection." Company officers are subject to several conflicting pressures.

The company itself was born an unwanted child of an outlying housing development. The builders of Essex Manor, a 300-unit garden apartment and home development, had to include sewage disposal in their plans for converting a large farm into a modern housing complex. Lewis Township[1] has no general sewage system—other than septic tanks for individual homes—but insisted on a biochemical plant for a population concentration like Essex Manor. To meet this need, Essex Creek Disposal Co. was formed.

Essex Creek Disposal Co. is a small, privately owned public utility, chartered to serve Essex Manor. It owns collecting lines, pumping equipment, and a treatment plant 2 miles from Essex Manor. Its effluent (which is potable) is discharged into Essex Creek. Initially the company was owned and operated by the promoter of Essex Manor. The promotor donated to the company about two thirds of the original investment and also set service charges low enough—$20 per quarter—to appear minor to prospective buyers of houses and apartments.

---

[1]Lewis Township is a subdivision of Clark County. The government provides all the local governmental services (education, police, etc.) for a 35 square mile area—except for two incorporated villages.

After the Essex Manor development was completed, the promoter wanted to move on to new ventures, and therefore sold all the common stock of Essex Creek Disposal Co. to a group of investors for a nominal amount. These present stockholders have diverse experience with local public utilities, and they bought the company with the belief that the state Public Utility Commission (which must approve changes in utility rates) would agree that the heavy investment justifies some increase in service charges. Mr. Boynton Boyd, Jr., president of Essex Creek Disposal Co., says, "The $600,000 invested in this company entitles the owners to roughly $36,000 income per year, even under the very limited profits allowed public utilities."

During its six years of operation the company has never made a profit. Costs of chemicals, power, and labor have risen while service charges remained constant—with a resulting increase in annual deficits. (The condensed balance sheet and income statement for the past year are shown below.)

Condensed Balance Sheet

Assets		Liabilities and Equity	
Cash....................	$ 540	Accounts payable	$34,170*
Accounts receivable	2,268	Accrued items	9,606
Total current assets	$ 2,808	Total current liabilities ...	$43,776
Utility plant & equipment:		Long-term debt	75,000
Cost $596,777		Contribution to aid	
Depr. 71,613	525,164	construction	379,752
		Common stock..........	100,000
		Retained earnings........	(70,556)
		Total liabilities and	
Total assets	$527,972	equity	$527,972

*$30,000 of notes due to company officers are subordinated to other claims.

Condensed Income Statement

Total revenue	$ 25,920
Operating deductions from revenue:	
Operating expense	$ 22,495
Maintenance expense	4,382
Depreciation expense	11,377
Taxes other than income taxes..........................	3,855
Total operating deductions	$ 42,109
Interest expense	$ 4,930
Total deductions	$ 47,039
Net (loss)...	$(21,119)

Obtaining approval to increase the service charges has proved to be more difficult than the present owners anticipated. Two current complications are new antipollution equipment and possible plant expansion to serve a new high school.

Who Pays What for Cleanliness?

Detergents used in homes for washing clothes and dishes have sullied our natural environment. First, in the 1960's high-foaming detergents that do not break down in the earth through biological action began accumulating at alarming rates; surface wells in some areas produced sudsy water! To correct this problem, detergent manufacturers substituted phosphates. Phosphates do a good job of cleaning and they foam only a little. But they do remain in disposed wash water, and this creates a different kind of pollution. Phosphates are excellent plant food—as their use in fertilizer attests. In water, phosphates stimulate the growth of algae and other plants, especially in warm shallow ponds and lakes. The algae die, rot, and use up the oxygen in the water, the fish die, and the whole body of water becomes a stinking mess. The more phosphates in the water, the greater the mess.

Phosphates in our lakes and streams were identified as a villain just as public concern with ecology accelerated. Since then, state health boards and others have demanded a reduction in the inflow of phosphates. One route is to ban the use of phosphates in detergents, but there is no convenient substitute that does not have its own polluting effects. (Besides, public authorities are embarrassed to ask detergent manufacturers to stop using an ingredient they were forced to adopt a few years earlier.) Another route is to remove the phosphate from the waste water before it is released back into the environment. It is this latter approach that complicates life for Essex Creek Disposal Co.

In response to the public outcry about polluted waters, the state Department of Health is urgently seeking ways to reduce the discharge of phosphates. And, the effluent from the Essex Creek Disposal plant is clearly high in phosphates (as are discharges from most other sewage treatment plants). An engineering firm, the Chemical Equipment Company, has invented a chemical process for removing phosphates from sewage, and the Department of Health is pressing Essex Creek Disposal Co. to install the process even though it is still in the development stage. Company executives feel that the company is being used as an experimental guinea pig, perhaps because the company is small, but state officials deny this.

Following negotiations with Chemical Equipment Company, Essex Creek Disposal Co. decided to pursue the plan urged by the Department of Health, provided the cost of doing so could be recovered in service charges to its customers. Toward this end the company petitioned the Public Utility Commission for permission to increase its basic rate for each living unit, or equivalent, from $20 to $75 per quarter. The requested increase explicitly included both an adjustment to overcome past deficits and projected costs of the new phosphate removal process. The key table supporting the request is summarized in the pro forma statement on pages 89 and 90.

This proposed rate increase of 275% was greeted by howls of protest from residents of Essex Manor, many of whom had already strained their financial resources when moving into the new development. The Public Utility Commission's hearing on the proposal was a stormy session. Shortly thereafter the Commission ruled the company was not entitled to relief for phosphate removal since the equipment was not

Pro Forma Annual Income Statement
Showing Effect of Proposed Rates and Phosphate Removal

	Present	Projected
Total revenue		
(324 residential units, at $80 and $300)	$ 25,920	$97,200
Operating expenses:		
Operating labor	$ 3,052	$15,600[a]
Power and fuel	3,633	5,433
Chemical expense	1,754	7,154
Miscellaneous supplies and expense	438	3,138
Administrative expense	8,458	8,458[b]
Office supplies and expense.	2,385	2,385
Professional services	2,275	588
Property insurance	500	945
Maintenance of plant and equipment	4,382	4,382
Transportation	——	750[c]
Depreciation	11,377	14,892[d]
Taxes—payroll, gross receipts, franchise, excise	3,855	15,242
Income taxes @ 22%.	——	2,927
Total operating expenses.	$ 42,109	$81,894
Operating income or (loss).	$(16,189)	$15,306
Interest charges:		
Interest on long-term debt	4,500	4,500
Other interest	430	430
Total income deductions.	$ 4,930	$ 4,930
Net income or (loss)	$(21,119)	$10,376

[a]Addition of full-time operator stipulated by Department of Health.
[b]Administrative expense includes part-time salaries of all officers.
[c]Station wagon for operating personnel.
[d]All depreciation charged at 2% per year, except 33% on station wagon and 20% on new laboratory equipment.

installed and working properly. However, the Commission did authorize an interim rate increase from $20 to $31.25 per quarter to overcome current cash deficits. The ruling also indicated that if and when the company had a phosphate removal system installed and operating properly,[2] and had experience with additional costs, a request for further increase would be appropriate. Of course, no commitment was made as to the amount that might be allowed under such conditions.

Now, the company must decide what to do about phosphate removal. (1) It can proceed as the Department of Health is urging—i.e., invest $78,000 in new equipment, hoping that the system will be effective, and then go back to the Public Utility

---

[2]Proper functioning is defined by the Department of Health as removal of at least 95% of the phosphate coming into the treating plant, and less than one part per million in its discharge.

Pro Forma Estimate of Return on Investment

Rate base:

Present plant and equipment, depreciated		$525,164
Add: New investment in phosphate removal		
Plant and equipment	$70,745	
Transportation equipment	4,500	
Laboratory equipment	3,000	78,245
		$603,409
Less: Contribution to aid construction		379,752
New rate base...		$233,657

Return on investment at proposed rates:

Projected operating income	$ 15,306
Divided by new rate base...................................	$223,657
Equals rate of return on investment	6.84%

Commission for a further rate increase. *Or* (2) it can stall. Under this second alternative the Department of Health will probably obtain a court order compelling the company to remove the phosphates. (The company could argue that a state or country prohibition of the sale of detergents containing phosphates would be more effective, but such action is unlikely because it would be unpopular with detergent users and opposed by manufacturers.)

The second alternative differs from the first primarily in four respects. Essex Creek Disposal Co. will be regarded as uncooperative by the Department of Health, Lewis Township officials, and ecology buffs. There is a possibility, though very small, that the order compelling Essex Creek Disposal Co. to install the new equipment will not be issued. The need for action will be postponed for about six months. The company's posture in appealing for a rate increase will differ, but whether the Public Utility Commission will be more—or less—considerate of the company if it is acting under court order rather than its own initiative is unknown.[3]

Either alternative is risky for the company. The process may not work satisfactorily; the company would then be stuck with ineffective equipment with no one to pay the bill. The Department of Health has much enthusiasm but no money to underwrite experiments. Even if the equipment works properly, there is no assurance that the Public Utility Commission will permit the company to pass off the entire operating and capital cost to users of its services. Yet everyone agrees that phosphate pollution of waters should be reduced.

New Customer on the Horizon

Essex Creek Disposal Co. has another opportunity that is related to its action on phosphate removal. Lewis Township is building a new high school close to the company's sewer line and clearly will need arrangements for disposal of sanitary sewage.

---

[3]The Public Utility Commission is an independent body with its own due process procedures. There is no possibility of a working agreement between the Commission and the Department of Health, especially on a very small case such as this.

When plans to build the school—to provide for a growing population—were first announced, Mr. Boyd recognized that a large potential customer would be created. However, he decided not to seek a tie-in of the school with company facilities for the following reasons: (1) The treatment plant would have to be expanded. Although some excess capacity exists, the addition of the high school would create a risk that the existing processing tanks might overflow into Essex Creek before treatment was completed. To maintain a comfortable safety margin, a 25% increase in capacity would be necessary. (2) The service charge to support this additional plant would look high to school and township officials. More than half of the construction cost of present facilities was donated by the developer of Essex Manor, and prevailing residential rates do not provide reasonable earnings even on the residual investment. So, charges that would provide a reasonable return on the added investment needed to serve the new school would appear high in comparison to residential rates.

The company charter does not require the company to serve new customers such as a high school. Since the company was created explicitly to solve a problem related to the Essex Manor development, it is not part of a scheme to serve the total township or county. In fact, the company has accepted about 30 residential customers located outside Essex Manor, but these could be easily handled with existing capacity.

Recently Mr. Boyd discovered that the school architect assumed that sanitary sewage would flow into Essex Creek Disposal Co.'s line. Contracts have been let and construction is under way based on this assumption.

Thus, the company is in an unusually favorable bargaining position. For the school to build its own treating plant would cost more than the addition to the Essex Creek Disposal Co. plant. Moreover, planning and construction of a separate plant would delay opening the school for perhaps a year, whereas no delay (though perhaps a short-run pollution risk) will be involved in a tie to company facilities.

The relation of the new school to phosphate removal is explained by Mr. Boyd as follows: "If Essex Creek Disposal Co. has already embarked on a phosphate removal program when school officials approach us—as they undoubtedly will—the school can be expected to bear a reasonable share of that expense. On the other hand, if we are still arguing with the Department of Health, then the school people will focus on our present costs and rates, and phosphate removal will come as a separate issue on top of that.

"As you know," Mr. Boyd continued, "I wish the high school problem had not come up, because I doubt that we can make a decent return on the necessary investment. It complicates our picture, and we'll end up having another group—the Board of Education—trying to tell us how to run our business."

Questions

(1) Who are the key actors with whom Mr. Boyd must deal in his present situation?

(2) For each of these actors, what are their primary motivations, power, and likely responses to actions that Mr. Boyd is considering?

(3) What should Mr. Boyd do to resolve his phosphate problem? Explain how your recommendations relate to social responsibility and to a longer-run strategy for Essex Creek Disposal Co.?

SELECTING BUSINESS-UNIT STRATEGY

For a short period a company may simply drift along just doing what is customary. Or if the competition is tough, it may react to each new crisis as seems best at the moment. Only if it is lucky and has a lot of resources will such passive or "fire-fighting" behavior enable the enterprise to survive very long in today's turbulent environment. The constructive alternative is to be *proactive* instead of *reactive*. This requires company managers to energetically forestall trouble and seize new opportunities. They must provide positive, future-oriented direction to company activities. An essential part of such proactive behavior is the development of a *master strategy* for the business-unit as a whole.

The three preceding chapters on dynamic environment, company strengths, and likely behavior of key actors outline the array of forces that should be considered in designing master strategy. They set the stage. The next step is for the central managers of the business-unit to decide how their companies can best adapt to the anticipated opportunities and threats. A business-unit strategy normally should indicate:

1. *Domain sought.* What products or intangible services will the business-unit sell to what group of customers?
2. *Differential advantage in serving that domain.* On what basis—e.g., access to raw materials, better personnel, new technology, or low costs and prices —will the business-unit seek an advantage over competitors in providing its products or services?
3. *Strategic thrusts necessary and their approximate timing.* For the business-unit to move from its present position to where it wants to be—as laid out in (1) and (2)—what moves will be made early and what can be deferred?
4. *Target results expected.* What financial and other criteria will the business-unit use to measure its success, and what levels of achievement are expected?[1]

---

[1]By listing targets as the fourth element, rather than the first, we place emphasis on the operational content of strategy. The more abstract goals, such as growth, usually serve better as criteria for acceptability than as guides for action. In practice, possible strategies are debated back and forth so often that no clear priority exists between target results and mission.

Too often statements of strategy deal with only a single dimension. A new market or a desired financial return on investment, for instance, may be labeled as "our company strategy." Such a goal may indeed be part of the strategy, but its narrowness robs strategy of a needed balanced operational quality. A company strategy should be a well-conceived, practical commitment. To achieve this realistic quality, all four of the elements just listed should be carefully considered. The resulting strategy will then be an *integrated,* forward-looking plan.

Although strategy has many dimensions to consider—domain sought, differential advantage, strategic thrusts, and target results—it need not be detailed and comprehensive. Rather, strategy should concentrate on *key* factors necessary for success and on *major* moves to be taken by the particular company at the current stage in its development. The selectivity of key points, and by implication the designation of other points as supportive, gives strategy much of its value as a planning device.

Full elaboration of plans is a necessary sequel to selecting company strategy, as we shall see in Parts 2 and 3. The role of strategy, however, is primarily to identify missions and to set forth major ways of achieving distinctiveness; this is the focus of the present chapter.

DOMAIN SOUGHT
Product/Market Scope

The starting point in clarifying the mission of almost any enterprise is to define the services it will provide. It may design and manufacture a broad range of physical products or it may merely sell advice. But to continue to exist, it must provide some package of services for which some segment in society is prepared to pay. For example, after carefully examining the anticipated growth in the use of computers for billing retail customers, two enterprising IBM salespeople set up their own firm that (1) leases time on a central computer and (2) assists medium-sized stores in adapting their records and procedures to make use of this service. Note that this young firm has a sharp definition of the kind of computer work it will undertake and the kind of customers it seeks. This definition is a key element in its strategy.

Attractive Industries

Most business-units have their resources and strengths so deeply committed to an industry that they have only limited choice in this matter. Nevertheless, a careful analysis of that industry outlook, as suggested in Chapter 3, provides an essential basis for deciding whether to harness a favorable underlying trend or to seek unusual segments in a mature or declining situation. For example, most companies dealing with mobile homes are trying to increase their industry position. In contrast, the senior managers of the former Illinois Central Railroad are seeking ways to get rid of their railroad operations. (In recent years less than 20% of I.C. Industries' operating profits came from railroading.)

A redefinition of one's industry sometimes suggests an attractive domain. A typical example is O.M. Scott & Sons which found the outlook for its grass seed business not very attractive. By redefining its industry from grass seed to "lawn care" it uncovered many untapped opportunities in fertilizers and herbicides. A glass-bottle firm has significantly shifted the nature of its business by thinking in terms of containers.

Finding Niche Suited to Company Strengths

The chief domain issue for most companies, however, is picking a "propitious niche" in its industry. The niche may be a segment of the total products (or services) offered by the industry, or it may be a selected group of customers defined in terms of size, income, location, or some other characteristic. Obviously, each business tries to select a niche where the growth and profit prospects are attractive, and also where it has strengths relative to competitors.

The Franklin National Bank switched the domain it sought during its exciting history. Starting as just a small country bank on Long Island (New York), it grew under the guidance of a single CEO to become the thirteenth largest bank in the United States. Its first domain was commercial banking serving consumers and local business in the limited area of Long Island. Having become the leading bank in this domain, Franklin National expanded its goals (as soon as the state law permitted). It then moved into Manhattan and sought to become a truly national and international bank with an array of services matching Citibank, Chase Manhattan, and the other giants. This enlarged domain drastically altered the character of the bank, with results explained in the next sections.

Even coal raises strategy questions. The Island Creek Coal Company, to cite a specific case, has large deposits of coal especially suited for the production of steel. Clearly the company should serve these metallurgical customers. But the recent growth in coal demand is in generating electricity. Island Creek is handicapped in serving this large market because its coal must be dug in high-cost underground mines and because electric utilities are unwilling to pay a premium for the high quality of Island Creek coal. So Island Creek must decide whether to (a) concentrate only on metallurgical customers who will pay a premium, (b) sell its high-quality coal to utilities at low prices, (c) try to capture some of the utility business by buying strip mines and learning a new technology, or (d) hold onto its reserves until techniques for converting coal into gas and gasoline become practical.

Clear identification of a desired domain enables a business to concentrate on the particular activities necessary to serve that domain well. Especially important is anticipating changes in demand, supply, and regulation in the domain and preparing in advance to meet these new requirements. A secondary benefit of a well-defined domain is that it provides a guide on what *not* to do. Activities which are irrelevant to serving the domain can be pushed aside.

The desired domain does not remain static. The nature of markets and competition in those markets frequently change. Products mature. A business may achieve a dominant position in one niche and have to look elsewhere for growth. But until a change is decided upon, the selected domain provides positive direction to other business-unit planning.

Multiple Niches

The strategic advantage of picking a niche very carefully does not necessarily mean that a company should confine its activities to a single niche. As a firm grows, it frequently spots an additional service it can provide effectively. Thus, an auditing firm may also do consulting on management information systems.

Such expansion is desirable because it secures synergistic benefits. *Synergy* arises when two actions performed jointly produce a greater result than they would if performed independently. A simple example is building a restaurant with a motel; the restaurant makes the motel a more convenient place to stop, and the motel contributes business to the restaurant; the total business is larger than it would be if the two units were located 5 miles apart. Often this is called the "2 + 2 = 5" effect.

Because synergy is often involved in considering multiple niches, a framework for thinking about it is desirable. The following *expansion matrix* suggests that growth arising from finding new customers for present products leads in quite different directions from adding different products for existing customers. Thus, the producer of Eveready flashlight batteries took virtually the same product from the United States to many developing countries; and expanded its use from flashlights to portable radios and toys. In contrast, Head Ski Company went from skis to ski-wear and then to tennis rackets and summer sport clothing—all to the same (or a closely related) group of customers.

With respect to synergy, as a firm moves further away from its present customers and/or its present products, the prospects for synergistic benefits diminish. At the extreme (lower right corner), if new customers are to require completely different products, synergy almost disappears; the firm is thus involved in unrelated "conglomerate" expansion.

Naturally, a firm will seek combinations of niches that supplement or reinforce each other in a synergistic way. Managers should be aware, however, that negative synergy can occur; perhaps "2 + 2 = 3." Such a possibility is the subject of bitter debate in the life insurance industry. Several aggressive firms have added variable annuities and mutual funds to the "products" their sales representatives offer policyholders. The contention is that the policyholder will be glad to deal with a person who can offer a full range of protection against future financial need; synergy will be at work. The other side, with equally strong convictions, has argued that a half century has been devoted to building up the image of life insurance as stable and sure, not a gamble and not associated with speculative ventures. The supporters of this view believe that the association of variable annuities with the established types of life insurance will lead to a substantial reduction in life insurance sales. Experience to date is too limited to indicate whether synergy in this instance will be positive or negative.

If a business-unit elects to serve two or more niches, it is highly desirable to analyze and plan for each separately. In this way, the benefits that come from concentrated attention will not be lost. When and if the volume of work in a single niche can support its own organization, and if economies of scale permit separate marketing and production activities, the creation of an additional business-unit may be wise. The desirability of having two or more separate but related business-units is discussed in Chapter 15 as a portfolio issue.

Early writers on business strategy gave almost exclusive attention to this task of finding attractive niches suited to company strengths, and to building a large market share in such niches. Indeed, selection of "domain" is crucial to success. Experience with strategic management, however, shows clearly that being well situated in an attractive market is not enough. Business-unit strategy should include three additional elements.

DIFFERENTIAL ADVANTAGE IN SERVING SELECTED DOMAIN

The second essential pillar in a company strategy is identifying one or more bases in which superiority over competitors will be sought. If our particular enterprise is to continue to attract customers and resources, we must perform at least some parts of the total industry task with distinction. New product design, quick deliveries, low production costs, better personnel policies, fewer fights with environmentalists—these examples only suggest the many possibilities.

Franklin National Bank, to return to that example, differentiated itself during its Long Island growth phase by (a) promptly opening branches in expanding residential areas, and (b) offering unusual services first. (E.g., its "firsts" included parking for customers, drive-in windows, evening hours, prompt FHA home mortgage loans, and the like.) However, when the bank moved to Manhattan, it found itself in a "me too" situation, running hard to catch up with the services offered by established competitors. Consequently, the primary differential advantage it found itself forced to adopt was the granting of higher-risk loans. And this latter practice led directly to the Franklin National's collapse.

A company may seek a differential advantage in *any* of its external relations or in its internal resource conversion technology. The resource converter model, discussed briefly in Chapter 1, suggests the possibilities. The strategic requirement is to become—somehow, in at least a few respects—a favorable supplier in the selected domain. Several commonly used ways of getting at least some comparative advantage are highlighted in the following paragraphs.

Products and Services Tailored for Selected Niches

Having selected a niche which is growing fast or is being inadequately served by competing suppliers, a company may adjust its products and services to suit the particular needs of customers in that niche. Familiar examples are radio stations which focus on sophisticated listeners by programming classical music, or on hispanic listeners by offering Spanish-language programs. Such stations then have a differential advantage for advertisers who want to reach those particular audiences.

Pioneer Life, a medium-sized insurance company, revamped a large part of its operations for a similar purpose. Pioneer could not compete successfully with large insurance companies for most *group* business (group life, insured pension plans, group health and disability, and the like). However, the large companies were giving little attention to clients with fewer than 200 employees. Such small clients usually lacked an insurance specialist on their own staff, and they were often confused by government tax and reporting requirements and by union requests for insurance as a fringe benefit. So Pioneer decided to cater to this niche.

To build a differential advantage in serving the smaller clients, Pioneer: (a) selected and trained agents (salespersons) to advise small companies on *all* aspects of employee insurance; (b) prepared an array of standard options suited to small companies from which an insurance plan for a specific client could be quickly assembled; (c) wrote computer programs which store employment and vital statistics on company employees, and quickly calculate costs of various kinds of insurance; (d) designed a monthly (or quarterly) report form for the client showing the contributions and status of insurance coverage on each employee; and (e) reorganized internally so that group insurance became a self-contained business-unit within Pioneer. Of course, this kind of service is expensive on a per employee basis, but Pioneer is now able to relieve smaller clients of almost all of their headaches in this technical area of employee insurance.

High Volume-Low Cost

A very different approach to differential advantage is to seek high volume which, it is hoped, will result in low cost per unit. The low cost, in turn, will enable the company to set a lower selling price—or spend more on promotion and service—than its competitors can afford.

The classic concept of high volume leading to low cost has been popularized recently by The Boston Consulting Group. B.C.G. talks of large market share, which gives a company higher volume than its competitors, and of the "experience curve," which explains why costs can be expected to drop as a result of that higher volume. More specifically, the argument is that a company (like a person) learns from experience; each time the cumulative output doubles, cost per unit should drop, say, 30%. Indeed, experience in production of aircraft and electronic components, two well known examples, conforms with the theory.

Fortunately, for small firms and newcomers the B.C.G. theory is subject to a variety of qualifications. For instance, with a new product or a new production technology, a company may start with as much "experience" as its more prominent competitors. Nevertheless, the central point remains. Using some relevant concept of volume, a company can seek a differential advantage by playing the high volume/low cost game.

Distinctive Research and Development

In some industries, such as pharmaceuticals or electronics, strong company research and development is regarded as the touchstone for success. Especially for firms that hope to serve new technical markets, an imaginative engineering department is vital. Two college professors, who set up a firm to design and install equipment to control air pollution of chemical processing plants, considered their research program as a key element in the firm's basic strategy.

But what is good for one firm is not necessarily wise for another. For instance, a leading British cement company relies on very good customer service, not on distinctive products, to win business from competitors. Hence it spends no money on product research; its engineering is focused on reducing operating costs. In contrast, many advertising agencies rely heavily on their ability to create unusual campaigns. For them, as for fashion dress manufacturers, creative design is the main way they try to differentiate themselves from competitors.

Favorable Strength in Resources

A company may gain an advantage in serving a particular niche by having greater strength in key resources, such as scarce raw materials, unusual people, or cash for investment. For strategic planning, an ability to acquire the resource quickly is almost the same as having it in hand. Of course, to provide a differential advantage the resource must be vital in serving the niche, and it must not be readily available to competitors.

Ownership of crude oil is currently a great benefit to a petroleum refiner. This is partly to assure that the refinery will run but also to assure that cost of raw materials, and thus of finished products, will be at least as low as competitors' products. Similarly, in times of inflation having timberlands can be a comparative advantage to a paper company. Whether owning a tomato farm places a catsup plant in a superior position depends upon the availability and price of tomatoes for competitors.

Access to capital creates a distinct advantage in some circumstances. For instance, large sums of risk capital must be available for any firm engaged in exploring the ocean floor. Small equipment companies have difficulties expanding in niches where end-products are leased rather than sold. Even urban renewal firms have discovered that one requirement for growth is equity capital. Again, the underlying question is, "Do we have, or can we get, the financing needed? And in this respect, will we be at any advantage or disadvantage relative to others serving the same need?"

In service operations personnel is *the* critical resource. For this reason one of the leading management consulting firms insists that staff members devote 10% of their working time to training and development, even though billable work for clients is available. The aim is to have the best staff in the profession fully informed on the latest developments. A secondary benefit is that this training appeals to the professional pride of the individuals, and that aids morale and recruiting. Of course, any enterprise can benefit or suffer from the relative capability of its management and technical team. Realistic strategic planning should always take this resource into account.

Choice in Emphasis

Many potential sources of differential advantages exist. The preceding examples only suggest the possibilities. As a practical matter, any single company becomes ineffective if it tries to excel on all fronts. Instead, a key feature of strategy is selection of a few ways in which the company seeks to distinguish itself.

A few examples will highlight this feature of strategy. IBM has always stressed customer service, customer orientation in product design, and liberal treatment of its employees. Humble Oil rose to prominence because it gave high priority to acquiring an advantageous crude oil supply. Merck and Boeing stressed building better mousetraps—ethical pharmaceuticals and aircraft, respectively. Conglomerates derive their differential advantage predominantly by the way they raise capital.

Each company singles out perhaps one, but more likely a few areas having synergistic ties. In these areas it tries to develop a relationship with the resources that is more favorable than that of its competitors. Typically, it establishes a new symbiotic relationship between a key group of resources and the internal technology of the company. If the company is wise (or lucky), it selects relationships for emphasis which will become especially important strengths in the future competition within its industry.

In the numerous external relationships not selected as a source of differential advantage, a company "satisfices"; that is, it merely seeks to be acceptable but not to excel. Often a company is too small to attempt any more than following general industry practice; its location, history, personal preferences of key executives, or existing resource base may not provide a good springboard; or management may deliberately decide that effort applied in other directions will be more rewarding. These secondary relationships cannot be neglected; they must be adequately maintained, like Herzberg's hygiene factors. Moreover, the secondary relationships should be designed so that they support or are at least compatible with the primary features of the selected strategy.

Of course, over time a company may shift its choice of areas in which it seeks differential advantage. Critical factors for success change; the company changes; new opportunities for distinctiveness emerge. Adapting to these opportunities by adjusting the emphasis placed on sources of distinction is a crucial aspect of successful strategy. Unless a business-unit can devise a strategy which couples obtainable differential advantage with an attractive domain, the domain is likely to be captured by a competitor.

STRATEGIC THRUSTS

Normally a gap exists between the present position of a business-unit and the domain and differential advantages it seeks. Obstacles to closing that gap will vary in magnitude and over time; and the business-unit will have

limited personnel, capital, existing external relationships, and other resources to use in dealing with these obstacles. Consequently, a third basic
strategic consideration is deciding what major thrusts to make and how fast
to press for changes. Besides identifying what these major thrusts should be,
this element of strategy also involves steering a course between too-much-
too-soon and too-little-too-late.

Major Steps to Be Taken

A few years ago, Crown Cork & Seal Company faced a threat to its strong
position in high-pressure cans. The aluminum companies began producing
a two-piece aluminum can. This new can had a differential advantage over
the conventional three-piece steel can such as Crown Cork, American, Continental, and National can companies were making: it was lighter in weight,
it had less possibility of leaky seams, it avoided the remote chance of producing lead poisoning from lead on the seams, and it produced printing on the
can that looked slightly better. Crown Cork did not want to switch to the
aluminum can because it would then find itself buying raw material
(roughly half the cost) from companies which would also be its competitors
for the end-product. A possible alternative was a two-piece steel can.

So a new thrust, vital to maintaining Crown Cork's position in the can
business, was forged: the development of a low-cost technology to manufacture a two-piece steel can. This involved high-speed drawing of a thin
steel sheet into the sides and bottom of the can, a task previously believed impractical. A complicating factor was that Crown Cork's low
overhead policy meant that it normally spent very little on manufactur-
ing-process R&D. So a joint engineering venture with steel companies,
which also had a substantial stake in the outcome, was launched. Five
years later a technology that involved both steel-making and can-making
emerged. The two-piece steel can is now a viable competitor with the
two-piece aluminum can.

A second issue then arose. How fast should Crown Cork convert to manufacturing two-piece steel cans? A large investment in machinery was involved; the technology could change; excess three-piece capacity would create price pressure in the total market; and the environmental agitation
against non-returnable containers could swing demand back to glass bottles.
In spite of these drawbacks, Crown Cork decided to beat its competitors in
building two-piece steel can lines. As a result of this second thrust, the
company already has over half of the installed capacity for making the new
steel cans.

Clearly, these two moves have been crucial points of Crown Cork's strategy. They illustrate what we have called "thrusts" and what some other
people term "initiatives," or "key programs." A strategic thrust is a vital,
positive undertaking which moves a company toward its differential advantage in its desired domain.

Failure to include thrusts in a strategic plan may leave the selected objectives floating; it is probably the major "missing link" in moving strategy from ideas to action. This was a contributing weakness in Franklin National Bank's move into Manhattan. In addition to taking risky loans, Franklin National failed to tool up to do the broader business it said it wanted. There was no thrust focused on developing and/or acquiring a pool of talented personnel necessary for the new tasks. And there was only slow recognition of the need to modify the informal centralized organization which had suited Long Island. The necessary shift to a complex, sophisticated organization needed by a major bank of world stature posed so many difficulties that it should have been set up as an explicit thrust. By contrast, note that when Citibank adopted its strategy to go after more business from "world corporations," it recognized the organization and personnel hurdles and established thrusts to overcome them.

Timing of Thrusts

The sequence and timing of thrusts may be tricky. Some actions obviously must precede others, for example land acquisition before plant construction. But often a strategic choice can be made. In the British Petroleum move into the U.S. market, the company deferred heavy commitment in marketing until a source of U.S. crude was in sight. To have started marketing alone and relied completely on local purchases of finished products would have exposed the company to very high risks. In this situation, we can also note that building or acquiring refining capacity came even later; clearly, refining capacity was not regarded as a critical factor and it could be manipulated later without paying high penalties.

A different sequence is being followed by a manufacturer of fiberglass boats. A low selling price is a key feature of the marketing strategy, and in order to achieve costs permitting this low price, a large modern plant is necessary. Starting up such a plant is clearly a strategic thrust. However, the company's current sales are not large enough to keep an optimum sized plant busy. Nevertheless, the management decided to build the plant so as to be in a strong competitive position. While market demand is being built up, the company has taken on several subcontracts at break-even prices and is even selling some boat hulls to another boat builder to help cover overhead costs of the plant. Here is an instance of moving first into large-scale production facilities, hoping that demand will catch up.

Even after a sequence has been selected, the manager has to decide how fast to move. It is quite possible to be too early. A leading East Coast department store, for example, correctly predicted a major shift of population to the suburbs, and it became a leader in establishing suburban branches. However, at the time it selected branch locations, few of the large modern shopping centers with their vast parking spaces were in existence. Consequently, the store established branches in locations that are now being passed by. The irony of the situation is that the management of this store had more foresight than several of its competitors, yet because it moved too soon, it is now at a relative disadvantage in suburban operations.

In the preceding examples, and in most other timing decisions, the likely response of other key actors to company moves is a significant consideration. As noted in the previous chapter, the possibility of gaining cooperation or provoking counter-moves depends upon the involvement of the other actors at the time we initiate our moves.

Although difficult to do wisely, the timing of thrusts does provide a desirable "flexibility" in the execution of strategy. Delaying or even shifting the sequence of major moves permits postponement of heavy commitments. This introduces a degree of flexibility without a total change in strategy with each shift in the wind.

In dealing with thrusts, even more than with differential advantages, a business-unit should be highly *selective*. Highlighting the critical moves, in contrast to all sorts of minor maneuvers, is a significant part of the guidance strategy provides.

TARGET RESULTS EXPECTED

The three elements of company strategy just described deal primarily with what to do, when, and by implication, what not to do. They are guides to more detailed planning and action which are to follow. This emphasis leaves out one important dimension of strategy. If these things are done (and the environment is largely as predicted), what results are expected?

A small manufacturer of testing instruments for metallurgical industries, for instance, adopted a strategy of major commitment to research in the use of lasers. Translated into targets or anticipated results, this research commitment meant aiming for (1) a breakthrough in testing equipment in two to five years, (2) a reputation as a technical leader in this field within three years, and (3) reaching a break-even point in company profit and loss during the next three to five years. Note how much clearer the strategy is when we state *both* the means (laser research) and the ends (the three targets).

There are several reasons why strategy should include some statement of anticipated results. The people who must endorse the strategy, especially those who contribute resources, can reasonably hold back until they get some feel for what the situation is likely to be as a consequence of all this activity. Also, the individuals designing the strategy will have their personal objectives and values, and they, too, will be concerned about how results are expected to match these criteria. By no means least important, target results set the stage for shorter-run goals and controls which are essential ingredients of effective implementation.

Taking the viewpoint of the senior manager who is responsible for the selection of strategy, how does this person decide, "O.K., that's it"? Fundamentally, the process involves: (1) selecting the criteria for judging the strategy, (2) translating and stating the expected results of the strategy in terms of these criteria, and (3) deciding whether the expected results (the targets) meet acceptable minimum levels of achievement and are better than expected results of alternative targets.

Criteria to Be Considered

Several criteria are often used to evaluate a strategy, such as:

1. Return on investment (usually this is profit related to financial investment, but it might be the return on any critically scarce resources).
2. Risk of losing investment of scarce resources.
3. Company growth (in absolute terms or as a percentage of the market).
4. Contribution to social welfare (in one or more dimensions).
5. Stability and security of employment and earnings (of all employees and/or of executives).
6. Prestige of the company and of company representatives.
7. Future control (or influence) over company decisions.

Different individuals naturally stress one or two of the above criteria—finance people the return on investment, research people the company prestige, marketing people the company growth, and so forth—and occasionally they may wish to add other criteria such as cash flow or international balance of payments. Fortunately, doing well on one criterion does not necessarily detract from all of the others. A specific strategy has not one but a whole set of results, and the only practical way to judge a strategy is to consider several criteria simultaneously. To expedite the evaluation process, three or four of these various criteria should be singled out as dominant in the specific situation.

Expressing Strategy in Terms of Criteria

Meaningful strategies must be conceived in *operational* terms, such as products to sell, markets to reach, materials to acquire, research to perform, and the like. However, such actions take on value only as they contribute to desired results. And the pertinent results are defined by the criteria just discussed.

So to relate a strategy to the selected criteria, a conversion or translation is needed. For instance, the actions contemplated in a strategy have to be expressed in anticipated costs and revenues, which give us an estimated profit. Similarly, the proposed actions have to be restated in terms of human resources to estimate their effect on stability of employment (if that is one of the key criteria). And likewise for other criteria.

These restatements of anticipated results become the targets at which the strategy is aimed. But since the success of any strategy is never certain, these targets will be surrounded by many "if's" and "maybe's." Often they should be expressed as a range, not a single point, with subjective probabilities attached. Nevertheless, tentative though the estimates may be, this is the basis on which a strategy will be evaluated.

Are Targets Acceptable?

Now, with criteria selected and the anticipated results of strategy expressed in terms of these criteria, the manager is in a position to say, "Let's go" or "That's not good enough." Rarely is there a choice among several strategies, each of which is quite attractive. Instead, the pressing question is whether any proposed plan is acceptable at all. The reason for this scarcity of attractive choices is that all of us have *high aspirations,* at least for one or two criteria. Thirty percent profits, no real risk, worldwide prestige, half of industry sales—any and all of these may be part of one's dreams. The blunt facts are that few of these dreams will be realized by any strategy we can conceive. So we have to decide what *level of achievement* will be acceptable for each of our criteria.

This picking of acceptable levels is complicated by differences in values held by key executives. For instance, Strategy A may promise a 30% return on capital but with a 15% chance of complete loss and a sure transfer of ownership; whereas Strategy B promises only a 15% return on capital but with small risk of total loss and little danger of change in control of the company. Many quantitative techniques exist for computing optimal combinations. Reality, however, indicates that personal perceptions and values strongly affect the decision. The chair of the board—say, a wealthy person and a large stockholder—may prefer Strategy A; while the president, who came up from the ranks and owns little stock, may prefer Strategy B. Or, if the chairperson likes the prestige of the position and the president thinks the chairperson is too conservative, the preferences may be reversed.

It is difficult to generalize about whose values will predominate. Generally, the most active and aggressive senior executives will establish the pattern, *provided* their objectives meet at least the minimum acceptable requirement of each interest group whose withdrawal of support could paralyze the company. In the language of Chapter 1, the "output" of the strategy must enable the company to fulfill at least minimum needs of resource contributors.

Thus, while there is no simple resolution of how high targets should be, we obviously should not evade the translation of operational plans into key targets (or vice versa). A strategy expressed in terms of targets alone is little more than wishful thinking. On the other hand, an operational strategy that is not translated into targets is primarily an article of faith. A well-developed strategy has *both* an operational plan and targets.

SUMMARY

Company strategy deals with the basic ways a business-unit seeks to take optimum advantage of its environment. As we saw in Chapter 2, changes in technology, politics, social structure, and economics create opportunities and problems. To bring these environmental factors into sharper focus, we urged in Chapter 3 that they be woven into industry analyses. Such industry studies identify growth and profit prospects, and also the key factors necessary for future participation in the growth. Still more pointed is an analysis of company strengths and weaknesses, and a matching of these against the key success factors for each industry. The final narrowing, proposed in Chapter 4, calls for an analysis of key actors and their likely responses to our moves.

Armed with this background, central management selects its strategy. The strategy indicates (1) the *domain* to be sought, (2) our *differential advantages* in serving that domain, (3) *strategic thrusts* necessary to move from our present position to the desired one, and (4) *target results* to be achieved. These elements interact and they should reinforce each other.

This master plan evolves, of course. As the environment changes, some uncertainties become realities and new uncertainties arise. And the company strategy may be shifted to take advantage of the new situation. Competitors are also responding to the same environment, and their actions may open up—or require—adjusted action. Meanwhile the company itself moves forward and/or runs into snags, so it has new internal information and modified strengths and weaknesses. Inevitably the strategy needs reassessment.

Nevertheless, at any point in time, and hopefully for a long enough span to translate plans into action, the main elements of strategy remain stable. With this overriding guidance, central management moves to elaboration and implementation of the scheme (as we do in the next parts of the book).

Small companies benefit from well-conceived strategies fully as much as large ones. Their strengths and options differ, but their flexibility and growth rate can be greater.

 QUESTIONS FOR CLASS DISCUSSION

1. The Mitsubishi group, a Japanese-based giant among the business companies of the world, both built and financed the small, imported cars and trucks— Dodge Colt, Plymouth Arrow, and others—which Chrysler Corporation

marketed and sold in the United States through its dealer organization. Spurred by Chrysler's financial troubles, the banks at the head of the Mitsubishi group pushed for an end to both the financial and sales arrangements with Chrysler. They contended that more money could be made by lending in Japan with less risk, or the funds could be used to help finance a separate, Mitsubishi-owned dealer organization in the United States. The bank's central managers argued that, in this way, the group could readily sell more than the 150,000 Mitsubishi-made cars sold annually to Chrysler and its dealers, that its own U.S. dealer organization would be valuable if import controls were placed on foreign-branded cars sold in the U.S. and, most important, that the risks of lending to a Japanese firm or a Japanese-based exporting company were less. The executives also argued that increased sales in the U.S. above 150,000 cars—probably 200,000 to 250,000 units—would considerably lessen manufacturing costs. What is your view of Japanese versus United States companies as a domain for lending for the Mitsubishi group? Do you agree that there are several differential advantages for a Japanese firm which owns and controls the U.S. marketing company? How might the matrix in Chapter 4 (page 78) be altered if the financial and lending domain changed as proposed?

2. (a) The number of farmers in the United States continues to decline (31 million in 1940, 16 million in 1960, and 8 million in 1980). Does this mean that there are no attractive niches in the farm industry? (b) Briefly outline what you believe would be a successful master strategy for a farmer in your home state.

3. Several airlines have purchased resort hotels at locations they serve. For instance, Eastern Airlines bought hotels in Puerto Rico. (a) Use this development to *illustrate* each of the four elements in company strategy discussed in this chapter. (The aim of the question is to show the meaning of strategy, so make assumptions about the local situation if you need to.) (b) Now assume the airline decided to go out of the hotel business (its hotels were losing money) and sold one of them to you. How would this change in ownership affect the strategy you would recommend for the hotel?

4. Use each of the boxes in the chart on page 96 to identify possible alternative ways of expanding for (a) a company in the office furniture manufacturing business, or (b) a medical "clinic" consisting of five doctors concentrating on pediatrics (care of children).

5. The speed at which tough, antipollution emission controls should be required for all autos has been intensely debated. (a) List the major arguments for quick and for slow national requirements. (b) Do the pros and cons in your answer to (a) suggest similar arguments for the speed at which: (1) a successful fried chicken fast-food chain should grant additional franchises; (2) an undergraduate college should establish a master's degree program; (3) a Hawaiian pineapple canning company should develop more economical Philippine and other foreign sources? In (1), (2), and (3), assume that central management has decided to make the change at some time.

6. Ms. Norton says: "I run a 100-bed retirement home. It is a non-profit enterprise started by a church group. Although we get complaints about quarterly increases in our residence charges (for meals, building operating costs, cleaning, social service, office, etc.), we still have more applicants than we can accept. Any suggestions for dealing with inflation would be very helpful. But I don't see how I can use 'strategy.'" Use the outline of this chapter to identify

strategy issues which Ms. Norton is likely to face within the next few years. How might awareness of these issues be helpful to Ms. Norton?

7. One company's statement of objectives calls for "a decent return to stockholders, an example to the community of corporate citizenship, payment of better than a living wage and stability of employment for all employees, honorable treatment of suppliers, and the willingness to undertake business risks to provide an example of dynamic management." How can the concept of a "strategy" as outlined in this chapter help sharpen the meaning and the focus of such a statement?

8. At one time the major U.S.-based oil companies considered production, transportation, refining, and retail marketing in the United States to be their domain. Then they dropped a major emphasis on retail marketing in the U.S. and, later, production only in the U.S. as major elements of their domain. Then, more recently, they have changed to emphasize refining abroad and marketing abroad as major strategic elements. Why have they done so, in your view? Is their domain still changing?

9. Assume that you have just been appointed manager of the leading bookstore on your campus, with a free hand to make any changes you believe desirable. Outline the strategy you intend to follow.

10. (a) Texas Instruments, beginning with transistors made and sold in the U.S., has moved on to make such advances in technology as integrated circuits and other solid-state electronic products and, a few years ago, began to sell digital watches. Now, at its plant in Lubbock, Texas, it manufactures somewhat over 50 percent of the watches (of all kinds) sold around the world. A key element in the Texas Instruments strategy has been to sell a product below cost in the first stage of its life-cycle and then to drop prices rapidly as volume increases. Does the diagram on page 96 of this chapter explain and, perhaps, predict what T.I. has done? How about the diagram on page 46 in Chapter 3?

   (b) What have been the reactions of the older major watch companies; i.e., Timex and Bulova (U.S.-based), Seiko (Japanese), and the jeweled-watch manufacturers of Switzerland? Does the diagram on page 78 of Chapter 4 look helpful to you had you been an executive of any of these companies?

11. "Job Offers Are Lavish in Competition to Hire Business School Grads . . . Consultants Up the Ante" (from a headline in *The Wall Street Journal*). One Stanford Business School graduate has signed with a consulting firm for 80% more than the average starting salary paid to MBA degree holders in the same year. (She also earned $3,500 per month in a summer job with the same firm while studying for her degree.) The cream of New York City's law firms will pay newly-minted attorneys as much as 100% more than the national average for new lawyers. A director in charge of recruiting for McKinsey & Company stated that some starting salaries for MBA's would hit $55,000 in 1980 dollars.

   Consulting firms are pushing MBA pay skywards. "Consider what we can sell," said one consultant, "so we pay top dollar to get the best. High salaries are almost viewed as a promotional expense . . . We concentrate on the best schools for a reason." Early acceptance bonuses ($10,000 to sign within a week plus $1,000 for every month prior to graduation the job is accepted), and "exploding" offers (a job and a salary are offered to a student on Friday but the student is told that on Monday the offer expires—or explodes), as well as other early recruitment efforts, are discouraged by some schools. "Commercial banks have been crowded out by the management consulting industry," say recruiters for large, international banks, "we can't touch the money (the consulting firms are offering) without throwing our entire salary schedule out of whack."

(a) How is "paying the top dollar" related to a differential advantage a consulting firm might wish to gain and keep? What domain is it seeking? (b) Do early recruiting and exploding offers demonstrate social responsibility on the part of the consulting firms? (c) Are the business schools engaging in socially responsible behavior when they try to discourage early recruiting? (d) Should the banks protest the salaries paid by consulting firms and use what influence they have to reduce these high offers? What responses could the banks predict? Where do they stand in the diagram on page 78 in Chapter 4?

CASE 5
Uniroyal Tires

A large chunk of modern society travels on rubber tires—in autos, trucks, tractors, buses, earthmoving equipment, aircraft (on the ground), bicycles, etc. Since the turn of the century we have become highly dependent on rubber-tired vehicles. And, the companies which produce tires are among the giants of industry.

Nevertheless, the industry is mature. Its growth prospects are dim and profit margins narrow. Billion dollar companies like Goodyear, Firestone, Goodrich, Uniroyal, and General Tire are all diversifying and struggling to cut costs. The 1980's will surely see major realignments, and probably some bankruptcies. Uniroyal, Inc., the third largest rubber company in the U.S., is one of the companies poised between success and failure.

Industry Outlook

Although the big rubber firms are diversifying to lessen their dependence on the highly competitive tire business, tires continue to dominate their outlook. The following table showing growth rates during the 1970's provides a backdrop for what can be expected in the 1980's. Among the most notable points shown are: (1) truck production accounts for more of the *increase* in tires for new vehicles than does auto production; (2) sales of replacement tires are almost level even though the number of autos and trucks registered rose from 108 million to 154 million during the ten-year period. Clearly tires are lasting longer.

Future demand for tires will depend on whether trends already present will continue throughout the 1980's. A major factor is a change in tire construction. Radial tires (developed by Michelin in Europe and introduced in the U.S. in the mid '70's) provide up to twice the mileage of bias-belted and bias tires. Although radials are somewhat more expensive than other tires, by 1980 they accounted for over three-quarters of original equipment sales and half of replacement sales. With retreads available for people who want a cheap tire, the trend toward radials is likely to continue. Moreover, elliptical tires are being tested and their proponents claim that they will have even longer life. Such longer life will cut the demand for replacement tires.

Past Trends Affecting Tire Industry—U.S.A.

	1971	1980*	Increase
Population (millions)	208	223	7%
GNP (billion 1972 dollars)	1,107	1,503	36%
Auto production (millions)	8.6	9.1	6%
Truck production (millions)	2.1	3.5	67%
Auto registration (millions)	89	121	36%
Truck registration (millions)	19	33	74%
Tractors on farms (millions)	4.4	3.7	−16%
Auto tire sales:			
Total (million units)	189	200	6%
Original equipment (million units)	49	57	16%
Replacement (million units)	140	143	—

*Partly estimated

The energy situation also affects tire demand. Driving at slower speeds reduces tire wear per mile. Smaller, lighter autos also reduce wear. And, of course, fewer miles driven (shorter trips, more car pools, and mass transportation) would cut tire demand. How potent these factors will be is as yet unclear. Incidentally, front-wheel drives probably increase tire wear somewhat. And small, temporary spare tires create short-run downs and ups in regular tire demand.

A profile of the tire market at the beginning of the 1980's is indicated in the following table.

Sources of Tire Demand
(in 1,000,000 units, 1980, partly estimated)

	Passenger	Truck	Farm	Other Off-Highway	Total
Original equipment	57	13	2	2	74
Replacement	143	32	3	4	182
Total	200	45	5	6	256

No marked change in retreading of tires is anticipated. For several years in the replacement market, about one in five passenger tires has been a retread and one in three truck tires has been a retread. About half the passenger auto retreads are snow tires.

Imports continue to be a potential threat to domestic producers. Michelin entered the U.S. market with imports, as did Bridgestone (a Japanese-owned company primarily focusing on the Far West). However, the decline in the value of the U.S. dollar made imports very expensive, and Michelin opened its own U.S. plants to continue its drive in this market.

Fairly stable total demand for passenger tires, coupled with increased production capacity for radial-type tires, has created excess capacity for bias and bias-belted tires. This excess capacity has contributed to severe price competition. Management search for ways to hold costs down, in turn, complicates relations with a strong labor union—with long and costly strikes being all too frequent. So it is not surprising that profit margins are meager. With inflation, prices must go up, but labor, materials, interest, and other expenses will probably rise at least as fast.

Company Position

The industry conditions sketched above pose a serious challenge to the management of Uniroyal, Inc. Uniroyal has total sales of over $2.5 billion, and a net worth well over $0.5 billion. Nevertheless, it is fighting for its life. About sixty percent of Uniroyal sales come from tires and related products, and it has $0.9 billion invested in this segment of its total business. But the operating profit on tires *before* corporate expense, interest on debt, and income tax has been hovering around 4% of sales. Unless the corporation can improve results in this section of its business, it probably will be unable to meet required payments on its financial obligations (about $20 million long-term debt repayment and $50 million interest on long- and short-term debt annually).

Uniroyal is clearly number three in U.S. tire production, behind Goodyear and Firestone which each about doubles Uniroyal's size. (See the following table.) This means that Uniroyal has less to spend on advertising and R&D. It has both old plants and modernized radial-tire plants—with overall costs about average for the industry. So, Uniroyal must find sources of distinctiveness which fit with its relative size.

Estimated Company Shares of U.S. Tire Production

	Passenger	Truck and Off-Highway	Total
Goodyear	25%	28%	26%
Firestone	23	18	22
Uniroyal	13	9	12
General	8	11	9
Goodrich	9	7	8
Armstrong	6	8	7
10 smaller producers	16	19	16
	100%	100%	100%

In original equipment for passenger cars, Uniroyal has been successful in obtaining the leading share of General Motors business. (See the table on supplies to auto producers.) These sales to General Motors give Uniroyal a larger position in original equipment than in replacement tires. Also they give Uniroyal a more prominent place in the passenger than in the truck market. (Generally, Uniroyal is not a major supplier of the various kinds of off-highway tires—except recreational vehicles.) Of

Estimated Company Shares of Original Equipment Market

	General Motors	Ford	Chrysler	Total U.S. Autos
Goodyear	21%	24%	62%	34%
Firestone	19	39	19	23
Uniroyal	36	9	0	19
Goodrich	11	10	0	8
General	13	9	18	13
Michelin	—	9	1	3
	100%	100%	100%	100%

course, this market position contributes to Uniroyal's thin profit margins because prices on original equipment orders are normally very close to costs.

Recommended Strategy

Several different people have considered what Uniroyal should do in the 1980's. Here is the summary of what one outside group of consultants proposes.

1. Select and concentrate on particular segments of the tire business where Uniroyal can be distinctive. Uniroyal does not have resources and momentum to compete with Goodyear and Firestone on all fronts. Instead, treat segments as separate strategic business units. Strategy for various units probably should differ.

2. The most promising segment is truck tires. The profit margins are somewhat better here than in passenger tires. There is some growth instead of stable or declining demand. The expense of gaining market share is less than cutting into entrenched strong distribution of the two leaders.

3. Within the truck tire segment, focus on replacements for medium and small size trucking firms. Original equipment manufacturers, and the large trucking firms that do their own servicing, buy tires on a competitive bid basis. However, the vast number of truckers purchase maintenance and tires from local dealers. For them prompt service coupled with dependable quality is more critical than small differences in price.

4. To build a differential advantage in this domain, establish a network of *truck-service-centers*. Locate these truck-service-centers in spots convenient for truckers. Such locations will differentiate Uniroyal from Firestone and Goodyear which locate their stores primarily to serve passenger car owners.

5. Shift R&D emphasis away from passenger tires to truck tires. Strive to be a leader in truck tire design and efficient production, and a fast follower in passenger tire design. This narrower R&D focus should enable Uniroyal to lead in its selected niche while also reducing total expenses. Distinctive service and quality, then, will be Uniroyal's competitive edge in the replacement truck tire business.

6. Start moving with the following thrusts:

   (a) Find and sign up managers of the co-owned truck-service-centers. Each will need only relatively low cost garage and warehouse space, about five servicing trucks, and about ten employees (dispatcher, 2 outside salespersons, 5 service workers, warehouse supervisor, office clerk). Each should produce $3 million sales per year (in 1980 dollars) with at least 12% incremental operating profit. By leasing space and renting trucks the investment and working capital per center can be kept down to $500,000. The aim is 30 such centers in the first year.

   (b) Revise the physical inventory control and regional warehousing so that truck-service-centers will be assured of prompt delivery of tires.

   (c) Reallocate R&D effort in line with point 5 above.

   (d) Prepare a campaign of local advertising and sales promotion to the trucking industry to back up truck-service-centers.

7. Target results related to this truck tire strategy include:

   (a) Thirty new truck-service-centers each year for next three years. These ninety centers should generate $270 million sales, $32 million operating profit, and move Uniroyal's market share in the truck tire business from 9% to 14%.

   (b) The redirected R&D effort should create a new line of truck tires within two or three years. (Single-ply, steel-belted radials are already being developed and may be ready sooner.)

   (c) Roughly $25 million of Uniroyal's R&D outlays are related to tires. The narrowing of focus may permit a $5 million reduction. This $5 million added to the $32 million operating profit from new truck-service-centers provides a prospective improvement in truck tire operating profits of $37 million per year by the end of the third year.

The consultants did not work out a specific program for passenger tires, but they did sketch one alternative to show how passenger tire and truck tire strategies might be coordinated. The main points are:

1. Acceptance or rejection of the following tentative proposal will not upset the preceding recommendations for truck tires. They can be treated as separate issues. However, a combination of the two does provide desirable cash flow balance and risk balance.[1]

2. In passenger tires a status quo or no-growth strategy was proposed. Uniroyal does not now possess unusual marketing strengths nor exceptional products. The total market may be shrinking. In the face of these conditions, to attempt to increase market position would be expensive and the benefits low. Instead, the long-run objective should be to convert assets (including market position) into cash—cash that can be more profitably invested in other areas.

3. This strategy does mean trying to retain the original equipment business. Also passenger tires for replacement would be sold widely through independent dealers at a somewhat lower price than Goodyear and Firestone (and Michelin). To succeed

---

[1] For the significance of these balancing issues, see Chapter 15.

in both markets Uniroyal must have quality products and low enough costs to be able to underprice its major competitors.

4. For product development, a "fast follower" policy appears feasible. A variety of experiments are being tried by large competitors and it is uncertain which will succeed. If any one tire company makes a breakthrough, the large auto companies will insist on a second supplier before adopting the innovation. Thus, know-how and patents will be available to Uniroyal. Being ready to grasp such an opportunity is much less expensive than conducting the original and risky research.

5. The marketing approach sketched in (2) above does not call for as much TV and similarly expensive advertising. Only enough to keep dealers and car owners recognizing Uniroyal tires as quality, dependable products is necessary. So, this strategy calls for less R&D and less advertising, and relying more on lower prices which such saving makes possible.

6. Over time Uniroyal may lose market position by following the above strategy. But if carefully done, it provides a means of reducing (in real dollars) the company's large investment in a mature business.

Executive Response

The preceding proposals have received very mixed responses by Uniroyal executives. Among the critical comments are: "We need more, not less, advertising." "It's odd to place our bets where our market position is weakest." "Michelin, Goodyear, and Bridgestone are already going after the truck replacement business." "Why not be creative in passenger tires as well as in truck tires?" "Sure, General Motors wants a second supplier, but as fast-followers we'd get 10% of their business instead of 36%." "How can I keep an enthusiastic field organization when they suspect we are liquidating the business?" "We beat Firestone in developing radials, and if you leave R&D alone we'll do it again on the next round." "With almost a billion dollars tied up in the tire business, a thirty-seven million dollar improvement looks small." "The 1980's will be different, so let's not yield an inch."

Question

What strategy do you recommend that Uniroyal follow in its tire business?

Part 2

DEFINING MAJOR POLICY

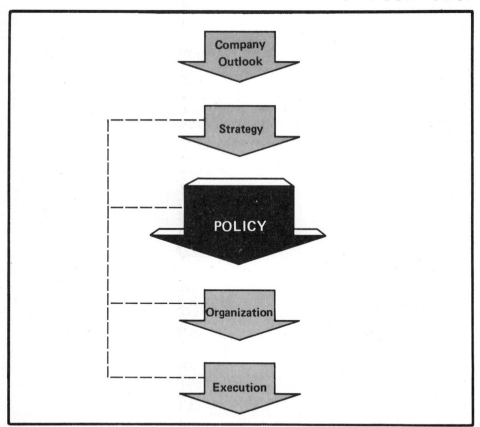

MARKETING POLICY— PRODUCT LINE AND CUSTOMERS

Relation of Policy to Strategy

Strategy, as defined in Chapter 5, takes a broad, total company view and singles out major targets for company action. Its strength arises from highly selective concentration on a few critical issues. To achieve this necessary perspective and emphasis, strategy sets aside a whole array of issues "to be considered later." Policy deals with an important group—though not all—of these issues that were temporarily set aside.

A policy is a standing plan; it is used over and over to guide specific actions. For example, if a company adopts a policy to sell only for cash, all employees give a consistent answer to any customer asking for credit. Every company needs policy covering many aspects of its operations in order to simplify decision-making and to give predictability and consistency to actions taken at different times by different people.

In addition, policy serves a key role in spelling out, clarifying, and testing strategy. Frequently strategy is stated in such general terms that its interpretation can be varied. A carefully selected policy sharpens the meaning of the strategy and guides specific decisions in a direction that supports the strategy. In a sense, no strategy has really been thought through until its implications for policy (and programs) have been explored. Sometimes as our planning follows through from a tentative strategy to more specific policy we encounter a stumbling block that causes us to go back and revise the strategy. In the end, each should support the other. To be sure, some policy is adopted for administrative convenience and is not affected one way or the other by a change in strategy; our focus here, however, is on policy that does directly help implement strategy.

Basic Policy Issues

Since each company has its own unique strategy, its policy will also be individually tailored. However, virtually every firm faces a similar set of issues, and an analysis of policy can be expedited and improved by a systematic exploration of these basic issues. A convenient sequence for analysis is:

1. Marketing policy.
2. Production and purchasing policy.
3. Personnel policy.
4. Financial policy.

These groups are interrelated, and it is impossible to make final decisions for one group without considering other groups. Some companies may have still other policies for specialized activities. Nevertheless, the sequence does provide a logical approach to overall company activities, so in this Part the chapters are arranged to illustrate this flow of analysis.

Within the marketing policy sphere, every enterprise needs general guidelines with respect to (1) product line, (2) customers, (3) pricing, and (4) marketing mix.

PRODUCT LINE

Although the domain part of company strategy defines the type of product or service to be sold—such as mobile home sites, textbooks, or sneakers—rarely does it provide answers to the following questions: How many *different* sizes, grades, and shapes of the product will be carried in the line? Just how can our products be made *distinctive* from those of competitors? Should we *change* product design frequently, say every spring, or stick with a tested model? We need standard answers—policy —on such issues for two reasons: first, to build a desired and consistent interpretation of strategy, and second because many marketing, production, and financial activities will be affected by the simplicity or the elaborateness of our product line.

Variety of Products

For each strategic niche, a company must decide what variety of products will be offered to its customers. This is a recurring and often controversial problem as markets change, competition grows, and new technology becomes available.

Cost of diversity. Customers are continually asking for products that are smaller, stronger, another voltage, or otherwise different from what is offered, and sales representatives will contend that the sales volume could be increased materially if they had a larger variety of products to sell.

One manufacturer of soaps yielded to this pressure. Whenever the sales manager noted that competitors were offering a new soap or that a number of customers had requested a new soap that differed in color, shape, fragrance, or composition, a new product meeting these specifications would be introduced. Examination of sales records showed that sales of most of these new products were satisfactory for several months but would gradually dwindle.

Apparently the initial sales were due to the enthusiasm of the sales representatives for a new product and a willingness on the part of the retailers to try an original stock to see how the product would sell. After this original

NARROW PRODUCT LINE
IN EARLY OR MIDDLE STAGES OF PRODUCT LIFE CYCLE
TENDS TO BE UNPROFITABLE

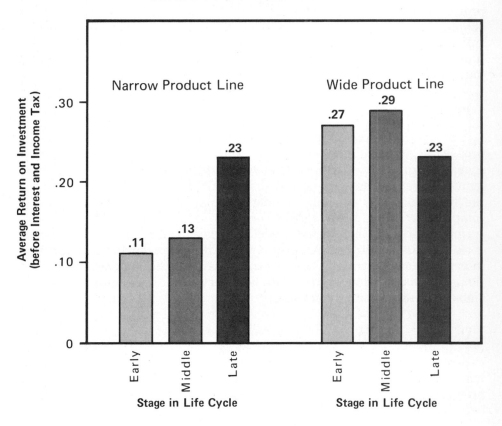

Source: Strategic Planning Institute.

distribution, however, most new products were discovered to have no unique appeal. This particular company, therefore, had a large number of products for which the sales volume was inadequate to justify the cost of manufacturing, warehousing, and selling. Only by careful study the company was able to reduce the number of items carried to comparatively few products that really had significant differences. It then concentrated its attention on selling these products rather than dissipating its efforts on new and unnecessary additions to its line.

One way to deal with this recurring controversy is to fix a limit on the number of items. Then any proposal for a new item must be accompanied by a recommendation to drop an existing one. While exceptions may be necessary, this plan has the advantage of forcing attention to pruning along with justifying the new item.

Need for complete line. In some situations the customer desires to buy a variety of products from the same source. For example, each of us expects the local druggist to be able to fill within a few hours any prescription our doctor may write. The druggist, in turn, expects the same kind of complete line service from drug wholesalers. Since a single slow delivery is likely to result in a long-time loss in patronage, a complete line is very important.

In contrast, a policy to concentrate on only a few items may be wise for a firm seeking distinction as a specialist. A paper company may sell only newsprint, for example, or a firm may specialize in putting out fires at oil and gas wells. By focusing on a narrow line, costs can be reduced; and if the product is sold in *large enough units* to warrant separate action by customers, the lack of a complete line may be no serious handicap. A narrow line policy relies on specialization to achieve a competitive advantage in pricing, unique service, or concentrated attention.

Ways of customizing products. A middle position may be feasible. Perhaps some variety can be offered without too much added expense. Common practice with automobiles or refrigerators, for instance, is to have basically a standard product but with two or three sizes and other options as to color and accessories. The number of variations is strictly limited, and the optional items are available only by paying a premium. While inventory and production scheduling are complicated by this practice, it does give the customer some choice.

Product Differentiation

Variety of products is one way to seek differential advantage. A related and perhaps less costly possibility is to offer "better" products; that is, better in the eyes of our desired set of customers. This raises a question: In what respects will a company try to make its products distinctive? Usually the company will have a standing answer, because it wants a continuing and consistent reputation in the market and because its engineers and production people need guidance on what to emphasize.

What is quality? Quality is not capable of an exact definition. The purchaser of garden tools may define quality in terms of *durability,* while the buyer of a dress who expects to use it only one season may be more interested in richness of *appearance*. For medical products, quality usually refers to *purity;* customers will pay a high premium for a product they feel confident is pure. *Dependability* is crucial in the space industry, and so forth. So, if a company seeks distinctiveness on the basis of product quality, it must decide the particular characteristics it will stress. Here, desired market segmentation is the key in setting policy.

In television programming there is doubt about how much basic difference the major networks really want. Likewise, universities would like to excel in accepted dimensions but are reluctant to change their services in any way that will be challenged by accrediting bodies. In contrast, Arthur Treacher's Fish and Chips outlets rely on product differences to attract customers away from the more common hamburger chains.

Consumer recognition of product differences. In deciding on the kind of distinctiveness to emphasize, the company must consider not only the desires of its customers but also their ability to appreciate variations in quality. Even purchasers of hi-fi sets have limits in ability to detect differences in tone quality. The company must therefore determine (a) what characteristics of its product its customers feel are important; (b) the extent to which its customers can appreciate the differences in such features and how much they are willing to pay for this extra quality; and (c) whether the cost of producing extra features is more or less than customers are willing to pay for them.

Frequency of Design Change

Related to the question of how product distinction is to be achieved is the troublesome issue of how frequently changes in design should be made.

Costs of change. Design changes are costly. First comes the technical and marketing research, engineering, testing, and tooling-up for the redesigned product. For simple products, such preparation expenses often amount to thousands of dollars; for complex products, like automobiles or airplanes, to millions of dollars. General Motors invested over $2 billion on its new line of front-wheel drive cars. Then, manufacturing costs tend to increase if frequent changes are made. New skills have to be learned, production runs are shorter, and overhead builds up.

Next, inventory problems are complicated. Enough but not too much of the old product is needed as it is being phased out, and stocks of the new product must be built for an uncertain demand. The same problem arises at each stage in distribution—wholesaler, retailer, and perhaps consumer. In fact, anticipation of new models often leads to wide fluctuations in distributors' inventory and irregular orders for the manufacturer. If the manufacturer wants to keep distributive channels well stocked, it may have to accept return of old merchandise or make price concessions.

Finally, service problems are complicated by frequent design changes. The user of the product will expect repair parts to be readily available and those servicing the product to understand the idiosyncrasies of each model. As users of foreign products know from bitter experience, adequate service on a product has a significant effect on its usefulness and its resale value.

But these costs of development, manufacture, distribution, and service are only one side of the picture. In setting a policy for frequency of design changes, the manager must also consider the benefits of changing.

Pressures to change. The most recent style may be so important to consumers that frequent design changes are inevitable. Today even staple products are styled according to the current mode. Kitchenware and bathtubs, which still render the same service they did thirty years ago, are streamlined and styled to the modern taste. Bath towels and sheets have blossomed out in all colors of the rainbow; even steam hammers are now streamlined.

Change may be necessary for more technical reasons. New developments are occurring every year in color television, microfilming, and solid-state controls of machines, to mention only a sample. If customers are to be well served, a company must from time to time adapt its products to such technological developments.

The pressures of style or technology are strong by themselves. Competitors' actions, however, may make the need to change irresistible. When a clearly preferred product is offered by a competitor, a company must respond in some manner, usually by redesigning its own products.

Frequency of change. Several alternative ways of reconciling the pressures and the costs of redesign of products are available to managers. Annual models are often used for consumer goods. Another tack, more common in industrial goods, is a policy of "product leadership." Here the firm wants to be first on the market with improvements, and new designs are introduced as rapidly as new technology is developed. But as one urban planner observed, "You don't tear down your house every time a new heat pump is invented."

A few firms try the leapfrog approach. Once they have a good design, they stick with it, letting competitors try various modifications. Then when significant improvements are evident, they make a major adjustment—incorporating not only competitors' advances but hopefully many more. The presumption here is that production and marketing economies of few changes will more than offset a temporary lag in improvements. In those fields where technological change has been slow, this policy works well.

Product Line Policy of a Service Company

The issues regarding product line are easier to grasp when we use physical products as examples. However, most service enterprises face comparable problems. Consider a university. What variety of courses should it offer—

aerospace, black studies, and Sanskrit? How should it differentiate its services from other universities? What characteristics of quality are significant, and can the consumer recognize the differences? How frequently should programs change? A similar set of questions confront advertising agencies, hospitals, and management consultants. Clearly, these issues are fundamental in developing a viable, continuing relationship between a firm and the people who use its product/service output.

CUSTOMER POLICY

Customer policy, like product policy, is broadly determined by company strategy regarding domain but it needs elaboration and refinement before it gives adequate guidance to day-to-day decisions. Three kinds of issues arise again and again: What body of ultimate consumers does the company wish to serve? What channel of distribution will be most effective in reaching these consumers? And, what limits on size or other characteristics should be placed on customers with whom the company deals directly?

Consumers Sought

Distinction between customers and consumers. Confusion sometimes arises because of failure to distinguish between "customers" and "consumers." The term *consumer* means the one who *uses* a product (or service) for personal satisfaction or benefit; or in the case of industrial materials, the one who so *changes* the form of the product as to alter its identity. A *customer,* on the other hand, is anyone who *buys* goods. A customer may be a consumer, or it may be a dealer who will resell the product to someone else.

The habits and the wishes of the ultimate consumer of a product (or service) are of vital interest to all businesses having anything to do with the product, for a major purpose of economic activity is to create consumer satisfaction. In the original design of a product, during its production, and throughout its distribution, consumer satisfaction is ever a controlling consideration. Consequently, a policy clearly defining the "segments" of consumers sought should be an early decision for every company, even though the company may use middlemen (for example, retailers) to actually sell to those consumers.

Types of consumers. Various kinds of consumers want services of widely different nature. Thus, the restaurant catering to business executives offers a different service from the campus kitchen seeking the trade of students. A patent medicine company found as a result of studying its market that a major group of its consumers were people who spoke only foreign languages. These groups were located primarily in large industrial centers and could be reached only by foreign language newspapers and circulars printed in foreign languages.

When a manufacturer of electric-powered hand tools decided to tap the do-it-yourself market in addition to its established market with the professional building trades, it failed to recognize the difference in needs of the two types of customers. The amateurs required more foolproof machines and elementary instruction sheets. After two years of losses, the manufacturer returned to its policy of focusing only on the professional market.

The relation of a company to consumers of its products is normally continuous over a period of years. Reputations are established, and expectations —so vital to careful planning—are built up. Consequently, a company cannot move in and out of a market from week to week. Instead, well-established and relatively stable policies regarding consumers to be served are very useful.

Location of consumers. The large mail-order houses such as Sears, Roebuck and Montgomery Ward built their businesses with rural consumers— people who had difficulty getting to cities to shop. But conditions have changed. Now there are fewer farmers, and they drive automobiles. One adjustment to this shift has been an impressive expansion of retail stores operated by these companies.

Nevertheless, the mail-order business also continues to prosper. How? Through a shift in definition of potential consumers. The largest mail-order market now is the suburban homemaker, whose children and other duties make shopping a chore, and the "do-it-yourselfer." They find the semiannual catalogs a storehouse of merchandise information and a convenient way to select many items. To be sure, the merchandise offered has been adapted to appeal to the nonfarm consumer, and telephone ordering is replacing the mailed order. But, vital to the planning of what will be offered is a clear concept of where the potential buyers live.

How about exports? In analyzing foreign markets, as any other new markets, the added or *incremental* costs should be balanced against the added income. Once a company has completed its product engineering and is "tooled-up" for production, the cost per unit of turning out an added 5% or 10% is less than the total average cost of the basic output. If the company has idle capacity in its plant, this incremental cost may be very much lower. So, even though there are difficulties in selling abroad, the net revenue received may still be above the incremental cost. Banks, advertising agencies, and consultants also seek clients abroad, but they are exporting only ideas and services.

Full utilization of an existing strength may be a factor. Most common is adoption of *national distribution* because national advertising of the company—already necessary for part of the market—is reaching consumers in all areas. In these cases, sales promotion considered to be desirable dictates the market scope, rather than consumer policy determining what promotion is feasible. A somewhat similar situation arises when a company invests heavily to acquire technical know-how for a specific problem and then feels impelled to serve all people having this problem regardless of where they are located.

Competitive tactics may also influence policy regarding location of desired consumers. For instance, Company A may immediately follow Company B into a new area—say the West Coast—because A does not want B to acquire a possible source of strength that might be extended to other markets. On the other hand, if a pattern of normal territories has evolved, Company X may not move into Company Y's home market for fear that Y will reciprocate. Such intangible considerations may result in a firm not pushing its territorial limits just to the point where incremental selling and delivery costs match incremental revenue.

Consumers of a "small business." Over the years small businesses have typically catered to local consumers. Dramatic improvements in transportation and communication, however, have undercut the local butcher, baker, and candlestick-maker. National concerns now reach even the remotest consumers, and consumers drive many miles to shop. Local semi-monopolies are fast disappearing. Consequently, most small businesses now are seeking more distinction in their products and services, while expanding the geographical location of their potential consumers.

Channels of Distribution

By *channel of distribution* is meant the *steps* by which products are *distributed* from the one who first converts them into usable form to the consumer. Many enterprises, of course, render services rather than manufacture products; for example, airlines, banks, public accountants, and all sorts of retail stores. Because of their nature, such services are almost always sold directly to consumers. But for manufacturers the selection of the proper channels of distribution is a very real problem.

Changes in buying habits, transport, communications, and market locations have modified methods of distribution greatly during recent years. This whole field is in a state of flux, and few companies are justified in assuming that their traditional channels are necessarily the most effective ways of reaching the consumer they prefer. The farsighted choice of the right channel of distribution sometimes becomes a major "differential advantage."

Through jobbers. Utilizing jobbers (or wholesalers) was long regarded as the orthodox method of distribution. They assemble products from many manufacturers, store them, and sell them to retailers. In so doing, they also assume risks of price change, damage, or obsolescence; they extend credit to retailers; and they sort and ship products according to retailer needs.

All of these functions are essential in the distribution of merchandise; regardless of the channel of distribution used, someone must perform them. When a large part of consumer purchases was secured through small retailers scattered over a wide territory, it was more economical for a manufacturing firm to have the wholesaler perform these services than to undertake them itself.

Today, retailers are larger and many manufacturers have set up distribution systems which deal directly with them. Nevertheless, there are auto supply jobbers who serve repair shops, plumbing supply houses that serve plumbers, and similar specialty jobbers for a particular trade or industry. A baffling issue for every manufacturer is the extent of the use of such distributors; they add at least 20% to the selling price of the products.

Direct to retailers. Distribution by the manufacturing firm direct to retailers has some distinct advantages. By using specialty sales representatives to concentrate on the sale of the products, the manufacturer may secure more aggressive selling efforts; a jobber's general-line salespeople sell a wide variety of products and cannot concentrate their efforts upon the sale of one particular product. This plan may also enable a manufacturer to ascertain better the consumers' desires, since it enables firsthand contact with the final "point-of-sale," namely the retailer.

The manufacturing firm exercises more control over the final sale of its goods if it has direct contact with the retailer. Personal relationships and goodwill are tied to the manufacturer, and consequently the firm is not so dependent on the jobber for sales volume. Also, the manufacturer has a better opportunity to influence retail prices, display, and other factors that affect the popularity of the product with the consumer.

The plan of selling direct to retailers, however, may lead to excessive costs if it is used unwisely. If the manufacturing firm eliminates the jobber entirely, it may incur unbearable costs because many retailers buy in such small quantities that the expense of selling and servicing them may exceed the gross profits on the goods they purchase.

Companies that manufacture a variety of products may set up their own *sales branches.* These branches perform in many respects like a jobber, except that they sell only products of the parent company. One firm, for example, has eleven separate manufacturing divisions—each operated like an independent company. The sales division is another fairly independent unit with several branches that perform the functions of a jobber. A sales branch with its own sales staff enables a company to secure improved selling effort and at the same time have a local distributing point.

Direct to consumers. This plan is usually employed when the product is of such a nature that the salesperson needs a high degree of technical training to sell it, and when technical services must be rendered in connection with the product after it is sold. For example, this plan is used by manufacturers of office equipment such as duplicating machines, postage meters, and computers. Salespeople must be able to operate such equipment to sell it, and the manufacturer must be sure that the equipment is kept in proper repair. For similar reasons most industrial equipment is sold directly to users.

Use of *exclusive dealers*, as is done by automobile manufacturers and many oil companies, combines many advantages of direct sales to consumers while retaining the initiative of local businesspeople. The dealers "run their own business," but retaining a franchise means joining in company sales programs and conforming to service standards set by the company. Obviously, the producing company must have a good enough line of products for the typical dealer to make a profit or competent people will not apply for dealerships and the whole system will collapse.

Through brokers or agents. The broker usually performs only one major function of distribution—selling. As contrasted with the jobber, the broker usually sells only one type of product, or at most only a few closely related products. Although brokers are employed most frequently in the distribution of producer goods, they may also be used in the distribution of consumer goods. For example, brokers are often used by small canneries that do not have sufficient output to justify a full-time sales force. Anyone who has publicly announced an intention to buy a house or a suburban lot knows that brokers are also used in the real-estate field. Here, again, it is difficult for buyers and sellers to get together without the aid of someone who is in close contact with the market.

Selecting a channel of distribution. Dr. Thomas L. Berg suggests that selecting a channel of distribution be viewed as an organization problem and that the activities analyzed include the total distribution system. More specifically, his approach involves:

1. Listing all actions necessary between producer and consumer—promotion, actual selling, transportation, financing, warehousing, repackaging, risk-taking, installation and repair service, and the like.
2. Grouping these activities into jobs that can be effectively and efficiently performed by separate firms. These firms may be banks or warehouse workers who also do other things, or they may be firms exclusively involved in this particular channel. The crucial matter here is to conceive of jobs (packages of activities) that are the most effective combinations.
3. Defining relationships between the jobs that will assure cooperation and necessary flow of information. Also define how each firm involved is to be compensated for its efforts. And work out necessary, minimum controls to be exercised by various members over other members.
4. On the basis of the organization design (the *policy* adopted by the designer), developing specifications for the firms that are to fill each job.
5. Then moving on to execution of the plan by recruiting people to take the specified jobs (some negotiation may arise here since independent firms will be participants), educating people on how the plan is to work, supervising the day-to-day operations, and exercising necessary controls.[1]

One of the significant aspects of this approach is that the channel of distribution problem is not viewed as a choice between a few predetermined

---

[1] See T. L. Berg, "Designing the Distribution System," in W. D. Stevens (ed.), *The Social Responsibilities of Marketing,* American Marketing Association, 1962.

alternatives. Instead, each company should work out a design that is the best way to get its products to the consumers it has selected. Also implied is the idea that tasks assigned to participants are apt to need modification as economic and competitive conditions change.

Since a channel of distribution typically creates a complex set of relationships, a policy is needed to provide consistency and stability of action. And top management is vitally concerned because—as experience in the automobile, watch, liquor, and many other industries testifies—a strong, well-designed distribution system may spell the difference between success and failure of the entire enterprise.

Size of Customers

Customers that a company deals with directly may buy in quantities either too small or too large. The company should know how much it costs to serve each type of customer and the amount the customers must buy if their business is to yield a profit to the company. One manufacturing concern, for example, was selling to 8,000 retail accounts. An analysis of these accounts revealed that 55% of the total number purchased only 5% of its entire sales volume and that none of these 55% purchased more than $200 worth of merchandise a year. The company decided to eliminate all such accounts, which, it was thought, would not develop into better accounts, and as a consequence the number of customers was reduced to 4,000. This enabled the company to reduce its sales staff from 82 to 43 and to make a number of other substantial reductions in selling costs.

In deciding whether to eliminate customers who purchase in small quantities, consideration should be given to the potential purchases of these customers as well as to the actual purchases now made from the company. If these customers have the capacity to increase their purchases substantially, it may be desirable not to eliminate them but to concentrate on securing a larger percentage of their trade.

On the other hand, a customer may purchase too much merchandise! If a concern is dependent on one or two customers for most of its business, its position is vulnerable because loss of patronage of one such important buyer will disrupt the entire organization. In terms of Chapter 4, those few customers exercise too much relative power.

Companies in the aerospace industry often depend upon one or two large government contracts for the bulk of their business. Cancellation of or failure to win a renewal of such a contract can spell disaster for the firm. Advertising agencies may develop a similar overdependency on one or two large accounts; when an account is "dropped," the agency has to lay off most of its talented employees and may close entirely. Consequently, companies may have a policy that says no more than 20% of their business will be done with one customer.

SUMMARY

Company strategy requires elaboration to give it specificity and to put it in more operational terms. Policy is a major instrument for thinking through and sharpening such elaboration. And in this chapter we started a systematic review of key policy that almost always is involved in this "filling in of the broad picture."

Two dimensions that shape the domain part of every master strategy are the products (or services) to be sold and the customers who will buy them. So the discussion in this chapter of policy covering product line and customers is a logical starting point for this phase of company planning.

Sharpening of the product area singled out in a master strategy involves policy regarding the variety of products, product differentiation, and frequency of design changes.

Central management should also set up policy regarding the types and the location of final consumers the company hopes to reach, the distribution system to be used in getting products to such consumers, and the upper and lower limits on the size of direct customers. These adjustments to the market are vital to success; they have to be nurtured over time; and they need wise policy guidance for consistency and dependability.

There has been frequent occasion in this chapter to note how customer policy is closely related to many other aspects of a company's activities. For example, the customers sought will affect the kind of sales promotion needed, the size of plant, the type of sales and perhaps production personnel, the need for large accounts receivable, and other phases of operations. These interrelations will become more apparent in subsequent discussion of the other aspects of management and in the analysis of the cases found throughout the book.

QUESTIONS FOR CLASS DISCUSSION

1. The following is from a *Wall Street Journal* article: " 'Sears Recession' Afflicts Many Suppliers After Big Retailer Cuts Back Its Orders. . . . Lots of small Sears suppliers went from feast to famine . . . some 12,000 manufacturers sell Sears more than $10 billion in goods a year. . . . They have tried desperately to drum up new business elsewhere. . . . Many potential customers are openly resentful and suspicious of Sears suppliers. A hardware-store buyer says, 'I suspect the reliability of these manufacturers as long-term suppliers for me. They have a great credibility gap.' . . . Another problem is that most suppliers have little

or no name recognition because Sears puts its name—not the manufacturer's name—on almost everything it sells. . . . A Plasto salesman who calls on retailers, laments that much of his time is spent explaining what Plasto is. 'The Sears supplier doesn't have any worries except one—that Sears might decide not to do business with me next month.' "

(a) Does policy on the type and size of customers affect the power of a company (as described in Chapter 4)? Explain how this applies to Sears, its suppliers, and the other customers of the suppliers. (b) How might policy on customers and policy on channels of distribution be shaped so as to increase the relative power of a company? Does anything restrain a company's shaping policy this way?

2. Possibilities for the product line of a filling station include, in addition to gasoline and oil, the following: batteries, tires, antifreeze, oil filters, fan belts, windshield wipers, mufflers, brake linings, tire chains, soft drinks, cigarettes, souvenirs, candy, and an array of repair services ranging from motor tune-ups, front-end repairs, body work, and transmission replacement to greasing and car washing. (a) If you owned and operated a filling station, how would you decide on your product line? (b) If you were the manager of a major oil company's nationwide chain of filling stations, what policy would you establish regarding filling station product lines? What would you insist on? forbid? leave up to the local operator?

3. (a) In what ways do television broadcasting networks try to differentiate their "products" from other networks? In what way do they not try to differentiate themselves? (b) Select a TV station close to your university and recommend: (1) the extent it should call upon its network affiliation for its programs, and (2) the kind of local (or independent) programs it should broadcast. (c) How frequently should the local station *change* its policy with respect to (b.1) and (b.2)?

4. Most people find it difficult to distinguish between the services of real estate brokers. How might a progressive broker apply to its business the concepts of market segmentation and of product differentiation related to each segment? Under what conditions should a broker utilize the segmentation and differentiation you have developed?

5. Name two or more industries (in addition to plumbing and auto supplies mentioned in this chapter) in which specialty jobbers play a major role in distribution. What factors explain this continuing importance of jobbers? If you were a manufacturer in the industries that you have named, what functions would you want the jobber to perform? What functions that jobbers often perform would you try to reserve for your own organization?

6. A producer of room air-conditioners for use in homes is having difficulty obtaining adequate distribution. Use the Berg approach outlined on pages 126 and 127 to build a model of the total distribution system of the industry. Then select places in that system where you believe a company with only 12% of the total market could develop some comparative advantage. Assume that the products of all competitors have about the same characteristics and quality.

7. What are the advantages and disadvantages of using annual models to make changes in a company's products? Illustrate your answer in terms of: (a) skis, (b) life insurance, (c) travel tours, (d) airplanes.

8. A highly successful U.S. motorboat manufacturer is considering international expansion. Two markets being considered are England and Mexico. To what extent will the company's product line and customer policies need to be modified in each country?

9. The converter-resource model used in Chapter 1 to discuss social responsibility implied that relationships with each resource group are somewhat similar. Test this notion by applying the product and customer policy issues raised in this chapter to (a) labor and (b) raw material suppliers.

10. American Motors, under the leadership of George Romney, narrowed its product line in the late 1950's to concentrate on its Rambler line of compact cars. Another central executive group turned back to a full line of compact and full-sized cars in the 1960's. Then American Motors once again narrowed its product line to the specialized group of four-wheel-drive cars, the Jeep line, and imported subcompact cars to compete in the decade of the 1980's. (a) To what extent does the diagram on page 118 in this chapter explain or justify these three changes? (b) Are there other factors in addition to the width of the product line which affect American Motors' average return on investment?

11. The Olde & Rubaiyat advertising agency has been encouraged by its two leading U.S. clients to establish offices in Mexico City and Sao Paulo, Brazil. These clients say that they cannot obtain in Latin America the quality of service they are accustomed to in the U.S. Also, dealing abroad with the agency which already understands their products and approach to marketing would be a convenience. Business from these two clients barely supports an office in either city. Assume that Olde & Rubaiyat has decided to open the offices. Should it: (a) simply concentrate on these two clients as a special service? (b) Also try to serve U.S. clients, but confine its efforts to companies that want—and will pay U.S. rates for—the same advertising agency in at least two countries? (c) Actively seek any clients it can get in Mexico or Brazil?

CASE 6
Steiger Tractor, Inc.

Steiger Tractor, Inc. makes distinctive four-wheel-drive tractors and must find the best way to market them to large farmers. A striking example of "small business" innovation, the company could get in trouble either way it moves.

Through luck or foresight, Steiger fits neatly with trends in farming. During the last twenty-five years, U.S. agriculture has far outpaced manufacturing in mechanization and productivity. The number of farms has been cut in half and workers on farms dropped even more. But physical output rose more than 50% during the same period. Several factors have contributed to this record: improved seeds and farm animals, more fertilizer and chemical treatment, larger farms, and—by no means least—major increases in mechanization.

U.S. Farm Trends

Year	Number of Farms (millions)	Acres per Farm (average)	Farm Population (millions)	Output per Man/hr. (index)	Tractors on Farms (millions)	Horsepower on Farms (millions)
1950	5.6	213	23.0	34	3.4	93
1960	4.0	297	15.6	65	4.7	153
1970	2.9	374	9.7	112	4.6	203
1980*	*2.3*	*450*	*7.3*	*164*	*4.3*	*245*

*Estimate.

Most of the trends are clear, although the rates of change are slowing down. The number of tractors on farms, for example, has passed its peak. Only an increase in the size and power of new tractors has permitted the rise in total horsepower to continue. In 1965, when Steiger was still struggling to produce its big tractors in a converted dairy barn, only 2% of all tractors sold had more than 100 horsepower; ten years later almost half the new tractors exceeded this power.

The demand for agricultural equipment, however, fluctuates sharply with the rise and fall of farm prosperity. These cyclical changes, coupled with the natural seasonal change, create a lot of instability in tractor sales.

Highs and Lows in Tractor Shipments

Year	Units (thousands)	Value (millions)	Average Unit Value
1955 high	326	$ 519	$ 1,592
1960 low	156	358	2,295
1966 high	270	1,006	3,726
1971 low	165	892	5,406
1974 high	234	1,785	7,628
1978 low	174	2,663	15,305

Steiger has carved out a small, distinctive niche in this $2 billion farm tractor industry. The company was founded in Minnesota by two farmers who wanted a versatile, powerful tractor. They were among the first to make a four-wheel-drive tractor. Since then the company has consistently led the industry at the top of the power range, and now produces fifteen models varying from 210 to 450 horsepower.

A Steiger tractor is a rugged, sophisticated machine, with a retail price of $40,000 to $70,000 each. Like other large tractors, it has power-steering, power brakes, hydraulic lifts, etc. The cab is equipped with air-conditioning, radio and tape-player, noise insulation, wide visibility, adjustable seat—all to ease the very long, strenuous days in the field.

Several of Steiger's large competitors now offer four-wheel-drives on some of their large tractors. However, Steiger has a unique construction which it claims enables its tractors to get the maximum benefit of a four-wheel-drive. A Steiger tractor is "articulated," which means its body has a joint in the middle which permits the front and rear axles to move independently of each other in both a horizontal and vertical plane. This articulated body can keep all four wheels on the ground in hilly or uneven terrain and thereby reduce slippage. Moreover, an articulated body significantly reduces a tractor's turning radius.

The advantages of four-wheel-drive, and especially Steiger's articulated body, are (1) reduced soil compaction, (2) improved ability to work in wet fields and otherwise act fast when planting and harvesting should be done, and (3) increased fuel economy. Steiger's 267-gallon fuel tank and lighting system allow twenty hours of uninterrupted running time.

Four-wheel-drive tractors are more expensive than conventional two-wheel-drives, and this hurt sales. In the recent cyclical downturn, from a peak market penetration of 6.3% of all tractor sales in 1976, four-wheel-drives slumped the following year to 4.7% of the total. Ten thousand units is a good year for four-wheel-drives, and Steiger is fortunate to market 20% of these.

A critical problem facing Steiger management is how best to sell its tractors. Clearly, sales must be made through agricultural equipment dealers because they have continuing contacts with farmers and are the source of local service. But there are at least three ways to reach the dealers:

1. Steiger can rely, as it now does, on its own dealer network. These dealers will sell other farm equipment and other kinds of tractors in order to have a sizeable and sustained volume of business. But their four-wheel-drive tractors will be only Steiger's. They should carry inventory and be prepared to service what they sell.
2. Other farm equipment manufacturers or even tractor manufacturers might sell Steiger tractors with the Steiger name, guarantee, etc.
3. Steiger could simply sell its product to other tractor manufacturers to be resold by them under their respective trade names. Steiger's primary efforts would then be focused on product design and manufacturing.

The marketing vice president wants to build his own dealer network. "We already have about 300 dealers in 38 states. Most are well established dealers for a big full-line company, and have simply added our tractors. But with a total of over 10,000 dealers in the U.S. there obviously are still many areas where we should be represented but are not. If we turn our marketing over to other companies we're sure to suffer. Either they will neglect the product and just carry it to make their line look complete; or if articulated tractors take off like we believe they should, the other companies will start producing themselves—and our patents are not strong enough to stop them."

The treasurer has doubts about "our own dealer network. It is very expensive to maintain contacts with dealers, many of whom may sell only one or two of our tractors a year. Also, we have a single product line, and to promote that alone we should spend up to a million dollars a year in advertising. Financing is another angle. Inventory and accounts receivable—including the floor stock which we want the dealers to carry—come to about half of annual sales. If we did sell 5,000 units at $30,000 each, we'd need $75,000,000 in current assets; our present equity of about $15 million is much too small to support that.

"I know," the treasurer continued, "that there are risks in tying up with other manufacturers, especially when they are much bigger than we are. However, they do have the capital and are already absorbing the expense of the dealer network. As long as no one of them sells very many articulated tractors, they probably will be glad to leave short production runs to us. Of course, they could undertake their own production; we buy 80% of our parts. But after years of experience we do have specialized know-how and a demonstrated record of dependable products."

The key actors in the agricultural equipment industry with whom Steiger might work out some kind of a relationship are:

Deere & Company,   largest company in the industry with farm equipment sales of over $2.5 billion. Already making and selling four-wheel-drive tractors. Most profitable company in industry.

International Harvester,   close second to Deere in agricultural equipment, but truck sales are even larger. Pushing diversification outside of agriculture. Sells four-wheel-drive tractors, although stresses two-wheel-drives.

Massey-Ferguson,   large Canadian company with world-wide sales. One of top three full-line agricultural equipment companies. Does have two four-wheel-drive models in lower power range. Recently serious financial difficulties are leading to some retrenchment.

Allis Chalmers,   a diversified company whose agricultural equipment sales are about 25% of each of the three leaders. Distribution is uneven. Sells but does not manufacture two four-wheel-drive tractor models.

J.I. Case,   formerly a full-line company that got into serious trouble switching its product emphasis. Now focusing on selective areas including several big tractor models. Also diversifying into industrial lines.

Ford,   for years a leader in small tractors, has been slow in adjusting to trend toward larger equipment. Does sell several models of powerful four-wheel-drive tractors. Auto parent gives financial strength.

Others include *Versatile* (a small pioneer-like Steiger in four-wheel-drives; financially weak) and *White Motors* (which bought up and is trying to rationalize three ailing agricultural equipment producers). *Hesston* and *North Holland* sell a variety of implements though not tractors.

Question

What distribution policy do you recommend for Steiger Tractor, Inc.?

MARKETING POLICY—
PRICING

An inescapable issue in building relationships with customers is price. Whether blazoned on a ten-foot sign swinging over a subdivision real estate office or discreetly noted in a bill from a doctor, the charge for products or services must be dealt with sensitively.

Inflation, changing fashion and technology, shortages, competitive jockeying, and union contracts all have an impact on pricing. Because price adjustments are often used to reconcile or "balance off" such diverse pressures, setting prices is a complicated task. This complexity and sensitivity make necessary some general policy to guide executives in their daily actions.

Important issues on which policy guidance is useful include:

1. How much emphasis will be placed on relative prices as a *competitive weapon?*
2. What will be the relation of prices to *costs* of production and distribution?
3. What adjustments will be made in *anticipating responses* to our initiatives?
4. Will all customers be charged the same price? If not, on what basis will *differences* be established?
5. What *protection* will be provided against price changes?

The above sequence of questions does provide a general approach to pricing. However, the issues are so interrelated only tentative answers can be given to one question until the others are considered.

PRICING AS A COMPETITIVE WEAPON

One way to think of pricing is as a competitive weapon. By setting our prices higher, the same, or lower than competitors' prices we are establishing a basic relation to the competitive market. We signal both customers and competitors how we intend to play the game. In this respect, pricing is one part of the total "marketing mix" (discussed in the next chapter) that we will use to attract customers.

Position Relative to Competitors' Prices

The extent to which a company can wisely establish its prices either higher or lower than those charged by competitors depends on the kind of products it is selling. Highly standardized products such as cotton or gold have such a competitive market that continuing differentials are not practical. At the other extreme, consulting services or art objects are so unique that only the most general comparisons with competitors are possible.

In between are the vast majority of products which are somewhat distinctive in their characteristics or services provided with them. For these the customer does perceive some difference, and there is an open question whether my products are worth more than yours. For instance, is an IBM computer with its reputation for quality and known availability of repair service worth 20% more than a physically similar computer offered by a new competitor?

When significant product or service differentiation is achieved, the company must decide whether (a) a higher price than that of competitive products will be charged, or (b) a comparable price will be set and the superior quality or service will be used as a means of building sales volume, or (c) a high price will be used initially to "skim the cream off the market" and then the price will be cut to competitive levels. The choice of one of these alternative policies depends, in part, upon how long the product or service distinctiveness can be maintained and how much premium consumers are willing to pay for the superior quality.

Marketing Benefits Sought from Pricing

If pricing is thought of as a marketing tool, as just suggested, then the marketing objectives being sought via pricing should be clear. Here are some of the possibilities.

Increased volume of orders from present customers is a common aim. For this purpose, prices somewhat below competitors' is an obvious option, especially for smaller companies trying to increase their share of the total market. Manufacturers of room air conditioners, for instance, often use relatively low prices with this aim. A serious drawback is that customers often assume that a lower price means lower quality, and many may not want what they believe is a lower-quality product.

Attracting new customers is another frequent goal. Since the target group is only a part of the total market, special prices for that group are typically devised. A low introductory price—commonly used by magazines —or even free samples may be a way to get new customers acquainted with the product. Or if the new group will consume the product in a different way, a continuing discount for them may be warranted.

Maintaining an attractive position is a normal view for well established firms. In these situations, keeping prices on a par with competitors' is the usual policy. "Don't rock the boat" is the goal.

Maximizing short-run cash flow is another possibility, but not a popular one among marketing executives. Here prices are kept high even though doing so results in losing some customers to competitors. When there is reason to believe that future demand for the product will fall regardless of our pricing, and we have good alternative uses for cash, then short-run return takes priority.

Markets for most products are much more intricate and sensitive than the preceding alternatives (and economic textbooks) imply. Of course, pricing policy must be tailored to fit these complexities. However, pricing also should give support to the broad strategy being pursued by the company. The theme of this section is that central managers should make sure that this linking between marketing goals and pricing practice is clearly understood.

PRICING IN RELATION TO COSTS

In addition to seeking marketing benefits, a second basic approach to pricing policy is relating prices to costs. Experts differ on what costs to consider, but no one argues that costs can be ignored.

Selling at a Normal Profit Above Cost

A policy to set prices at cost plus a normal profit is much more common than economic textbooks imply. It suits three kinds of situations especially well. (1) For unique services—a consultation with a doctor or the repair of furniture, for instance—there can be no market price, and the benefit received by the customer is hard to measure. So a "professional" relationship is established in which the fee is based on time spent. (2) Public utilities, other monopolies, and diverse nonprofit enterprises basically aim to set prices that cover costs and enough margin to attract capital needed. (3) Other firms may choose to subordinate price as a sales appeal and, if competition will permit, simply charge what both buyer and seller feel is a "fair" price, which typically is cost plus a normal profit.

In all such situations mutual confidence and normal expectations are essential. Consequently, policy that introduces consistency and predictability into the pricing serves an important role. Of course, from time to time the policy may be changed, in which case a new mutual understanding must be established. And there will be occasional questions about the applications of the policy to unusual transactions. But clearly the aim is to remove price as an issue for negotiation, while retaining flexibility in the actual charges.

In practice, measuring cost and profit may be complex. (The federal government has a library of manuals and thousands of accountants devoted to measuring costs on its "cost plus fixed fee" purchases.) Standard guides are needed for (a) the per diem rates to be charged for labor, (b) the way prices for materials will be determined, (c) the allocation of overhead, (d) the treatment of idle capacity, and (e) the level and base for computing normal profit.

Setting prices at cost plus a normal profit is a comfortable way to deal with a troublesome problem. But it may be too comfortable. Opportunities for more effective use of resources may be overlooked, and new competition may be invited. Moreover, a cost plus normal profit policy does not resolve issues of price lining, protection, and frequency of change, and it is hard to apply to market segmentation.

Selling Below Cost

Pricing on the basis of out-of-pocket expenses. A number of conditions may lead a company to establish prices below the total cost of a product. Every firm has certain expenses such as interest, rent, and executive salaries that must be paid regardless of the volume of sales. Other costs, such as materials and direct labor, vary with the volume of activity. These latter costs are *out-of-pocket expenses,* and theoretically any sale above such incremental costs will make some contribution to overhead and profit. Especially when a company is trying to gain market position, selling at incremental costs is appealing.

Strong feeling exists in many industries against selling goods at a price below the total cost. The manager of a printing establishment, for instance, recognized that he might secure additional business if he reduced his price to slightly more than his out-of-pocket expenses, but he refused to do so because he did not want to "spoil the market." He pointed out that if he reduced his price, competitors might follow suit and soon all business would have to be taken at the low price. Moreover, after the price had once been generally used throughout the market, it would be difficult to return it to the present level. In other words, pricing followed at one time may materially affect the price structure for subsequent sales.

Loss leaders. Still another reason why retail stores occasionally sell below cost is to attract customers to the store. In such cases one or more standard products are sold at a loss; and it is hoped the loss will be more than offset by the profit on the sale of other merchandise to the customer while in the store, or on subsequent visits resulting from the contact established by the special sale. In many states there is agitation to prohibit the use of loss leaders, but from a strictly business point of view it is difficult to see any valid distinction between incurring a loss on certain types of merchandise and spending money for other forms of advertising. (Misrepresenting the

reasons for selling below cost or selling below cost for the purpose of eliminating competition are already contrary to federal law.)

A company may sell some minor item at a price below the total cost just
to render a service to its regular customers. This may be done on a certain
part of the product, or it may be done on a particular item necessary to
complete the line. Such a practice is distinct from using loss leaders in that
it is done as an accommodation and is not featured.

Pricing Above Cost During Inflation

During inflation most costs and prices are rising. Trouble arises when
costs go up faster than prices. Such a squeeze is likely to occur in two quite
different ways.

A company may set prices in, say, January for goods or services that are
produced in June. When the prices were set the margins above costs at that
time were satisfactory, but by June wages and raw material and energy
prices have risen so much that the margins evaporated. Of course, the
January prices could be set higher in anticipation of rising costs. The problem is that in January we do not know how rapidly costs will go up. If we
overestimate, our prices may be seriously above competitors' prices, and we
thereby encourage loss of business. Also, too much anticipation may be
contrary to the prevailing government control on price increases.

Note that the more we and everyone else raise prices in anticipation of
higher costs, the faster will actual costs rise. Moreover, the longer the time-
span between price-setting and shipment of goods, the greater the potential
squeeze.

The second way prices and costs get out of line is hidden. Part of our costs
—notably for machinery and inventory—may be incurred when prices are
set or even before. The margins of selling prices above these actual outlays
may be attractive, and the resulting profits reported by normal accounting
look fine. The catch is that the machinery and inventory have to be replaced
if we are to continue in business. During inflation the replacement cost will
be substantially higher, and the normal profits on the previous transactions
may be quite inadequate to cover the added sums needed to remain in
business. A depletion of real capital has occurred.

The pricing policy issue is deciding how much of these inflated costs to
try to recover by prompt price increases. *Assuming legal restraints leave the
company some flexibility,* a reasonable answer can be found in the marketing
objectives discussed briefly earlier in the chapter. What does the company
prefer to accomplish? During the uncertainties and tensions of inflation,
customer-supplier relationships are more volatile. Therefore, more opportunities to increase market position arise for firms that are prepared to
sacrifice profit margins. Likewise, more care is needed to maintain an existing customer base. Cash may be generated—probably at the loss of goodwill
—if that has top priority.

Inflation greatly increases the difficulty of estimating costs, and of keeping track of competitors' prices and costs. But for the firm that does know where it stands, opportunities to improve its relative position are likely to arise.

EFFECT OF PRICES ON VOLUME/COSTS/PROFITS

In most companies the total cost of products varies with the volume sold. A partially filled airliner (or classroom), for example, may handle a substantial increase in passengers (or students) with little change in total operating cost. In the production of many metal products, the cost of making dies and setting up machinery for production is often half of the total expense of producing a normal volume. This fixed expense will remain the same whether the volume is cut in half or doubled. Thus, there will be a substantial variation in the *average cost per unit*.

Note that the foregoing tendency holds true only when the production capacity of facilities is not fully used. If a motel, for instance, had to build an addition and increase its staff in order to handle additional customers, its profit on each customer might not increase at all.

There are, of course, many companies in which the fixed expenses are comparatively small and consequently the unit costs do not change greatly with the changes in volume. For example, the expenses of a commission merchant dealing in fruits and vegetables consist largely of material costs. Similarly, contractors building homes have low fixed expense. Nevertheless, for most companies the effect of price levels on volume and via volume on average unit costs should be weighed when establishing pricing policy.

Estimating Profits for Different Price Levels

When per unit cost varies with volume, the manager should estimate the quantity of output that can be sold at different prices; the effect of change in volume on the cost of goods produced as well as on the cost of selling; and the combined effect of changes in the price, the volume, and the cost on total net profits.

A hypothetical illustration will indicate the possible variations resulting from changes in price. A company may be able to sell 800 dresses at $40 a dress. By reducing the price to $36, 1,200 dresses may be sold; and at a price of $32, 2,000 dresses may be sold. Additional reductions in price may increase the demand for the product further. The possible effects of variations in price on the sales volume, the cost, and the net results are shown in the table that follows.

In the example the cost per unit decreases as the volume increases—a typical experience for many companies. In most instances, however, unit costs do not decline as rapidly since the prices must be reduced in order to secure the additional volume. Consequently, the *profit per unit* diminishes as is indicated in Column 4 of the table.

Profit per unit, however, is not the final answer regarding the desirability of a particular price because recognition must be given to the number of units on which this profit is earned. Thus, if an increase in price results in a significantly higher profit per unit and a comparatively small reduction in volume (from $28 to $32 in the illustration), the total profit will be increased. But if the drop in volume is sharp, it may more than offset the higher profit per unit (from $32 to $36 in the illustration).

The Effect of Price on Volume, Cost, and Profit

(1) Price	(2) Number of Units Sold	(3) Cost per Unit	(4) Profit per Unit	(5) Total Profit (2) × (4)
$40	800	$28.00	$12.00	$ 9,600 .
36	1,200	23.00	13.00	15,600
32	2,000	22.00	10.00	20,000
28	2,500	21.60	6.40	16,000
24	3,000	21.20	2.80	8,400

Factors Affecting Response of Volume to Changes in Price

The total profit secured at each price, as can be seen by the preceding table, depends upon the volume of sales as well as the average cost per unit. Clearly, management must estimate as best it can not only the effect of volume on the total cost but also the volume of sales that will be secured at different prices. In practice the response of volume to price changes depends upon many factors, such as the following.

The effect of a price change on competitors will depend significantly on the *size of the company quoting low prices.* Price changes by a large and dominant firm in an industry are very likely to affect the prices of the entire industry. Thus, in the farm machinery industry a recognized *price leader* must anticipate that its price changes will be copied by most, though not all, of its competitors. On the other hand, a small company may be able to quote prices lower than those of the large competitors because its total sales volume is not important enough to the large company to warrant an adjustment of its entire price schedule. In the steel industry, for example, several small concerns have been able to increase their business by shading the prices quoted by the leading companies.

If there are two or three price leaders (oligopolistic competition), any one of them typically will raise its price only when it predicts that major competitors will follow. Such predictions are based on rising labor and material costs throughout the industry and on guesses about the competitors' desire to increase their volume—to fill up plant capacity and/or to gain market position—even at the sacrifice of profit.

Another factor in the response of volume to price changes is the *elasticity of the demand*. We have observed that if a retail store has a big sale with prices on standard articles significantly reduced, the volume of sales will be greatly expanded. In fact, the sale of certain articles will be doubled and trebled. The use of synthetic fibers has expanded greatly as its real price has declined. On the other hand, a doctor would not greatly increase the volume of his business if he were to make a 25% reduction in his charges, nor would an electric power company sell much more current for household use if it were to make a similar reduction in its rates.

The behavior of the price of one product may affect the response of volume to price changes in another product. Packing companies have observed that if the price of pork rises while the price of beef remains constant, there will be a significant decrease in the consumption of pork. Should beef prices rise at the same time pork prices are increased, there will be a much smaller drop in the volume of pork consumed.

Professional buyers for industrial concerns, as well as retail stores, *adjust the volume of their purchases to anticipated prices* as well as to changes that have actually occurred. Thus, if a company reduces its price and the buyer anticipates that this is just the beginning of a series of price reductions, the buyer may actually diminish the volume rather than increase it. Contrarily, if an increase in price is interpreted as a sign of future scarcity of goods, the buyer may place large orders so as to be assured of an adequate supply at the current market price. This is one of the reasons for temporary spurts in business activities during periods of business prosperity and a sharp contraction in activity when a decline in prices is anticipated.

Clearly, pricing is not an exact science. Responses of competitors to our changes must be anticipated (as recommended in Chapter 4). Then the impact of our new prices and those of competitors on purchases by customers should be estimated. Next the effect of the estimated volume on our costs is predicted. Finally, the combined impact of new prices, costs, and volumes on profit should be estimated. And this calculation is only a start because, as already suggested, much pricing is aimed at longer-term market position when still another combination of price/cost/volume will be relevant.

These anticipated responses to various pricing alternatives do not call for separate pricing policies. Rather, they extend the analysis which should back up the policy choices already discussed in the earlier parts of this chapter.

Composite Policies

Often companies use both competitors' prices and their own costs in formulating their general pricing policy. A local manufacturer of electrical fixtures who uses price as a sales appeal, for example, follows a policy of (a)

10% below prices of a well-known competitor, except (b) this differential is narrowed to avoid selling below "cost" (total manufacturing costs at estimated sales volume), and (c) sales below "cost" are made only temporarily to close out an item or to combat a "price leader" of a competitor. In contrast, a company producing high-quality, shortwave intercommunication systems relies on technical service and quality to attract customers. This firm normally quotes prices on the basis of total engineering, manufacturing, and selling costs (with a liberal allowance for overhead) plus 15%. However, downward adjustments are made when it is known that the normal price is more than 20% above either of two reputable competitors.

DIFFERENT PRICES FOR DIFFERENT CUSTOMERS

One-Price Policy

Every enterprise must decide whether its products will be sold at the same price to all customers. In the United States the so-called one-price policy has wide acceptance, particularly in retail transactions. Retail stores typically have a set price marked on the merchandise, and every customer coming into the store must pay this set price. In fact, an American is frequently at a loss when buying goods in foreign countries where dealers name a high price and expect to haggle before the sale is finally made.

The horse-trading days in the United States, however, are by no means over. New automobile prices are not rigidly fixed, and the secondhand market and trade-in values retain many opportunities for deception and bargaining. A wholesale fruit company considered a one-price policy but rejected the plan because the prices in the market changed so frequently and the products were so perishable that standardization of prices would have prevented the flexibility for success in this type of business.

Discounts from Established Prices

Many manufacturers and other concerns wish to have the benefits of a one-price policy, but they find it desirable to have different prices for different types of customers. This is often accomplished by maintaining a list price and then granting discounts to certain classes of customers.

Discounts are necessary when a company wishes to sell to wholesalers (jobbers) as well as to retailers. A wholesale firm performs services for which it must be paid, and unless it can buy products for a lower price than the retailer, its resale price for the products would be so high it could not get business. This need for *trade discounts* is generally recognized, but there is much debate as to how large such discounts should be and who are entitled to them. For example, one firm with three retail stores set up a "wholesale department" in an attempt to get an extra 20% discount. Most manufacturers would refuse to grant a wholesaler's discount to such a firm because it is not really performing wholesaling functions. In some industries, such as tires, it is a common policy to have a whole series of discounts that presumably reflect the differences in actual services performed by the various distributors. Clearly, a company's discount policy will have a marked effect on its success in winning patronage from different types of customers and hence should be coordinated with customer policies.

Quantity discounts are commonly offered to anyone who purchases in large volume. Here, again, the difficult questions are under what conditions the discounts will be granted and how large they should be. Large customers may be so important to a company that there is a temptation to give them very high discounts. Under the Robinson-Patman Act and related legislation, however, quantity discounts are limited to actual savings in producing and selling the larger orders.

There are, of course, other forms of discounts, such as cash discounts and advertising allowances, that are not intended to be price reductions. In actual practice, however, they are sometimes so large and are granted in such a way that their effect is a price reduction in a somewhat disguised form.

In addition, a company may offer price concessions in an effort to build up volume in slack periods. A 10% discount for early orders of Christmas cards is not uncommon; airlines have lower fares in slack seasons; electric utility companies offer special "off-peak" rates. When a well-recognized policy has been set up, such discounts can be granted without upsetting the basic price structure.

Regional Differences in Prices

Still another pricing problem deals with regional differences in prices. If the cost of shipping the finished goods from the plant to the customer is a significant part of the cost, as is true for most heavy or bulky articles, this problem can hardly be avoided. A manufacturer who pays the freight will receive a lower *net price* from the most distant customer.

The policy of many companies is to absorb most or all of the shipping costs to distant customers whenever a competitor is located in that territory. In some cases the courts have ruled, however, that this is an unfair price discrimination, and there are legal questions as to how far a company may go in regional pricing. Clearly, a producer who wants to sell products in a highly competitive, distant market at a *lower* price than what is charged locally will be on sounder ground if he or she differentiates the products sold in the two areas.

PROTECTION AGAINST PRICE CHANGES
Holding Costs Down

For years various arrangements have been made to protect customers against sharp increases in their costs (our prices). Changes in prices on industrial raw materials create a special problem because these products are often an important item of cost to the customers. To get orders on the books and thus facilitate production planning and also to assure the customer of a supply of material at a known price, it is customary to plan orders for such material a long period in advance. The order specifies the price and protects the customer against an increase in the price of its raw materials. In practice, the customer is often permitted to defer the contract if the price falls. Thus, the customer is in a position to take advantage of a falling price or is protected against an increase in price as circumstances may warrant. The raw material producer follows such a pricing policy because it is the only way to secure advance orders that greatly assist in production scheduling, and also because it is necessary if the goodwill of the customer is to be maintained.

Sometimes price increases are announced several weeks before they become effective and customers are encouraged to place firm orders at the old price. This builds volume temporarily and gives customers an opportunity to protect themselves against the rising costs.

Indexing of Prices

With widespread inflation, however, the frequency and amount of price increases become hot issues on many fronts. In addition to dealing with equity, ways must be found to permit business exchanges in spite of unstable prices.

One arrangement is to agree that the sellers may *pass-through* any increases they encounter in prices of large items which they buy. For instance, travel agents selling package tours—often months in advance—now normally stipulate that increases in airfares or adverse fluctuations in foreign exchange rates will be added to the original price of the tour. Similarly, aluminum wire for electric transmission lines will probably be sold at a price which will automatically rise to offset increases in the market value of the basic aluminum content.

The pass-through plan has sharp limitations. It covers only part of cost increases and is applicable only for well defined items with easily measured prices. So we turn to *indexes* which at least roughly reflect changes in the relevant costs. Best known is the pre-set adjustment of wage rates and social security payments on the basis of a cost-of-living index. Occasionally the interest rate paid on a loan is regularly adjusted to reflect changes in rates in the money market; in Brazil, with its high inflation, even the principal amount that must be repaid is indexed.

Any company that tries to insert indexing into its prices confronts two problems. Which of its cost increases will it try to cover? And, what objective index will reflect these changes with acceptable accuracy? In construction work where the work inherently extends over a long period, a general construction cost index is sometimes used. However, such an index rarely fits accurately any one specific project; for large contracts, a specially designed index may be used. But to apply indexing to more typical transactions, some more remote industrial price index is probably the best alternative.

Of course, the customers must be willing to accept any indexing of prices, because the onus of the increase is being transferred to them. Their response will depend, in part, on whether they can pass the increase on to their customers. It will also depend on what our competitors are offering, and on the overall supply and demand situation.

So, while indexing is, indeed, an attractive pricing arrangement during inflation, it is only a mechanism for guiding price increases. Each company in its own setting will have to assess the workability of indexing, or pass-through pricing. The more basic issue of how hard the company wishes to push for higher prices goes back to considerations discussed earlier in the chapter.

SUMMARY

Every company needs policy covering the prices to be charged for its products and services. Often the setting of this price policy is one of the most complex problems central management faces.

An orderly approach to pricing has been suggested in this chapter. First, pricing is viewed as a competitive weapon. The relation of our company prices to those of competitors should be established, at least tentatively, to achieve selected marketing benefits. Second, this viewpoint should be tempered by the relation between our costs and prices. In practice, especially during inflation, these cost considerations may dominate pricing policy. Third, a consolidated picture of the effect of price on volume, costs, and prices is required. Both short-run and long-run estimates are needed, and particularly the long-run view should be matched with broad company strategy. Fourth, the underlying pricing policy which comes out of the preceding analysis must be tailored to a variety of specific situations. Important here will be a discount structure and regional differentials which adjust prices to various types of customers. Finally, the way prices can be most readily adjusted to inflation has to be fitted into the general scheme.

Pricing is closely connected with many other aspects of managing a firm. It should reflect and support the master strategy with respect to the domain sought, the differential advantages to be emphasized, and the particular thrusts into new markets or new product lines. And at the operating level, pricing policy ties closely to purchasing, timing, and quality of production and the like. The most intimate connection, however, is with various other elements of the "marketing mix," which is the subject of the next chapter.

QUESTIONS FOR CLASS DISCUSSION

1. Not too many years ago, automobile companies set prices on their cars by following a procedure worked out at General Motors in the 1920's under Alfred P. Sloan's direction. First, the break-even level for production was calculated, then a long-run "target rate of return" was determined and prices were set above the break-even point to provide this return at an expected amount of production. Then, in the second half of the decade of the 1970's during the long, continuous and sizable recovery from the 1974–75 depression, automobile makers and companies in other industries changed to a pricing strategy that was flexible in every respect. Prices have been raised on larger cars and lowered on sub-compacts. General Motors and Ford began to price by location, with geographic price cuts considerably exceeding transportation cost differentials. Options are available to run up prices well above the basic car costs. GM, Ford, and Chrysler have given large factory rebates which cut revenues to less than costs on some models. The price-leader, price-follower pattern (common in the steel and main-frame computer industries) is no longer followed by automobile companies. What, in your opinion, has led to these changes in pricing strategy? What marketing benefits have been gained?

2. As a way of dealing with rising costs, do you recommend that tuition and fees at your university or college be "indexed" with the consumers' price index to help adjust to inflation and deflation? How about board and room in university- or state-owned dormitories? Parking fees? Are any other indexes appropriate for any of these items?

3. From a letter written by Mr. B. Charles Ames, president, Reliance Electric Co., Cleveland, to *Business Week:* "There is nothing new about the notion of cutting a price to get additional volume . . . professional consultants . . . contend that short-term profits should be sacrificed for market share. This is the kind of 'sophisticated advice' to avoid like the plague. This approach may pay off in an unusually strong growth market or one where demand is highly elastic. But . . . it doesn't make sense to seek added volume in a mature business (the industrial markets I know) by cutting price(s). . . . Doing so will result in a plant full of unprofitable business and an untenable profit structure. Any of our competitors (who) want to take a larger share of a mature market can have it. And any of our managers (who) resort to price-cutting to pick up added volume better start looking for another company to work for." (a) Can you explain when and why short-term profits might be sacrificed for market share? (b) Why would Mr. Ames say "it doesn't make sense to seek added volume in a mature business by cutting prices"? What would be untenable about the resulting profit structure? (c) If you were a product manager for Reliance (which makes

small motors and other electrical equipment and which was ranked 75th in its rate of profitability in a ranking of 1032 U.S. business corporations made recently by *Forbes,* Jan. 7, 1980), would you start looking for a job in another company?

4. As part of its program to control inflation in expansion periods, the federal government often urges business firms to refrain from raising their prices. (For some key products such as steel and oil, government pressure is intense.) How much weight do you recommend that a company give to such governmental requests when setting the prices of its services or products?

5. (a) In a period of general inflation, many companies will own buildings and equipment that cost a lot less than their current replacement costs. Also, inventories will often have been purchased at less than replacement costs. In pricing its products, should such a company use actual costs or replacement costs when thinking about its cost/price ratio? (b) How would you answer the question if replacement costs of equipment and of inventory were below actual costs?

6. How do you explain the wide range of prices charged by airlines for an almost identical service—transporting someone from X to Y? What policies seem to be in effect? Is there a better way of pricing?

7. In the automobile tire business, wages constitute approximately 15%, materials 43%, and overhead 42% of total costs. The typical costs of sugar refining are: labor 4%, materials 85%, and overhead 11% of the total costs. Suppose that the X Tire Company and the Y Sugar Company each suffered a 33-1/3% decline in volume of business. (a) Which company would have the largest increase in average total unit costs? (b) Should each company raise its price to cover the increased costs? Why?

8. Five medical doctors with diverse specialties have established in Cheyenne a private clinic for their joint practice. From society's viewpoint, how should they price their services: (a) On the basis of time devoted to a patient? (b) On the value of the services to the patient? (c) On ability of patients to pay for services? (d) On an annual service charge for all care needed? (e) On an annual service charge, with quantity discounts for families? (f) On fixed charges for each specific kind of service—tonsillectomy, broken arm, obstetrical care, infected toe, case of pneumonia, etc.?

9. The Amsterdam Petroleum Transport Company owned and operated eight T-2 tankers. By today's standards these tankers were small and slow, and they had been operating at a substantial loss (except for brief periods of acute tanker shortage). Estimates showed that a cut in freight rates might increase the volume of business but that, even with the increased volume, depreciation and interest on the capital investment would not be earned; consequently, the vessels were sold at substantially below their book value to an Algerian concern. The Algerian concern proceeded to cut the freight rates to a point where the tankers were kept reasonably busy. Amsterdam Petroleum Transport protested strongly against the low rates. The Algerian concern replied that, because of the low purchase price and the resulting low depreciation and interest, it was able to operate at these low rates and show a profit. Assuming equal efficiency of operation, should Amsterdam Petroleum Transport have sold the vessels or should it have cut rates to the same level as the Algerian concern?

10. The *Guinness Book of World Records* has accepted Barnes and Noble, a New York City retailer of books, as the biggest bookstore anywhere. This world record was achieved by the lure of low prices in a store with shopping carts, check-out counters, and cavernous salesrooms like those of an off-the-rack discount house. Tables are loaded high with books and signs saying: "Books for a Buck." The *Random House Encyclopedia* is discounted about 30%, J.K. Lasser's *Your Income Tax* sells at 13% off the newsstand price, the fifteen best-sellers (both fiction and non-fiction) go for 35% less than the prices on their covers, and the latest paperbacks are knocked down 20% each from their newsstand prices. The president of Barnes and Noble has a theory that any book can be sold if it is priced right and that, overall, the store will be profitable. This theory is general enough to include treatises on agriculture in prehistoric times or tomes on biliary-duct surgery. About 4,000 customers per day go through the check-out counters, each person with an average of 4.5 volumes. Most large bookstores are satisfied with traffic of 25,000 to 30,000 customers per month. Some of these bookstores are discounting best-sellers from 10% to 15% in order to bring in customers. The president of Bantam Books, a big paperback publisher, said that he expects Barnes and Noble to inspire imitators in many cities. Has this happened in your city? Is price-discounting a way to stop the erosion of sales volume in units being felt by U.S. publishers? Publishers claim that the rise in the list prices of books has not exceeded the rise in the nation's consumer price index, but they are nonetheless selling fewer books and facing sales resistance. Are bookstores on or near your campus discounting best-sellers? Textbooks? Reference books? What marketing benefits might Barnes and Noble, Inc. be trying to gain by discounting list prices so heavily?

11. "Isn't this remarkable! Thirty-three years ago, when Jeanie was one year old, I paid ten dollars for a new, portable, electric beater and mixer. The beater blades just now broke so I bought a new one. And the price of this new G.E. mixer is the same—just ten dollars." What factors in the small appliance industry would lead to the General Electric Company's setting prices this way? What has happened to the general level of costs of wages and materials in thirty-three years? Will G.E. index its prices to the consumer price index with heavy inflation?

CASE 7
North-Central Standard Oil Company, Inc. (R)

North-Central Standard, a major domestic oil refining and marketing company, sells gasoline and other oil products throughout the United States west of the Appalachian Mountains. The company has had several different pricing policies during the past sixty years. Now the Vice-President for Finance is concerned about future company earnings and is making a statement to the Committee for Pricing Policy. Two other executives are also appearing before the committee.

Company policy during the firm's early history was to base its wholesale (tank wagon) prices on costs plus a desired profit margin. After some years, when marketing executives gained greater influence in the company, policy shifted to meeting the prices of the largest competitor in each city or district. More recently, pricing policy has been modified to be based upon the entire competitive situation in any one locality, which includes considering the costs of various products and the types of marketing that characterize the individual local markets. (Some cities have had price competition from local refiners plus rebates, premiums, trading stamps, sales contests, and giveaways—others have not.) Pricing policy is now stated as meeting competitive conditions on both a broad industry basis and on a local market basis. If necessary to meet local competition, prices in a local market may be unrelated to company costs and primarily influenced by the local wholesale market price.

By analyzing market prices at different stages of production (crude oil, refinery door, major shipping point), the company attempts to determine what it will cost a competitor to serve a given market. Shifts in costs do not automatically affect prices but are weighed along with market trends in determining whether changes are warranted in the company's overall price structure.

The Vice-President for Finance's statement is: "Company profits have been hurt by legislative action that changed depletion and depreciation allowances and that relaxed import restrictions on foreign crude oil. Profits may even be damaged further by changes in excise taxes or tariffs. We have to buy foreign crude at the spot market price. That puts our costs well above those who are a part of Aramco in Saudi Arabia or who have made a deal with the British or Norwegian governments in the North Sea. We also are paying the higher domestic price on 'new' oil. Increases in material costs due to these factors are not under our control.

"However, we have done our best to reduce controllable costs. Our refineries have increased output over the past ten years from 300,000 barrels per day to 450,000 barrels per day. We have reduced the number of employees from 22,000 to 15,000. We have recently negotiated a three-year labor contract that will keep us free from strikes and allow us to stabilize wage costs as a percent of prices.

"The big question that remains is whether demand is increasing and will increase. If so, a price increase is warranted. The accompanying tables and financial statements explain the demand situation and fully warrant, I believe, the kind of price increase I have in mind to restore our return on assets and return on equity to acceptable levels.

"We all know that government policy and action is uncertain and will change with regard to tariffs, excise taxes, import quotas and/or license fees for imports; but some forecast has to be made, so I have used a median forecast based on analyses by the Department of Energy and by Resources for the Future, Inc.

"Gasoline prices have stabilized and even declined slightly in some markets over the past six months. And, over the past decade, gasoline prices have risen much less than crude oil prices. So, despite the increases of not too long ago, we still have not caught up and are justified in raising our prices further.

"It is necessary for us to maintain our oil exploration program to survive as a company. We can't cut that expense. We need to explore in northern Canada to supplement our Alaskan North Slope discoveries.

"To show the benefit of raising prices which I am recommending, I have made some five-year estimates and compared these figures with our present situation. (See income and balance sheet statements below.) Each set of figures—current and *pro forma* five years hence—assumes that the company will be running at the same throughput. The *pro forma* statements show the effect of the 10% increase in our prices. They also show the effect on costs of purchasing and refining of a 2% per year increase in productivity. Some other cost changes are shown because these are necessary for improved management of the company or because taxes and allowances are just going to change. All these data are shown in *real dollars,* without reflecting dollar increases due only to general inflation. I can't predict what inflation will do to the dollar amounts reported five years from now.

"To properly manage the firm and to take advantage of successful exploration efforts, we need to increase our assets, as I have shown. We also need a return on investment at least equal to all industry. The solution to our problems of return on investment, financing exploration and finding more capital is to raise prices. We should increase our prices 10% as rapidly as possible.

"As to the reactions of our competitors, the changes in depletion allowances and import quotas and other legislative action will affect us all about equally. Demand studies estimate national price elasticity at various amounts from −.2 to −.8. As the price goes up, revenues will also rise because demand is not elastic. The quantity

INDUSTRY DATA

U.S. Liquid Petroleum Supply and Demand
(millions of barrels per day)

	Domestic Production	*Imports*	*Total U.S. Demand*
Ten years ago	11.3	3.4	14.7
Five years ago	10.5	6.1	16.6
Current	10.0	9.0	19.0
Five years hence	10.0	11.5	21.5
Ten years hence	10.0	12.0	22.0

Rate of Return on Equity

	All Industrial Companies	*Oil Industry*
Current year	16.7%	20.2%
Past five years	15.1%	15.3%

Domestic Tax Burden

	Percent of Gross Revenue
Petroleum	5.43
Mining and Manufacturing	5.50
All Business Corporations	4.62

taken will decrease a bit, but not as much as the price increases. So, I recommend an immediate price increase and the policy shown in the *pro forma* statements."

Income Statements
(in millions)

		Current	Pro Forma (Five Years Hence)
Sales		$2,275	$2,502
Costs			
Production, Purchases of Crude			
Oil and Refining	$1,235		$1,117
Exploration	104		108
Selling and Administration	360		432
Taxes	150		202
Depletion	188		91
Interest	31		57
Total Costs		2,068	2,007
Net Earnings		$ 207	$ 495

Balance Sheets
(in millions)

	Current	Pro Forma (Five Years Hence)
Current Assets	$ 845	$ 930
Net Property	2,112	2,324
Total Assets	$2,957	$3,254
Current Liabilities	$ 413	$ 416
Long-Term Debt	546	437
Deferred Taxes	117	195
Equity	1,881	2,206
Total Liabilities and Equity	$2,957	$3,254

The Marketing Vice-President says: "In my judgment, the rest of the industry is not in the same position as we are. Look at the facts. We don't have guaranteed sources of foreign crude so we have to buy at the spot-market price which has been well above long-term prices. For domestic oil, we have to pay for 'new' oil bought from independents who are undertaking the very high costs of domestic exploration. Thus our competitors' costs don't change as do ours and they don't need to follow up our selling prices in an attempt to hold or gain any particular profit margin.

"We should price to hold market share and regain markets. Pricing to attain a fixed target return on assets or on investment is wrong. The price we can charge depends entirely on competition. Profitability should be determined by the way we manage the company—by continuing efforts to improve efficiency and lowering our costs so that the market price will yield a satisfactory return. If we maintain the

current price and don't raise future prices more than enough to offset general inflation, we will be close enough to the lowest seller and yet not highest in our markets
so that we will hold our proper market position. I have prepared projections to show
this—a 13% increase in physical volume over the next five years. (See the statements
below.) The production, purchasing, and refining costs shown reflect the productivity
increases mentioned earlier as well as the 13% gain in volume. I agree with your
earlier statement that gasoline prices have stabilized over the past six months. So
it is not wise to increase ours now."

The Vice-President for Finance responds: "I disagree. It seems to me perfectly
satisfactory and the wise course to follow to have a higher price and higher margins
with a lower volume and even a declining market share if this means that we can
have the highest return on investment. Let those who want to run a profitless
treadmill do so. We were the price leader in the past. Let's return to that policy now."

The National Sales Manager says: "Think back on our history. For years we lost
market share and then went below 10% in our three big markets. We have won back
some of our position and are now up to 13% and 14% in the Twin Cities and southern
Wisconsin. Currently our prices are 4% to 5% *above* the lowest seller in the market.
To move toward regaining our historically justified market position of about a 20%

Pro Forma Statements (Five Years Hence)
(in millions)

	Marketing (Vice-President)	National Sales Manager
Income Statement		
Sales	$2,571	$2,874
Costs:		
Production, Purchases of Crude		
Oil and Refining	$1,262	$1,481
Exploration	122	210
Selling and Administration	525	531
Taxes	150	100
Depletion	100	88
Interest	86	154
Total Costs	2,245	2,564
Net Earnings	$ 326	$ 310
Balance Sheet		
Current Assets	$ 955	$1,211
Net Property	2,387	2,909
Total Assets	$3,342	$4,120
Current Liabilities	$ 467	$ 771
Long-Term Debt	617	1,025
Deferred Taxes	132	156
Equity	2,126	2,168
Total Liabilities and Equity	$3,342	$4,120

share, we need to *decrease* prices 5%, not increase them. This increase in market share plus the generally predicted sales growth of 2% to 2.5% per year in total oil and gasoline barrels demanded should bring sales up to about $3 billion in five years (a 33% increase in physical volume after a 5% cut in prices).

"You will see this volume increase reflected in the *pro forma* statements I have prepared. Look at the size I believe we can attain. Physical plant increases as the result of finds from exploration and from the increase in output. Other costs have changed as they should. The interest rate I show is more realistic (15%) than are the rates shown on the other two *pro forma* balance sheets. Also note the amount I allocate to exploration. To grow we need more oil. The profit amount shown is good and will increase considerably in later years as we gain market share. The best thing that we can do is to lower prices 5% to achieve the strongest possible consumer franchise and thus protect the company in the market.

Questions

(1) Explain the effects of the three pricing policy proposals.

(2) What economic reasoning underlies the statement of the Financial Vice-President?

(3) What is your decision as to wise company policy? Explain.

MARKETING MIX POLICY

Strategy and the Consumer

The strategy of a company identifies the domain it seeks—its product line and preferred market niche(s). And perhaps, though not necessarily, the selected differential advantage will further define the way the company will deal with customers. Then product, customer, and pricing policy do expand and specify the marketing efforts. Essential as all this planning is, however, it is not enough.

The analysis and planning should also take a consumer viewpoint. Management should envisage all the actions necessary to complete the full transformation of company products (or services) into consumer satisfactions.

Rarely does a consumer merely buy a physical product. Instead, the consumer purchases a *package* that fulfills some "need," that provides a psychological pride of ownership and/or consumption, that involves a minimum of anxiety about breakdown or damage, that is considered a "good buy at the price," that can be acquired without great financial upset, that will be delivered when wanted, and so forth. An essential part of a marketing plan, then, is to conceive of a practical package of satisfactions that will appeal to a significant number of consumers.

Normally, providing each of these consumer satisfactions involves a cost. The cost may be a direct expense incurred by the producing company, or it may be a fee or margin charged by a distributor. Keeping these costs within acceptable bounds is, of course, an inherent aspect of designing a viable package of satisfactions.

Marketing Mix

In addition to seeking a winning combination of consumer satisfactions, the central manager must consider how to communicate with the consumer to present an offer. A whole array of alternative forms of advertising are available for this purpose. And the role of sales representatives and agents in this total distribution process has to be defined.

But, advertising and sales staffs involve costs, just as do the satisfactions discussed in the previous section. Inevitably, a choice must be made. How much of each—consumer services, higher quality, convenient packages, lower price, advertising, or personal solicitation? This allocation among such competing uses for the distribution dollar is called the *marketing mix*. Of course, the particular marketing mix that fits one product in one market will differ from the combination suited to other product-markets. Selling life insurance differs from selling automobile insurance; a marketing mix suited to electric typewriters differs from one for computers. Also, a company may elect to seek a distinct differential advantage. Key decisions are needed with respect to:

1. Selecting *sales appeals* that are important to the customer.
2. Determining the use that will be made of *advertising*.
3. Deciding the role of *personal solicitation*.
4. Combining all marketing plans into a practical *marketing mix*.

SALES APPEALS

A variety of dimensions are available for the total service a company provides its customers. The role of policy on sales appeals is to clarify the emphasis that management believes will be most effective. Among the possible appeals often featured are:

1. Customer services.
2. Quality.
3. Style and packaging.
4. Price.
5. Reputation of company.

Customer Services

Personal assistance. A recurring question is how much personal assistance to the customer should be a part of the total sales package. For example, in Honolulu a car driver who pulls up to a gas pump finds someone washing all the car windows, checking tire pressure, filling the radiator, and inspecting the battery while the gasoline is being pumped; this requires two or three attendants working simultaneously. In contrast, in a New York City service station the driver has to ask to have the windshield washed, and checking tire pressure is clearly a do-it-yourself operation. Many filling stations in London are on a complete self-service basis—except for paying the bill (and even that function may be taken over by an automatic credit card device). Maps, touring advice, washrooms, and soft-drink dispensers provide still other variations. Clearly, filling station operators must estimate

which services their customers really want and whether they are prepared
to pay a differential to get them.

Similarly in industrial products, some companies give their customers a
great deal of free advice. Some sales representatives of dairy equipment, for
instance, advise milk plant operators on their total production activities.
The commercial banker, to pick another example, frequently counsels with
important customers about all sorts of financial matters that may not directly relate to the bank. In contrast, the homemaker does not expect to get
cooking advice from the clerk in the supermarket.

A shift is occurring in personal service in the hotel field. Motels grew
up with a minimum of personal service, in contrast to the traditional hotels with doormen, bellhops, and room maids. But as motels are becoming more luxurious, they are adding more personal assistance; meanwhile, the large downtown hotels will permit guests to carry their own
bags and to find their own rooms. With changing attitudes about personal assistance, matching services to a particular desired clientele calls
for sharp perception.

Buying convenience. How far should a company go in making it easy for
a customer to buy? A wide range of answers are found in the retail field.
Department stores, for instance, provide attractive displays, wide selection,
sales help, gift wrapping, home delivery, charge accounts, and return privileges. In contrast, discount houses provide few or perhaps none of these
services. When discount houses were first started, the differences in their
prices compared with those of the department stores were almost as great
as the differences in buying convenience. More recently, the spread between
prices and between services has tended to narrow. Department stores have
trimmed their services somewhat and have reduced their margins, whereas
the larger discount houses have done just the opposite. Obviously, retail
managers believe that the differences in convenience desired by various
groups of customers is becoming less sharp.

In industrial fields, buying convenience takes the form of descriptive catalogs, telephone ordering, stock held for future delivery, and acceptance of
rush orders. Companies differ greatly in their policy on the extent to which
they provide such services.

Maintenance and repair. One of the central pillars of IBM's marketing
success is its maintenance service policy. Most of its machines are covered
by a contract under which IBM provides regular maintenance service and
is available for prompt repair work in the event of breakdown. Other manufacturers have a less elaborate service organization but do maintain a stock
of repair parts for all equipment sold during, say, the past twenty years. The
importance of repair service for durable equipment is illustrated by foreign
automobiles. Neither a low price nor the latest sportscar model is an adequate substitute for keeping the car running. Consequently, foreign car sales
are closely correlated with the availability of good repair service.

Policy on customer service and policy on channels of distribution are closely related. The further removed manufacturers are from the final consumers of their product, the more difficult is control of customer service. Companies that stress service often find it necessary to maintain their own branches; some television and hi-fi manufacturers establish exclusive distributorships in order to improve the quality of repair service available to ultimate customers.

Installment credit. The day is gone when installment credit is available only on durable goods in an amount less than the resale value. Now financing may be arranged on almost any large purchase, and mail-order houses —among others—extend installment credit on an accumulation of small purchases. However, the ease of obtaining credit and the terms on which it is granted do vary. Also, manufacturers give more or less help to their distributors. Part of the marketing mix, then, is the extent to which a company gets into the financing business. Recently, companies have been turning over more and more of this function to banks, finance companies, and credit card companies; this tends to remove installment credit as a competitive factor.

Leasing equipment instead of selling it is a service provided by some manufacturers. Computers, postal meters, shoe machinery, and automatic bowling-pin setters are all available under lease. Many of these lease arrangements are similar to installment credit, calling for periodic payments during the period when the product is being used and giving the customer an option to buy the equipment at the end of the lease. The major difference is that the customer may return the equipment to the manufacturer when it is only partially used. For customers with limited financial resources or fluctuating needs, such leases can be quite attractive.

Often leasing and maintenance service are combined. This has an added attraction to the manufacturer who then knows that the equipment which may be returned is being kept in good repair.

Prompt availability. This is a valuable dimension for both products and services. An employer with a potential strike, or a mother about to give birth to an offspring, wants consulting advice promptly—not next week. Similarly, a loan from the bank or a delivery of fuel oil have much greater sales value if customers know they can depend on the services being available when needed. Advance planning helps, of course; but rarely can requirements be precisely predicted, so prompt availability becomes an added aspect of service.

Small local companies can often gain significant advantage by providing this prompt delivery. They can reach the scene of action quickly, they are already familiar with local conditions, and their small size permits considerable flexibility. If larger firms choose to stress availability, they have to set up local representatives or branches and then give the local units both the incentive and the authority to meet unusual customer requirements.

Considerable choice and opportunity for creative variation is available in customer services that a company provides, as the preceding examples show. Some of these services may be so important to customers that they are regarded as part of the product itself. Since they are intimately tied up with the product in the mind of the customer, it is important that policies regarding their use be integrated with product, customer, and other marketing policies.

Quality as a Sales Appeal

The importance of quality in certain types of services has already been indicated in the discussion of product policies. Minimum quality standards are essential for many products, and here we are assuming that such minimums are being met. The issue in terms of sales appeal is whether quality higher than the prevailing level will be used to attract customers.

Extra quality involves extra effort and cost. Strawberry jam made with only pure sugar and no corn syrup has added raw material cost; handrubbed furniture has extra labor cost. A policy to build extra quality into our products, therefore, has to be matched up against other ways to differentiate our total marketing mix. The question is: Does distinctive quality hold strong appeal to the particular customers we are trying to reach?

One limitation to using quality as a sales appeal is that consumers may be unable to detect the difference and may be skeptical about the claims made. So, to clinch the appeal, some companies *guarantee* their products. For instance, an automobile manufacturer recently extended its guarantee from one year to three years (and on some parts to five years). The move attracted so much attention that competitors were forced to follow. In the meantime, the first company added to its reputation for producing dependable products.

Guarantees must be carefully worded to keep liability within reasonable bounds. One arrangement, common for automobile batteries, is to adjust the allowance made on a replacement downward as the normal life expires. Actually, most customers never expect to make claims under a guarantee. The fact that a company is willing to make it is the significant appeal.

Professional ethics prevent doctors or lawyers from guaranteeing the results of their services. Nevertheless, quality is especially significant in intangible services, so a professional person's reputation for quality work becomes very important.

Emphasis on Style and Packaging

"Pick the right style" is merely a pious wish, not a policy. However, the degree of emphasis on style in the total selling effort may be a significant policy. A French restaurant, for instance, may go to great lengths to create a Louis XIV decor and atmosphere. A few men's shoe manufacturers stress the latest style, at the sacrifice of durability. Producers of household items —from hand tools to garbage cans—need some guidance on how much to add to design and production expense to have currently popular styles and colors.

Packaging is one means of giving a product stylish appearance, but it may play a more important role in the marketing mix. Packaging can affect the product-service itself, as in the use of aerosol cans for paint. If a product is to be sold through self-service stores, the size, sturdiness, and shelf appeal of the package are critical to success. Continued usage of a returnable glass milk bottle is primarily dependent on the use of home versus store delivery. So, while a package may add significantly to the unit cost, the right kind of package can be an integral part of providing distinctive service for a group of consumers.

Typical Use of Price Appeal

Price has some influence on the sale of all products. However, the emphasis placed on price varies widely. Large mail-order houses stress the price appeal throughout their catalogs. For some products, such as pianos, where quality rather than price is the normal emphasis, one or two manufacturers will try to tap a segment of the market by stressing their low prices.

Of course, as discussed in the previous chapter, price enters into the marketing mix decision in two ways. If lower than competitors', price may be used as a sales appeal. At the same time, price influences the amount of income that is available for other appeals and for sales promotion. Perhaps a relatively high price (to some extent a negative appeal) is warranted if this finances a service which a segment of the market finds particularly attractive.

Effect of a Company's Reputation on Sales

Banks, insurance companies, and other financial institutions must guard their reputations jealously because this is a major factor in the business they secure. Some manufacturers have developed a reputation for well-designed and reliable products, and they use this reputation as one of their important sales appeals. For instance, a well-regarded brand name is so important in the sale of large kitchen appliances that an unknown company has a hard time breaking into the market. The Whirlpool Corporation, to cite a specific case, for years made appliances for Sears, Roebuck & Company but was unknown to the general public; lacking a reputation with consumers and dealers, it entered into a long-term agreement to use the highly regarded RCA label. Several years later, after the Whirlpool reputation had become established, the association with RCA was dropped.

Even the highly competitive bidding process of the federal government makes allowance for company reputation. A low bid may be rejected if the bidder lacks a demonstrated ability to perform. And for high technology contracts, as in aerospace, reputation is often the deciding factor.

Good reputations are not bought on Madison Avenue. They arise primarily from a sustained willingness to devote extra effort to assure dependability and use of the latest state of the art, to avoid exaggerated claims, and to adjust such errors as do occur in a prompt and liberal fashion. Since conducting activities in this manner is sometimes inconvenient and costly, a policy on the kind of reputation the company desires is necessary. (We might note in passing that a policy on company reputation is very difficult to state in writing; here especially the policy takes on operational meaning through a succession of specific decisions that become a traditional way of operating.) If a company has earned a distinctive reputation, then it is appropriate to publicly reinforce this posture and to incorporate it in the total marketing effort.

Concluding briefly, no company can stress all the sales appeals we have discussed. Some are incompatible (for example, low price versus high quality and service); others are inappropriate; all involve some expense. In thinking through what combination of appeals makes sense for a particular company, central management should recognize (1) the differences in attractiveness of various appeals to the groups it seeks as customers, and (2) the compatibility and perhaps synergistic effect of a particular appeal policy with the product-market emphasis and the differential advantage selected by the company, and with other aspects of its master strategy.

ADVERTISING

Today we are bombarded on all sides by many types of advertising. No matter whether we walk on the streets, drive an automobile on the highways, ride a bus, watch television, read a newspaper or magazine, or open our mail, we are brought face to face with advertising. This creates a difficult situation for management, for it must determine what advertising on its part will justify its cost amid the bewildering array of advertisements by other companies. Major questions of policy with reference to advertising are (1) the purposes for which it is to be used and (2) the media employed to accomplish these purposes.

Analysis shows that advertising is employed for numerous purposes. It also shows that many companies have not given adequate thought to the question of exactly what they are trying to accomplish with their advertising. Let us, then, take a closer look at the major options.

Bringing Customers to the Place Where Goods Are Sold

Retail stores frequently use advertising for this purpose. In such cases the display of merchandise and the efforts of salespeople are depended upon to close the transaction. We are all familiar with advertisements of special drugstore sales that feature twenty-five or fifty different items. The store usually hopes to sell substantial quantities of the merchandise advertised; but more important, it hopes to get customers into the store so that they will buy other types of merchandise and will develop a habit of coming to that establishment for their subsequent requirements.

Stores desiring to use a prestige appeal may have the author of a popular book give a lecture or may secure designers of furniture, dinnerware, or clothing to talk about these particular products. A number of stores provide space for local art exhibits or a showing of crown jewels; a pair of unusual and very expensive fur pelts or the elaborate doll houses of a well-known TV actress may be featured for the purpose of attracting customers to the store.

The point is well illustrated by a story told of two keen partners operating a store located in a very low-income neighborhood. Upon observing that a large number of customers were patronizing their nearby competitors, they set up a table filled with small articles, such as pickle forks, salt shakers, and cigarette holders. This table was placed near the front door where it would be passed by everyone entering or going out of the store. The sales of the articles proved to be very unprofitable, however, since they could easily be slipped into a pocket and the nearby door allowed easy escape for would-be purchasers. According to the story, however, there was a substantial increase in customer traffic. When asked to explain the situation, one of the partners said, "We call that our steal table. We place $25 worth of merchandise on the table each morning and know that most of it will have disappeared by evening. But when people come in to steal from this table, they have to act like customers and look at other merchandise, and sometimes they buy. They like to come to the store because they can go home with an extra 25-cent article that probably cost us 10 cents. All for $25 a day—it's cheap advertising."

Persuading the Customer to Ask for a Specific Product

This function of advertising is the likely aim of manufacturers who wish to create consumer demand, or at least consumer acceptance, for their brand of products. For example, a number of children's television programs are sponsored by manufacturers of food products. The program may consist of adventures in space, a detective serial, or anything that arouses the intense interest of a child. Somewhere in the program the youngsters are instructed to insist that their mothers buy the product of the sponsoring manufacturer.

This kind of advertising has proved very effective under certain conditions. In fact, almost the entire advertising programs of the large cereal companies are directed towards ultimate consumers for the purpose of getting them to ask for that specific product. Although the goods are usually sold through a jobber, who in turn sells them to a retailer and thence to the consumer, it is the policy of these companies to advertise only to the consumer and thereby to create such an active consumer demand that the retailer and the jobber will be glad to carry the products and benefit from the quick turnover resulting from the strong demand.

Any of a number of advertising techniques are used to induce the customer to purchase specific products. Some have a rational basis while others are largely psychological or emotional. Thus, when you buy aspirin, you are to insist on a given brand because it is pure, it dissolves, and it acts more quickly. At other times reliance is placed primarily upon repetition of the brand name so that the consumer will automatically select that particular product. The Coca-Cola Company follows this technique extensively. Whatever the technique, the purpose is to get the consumer to ask for, or at least willingly accept, a particular brand of product.

Assisting the Sales Representative in Making Sales When Calling on Customers

Manufacturers use advertising extensively for this purpose. The objective is to familiarize the customer with the products and to create a favorable attitude toward the company before the sales representative approaches the customer. For example, concerns producing basic metals frequently advertise in trade papers that are read by their customers. The advertisement itself will not induce the potential customer to take any action, but it is hoped that the sales representative will receive a more cordial welcome as a result.

A firm manufacturing a line of luggage had for several years advertised extensively in national magazines. This advertising was discontinued when a special study convinced the management that style, design, quality, and price were so much more important to the ultimate consumer than a particular brand name that directing advertising toward the ultimate consumer was not economical. Nevertheless this company does a limited amount of national advertising because retailers are more inclined to stock a product that is nationally advertised. Thus the primary purpose of the national advertising campaign of this company is to assist sales representatives in their negotiations with retailers.

Other companies provide the retailer with attractive window displays and store decorations that serve the dual purpose of creating consumer interest and providing the sales representative with a favorable reception by the retailer.

Producing Direct Sales

In some circumstances advertising is used for the purpose of persuading the customer to submit an order as a direct result. The catalogs of mail-order houses, for instance, present merchandise in such a way that the consumer can write out or telephone an order without going to a shopping center and without further promotional effort on the part of the vendor. Similarly, motels expect their outdoor advertising along highways leading toward a specific building to attract guests.

One company has been successful in selling men's shirts as a result of direct-mail advertising to the consumer. This company stresses a price appeal that, it claims, is justified by its distribution "direct from the factory to you." How-to-do-it and reference books that appeal to a particular type of reader are often sold by direct mail or magazine advertising.

Building Institutional Goodwill

Practically all advertising is expected to build institutional goodwill to some degree, but in some cases this is the primary objective. The advertising by telephone companies is largely for this purpose.

One of the leading personal finance companies has made extensive research on the problems of consumer buying and distributes a large number of pamphlets guiding homemakers in the selection of merchandise. Intelligent expenditure of a limited income is, of course, related to the collection of small loans made to individuals for personal use. Nevertheless, the primary purpose of the distribution of these pamphlets is the development of goodwill toward the company.

Enough illustrations have been given to indicate that advertising may be undertaken for widely different purposes. Central management normally does not become involved in detailed aspects of advertising, but it can and should exercise a significant influence by setting policy regarding the purposes of the expenditure.

Choice of Advertising Media

After a company has decided on the purposes of its advertising, the media must be determined. The principal media include:

1. Magazines.
2. Newspapers.
3. Trade papers.
4. Television and radio.
5. Billboards.
6. Direct mail.

This list is not intended to be complete. Other types of sales promotion that might be included under the general heading of advertising are displays, dealer helps, and sampling.

Rarely does a single company use all of these media. It must select those that will accomplish its objectives most economically. For example, one large hosiery company that used advertising primarily to influence retailers formerly spent approximately $800,000 annually advertising in magazines having a national circulation. A survey among retailers showed that, while dealers liked nationally advertised products, they were influenced to a greater degree by dealer helps, such as counter displays and leaflets, and by cooperative advertising in local newspapers in which the name of the local dealer was mentioned along with the company's products. The expenditure of the company on magazine advertising is now less than $50,000 a year.

An airline company faced a serious problem in the selection of media to build familiarity and goodwill among a large number of people. Advertising that would produce traffic on its planes immediately was also wanted. For this latter purpose expenditures were confined primarily to direct-mail letters, TV commercials, and announcements to business executives and other people believed to be potential passengers in the near future. Considerable effort was directed toward passengers on its planes because these passengers as a general rule do not travel by air as much as they might, and the fact that they do use planes occasionally indicated they were interested in this method of transportation. The institutional program consisted largely of magazine advertisements and general newspaper publicity.

We see in both of these cases the need to match media and purpose carefully. Too often the virtues of a particular medium are advanced without reference to the mission of the advertising.

The chart below shows the relative importance of the major types of media for all U.S. advertising total annual expenditures for advertising recently passed $45 billion.

**ALLOCATION OF U.S.
ADVERTISING EXPENDITURES
AMONG TYPES OF MEDIA**

Other Advertising Problems

Problems of advertising are by no means limited to a determination of the major purposes and selection of media. In addition, decisions must be made as to the general type of advertising to be used. Some companies feature testimonials; others employ cartoons to a large extent. Some use flashy advertisements and large print; others make their advertising more dignified. The use of premiums and of contests can open up many additional possibilities for the imaginative copywriter. Then there are numerous questions regarding such things as layouts. Primarily these are questions of advertising techniques rather than general sales promotion policy.

PERSONAL SOLICITATION

Although sales representatives must be used to some degree in nearly all types of selling, the extent and the purpose of personal solicitation vary greatly.

Differences in the Use of Sales Representatives

The nature of the product to be sold, the type of customer to be solicited, the channels of distribution to be used, and the types of sales appeals to be employed all affect a company's policy regarding personal solicitation. An accounting firm, for example, operates on a professional basis and consequently is prevented from using advertising beyond a few dignified announcements. Such a firm secures its business primarily through personal solicitation. As a general rule, specialized representatives are not employed. The partners and the supervisors are expected to seek new business among their acquaintances, but in so doing they must maintain the professional dignity of the firm.

The selling activities of a clerk in a variety store consist of little more than making change and wrapping packages; therefore, the amount of constructive selling such a clerk can perform is very limited. In contrast, good insurance salespeople are usually well-versed in problems of personal finance in addition to knowing facts regarding insurance premiums, cash reserves, cash surrender values, mortality rates, and contingent beneficiaries. They must also have considerable skill in approaching people and developing their interest in insurance to a point where a policy is purchased.

Some companies use what are known as missionary sales representatives. Most of the leading cracker manufacturers, for instance, distribute their products through grocery wholesalers. Experience has shown that the sales staff of these jobbers handle such a wide variety of products that they do not effectively promote the sales of a particular brand of cracker. As a result, cracker manufacturers employ sales representatives to travel among retailers, sometimes with the jobber sales representatives, to advise retailers regarding their problems connected with selling crackers and to secure their cooperation in promoting the company's products to the retail consumers. The jobbers fill orders, keep the accounts with the retailer, and make collections; they also contact the retailers at more frequent intervals than is possible for the specialty sales representatives. The missionary sales representative, however, is an essential part of the sales promotion program of the manufacturer.

Sales Personnel, Organization, and Techniques

From these examples it is evident that every company should adopt definite and clear-cut policy regarding its use of sales personnel. The company must not only decide the extent to which sales representatives are to be used

HIGH MARKETING EXPENDITURES HURT PROFITS ESPECIALLY WHEN QUALITY IS LOW

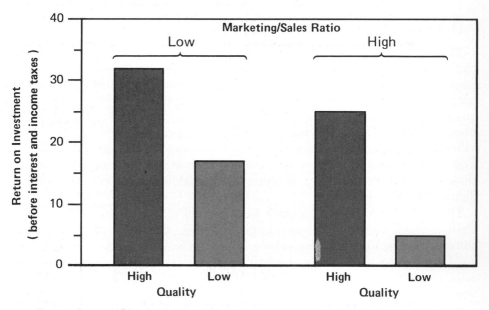

Source: Strategic Planning Institute.
Quality of products is relative to those of competitors. Marketing expenditures include:
salesforce expenses, advertising, sales promotion, market research, and related outlays.

but also must clearly define the purpose of their activity. Unless such a program is adopted, a considerable amount of misdirected sales effort and expense will result. The administration of a sales force involves, of course, many problems in addition to the establishment of general policy. There will be personnel policy relating to selection, training, and compensation of these salespeople. A sales organization must be provided, and detailed techniques must be worked out for specific activities to be performed. These problems are discussed in later chapters of this book.

MARKETING MIX

Finding an effective balance among the alternative measures a company can take to build sales volume involves analysis, imagination, and judgment.

Too often the task is done a piece at a time without relating the pieces to a grand design.

An Approach to Sales Promotion

At a minimum, the various facets of sales promotion should be tied to a common purpose. One analytical method that helps put various promotional devices in perspective is to answer these four questions:

1. *Who consumes the product to be sold or alters it so that its identity is lost?* The answer to this question should be found by a study of the customer policy of a company.
2. *Who makes the final decision as to the products that the ultimate consumer buys?* A study of this question will often lead to interesting results. Clearly it is the doctor who selects the medicine, not the patient who actually buys the prescription at the drugstore. Usually a mechanic, rather than the car owner, decides what brand of sparkplugs to use for replacements. In the same way the student buys the textbook specified by the instructor, and consequently sales promotion efforts of a textbook publishing company are directed toward the teacher rather than the student.

    On the other hand, the ultimate consumer usually makes the decision in the selection of the brand of cosmetics bought. The purchaser of producer goods is often influenced by several individuals. For example, the engineering department, the production department, and the purchasing department may all exercise an influence in selecting the company from which steel or coal is bought.

    The answer to this question is often the key to a proper sales promotion policy. It certainly was for a company manufacturing piston rings for automobiles, since the entire advertising program depended upon whether the car owner or the garage manager actually selected the brand of piston rings that was to be used in the repair job.
3. *What factors influence those who make final decisions?* Note that this question focuses attention upon the factors that influence the person making the decision. The more common factors have been discussed in detail under sales appeals, and added illustrations are not necessary at this point. For example, a small difference in the price of piston rings is of little importance to the ultimate consumer, nor is he or she concerned with the delivery service of the manufacturer since the consumer depends upon the local garage owner to carry a supply of such parts. If, however, the garage owner makes the decision regarding the rings to be used, then some of these things become of vital importance.
4. *How is it possible to influence these factors by means of sales promotion?* To what extent is it possible by national advertising, by sampling, or by personal solicitation to influence the thinking of those who make the final decision regarding the purchase of the product? There are some factors, such as the price or delivery service, that no form of sales promotion can change. On the other hand, an explanation by a salesperson may be effective in pointing out the distinctiveness of quality and design of a particular product, and an advertising program may greatly affect the reputation of the company.

The approach to sales promotion problems indicated by a discussion of the foregoing questions does not provide a ready answer, but it will often lead to very significant conclusions. As the advertising manager of a company securing annual sales of approximately $100 million said, "I have asked a large number of advertising people those four simple little questions and frequently found a lack of adequate understanding of the problems they were pretending to solve. The questions are keen because they go right to the heart of the problem."

Relating Marketing to Other Policy and Strategy

The effectiveness of sales promotion is improved by synergy. We have already noted how, say, technical bulletins and engineer-trained salespeople or well-styled products and magazine advertising can reinforce each other. Likewise, sales promotion and other policy should be synergistic. IBM's repair service, leasing machines, capital financing, and high wage policy, for instance, each gives added impact to the other.

The final marketing mix selected need not be complicated if a relatively simple combination fits the basic mission of the company. Here are three examples:

1. Handy & Harman, a leading processor of silver, makes bimetals, brazing compounds, and a variety of other fabricated silver products for industrial uses. To reach the industrial users, stress is laid on (a) closely controlled quality, (b) engineering advice to customers by sales representatives backed up by technical bulletins, (c) sales representatives who understand the problems of their respective industries, and (d) company reputation built up over a hundred years. A relatively high amount of money is spent on the first two appeals. In contrast, advertising is very low (occasional ads in trade journals and Christmas greetings), price is simply kept "in line" with competition, and no thought is given to style.

2. A prominent correspondence school offers courses in computers, programming, mathematics, and a wide variety of semitechnical subjects. It concentrates heavily on advertising in trade and do-it-yourself magazines and by direct mail. A low price is featured, that is, low in relation to potential earnings resulting from a course. Also, considerable effort goes into "product design" so that courses are up-to-date and easily grasped by the students. The school has no sales representatives, quality of performance is not stressed, and reputation of the institution is not a major appeal.

3. The Paper Wrapper Company prints and finishes wrappers for bread, candy, and other food products. It obtains business primarily on the basis of low price, willingness to accept short runs, and personal friendships of sales representatives. It does no advertising, provides no technical advice, and gives no special emphasis to style, reputation, or quality.

Each of these companies has a marketing mix carefully designed to fit its master strategy. They differ sharply, but this is a reflection of very different jobs to be done. In each example the marketing approach builds on company strengths and avoids efforts that would create internal strain with other activities of the company.

SUMMARY

In moving a product from the plant to consumers, a variety of activities are undertaken—and each of these involves an expense. The marketing mix policy of a company guides the selection of these activities and the allocation of marketing funds. The aim, of course, is to create a final package of satisfactions that are attractive to the specific groups of customers identified by customer policy.

Services cannot be stored, and so they move directly from their creator to the user. Nevertheless, an array of attributes also surrounds each service. Here, too, there is a marketing mix, and the customer is attracted by the total package of attributes provided.

Components of a marketing mix policy include: (1) the sales appeals that the company will stress, such as customer service, unusual quality, style and packaging, low price, and company reputation; (2) the nature and the use of advertising; and (3) the functions to be performed by sales representatives. Selection of an optimum combination is crucial. It calls for empathy with various target customer groups balanced against realistic understanding of incremental expense.

Policy regarding marketing mix should be compatible—hopefully also synergistic—with production, purchasing, personnel, and financial policies. For instance, stress on quality affects production, delivery service is related to purchasing, leasing increases capital requirements, and so forth. So, as we examine these other types of policy in the following chapters, we will often need to think back to the package of consumer satisfactions that has been adopted for our marketing mix.

 QUESTIONS FOR CLASS DISCUSSION

1. Wilkinson Sword, Ltd. (the British manufacturer of razor blades and other cutting instruments) poured $8,000,000 cash into the U.S. division of Scripto, Inc. as part of the acquisition agreement when Wilkinson bought majority ownership of Scripto. Some of the money went toward refurbishing the manufacturing facility that produced and packaged Scripto's ballpoint pens, fiber-tipped pens, and mechanical pencils, some went to badly needed working capital and some, perhaps $2,500,000, remained for marketing. Scripto had been trying to regain market share and earn some profits in an industry dominated by BIC Pen Corporation, the French-owned leader in the U.S. market, and by the Gillette Company through its Paper-Mate division. BIC's market share was

about 66% of all ballpoint pens sold at retail, Gillette's share was about 35% of the porous pen segment and 15% overall, while Scripto limped along with a 2%–3% share. Scripto had spent about half a million dollars a year on consumer advertising (network TV, spot TV, and consumer magazines), while BIC's expenditures were $7,000,000 and Gillette's $9,000,000 on the same media. Scripto had stayed with its drug, tobacco, and food distributors to market its pens and pencils while the two major firms moved rapidly into selling direct to discount houses and mass-merchandising chains. Scripto had existing plans to about double expenditures on consumer advertising. One million dollars might be spent on gearing up a field salesforce to sell direct to about 225 national chain accounts. Other retail sales would then be carried out by the currently used specialized distributors—well over 4,000 of them—and by 40 food brokers. Beyond these plans there were thoughts about spending another $1 million on designing packages and building machinery for multiple-packaging of pens and pencils. The multi-packs might increase sales volume even though the price per item was lowered.

(a) What is your appraisal of these three ways to approach Scripto's marketing mix? Do multiple-packages seem to you an effective way to gain a larger share of the market? What does this kind of marketing do to profits? (b) Would it be more effective, in your opinion, to attempt to "push" pens and pencils through distributor channels by advertising to the trade and increasing dealers' margins, or to "pull" them through by persuading customers to buy Scripto by consumer advertising and low retail sales prices?

2. Two of your friends like outdoor work and have decided to set up a landscape gardening business. In the beginning they hope to get regular customers for whom they will mow the lawn weekly, trim shrubbery, fertilize, etc. Their location will be in an upper-middle class suburban area north of Cincinnati, hopefully focused in a five-mile radius to reduce travel time. They have enough capital for necessary equipment. "You've studied business," they say, "How should we market our services? Will advertising pay?" What marketing mix do you recommend?

3. (a) During periods when gasoline is in short supply and consumers are unsure whether they can buy as much as they want, what marketing mix policy should a major integrated oil company adopt for its gasoline? (b) Should it advertise at all? If so, for what purpose and through what media?

4. "In the typical product life cycle (see page 46) a manufacturer should stress market position during the growth phase and then stress total profits—volume X margin—during the maturity phase." Assuming that a company producing electronic pocket calculators accepts this advice, what changes, if any, should it make in its marketing mix when it decides that its product has moved from growth to maturity?

5. Contrast the marketing mix policy that you would recommend for two companies; both make men's shirts but differ in their strategy regarding domain sought. Company C-P sells only high-quality shirts under the brand name of "Arrow." Company E-Z sells much less expensive shirts under any brand name that a wholesale distributor likes.

6. Explain how a change in strategy of a company making automobile air-conditioners—from (a) sales only to automobile manufacturers to (b) sales also to car

owners for installation after the automobile has been driven—affects the market mix that is appropriate.

7. Do you recommend that the sales appeals and sales promotion activities of a motel located close to an airport differ significantly from those of a motel at a resort such as the Grand Canyon? Explain specifically.

8. In the pharmaceutical industry products are divided into proprietary drugs (products with brand names often widely advertised and readily available to consumers) and "ethical" drugs (products sold by drugstores only on prescription from a doctor). Since the purchaser of ethical drugs does not decide which product to buy, special problems of marketing mix arise. Pharmaceutical manufacturers spend large sums sending representatives, called detail persons, to doctors to explain the merits of their products and to encourage the doctors to prescribe such products by the company trade name. (It is strictly unethical for a doctor to accept any financial inducement from a manufacturer or a drugstore.) The cost of detail persons is subject to much debate. Manufacturers of ethical drugs contend that such persons perform a vital educational function; critics recommend use of generic (not company) names and reliance on professional journals to keep doctors abreast of new discoveries. In addition to detail persons, ethical drug producers can promote their products by publishing research reports and by direct-mail advertising to doctors with stress on quality, pricing, service to drug wholesalers and retailers, etc. (a) Which sales appeals and forms of sales promotion do you believe will be most effective and profitable for a manufacturer? (b) Is the marketing mix you recommend in answer to (a) in the best interest of the consumer? If not, what can be done about it?

9. In Europe the chain-store operator, Tengelmann Warenhandels, has been quite successful with a separate kind of grocery supermarket which: (a) stocks only a limited variety of fast-moving items; (b) provides very few services (e.g., displays merchandise only in opened cartons, provides no paper bags or bagging service, accepts cash only, has side-street locations and minimum fixtures); (c) has low prices. Tengelmann Warenhandels recently became the largest stockholder of A&P, and is urging A&P to try its supermarket plan. Do you think such a marketing mix is transferable from Europe to the U.S.? Explain.

10. Barnes and Noble, the world's largest retail bookstore, discounted books aggressively as its primary appeal to buyers (see question 10, Chapter 7, page 148). Other elements of a marketing mix policy already used include self-service, shopping carts, and check-out counters. Possible additional elements include: a huge inventory of all kinds of books from medical treatises to popular fiction and children's books; publishers' closeouts and used books; aggressive advertising on the radio and via 30-second TV spots; benches scattered through the store to encourage browsers; a play area equipped to occupy children; free copies of book review sections of newspapers; a book-finding service for out-of-print, rare and scholarly books; a gift-wrapping counter; a bibliographic reference service to furnish titles of books and articles devoted to one subject; a book-binding service; lines of drafting supplies, scientific supplies, and small calculators; a translation service for foreign languages; special collections of scientific books in Russian, German, and Japanese. Which of these elements

are suitable in a marketing mix policy designed for the satisfaction of book buyers and for the profits of the bookstore?

11. A method of approach to sales promotion problems has been outlined on page 167. Apply this outline to the development of a sales promotion program for (a) a breakfast cereal, (b) tents for camping, (c) sightseeing tours in San Francisco, and (d) a World Trade Center (office building) in New York City.

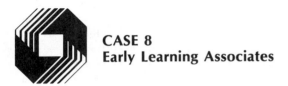

CASE 8
Early Learning Associates

Early Learning Associates is a relatively large supplier of equipment and materials to kindergartens, nursery schools, day-care centers, and other preschool educational programs. Its product line embraces most of the things used within the classroom, including: (a) environment for learning—tables, chairs, mats, lockers, storage units, etc.; (b) active play—vehicles, sand and water, woodworking, slides, etc.; (c) dramatic play—dolls, utensils, hand puppets, etc.; (d) block-building—large, small, etc.; (e) creative art—easels, paint, scissors, paste, etc.; (f) sound and rhythm; (g) puzzles and games; (h) perception-measurement, eye-hand coordination, etc.; (i) sciences—biology, chemistry, math, etc.; and (j) reading readiness.

"Our emphasis is on education, not merely entertainment," says Ms. Mary Gleason, the president. "The founder of Early Learning had the vision of being more than a toy supplier, and in twenty-five years he built up a million dollar business. Unfortunately, he ran a one-man show, and when I came over from juvenile book publishing there was no other professional backup here. Catalogs were mailed at irregular intervals to 12,000 institutions, and that was about it.

"Three years ago the company was acquired by a large conglomerate that believes education is a growth area. Mr. Early retired, and we were given the encouragement and the capital to expand. I'm a strong advocate of preprimary school child development, and I am convinced that we can be of real service to thousands of teachers who feel the same way.

"We now have a strong team. Dr. Ann Brewington is a full-time educational consultant; she helps with product selection, counsels with our school representatives, and represents the company at all sorts of meetings. Then we convinced Hilda Hirsh that she could do more good with us than in a school system; her enthusiasm and drive help her supervise our growing field force. Michael Sherman gives our catalogs a real professional tone; he knows how the products can be used and has a gift for selecting pictures that communicate to teachers. The work of these people and their associates shows up in results. Our sales last year were over four million. As volume grew, we soon discovered that our warehouse and shipping procedures were antiquated, so we brought in a new warehouse coordinator. Also we added a supply coordinator to pick up part of the buying responsibility.

"Of course, we're not alone," Ms. Gleason continued. "Childcraft and Novo on the East Coast, for example, also push education. But our location in Ann Arbor,

Michigan, gives us better contact with the Midwest. The local jobbers—and there must be several hundred of them—pick up the routine supply business. Someone estimated that they sell 10,000 different items, seven times what we carry, though they don't actually stock anywhere near that number. As a matter of fact, jobbers don't attempt to give professional service. They are just order-fillers; many are small family firms, and they may do office supply as well as school supply. A few manufacturers sell their products directly to schools—Creative Playthings, for instance, and there is even a harp maker going direct—but most manufacturers rely on firms like ours and on jobbers. Outdoor equipment is different; we're not in that business.

"We work closely with our major suppliers and check their quality very carefully. We may suggest changes to fit school needs better. Then we work out annual supply arrangements. Of course, we try to get exclusive designs, but products are quickly copied so we don't insist on it. Our products are distinctive because they are carefully selected by people who understand education and because we are very particular about quality—durability, good colors, safety, designed for school use, and the like. By dealing with Early Learning, the teacher gets sophisticated professional help in creating an attractive learning situation."

Dr. Ann Brewington, the educational consultant of Early Learning Associates, in a speech to the Illinois State Conference of Social Workers predicts continuing growth in the company's market:

"Several social factors bear on the future of preschool education:

1. Kindergarten attendance will remain stable. Although the drop in national birthrates will lead to a continuing decline in the number of children of kindergarten age, urbanization and other social forces point toward an increase in the percentage (now about 75%) of such children who will attend preschool.
2. The percentage of 3- and 4-year olds in nursery schools and other programs is still small—less than 15% for the 3-year olds and below 35% for the 4-year olds.
3. The Head Start program established a precedent for federal support of preschool education for the underprivileged. Our nation is committed to external supplements to inadequate home training.
4. Mothers of children under 6 are entering the work force in increasing numbers. Children of such mothers are expected to increase from 4.2 million in 1970 to 6.6 million by 1985.
5. Educators are stressing early learning as never before.

"For these and related reasons, we expect that the proportion of 3-to-5 year olds participating in some formal preprimary educational program will increase from two-fifths to one-half over the next 10 years."

In an estimate for Early Learning, Dr. Brewington states: "Examination of kindergarten and nursery school budgets indicates that expenditures for the kinds of products we sell range between $12 and $15 per pupil per year. Over the next 10 years the total population of 3-to-5-year olds probably will drop from about 10,500,000 to 10,000,000, and program participation probably will rise from two-fifths to one-half. These estimates indicate an increase in market potential from $50,000,000–$63,000,000 to $60,000,000–$75,000,000, with no allowance for inflation. If we assume inflation at 5% per year, the 10-year projection becomes approximately $100,000,000–$125,000,000."

Ms. Hilda Hirsh, the school service director, explains: "Most school suppliers rely solely on their catalog to explain what they have to offer. Early Learning is one of the few companies that sends people into the field to counsel teachers and supervisors. We now have 15 representatives, all experienced educators. Their service to teachers is helping to build a distinctive reputation for Early Learning.

"Each representative has a territory with about 200 key schools—schools with at least 150 pupils. The representative is expected to know personally the main people in each school and to help them in any way possible. In addition, if we receive a request for help from smaller schools in a territory, the representative follows up with a visit or at least a phone call. You'd be surprised how this sort of personal attention helps. Naturally the representatives are present at conferences and meetings attended by teachers from their territory, especially if we have an exhibit there.

"Of course, this kind of service costs money. We are now paying a base salary of $16,000—somewhat more than most representatives earned at their previous school jobs. And then they receive 6% on all Early Learning sales to their key schools, plus 6% on sales to schools requesting help during the 6 months after the request was serviced. We expect these commissions to build up as a representative becomes better known; even now commissions already average $4,000. We pay all travel expenses from the representative's home to her territory—about $6,000 per year. So we provide a stimulating and rewarding job to an energetic person.

"I believe we should keep on expanding this kind of service as fast as we can find and train good people—say, 5 to 10 per year as we have done. It clearly pays off. Even at the present level the typical representative earns commissions on $67,000 sales. The gross profit on that alone is $31,500 compared with total cost of a person in the field of $26,000. That's right now, in the short run. But those representatives are building goodwill for Early Learning that will last for years to come.

"We're still learning ourselves. Maybe after a territory is well established a representative can cover more than 200 key schools—but when you consider the number of school days in a year and the need to see teachers when they are not busy in the classroom, I have my doubts. One point is clear—we must have inventory to ship when an order is received. It's terrible when a representative has generated enthusiasm for a type of program and then has to return an order with, 'Sorry, out of stock. Will ship in two months.' The next time our representative shows up, she gets a chilly reception."

Viewing the national market, Michael Sherman, the communications director, says: "There are about 200,000 teachers working with the kindergarten and nursery school group. Some teachers in nursery schools are only baby-sitters, but most recognize that the 3-to-5-year old is learning fast and developing lifelong attitudes and skills.

"Communicating with those teachers is a challenge. Nursery schools are held in churches, homes, community buildings, and empty storefronts. They come and go much more than kindergartens, which typically are attached to a public school system. Nursery school programs also vary more than kindergarten programs. Some stress social development, others ooze child psychology and psychiatric adjustment, while many try to speed up first-grade reading and arithmetic—just like the fourth grade now teaches calculus. Usually a teacher has no more than 15 to 20 children, and she either determines or strongly influences what happens in her classes—and what supplies she uses. There may be a director if the school has two or three classes, and the director sets the tone, largely by selecting teachers who are sympathetic with her views on education. Often the parents get into the act.

"Now, to reach that highly dispersed market we use catalogs. Over half the products are pictured, preferably in use by a happy child. The teacher should grasp quickly how the product would be helpful to her. Our catalog has over 500 such messages to get across. (Different sizes or colors add up to 1,400 items sold.)

"Each year we have sent out more catalogs to teachers, with a 120,000 nationwide mailing last year. Also last year we experimented with a smaller catalog mailed to 10,000 consumers. Our sales results show that the catalog to teachers pays off. The current costs of preparing and mailing a catalog break down like this:

Catalog Costs

	To Teachers	To Consumers	
	Large catalog* (148 black-white pages, 4-color cover, 4 photos per page)	*Large catalog* (148 black-white pages, 4-color cover, 4 photos per page)*	*Small catalog (48 black-white pages, 4-color cover, 3 photos per page)*
	120,000 copies	*10,000 copies*	*10,000 copies*
Preparatory costs (copy, photography, layout, typography, mechanical preparation)	$46,000	$46,000	$16,000
Reproduction costs (plates, makeready, printing, binding)	110,000	23,000	8,000
Mailing costs (envelopes, addressing, stuffing, postage)	47,000	4,000	3,000
TOTAL	$203,000	$73,000	$27,000

*Preparatory and reproduction costs could be reduced $20,000 and $5,000, respectively, if the company chooses to put out an ordinary catalog. A large catalog for consumers was never prepared; the estimated cost figures given above are shown for comparative purposes only.

"Since the marginal cost of an additional catalog is low, we might as well send to all the good addressees we can get. Of course, we do pay something for use of mailing lists.

"We went west of the Rockies for the first time last year, and returns were low. But that was the first those people ever heard of Early Learning. Also, we have a lot of competition in New England and the Atlantic States, and the f.o.b. warehouse pricing puts us at a disadvantage there.[1] Nevertheless, the gross margin on shipments to the East is double the related catalog costs.

---

[1]Early Learning's selling terms are like those of its competitors: no discounts to anyone; customer pays shipping charges; 30 days credit to established customers; $15 minimum order.

"Inflation creates pricing problems. An annual catalog commits us to fixed prices for a year. Since we don't want our prices to be clearly out of line with competitors, we hesitate to anticipate future increases in costs to us. So we have been absorbing suppliers' price hikes made during the year. We tried sending out price change notices, but nobody paid any attention to them and we just had a lot of confusing correspondence. One very real possibility is to issue semiannual catalogs.

"Actually, small differences in price are not critical to making a sale. The typical teacher has an annual budget of, say, $300 for everything, and she can't save enough by shopping around to enable her to vary her program. As I see it, so long as she has confidence in the supplier and feels that its prices are fair, other selection factors predominate—the appeal of the product, the way it is presented, confidence in durability and quality, good experience with delivery, and the like. But if we increase prices after a catalog is issued, and then either hold up shipment while corresponding about the higher price—or ship goods that create budget problems for the customer—we're in trouble. From the teacher's viewpoint, we have failed to give good service."

3-Year Increase in Expenses Under New Management

Sales representatives	$ 390,000
More catalogs	250,000
Order handling (10% on increased volume)	290,000
Salaries and related office expenses of 5 new executives	200,000
Increased promotion at conventions and meetings	100,000
Other	85,000
Total increase under new management	$1,315,000

Comparative balance sheets and income statements for the last year under the former management, the transition year, and the two years under present management are on the following page. In commenting on these, David Rubin, the chief accountant, says: "Customers in this industry are inherently slow pay. Our accounts receivable ratio to sales is in line with those of our competitors. But the inventory is running wild. In the name of 'service' our stock turnover has fallen below 3. As a consequence, Early Learning is just soaking up capital. The treasurer at the holding company—really my boss—is about to blow the whistle, and some heads will roll. Here's a rough breakdown I prepared for him on increase in expenses during the last 3 years."

Question

What should Early Learning Associates do to improve sales and profits?

Balance Sheets
as of December 31st
(in 1,000's)

	Last Year	Preceding Year	2nd Preceding Year	3rd Preceding Year
Current Assets:				
Cash	$ 147	$ 49	$ 48	$ 17
Accounts receivable (net) . .	892	711	326	254
Inventories	981	557	217	148
Prepaid expenses	85	119	23	—
Total current assets	2,105	1,436	614	419
Fixed Assets:				
Office and warehouse				
equipment (net)	273	287	141	16
Other	64	41	19	19
Total assets	$2,442	$1,764	$ 774	$454
Liabilities:				
Accounts payable	$ 223	$ 146	$ 91	$ 73
Bank loans	500	500	—	100
Accrued items	106	72	43	114
Total current liabilities . . .	829	718	134	287
Term loan from affiliate . . .	600	100	250	—
Total liabilities	1,429	818	384	287
Equity:				
Common stock	200	200	100	20
Capital surplus	800	800	400	—
Retained earnings or (loss) .	13	(54)	(110)	147
Total equity	1,013	946	390	167
Total liabilities				
and equity	$2,442	$1,764	$ 774	$454

Income Statement
(dollar figures in 1,000's)

	Last Year		Preceding Year		2nd Preceding Year		3rd Preceding Year	
	Amount	%	Amount	%	Amount	%	Amount	%
Net sales	$4,112	100	$2,871	100	$1,423	100	$1,260	100
Cost of goods sold	2,181	53	1,548	54	867	61	741	59
Gross profit	1,931	47	1,323	46	556	39	519	41
Selling and admin-								
istrative expenses	1,765	43	1,213	42	651	46	450	36
Interest charges	99	2	54	2	15	1	6	—*
Profit or (loss)								
before income tax	67	2	56	2	(110)	8	63	5

*Less than 0.5%.

INTEGRATING CASES

Strategy and Marketing

HYGEIA INTERNATIONAL

Expansion in Nigeria is the issue. Henry Livingstone, vice president of the Africa/ Middle East Region of Hygeia International, has just received a proposal from his Nigerian managing director for a major move into poultry production. This would extend Hygeia's profitable agricultural activities even more in that west African country.

Corporate Base

Hygeia International is a pseudonym for one of the ten leading pharmaceutical companies of the world. Based in the United States, Hygeia also has laboratories and plants in many countries. Over a third of its net income is earned outside the U.S.; and because of growing federal regulation, Hygeia looks abroad for a rising percentage of its future income.

Like other large pharmaceutical firms, Hygeia has converted drugs designed for humans to use in farm animals. This opens up a large market with relatively low R&D expense. In addition to veterinary products for the control and treatment of disease, Hygeia produces a variety of feed supplements. Now about 15% of Hygeia's total sales of over a billion dollars come from "agricultural" activities!

Hygeia's agricultural business includes active participation in mass production of poultry. Today in this industry frying chickens are raised in 100,000-chick batches. Thanks to genetic selection, scientific feeding, and strictly controlled environment, friers can be ready for market in ten weeks. Egg production is similarly engineered. Significantly, these mass production methods provide one of the most efficient conversions of cereal grains into protein known on earth.

Of course, two essential features of such operations are drugs for disease control and feed supplements. Hygeia makes both (as do several competitors). Moreover, to keep in contact with the latest developments, Hygeia has a subsidiary focusing on development of new genetic strains in chickens—for faster growth, larger proportion of white meat, more eggs, disease resistance, or other desired characteristics. In the U.S., Hygeia itself does not produce chickens or eggs commercially nor sell chicks for this purpose, but it does have experts familiar with the entire technology.

As part of its international expansion, Hygeia has helped promote modern poultry technology in Europe, Latin America—and now Nigeria.

Potential Market

A British colony until 1960, Nigeria is growing dramatically. It is by far the leading black African country economically. Its large population of over ninety million (growing 2.7% per year) coupled with massive foreign exchange from its crude oil exports (15 billion dollars in 1980) provide a base for all sorts of expansion.

At the time of independence, Nigeria was a relatively poor developing country with only modest agricultural exports. Probably ninety percent of its population relied on the small village economy, almost unchanged for centuries. Political independence provided the drive, and oil the financial means to modernize. Even now the average annual per capita income of about $500 is unevenly distributed, with many village people being very poor.

National plans call for universal education, hospitals, roads and airports, electricity, radio and TV, industry, etc. Lagos, the capital, already has a population of over a million and so many automobiles that new bridges and a fine elevated highway can't cope with the traffic.

Such a rapid transition naturally creates strains. Politically, the major task is to unite three major tribal groups: the Hausa-Fulani in the north, Ibo in the east, and Yoruba in the west. They speak many different languages (English is the common language!), and traditionally are suspicious of each other. A serious civil war occurred in 1967–1969 when Biafra tried unsuccessfully to secede. The constitution provides for democratic government, but a series of military coalitions has been necessary to maintain national unity.

Although significant European influence in Nigeria is only about a century old along the southern coast, the Moslem religion and associated ideas have been present in the northern, more arid, regions since the twelfth century. (Kano, for example, was a city state when Europe was still in the Dark Ages.) Nevertheless, society continues to center around the simple village economy with strong emphasis on loyalty to the extended family. Today over three-quarters of the population relies on localized agriculture. The great movement now occurring is from the village to the city, with all the social and economic adjustments tied to such a shift.

The total population growth, and especially the movement to the cities, has created problems of food supplies. Nigeria has much fertile land, but sugar and cereals are being imported. The village society is unsuited to large-scale agricultural technology, and marketing channels are poorly developed. Particularly serious is the shortage of protein foods. The production of peanuts is rising slowly, but the amount of meat going into markets is stable at best.

Therefore, one facet of the national plan is to increase agricultural output. A system of agricultural agents to advise farmers is being established; some research on products and technology is underway; and loans to farmers are available on favorable terms. A major bottleneck in this effort is trained human resources. The number of experts capable of dealing with local farmers is very limited; and farmers with knowledge, skill, and capital needed for modern agriculture are scarce. As usual, pricing is also a dilemma. High prices which will stimulate farm output also lead to high food prices for the city dweller who is already caught in inflation. Nigeria, like the U.S., has basically a free price system but resorts to some political control of items that are important in the worker's cost of living.

In this situation, government officials would like to increase substantially the supply of eggs and chickens. And if this can be done without raising the real (adjusted for inflation) prices, that is even more attractive. A relatively small technical staff in the Ministry of Agriculture is working on poultry and low-interest loans are available to farmers who wish to install modern poultry raising equipment. A few demonstration farms are in operation, and their results show the advantages of mass production methods. However, the response to date has been limited. The concept of producing eggs or chickens in large quantities is new, and few farmers have a technical background in scientific feeding, disease control, and mechanical equipment.

Product/Customer Issue for Hygeia

Hygeia International is already well established in Nigeria. It has built a "dosage" plant where several hundred different pharmaceutical products (imported) are put into pills, capsules, bottles, and other forms suited to local use. These pharmaceuticals are sold to hospitals, clinics, and drugstores in much the same way as ethical drugs are sold in the U.S.

The sale of Hygeia products is helped by the local company's full cooperation with the "indigenization program" which requires the employment of Nigerians for virtually all positions. Also, to comply with recent laws, 40% of the shares of the local company have been sold to Nigerians. A substantial amount of training and technical advice continues to be provided for a fee by Hygeia offices in Europe and in the United States. Hygeia's policy is to cooperate as fully as it can in the development of medical services in Nigeria.

In the agricultural area Hygeia follows a similar practice. It imports and sells unique medicines and feed supplements, and it is active in technical development. Working closely with government and trade association officials, Hygeia helped set up demonstration sites for poultry colony housing and displays on lighting, ventilation, and feeding routines. It trains farmers on disease control and forecasts epidemics or disease frequency. Also, it has helped establish reliable regional feed mills. As a result of the total cooperative program, the number of egg-laying hens has increased to perhaps three million.

As with human products, Hygeia uses a wide range of services to build a market for its veterinary and feed products. Note, however, that the company does not now operate its own egg-laying colonies nor meat colonies. Nor does Hygeia maintain colonies of "parents"—pedigree chickens which produce the millions of first-line workers. In the U.S. parent colonies are usually operated by separate companies closely linked to genetic development; then fertile eggs or chicks are sold to companies in the meat or egg business. The question now facing Hygeia is whether to integrate forward in Nigeria; that is, to actually produce eggs or meat (sold as live chickens or dressed meat), or perhaps stop with fertile eggs or chicks sold to farmers.

Proposal from Nigeria
Dear Mr. Livingstone:

This letter outlines a proposed expansion of the agricultural division of our company. Estimates show that this would be a very profitable venture, and it would help meet the food needs of our growing population.

The basic plan is to become a large-scale producer of eggs and of chickens to be sold for meat. The reasons supporting this move are:

1. We already have the necessary technical staff who are fully acquainted with adapting the latest technology to local conditions.
2. There is high potential demand for protein foods, especially eggs which are less perishable than fresh meat. Considering only our urban population of 15 million people, Nigeria now markets only about 36 eggs per person per year compared with 335 in the United States.
3. Government support is available. Much of the plant cost can be financed with low-interest loans, and other cooperation can be expected.
4. Our success will attract others into the poultry business. Some of the people we train will leave and start their own operations. This activity, in addition to our own, will increase the demand for veterinary products and feed supplements.
5. Facilities for egg production can be shifted to birds for meat as marketing channels for live birds and/or frozen birds develop.
6. During inflation there is some risk that price controls on eggs might squeeze the profit margins. However, if eggs become a stable part of urban dwellers' diets, we doubt that the government will permit sharp reduction in egg production. Therefore, the increased demand for veterinary and feed products will continue.
7. To attract and retain good local managers, we plan a series of joint ventures with the local manager sharing in the ownership and profits. Each will be a separate corporation. Tentatively we are thinking of ten ventures located in the environs of the following cities: Lagos (3), Ibadan (2), Benin (2), Kaduna, Kano, Makurdi. Three will be parent-stock farms—one each in Lagos, Ibadan, and Benin; the others will be commercial egg farms.
8. The financial projection prepared by R. Akobo, our agricultural manager, and checked by M. Suleman, our financial manager, is attached. You do not have to send us cash; we can simply withhold capital as it becomes needed from remittances due on shipments made to us.

I hope you will telex your approval of this proposal in the near future so we can start negotiations with government officials and possible venture managers. I feel confident that local stockholders will approve the expansion.

Sincerely yours,

E.P. Murtala, President
Nigerian Hygeia, Ltd.

When Mr. Livingstone received Mr. Murtala's letter, he immediately asked Hygeia's treasurer and the corporate vice president for agriculture for their comments on the proposal.

Financial Summary
(Based on detailed estimates—
amount in thousands of dollars.)

	Parent Stock Farm (day-old chicks)	Commercial Egg Farm (eggs for food)
Land	40	25
Buildings & Equipment	960	440
Development Expenses	100	60
Total fixed investment	1,100	525
Working Capital	500	175
Total investment	1,600	700
Sales[a]	2,300	850
Direct Expenses	870	685
Administration, Sales, etc.	150	45
Operating profit	1,020	120
Income taxes @ 50%[b]	510	60
Net profit	510	60
Government and Bank Financing	1,000	450
Equity	600	250
Total investment	1,600	700
Return on Equity before Taxes/yr[c]	170%	48%
Return on Equity after Taxes/yr	85%	24%

Notes:

(a) Sales figures, but not expenses, reduced 20% to allow for contingencies.
(b) Actually most Nigerian taxes will be rebated during first four years.
(c) Figures converted from naira to dollars at rate of 1N = $1.5
   Inflation will increase all estimates, but the proportions should remain the same.

   Estimates are for fullscale operations. It will take two to three years to reach this level. Estimates show both cash and net income break-even by end of first year, and with tax rebate full recovery of equity by early in third year.

The treasurer noted that "the estimated return is well over the 30% hurdle-rate used for domestic investment. Also, with Nigeria's favorable foreign exchange position, the danger of exchange rate losses is not high. So the main question relates to political risks—revolution, confiscation, controls on repatriation of profits, arbitrary actions to promote diplomatic ends (e.g., South Africa), etc. And you are in the best position to assess these risks."

The agriculture vice president replied, in part: "My chief concern is whether Hygeia should enter into agricultural production. In the U.S., Europe, and most other locations we confine our activities to *helping others* (local people who know local problems) improve their output. That posture keeps us out of a lot of trouble.

In particular, we must be sure that what we do in poultry does not upset sales of livestock veterinary and feed products, or more important, sales of products for humans. My preference is to enter production only when that is the only feasible way to start the use of our regular line of products, and to pull out as soon as local operators are ready to carry on. So I urge you to think of the Nigerian proposal only as a sales promotion device. You can decide whether there are better ways to promote sales."

Question

Assume that you are a personal assistant to Mr. Livingstone, and that he has asked you to study the total Nigerian situation and recommend what he should do regarding Mr. Murtala's proposal. What do you tell Mr. Livingstone?

THE ARCHITECTURAL GROUP, INC.[1]

Four years of nearly steady growth in its number of projects has brought enough financial success so that the two founders of The Architectural Group, Inc. believe that their original investments are now safe. Their earnings are also high enough so that their standard of living equals that which they would have enjoyed had they remained as employees of other firms.

The Architectural Group has succeeded mainly in marketing its services for the design and building of churches, small office buildings, retail stores, apartments, and expensive, individually-designed houses. It now does work in towns up to 100 miles distant from its home city (Albuquerque). The Group participates in about 25% of the available construction projects in this particular part of the architectural market. The owners find it difficult to envision capturing a larger share of these kinds of jobs since they compete with seventy other architects or architectural firms in the city.

During the past three years, three more architects have invested in the company and become active principals. Along with the growth have come questions about what directions to follow in the future and, indeed, whether to attempt to expand at all.

The Beginnings

Rather than starting small in a backroom or a basement (the usual practice), John Givens and William Walton, the founders, rented substantial office space in one of the city's secondary office centers that had a large volume of traffic pass its doors.

Their original idea—the basic service offered—was, as they called it, "the team concept." Externally, their efforts would closely involve the client and the contractor in design and construction decisions. Internally, they would support one another.

---

[1]See the Appendix to this case for information about the work of architects, pricing of their services, and professional certification.

They tried to time their entry into the market to catch the beginning of a recovery by business in general from a recession and to be on the upswing of a construction cycle. This meant a year's wait after their decision to found the firm.

Two of the rules-of-thumb for new architectural firms are: (1) bring some clients with you when you begin; (2) work weekends and evenings at the new business—keep your old job as long as you can. The Architectural Group broke both of these rules. Givens and Walton believed it morally wrong to attempt to bring old clients with them. They assumed zero revenues for their new firm for six months. Each provided his own funds for living and provided the firm's working capital in exchange for common stock.

Early on, potential clients came in with 1, 2, or 3% commission jobs. It was hard to turn these jobs down when the firm had no revenue. But an early decision had been to turn down jobs at below standard rates. Eventually one client walked in off the street with a house he wanted designed—at the full rate. A few others followed.

Little revenue and a relatively large organization expense forced the founders to search for work. Fortunately, in a way, an urban development project was partly—but incompletely—planned. Decisions already made by city planners and elected officials had frightened off established firms. Concepts firmly fixed included adaptation to territorial and mission styles and a made-from-adobe look for the finished buildings. Plazas, shops, and individualized offices were to be on a small and intimate scale analogous to those of the Chocolate Factory in San Francisco or the shopping terraces and courts of Sydney, Australia, and Singapore.

When the Group became interested in the project and began to sell their efforts, they found that, although they were technically well prepared for designing and producing buildings, they were not well prepared for managing an architectural firm in the sense of making client contacts and actually carrying out effective relationships with the client and the contractors.

The Architectural Group's idea for Urban Center (as the project was called) was finally sold basically on its character as a solution to the three design criteria mentioned above and as an attractive way to refocus the interest of the city's people on the Urban Center area. No overriding systems approach could be used because decisions already made had led to the need for a complex set of services. But there was a great deal of architectural design work needed to carry out the character sketches for the 335,000 square feet of the Center.

The Product

John Givens said: "Communication with the client is a major part of our concept of the provision of architectural service. A frequent problem is keeping clients in a position so that they know what is occurring. We build models to do this and provide blueprints and perspective drawings. With each client it is a continuous educational process. A second problem is to bring clients into the decision-making for the development stage.

"We work hard to educate owners to the fact that they must tell the architect—rather than the contractor—about changes. On small jobs this is a major difficulty.

"The architect's true role when construction begins is to represent both the contractor *and* the client. Clients do not understand this even though it is spelled out in the contract.

"Every client turns out to be different. Our standard approach works, but we might do more if we could develop a way to understand how to handle the differences and then carry out the understanding.

"Everyone in the firm is attempting to reach one goal—'trying to do better architecture.' On one level this means winding up with a happy client. If we have not done this, then we have done no good. But a client may want to use a bad color. This leads to the second level, which is to satisfy our own ideas about what is good."

Organization

Mr. Givens and Mr. Walton found almost immediately that they could not do the necessary promotional work or even send out letters without a secretary. One was hired and the staff grew as the workload increased. The principle was to keep a stable staff and to feed it with work. A second principle was to select people to fill voids in the services and do the selection so that those hired would work together. An interiors group (not just one specialist) was opened within the firm, as was a planning and scheduling group.

For work not related to architectural skills, the firm used consultants. In establishing the firm, the partners attempted to find the best legal organization in the city. The benefits from using high-priced talent were expected to outweigh the costs. Then the founders met with the lawyers at least once per week so that they could understand just what the legal firm was doing or attempting to do for them.

The founders and the principals in the firm each take a direct part in the work of the firm. For example, Mr. Armando is responsible for all promotional activities, but he also spends half of his time working as an architect on specific projects. As new projects come in, they are assigned to be the responsibility of one officer or another. A fixed principle of the practice of architecture appears to be that "clients want to talk to principals."

The five officers all like to think that they will always be doing professional work as architects and project managers as well as having their functional responsibilities for promotion, production, design, accounting, and office management. But, if growth continues, how will additional officers and owners fit into this idea of executive tasks?

General policy decisions are now made in round-table discussions. Since the five officers were trained the same way and have the same goals and ideas, there are few matters on which they disagree. Often matters need not come to a vote but are settled by consensus or by relying on the particular expertise of one officer. Mr. Wilks commented: "I take the attitude that I am responsible to my partners for the work I do for the firm."

Promotion

Mr. Drollinger said: "When we first started the firm, we were continually being asked what experience we had. This still continues in some markets such as schools. Our experience with schools has been zero to this day."

Developing contacts with clients was, naturally, a major early concern. The plan was for everyone to devote a major share of his attention to promotion through these activities: (a) legwork—visiting every contractor and mortgage banker within the city; (b) ears open—using all social occasions to briefly chat about their new group and to listen for any response; (c) media—press releases, visits with broadcasters of local news and with feature writers; (d) public agencies—contact with all city, county, state, and federal agencies that had anything to do with housing in the city; and (e) hope—that a client would walk into the office unsolicited.

The point of most of the contacts was to find out who was the decision-maker or the decision-making committee in an organization with whom they might potentially work, to submit the Group's name or sketches and models, and to maintain an up-to-date list of the decision-makers and the status of any projects with which the potential client organizations might be concerned.

At one point, the Group made a special study of libraries since none of them had had experience in designing and building a library. They learned how to handle the problem of getting ready to construct a library. To date, no library job has been obtained. One principal said, "We must have a constant attitude of promoting ourselves. This is uncomfortable at first, but we have to get accustomed to it."

Presentations to potential clients include not only sketches, drawings, and models, but also specific attempts to explain how the architects hope to work with the client and what architectural, space design, and space-use goals they have with and for the client. They attempt to sell the idea that the job is going to be interesting to the client and that the client has information that will be needed regularly during the project but mainly as input at the design and scheduling phases.

The team concept is used on all jobs. Some clients are surprised to be called upon continuously. A significant minority of clients object to more than a few meetings with the architect at the onset of a project.

Issues to Be Faced

What roles, as architects, can the members of the firm play in society today? They have consistently attempted to be public relations men for an idea—to convince people that they can function better in a good space. Thus they have been promoting architecture that is promoting an ideal. Is this useful socially?

Projected growth, if it continues, will mean adding three more principals within the next two years. Then not all will be able to work in two roles. "We now have considerable momentum," John Givens observes, "and are regarded by people who know us as a progressive, growing firm. Naturally we would like to take advantage of this image. Adding principals and staff to support them will increase our fixed costs substantially, which could be serious to all of us if construction hits a tailspin. On the other hand, with a larger volume of work we should be able to utilize our existing staff support more effectively." The five officers can, of course, agree not to attempt further expansion of projects and activities. This will leave them in comfortable positions. And they will be able to be selective to some extent about their future work.

If new officers or principals are added to the firm, they will have to make a financial investment by buying a share of the common stock. Each man thus sees his work as, in part, a contribution to the firm's return on the financial investment. But, as one of the original architects said, "Not one of us would stay if we did not like to work together."

The Architectural Group has decided, for individual homes, to change its pricing system from the customary practice of charging a percentage of the total construction costs—a higher rate for smaller projects—to a fee system. Present practice includes making presentations on speculation at the expense of the firm. The fee system for individual homes is now 2.75 times the direct hourly payroll of those who work on the project with a maximum of 10% of total costs. This maximum is 2 percentage points less than the recommendation of the American Institute of Architects, but The Architectural Group believes it to be more just.

Should the Group change to a system with fees specified for all tasks undertaken, including an hourly charge for developing presentations or space concepts? The historical method is understood and generally acceptable to clients. The fee system is not widely known but is much more flexible for the architects and is thought to be more suitable for the presentation of a wider range of ideas and architectural choices to existing and potential clients.

The present physical space is just adequate for the number of architects, drafters, technicians, and office workers now in the firm. Finding more space will not be difficult nor will it impose any financial strain. But a lease commitment would mean a choice for continued growth.

Since architecture, tied as it is with construction, is cyclical, the five have considered other kinds of ventures. "When you work on your own, you begin to think of all sorts of things you never thought of before. We have wondered whether it would be wise to try other cities, repeating the kind of work done here. Or should we attempt land development—which requires a considerable financial commitment, much negotiating, a long-term plan, and close supervision of contractors as well as costs?"

Questions

(1) What promotional, pricing, product, and customer policies might The Architectural Group follow to be consistent with continued growth?

(2) Do you see an advantage for the firm in remaining at its present size? Explain. What policies will then be useful?

Appendix
Nature of Architectural Work

An architect plans buildings (houses, apartments, schools, factories, office buildings, churches, synagogues) to serve the many purposes of the owners and the inhabitants. An architect may, on a large scale, design useful and beautiful neighborhoods, cities, and metropolitan areas. An architect is, first of all, an artist who tries to provide beauty in the shapes, forms, and spaces of the buildings as well as usefulness to those who live and work within them. But an architect also needs the skills of a person in business and an engineer to keep the costs of the buildings reasonable, to meet project deadlines, to use materials effectively, and to work within building codes.

To provide usefulness for clients (who may be private individuals, governmental officials, contractors, or business executives), the architect works with them to learn their goals—expressed and unexpressed. The architect helps in the acquisition of a site or studies one chosen by the client so that the plans may be related by comparison or contrast to the form of the land and to nearby structures. With the client, the architect prepares a detailed program that outlines the requirements to be met as to a building's size, location, and general appearance as well as the proposed budget.

Following a sequence of decisions made by the architect and the client on the basis of rough sketches, room plans, section drawings, and elevation and perspective drawings, the architect prepares a basic design for the client's approval. The presentation may also indicate why and how the design meets the standards of good architecture.

The basic design is reviewed again for costs, alternative methods of construction, building code standards, and acquisition of a building permit. On large jobs the architect may call in specialists in interior design, heating and air-conditioning, foundations, or landscape design at this stage of the project. Once the design is accepted by the client, the architect prepares working drawings, specifications for materials, and the document of general conditions that describes the rights and duties of the client, the architect, and the contractor in working together. During construction, the architect evaluates progress against the plans, checks on materials and equipment used, approves subcontractors, and makes large-scale drawings of decorative details to guide the workers. After a final review, the architect's responsibility to the client for administration of the contract ends. The architect then, hopefully, receives the fee.

Fees, customarily, are negotiated as a percentage of the construction cost. Typical fees are 12% for an individual, custom-designed home; 8% for a church; 6% for a privately-owned building costing $1,000,000; 6% maximum for any state-owned building; 1% for a tract development of 40 to 50 houses selling for over $50,000 each.

Those architects who have changed their pricing to either the cost-plus or the fixed-fee basis submit bills to the clients at various stages of the project. Ordinarily the amounts billed under a fixed-fee contract are: schematic phase, 15%; development phase, 20%; construction contracts document phase, 40%; the bid-negotiating phase, 5%; contract administration, 20%.

Since new buildings are, ordinarily, rare events for the owners, architects seldom work with a particular client more than once. Even if they do so, the relationship is not continuous but sporadic, with jobs for the architects occurring at varying intervals of several years. Construction cycles add another dimension of complexity to the flow of work available for architectural firms.

In most states, architects must pass a licensing examination to open an office. Qualifications to take the examination ordinarily include five or six years of professional training beyond high school to earn a degree in an accredited architectural school and three years of practical experience in an architect's office.

RESEARCH AND DEVELOPMENT POLICY

The creation of services is just as indispensable as their distribution, which we have been examining in preceding chapters. Company strategy embraces both. In fact, it is often the ingenious marriage of producing and marketing that gives a company unique strength. And as with marketing, policy is needed to elaborate and sharpen the broad strategic choices that have been made for the production of services that are to be sold. This amplification of directions for creating services will be discussed in this chapter on research and development policy, and in the following two chapters on production policy and procurement policy.

ROLE OF RESEARCH AND DEVELOPMENT

Some firms quite wisely do virtually no research and development. Others rely on their "R&D" for continuing survival. Between these two extremes there are many variations in purposes and emphasis. Because of this array of options, policy guidance on the role of research and development is sorely needed.

Scope

This chapter deals with activities from basic research to placing a product on the market or utilizing a new process. We are primarily concerned with *innovation*—the effective application of a new idea. Innovations occur in all kinds of human activity, but here we are focusing on technological changes in products and processes.

Clearly, the business manager is concerned with more than *invention*—the conceiving of a new and useful idea. Invention is an essential part of the total process, but it is only a part. Companies may engage in activities that lead to inventions; but if they do, they must also devote a great deal of effort to converting the invention into a practical application.

Stages

When planning for R&D, a recognition of the stages involved in innovation is helpful. The normal stages of technological innovation are:

1. Basic research—the scientific investigation of a physical phenomenon without any defined use that might be made of the resulting knowledge.
2. Applied research—studies designed to identify specific potential applications of general knowledge.
3. Development—testing and elaborating a potential application into a model
   or a set of specifications that demonstrates the physical "doability" of a new
   process or product.
4. Pilot plant or prototype testing—testing the economic as well as the physical
   feasibility of actually using a model or specifications emerging from the
   development stage.
5. Manufacturing, tooling, and debugging—designing and assembling new
   manufacturing equipment, then testing and modifying it until full-scale
   operations at acceptable efficiencies are possible.
6. Marketing start-up—overcoming any new technical problems of physical
   distribution and customer use.

The following table presents an outline of the six stages of technological
innovation with respect to output, predictability of results, and types of
personnel involved:

Normal Stages of Technological Innovation

Stages	Output	Ability to Predict Results	Kinds of People Involved
1. Basic research	Knowledge	None	Idealists and dreamers—young, professionally oriented
2. Applied research	Directed knowledge, leading to identified applications*	Little	May be prickly personalities
3. Development	Product or process model—operational feasibility		
4. Pilot plant	Cost knowledge—economic feasibility	Some	Engineers—organization oriented
5. Manufacturing, tooling, and debugging	Total operating system, specifications, and process costs	High probability	Persons with efficiency and effectiveness as values
6. Marketing start-up	Product acceptance		

*Many inventions by individual tinkerers arise without knowledge from basic research; all major
inventions sparking the Industrial Revolution were of this sort.

In practice, the separation of these six stages of technological innovation is fuzzy. Problems encountered at any one stage may require backtracking to a previous stage. For instance, a difficulty uncovered in a pilot plant may signal the need for further development or even applied research effort. Similarly, good management practice requires forward bridging. Thus, basic research shades into applied research, and applied research shades into development. Especially important in private R&D work is a frequent checking of market potentials and market requirements during all of the stages except basic research.

In setting policies for R&D work, it is important to recognize that research expenses are normally very much smaller than development expenses for a successful project. Statistics on this point are far from precise, but the following chart does indicate the range in three important industries.

COST DISTRIBUTION OF SUCCESSFUL INNOVATIONS IN CHEMICAL, ELECTRONIC, AND MACHINERY INDUSTRIES

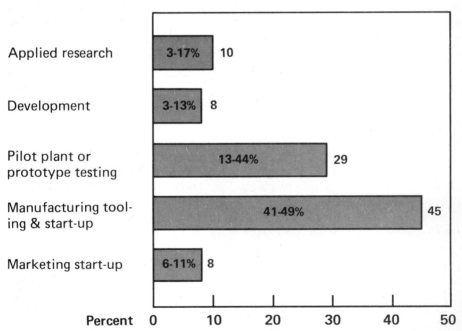

Source: Edwin Mansfield *et al., The Production and Application of New Industrial Technology,* (New York: W.W. Norton & Co., Inc., 1977), p. 71. Lengths of bars show mean percentages of sample cases; numbers within bars show the range.

The reasons for high expense in later stages are not hard to find. Many work-hours are required to design and test each of the subparts of a new product or process. Moreover, as the work progresses it must be done on a larger and larger scale, requiring greater inputs of materials and machinery. In some instances, such as the development of penicillin, entirely new processes for acquiring raw material in the quantity and the quality desired have to be invented. The identification and the recording of all the specifications in an experimental model is time-consuming. Clearly, any company that engages in applied research must be prepared to invest substantially larger additional amounts if it is to reap full benefit from its research efforts.

Progress by Increments

A single dramatic invention such as Carlson's Xerography or Land's Polaroid camera catches our attention when we think about innovation. However, it is a mistake to assume that the success of all R&D work depends upon major discoveries. Much more common is a succession of small improvements, one built upon another, that in total add up to a major change. The development of mobile homes and self-service stores are examples of innovations that occurred in this incremental fashion.

This incremental process permits several different companies to participate in an innovation. Frequently one firm builds on the advances of another, and it is possible to enter the game late and still be successful. Of course, a basic invention protected by a patent is of great competitive value, but a great majority of R&D work is not of this character. Most firms advance a step at a time, and R&D success is measured by who is stepping fastest.

Risk Entailed

Both uncertainty and expense permeate the design of all R&D policy. Of course, business expenditures in R&D of about $40 billion per year (one-half of this in government money) produces a stream of new products and processes, but the output of a single company laboratory is by no means sure. For example, laser theory was discovered and published by Charles Towne early in the 1950's. Many different laboratories started applied research with this new concept, but twenty years later only a few significant industrial applications had appeared. R&D managers estimate that less than 20% of the ideas that look good enough to move from applied research to development actually end up in a marketable product (or applied process), and only a part of these are commercially successful. Uncertainty in R&D is real.

Moreover, R&D work is expensive. When technical assistants and other laboratory expenses are added to salary, a scientist or a senior engineer may cost a company from $90,000 to $150,000 a year. Of course the cost of routine engineering is lower, but so is the useful output. Projects that call for a team approach quickly entail a significant investment. Such cost, coupled with uncertainty of outcome, puts pressure on central management to think through carefully how R&D should be used.

Among the key issues for which policy guidance is needed are the following:

1. Targets for improvement.
2. Depth of research effort.
3. Offensive versus defensive R&D.
4. Getting R&D done by outsiders.
5. Limits on total commitment.

TARGETS FOR IMPROVEMENT

R&D activities tend to wander. Researchers and engineers must be given considerable freedom to organize their own work, and each person prefers to move in directions that are intellectually exciting to that individual. No company can afford such a diffused effort on a large scale, although occasionally a company does permit its researchers to devote, say, 20% of their time to anything that intrigues them. Instead, guideposts—policy—are established to focus the effort. The guides should be directly derived from company strategy.

Product Versus Process Focus

A recurring question is how R&D effort will be divided between developing new and improved products and seeking improvements in production processes. The key to a policy on this matter lies in the *industry analysis,* which we have urged as a prerequisite for drawing up company strategy. In a mature industry where low cost is necessary to meet price competition, for instance, R&D effort on processes may be crucial. On the other hand, newly designed products may be the primary success factor in another industry, so here R&D should focus on products.

A large chemical company used this simple but fundamental approach to sharply alter its R&D targets. For years this company had focused on tonnage production of carbon compounds. It was an efficient producer and maintained a steady position in its segment of a growing industry. Good process R&D was an important contributor to this achievement. Then the oil companies entered the chemical industry on a large scale. In terms of tonnage and low cost, the oil companies had some relative advantages: ready access to low-cost carbon inputs in the form of oil and gas, and a large cash flow available for the huge investments needed for new plants. Analysis of these developments led the independent chemical company to conclude that maintaining its position in the tonnage business would probably yield a declining return on its invested capital. Prospects were brighter for complex products that produced special effects and carried greater added value. Consequently, a new strategy was adopted of gradually phasing out the heavy petrol chemicals and replacing this business with newer complex products. To implement this strategy the R&D policy was sharply altered. New products became the dominant theme, whereas process research was confined to modifications of existing plants.

Adoption of the policy change just cited was no easy matter. For years the company had prided itself on being an aggressive, successful competitor. The personal careers of several of the key executives were based on this success. To them the policy change was like forfeiting a football game in midseason. Of course, the firm would continue to be a major factor in the segment of the industry these individuals knew so well, probably beyond the date of their retirement, but they were well aware that the change in the R&D policy would probably shape the character of the company in the future.

Existing Lines Versus New Lines

A decision to support product research still leaves open the question of what type of product to concentrate on. For example, a jet engine manufacturing company sticks to its existing products. It believes that the future market in this line alone is very large and that technological improvements from company R&D will be the key determinant of who gets the lion's share.

In contrast, Minnesota Mining and Manufacturing Company, makers of Scotch tape, photographic material, and a variety of other products, has achieved considerable success with R&D focused on new lines. The company does have a clear policy about the kinds of products on which money is to be spent. The emphasis is to be on products that are (a) new, (b) patentable, and (c) consumable (heavy repeat business). Here again, the R&D policy is a direct extension of the expansion strategy that this particular company has selected.

One dimension of a product line sometimes covered by R&D policy is the amount of forward integration. For instance, should a transistor manufacturer do research on products using transistors? In its fiber division, the Du Pont company has stayed away from end-products such as hosiery, shirts, rugs, and the like. The R&D people must know enough about the subsequent processing and final consumption of its fibers to build desirable characteristics into its products, but that is as far as its R&D people are expected to go. Incidentally, when there is no clear breaking point, Du Pont does carry its research clear to the consumer level, as in paints. Nevertheless, for years the company's basic policy was to stick to chemical manufacturing. This forward limit has had a significant effect upon the character of Du Pont research and the innovations it has produced.

Process Improvements That Count

In process R&D, as with product R&D, policy guidance is needed on where to focus attention. One approach is to deal only with those aspects of production where significant savings are possible. Thus a farm equipment manufacturer turned down a proposal from its engineering department to develop a new way of heat-treating a special type of steel. Even if the project had been as successful as hoped, it would have cut total manufacturing costs only by a fraction of one percent. The company preferred to concentrate its limited resources where the potential payout was greater.

The number of units affected by a process change is also critical. A large copper company, for instance, devoted substantial effort to finding ways to improve the recovery of copper from its ore crushing process by just a small percentage. Since literally millions of tons went through this process, even a small improvement in recovery could be significant. Unfortunately, a special study showed that the R&D department of this company was proceeding with equal zeal on the recovery of other metals that were produced in minor amounts as by-products of the copper operation. The study resulted in a sharper definition of what kind of process improvements to seek.

Policy defining the direction of R&D effort should provide for some degree of freedom, especially in the research stages. Many new discoveries have come through serendipity—finding one thing when looking for another. Penicillin and X-ray are examples. However, an interest in bright ideas that may be unrelated to the purposes of the project at hand does not diminish the value of policy about where to put the major effort. With such policy, most of the output will be directly usable by the company. Additional insights are welcome by-products, but they should be treated as by-products.

DEPTH OF RESEARCH EFFORT

Identification of a promising research area still leaves management with a question of depth of effort. For example, does a research interest in vertical takeoff planes mean that the company will undertake theoretical research in aerial dynamics or structural properties of lightweight metal? Where in the continuum from a search for new knowledge to practical specifications for a marketable product should the XYZ Company focus its efforts?

Basic Research Versus Applied Research

No company authorizes its research department to study anything that intrigues its scientists. Even basic research will be in areas related to the company's strategic mission—biochemistry for pharmaceutical companies, geology for oil companies, and the like. The issue is whether (a) simply to investigate a phenomenon without any specific idea of how the new knowledge acquired will be used (basic research), or (b) to pick a potential application of knowledge—human need—and try to devise ways of meeting this need (applied research). The distinction is like studying the geography of Central Africa just to learn more about it versus identifying attractive sites for hydroelectric power plants in Central Africa.

Exceptional companies in basic research. A few companies have had outstanding success with their policy of doing basic research. A notable example is the work at Bell Telephone Laboratories on semiconductors. Because of a possible connection with solid-state amplifiers, Bell Labs set up a semiconductor basic research group of physicists, chemists, and metallurgists in 1946. In the process of their investigation they discovered the transistor in 1948, and by 1951 they had developed the theoretical knowledge on which transistors with all their manifold applications are based. In passing, note that the initial effort took over five years of basic research by a whole group of scientists and that ten to fifteen years elapsed before the transistor was in widespread commercial application.

The Du Pont discovery of nylon is another classic example of where basic research paid off. Here, the research was on polymerization and by accident one of the researchers discovered that the fiber formed by pulling a stirring rod out of an experimental batch had unusual flexibility and strength. This led to a change in the direction of the research; but after two years of intensive work, the results were so discouraging that the entire project was almost abandoned. It took seven years after the initial discovery before nylon could be produced on a commercial basis. Just when this undertaking moved from "basic research" to "applied research" is hard to define. But it is clear that the basic research provided the situation in which the initial discovery was possible.

Occasional commercial success growing out of basic research, however, does not mean that all companies interested in new products and processes should embark on basic research. In fact, most companies have concluded that the costs and the hazards of basic research make it an unwise investment of company funds. Even large research-minded companies like Union Carbide Corporation and Monsanto Company have recently redirected their R&D effort to applied market-oriented projects.

Policy criteria for basic research. If a company is going to undertake basic research, it should meet the following criteria: (1) be prepared to take the risk of long periods of research without discovering ideas that have commercial value; (2) have a "payout" period threshold that permits a long time between investment and return (over twenty-five years elapsed between Fleming's discovery of penicillin and its large-scale production); and (3) possess enough capital to exploit discoveries when and if they are made —often millions of dollars are needed after the discovery to bring it into commercial use.

In addition to the three preceding criteria, which are essentially financial, a fourth operating consideration is usually necessary to justify basic research: (4) be sufficiently large in the industry where the discovery is applied to take full advantage of the new concept. This means that the company should have an existing position that will permit it to obtain synergistic benefits when the new product or process is introduced. Of course, a company can license or sell its patents to other companies, or it might enter a new industry in an effort to exploit a discovery it had made; but the return from such use of a new idea is much smaller than enhancing an existing market position or production capability.

Government financing of research can mitigate these rather severe criteria. In the aerospace industry and some other industries, government financing does permit a lot of *applied* research and development. To a much smaller extent, this same approach can be utilized for basic research (typically, however, government funds for this purpose go to universities or other nonprofit research institutes). Of course, government financing means that the company will not have exclusive use of the knowledge obtained, but direct access to scientists familiar with the latest developments might be advantageous for the company.

Applied Research Versus Development

If basic research looks nebulous for a company, maybe it should also back away from applied research. Instead of spending time and money in finding how to accomplish a desired end, perhaps effort could better be concentrated on developing economical methods of utilizing ideas that are already known to work.

The considerations in making this choice are similar to those just listed for basic research, but here the risks are less and the payout periods somewhat shorter. The main advantage of sticking to "development" is assurance that results will reinforce existing activity. Thus the outcome can be directed toward strategic objectives (new products or production economy) rather than toward less predictable outcomes of applied research, which at least occasionally go off on tangents.

One category of applied research has a different twist. A company may develop a store of background knowledge about a phenomenon it often confronts. Then, as specific problems are faced, the research findings expedite solutions. For instance, a relatively small company making automatic materials-handling systems frequently needed to know how different materials (flour, paint, pigment, fertilizer, and cement) flowed; any tendency to lump, dust, or bridge required special design modifications. A research project on all factors affecting the way materials in general flow created a bank of information that enabled the company to give its customers distinctive advice on materials handling. The desirability of such applied research depends, of course, on the kind of service a company seeks to provide. One oil company may study the behavior of lubricants in Arctic temperatures, whereas an oil company selling only to Midwest customers would not bother. Policy guidance, geared into strategy, on how far to push such research is needed.

OFFENSIVE VERSUS DEFENSIVE R&D

Company strategy strongly influences R&D policy in terms of its emphasis on being a leader or a follower.

First with the Best

If company strategy endorses a strong leadership position in any industry where technological change is a significant factor, an aggressive R&D program is essential. Money, time, and executive effort must be devoted toward this end.

Maxwell House Coffee, the largest division of General Foods Corporation, illustrates the price of such leadership. Having won a preeminent position in the U.S. coffee market by pioneering instant coffee, the division might have concentrated on maximizing short-run profits. Instead, the basic strategy was to retain this strong position over the long run, and this required product leadership. Consequently, Maxwell House retained a large research effort on ways to improve its product—notably to capture the aroma of freshly ground coffee. The freeze-dry method of making instant coffee was finally perfected in the laboratory and, despite the company's existing market leadership, additional millions of dollars were spent on tooling-up and introducing this new type of coffee to the consumer. Incidentally, Nestle's developed a freeze-dried coffee about the same time, and if Maxwell had not engaged in "offensive R&D" during the preceding ten years Nestle's probably would have captured a large piece of the Maxwell House business.

The fact that a company adopts an offensive R&D policy does not, of course, guarantee a dominant position such as Maxwell House gained. RCA, for instance, spent millions of dollars pioneering in color television. It was successful in being an early entry into this vast market but other companies quickly followed, each with its own modifications, so the market has always been shared with half a dozen other leading manufacturers. Also, even a successful R&D effort, to be effective, must be combined with good production and marketing for the investment to pay off. We noted in Chapter 3 that Univac did very well with its offensive program in computer research but then failed to capitalize on its initial technological advantage.

Running a Close Second

The price of being first is high. Many firms, especially those not giants in their industries, adopt an R&D policy that they hope will enable them to defend themselves against advances made by competitors. The policy has two phases. First, a systematic scanning—including planned intelligence—of research effort and results by others is maintained in all fields that could seriously upset present competitive strengths. Such surveillance requires a few people of high technical perception but does not require large outlays of money for laboratory and staff. Second, the company needs unusual competence to perform development work; its engineers must be able to move rapidly and be ingenious in devising methods of accomplishing results someone else has demonstrated as possible. The aim is to match competitors' offerings before the delay seriously upsets market positions.

Such a defensive policy has advantages. The most obvious is avoiding long, unproductive expenses for applied research and perhaps basic research. In addition, typically a new product does not work well in all its early applications; these initial problems create customer dissatisfaction, delays, and perhaps makeshift remedies. For instance, despite all the testing, a really new model of an automobile usually develops a series of weak points that require tedious trips back to the shop. If a second-runner can avoid these difficulties, it may rightfully claim it has the more dependable product. So, for that very large part of innovation that is developed by a series of modifications rather than a dramatic "breakthrough," a defensive R&D policy may not be a serious handicap.

Patents do create difficulties for the company using a defensive R&D policy. Basic patents are the serious ones because they may cut off an entire new area; for example, Hall's patent on electrolytic reduction of aluminum prevented new entry into the basic aluminum business until the patent expired. Patents for modifications or refinements are less troublesome because often the same effect can be achieved in a slightly different way. In some industries, such as pharmaceuticals and automobiles, cross-licensing of the use of patents is fairly common. Nevertheless, the possibility of a patent block is one of the hazards that must be weighed in considering the defensive policy approach.

A Varied Attack

The R&D policy does not have to be the same for all product lines. A medium-sized pharmaceutical company, for example, concluded that it could afford applied research only in two fields—tranquilizers and anesthetics. In seven other areas it adopted a defensive policy of follow-the-leader, and for two older product lines it simply continued production of established items with existing facilities, doing no R&D.

In practice, this mixture of defensive and offensive R&D created some internal misunderstandings. The need to select a limited area for concentrated research was understood, although not everyone agreed on the selections made. Confusion sometimes did arise when high priority was given to intensive development effort on one side of the other lines—to catch up with competition. "Why don't they make up their minds whether to stay in that business or not? For six months, all hell breaks loose and then we lapse back into our 'do-nothing' policy." The idea that the company was playing *both* an offensive and a defensive game was hard to accept by people who found themselves shifted suddenly from one project to another. But, to the executives who wanted to get maximum return from a limited R&D budget, the mixed policy made sense.

GETTING R&D DONE BY OUTSIDERS

R&D does not have to be done "in house." As with other inputs desired by a company, the R&D results may be acquired from outsiders. This is the familiar "make-or-buy" issue.

A firm may consider the use of outsiders for several reasons. Much R&D work requires a minimum-sized effort to be effective; the minimum "critical mass" usually consists of at least two or three scientists, some laboratory technicians, physical facilities, a flow of information and raw materials, travel money, and overhead services. Also, while an improvement in a product or process may be desired by an industry, the potential use by a single company may be too small to justify the cost of the necessary R&D. Or, a company may have more attractive use of its funds; a quicker cash flow return will be preferred, particularly by a company in a tight capital position. For any of these reasons, a company may hesitate to back a proposal with its own R&D effort, yet strongly desire the result.

Buying R&D Effort

Like preparing advertising copy, making a computer analysis, or running a training course, R&D effort can be purchased outside the company.

Tapping expertise of others. In many fields, good independent research laboratories have been established to do special research for people who lack their own facilities. The Battelle Institute, for instance, did development work on Carlson's Xerox invention (the patent was subsequently sold to what is now the Xerox Corporation). The staffs of these institutes often include a wider array of specialists than many companies can retain on their permanent staff. Especially when a company only occasionally needs a particular type of R&D work, temporary access to such experts may be of great help.

Universities are a second major place to buy research effort. Occasionally a contract is made with the university itself, but more often individual faculty members are employed to work on projects in their special field of expertise. Pharmaceutical companies, for instance, frequently support the private research work of professors in the biochemistry field. The development of one of the oral contraceptives, to cite a specific instance, was done by university professors on sponsored research projects. Normally when university facilities are used, the results of the research must be made public; the sponsor gains by having the task done and being among the first to know about the results.

Joint ventures in R&D. If a project will be of value to several companies or perhaps an entire industry, several companies may join in financing the study. Currently, several studies on the control of pollution are being handled in this fashion. In some industries, such as coal and cement, a trade association conducts research for the entire industry. Incidentally, the common practice in the oil industry of several companies sharing the cost of an exploratory well is a variation of this general policy of joint ventures in research. In all these instances, the research cost to a single company is lowered and frequently the quality of research is improved; the disadvantage—which may not be serious—is that the results of the research must be shared.

Relying on Others to Do Desired R&D

A firm's outlay for R&D can be even further reduced without sacrificing all of the benefits from such effort. This policy need not be passive; a company can actively encourage and assist work in particular directions.

Pay license or royalty fee. In industries where cross-licensing is an established practice, a company can make known in advance its willingness to enter into such agreements. This knowledge, combined with similar assurances from other firms, may encourage a member of the industry or an outsider to conduct research in desired areas. A medium-sized oil company, for instance, concluded that the research it could afford in refining technology was too small to keep it abreast of its competitors. Instead, it publicly announced its willingness to pay substantial royalties for improved technology developed by others. After two decades of experience, the management feels that it has been at no serious technical disadvantage to competitors and that royalty payments, while high, total considerably less than would have R&D effort to achieve similar results. Obviously the feasibility of this policy rests upon a prediction that licenses will be available.

Seek foreign licenses or patents. Technical know-how is a significant item in international trade. U.S. companies receive over $1 billion annually in payment for their technical know-how, patent royalties, and the like. The flow into the United States is only about a fifth of this size, but it does reflect a potential source of technical ideas.

Often a foreign company lacks the desire or the capital to enter the U.S. market, and it may welcome an opportunity to get some additional return on its technical knowledge and designs. The U.S. company will probably have to take some initiative in working out the agreement, and it must be prepared to do considerable engineering work to adapt the foreign concepts to local conditions (just as is necessary in the reverse flow). Nevertheless, our debt to foreigners for important contributions to products ranging from helicopters to ballpoint pens indicates the potentiality of this approach.

Encourage equipment or materials suppliers. In a number of industries, the suppliers rather than the fabricators themselves provide most of the innovation. This is clearly true of the textile industry where most R&D activity has been carried on by producers of manufactured fibers and by equipment manufacturers.

A company can encourage such external developments. For equipment, the most common practice is to place an order for an experimental model or to agree to pay a rather high price for the first two or three units of a product that meet certain performance specifications. Vast sums are spent by the U.S. government in this fashion, and most of the high-speed railroad equipment has been developed on this basis. The amount of premium a company must pay for newly designed equipment naturally depends upon the size of the market the manufacturer anticipates if the equipment works well. Incidentally, from the equipment manufacturer's viewpoint, it is getting a customer to help underwrite its R&D expense.

Similar cooperation between customer and supplier can relate to raw materials. If the materials supplier sees a large and continuing market, it will foot most of the development expense. Even in such instances the supplier often wants trial runs in actual production conditions. The user contributes its plant for such testing. In return it hopes to have an edge in the early use of the new material.

Promote government research. The federal government spends over $20 billion a year to finance R&D work. Most of this goes to defense and space projects, but the remaining amount is still very large. The pressure for use of these funds is tremendous and the allocation is based primarily on potential contribution to public welfare. However, since many companies wish to pioneer in the same directions that the government is promoting, the possibility of having government finance expensive research exists. The production of gasoline from oil shale, improved means to control injurious insects, better urban transportation, use of plankton from the ocean, and less expensive hospital services are merely illustrations of the diversity of government interest in R&D work. A company can actively encourage the government to sponsor research that may make technical contributions of interest to the company.

Of course, if a company's strategy includes seeking the government as a customer, possibly the government will also underwrite company R&D effort. Usually this possibility is open only to companies with strong R&D departments. In this section, however, we have been exploring ways a company could obtain R&D results without having a large research operation of its own.

In conclusion, enough alternatives to in-house research have been mentioned to indicate that a company need not abandon all interest in R&D if it cannot do the work itself. Most of the possibilities for getting others to do desired research involve sharing the results. Nevertheless, when the magnitude or the duration of the necessary effort is beyond the resources of a single company, initiative in getting others to help share the load may bear fruit.

Finally, a mixed policy is again possible: a company can do its own R&D in some fields and work with outsiders in others.

LIMITS ON TOTAL COMMITMENT

The wide range of possible R&D effort, which we have already indicated, adds up to a substantial undertaking for most companies. Like most budgets, when one totals all the things it would be desirable to do, the sum can be staggering. Central management has the task of setting some kind of a limit that maintains a desired balance of R&D work with other activities of the company. This decision as to "how much" probably involves as much subjective judgment as any faced by central management. The uncertainty of results, what competitors will do, and the contribution of technology to long-range strategy—all are based on intuitive judgment more than on objective facts. Nevertheless, if R&D is to proceed with vigor and on an even keel, guidelines for the magnitude of the effort are needed.

Policy regarding the size of R&D commitment is usually stated in terms of the key considerations that will be used in setting annual appropriations. A useful approach is the following.

Use Percent of Sales or Gross Profit for Maximum Range

To get some kind of a handle on R&D expenditures, central managements often use "percent of sales." Sales volume does indicate the principal cash inflow of the company and thus provides a gross measure of the total annual resources from which outlays for R&D will be drawn. For example, a company with $100 million in sales can undertake more R&D than a company with $10 million in sales.

At best, this is a crude guide. The gross profit on a dollar of sales may be only 15% in a distribution firm compared with more than 60% in a pharmaceutical firm. Indirect expenses like R&D obviously must come out of the margin remaining after the costs of materials, labor, and other direct expenses are met. Consequently, it makes more sense to relate R&D outlays to gross profit rather than to sales.

Clearly, there is a limit to what proportion of this gross profit a management can allocate to R&D without eroding current profits so much that the company's financial strength is in danger. The permissible maximum depends upon the urgency of other claims upon the company's "discretionary income." Somewhere in the range of 5% to 20% of gross profit—depending upon the industry—is a limit beyond which a company cannot prudently go. While imprecise, this consideration does establish the order of magnitude for the maximum R&D expenditure in a normal year.[1]

---

[1]For an exceptional project, *new capital* may be brought into the company just to finance the necessary R&D. This is an unusual situation and goes beyond a policy for internal growth.

Use Competitors' Actions for Minimum Range

In technologically based industries, any company that wishes to maintain (or achieve) a particular position in the market must do enough R&D to keep up with the parade. In other words, the magnitude of the research effort by competitors sets a minimum floor below which it is hazardous to go. Such a minimum is an approximate figure. No two companies have exactly the same product line. Based on its technological forecasts, a company may decide to pursue an offensive policy with respect to some products, a defensive policy with respect to others, and the phasing out of its remaining products. Allowances must be made for differences in this mix when comparing research efforts of competitors. However, after making such adjustments, a study of competitors' actions does provide some guidance as to the minimum level of R&D that a company with given market targets can safely undertake.

Use "Expected" Profit Between Minimum and Maximum

A third way to set limits on R&D is in terms of "expected" profit. If no uncertainty were present, this would simply involve estimating the total outlays and the total incomes for each project and then, using discounted cash flow or some other appropriate procedure, computing the rate of profit. Unfortunately, both future outlays and incomes are highly uncertain. Theoretically, the decision-maker should think in terms of a frequency distribution for each of these figures, compute "expected" value, adjust for differences in time, and compute the "expected" profit. Rarely does the accuracy of the estimates justify this refined estimating procedure, but the underlying concepts can be used to size up the attractiveness of a series of proposed R&D projects.

Then, if the major R&D projects a company contemplates are ranked according to their attractiveness in terms of expected profits, a cumulative total may be computed running from highly desirable to least desirable proposals. The final step is to see where the cumulative annual expense for these projects falls within the previously established maximum and minimum. If the analysis shows that the company has an ample supply of very attractive projects to utilize the maximum that can be allocated for R&D, a strong case can be made for a policy of spending this maximum amount. On the other hand, if the company would be undertaking projects of marginal attractiveness with an outlay, say, halfway between the maximum and the minimum, then the policy should set an overall limit close to the minimum outlay. The reason for setting the combined total somewhat lower than the expected profit analysis of individual projects suggests is the optimistic bias that almost always exists in such estimates. Experience indicates that the ceiling should be low enough to encourage frequent review of projects in process so that the ones turning out badly can be dropped promptly to make room for exciting proposals that had to be temporarily deferred.

Adjust for Stability and Capacity to Absorb

Two further considerations are important in setting a limit on the total R&D effort. Some stability in the level of activity is highly desired. Effective R&D cannot be expanded and contracted on short notice. Time is required to hire good scientists and engineers, to build facilities, to establish working relationships, and to get a program underway. Consequently, central management should establish a policy that it expects to continue for several years, and the value of momentum should be recognized when changes in policy are considered.

A final factor in setting a limit is the capacity of the company to absorb the output of its R&D department. If the company lacks the capital, the managerial talent, or other resources necessary to exploit, say, two new products a year, then an R&D department that is likely to produce five such ideas is out of balance.

Subjective judgments and imprecision permeate the approach we have just outlined for establishing policy limits on total R&D commitment. Unfortunately, this is inherent in the nature of the problem. Our contention is only that the proposed approach is far better than dealing with this important subject on purely an intuitive basis.

SUMMARY

R&D very much needs policy direction in terms of (a) targets for new products and/or processes that are important to company success, (b) the areas in which the company wishes to push back from development work into applied research and possibly basic research, and (c) the areas where an offensive effort is called for and the areas where a defensive posture makes more sense. These guidelines define the mission of R&D activities.

Part or possibly all of this R&D mission can be met through the use of outsiders. So, policy is needed on subcontracting, joint ventures, licensing, and encouraging suppliers or governmental research. Here, as in each facet of the mission, a mixed response may be dictated by policy—the approach to be taken depending upon the kind of R&D being considered.

With the scope of R&D effort thus defined, limits on total resource commitments provide a third dimension. Financially, a policy maximum often is a percent of gross profit, the minimum is a sum necessary to keep up with competitors, and within this range "expected" profit of projects sets the level. The capacity of management and other aspects of organization may also set limits.

We have stressed repeatedly the need to relate R&D policy to master strategy. The R&D mission finds its *raison d'etre* in company strategy; the use of outsiders is a special aspect of the fundamental make-or-buy issue; and overall limits on R&D take their cue from strategy for the inevitable rationing of scarce resources. By interlacing strategy and R&D

policy, we harness the potentialities of modern science to the management of an enterprise.

QUESTIONS FOR CLASS DISCUSSION

1. A U.S. manufacturer of small turbine and jet engines was falling back in the race to sell engines designed for executive and commuter aircraft. Company executives believed that it had high-quality engines, but was losing out to the Garrett Corporation because its salesforce, its service facilities, its ability to sell on extended credit, and its supply of parts were limited since it did not have the financial strength to fund these needs. The firm sold some engines to Cessna and Beech aircraft companies, one British manufacturer, and a German-French consortium, but prospects abroad were not good in the future—even in Europe. The company has been approached by one of the huge Japanese manufacturing and financial conglomerates with an offer to buy its unissued stock. The offer will give the Japanese firm ownership of 35% of the U.S. company's common stock and will provide all the capital needed for continued engine development work as well as the manufacturing and marketing requirements. The Japanese also insist that the U.S. firm license its patents and know-how to a newly-formed Japanese company, at a royalty rate of 2% of the costs of goods manufactured. But the Japanese refuse to engage in a joint venture to make engines in Japan even though they foresee (as does the U.S. company) the rapid development of a Japanese aerospace industry. The U.S. firm prefers to manufacture and ship goods because that is where it creates the value added. But it estimates that the probability of exporting engines to Japan will be very small. Import restrictions will prevent such sales. (a) Does the proposal have any advantage for the U.S. firm? Drawbacks? (b) Will the proposal contribute to technological development in the U.S. and Japan? (c) What stages of the processes of technological innovation are involved in the proposed arrangement? (d) As an executive of the U.S. firm, what is your attitude toward the proposal?

2. Because American Motors is relatively small compared with General Motors, Ford, and Chrysler, it can afford much less product and process development work. Recently, General Motors agreed to make its new developments on auto safety available to American Motors. Possibly this move is a forerunner of other technological aid to American Motors. (a) Do you believe General Motors *should* share its technological advances with American Motors? Why? (b) Should American Motors rely on sources of this sort for its R&D work? What other alternatives does it have? (c) Should the U.S. government require cross-licensing of R&D output among U.S. auto producers?

3. More people in the United States are engaged in service industries than in "production" industries (manufacturing, mining, and agriculture). (a) Do you believe as many opportunities exist for innovation in services as in

"production"? Give illustrations. (b) What does your answer imply regarding the nature and the directions of R&D work in service industries?

4. Assume that the U.S. Congress passes two laws encouraging the use of generic drugs (that is, drugs described by a technical name available to any manufacturer, in contrast to copyrighted names available only to one company). One law requires the holders of a product or process patent to cross-license other drug companies to use the patent for a reasonable fee; the other law prohibits any U.S. agency from paying directly or through reimbursement (e.g., Medicare) an amount above the prevailing generic drug price. The first law encourages the manufacture of generic drugs, and the second law encourages the sale of generic drugs. Now, if you managed a large pharmaceutical company that for years had had a large R&D effort leading to the sale of patented products under copyrighted names, what changes in R&D policy would you make because of the new laws?

5. A small group of scientists and engineers have formed a company to design, manufacture, and sell an atomic-powered heart pacer. Thousands of people already have battery-powered heart pacers in their chests; use of atomic energy will reduce the size of the pacer and avoid biannual operations to replace the batteries. To date the company has focused entirely on the very exacting design problems and on obtaining FDA (government) approval of the device. (a) Assuming this effort is successful, what major problems will the company face? (b) What are the pros and cons of continuing the manufacture and sale of the device as an independent company versus selling or licensing the device to a large established firm already serving the medical profession? (c) If the company decides to undertake the manufacture and sale of the heart pacer, should it also continue R&D effort on other complex health devices?

6. McDonald's Corporation operates 5,400 outlets which sell its hamburgers and is the leader in the growing fast-food industry. What R&D policy do you recommend that McDonald's pursue?

7. The Strategic Planning Institute finds in its analysis of the experience of over 1000 business-units that high R&D spending hurts profitability when the business has a relatively low market share. More specifically, the return on investment (before interest and income taxes) for firms with a high R&D/sales ratio is: 30% if the firm has a high market share, but drops to 4% for firms with a low market share. The drop in return on investment which is associated with market share is much less severe for firms which have a low R&D/sales return: 27% for high market share firms and 17% for low market share firms. (a) What do you think is the explanation for this impact of R&D spending? (b) What are the implications for R&D policy?

8. One offshoot of work with cable TV is the idea of eliminating the need for meter readers. Electric, gas, and water companies face high expense getting their people into homes to read meters as a basis for charging customers; with more women away at work, finding someone at home is increasingly difficult. Several technically possible ways are known that would automatically "observe" a meter in a home and transmit the information via telephone lines to a central recording station. However, much development work remains to make such a system economically feasible. Assume that you had to decide for your company whether to invest in such development work, and that your president wanted to know the *expected value* of an investment on this R&D project. Explain (a)

what factors you would consider and (b) how you would combine estimates regarding each of these factors into an "expected value."

9. Several of the more innovative companies in the mobile home industry are subsidiaries of lumber concerns or metal producers. Assume that you are president of one of these subsidiaries and have been given a free hand to develop your company as you think best. In what ways, if any, would you want your affiliation with a materials supplier to influence your R&D effort?

10. A "hot potato" at the United Nations is the transfer of technological know-how. Developing countries criticize advanced countries for holding back technology secrets through patent control and other ways. "The advanced countries make profits from our raw materials, and they sell us manufactured products which we could make ourselves if permitted to." (Claims similar to those of the American colonies against England 200 years ago.) On the other hand, organized labor in advanced countries charges that big business is "exporting jobs" when production processing is transferred to developing countries—to save on transportation, use less expensive labor, or comply with local country regulations. From a company viewpoint, under what circumstances should it permit and train people in less developed countries to use the fruits of its R&D activities? How should the company be compensated?

CASE 9
Coated Optics, Inc.

A lull in military orders has led to a debate about what assignments to give available engineers. "Experienced engineers are our most precious asset," says C. Barnard, *President* of Coated Optics, Inc. "The way we use them comes close to determining where the company will be five years from now." Alternatives being considered include frontier research for COI's own account, product refinements likely to lead to orders from customers in the near future, or study of manufacturing processes which would prepare COI to mass-produce one or more of the products it now makes in small batch lots.

E. Fermi, *Technical Director,* explains: "Our company is a leader in a field of great potential. We know how to deposit an extremely thin coating of a metal or dielectric material on a surface such as glass. Such coatings are vital for lenses and mirrors in optical instruments, color filters in color television cameras, solar energy collectors, laser applications, fiber optics, and many other situations involving the transfer of light or heat.

"The production process involves placing the workpiece to be coated into a vacuum chamber and allowing vaporized materials to condense on the surface. Vacuums equivalent to the vacuum in space outside the earth's atmosphere are often required, as well as temperatures which will change, say, silver or silica (sand) into vapor.

By controlling these conditions, we can deposit a uniform film only a few atoms thick.

"COI was established about fifteen years ago, just when coated optics and lasers really began to take off. We have always had very able people, and have stayed at the forefront of the technology—learning as we went along. Consequently, we have a reputation of being able to do difficult, high-quality jobs for both military and civilian customers. Advanced technology is our forte.

"Normally, our customers pay us to do our R&D work. For example, the Space Agency may give us an order for an unusual lens that they want to try in satellite communication. In a sense the customers also do our market research because they know how the surfaces we create will be used.

"Now, when there is a temporary lull in orders, as at present, I think we should experiment with new combinations. We know pretty well the new performance characteristics that will intrigue customers, so if we have some promising results to point to we can improve our chances of getting some customer to underwrite further development. I doubt that we could discover an entirely new process which could give us an exclusive patent. Trying that would be very risky and expensive. Instead, my thought is to stay a bit ahead of what our competitors can do."

E. Caruso, *Marketing Director,* says: "COI must decide what part of the action it wants. Sure, we're a good-sized duck in our pond, but it's a limited pond. My guess is that we did almost 20% of the $200 million total contracted coating work done last year. A few big users like Bausch & Lomb, Kodak, and Perkin-Elmer have internal departments which do most of their own work. Then we have about 100 competitors ranging from garage operators to a couple of outfits about our size. That's a lot of competitors and the number is increasing.

"Over half our work goes indirectly to the military—for lasers on tanks, infrared spotting scopes, high-power night-viewing instruments for satellites, and the like. Most of these orders are for prototypes or pilot operations, so there is a small number of any one thing. The civilian part of our business is also mostly small orders—special filters, coating of telescope lenses, mirrors for lasers, special coatings of glass tubes used in fiber optics, and so forth. There is some good repeat business here, but we are not set for the big play.

"The biggest prospect right now is the use of glass fiber optics to replace copper telephone cables. Stretched very fine (five-thousandths of an inch), a hair-like glass fiber can carry communications on a beam of light. Its capacity is thousands of times that of copper wire. Both GTE and ATT are installing such cable, especially to carry color TV programs and computer 'conversations.' No one knows how many *miles* of such cable will be wanted soon. Also, fiber optics can greatly simplify photocopying machines, and these sell by the thousands. Owens-Illinois has a glass-coated tube which is unusually efficient in catching solar energy, and might be used in hundreds of thousands of homes.

"These are just examples of big volume applications of the coating processes we know so well. The question is whether COI is going to sit on the sidelines and watch other companies take the tremendous growth which lies ahead. We should put our engineers to work figuring out where we can cut into this large-volume business. With all our know-how, it is criminal not to stake out a position where the big growth lies."

G. Atlas, *Production Director,* has a different perspective. "In the early days our organization was quite informal. Each new order would be assigned to an engineer and a few appropriate technicians to help. They would work out the necessary processing and then get the shop to run the order. If it was a pioneering job, the engineer would call on colleagues for their help and hover over actual production. On the other hand, repeat business could be quickly turned over to technicians. Our small size made it easy to work as a team.

"However, when we reached thirty to forty engineers and maybe two hundred employees in all—half our present size—priorities on the use of equipment became real headaches, and marketing had to have more reliable information about delivery dates. So we reorganized. We now have what we call a civilian plant and a government plant (based on the kind of jobs they run). Each is fully equipped, and has its own production scheduling and cost control. Also, engineering has been split up and placed under the plant managers.

"Cost control, as well as scheduling, was a reason for this reorganization. For example, ten years ago when lasers were just getting into industrial processing, we could sell a set (2) of half-inch laser mirrors for $25. Now competition has driven that price down to $5. Sure, our costs have dropped, but not proportionately. Our margin on that kind of business is quite narrow. More and more of our orders have moved from frontier or experimental projects where price is secondary to components that a purchasing agent puts out for bids. This means the engineer on such jobs must think more in terms of lowering processing costs than making a unique product; and, the total amount of engineering charged to the job has to be low.

"If we should move into mass production, processing costs would become even more critical. Mechanical conveyors, electronically controlled pressures and temperatures, and very sensitive speeds are essential for an efficient production line. This would be a new ballgame for us. Also, at present our customers ship materials to be coated to our plant. Maybe coating—our contribution—should be done at the same place the substrate material is made. Does that mean COI should start making glass fibers or ceramics? If we are going to move into long production runs, I recommend that we do it in a separate plant with a separate group of people devoted to making it a success. And, before we make that leap, we need some solid research on production processes to know just what we are getting into."

J. Addams, *Personnel Director,* is concerned about morale of the present engineers. "We have to develop our own corps of optical coating engineers. Only two schools in the country, U. of Rochester and U. of Arizona, give specific courses in optics and they graduate only one or two coating experts a year. So we recruit physicists and chemists and help them learn on the job.

"These people are intrigued with moving molecules around, and also with working on the frontiers of technologies in optics, lasers, radar, and other fields. Sure, they also like to live in Arizona and we pay what good engineers generally are earning. But the excitement and pride in being an important contributor to a wave of new products is also rewarding. We have attracted capable people because of the prestige of being associated with COI.

"As COI grows, it is difficult to maintain the morale of the past. The reorganization didn't help because the engineers were separated organizationally and physically. On many jobs they now feel more pressure to keep expenses down, and more time must be devoted to fitting into the production planning and control system. As a result, we have had more turnover of 'free spirits.' They often go to small competitors.

"An R&D policy which gives the engineers more chance to experiment with frontier problems would help overcome the somewhat negative reaction to the steps being taken to control costs and deliveries. If we could rotate our imaginative people onto projects where they think breakthroughs might be made, I'm sure we'd stir up enthusiasm.

"Of course, such a policy would not do much toward cutting costs or moving into what we loosely call mass production. If these latter skills are to be our aim, we need people with different interests. The focus shifts from new coating techniques to designing a system—involving machines and people—that can apply known techniques in a reliable and economical way. In such a system materials handling is just as important as coating. A few of our engineers may be able to shift their interests to system design, but that has not been their reason for joining COI. We would have to bring in some new, experienced people to spark such a development. Also our whole company thinks in terms of *physical* processes. We do use a lot of technicians, but we have never thought about the interface between machines and people in a production system."

Question

What R&D policy do you recommend for Coated Optics, Inc.?

PRODUCTION POLICY

Company strategy, as we saw in Chapter 5, involves effective integration of the supply of goods (or services) with their marketing. Somehow, someplace, the goods must be procured. In the preceding chapter we discussed the creation of *new* products and processes. Now we turn to key issues in buying and/or making all the products that a company sells.

Many firms have separate departments for purchasing and production, but the basic problems that demand attention of central management are so entwined that it is simpler to consider production policy and purchasing policy together. This chapter and the next chapter should be considered as a unit.

Although our discussion of production will deal primarily with manufacturing (the physical fabrication of products), a comparable set of problems arises in the creation of intangible services. Banks, brokerage houses, consulting firms, and retail stores, for instance, face issues of capacity, technology, make-or-buy, and purchasing that are just as vital as production problems in a factory. With relatively minor adjustments, the points raised can be applied to intangible as well as tangible "production."

Historical Changes in Procurement Problems

For many years procurement of merchandise was the primary problem of business people. The rounding of the Cape of Good Hope and the discovery of America were actually attempts to find new trade routes. The enterprising merchants of those days were seeking products of the Far East because these products had a ready market in European nations. For centuries thereafter merchants searched the four corners of the earth for goods that they might bring back to sell in their home markets. These early merchants had some sales problems, but their major task was that of finding goods to bring to the markets.

Following the Industrial Revolution in the latter half of the Eighteenth Century, with its application of power and large-scale production methods to the processing of goods, more attention was given to the production than to the buying of goods. In the United States particularly, businesses gave their energy to exploiting natural resources, developing more efficient methods of production, and harnessing steam and electric power. Nevertheless, the problem still remained one of securing goods that could be offered for sale.

During the last fifty years problems confronting central management have shown a still further change in emphasis. The great increase in variety of goods produced and the improvements in transportation have compelled businesses to give added attention to marketing their wares. This increasing attention required by the marketing end of business has changed procurement problems in some respects but cannot be said to have diminished them. Because of the increased competition for markets, more attention must be given to timely production, keeping costs low, and maintaining quality standards.

In the future, world shortages of basic resources will raise the strategic importance of production. The supply of energy, mineral deposits, fresh water, even fresh air cannot expand at the fast-accelerating rates of use. And these restraints will create other shortages. Moreover, environmental protection will slow up readjustments. In our opinion the industrial system will not collapse, but resource availability and efficient use will certainly command closer attention.

Issues Requiring Central Management Attention

Production and purchasing, like other phases of a business enterprise, involve a myriad of detailed problems. At this point, however, we will focus on broad policy issues that need the attention of central management. Many, if not all, of these issues have a profound effect on the destiny of virtually every firm.

These major production and purchasing policy issues will be discussed under the following headings:

1. Deciding the extent to which vertical integration is strategic.
2. Selecting the general processes to be used in production.
3. Setting total capacity and facility balance.
4. Providing basic guides for maintenance and replacement.
5. Resolving make-or-buy questions regarding services and supplies.
6. Selecting vendors from whom purchases should be made.
7. Correlating purchasing, production, and sales.

The first four sets of problems will be considered in this chapter; the last three in the next chapter.

EXTENT OF VERTICAL INTEGRATION

"Should we manufacture what we sell or should we buy it? If we manufacture, should we just assemble purchased parts or should we make the parts? Should we make or buy raw materials for the parts? Should we produce the supplies needed to make the raw materials?" These are questions of vertical integration. Every firm faces them, and for many firms a sound answer is the key to long-run success.

Vertical Integration in the Aircraft Industry

The problem of whether to make or buy products is well illustrated in the aircraft industry. Clearly, Boeing will design and assemble its planes. Just as clearly, it will buy engines and navigation equipment from suppliers who specialize in those products. In between is a whole array of landing gear, subassemblies, galleys, and other equipment which Boeing could manufacture itself but typically does not. In fact, to simplify its production tasks and to draw on the most advanced ideas of suppliers, seventy percent of Boeing's material costs is likely to be outside purchases.

The Air Force, to move back one step, buys all its planes. However, the Air Force does have its own designers and testing capabilities, so it plays a more active role in overall design than, say, Boeing does in engine design. In this way, the Air Force promotes competition among suppliers and retains a high degree of flexibility in what and when it will buy.

Combining Publishing, Printing, and Paper Making

The sharp differences in vertical integration in the publishing field throw more light on the issue. Most book publishers do not print or bind their products. Their printing needs fluctuate in volume; one week they may have six printers working for them and the next week none at all. Also, being free to get printing done anywhere gives them greater flexibility in the design of their books. On the other hand, contract printing is expensive. The former president of the company publishing this book, for example, often said as he passed the plant that did most of his printing, "My business made the owner of that company wealthy. But, I have enough worries already."

In contrast to book publishing, larger newspapers always do their own composing and printing. Probably this saves them money. The dominant consideration, however, is the need for very close coordination—literally down to a few minutes—between writing copy, setting it in type, proofreading, headlining, layout, and printing. And when a hot story breaks, much of the work may be redone in an hour or two. Such fast coordination can be best supervised by a single management.

Also newspapers own paper mills and timberlands. The big papers and the chains have a large, fairly steady need of a single product. Production economies are a natural result. To be sure, these same economies might be obtained by an independent supplier under a long-term contract, but some risk would remain for both newsprint producer and newspaper. So, at least those papers that predict a long-term rise in newsprint prices and that have capital for investment try to reduce supply risks by integrating clear back to the forest.

To Farm or not to Farm

Still unsettled is the extent to which frozen food companies should raise their own vegetables and fruits. Seabrook Farms, to cite one case, is heavily engaged in farming. Most firms, however, rely on local independent farmers. Farmers tilling their own land conform to the centuries-old cultural pattern; and reliance on independent growers presumes that the resourceful, close supervision of farmers over their crops will be more effective than hired management. But the frozen food packers must be assured of a supply of quality produce suitable for freezing. So they sign annual contracts with farmers well in advance of planting, provide selected seed, and offer advice. We see here, not vertical integration in the usual sense, but an arrangement with supply sources that accomplishes several of its benefits.

For poultry, however, the advent of "factories" which often process a million birds a season has led to substantial vertical integration, including genetic design, chick production, scientific feeding, and automated processing. Only the actual rearing of the birds is contracted out.

Key Factors in Vertical Integration

The examples just discussed show that a variety of factors may influence a decision on when to integrate. Among the many possible considerations, the following are likely to be key ones.

Possible savings resulting from coordination. If a company manufactures the products or the materials it needs, the promptness of delivery and adjustment to emergencies may be easier. When the parts have to fit together into a complex balance, the engineering may be more easily coordinated. Unusual quality requirements may be easier to meet. A firm knowing its own needs and being assured of continued use of equipment may develop more specialized machinery than is feasible for an outside supplier.

Elimination of marketing expenses. If a firm produces its own materials, the selling expenses incurred by the outside vendor are automatically avoided.

Lower supply risks. If there is reason to doubt that raw materials will be readily available, then a company may acquire its own sources as a means of protection. For example, virtually all the basic metal processors mine their own ore, and the leading oil companies want a controlled supply of at least part of their crude oil requirements.

Effect of patents. The control of patents by other companies may make economical manufacture impossible; but if the company itself should obtain control of patents, then a policy of manufacturing may be particularly desirable.

Flexibility. Vertical integration tends to limit flexibility in product design. Heavy investment in plant or raw material sources hampers the shift to completely new designs or materials, whereas the firm (or Air Force) that buys its requirements is not so concerned with making a large investment obsolete.

In the short run, too, the nonintegrated firm may cut down its purchases or shift to another supplier, whereas the integrated firm must recognize the effect of such action on unabsorbed overhead. To guard against such a stultifying effect, General Motors has a longstanding policy that none of its divisions is required to buy from another division if the profit or the long-run development of the first division would suffer from doing so.

Volume required for economic production. Many small companies simply cannot consider backward integration because the volume of their requirements for any one part or material is too small to keep an efficient plant busy. Also, the requirements may be so irregular that a plant (like a college football stadium) would be kept busy only part of a year. Occasionally a company builds a plant larger than needed for its own use and then sells the balance of the output to other users. Such an arrangement, however, does divert both financial resources and managerial attention from the major activity of the firm.

Financial status of the company. Many firms have only enough capital to operate their principal line of business and may not be in a position to acquire new capital under favorable conditions. This precludes substantial investments in manufacturing facilities for the production of parts or raw materials. On the other hand, financially strong companies may undertake vertical expansion because their suppliers are financially weak. In such circumstances, the added financial strength may permit substantial improvements in the manufacturing operation.

Capacity of management to supervise additional activities. In a great many instances, a decision to produce products that formerly were purchased means that the executives of the company are undertaking activities of a distinctly different nature from those with which they are familiar. While they can employ an executive from that industry, central management cannot escape giving some attention to the new undertaking and bearing responsibility for making final decisions regarding it. Sometimes central management becomes so absorbed in directing the new activity that it fails to give adequate guidance to the older part of the business where it has demonstrated competence.

On the other hand, if inadequate managerial attention is given to the new venture, expected savings may not be realized. Perhaps low cost will exist when production is first started because the new plant will have new equipment and the latest methods; but with only secondary attention by central management and the opiate of an assured market, there is real danger that the plant will fail to keep up with other concerns.

General conclusion. Vertical integration decisions of the type that we have been considering in this section are of substantial magnitude. Each proposal should, therefore, be thoroughly examined in terms of the key factors listed, estimated ratio of savings to investment, and unique considerations such as idle plant or lack of technical knowledge. But underlying such a detailed analysis—and guiding a decision to devote time and energy to the study in the first place—should be a consciously determined disposition (policy) to move toward vertical integration or to stay away from it. Such a general policy should be based on an appraisal of what is required for success in the industry, the distinctive competence and resources of the company, desire for diversifying economic risks, and similar factors reviewed in Part I. Few policies are more crucial to the long-run development of a company.

PRODUCTION PROCESSES

Closely related to decisions on what production activities the company itself will perform are choices of processes to be used. Broad issues in this area are:

1. Choice of technology.
2. Extent of division of labor.
3. Extent of mechanization and automation.
4. Size and decentralization of plants.

Choice of Technology

In the production of many products the manager has no choice regarding the process to be used. Thus, a company that manufactures wallboard, using fiber of sugar cane as its primary raw material, need be in no quandary about the process to be employed in removing the small quantity of sugar remaining in the cane after it passes through a sugar mill. The only commercially practical method is fermentation. By allowing the sugar to ferment, it can be almost completely removed and the remaining fibers are then in a light and workable state. Since this is the only feasible process, the manufacturer promptly turns attention to the detailed methods and facilities for carrying out the process.

Not all manufacturers can solve their production process problems as readily as the wallboard company. For instance, small airlines that provide local feeder service to major cities must decide whether to use jet or prop planes. In the same way a company manufacturing steel must decide upon the extent to which it will use electric furnaces, open-hearth furnaces, or oxygen inverters. Stemming from such basic decisions will come a whole array of plans for equipment, personnel, methods, and organization.

Technology is not confined to physical processes. Universities, engineering firms, and mental hospitals—to mention only a sample—face similar choices. A management consulting firm, for instance, can either design standard solutions (statistical quality control, sales compensation plans, budget procedures, and the like) and adapt them to each client, or it can make a fresh analysis of each situation with no preconceived ideas about the solution. The choice here does not involve large investment in facilities, but it does affect personnel, organization, sales appeals, and other facets of the business.

A recurring issue of "production technology" in a business school revolves around the use of cases versus lecture-discussion. And in elementary education the busing of white children to black neighborhoods and vice versa is even more controversial. These examples suggest that when output and processes become more human and less physical, choice of technology has a lot of subjective value overtones.

Extent of Division-of-Labor

Practice differs among manufacturers of inexpensive dresses as to the use of the "section system." Sewing constitutes a major part of production activity, and under the older system each sewing machine operator did a whole series of operations on either the blouse, the skirt, or the other parts of the dress. The newer system has each operator do a much smaller piece of the work and then pass the garment to the next operator for another small seam. Thus, when work can be standardized and secured in sufficient volume, the idea of line production is applied. While not so called by people in industry, students of economics will recognize this as an example of the *extent of division-of-labor.*

Fine division-of-labor has been a common, and usually productive, policy in business operations since the establishment of pin factories in the early days of the Industrial Revolution. Recently it has faced two challenges— mechanization and automation of routine work, and "job enlargement" in which the duties of workers are deliberately diversified to give them more nearly a "whole" operation. In deciding how much emphasis to give division-of-labor, then, managers should weigh their policies regarding standardization of products, mechanization, type of labor to be employed, and style of motivation.

Extent of Mechanization and Automation

Some companies adopt definitive policies regarding the extent to which they will automate their operations. One manufacturer of automobile frames, for example, established a policy that operations would be mechanized from start to finish. As a result, the final product might carry the same label as appears on some food products, "Not touched by human hands." Most banks use computers to clear checks and to post to checking accounts; but the extension of such mechanization to trust accounts and noncash items is a debatable economy.

The rising cost of labor and the inflexibilities in the use of labor that are being introduced as a result of unionization and government regulations are leading more and more companies to mechanize wherever practical. They recognize that machines also are often inflexible, but machines are tractable and their costs do not rise after they are placed in operation. Moreover, ingenious electronic controls now can instruct some machines to make short runs of various dimensions, thereby overcoming the inflexibility.

A similar decision regarding mechanization has been followed on the large collective farms in Russia and the large farms in the United States. In the South, crop dusting from the air, flame throwers for killing weeds, mechanical harvesting equipment, and other power-driven machines are creating a change that alters the plantation more than did the Thirteenth Amendment.

The chart on the following page, however, shows that high mechanization, which results in a high investment per dollar of sales, does not lead to high profits. Just the reverse occurs! Further analysis of these data by the Strategic Planning Institute suggests that mechanization usually does lower costs, as expected, but that the associated high fixed overhead creates such strong pressure to obtain volume that the savings are passed on to consumers in the form of lower prices. The competitive pressure to lower prices and obtain volume is especially severe for firms having low market share.

Consequently, any policy to highly mechanize should be accompanied by other plans which will assure the company that it will be able to retain enough of the benefits to pay for the costs of mechanizing.

Size and Decentralization of Operating Units

Large manufacturing companies have considerable choice in the size and the location of their plants. For many years, most of them assumed that the larger the plant, the more economies would be possible; transportation costs of raw materials or finished products were usually considered the limiting factors on the size of a plant. Present thinking challenges these assumptions. At least the advantages of large plants are not taken for granted.

A firm in the clothing industry has a clear-cut policy toward separation of production into several operating units. Production technology does not require large-scale operations, and the company believes the optimum size plant is one just large enough to support specialized service divisions such as accounting, personnel, and maintenance. In this case, plant location is determined primarily by nearness of consuming markets and availability of women workers—but again, not in a big city.

DESIRABILITY OF MECHANIZATION IS INFLUENCED BY COMPANY'S SHARE OF ITS MARKET

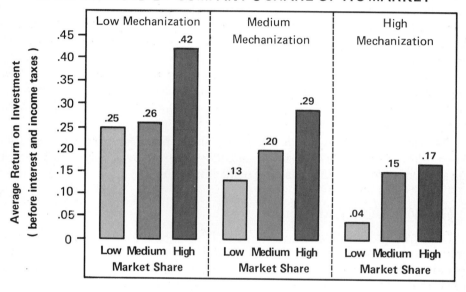

Source: Strategic Planning Institute.

In some industries, such as the chemical industry, technology requires a large-scale plant. However, once a plant is large enough to use economical processes and to support specialized service divisions, there is a question whether expansion should be at the same plant or at a new location. Smaller plants, especially those in smaller communities, have advantages of closer and friendlier relations among all employees (operators and executives), easier identification of the worker with the product being produced, less bureaucracy, more face-to-face contacts in place of expensive and impersonal communication systems, executives who have first-hand knowledge of what is going on, less commuting time and expense for employees, and so forth. Moreover, modern means of communication and transportation have reduced the disadvantages of having several plants separated from the home office.

The dispersion of plants and offices out of urban centers does contribute to unemployment difficulties in depressed areas. Recognizing the seriousness of the urban crisis, several companies are experimenting with a policy

of locating some production operations in city slum areas. Initially such
plants usually are high-cost units, but the hope is that the new ways of
training and supervision will turn the plants into economically sound ventures. Again, small-sized plants are better suited to this policy.

A similar challenge to size of operating unit is occurring in the retail field.
Here, traffic and transportation congestion in large cities has led department stores to open branches in suburban locations. These branches cannot,
of course, offer customers the same selection of merchandise as the larger
downtown stores. Several different policies are used to overcome this limitation. Some firms have their branches carry only certain lines, such as
women's ready-to-wear and domestics, and do not attempt to stock all kinds
of merchandise. Other companies place at least samples of a wide variety of
goods at their branches and rely upon the main store to supply a full range
of sizes and colors. Still other firms have only large branches and stock each
with almost as wide a selection as the main store. The decision as to which
of these policies to follow makes a fundamental difference in the branch
operation.

The smaller company with a single place of business does not face this
issue, but for larger companies a wise policy regarding the optimum size and
location of operating units is of crucial importance.

HOW MUCH CAPACITY

Data from a variety of sources must be brought together to estimate the
productive capacity a company needs. Sales forecasts of physical volume,
policy decisions on what will be purchased instead of made, engineering
estimates of machine productivity, and production plans on how equipment
will be used all contribute to projections on size of plant needed. In addition
and overriding such data are several central management policies regarding
capacity desired. These policies deal with provisions for peak versus normal
requirements, backward taper of capacity, allowance for growth, and balance of facilities.

Peak Versus Normal Load

A completely stable level of operations is virtually impossible. All types
of business activity are affected by cyclical fluctuations, and most industries
experience seasonal, daily, or even hourly variations in volume of business.
In addition, the demand for a company's product may increase or decrease
because of wars, government regulations, inventions, floods, changing fan-
cies of the consumer, and many other influences. Moreover, mere random
distribution will lead to peaks and valleys. Management must decide
whether it will provide capacity large enough to satisfy all demands during
peak periods, knowing that some of this capacity must remain idle during
slack periods, or whether it will maintain a smaller capacity and hope that

failure to render service during peak requirements will not have unbearable consequences.

A leading example of a company that tries to meet peak requirements is found in the electric utility industry. On dark winter evenings or hot summer days, we hope to have current available on the flip of a switch. Utilities have a policy of building capacity to meet such peak demands (occasionally there are some restrictions on industrial customers). Fortunately, the demand is predictable; nevertheless, the investment made for peak needs is tremendous.

Most companies follow a policy of letting the customer bear part of the peak load burden. This is obvious to the subway or bus commuter during rush hours and to the Christmas shopper on December 24. Neither the bus company nor the retail store is indifferent to crowds of customers. They provide capacity several times their volume during slack periods. The problem is one of balancing the amount of delay and inconvenience of X% of the customers versus the cost of providing the increment of capacity to meet the peak. Perhaps the policy will be to meet 90% of the requirements without delay. (When peaks occur in random fashion, queuing up theory is useful to estimate customer inconvenience.)

Other means of meeting peak capacity will, of course, be incorporated in the policy regarding maximum capacity. (a) Manufacturers of standard, durable products may manufacture stock during slack periods. This arrangement is explored in the next chapter. (b) Overtime work may be feasible for operations not already run twenty-four hours a day. (c) Obsolete or high-cost equipment may be maintained on a standby basis and placed in service just during the peak. (d) Some of the work may be subcontracted, although this is often difficult because potential subcontractors are likely to be busy during the same peak period. (e) Off-peak discounts, "mail early" campaigns, and other measures may be used to induce customers to avoid peak periods. These devices also involve extra expense and may be more or less satisfactory to customers. Clearly, policy guidance is needed to indicate the reliance on these various ways of responding to peak needs.

Backward Taper of Capacity

Vertically integrated companies may deliberately follow a policy of backward taper of capacity. Such firms normally perform final operations on all their finished products, but they manufacture only parts of their material requirements. A tire manufacturer may have its own textile mill in the south to weave tire fabric. This mill will probably have the capacity to supply only the minimum needs of the tire manufacturer. Additional fabric for peak requirements will be purchased from outside concerns. Such an arrangement has the obvious advantage of keeping the units in the earlier stages of production operating near their productive capacity. The feasibility of this policy depends on the presence of potential suppliers who are willing to supply fluctuating amounts of material.

Provision for Growth

Experience indicates that a business enterprise does not stand still. In economies or industries enjoying strong growth, time rescues executives who overestimate the capacity they need. But with a slowdown in overall growth rates, excess capacity becomes a continuing burden.

It is both expensive and inconvenient to customers and employees to have additions to facilities made at frequent intervals in piecemeal fashion. On the other hand, the financial downfall of many firms can be traced to the construction of excessive facilities, construction which absorbed a large part of the company's liquid capital and entailed annual charges that further depleted the company's resources.

Again, some middle ground is desirable if it can be arranged. Often provision for expansion may be included in the amount of land purchased and the shell of the building, while only part of the equipment is purchased initially and a work force is hired as needed. Perhaps the original plant can be used for both manufacturing and warehousing, and then a warehouse may be added later. Offices may be treated in a similar fashion. Whatever the specific scheme, the basic decision to be made by central management is how much growth to anticipate and the extent to which investment will be made now in anticipation of that growth.

Balancing Capacity

Each phase of an operation—materials handling, office processing, warehousing, selling, and the like, along with their subdivisions—has its own capacity. A recurring task is trying to keep the volume of business that each subdivision can perform about equal.

Lack of balance shows up quickly in a cafeteria line when customers stack up at perhaps the sandwich counter or the cash register. The difficulty here —and on a larger scale in hospitals, plants, and offices—is that the optimum size unit for various activities differs. Several stock brokerage firms, for instance, got into serious trouble because their optimum size selling activity was larger than the conventional "back office" (paper processing) could match. Deliveries were slow, accounts were not posted daily, and errors could not be located. To avoid catastrophe, sales had to be restricted until a new system permitted enlarged capacity of the back office.

Even if balance is achieved through careful planning, it is hard to maintain. Over time, the character of work may change, small modifications will be made in the techniques employed, and people will move about. With such shifts, some one operation becomes the bottleneck. Consequently, there seems to be a never-ending task of overcoming one bottleneck after another.

On the other hand, there is the task of trying to reduce the expenses in those phases of operations where the workload has dropped off.

Most of the examples of problems with capacity have been in terms of physical facilities. Nevertheless, similar issues arise in stores, offices, and firms dealing with intangibles. How to deal with peak requirements, what provision to make for growth, and how to balance capacity are questions likely to arise in any kind of enterprise.

Integrated Systems

Often process, capacity, and make-or-buy choices are interrelated. We must look at the total system. At McDonald's and most other fast-food restaurants, for instance, the amount of work done on the premises, the way food is prepared, and the size and location of each outlet all fit into a whole system. Similarly, in branch banking the optimum size of a branch depends partly on the technology used, and the best technology depends on how self-sufficient the branch is to be.

A specific production system is good only when it supports company strategy. McDonald's system would be a disaster in Maxime's in New Orleans.

New systems can be devised by combining the elements in fresh patterns, of course, but time is required to discover and learn the new harmony. For example, one-room schools, regional graded schools, and open-classroom schools each fit particular needs. However, if we decide to switch from one to another, pupils, teachers, and facilities all have to be adjusted. So in each situation we need a well-conceived policy for general guidance and consistency of action.

MAINTENANCE AND REPLACEMENT

Closely associated with issues of how much capacity should be provided and the design of an integrated system are questions of maintaining and replacing existing capacity.

Levels of Maintenance

The statement "Captain Svenson runs a tight ship" conveys meaning to any sailor. It refers to much more than caulking the hull; everything throughout the vessel—engines, galleys, winches, and whistle—are kept in excellent running condition. Sloppiness and procrastination are not tolerated.

Similarly, a tourist driving through Kansas can easily tell when he or she is in a Mennonite section. The fences are mended, the barns are painted, the fence rows are weeded, and the crops look good.

Plants and offices, likewise, may be run like a "tight ship" or in a more casual and relaxed fashion. The level of maintenance results partly from the personal preferences of key executives, perhaps a cultural value inherited from their forebears. It may also reflect a calculated decision on the kind of maintenance that will most effectively support the other objectives and policies of the particular company. Maintenance involves expense (the Mennonite farmer in Kansas works hard and long). And the "tight ship" approach may be unwarranted in, say, a sawmill located on a tract that has just been cut over. Railroads appropriately vary the level of track and right-of-way maintenance on their main lines compared with a branch line soon to be abandoned. Incidentally, railroads also accelerate or hold back on deferrable maintenance depending upon their financial condition from year to year.

Preventive Maintenance

In atomic energy plants, avoiding accidents through preventive maintenance is even more important than keeping the equipment running. In fact, an accident at the Three Mile Island plant, while involving no casualties, so frightened the general public that the use of atomic energy to generate electricity was set back at least five to ten years.

Preventive maintenance has many applications, though less dramatic than in atomic energy or air travel. We are all familiar with this approach in the care of an automobile—regular greasing and oil changes, driving within prescribed limits, 5,000-mile checkups, prompt inspection of unusual noises or performance, and replacing tires when they are worn. Observing such practices enables us to depend on the automobile instead of wondering when we will have a flat tire or whether the motor will start.

Proper care, regular inspections, and scheduled repairs—all are designed to avoid unexpected breakdowns. The same general concept can be applied to a sales organization or an accounting office, except that here we deal with people, social relationships, paper forms, and procedures.

Again, there are questions of degree. The attention given a fire engine should differ from that given a wheelbarrow; an integrated chemical plant, from that given a roller rink. If a breakdown can be repaired quickly without serious interruption, the intensity of preventive maintenance can be relaxed.

Scheduled Replacement

In this day of mass production, regular replacement may be simpler than careful maintenance. The typical trouble-free life of electric bulbs, autos, water meters, and airplane engines can be measured and replacements made regardless of the apparent condition of a specific piece of equipment. Compulsory retirement of air pilots at age 60—or professors at age 70—was based on the same logic. The replaced item may be salvaged for use, or it may be rebuilt, but the aim is to make the change before performance falters.

Central management rarely becomes involved with maintenance or replacement of specific units. To maintain effectiveness and efficiency, however, senior executives need to provide guidance on how tight to run the ship, when and where to slow down or push ahead maintenance, the level of preventive maintenance desired, and the extent of scheduled replacements.

Purchasing policy, also intimately related to productive capability, is examined in the next chapter.

QUESTIONS FOR CLASS DISCUSSION

1. Fayette Grain & Produce Co., a major chicken-growing and processing firm, is continually squeezed between increasing costs for feed and breeder chickens and the much more slowly rising wholesale price for frozen birds. The company already has automated hatcheries and processing plants which are at an optimum size given present and foreseeable technology. One alternative is to integrate further back into growing the chicks and eggs which it now buys for its breeder flocks. This would involve Fayette in genetic research as well as in growing disease-resistant, rapid-growth strains of chickens. Federal government support provides most of the funds and some of the ideas for the research work. So results and improvements with the chicken strains are usually not patentable and are freely shared in the industry. From work done entirely on its own, Fayette might perhaps develop a superior strain of chicken which would give it a cost advantage in egg-laying for maybe a year or two.

   Another possibility is to lower the firm's intensity of mechanization along the line pointed out by the Strategic Planning Institute (see page 221) and try to build a flexible organization that could contract or stop operations when profits dropped toward zero. Leasing, rather than owning, the hatcheries and processing plants, or even hiring out only as an operating organization (running plants owned by others), as well as making only short-term (three months or less) contracts with the "grow-out" farmers who raise and feed the chicks (using Fayette feeds, of course) all might give flexibility and allow Fayette to move in and out as costs and prices changed. One unknown is the willingness of the "grow-out" farmers to expand and contract the work they do.

   A third possibility for improving profits seems to be transferring know-how of breeding, feeding, and processing to raising catfish. The fish eat grain while growing, but unlike chickens, they eat very little when grown so that the grown fish can be held in the farmers' ponds awaiting favorable prices. Catfish-raising is on a small scale now, but Fayette might make it big business. Should Fayette pursue any or all of these three alternatives to help in getting its costs under control?

2. Vertical integration in the oil industry is being challenged by some members of Congress. Their underlying argument is that having crude oil production combined with refining and marketing, places too much power in the hands of a single company (even though no one company controls over 5% of the total U.S. capacity at any stage). (a) Which of the potential benefits of vertical integration listed in this chapter do you think apply to vertical integration in the oil industry? (b) In light of your answer to (a), do you think the oil companies should be "dis-integrated"? (c) What measures, if any, should be taken to allay the fears being voiced in Congress?

3. Legislation requiring tighter control on air, water, and other forms of pollution has limited processing options and added over 40% to the investment and operating costs of numerous manufacturing processes. New safety laws have the same effect. (a) Do you think this kind of regulation will be a more serious obstacle to large or small businesses? (b) Who will ultimately bear the added cost? (c) Under what conditions is such regulation likely to lead to significant modification in a company's strategy?

4. Seaboard Utilities must expand its electric generating capacity substantially if it is to meet peak demand five years and more hence. The alternative processes for a new plant are: (a) oil-fired steam plant—with highest estimated operating costs, dependence on foreign oil, and adding to U.S. foreign exchange deficit; (b) coal-fired plant—with medium operating costs, significant air pollution hazards, and adding to ecology problems in mining areas; (c) atomic energy plant—with lowest operating costs, widespread public fears of a serious accident, and likely construction delays. Power in the quantities needed cannot be purchased from other utilities. What should Seaboard Utilities do about meeting the anticipated peak demand?

5. (a) Which of the potential advantages and disadvantages of vertical integration discussed on pages 215–218 apply to a chain of food stores? (b) Why are most of the items carrying the private label of a retail food chain purchased instead of produced by the chain?

6. The new autos coming out of Detroit will have an increasing number of electronic controls. If one of these controls breaks down, the local auto mechanic will simply replace it—if the source of the trouble can be found—because the mechanic will be unable to fix it. Assume that Ford Motor Company has asked you to devise a general plan to minimize complaints from Ford owners about electronic maintenance problems. What do you recommend?

7. Does a trend toward increasing freedom of trade among nations add to or detract from the attractiveness of vertical integration? Illustrate in terms of a company dealing (a) in watches, (b) in paper, and (c) in men's and women's clothing.

8. In home construction the use of specialized subcontractors and of prefabricated materials is increasing. Separate contractors are often used for excavation, masonry, plastering, roofing, painting, plumbing, tile-laying, flooring, and electric wiring. Prehung doors, glazed windows, finished cabinets, finished stairs,

and installed garage doors illustrate prefabrication. (a) How do you explain this trend toward buying rather than making by the general contractor? (b) How does the trend affect the contractors' cash flow, capital requirements, and potential sources of capital? (c) What are the principal services now rendered by a general contractor; that is, what has happened to the contractor's economic mission?

9. Among the possible ways of improving the ratio of actual operation to theoretical maximum capacity are: (1) not accepting peak business, (2) manufacturing to stock, and (3) buying goods or otherwise using idle capacity of another company in the same industry. To what extent can these three ways of reducing necessary capacity be used by: (a) a typical electric utility plant, (b) a dress factory, (c) a restaurant, and (d) a brick factory?

10. The good news is that Ultra Hydro and Machinery Company has concluded an agreement with Toygo Manufacturing of Osaka: the Japanese Company is to license one of Ultra's patents and some proprietary information about making parts for hydraulic equipment for an immediate $2 million payment and then a 7% royalty on sales of these parts. The $2 million can be used to expand the plant of Ultra's Spanish subsidiary, which can then supply 100% of the parts needs of Ultra's French and British subsidiaries, and also send some parts to the U.S. The bad news is that productivity in Ultra's Eureka plant has declined for the twelfth straight year (while productivity has been rising in Spain) to the point that the Eureka plant no longer has any cost advantage over German, Japanese, and Spanish parts manufacturers; and it has some quality deficiencies because the older machinery there cannot always hold to the tolerances required. Ultra's vice president for production is contemplating using the Spanish plant to supply 100% of the parts needed by the two European machinery manufacturers (rather than 50% as before) and using a combination of supply from the Spanish plant and the Japanese licensee to bring in parts needed in the La Jolla, Mackinack Island, Bar Harbor, and Hilton Head assembly operations in the U.S. Backward taper would be given up in Europe, but introduced in the U.S. The future of productivity gains in Spain and Japan indicates some promise of dropping the cost of parts for the U.S. plants. Shutting down the Eureka plant would decrease the maintenance expense account in the company's consolidated statement of profits and losses. Should these proposed changes in production facilities be made?

11. An Eastern railroad in financial trouble had postponed and slowed down expenditures on maintenance-of-way until it would be necessary to reduce freight train top speeds from 60 to 50 mph over the system, if a sustained maintenance improvement program was not introduced immediately. Train schedules and interchanges with other roads would be considerably affected by the reduced speed. How much could not be completely determined. A maintenance program could be carried out (1) by the old system of section gangs using temporarily hired labor or callbacks from the layoff board; or (2) in half the time by investing heavily in mechanized equipment that would have to be financed by borrowing at high interest rates. Detailed quantitative studies had led to the qualitative conclusions just stated. What would you recommend?

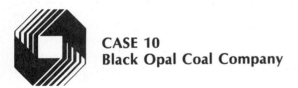

CASE 10
Black Opal Coal Company

In their long-range planning for Black Opal Coal Company, executives are considering (1) ways to meet the increase in demand expected over the next ten years, and (2) ways that will help resolve a major problem for the country as well as for the industry and the company—declining productivity. Output per worker hour in bituminous coal mining is now 70 percent of its 1972 average. Costs have risen substantially as a result. Black Opal Coal Company, like other major competitors, has lost markets and customers to both imported coal or coke and to non-union, U.S. mines.

The Industry. Bituminous coal has, it is generally believed, a sound future in the long-run. This is based upon its economic advantage in generating power over competing fossil and nuclear fuels. Total operating, fuel, and overhead costs of a utility company burning coal and using the very best pollution-control gear are about 3 mills a kilowatt hour, while the total costs of burning oil amount to about 4 mills a kilowatt hour.

The President of the United States has been urging public utilities to convert power plants from oil to coal. New technologies, such as fluidized-bed burning, show considerable promise in removing sulfur, ash, and other pollutants from coal as it is burned, thus preventing their escape into the air.

In the short-run, there is an excess of coal supply over demand—about 75 million tons excess capacity in a market using about 760 million tons per year. With the expected rate of growth of demand for coal at 5 to 7 percent a year and with the expected withdrawal of marginal mines from the market, the excess of supply is commonly predicted to disappear within two to three years. Tighter regulation through the strip-mine law will have an effect by eventually wiping out 50 million tons per year of Appalachian coal production.

The Company. Black Opal Coal Company (B.O.C.) has three operating divisions: Eastern (West Virginia, Pennsylvania, and Kentucky), Midwestern (Indiana, Illinois, Iowa), and Western (Wyoming and Montana). The Western Division, at present, operates one large strip-mine in Montana and has leased land in Wyoming for possible future mines. The other two Divisions operate both underground and surface (strip) mines.

An old, established firm with a long history of paying steady dividends to its stockholders, B.O.C. has these financial results: A current ratio of 1.6 to 1; long-term debt is 60% of total long-term debt and equity; the net profit to sales ratio is 5% (a bit better than the industry average); the turnover of total assets is 1.7 times; depreciation charged is $33 million; the current, post-tax rate of return on equity is 28%; and stockholders' equity is $150 million. Financial analysts call B.O.C. "very liquid, a solid performer, not likely to go up in smoke."

The company has a market share in its operating regions of 5% in the East, 6.5% in the Midwest, and less than 1% in the West. It has enough unmined coal in the ground to hold these market shares for 200 years.

The Opportunity. Reaching its first goal of maintaining market share east of the Mississippi River means a 35% increase in output over the next five years. The long-run goal is to produce 30 million tons of coal per year, one-fifth of it in the West. This will about double the present output and increase total market share by 3 percentage points.

Executives see three possible ways to increase output and productivity: (a) Changing compensation of the miners to an incentive plan, (b) continually improving equipment, machinery, and production methods, and (c) expanding only by opening strip-mines in the West. These three possibilities are explained in the following highlights from presentations by the Personnel Vice-President, the Labor Relations Vice-President, and the West Regional Operations Vice-President.

The Personnel Vice-President: "We have 8 percent more people in the mines than we need just because of absenteeism.

"Eighty percent of the total tons we can produce at current productivity levels is already sold and committed for 1989. One hundred percent is committed for the coming two years.

"Non-union mines of comparable situations to ours and whose market share has increased in five years from 20 percent to 35 percent of total production, have a 20 to 30 percent higher rate of output per worker hour.

"Tons per worker day are now 69 percent of the rate we had six years ago. Our productivity is dropping steadily. The industry was down 24 percent over the same period.

"Under the new union contract we now have an opportunity to install an incentive payment plan.

"Data from the Strategic Planning Institute (see the text, page 221) show that improving our market share and improving our capital utilization should improve our profits and return on investment.

"This is a major departure from all our past union-management relations policies and practices, so the board of directors will want to consider it. Three months after the Board's approval we can get the plan going in one mine. After one year, and necessary adjustments, it can be expanded to five mines. Then, in another year, it can be used in an entire region.

"The formula is technical but it will pay off for the miners in three ways: (1) A bonus of one percent of the hourly rate will be paid for each one percent of increase in output per worker above present standards—up to a 20 percent maximum. (2) An added amount will be paid for reductions in lost-time accidents. (3) The bonus will be reduced by one percent for each percent of absenteeism—to a limit of ten percent.

"The effect on profits will be a 43 percent improvement since overhead will not increase. The bonus can be taken in cash—three weeks later—or by buying shares in any one of three different investment and savings opportunities, including the company's common stock.

"The plan is not traditional for hourly wage earners. But it will improve productivity and safety and lessen absenteeism at the mines because the workers will be aware, for the first time, of the effect of actual output results in their pay. With this plan we do not risk any investment; the only risks are lost operating time and perhaps a changed state of union-management relations."

The Labor Relations Vice-President: "My plan is to continue what we have been doing—making continual improvements in our technology which will, eventually, increase productivity. These process improvements should be focused on underground mining where the problem is. Output per worker may increase slowly, but it will be up and it will allow us to keep up with the predicted rate of growth for the industry. This method is tried and true. It has no time delay. In the near future we can extend the use of high-pressure water to cut the coal and go to emerald nozzles on the high-pressure hoses. We can complete testing of an hydraulic haulage system which uses a slurry to move the coal. We can extend further the use of the long-wall technology in the Eastern underground mines. The increasing use of machinery and the specialization and complex jobs which result match the kind of miner who now works for us—young, better educated, and very mobile. The average age is becoming much younger. These people do not want pick-and-shovel jobs. The yearly investment required will be no more than our present capital budget—depreciation plus one-third of profits.

"Our safety record is already good—9.9 lost time accidents per million worker hours. The industry is at 37.3.

"An incentive pay plan is not traditional for hourly wage earners. The union is against it. Incentive plans were one of the major reasons behind the 1978 110-day industry-wide walkout. That cost us $150 million in lost sales and $11 million in lost profits. A strike means lost market share, damaged employee relations, and damaged plant and equipment.

"This is a high-risk area. Since the '78 strike we have had at least three wildcat walkouts each year—one for eleven days. And fifty grievances have been taken to arbitration in one state in which even Peabody and Big Ben had no more than twenty. Strikes cost. We have to ask what will happen when we reach the output limits of our present technology and bonuses no longer rise.

"Grievances under an incentive plan will be numerous. Other problems will be numerous. The president will have to spend a lot of time deciding who is to administer the plan since both the personnel department and the mine superintendents will have to make it work. Any conflicts between the mine management and personnel will go to the president for resolution.

"I cannot see making negative investments in an incentive plan which will inevitably mean wildcat walkouts like the big one in 1978."

West Regional Operations Vice-President: "The answers to our concerns about output, appropriate technology, and productivity can be found in Wyoming, Montana, and Utah. Demand that is increasing more rapidly than it is in the East, plenty of non-polluting coal, and high productivity in surface mines are the factors that make it wise for us to open more strip-mines as rapidly as possible.

"Output in our Montana mine is two to three times more productive than it is in the eastern undergrounds—35 to 40 tons per worker day as compared to 14 tons per worker day at best. The technology is different. Strip-mines in the West resemble huge construction sites. They are capital-intensive rather than labor-intensive and use huge draglines to remove the cover and dig the coal. Transporting by truck and rail, sorting plants and cleaning plants are all highly automated.

"Population growth and industry moves to the Sun Belt—the Southwest and the West—lie behind the increases in demand. Will these trends slow and die? No.

"Bringing in a mine in Wyoming will take no more than two to three years on land on which we now have leases. Annual output can be anywhere from one to three million tons per year, depending on how much we invest. Additional surface mines can be opened in five to six years from the time we start to negotiate leases.

"We can finance the investment of $70 per annual ton of production by using the present cash flow. In two years that would double the output of our West Region."

Questions

(1) What are the strengths and weaknesses of the three proposals?

(2) What goals of Black Opal Coal Company can be attained by the various alternatives?

(3) As a director, what proposal do you favor?

PROCUREMENT POLICY

MAKE-OR-BUY SUPPLIES AND SERVICES

Every company uses a variety of supplies and services—heat, power, packaging, transportation in and out, telephone, electronic computing, and many other items. Time and again the question arises of whether to make or buy these supplies and services. The following examples suggest the nature of the problem.

Production of Containers and Printed Forms

All firms must decide whether to purchase or manufacture printing and packing supplies such as plastic containers, cartons, and seals. Some companies have a small printing shop in which they print their own forms, circulars, and notices, and do other job printing. While this practice is convenient, a single firm rarely has enough printing of a similar type to justify the most economical machine methods. Consequently, the wiser policy usually is to have such printing done by an outside firm that has a large number of customers.

A similar situation exists in connection with packing boxes. For example, the Taft Pharmaceutical Company, which had its own box shop, needed boxes in a considerable range of shapes and sizes for the packing of its various products. Because of the variety, several different machines were needed; however, most of these machines were used only part of the time. While the boxes made in the local shop were satisfactory, an independent check showed that it would be less expensive for the company to purchase boxes from a manufacturer specializing in this type of work. This also gave the company more flexibility to shift to plastic containers.

On the other hand, a leading manufacturer of prepared breakfast foods concluded, after an exhaustive study of the relative costs of manufacturing and of buying packages and cartons, that a considerable saving would result from its own manufacture of these products. In this instance large quantities of identical boxes and cartons were required, and the cereal company was able to install as efficient machinery as the independent box companies. Furthermore, under this arrangement the company was able to exercise direct control over all phases of production and to coordinate under the same roof the manufacture of the packing boxes with the packing of the final product. This same company, however, decided that its job printing could be done more economically by an outside concern.

Company Power Plants

Larger companies must decide whether they will produce their own power and light or buy all their electric current from a public utility. The policy sometimes followed in this case is to manufacture the minimum load and to purchase from the public utility only for the purpose of meeting peak requirements. Thus, the company plant can be operated continuously and the burden of fluctuating demand can be shifted to the public utility. The feasibility of such a plan depends, of course, upon the rates charged by the public utility. If the peak demand for a particular company occurs at the same time that other utility customers have peak demands, the rates charged are likely to be high.

Emergency power supply for hospitals, alarm systems, dairy farms, and the like is quite a different issue. For safety, in-house generators or batteries are needed.

Guides to Make-or-Buy Policy

The following line of analysis provides an answer to most make-or-buy questions relating to supplies and services.

1. Does a dependable outside source exist? If the answer is "no," then we presume that our own production is best unless unforeseen obstacles arise. For instance, a cement plant in Chile has its own foundry and machine shop because no reliable source of repair parts is within reach. Similarly, most large industrial plants in Argentina have their own power plants because public power is unreliable.
2. When a dependable outside source does exist, we will use it unless a strong case can be made for not doing so. The reasons for this preference include simplifying the total managerial burden, focusing executive attention where major opportunities lie, reducing capital investment, retaining flexibility regarding sources, and—in competitive markets—gaining some of the economies that suppliers serving several customers will obtain.
3. Possible reasons for making exceptions to the preference for buying, just stated in (2), are: (a) Coordination with outside sources would be very cumbersome; for example, although office buildings frequently contract for janitor service and window washing, industrial plants rarely do so because cleaning up is intimately related to plant operations. (b) A large volume of a uniform item would result in unusually low costs. (c) The supply source

is unwilling to provide special services (for example, speedy delivery or unusual sizes) we desire.

This approach at least puts the burden of proof on the executive who suggests deviating from the main activities on which the firm is staking its success.

SELECTION OF VENDORS

Regardless of how a company resolves its problems of vertical integration and of make-or-buy supplies, some sorts of goods must be purchased. The manufacturer must buy raw materials and factory supplies, the retailer must buy finished goods, even the professional firm must buy office supplies. In most businesses it is possible to purchase satisfactory products from several vendors; these may be local or foreign. This raises the question of whether purchasing from several vendors is wiser than concentrating the business on only one or two. Even after this policy is settled, the type of vendor that will be the most satisfactory source for materials has to be resolved.

Number of Vendors

The number of suppliers of at least the essential products purchased by a firm should receive careful attention. Entire operations of the firm can be jeopardized if this issue is not wisely handled.

Allocating buying to secure vendor's services. A school supply jobber, for instance, followed the practice for a number of years of buying from as many different manufacturers as possible so that the firm name might be widely known. The company later became involved in financial difficulties and regretted its policy of using a large number of vendors. The purchases it made from any one manufacturer were not important enough to that manufacturer to justify granting special credit terms, and each vendor sought to collect bills promptly. Had this firm concentrated its purchases to a greater extent, it might have induced its vendors to be more lenient in making collections during the period of financial stress.

Advantages and dangers of concentration. A few companies that buy large quantities of merchandise concentrate their purchases to such an extent that they buy the entire output of the supplier. By doing so, they are able to secure favorable prices because the manufacturer is relieved of all selling cost and is able to concentrate its production operations on just those commodities desired by its one customer. The danger in this practice is that the manufacturer may fail to make delivery because of labor troubles, lack of capital, fire, or some other catastrophe, thus leaving the company deprived of its supply of products at a time when they are sorely needed.

A large mail-order house that was buying the entire output of a refrigerator plant guarded against this danger to some degree by having at the plant its own representative who watched accounting records and was familiar with plant operations. Such a representative could warn the mail-order house of any impending difficulties. Another large firm followed the policy of buying no more than 25% of its requirements of any one product from the same manufacturer. If for any reason something happened to one of these sources of supply, the company would be able to continue to get at least 75% of its requirements from its other vendors. When buying abroad, use of several alternative sources gives protection against political interruptions— as petroleum companies using Middle East crude oil well know.

Many firms follow a policy that seeks to gain the advantages of both concentration of purchases and multiple vendors. They find that buying most of their needs of a particular material from one source is desirable; the quality, price, delivery service, or some other factor makes concentration clearly the best arrangement. So, they give 70% to 80% of their business to this one vendor. The remaining part of the business is divided among several other suppliers. In this manner, business relations are established, specification problems are met and resolved, and the way is prepared for much larger purchases at a later date. Placing these small orders with several vendors is probably more expensive than buying all requirements from the chief source, but it serves two important purposes: (1) if a strike, fire, or other catastrophe hits the main supplier, the firm can shift to other suppliers much more quickly than it could if no relationship had been established; and (2) the main supplier is "kept on its toes" because the buyer is in close touch with the market and in a position to shift to other suppliers if the price, quality, or service from the main source does not continue to be the best.

Buying distress merchandise. Some retail stores appeal to their customers primarily on the basis of price, and in order to make a profit they continually seek to buy merchandise at "distress" prices. These stores usually offer to pay cash for merchandise, and they are not particularly concerned about being able to secure additional products from the same company. Such stores will deal with any vendor who has merchandise to offer for sale at a reasonable price, and they are continually "shopping around" for more favorable terms. Although such a policy appears to be good for companies operating on a purely price or cut-rate basis, most concerns have learned by experience that it is preferable to cooperate with vendors. A cooperative relationship will not be disrupted by either party because of apparent temporary advantages that may be obtained from time to time under special conditions.

Factors determining number of vendors. These illustrations show that there are both advantages and disadvantages to limiting the number of vendors from whom purchases are made. It is often necessary to balance the advantages of better service and quantity discounts that can be secured by concentrating business with a few vendors against the disadvantages of possible failure of supply and the passing up of occasional bargain merchandise. The problem often resolves itself into the following questions:

1. Can a limited number of vendors supply the variety of products required?
2. How much special service and price concession will result from concentration?
3. How important is such service to the purchaser?
4. Is the company too dependent upon any one company for materials?

Type of Vendors

The type of vendors selected by a company will depend on the company's requirements in regard to quality, service, reciprocity, and price.

Importance attached to quality. Selection of vendors by a company will be influenced, in part, by the quality of the products that it wishes. Thus a publishing house, desiring all its books to be made of a high-quality material, buys only from mills that make paper of dependable quality. Although the paper is purchased according to detailed specifications, the company is aware of the difficulty every paper mill has in controlling the quality of its product. The publishing house therefore prefers to pay somewhat higher prices to those mills that have a reputation for exercising care in maintaining the quality of their product.

Even a product that is highly standardized and that has a recognized market price may be purchased from one vendor rather than another in order to secure certain intangible qualities. Operators of textile mills, for instance, point out that there is considerable variation in the way raw cotton of identical staple and grade will work up in cloth. Consequently, when a textile mill discovers that cotton coming from one region through a given broker is more easily handled on their equipment than cotton from any other region, that mill will try to concentrate its future purchases on cotton coming from that particular section.

Service of vendors. Vendors may be selected because of the service they render their customers. For example, companies manufacturing computers, duplicators, and other types of office equipment often give their customers a great deal of aid in designing office forms and in establishing new systems. Most of these companies also maintain an extensive repair service. If a machine should break down, it may be quickly repaired without serious interruption in the work of the office using the equipment.

The importance of such service became striking in Brazil when that market was flooded with relatively inexpensive office equipment of German manufacture. The machines had entered Brazil under a barter agreement in which Brazil exchanged coffee and other raw materials for a specified quantity of machinery from Germany. Inadequate provision had been made for servicing the German machines, however. Consequently, when one of these machines broke down, it was both expensive and time-consuming to get it back into working order. As a result, many of the office managers were turning to more expensive American machines because of the repair service maintained by the American manufacturers.

Under some conditions promptness of delivery is a controlling factor in the selection of vendors. This has been one of the primary reasons why small steel companies have been able to secure in their local territories business that otherwise might have gone to the big steel companies. With standardized products and uniform prices prevailing in the industry, such special services as delivery often become controlling influences. The large companies have recently given more recognition to this factor and have spent substantial funds in an effort to expedite the handling of customers' orders.

Reciprocity. Under special circumstances vendors are selected on the basis of reciprocity. Thus, railroads are careful to place orders with concerns that are in a position to route a large quantity of freight over their lines. Sometimes the reciprocity may be a three-cornered deal. For instance, a Great Lakes steamship company decided to place a large order for motors with a particular manufacturer as a favor to a pig-iron producer. The pig-iron producer shipped large quantities of ore and could therefore demand favors from the steamship company in exchange for a contract to transport ore. To complete the circle, the pig-iron producer used its controls over the order for motors in selling pig-iron to the motor manufacturer. Hence, each of the three concerns selected vendors with an eye to the indirect effect such selection would have on sales.

Formal reciprocity agreements have been challenged legally as a restraint of trade, but this aspect is very cloudy. Much more common is the objection of "professional" purchasing agents. In fact, a policy on reciprocity is often necessary to keep peace between the purchasing department and the sales department.

Role of price. Thus far, no mention has been made of price in connection with the type of vendors. Prices for many products are uniform, and for other products the differences are not of sufficient importance to offset such factors as quality and special service. It should be clear, however, that price is an ever-present consideration, and if for some reason one vendor charges higher prices than another, the former is automatically eliminated unless there is some special reason for dealing with that particular vendor. As already noted, the significance of differences in prices depends partly upon the emphasis that the company buying the material gives to price in reselling the material, and also upon the importance of that particular product to the total cost of the company.

Gifts and friendship. Especially when large purchases are to be made, gifts and lavish entertainment may be offered to the person who selects the vendor. In its gross form this is clearly bribery. But the line is hard to draw; for instance, is a free lunch unacceptable? While not so strict as government on rules regarding favors, most companies do have a clear-cut policy forbidding the acceptance of any significant gifts from vendors.

More subtle is the question of friendship. Business relationships naturally lead to numerous contacts and mutual dependence—as we noted in Chapter 1. Friendship often grows out of such contacts. And cooperation between friends typically flows in both directions. In the United States the principle that we assume should guide business relations between friends is clear enough: cooperate to the hilt as long as the interests of the two companies are compatible (and such action is legal), but when interests conflict always give one's own company uncompromising priority. This norm is so widely understood it is rarely stated as a policy.

Summary Regarding Selection of Vendors

In selecting vendors a company is responding to the *sales appeal* of the numerous companies desiring to sell merchandise of the type used by the company. The point of view, however, is essentially different because the purchasing company is concerned only with its own specific problems and has no interest in the sales activities of the vendor unless these activities are of some value to it. There are also a number of questions, such as the number of vendors that do not have an exact counterpart for the seller. The more important factors that should be considered in making vendor selections are indicated in the following table:

Factors Influencing Vendor Selection

Capacity and Willingness of Vendor to Meet Company Needs	General Characteristics of Desirable Vendors	Factors Limiting the Choice

Quality of product:
  Specifications
  Dependability
	Size of vendor:
	  Interest in our
	    business
	  Financial stability
		Reciprocity
		
		Time and expense of
		  locating and dealing
		  with new vendors

Services offered:
  Delivery
  Technical aid
  Repair
  Credit terms
  Guarantees
  Adjustments
	Geographic location:
	  Support of "local"
	    industry
	  Dispersion of risks
	
	Manufacturer *vs.* jobber
		Habit and conservatism:
		  potential "headaches"
		  in new relationship
		
		Friendship and loyalty

Price:
  Competitive level
  Inclination to squeeze
  Protection on changes
	Maintenance of alterna-
	  tive sources:
	    Divide equally
	    One main source,
	    others minor
		Willingness of using de-
		  partments to try
		  new vendors

Company policy is needed to show which of these factors should be given primary consideration and which should be disregarded.

COORDINATION OF PRODUCTION, PURCHASING, AND SALES

Even after policies regarding integration, capacity, processes, procurement of supplies, and selection of vendors are clear, a cluster of problems on *timing* of purchasing and production remains. We are concerned here not with specific programs—a topic explored in Chapter 21—but with several underlying guides that must be established before programs can be built. As a basis for coordination of purchasing and production with sales, central management should set policies regarding:

1. Procurement "to order" or for stock.
2. Minimum inventories.
3. Size of production run or purchase order.
4. Stabilization of production operations.
5. Adjustments in inflationary periods.

Procurement "to Order" or for Stock

The made-to-order policy. Coordination of procurement with sales is accomplished in some industries by buying or making goods only if the customer's order is already received. The purchase of raw materials and supplies is not undertaken and production is not started until the order is actually in hand. Manufacturers of heavy machinery—or space ships—almost always follow such a make-to-order policy.

Other companies, such as producers of radio and television broadcasting equipment, make finished products only "on order"; but, in fact, they produce many parts and even subassemblies for stock. Then when an order is received, only the final assembly operation has to be done according to customer specification.

Concerns manufacturing high-class upholstered furniture may follow the same policy to even a lesser extent. In this industry, it is customary to manufacture the furniture up to the point where the upholstery is to be put on. This final covering is not applied until a specific order is received from a customer designating the kind of cover desired.

While a policy of making-to-order does reduce inventory risks and gives customers just what they want, it also has serious drawbacks. Delivery is inevitably slow and costs tend to be high because mass production techniques cannot be fully utilized.

Carrying stock. The majority of products are purchased or produced long before the customer's order is received. Orders are filled from inventory already on hand. This is true of most of the products that we, as ultimate customers, purchase, and it is also true of a great many products purchased by industrial concerns.

A compromise policy is followed by some firms that carry only standard products in stock. If their customers want an article that is not standard, the merchandise will be purchased or produced according to the customer's choice. For example, a shop dealing in dinnerware and glassware may carry an open stock of certain popular patterns. Should a customer wish other patterns, the manager of the shop will be glad to order them from the factory.

Since there are various degrees of making-to-order and of carrying stock —as the preceding examples show—and the degree affects purchasing, production, and selling activities, management should provide policy guidance. This is not a decision to be made from the viewpoint of any one department alone.

Minimum Inventory

If stock is to be carried, a company must establish some general guide to assist the purchasing and production departments in determining how much inventory to have on hand at any one time. Let us look first at the more mechanistic aspects of the problem—ordering points, size of production runs, and purchase quantities—and then note two main reasons for further adjustments, namely, stabilization and speculation on price changes.

How low should inventories be permitted to go before they are reordered? Each retail store in a modern grocery chain, for instance, is expected to maintain a minimum of all items regularly sold. Since the store gets frequent deliveries of additional merchandise, the minimum may be only a week's supply. In contrast, because of slow turnover the minimum inventory carried by many independent furniture stores is equal to a full year's sales.

Manufacturing firms must establish some general policy for minimum inventory for both finished goods and raw materials. Thus, a company manufacturing rugs had a policy of carrying finished merchandise only at the beginning of each selling season and gave no assurance to its customers that it would carry an inventory throughout the year. On the other hand, it did wish to carry a minimum stock of raw materials so as to avoid possible delay in production operations. Here the policy was to carry approximately three months' supply of yarn and other raw materials.

A general rule for finished merchandise is that the stock level at which replacements will be ordered should approximately equal the sales of that merchandise during the period required for replenishment. Thus, for stock that can be replenished within two weeks, the reordering point would be approximately two weeks' sales. If it takes three months to procure new inventory, then the minimum at which orders should be placed would be correspondingly higher. The same general idea can be carried back into the inventory of raw materials. Of course the rule does require estimates of future sales and of the speed of procurement, and these may be quite unstable.

Since the sale or the use of stock on hand will continue during the period of replenishment, it is customary to add a reasonable margin of safety to any such reordering point as a protection against possible contingencies. The size of the safety margin will depend upon the likelihood of delays in getting replacements and the seriousness of the delay to production operations or customer service. These considerations lead many firms to follow a policy of carrying a minimum inventory much higher than strict interpretation of the replenishment rule requires.

Size of Production Run or Purchase Order

When reordering is necessary, how much should be ordered? Primary considerations are economical production runs in a company's own plant or quantity discounts offered by vendors due to economic production runs in the vendor's plant or warehouse.

A company producing printed plastic bags for bakeries and candy companies, for example, found that the cost of preparing plates, setting up plates in the printing presses, threading the proper weight of plastic film through the presses, and making other preparations necessary for actual printing was often a substantial part of the total expense incurred on small orders. It was found that labor and idle machine charges were often $200 per order, and when this cost had to be charged to a few hundred bags, the cost per unit was quite high. If the order was for several thousand, the expense could be spread over the entire order and thus the cost per unit could be lowered.

To meet this situation, the company often printed more bags than were actually on order by the customer, thereby securing a low production cost per unit. The extra stock was then held until the customer placed a reorder. This policy substantially increased the company's inventory but was the only way that the company could secure satisfactory production costs.

Policy regarding size of purchase orders, like policy regarding size of production runs, may be stated in total quantities or in so many weeks' or months' supply. Then order standards for specific items may be computed, giving effect to economy of large lots, cost of storage, perishability and obsolescence, and related factors.

If the time at which sales orders will be received (or supplies needed) can be predicted with reliability, at least for a frequency distribution, and dollar values can be attached to carrying inventories, to savings on large quantities, and to loss resulting from failure to accept or deliver a sales order—then minimum inventories, ordering points, and size of production runs or purchase orders can be calculated statistically. Even then, however, the judgment of central management is needed to establish safety margins on receipt of goods and to evaluate the seriousness of disappointing a customer. These judgments are often stated as policies. Moreover, management may choose to modify statistically optimum schedules (a) to stabilize production or (b) to adjust to price changes.

Stabilization of Production

The business of every company fluctuates by seasons and by cycles. For example, a firm manufacturing electric blankets may find that it sells two thirds of its products in the last half of each calendar year, and a company manufacturing gloves may find that it sells 45% of its products in the last three months of the year. Even articles in daily use, such as cosmetics, have a seasonal fluctuation.

Production for stock. Faced with such a seasonal fluctuation, a company may decide to synchronize procurement with its sales volume so that it will not carry inventory in excess of its sales needs at any time. Most women's glove manufacturers, for instance, do not attempt to produce very far ahead of the season in which they will sell their gloves. Frequent style changes may make gloves produced in advance of the season unsalable, or salable only at a reduced price. But, unfortunately, seasonal production means unstable employment.

Other firms produce at approximately a level rate throughout the year. This means that they accumulate during the seasons of slack sales an inventory to satisfy demand during the peak periods. One of the leading manufacturers of skis follows this policy to avoid having an idle plant during part of the year and to keep a group of efficient workers employed the entire year.

Theoretically, a similar policy of production stabilization could be applied to cyclical fluctuations. But few companies have financial strength to do more than stretch out a product for a few months while looking for a prompt recovery in sales. (The massive stabilization programs undertaken by the federal government for agricultural products involve resources far greater than any company possesses.)

Any company that considers producing during slack periods for sales in later boom times must reckon with obsolescence, deterioration, storage costs, and financing. Fully as important is the ability to forecast the duration and the amplitudes of downswings and upswings. Even seasonal drops are difficult to interpret during the downswing because a manager usually cannot tell *at the time* how much of the change is random, trend, or seasonal. So, an important aspect of a policy to stabilize production is how long production will be maintained above sales—or how large an inventory will be built up—in the face of below-normal sales.

Other ways of dealing with fluctuations. Production in excess of demand during slack seasons is not the only way companies have sought to adjust to fluctuations in sales volume. We have already seen that some companies have been successful in adding to their line products that have complementary seasonal fluctuations. The combination of the TV and electric refrigerator business is an illustration.

Subcontracting at times of peak demand has been used by some companies in place of a temporary expansion in their own work force. This is not always practical, however, since subcontractors are likely to be busy just at the times when the prime contractor has a peak load.

The automobile industry changed the date for bringing out new annual models from the spring to the fall in an effort to level out seasonal fluctuations. A large number of people prefer to buy new cars in the spring of the year. When the new models were brought out at this time, there was a double incentive to buy during the months of March through June. By changing the time of introducing the new models to the fall, the companies were able to attract customers in the fall of the year who otherwise might have purchased in the spring.

These methods, like almost all stabilization devices available to private enterprise, apply best to seasonal fluctuations and have only limited application to cyclical changes.

Adjustment in Inflationary Periods

Many companies adjust their purchasing and production schedules in anticipation of changes in prices of raw materials and finished products. When price increases are anticipated, goods will be procured in excess of immediate requirements; and when declines are forecast, inventories will be reduced. In this way the companies hope to secure additional profits. This practice is so hazardous—and yet in inflationary periods so necessary—that the elements involved should be separately evaluated.

Total inventory position. Exposure to inventory price risks involves commitments as well as physical goods in the warehouse. Firm orders to purchase entail just as much price risk as goods in-house. On the other hand, firm orders from customers with fixed prices are an offset against goods on hand. The amount of exposure is the net total of these commitments and goods on hand. In fact, a company making products such as aircraft, which are ordered several years in advance, may have a negative inventory exposure. When we establish policy regarding inventory price risk, the focus should be on net exposure.

Case against speculation. There are three main reasons why merchandising, manufacturing, and nonprofit enterprises should not vary the size of their inventory in an attempt to buy-low-and-sell-high. First, it detracts from the primary function of the enterprise, and most managements have all they can do to accomplish their primary mission. Second, every enterprise is exposed to a wide variety of risks that cannot be avoided; it is desirable to try to minimize these risks rather than add others. Third, someone within the company who has exceptional price forecasting ability should resign and concentrate all his or her talent on speculation. Perhaps this person can join a trading firm where speculation is part of the mission.

This injunction against speculation is generally accepted. But it applies to the more extreme situations, and it leaves unresolved a lot of inventory variation that most managers insist is not "speculation." These remaining price risks arise directly from performing the regular business. The question is how to deal with them prudently.

Assuring uninterrupted operations. Availability of goods often fluctuates with price. At times of rising prices, demand is brisk and it may take twice as long to get delivery as is necessary when business is dull. Consequently, purchasing agents who are responsible for having an adequate supply of inventory on hand may buy ahead in boom times just to make sure that they get goods on time. On the downswing, prompt deliveries are easier to get and the purchasing agents may safely cut back their inventory.

Thus, in times of material shortages—and these are likely to occur during a period of general inflation—a company quite properly protects itself by building inventory. However, practical limits arise because some inventory may become obsolete—due to changes in style or engineering specifications —or may deteriorate as do many food products and sensitive chemicals. Also storage and other carrying costs may be quite high. These factors place an outer limit on the physical supply it is practical to hold. But within these limits, inventory accumulation is desirable if it is needed to assure uninterrupted operation.

This kind of inventory buildup is not really an anticipation of price changes. The underlying reasons for expansion and contraction are so entwined with price fluctuations, however, that they are difficult to separate. The motive is availability of supply, but an accompanying side effect is exposure to inventory price fluctuation.

Known risks of not buying. Interwoven with problems of having inventory when needed are adjustments to "known" price changes. Sometimes suppliers announce price increases in advance of an effective date. Clearly, when this occurs, a company should buy its future requirements as far ahead as it is practical to store goods.

More common are situations where the odds are, say, 80% that prices will rise in the near future. For instance, the supply may be known to be tight, a labor contract providing higher wages has just been signed, prices of competing products have already gone up, or the world price may have firmed. And there is certainty the price will not fall in the near future. Under these conditions a firm is assuming greater inventory price risks from not buying than from buying.

Limits on exposure. Inventory buildup for the two reasons just discussed —assurance of uninterrupted operations and reduction of "known" risks— should be subjected to one other influence. A company's total risk posture may place constraints on the amount of inventory risk assumed. Overall business uncertainties usually set a time span beyond which it is dangerous for a company to cover its specific needs. Just as we consumers don't buy an oil filter replacement that our car is likely to need two years hence, there are limits on how far ahead a company has full confidence in its detailed projections. In turbulent periods the possibilities of an international monetary crisis, war, overthrow of the government, drastic government intervention, or comparable events may make firm commitments beyond six months unwise. Under more favorable conditions management may feel reasonably confident about the shape of events for a year or more ahead. Regardless, then, of specific expectations about a particular material or part, management often sets a general horizon beyond which commitments should not go.

Likewise, as we shall see in Chapter 13, the scarcity of capital may require a company to set some limits on the total sums tied up in inventory.

Summarization. A strong case can be made against out-and-out speculation on inventories—except for a trading company organized for such a purpose. Nevertheless, especially in periods of inflation, adjustment of inventories in anticipation of external shortages and price shifts may be prudent. An approach to this troublesome issue is (a) to focus on inventory necessary to assure uninterrupted operations—within the practical limits of holding such inventory. In addition, (b) inventory may be built up when the price outlook makes the risk of not doing so quite high. Here, again, the inventory is confined to future operating needs. Finally, (c) the accumulations for either (a) and/or (b) should be restricted to a general commitment horizon and financial allocation set by central management.

Conclusion Regarding Timing of Procurement

In producing and in buying, wide differences exist in anticipating consumers' actions or waiting until orders are in hand. Many companies carry larger stocks than are required for customer service to secure economic production runs or to obtain discounts from vendors. Sometimes the procurement of merchandise is adjusted in an effort to stabilize production operations, but more frequently it is adjusted in anticipation of price changes or to assure adequate supply.

The more important factors that an executive should consider in dealing with such timing issues include:

1. Customer requirements for specially designed merchandise or for prompt deliveries of standard merchandise.
2. Economies possible from larger production runs.
3. Economies that may be secured from level production, including maintenance of a well-trained labor force, more complete utilization of facilities, and possible reductions in tax burdens.
4. Expenses of carrying goods in inventory, including the storage charges, the financial cost, the insurance expense, and the deterioration or obsolescence of merchandise.
5. Accuracy with which price changes may be predicted.

6. Accuracy of prediction of the volume and nature of products demanded at a subsequent period of time.

This list, though incomplete, does indicate that the timing of procurement is a complex problem. Central management should provide policy guidance in this area because actions will affect the company's ability to render good customer service, influence its operating costs, change its circulating capital requirements, and bring about special losses due to adjustment in inventory valuation.

SUMMARY

Every business enterprise will face many of the production and procurement issues discussed in the last two chapters. There is the inevitable question of "make-or-buy," and this applies to the whole range of finished products, parts, supplies, and raw materials used.

Production processes must be selected, and here policy regarding division of labor, automation, size of plant, and process research is needed.

Then comes the issue of how much capacity. Plans for meeting peak loads should be set up. Provision for growth, balance between departments, and backward taper of capacity also have to be fitted into the general scheme. Guidance on the level of maintenance and on replacement should be correlated with product line, customer service, and financial policy.

For goods to be purchased, policy dealing with the number and the types of vendors is necessary. And there are basic issues of when and how much to buy and to produce.

In this array of issues we are concerned with the company's basic strategy for generating the goods and the services that its marketing strategy requires. Each part of the total production plan should support the other and also should be consistent with personnel and financial policy—to which we now turn our attention.

 QUESTIONS FOR CLASS DISCUSSION

1. Envirometrics, Inc. makes trash compactors that compress all sorts of refuse into small, heavy bundles. A co-founder also owns another company, Baruch Steel Works, that was of major help in designing the first compactors and that originally provided space for Envirometrics. Baruch still helps with rush orders, with the design of new parts for the compactors, and with any general questions about manufacturing. Envirometrics buys 75% of its parts and

materials from Baruch. Prices charged Envirometrics are "our cost plus the normal markup." No thought has been given to date to finding and buying from other suppliers. But now, after another increase in Baruch's charges has put pressure on Envirometrics to raise its prices again, the marketing vice president of Envirometrics has objected. "Are production costs as low as they should be?" This question has been reported to the board of directors. As a director, what is your opinion about using the Baruch company as a source of 75% of items purchased? What would be your answer to the questions on page 238?

2. In several Far Eastern countries, the local culture calls for the sending of substantial gifts to individuals (often part owners) who place large orders with a company. These are regarded as expressions of friendship and tokens of appreciation. What should be the policy of a U.S. company with a branch in such countries (a) if it is buying goods or services? (b) if it is selling goods or services?

3. Which of the factors listed in the table on page 240 do you think should carry the most weight in selecting vendors by (a) a woman's specialty dress shop? (b) a good restaurant noted for its seafood? (c) a hospital? (d) a specialty store selling personal computers and programs for them? (e) a city such as El Paso, Texas?

4. Assume there is a popular belief that the prices of automobiles will rise 12% per year for at least the next three years. How would that expectation affect your decision, if you were considering buying a car for your personal use? Should a company that operates a fleet of cars respond as you would personally? Explain any differences.

5. In all large cities, firms selling computer time have sprung up. The services of most kinds of computers are available; consequently, a company need not buy or rent its own computer in order to be able to use one. If you were advising the president of a company regarding the advisability of having its own computer(s), what factors would you consider?

6. Most discussions of stabilization of production, including that in this chapter, accept fluctuations in sales and consider ways of adjusting production to those sales. An alternative approach would be to set the production volume—at a stabilized level—and consider ways of adjusting sales to production. The second approach (widely used in Japan) enables companies to provide stable employment and helps maintain the gross national product. Would such a practice be socially desirable in the United States? What would companies have to do to operate in this manner?

7. (a) At what point should company policy bar the acceptance of gifts and entertainment from vendors: lunch at a local restaurant, golf game at an exclusive club, three-day technical seminar at a comfortable inn, Christmas calendar, bottle of Scotch, electronic watch, theater tickets, mink coat, opportunity to invest in Florida real estate, assistance in getting son a seat on a booked-up plane flight, employment for Uncle Ben, $10,000 to a pet charity, $50 bet at favorable odds, or you name it? (b) Should the company policy be the same with respect to company bankers? union leaders? advertising agents? customers?

8. "When selecting vendors, we carefully consider service, price, and other factors affecting our operations. However, we do not feel that we should interfere with

the way the vendor runs its business. Specifically, its decisions on equal employment opportunity, pollution, foreign military contracts, and such matters are not our responsibility. We run our company as we believe is right, and the other company is entitled to the same respect." Do you agree? Does a bank have any more obligation to "interfere" with the way its customers operate than a steel company does its customers?

9. (a) A Wall Street analyst says: "During a period of inflation the smart person owns things, even if it means going into debt to do so. A company has an even better built-in opportunity to own things and should buy inventory to the extent of its financial capacity." Do you agree? Why? (b) How should a company take advantage of inflation?

10. "When is a price break a real break? When it will not overload our inventories and increase our financial investment in materials." Mr. Conrad Lloyd, vice president of production for Runner Manufacturing Co., used this explanation to justify the pressure he put on the buyers at Runner's eight plants in Canada, the U.S., and Mexico to move steel deliveries scheduled for October forward to September. Mr. Lloyd used the same explanation to justify his refusal to authorize one of the buyers to load up an extra 3,000 tons of steel the previous May at a price break of $20 per ton. (Runner's six regular steel suppliers had all announced a price increase of $20 per ton to take place October 1. Moving delivery of about 6,000 tons from October to September gave Runner a "substantial saving," according to Mr. Lloyd). "Last May we were still reducing steel inventories and could not have brought in an extra pound whatever the price." So the Runner Co. also passed up another offer from Sharon Steel Corp. which promised hot- and cold-rolled sheet through the third quarter at $40 a ton below the going price. "It was a tough decision. Sharon is a U.S. company but is not one of our six major suppliers who had not received many orders from us all year. . . . I believe that, over the next ten years, we will have more times of short supply in steel than of excess. . . . Therefore, price becomes secondary to harmony.

"We have an offer right now from a European supplier of 1,500 tons of galvanized steel at $67 per ton below domestic prices. I am recommending that we not be overawed by the amount because, in a tight market, we'd lose that savings so fast you wouldn't believe it. By investing with our regular domestic mills, we won't have to sit down next year in the next tight market and reinvent the wheel." In line with this policy, the share of Runner's steel supplied by foreign mills has been slashed to about 3% this year from 20% three years ago when Mr. Lloyd was named vice president.

(a) Many steel buyers agree with Mr. Lloyd about long-term interests. Many others do not. "The quality of Belgian and Japanese steel is certainly as good as that of Canadian and U.S.; Mexican steel and transportation is no problem at all. The savings from 1,500 tons of steel at $67 per ton below domestic prices would go a long way toward paying Lloyd's salary for the year. How else does a purchasing agent find justification?" So said a friend. Do you agree? (b) The price break offered by Sharon Steel was 13% below the market for one quarter "which is not a bad return on the money that would have been invested in the steel." Do you agree?

CASE II
Hammond Engineering Company (R)

For the past half-decade, John Sorenson, president of Hammond Engineering Company, has been buying copper ingots on the open market for his company to use as its major raw material. This work has taken a large amount of his time, but has been necessary, he believes, because a sound vision and a sure touch on the London Metal Exchange or the New York Commodities Exchange (COMEX) is needed to keep raw material costs for his company to a minimum.

Hammond Engineering is in the heating and air-conditioning business. More specifically, it manufactures valves, fin pipe, cooling units, radiators, heat exchangers, and copper tubing for the air-conditioning and chemical industries. Copper is a vital raw material, accounting for about 40 percent of the cost of goods sold. In his attempts to pay no more than his competitors do for copper, Mr. Sorenson has bought in both the spot market and the futures market.

Recent major changes in the copper industry and some likely future changes have raised questions about Hammond Engineering's use of the spot and futures markets as its sources of copper and have called for an analysis of other possible sources of supply.

Over the past five years, copper prices have been depressed relative to other materials and product prices. Despite the long recovery of general business from the major depression of 1974 and 1975, copper prices have taken little part in the widespread inflation of most industrial prices. This history of prices has led to the closing of many U.S. copper mines because their costs of wages and materials have risen much more rapidly than has the price of copper.

High inventories of copper on a worldwide scale (about three million pounds or one-half of yearly usage), and the policies of Peru, Zambia, Zaire, and Chile to keep their mines open at almost any price to provide employment, have kept copper prices down.

But now it appears that excess inventories may well be worked off, that big new mines in Mexico and Brazil are delayed in reaching their planned output, and that direct contracts with producers might be a safer and lower-cost way for Hammond Engineering to obtain its copper than are the spot and futures markets.

The former practice by U.S. copper producers (Kennecott, Anaconda, Phelps Dodge, American Smelting and Refining, and others) of maintaining a firm price (known as the producer's price) for many months was discontinued in 1978 and 1979 after some of these firms were purchased by other companies, including Cities Service Co., Atlantic Richfield Co., and Tenneco Corporation. Current pricing policy is for these U.S. copper-producing firms to base their prices upon recent quotations on the New York Commodity Exchange. Thus, the opportunity for Mr. Sorenson to buy copper cheaply by playing on the differences between the producer's price, futures prices, and the London spot market has disappeared.

There appear to be five possible ways for Hammond Engineering to obtain the 12,000 tons of copper which it uses each year: (1) to continue buying on the spot and futures markets, (2) to take up an offer for Hammond to purchase some additional tonnage being brought on to the world market by a government-owned company in the Arabic state of Al Adraman, which borders Saudi Arabia, (3) to develop an open-pit mine in the huge Arizona, New Mexico, and Mexican ore-body, (4) to build a leaching plant to extract copper from tailings dumps of old mines, and (5) to build an electrowinning plant for refining copper.

1. Continuing the present practice of buying on the open market has the advantage of using Mr. Sorenson's skill in buying which has been highly developed over the past ten years. He has an intimate knowledge of the spot and futures markets and has generally been successful at paying a price for the company's copper which has been two to three cents per pound less than the spot market price at time of delivery. An added advantage is that this course of action requires no capital investment and little operating expense other than the 40 percent of Mr. Sorenson's time which he spends on buying refined copper. Of course, this arrangement does reduce the president's attention to other aspects of his firm's operation. Hammond Engineering has been growing in real terms at close to one percent per year. Since this rate is one-fourth to one-tenth the real growth rate of other subsidiaries of Hammond's parent firm, executives of the parent corporation have been urging Mr. Sorenson to find ways to recoup and increase Hammond's market share.

2. The government of Al Adraman has been a small factor in the world copper market for some time, ever since the sultan decreed the construction of an integrated facility including a mine, a concentrating mill, a smelter and refinery—with an output of about 30,000 tons per year. The operating company, Al Adraman Mining, is owned by three groups: the government (70%), a U.S.-based copper firm (28%), and a Tucson-based mining and consulting company (2%). The operating company has produced steadily at its rated capacity for the last six years.

Recently, Al Adraman Mining has demonstrated an expanded ore-body and, with the help of financing from Saudi Arabia, intends to increase output by one-third (10,000 tons per year). Friends in the Tucson firm have approached Mr. Sorenson with the idea that Hammond Engineering buy ten percent of the stock of the operating company (about $15 million) to gain a preferred position for all or part of the added tonnage. The friends propose a contract which includes: a beginning price per ton equal to the present price on the London Metal Exchange; a ten percent share of dividends when payment of dividends begins following the repayment of the loan to Saudi Arabia (five years after production of the added tonnage begins); all payments in U.S. dollars; an inflation clause which guarantees that the price charged Hammond Engineering will rise no more than six percent per year and less than that if the rate of inflation in the sultanate is less; the price never to be less than the opening price unless the world price drops 10 percent or more, in which case the contract price will be renegotiated; and shipments of refined copper to begin 15 months after the agreement is made. Dividends paid so far have been a steady 15 percent of the equity capital.

3. Almost all long-term forecasts of copper demand and supply over the next ten years indicate a steady increase of 4 percent per year in the world demand for copper in real terms, and a worldwide shortage of supply to begin in five years. This outlook

has led Mr. Califano and Mr. Schlesinger of Hammond's parent firm to make a trip to the Southwest to explore the possibility of developing an open-pit mine.[1]

This study revealed that the normal course of exploration, development, and stripping the over-burden to bring a new open-pit mine into production would require four to five years and an investment of $250 million to $300 million. Such a mine would include the digging, crushing, and concentrating stages. Its output would then go to a smelter and refinery for production of copper electrodes that are 99.90 percent pure. Mine production would be 45,000 tons of copper annually for about twenty years with present-day technology. At the start, the average total manufacturing cost would be about $0.88 per pound (in 1981 dollars) for the refined copper. With normal luck and good management, the return on investment for such a mine would be thirteen percent after all taxes.

4. Refinery time is not entirely impossible to obtain provided Hammond Engineering can offer the necessary semi-processed copper to the refiner. Mr. Sorenson knows a Belgian refinery which will take any smelted-ore concentrates Hammond may have in a substantial quantity and trade refined copper for it at the relevant free-world prices. Transportation costs overseas are about $.03 per pound one-way.

To supply semi-processed copper to an independent refinery, Mr. Califano and Mr. Schlesinger have located an old mine with an exhausted ore-body but with substantial tailing dumps from which copper can be leached by trickling sulfuric acid down through the dump. The resulting solution can be treated to remove the copper for later stages of refining. The quality of such copper is not as good as that obtained from virgin ore-bodies, but it is satisfactory for making tubing. The copper would be produced at a cost of about fifteen cents per pound below the present price on the London Metal Exchange after refining and before any shipping costs. Required initial investment in the land and associated chemical plant will be $12,000,000 to $15,500,000, depending on the desired output which could range from 10 to 20 tons of copper per day. Development time is one year and useful life would be ten years.

5. During the directors' search, Hammond engineers have been busy designing and building a pilot plant for a new method—called "electrowinning"—of extracting copper from ore-bodies which can be leached. The engineers believe that the equipment design has overcome the problems of corrosion that have been a stumbling block to other developers attempting to do the same thing. A pilot plant, which can be moved on a railroad flat car, is under construction at the factory. The engineers' cost estimates indicate that 99.90 percent pure copper may well be produced at a total manufacturing cost which will be about $.20 per pound below world prices by

---

[1]The parent corporation makes and sells electrical, mechanical, and hydraulic machinery throughout the world. Both its plants and its customers can be found in North and South America, Europe, and the Far East. An investment by this corporation in a new open-pit copper mine would force a re-examination of its present strategy of diversifying in machinery industries. This diversification aims at growth in sales, assets, and market share. The present position of the corporation in machinery industries has been achieved by very active product development in a strong internal design staff and by acquiring other firms. Most of such expansion has been financed by internal sources of funds. Currently, there is sharp internal competition for available funds for (a) dividends, (b) expansion of the machinery business, (c) international growth of warehousing, repair and service operations, and (d) building a central research group specializing in metallurgy.

this process of leaching, concentrating the solution, and then precipitating the copper electrically.

	Financial Information	
	Hammond Engineering Company	**The Parent Corporation**
Sales—last year	$86,000,000	$900,000,000
Profits—last year	1,720,000	54,000,000
Stockholder's equity	41,000,000	415,000,000

This process avoids all pollution problems usually associated with smelting and refining. The necessary investment for full-scale operations will be about $13,000,000 to $14,000,000 (in 1981 dollars). Finding a surface ore-body which could produce 6,000 short tons of copper per year for ten years in total from ore containing 0.6–0.75 percent copper in acid soluble form, delineating the ore-body, developing the mine, and building the plant will take three to four years, provided the process proves out.

Questions

(1) Prepare a table showing a comparison of the alternatives available to Hammond Engineering Company.

(2) What decision would you make about the supply of copper for the company?

(3) Explain how your decision would be useful in meeting corporate objectives.

PERSONNEL AND INDUSTRIAL RELATIONS POLICY

Every enterprise requires labor inputs. Survival depends upon continuing cooperation of the men and women who convert resources into services. Moreover, any strategic redirection of a company's mission is possible only if human resources can be focused on the new tasks.

—When central management turns its attention to mobilizing personnel resources, three underlying issues are always present:

1. Will the necessary labor force be available? More specifically, what must the company do to develop the number and type of workers needed to carry out its proposed strategy?
2. Can the company afford the cost? Are the satisfactions—monetary and others—that may be necessary to attract and retain such a workforce within the company's ability to provide?
3. Can viable relationships with unions representing the workers be maintained?

In addition, an array of problems bearing on the effective use of labor must be confronted. Organization design, motivation, informal relations are examples. But these are largely internal matters. We will deal with them briefly in Part 4, and a large body of "organization behavior" literature is available on various aspects of internal relationships. The focus of the present chapter is on the company's boundary looking outward, on mobilizing human talent suited to the specific strategy that a company hopes to pursue.

Because of its importance, executive personnel is discussed in a separate chapter (Chapter 20). Here we will deal with policy guides covering personnel as a total resource.

SELECTING AND DEVELOPING PERSONNEL

Each person has distinct abilities. Each job has particular duties. One must fit the other. For convenience, we often talk of labor in general, but within that broad resource highly individualistic matches with jobs are essential.

Skills Matched to Strategic Requirements

Are suitable people available? A large labor pool is only a start. During the great depression, for instance, millions of people were looking for work. However, it was a very unusual group of refugees from Nazi Germany who had the exceptional intellectual skills and training which enabled them to become the founding nucleus of the New School for Social Research, an unusual graduate school in New York City. Or, to note another educational example, the Nigerian government has both funds and desire to build a full-fledged medical school in the northern city of Kano. But there are not yet enough trained medical professors available to make more than a small start. In each example, suitable personnel became a key to the execution of strategy.

Finding pools of talent. A company may have to move to find qualified workers at competitive wages. The scarcity of laboratory personnel in the U.S. has forced several pharmaceutical firms to shift parts of their research work to Europe. The movement of textile firms to Korea and Taiwan reflects a search for cheap, though dexterous, labor. Publishers have located part-time editorial staff in middle-class suburbs.

This searching for more favorable sources of labor is similar to marketing executives looking for attractive niches for products. The aim is to establish a strong position before competition becomes tough.

Adjusting to a changing labor market. Of course, sometimes it is practical to modify company operations to fit available labor. For example, for years a drug wholesale company followed a policy of hiring high-school graduates to staff its large warehousing operations. These people stacked, marked, and kept track of the thousands of different items involved; assembled orders for prompt delivery to retail druggists, priced the order, and computed the bill; kept track of back orders; and helped maintain records needed for buying new stocks. High-school graduates were found to have the accuracy and the dependability required, and at the same time they did not find the highly standardized operations offensive. The more energetic employees became supervisors, sales representatives, buyers, and perhaps branch managers.

The company now finds that most of the more able and energetic high-school graduates go to college. Efforts to use men and women who want a full-time job while working their way through school have shown unsatisfactory results because many of these people become bored with their routine work. So, some modification in hiring policy clearly was called for.

A modification in the *structure of jobs* was the first move. Instead of assuming that everyone would have a basic competence to perform a variety of tasks, the work has been more sharply graded in terms of reading, writing, and arithmetic skills. This permits relaxation of the high-school graduation requirement. Also, more minorities have been hired even though some are weak in desired basic skills at the time of employment. This new type of employee is given intensive training on limited tasks. Turnover is high during the early months of employment, but out of the group come a significant number who can do the simpler tasks well and quite a few who quickly move on to the more skilled jobs.

In addition, provision has been made for hiring a few college graduates and moving them rather quickly through various operations with the expectation that they will qualify for buying, selling, or supervisory jobs.

The revised policy has some disadvantages. It is more difficult to move people from task to task to meet peak requirements. More significant, lost is the feeling that everyone starts out on an equal basis and progresses to more difficult positions on the basis of demonstrated merit. Even though it is now possible to move up through the hierarchy, and some people do, new employees enter the company at different levels. This generates an undercurrent that some people—because they are lucky enough to get more education—continue to receive favored treatment.

How much provision for growth? Communications Systems, Inc. is a growth company centered around some patented devices that transmit and receive multiple electronic messages. These devices are particularly well suited to handle communications between branch offices and a centralized computer. The company founder and president, however, regards the equipment merely as the base from which all communications systems can grow. Among the possibilities already worked on are central inventory control of multiple warehouses, central payroll records for all branches of a state government, logistic systems for the Air Force, a nationwide bidding system for commodity exchanges, and complete integrated data processing systems for business firms.

With these possibilities in mind, the firm expanded rapidly. Its stated personnel policy was "to attract the best brains in the country." The glamor of the company objectives enabled it to hire both theoretical and applied experts in systems design, communications equipment, computer technology, and the activities to which the systems might be applied.

The match between the mission conceived for the company and the kinds of people employed was excellent. But serious difficulty developed in terms of the rate of growth. Communications Systems was employed to make a variety of pilot studies, but full-scale applications proved to be complex and costly. Concepts such as national bidding on commodities require legal and institutional changes that probably are several decades away. The result was that many members of the high-powered staff that was employed became frustrated. The high morale in the early stages turned to internal criticism and disappointment with lack of personal advancement. Since many of the people employed were indeed very capable, they began taking other jobs. Turnover accelerated. Hiring mistakes during the initial expansion became conspicuous because these individuals tended to stay with Communications Systems. The company is still in business, but it now has a poor name rather than a good name in its particular labor market.

Hiring policy has a quantitative as well as a qualitative aspect, as we clearly see in the preceding example. While this was an extreme case, other companies have discovered they moved too fast in the right direction. (It *is* possible to have too many bright young MBA's.) Excess inventory of talented human resources is both hard and expensive to keep in storage.

Constraints on Selection

In addition to policy guides regarding types, sources, and numbers of employees it intends to attract, each company must decide how it will cope with "thou shalt not" laws.

Hiring, promotion, and discharge of employees are surrounded by increasing government regulation. Equal opportunity for blacks has been extended to other minority groups. Women likewise are guaranteed explicit rights. Discrimination on the basis of age and compulsory retirement ages have been outlawed. And the list is increasing.

In each of these areas there are past injustices to be corrected and worthy social goals to be achieved. The perplexing challenge for managers is that the new laws, and regulations supporting them, are inconsistent, and no consensus exists on how rapidly the "equal opportunity" norms are to be evident in various occupations and levels of the organization. Preferential treatment must be given to blacks, women, and other under-represented segments of society; but such preferential treatment obviously involves reverse discrimination against still other workers. Or to cite another example, jobs retained by elderly white males block the promotions of younger women or blacks.

Broadly speaking, companies can respond to these—and similar—issues in one of three ways. *Minimum compliance* just to stay within the law is a short-run option. Meanwhile, several of the inconsistencies and uncertainties may be resolved. Conscientiously carrying out the *underlying intent* of laws is a second alternative. Here a company seeks to move with changing social norms. It recognizes that changes are appropriate, and tries to be a good citizen. *Pioneering* is a third possibility. This involves being a leader in social reform, perhaps to the extent that favorable ties to particular segments of the labor market will become a "differential advantage."

Reliance on Internal Development

Interwoven with decisions on who and where to hire are questions about "promotion from within." One source of specialized talent is to "raise your own." This is like the "make" option in make-or-buy policy regarding materials.

Companies vary in the degree that they expect to fill better jobs and managerial positions by promotion. General Motors, like the wholesale drug company referred to earlier in this chapter, relies almost entirely on internal sources. Such a policy, of course, requires the company to do a lot of internal training if people are to be fully prepared for new assignments. And in fact General Motors has the equivalent of a college, the General Motors Institute, for this purpose. Training on the job and horizontal transfers are even more important. A major hurdle in such internal development of personnel is the lack of opportunity for injecting new ideas, especially when a company's external environment is turbulent.

The primary factors in choosing between "raising your own" versus "hiring seasoned workers" include, first, the probable length of employment. Industries such as construction or the theater, which work on relatively short projects, typically assemble the talent needed for immediate purposes and leave the task of training to the individual and to other institutions. Staffing of government contracts in the space and defense industries largely falls into this category. Of course, any company that undertakes to enter a different industry on a large scale lacks time to do very much training. Second, the existence of well established skills or professions affects the need for in-company training. Thus, printers, doctors, and welders are usually hired as experienced individuals. By comparison, if the work of a particular company is primarily unique, internal training is necessary to assure the skills required.

Companies that are technological leaders in their field are always faced by a problem of training people who then go to work for competitors. A substantial number of engineers and sales representatives in the computer industry, for instance, have been trained at IBM expense. If a company's strategy is to be a leader, it should anticipate not only the cost of overcoming the pitfalls of a new product or process, but also a personnel development cost. Moreover, the company will probably have to be a leader in compensation and supplemental benefits in order to keep its turnover low.

DESIGNING A REALISTIC COMPENSATION PACKAGE

Recruiting and developing personnel, as was just discussed, focuses on the inflow of a vital resource to the company. The other side of the coin is an outflow of compensation that will retain this talent. And as noted in Chapter 1, this outflow must be of a size and nature that the company can afford to pay.

An attractive job includes a whole set of factors: the work itself, future opportunities, security, status, hours and working conditions, fringe benefits, as well as monetary compensation. The ability of a company to provide most of these attractions depends especially on two conditions we have already stressed: (a) an economically strong business is crucial. No personnel policy or government regulation can be a substitute. Security, growth opportunities, status, and many other benefits are possible only when a company has a sound strategy well executed. (b) People must be well matched to the jobs they hold. Individuals vary and jobs vary. Unless a good fit is achieved, the employment situation will be unstable and probably unsatisfactory.

Assuming that these preconditions are met, there will still remain important issues about both direct compensation and supplemental benefits.

Level of Pay

Relation to prevailing rates. Many firms simply decide that they will pay "going rates" for each occupation or level of job. Such a policy seeks to neutralize pay as a competitive factor. Employees will have to be attracted and motivated in some other way.

Paying above the market is an alternative that has popular appeal. Here a firm may seek to get the "cream of the crop," to give customers distinctive service, or perhaps to reduce turnover. Of course, if too many companies are prepared to pay above the average the policy loses its distinctiveness (and the actual average being paid keeps moving up). Moreover, unless the company's technology gives it low labor expenses relative to the total, or unless it has some offsetting cost advantage, a high wage policy cuts into the company's ability to attract other kinds of resources.

Few firms admit that they consistently try to pay less than market averages, but it is an option which suits some situations. A small, remote firm drawing from a local labor pool is a convenient place to work; commuting time and expense are low. Or the enterprise may offer offsetting attractions, such as prestige (working for the leading bank in town) or service opportunities (hospitals). Also, if a company does not need high skills its wage rates may look low when, in fact, it is paying reasonably well for what it needs.

Keeping up with inflation. Pay rates are not viewed just in terms of comparable jobs elsewhere. They also have a history. What is good pay today depends partly on what was paid last year. Especially during inflation these historical comparisons loom large.

Periodically raising wages to match increases in living costs is a straightforward basic policy. Its application, however, raises prickly problems. Accurate and acceptable measurement of relevant price increases is not easy. Leads and lags become important; in Brazil, for example, real wages fell during a period of 50% inflation per year simply because the indexed adjustments lagged a couple of months behind actual price rises. By no means least important, a company's selling prices and hence ability to pay often does not rise as fast as living costs. Commitment in advance to match cost of living increases could (and has) forced companies to shut down. A popular compromise is to commit to matching costs of living increases only up to a maximum percentage per year; this is widely known as a "cap" on cost of living adjustments.

Internal alignment. Workers—from janitor to president—are also sensitive to how their pay compares with their fellow workers'. Because internal alignment is such an emotional issue, most companies have an explicit method for setting differentials in pay within the organization. Job evaluation to place jobs into standard pay grades, and a fixed relationship between grades, is the usual technique.

A serious drawback to such schemes for internal alignment is inevitable inflexibility in recognizing outstanding performance of specific individuals. Attention to equity—equity that can be proven objectively in this age of government regulation and union surveillance—tends to stifle recognition of individual merit. So in setting a policy of maintaining fair internal alignment, each company must also consider how it will reward its stars.

As with other policy issues, central management must attempt to find a compensation policy that gives positive support to company strategy. Just the opposite effect is all too common. The combination of trying to keep payscales in line with external rates, make some but not catastrophic adjustments for inflation, maintain acceptable internal alignment yet reward outstanding performance, observe government regulations regarding discrimination, maintain maximum permissible increases, and keep those fast-track MBA's happy—all becomes so complicated that compensation can be a hindrance rather than help in pushing for selected goals.

Supplemental Benefits

In today's labor market every company must offer supplemental benefits that are at least in line with general business practice. These benefits typically provide for (1) paid vacations and holidays; (2) protection against risks of illness, unemployment, premature death, and old age; (3) social and recreational activities. Incidentally, the cost of these benefits plus the company share of social security taxes often exceed 25% of an employee's base pay.

The basic policy question is whether merely to follow general practice as it develops or to take the lead in one or more of the various areas we noted above.

Sharing the costs of pioneering. The company that pioneers in liberal pensions, early retirement, or guaranteed annual wage may find itself at a competitive disadvantage because of high costs.

One policy is to have the employee share the cost of a new benefit. This has been done for medical insurance, pensions, and even recreational activities. In addition to cutting cost, an advantage of this arrangement is that most of us prize those things for which we have made some sacrifice. Thus, employees may appreciate major medical insurance more if they contribute to its cost.

Employee expectations. Not so long ago all regular employees expected to work at least half a day on Saturday. Now, an employee who doesn't get a 2-day weekend feels abused. The attitudes toward other supplemental benefits follow this same pattern. Consequently, if a company expects to generate strong employee enthusiasm because of its supplemental benefits, it must be prepared to keep adding new ones.

Also, what interests an employee shifts over time. The automobile and the television set have radically changed the social structure and the recreational patterns at the place of employment. Suburban living segments a person's life. Added purchasing power permits diversified and dispersed recreation. Living patterns diminish the feasibility of mutual family assistance. Government aid reduces the tradition of self-dependence. Because of such changes as these, a supplemental benefit that was heralded a generation ago may generate little excitement today. Consequently, leadership must be sensitive and imaginative.

Showing genuine concern. Mayo found in his famous Hawthorne studies that the employee's belief that the company was concerned about him or her as an individual was more important than the particular actions the company took. This insight suggests that supplemental benefits cannot be passed out with the assumption that the employees will be grateful. A policy of pioneering in this area must be accompanied by other demonstrations of genuine concern about the employee as an individual. Organization, personnel development, and supervision—discussed elsewhere in this book—are all part of the picture. In the proper combination they give synergistic effects.

Coordinating supplemental benefits with operations. For reasons just outlined, central management must carefully analyze the particular operations of its company when deciding what supplemental benefits to stress. Generally speaking, companies that want to hold their employees over long periods and have low turnover will probably find their employees more responsive to supplemental benefits. In contrast, companies that use many part-time employees or have wide fluctuations in employment, as in the space industry, are more likely to find their employees saying, "Put it in the pay envelope." Location in or outside a big city will also affect the social and recreational activities that are attractive to employees. The general age of employees is still another factor. In personnel, as in marketing or research, being a successful pioneer requires keen discernment.

INDUSTRIAL RELATIONS

For managers and employees to work together to accomplish the objectives of an enterprise, they must agree on wages, hours, and other conditions of employment. For many years these agreements were made primarily between managers and individual employees. Even today, over two-thirds of the employees in the United States bargain individually with their employers. However, there has been a dramatic rise in the power of labor unions, and the agreements reached with the unions set the pattern for many of the individual agreements.

Some people contend that the existence of a union makes the objective consideration of personnel policies futile. The assumption is that if management is not entirely free to make final decisions on such matters, the alternative is an irrational patchwork of agreements based on the bargaining surrounding each issue. Such a view is both unrealistic and unproductive. The manager designs products in terms of what customers will buy, sets prices on the basis of competition and within the limits permitted by law, and buys materials and borrows money under terms negotiated with the supplier. The views and the strength of the union will, of course, influence the personnel policy finally established, just as the operating situations influence other policies. But the fact that the decisions are not made by the manager alone does not remove the desirability of a workable, integrated plan of action. The need for unemotional, careful analysis remains unchanged.

Policies regarding the selection and the development of a work force, compensation, and supplemental benefits have already been discussed; consequently, attention here will concentrate on the way relations with unions are conducted. In this connection, a company should establish its policy regarding:

1. Character of union relations.
2. Scope of bargaining.
3. Recourse to outside agencies.

Character of Union Relations

A key aspect of all union relations is the underlying approach of a company to its relations with the union. The following examples illustrate the wide choice and the importance of this policy.

Belligerent policy towards unions. Companies engaged in interstate commerce are required by federal law to bargain with unions that represent a majority of their employees. Similar state laws require collective bargaining by most local businesses. Nevertheless, some employers balk at union activities whenever possible and do anything in their power to weaken the union.

Such a policy usually stems from a conviction that unions are antisocial. It may be supported by experiences with corrupt union officials, or communist-led unions, or unions that fail to live up to their contracts. Whatever the causes, there is strong dislike and mistrust of the union by the company executives. They try to conduct themselves so as to discredit the union in the eyes of the employees. They hope that sooner or later the employees will repudiate the union and it will no longer have to be recognized as the bargaining agent.

Obviously such a militant policy keeps the union stirred up; it will probably continue to use scurrilous tactics in its organization efforts. At best there will be only an armed truce between the two factions.

The horse-trading approach. Another view accepts the union as being inevitable but conducts relations along horse-trading lines. The union is assumed to be unreliable and conniving; consequently, negotiations are conducted in an air of suspicion and sharp bargains are quite in order. In keeping with this approach are deals that resolve immediate difficulties but that violate sound principles of human relations. As one advocate of this policy said, "It is just a question if you can outsmart the other guy."

Follow the leader. Often smaller companies try to establish an understanding with the union that the company will grant any wage increase or fringe benefits that have been agreed to by the leading companies of the industry, or sometimes in the local labor market. These firms feel that they are too small and weak to stand out against the union. The most they hope for is to be no worse off than their large competitors.

This is undoubtedly a practical policy in some circumstances. It does, of course, have the weaknesses of any policy of appeasement. Naturally, the union is going to ask for, and probably get, the most favorable clauses that are granted by any of the leading companies. Having won these points, the union leaders may ask for even more, particularly if they face political problems within the union and feel they must win further concessions to strengthen their own position. Moreover, one important way a small company competes with a large one is by making special adaptations to the local situation. The follow-the-leader policy sacrifices this potential strength insofar as industrial relations are concerned.

Straight business relationship. When both company executives and union leaders take a mature view of their relations, a company may approach union negotiations as a straight business proposition. This can occur only after union recognition has been accepted and the bitterness so often associated with such activities has passed into the background. There is mutual confidence, respect, and trust, just as there should be between the company and its major suppliers of raw materials.

This sort of business relationship does not mean that there will be no disagreements. The company may take a firm, even tough, position on certain matters; but the positions it takes are based on long-run business considerations, and there is a strong undercurrent of sound personnel relations.

Company executives must recognize that union leaders hold elected offices and that at times they must press grievances simply in response to pressure from some of their constituents. Under the straight business policy, this does not create a strong emotional reaction but is regarded simply as a normal part of the relationship. This type of relationship is often found in industries that have been organized for several years by a union which itself is stable and follows a bread-and-butter philosophy.

Union-management cooperation. Still another policy is to regard the union as an ally in improving the efficiency of the business. One of the best examples of union-management cooperation is the agreement developed over a generation ago between Hart, Schaffner & Marx and the union representing its factory employees. The union recognized that the company was in a highly competitive industry; consequently, it helped make improvements in labor productivity. On the other hand, the company acceded to demands for higher wages and better hours.

From the start there was emphasis on settling disputes by arbitration. The arbitrators have been highly respected individuals and always insist that questions regarding interpretation of an agreement be examined objectively. Even more important than wise administration of fixed agreements, however, are the methods developed to deal with technological and economic changes in new agreements. The actual operation of the plan has required a great deal of patience. Nevertheless, there is substantial evidence that employer and employees alike have benefited by the spirit of cooperation and tolerance created by working together under such circumstances.

Union-management cooperation has taken different forms in the steel industry and in other places where it has been tried. In some cases a sharp distinction has been made between cooperative activities at the plant and bargaining over a new contract. In other instances, as in some agreements in the hosiery and ladies' garment industries, plans for improving productivity have become part and parcel of the basic contracts. Whatever the form, the important point here is that the company followed a basic policy of union-management cooperation.

The foregoing illustrations, ranging from a belligerent policy to union-management cooperation, are among the more common policies followed in union relations. Of course, many other variations are possible. Until a company formulates some kind of policy on the character of its union relations and gets this policy thoroughly accepted through its executive ranks, there is little hope for consistent and really effective industrial relations.

Scope of Bargaining

Recognition of a union does not, of course, indicate what activities are to be covered in the union-management relationship. By tradition and law, questions of wages, hours, and physical working conditions are normal subjects of collective bargaining. More recently, employee pensions and similar benefits have been added to this standard list. Most companies would also agree that job assignments, the use of seniority or other factors in selecting employees for layoffs or promotions, and other supervisory activities were legitimate subjects for discussion, although they might firmly oppose any written agreement as to how these matters were to be handled. As soon as discussions extend beyond these traditional subjects, questions arise as to whether the union is interfering with "management prerogatives."

Employees clearly have a real stake in the stability of their company. Their income and their economic future are strongly influenced by the prosperity of the firm for which they work. If the union function is to protect the worker's interests, is it not reasonable then that the union should participate in decisions regarding pricing, new customers, product line, and similar matters?

This line of reasoning led unions in postwar Germany to insist on membership on boards of directors and other means of co-determination. With a few exceptions, American unions have shied away from such arrangements. Union leaders have recognized that if they participated in such decisions, they would share responsibility for them. By staying away from such matters, they avoid managerial responsibility and continue to be in a position to criticize (a significant weapon in union politics).

While neither union nor management leaders want unions to become involved in the entire managerial process, it is likely that an increasing number of topics will fall within the orbit of union-management relations. Unions can be helpful on such matters as absenteeism, productivity, and installation of new processes. They are concerned about changes in plant locations and mechanization.

Some firms follow a policy of keeping unions as far away from such matters as possible. In other cases, such as the union-management agreements on mechanization of hosiery mills and contracting in the garment industry, union contracts deal with what typically are regarded as management matters. A more common and more flexible policy is to restrict the formal collective bargaining process to conditions of employment and to work out other matters of mutual interest in a much more informal manner.

Recourse to Outside Agencies

Union-management relations are not confined to an individual company and the unions representing its employees. Other parties may enter the picture, and a company will do well to clarify its policy on recourse to outside agencies.

Impartial arbitration. Most union contracts provide for arbitration of disputes over the interpretation and the application of the contract. Typically, a dispute follows a grievance procedure moving up from the worker and the first-line supervisor through several administrative levels. If the matter cannot be settled by management and union representatives, an impartial arbitrator is called in to make a decision that becomes binding on all parties concerned.

Some such provision is necessary if strikes are to be avoided during the period of the contract. Where a single impartial arbitrator has been used over a period of years, a sort of "common law" develops. Once this common law becomes accepted, many potential disputes are settled without ever reaching the arbitrator. Many companies take the position that minor disagreements can be worked out best by the parties directly concerned and follow a policy of minimum use of outside arbitrators.

Group bargaining. The negotiation of a new labor contract is quite a different matter than its interpretation, which has just been discussed. The distinction is like that between the legislative and the judicial branches of the government. Usually the company itself works out the new agreement with its employees. To an increasing extent, however, employers are joining together in groups to negotiate new contracts with labor unions. Roughly a tenth of all contracts in effect are negotiated through employer groups, and these cover approximately a fourth of all workers under union agreements.

Industry-wide bargaining is used in a few industries, such as coal mining and glass. More often, group bargaining covers employers in a city or a region. A company might want to join such a group for several reasons. The executives in small firms lack the time typically consumed in negotiations. In many instances they are not as skilled in the process as the professional union representatives with whom they must deal. Even the larger companies that have full-time industrial relations staff may join an employer group in an effort to increase their bargaining strength. Moreover, the union has less opportunity to play one company against the other, pushing for different concessions with the several companies and then requesting everyone to agree to the most favorable concessions any competitor made.

On the other hand, such group bargaining makes it much more difficult to adapt the agreements to the particular situation of a given company. Also, at times the company may find itself being pushed into agreements that it would not make had it bargained alone. Consequently, companies whose industrial relations policy differs significantly from others in the industry, or whose economic position is distinctive, are often reluctant to participate in group bargaining.

Government mediation and arbitration. When a company and a union cannot agree upon a new contract and a strike threatens or actually begins, it is possible to call for assistance of a government *mediator*. This person explores the dispute and tries to find some basis on which the two sides may agree. The company will determine in part when a mediator should be called in and how effective the mediator is likely to be. Some companies believe that this type of mediation is very helpful, while others resent the intrusion of an outsider.

If the impending strike is of sufficient importance to the public interest, the company may face other forms of outside assistance. Public utilities and basic industries are subject to fact-finding boards and impartial commissions of various kinds, depending upon the state or federal laws under which they fall. In this country we have not yet adopted *compulsory arbitration* in which parties to such a disagreement have to submit the dispute to an arbitrator whose decision is binding. But government seizure and other forms of pressure bring us pretty close to that point.

Each dispute has its own unique problems, and a general policy governing the way a company will conduct itself in this type of negotiation is difficult to establish. Nevertheless, some companies very carefully steer away from government intervention, whereas other firms either are willing to submit to government decision or they permit themselves to be jockeyed into that kind of position. The reason why the general policy of resorting to government intervention has detrimental value is that the whole preliminary bargaining process tends to break down if it is assumed that the dispute will be carried to mediators, political bodies, and public opinion. Strong pressure for the negotiators to arrive at agreement is lacking if they feel that a final settlement will not be reached at their level. On the other hand, if the feeling is that some type of an agreement must be hammered out without recourse to outsiders, then local negotiations can be carried on in an atmosphere where results are likely to be achieved.

SUMMARY

The resource converter model of a company, sketched in Chapter 1, shows labor as one of the essential resources. If a company's strategy is to be carried out, personnel suited to that strategy must be available on a continuing basis. In this chapter we have looked at three broad issues involved in obtaining such an adequate flow.

Selecting and developing a workforce that fits company needs raises several questions. Policy is needed regarding the main sources to be tapped, the size of staff to be assembled, the way "equal opportunity" constraints will be dealt with, and the extent of reliance on promotion from within.

At the same time consideration must be given to how the company will attract and retain the personnel it desires. Fair compensation is vital. Here policy must deal with (a) an optimum alignment with what other companies are paying, (b) provision to keep up with inflation, and (c) reasonable internal alignment which also permits recognizing individual merit.

In addition to financial remuneration, every company must decide how far it wishes to go with supplemental benefits. Vacations, holidays, recreational activities, and a whole array of protections against economic risks such as sickness, old age, and unemployment should be appraised. Few companies dare lag behind general practice in such matters, so the major issue is in what ways a company wishes to be a leader in granting special benefits.

Finally, relations with unions must be considered. The underlying approach of a company, which may be anywhere from a militant policy to union-management cooperation, will permeate all union contracts. Within this general policy, more specific guidelines regarding support to existing union organizations, the scope of topics that will be discussed with the union, and the extent to which the company will join in group bargaining and use outside arbitrators need to be clarified.

Just as viable, continuing relationships with customers and suppliers are essential to a firm's existence; so, too, are its relations with its employees.

The ritual of collective bargaining in no way diminishes the value of objective analysis in formulating a pattern of relationships with employees that are suited to the mission and the technology selected by central management.

Having discussed policy issues in three areas vital to every business enterprise—marketing, production, and personnel—we turn in the next chapters to a fourth inherent dimension—finance.

 QUESTIONS FOR CLASS DISCUSSION

1. For years Northwest Airlines was one of the most profitable of U.S.-based airlines. It was also known for its hard-nosed bargaining with various unions and for its insistence on keeping flight crews to a minimum size. Passengers riding the airline's 747's have been known to call it "Northworst Airlines" when they were served by eight flight attendants rather than eleven or twelve (close to the industry standard). Extensive grievance reviews did not solve a substantial number of back-logged grievances. Executives regularly rode planes to check flight attendants' compliance with company rules and to keep hidden logs of "things the employees did wrong." These policies and practices led to Northwest's being among the least-liked airlines as well as among the most profitable. However, deregulation of the industry by the Civil Aeronautics Board has increased competition substantially in the territory served by Northwest and has also ended the mutual aid payments that strike-bound airlines received from their competitors. No more will Northwest be able to show a $62 million profit as it did one year with the help of $105 million in mutual aid payments it received during a strike by its pilots. To accommodate to these changes that resulted from deregulation, some central executives have proposed that Northwest change its attitude toward the unions and be more prone to compromise. One executive stated: "We can solve a great majority of the grievances by a more lenient attitude without changing the substance of our union contracts. We can increase the number of attendants on our flight crews. We can give bonuses—say $100 each—as have other airlines for handling heavy traffic during the United strike." One attendant commented: "I'm overworked and underpaid. After 16 years on this job, I'm hopeful but not encouraged." Should Northwest Airlines change its policy on the character of its union relations?

2. American State University wishes to increase the proportion of blacks and women in its law school, medical school, business school, and engineering school. Target quotas have been informally agreed upon. Several white students allege that they are being discriminated against in (1) admissions, and (2) financial aid, while the target quotas are in effect. (a) Do you believe such discrimination should be made? (b) How else can the targets be met?

3. For the following positions do you recommend a hiring policy giving preference to women, giving preference to men, or based solely on objective measurements: (a) Taxicab driver? (b) Hospital dietitian? (c) Coal mine superintendent? (d) Office secretary? (e) Army officer?

4. A manufacturer of stainless steel tubing plans to open a small plant in the Piedmont region of North Carolina. The new plant will concentrate solely on automated production of quality tubing for hypodermic needles. Thus the new plant will avoid problems of frequent shifts in sizes and materials that occur in the main plant. Should the selection and training policies of the new plant differ from those of the main plant? If so, in what respects?

5. Most large book publishers have moved their main offices to the suburbs. Here the primary functions are editorial, warehousing, bookkeeping, and sales promotion (typesetting, printing, and binding are almost always subcontracted). Most publishers hoped to tap a new labor supply in the suburbs—mostly women living within easy commuting distance. They now find that many potential employees are second wage earners in the household and want only part-time jobs, often with irregular hours. How do you suggest the publisher utilize this potential resource? What are the implications of using such personnel on the way the business is run?

6. In selecting an employer after you graduate, will you give preference to a firm that has a strong policy of promotion from within? Explain your answer.

7. The regional manager of a franchised chain of Pancake Shops (fast-food restaurants) says her only personnel problem is finding good owner-managers and training them to train their workers. "Each shop is an independent enterprise. It has its own employees (15 to 30 people, since we are open 24 hours a day, 7 days a week, and use some part-time help), and sets its own pay. The turnover is fairly high, and we have no unions. It would be a mistake for us to try to develop personnel policies, because one of the advantages of a franchise system is to let local managers run their business in a personal way like all the early business enterprises in this country did." (a) Do you agree with this viewpoint? (b) Is this a good example of the advantages of a small business with respect to personnel and industrial relations?

8. Several large companies recruit business school graduates (both four-year graduates and MBA's) as potential candidates for key jobs. Starting salaries are high, often equal to those of good employees with ten years of experience occupying second-level supervisory positions. (a) What problems will such salaries create for the company? (b) What problems will such salaries create for the newly hired business graduate? (c) What should companies do to utilize these young people most effectively?

9. "Business firms and other employers should get out of the welfare game. Let the U.S. government follow the lead of other Western nations and finance more and more of health care, old-age benefits, and the like. Business can't compete in playing Santa Claus. Instead, it should put all it can in the pay envelope. And inflation will provide an opportunity to withdraw gracefully. By freezing existing dollar commitments, the percentage cost

will drop as prices and wage levels rise. Any increase in compensation can then go into immediate pay, which employees will need very much to cover rising living costs." (a) Do you think this proposal is wise policy for a company to follow? (b) Does the proposal make more sense for some types of companies than others? Explain.

10. Should unions as representatives of employees have more, or less, participation in company discussions regarding expansion, product lines, mechanization, location, and vertical integration than representatives of (a) customers, (b) major suppliers of materials, (c) government, (d) bondholders, and (e) stockholders?

11. (a) Home and Business Finance Corporation has had a steady growth of about 5% per year for the past twenty years, when measured in real sales volume or real dollars of profit. "This underlying growth has meant both happiness and problems for the company," said a personnel director. "Much of it has come about because we have been buying out smaller firms that were family-owned or that were financially troubled and were turn-around situations for us. We have had to absorb family members and some executives in ways that have caused trouble with our middle-level managers. Outsiders have been brought in for positions that blocked promotion chances for insiders and many insiders have had to move to new (for them) regions and cities if they wanted promotions. Surprisingly enough, many did not want to move. Either their spouses had good jobs and would not change locations or their children were at the wrong age to move. One thing we are thinking of doing is to introduce a package of perquisites— company-paid life insurance; health, hospital, and dental care programs for the entire family; executive dining privileges; company cars and personal financial counseling. These perquisites are perfectly legal and would cost the company at most $5,000 in after-tax income but the executive would have to generate at least $20,000 in pre-tax earnings to duplicate what is provided in the company's package. A middle-level executive earning $50,-000 a year might be induced to move by this package when he or she would not be enticed by a 20% salary increase, all of which would go right out in taxes. What do you think?

(b) "Also, a group of the middle-managers has been promoting the idea that we retain an executive recruiting firm to assist in out-placing some executives and in finding others for the turn-around situations. Their point is that our promotion-from-within policy will be made meaningful at last if the acquired family members can be well placed elsewhere and those few insiders who might want to look elsewhere be given help so that channels can be freed for promotion of loyal, long-term employees.

"We have approached a couple of executive recruiting firms informally and one has given us an idea. It is to promote line managers from the inside and bring in outsiders to fill staff functions. Attorneys, human resources vice presidents, public relations executives, and computer science managers have a particular expertise that cannot be developed quickly through training. They have transferable skills. Would this be a way to clean up some of our troubles?"

CASE 12
Stornford Corporation

The present policies of Stornford Corporation as to types of workers hired, skills sought, wage rates and pay methods, and character of relations with its union (United Automobile, Aerospace and Agricultural Implement Workers of America, U.A.W.) are a consequence of changes in company strategy over a period of years.

These policies are continuing issues. Recent events have led to a focus on three technical matters in the union agreement—cross-equating of jobs,[1] pattern-bargaining,[2] and supplemental unemployment benefits (S.U.B.'s).[3] Actually these three problems are directly related to the company's diversification moves.

History

The company began, in 1926 in Evansville, Indiana, as the Stornford Machine Tool Company. The domain first sought was a line of metal-cutting equipment (including lathes, grinders, and milling machines) sold to the metal-working and manufacturing industries.

Sales and profit results of the 1930's persuaded Stornford executives to change company strategy by diversification. The first new domain sought was oil burner pumps to be sold to makers of residential heating equipment. An early attempt to sell these pumps was not successful because Stornford did not have the marketing capability to sell 400,000 to 500,000 pumps annually, a volume necessary for an adequate level of unit cost.

This led the company to set up a separate division to make and sell products other than machine tools. In this way, the organization was reshaped to follow through on the diversification strategy. The division, the "Air Comfort Group," grew through acquisitions until it now makes and sells compressors, coils, water circulator pumps, and other items for both home and automotive air-conditioners as well as the oil burner pumps.

---

[1]"Cross-equated jobs"—those jobs which are in different divisions of the company but which have work content so similar that an employee should be able to move from one to the other and perform effectively without additional training.

[2]"Pattern-bargaining"—a practice, by a union, of attempting to impose on one company, or one industry, the contractual agreement reached with another company or industry; for example, using the contract reached with the automobile firms in Detroit as the contract to be reached in bargaining with machine-tool manufacturers in different cities and states.

[3]"Supplemental unemployment benefits"—money paid to out-of-work union members which is an addition to (an extra above) the money these members receive for a number of weeks from the state and federal governments as unemployment compensation.

The old machine tool operation also grew through acquisition and internal development. Much of the machine tool activity is now focused on Power Transmissions and Fluid Handling equipment. Another major segment is now spun off as the Aerospace Group which makes basic equipment for commercial aircraft and for many military planes and missiles.

Recent activities by major business segments are shown in the following table.

Stornford Corporation
Financial Results by Major Segments
(in millions)

Net Sales

	Aerospace	Air Comfort	Machine Tools Power Transmissions & Fluid Handling	Total Corporation
1970	137	56	95	287
1972	123	68	113	304
1974	190	71	195	456
1976	229	91	275	595
1978	266	139	326	732

Operating Profit

	Aerospace	Air Comfort	Machine Tools Power Transmissions & Fluid Handling	Interest and Corporate Expense	Corporation Profit before Tax
1970*	24	7	16	−30	17
1972*	23	5	18	−37	9
1974	25	−1	29	−25	28
1976	28	−3	40	−14	51
1978	40	6	52	−21	77

*R&D and some other expenses not allocated to business segments in these years.

Current financial ratios for corporation: sales to assets: 1.17; current assets to current liabilities: 2.51; long-term debt to stockholders' equity: 1.14; net profit to equity: .126.

Labor Relations

Stornford employs approximately 13,800 persons, 12,500 in the U.S. Of these domestic employees, approximately 2,500 employees are covered by collective bargaining agreements. All of the agreements have been renegotiated without a work-stoppage of any kind, with the exception of the May 15, 1977 agreement which followed an 11-week strike. Recently, two of its four agreements were negotiated six months in advance of their normal expiration dates.

Production

Labor skills and attitudes toward the work to be done varies among the production shops. For example, manufacturing machine tools requires years of experience by employees to understand the complex designs. It also depends upon skilled assemblers to carry out instructions which are, at times, nebulous. Three or perhaps four items are the maximum made of any one type of machine.

Pump manufacturing, in contrast, requires dependable production at a high rate of output with close attention to minimizing costs.

Parts and subassemblies made for airplane and aerospace customers are designed to save space and weight, the most important purchasing criteria. Also of major importance is a record of meeting promised delivery dates without fail. For these customers price comes in third.

Equating Jobs and S.U.B.'s

This practice of attempting to find jobs in the various divisions of the company which are equal in their characteristics (skill necessary, experience required, pay, attitude toward what is important on the job, and the like) came about as the union reacted to Stornford's policy of diversification.

When Stornford added heating pumps (a high-volume, low-cost item) and airplane parts and subassemblies (a job-shop) to the machine tool line (capital goods with wide cyclical fluctuations and accordion-like results for the labor force and for the use of equipment), the machine tool makers' union continued to represent all employees despite the differences in work caused by the diversification strategy. This seemed to be the easiest policy to carry out at the time since the new items were, to some extent, a development within the machine tool company.

Difficulties arose when union negotiators brought the idea of cross-equating jobs to the bargaining table. Their notion was that a skilled assembler of machine tools was equivalent to a skilled assembler of heating pumps and their claim was that the machining accuracy required was about the same for pumps and machine tools.

Each time the contracts for the persons in the bargaining unit in the three different plants in Indiana came up for renegotiation, the union bargained harder for the cross-equating of jobs. The aim of the union negotiators appears to be to stabilize the total workforce and especially to save jobs for the senior workers.

When machine tools were moved to a different plant in Boonville, the management asked the union to establish another local and to take a part of the cross-equation out of this plant. Negotiations over these changes were expensive because more money and more assurances on job retention were asked for by the union. At this point, the idea of supplemental unemployment benefits was brought over from the automobile industry. The company pays about fourteen cents per hour worked into a separate fund.

Point of View: Vice-President for Personnel & Public Relations

The vice-president states: "I am not one who believes that unions are all bad. That is not to say that unions are needed by all employees everywhere, nor to say that union leadership of today is always interested in the legitimate interests of employees as opposed to their own political interests. I think 'pattern-bargaining' is a good example of this latter point . . . it is virtually impossible to get an international representative of the U.A.W. to deviate from the Detroit pattern . . . 'I got the pattern' is a satisfactory answer to the boss and . . . defensible . . . to the local membership.

"From an employee viewpoint, our basic employee relations goal is to create, to the highest degree possible, jobs for all employees which are rewarding . . . and which will give the employees a degree of job security. . . .

". . . comment on . . . the equating of jobs . . . we have to consider seriously the desire of employees who want to continue practicing the skill they have acquired and who want to stay with a company with which they have invested a number of years of their life. We accept these desires as being very natural, in spite of the operational problems that fulfillment of those desires creates. In a 'loose' labor market, when needed people are readily available, there is no question that the equating of jobs, and the resultant bumping rights of employees, causes many extra personnel moves and, therefore, additional costs.

"On the other hand, in a tight labor market, where skilled people are scarce, we would rather bump our skilled class A people across divisional lines to keep them with the company. . . .

"Also, the U.A.W. is very dedicated to 'pattern-bargaining' insofar as economic terms are concerned. . . . In the auto industry people with many years of service found themselves without a job for approximately 4–6 weeks each year merely because of the need to prepare the factory for the new models. No such annual temporary layoffs were part of Stornford's history, but . . . we had to accept the concept of S.U.B. . . . Our (S.U.B.) benefits to short-service employees dried up the fund by the time long-service employees were laid off. Likewise, none of our operations have the repetition and boredom of an auto assembly line, which was the rationale used for '30 and out' pensions. Yet we are asked to agree to that Detroit concept. . . ."

Point of View: Production and Operations Managers

In summary, these views are: "With seniority rules and equating jobs, we often have five bumps before a person is laid off, whenever we have a slowdown in production. . . . With re-hires, we have five bids for re-opened jobs. . . ."

"The union leaders don't know the work in detail of many of the skilled jobs in the various divisions. So it is difficult to negotiate with them sensibly over equating jobs."

"We have had a few strikes in the past—and long ones over important provisions of the agreement. But I don't think that we can afford one now. Machine tool profits may be well down, but my division does a lot of subcontracting in the airplane and aerospace businesses. Those sales depend upon meeting target dates."

"Some vice-presidents want us to look at cross-equating as a fact of life. The facts that stare me in the face are the extra costs."

"When will we start to negotiate differently for each division with the union? This is the big question. We need an answer."

"We either have to decide to live with pattern-bargaining and cross-equating or to take a big, long strike and get rid of one or both."

Financial Point of View

Stornford Corporation has had two strikes in the last ten years. In the year of the first strike, sales declined by $37 million and profits dropped by $4 million from the year before. In the year of the second strike, sales increased by $73 million and profits went up to $5 million over the year before.

In the long run, costs must come down. Stornford faces strong and continual competition from both U.S. based and foreign manufacturers. Imports of general industrial machinery, which grew over 10% per year in the latter 1970's, are still growing but at a slower pace due to troubled business conditions in the U.S.

The industries in which Stornford competes are generally thought of by analysts as "stars" (see text, page 353) since real growth rates for machine tools, aircraft and parts, and guided missiles and parts are predicted to be three times or more greater than the U.S. manufacturing average over the next five years. So foreign competitors are working hard to increase their market share.

Questions

(1) What are the advantages and disadvantages to Stornford Corporation of negotiating with the union to halt cross-equating of jobs between divisions? to get away from pattern-bargaining?

(2) How did cross-equating arise? Why is it troublesome to some executives?

(3) What are the advantages and disadvantages to the union members and also to the union's officers and international representatives of cross-equating jobs? of pattern-bargaining?

(4) What would you recommend to the company?

INTEGRATING CASES

Strategy and the Creating of Goods and Services

DOVER APPAREL COMPANY

"The apparel industry is a critical source of jobs in the United States, over a million of them," explains an industry representative. "Traditionally staffed by poor immigrants, today many garment workers are women and minorities. They are on the borderline; for most of them, if they lose their jobs unemployment and welfare are their only alternatives.

"In fact, the industry has already lost about 200,000 jobs —from a peak of 1,400,000 in 1973—because of foreign imports, and the trend will continue unless steps are taken to stop it. Apparel imports mean more unemployment. The country can't stand more unemployment. So from an economic, as well as a humanitarian, view imports should be reduced."

The issue expressed in the above quotation is only one of the factors Dover Apparel Company must weigh in deciding whether to go abroad for expanded production capacity.

Need for Expansion

Dover Apparel Company is a successful producer of children's clothing, especially girls' dresses. Under the leadership of Irving Perlman, son of the founder, Dover has become a recognized leader in higher-quality girls' dresses and related outer garments. Its Princess line is regularly carried by better stores throughout the country. Styling is good; also, stores have learned to depend consistently on high quality products, and on dependable deliveries. In a volatile industry, this kind of dependability is a basis for repeat business.

Dover's reputation is no accident. Twenty-five years ago, Irving Perlman (now 58) convinced his father to shift emphasis from women's to girls' dresses, and they were fortunate in hiring a very good designer. Irving then switched his attention to production. Hoping to get a relative cost advantage, a new plant was opened close to Atlanta, Georgia. And as the relative sales of girls' dresses grew, the Georgia plant was expanded. Production in New York City was completely stopped by Dover in the early '70's.

Actually, the expected low southern labor costs were not obtained. To ward off unionization, Dover kept its wage rates and benefits almost equal to those in New York City. And to maintain quality and assure delivery, Dover employed technical staff and bought new equipment. Within the last few years the company went even further into "modernization." It has invested over $1 million in recently devised electronic pattern-making equipment and electronic cutting equipment. This equipment greatly speeds up the making of patterns for various sizes of a basic design; it speeds up and probably improves the laying out of the patterns on stacks of cloth so as to reduce waste; and the actual cutting is also faster and more precise. Only large and financially strong manufacturers can afford such equipment.

In addition, Dover has fully computerized its production scheduling and inventory control. While adding to overhead, this computer set-up aids in stabilizing the sewing operations and it is especially valuable in helping the company meet its delivery promises.

As a result of these and related moves, Dover is on the leading edge of production technology. But its costs are not low. Assuming good volume, it can match New York City costs for comparable quality. However, other southern shops which keep overhead and labor rates low, can produce for 5% less.

Last year, profits were just over 2% of sales. On $51 million sales net profits were $1.1 million. The condensed balance sheet at year-end was (000's omitted):

Cash	$ 1,350	Accounts payable	$ 6,040
Accounts receivable	6,580	Other current liabilities	1,100
Inventories	7,260	Long-term debt	3,040
Fixed assets (net)	3,090	Equity	8,100
Total assets	$18,280		$18,280

A third generation Perlman, Joseph (age 32), is being groomed for management and he is spearheading an expansion. Dover does not now sell knit slacks, knit skirts, shorts, or sportswear. Joe has convinced his father that this is a natural expansion of the present line. Although such products are often sold at low, highly competitive prices, the Perlmans believe that well-styled, color-coordinated numbers could be a good complement to their Princess line—and might be extended to boys' wear. Even when treated as a supplement to the Princess line, knitwear sales could add 10% to 20% to total sales. And the potential knitwear market is much larger than the niche Dover now serves.

The main difficulty with this expansion is production costs. Typical children's knit clothing does not have clear quality differentiation. Production is simpler than for dresses. So low-cost products provide keen competition. Foreign competition is especially severe. More than one-third of children's knitwear clothing is imported, chiefly from Korea, Taiwan, and Hong Kong. Although Dover hopes to sell its knitwear at premium prices (because of styling and company reputation for quality, etc.) a wide margin above prevailing prices would severely limit the volume of sales. Success of the new line requires, among other things, production costs which are no higher than costs which other dependable suppliers will have in the future.

Sourcing Options

Joe Perlman has explored alternative locations for the production of the proposed knitwear products. He summarizes his present thinking as follows.

1. U.S. production. "Wherever we go we want to take advantage of our modern pattern-making equipment and our computerized production scheduling and inventory control. We're ahead of our competitors and must reap the benefit of the investment we have made. There is ample capacity in these operations.

"On the other hand, we are short of space in sewing. Besides, sewing knit goods takes different machines and somewhat different skills. So we do not plan to sew the new products in the present plant.

"The simplest arrangement, especially when the volume is still small, is to subcontract sewing of all knitwear and do everything else in the present plant. Or, if we found the right subcontractor, he could also finish and pack. We have subcontracted girls' coats with good results, and there are even more shops looking for knit goods contracts.

"An alternative is to set up a separate knit goods plant of our own. It's just a question of where to send the cut pieces for sewing and finishing.

"The obvious trouble with either subcontracting in the U.S. or opening our own shop here is high labor costs. Labor rates in developing countries are a fifth to a tenth of what we pay. In the U.S., labor is about 30% of total costs, so foreign producers may have a 25% overall f.o.b. cost advantage. Of course, there is freight, tariff, and time to consider. Nevertheless, for as long as we can see, smart foreign competitors will be able to sell in U.S. markets with lower costs than we will have if we manufacture domestically."

2. Latin American production. "How about subcontracting in Latin America instead of in the U.S.? Incidentally, we have reluctantly dropped Puerto Rico from consideration because their cost advantage is narrowing. If we go into a non-English speaking country, we might as well go where the labor differential probably will continue to be substantial.

"The political climate in most Central and South American countries is not attractive for new investment. Governments are unstable, inflation is causing unrest, socialism if not communism is becoming common, and Yankee business is a popular target for nationalistic politicians. I think Colombia has one of the least troublesome situations right now, and that country seems interested in more textile business.

"We have been advised that using a local subcontractor in Colombia would involve much less political risk than setting up our own subsidiary. But that raises other problems. The prospective subcontractors we have contacted so far do not have a long record of dependable, quality work. And if the one we selected got into difficulties, we would be in a poor position to step in to help. We hesitate to be so dependent for a supply of products which we are just launching into the market."

3. Far Eastern production. "Of course, most apparel imports come from the Far East. Japan is no longer competitive; its labor rates have risen so that it is importing products like knitwear much as the U.S. is doing. And the costs in Hong Kong—long an apparel center—are beginning to rise. Taiwan and Korea are now the major sources of low-cost products imported into this country. In the U.S., we can't come even close to their costs.

"Frankly, I'm leery of both Taiwan and Korea on political grounds. Both countries need strong U.S. support to prevent a communist takeover. As we build closer ties with China, our commitment to these buffer-states could diminish.

"There is an interesting alternative. Sri Lanka (formerly Ceylon) has unused capacity and is highly interested in establishing new foreign markets. This island, about the size of West Virginia, lies to the southeast of India. Known for centuries as a source of tea, spices, gems, and rubber, industrialization has passed it by. Its 16 million population has a very low average income, and because much food is imported, the country often has an unfavorable balance of trade.

"A study by the World Bank recommended establishing a textile industry, and the Bank advanced funds for training and for equipment. Apparel cut and sewn in Sri Lanka soon flooded the European markets. However, at just this time an 'orderly marketing agreement' was negotiated (under GATT auspices) which sets quotas for textile imports into Western Europe. These quotas are based on historical trade and sharply restricted permissible imports from newcomers like Sri Lanka. As a result, textile plants which started with high hopes and grew rapidly for two or three years now are closed or cut way back.

"Dover Apparel Company could easily form a joint venture with a Sri Lanka mill. I know of two enterprises eager to join with us, and the government is encouraging such a scheme. We could lease existing plants and equipment (though additional machines would be needed for our specific requirements), and have low taxes. Probably $200,000 is all we would have to invest in the joint venture.

"Air freight makes production in a country on the opposite side of the world possible. Only three or four days, either way, are necessary for transportation. We might cut cloth here in the U.S. and ship pieces out for sewing—as mentioned for Colombia. The import duty on such work applies only to the value added abroad. More likely, however, we would purchase fabric on the world market (possibly in the U.S.) and have it both cut and sewn in Sri Lanka. They have facilities for cutting and would use the patterns we supply.

"Wages of three dollars a day look attractive to many Sri Lankan workers. In fact, that additional cash income can raise an entire family out of poverty. However, a direct comparison with U.S. rates of four dollars an hour is not warranted because of differences in the social structure and in productivity. Most Sri Lankans are Buddhists, and I understand they have even more holidays than we do! Nevertheless, at present exchange rates, preliminary estimates do indicate that after paying freight and import duties garments made in Sri Lanka would cost us 15% to 20% less than comparable products made entirely in the U.S. Estimates for sewing in Colombia show a 10% saving.

"The government of Sri Lanka, formed with a new constitution in 1972, is still developing its traditions and institutions. However, the country was ruled by Great Britain from 1796 (as a self-governing dominion of the Commonwealth from 1948). English is commonly spoken, and it should be as easy for Yankees to do business there as in India. As governments of developing nations go, Sri Lanka's is reasonably stable.

"Incidentally, the U.S. government has negotiated some bilateral 'orderly marketing agreements' for textiles with Korea, Taiwan, Hong Kong—like those restricting imports into Europe. However, Sri Lanka has been such a minor source of textile imports into the U.S. there is currently no prospect of quota restrictions between these two countries."

Other Views

Dover's production vice president is skeptical about foreign production. "I have to admit that I can't get costs down to match foreign competition. But I'm afraid we are heading for trouble. We have to work hard to keep on schedule with good quality right here in our own plant. How can Joe or anyone else do that thousands of miles away?

"Even more serious is what may happen to our labor relations. Our workers aren't dumb. They know that importing means fewer jobs here in the U.S. When Dover starts importing even knit garments, some workers will start thinking that their jobs might come next. And that's the kind of issue which labor organizers can exploit—no matter how much we deny it. I'm sure we could learn to live with the ILGWU, but we would have had a rough time installing our new pattern-making and cutting equipment if each move had to be negotiated with a union. We have good relations now. Is it wise to rock the boat?"

Irving Perlman is more venturesome. "When I came into the business my father gave me a chance to try something new. And it succeeded. Now I've told Joe that he should develop a way that we can live with foreign competition. He will have to make whatever plan we adopt work—even if that means spending months abroad every year. We now have many more dollars at stake than I did, but it is much the same. Now, as then, the company might be ruined or it can position itself to be strong for the next couple of decades."

Questions

(1) What is Dover Apparel Company's social responsibility in this situation?

(2) Assuming that Dover does add knitwear to its line, what procurement policy should it follow? If you wish, consider variations or additions to the alternatives discussed in the case.

(3) On the basis of the information that you have and your answers to questions (1) and (2), do you recommend that Dover add knitwear to its line?

WARDWELL VINYL COATINGS, INC. (R)

Wardwell Vinyl Coatings, Inc., of Charleston, West Virginia, designs and makes vinyl-coated fabrics for the automobile, luggage, shoe, and furniture industries. Wardwell's fabrics cover interior panels of the Ford Thunderbird and the Cadillac Seville, and they grace Knoll Associates' line of Saarinen-designed chairs.

Wardwell Vinyl Coatings is directed by Beckley Wardwell, the president, who started in the firm as a salesperson on house accounts. Even though his duties in the organization have since changed, Beckley has continued to sell to some customers; in fact, at present he still does all the sales work with the two largest customers whose purchases are now $2,950,000 annually. Under Beckley Wardwell's supervision, the company's sales have grown and profits are at such an all-time high that he is thinking about a political career. With some satisfaction, he contemplates reducing his operating responsibilities, changing his position to chair of the board of directors, and beginning an effort toward a higher post in the state legislature. Occasionally Mr. Wardwell muses: "If Winthrop, Nelson, and Jay Rockefeller can be state governors, why not a Wardwell?"

The family-owned firm has competed successfully for years in the fabric coating industry with subsidiaries of B.F. Goodrich and the other major rubber companies, with divisions of General Motors and Ford Motor Company, with departments of E.I. du Pont de Nemours, Monsanto, Eastman Kodak, and Dow Chemical Company, and with a host of smaller competitors.

Within the past month, the firm has received a proposal from a European company that is a chance to broaden and diversify Wardwell's product lines.

Marketing

Harleton Rowe, the sales manager, came to Charleston four years ago after a fifteen-year career as salesperson and product manager with eight garment manufacturers and textile producers. His first move was to add a person who specialized in sales to the furniture industry. Earlier, Wardwell Vinyl Coatings, Inc. had sold only through manufacturer's representatives whose total compensation was an 8% commission.

Half of the manufacturer's representatives have now been replaced by six company salespersons who specialize by industry. They are guaranteed an annual draw of $30,000 and are then paid by commission at an increasing rate when their sales exceed $1,000,000 annually up to a maximum rate of 8%.

Beckley Wardwell approved the changes in sales representatives and their compensation as being consonant with his belief in putting great trust in his senior managers and in allowing them all the responsibility they are willing to take. Harleton Rowe had come highly recommended by some old family friends of the Wardwells who were associated with the J.P. Stevens Company.

Mr. Rowe commented that he attempted to give some direction to the selling effort. "In the past, for the most part, we took any order that came along. We did well because of the quality of our products. I don't reject orders that come in, of course, but I believe that it is also possible to define certain industry groups that will naturally want to buy what a small firm like this can best sell—fast delivery, a short order cycle, design help, and a quality product. It did not take any particular marketing skill to figure this out, just a look at those customers whose buying characteristics and buying decision-making fitted our demonstrated skills.

"I did this on my own. Beckley Wardwell does not question what you are doing and lets you alone so long as you keep him informed. On any scheduling problems with new orders I talk directly with him. Leon Torbit, the plant manager, listens to Beckley but runs around the factory so much that I have found it difficult to reach him, let alone work out a decision with him."

Products of the vinyl resin coated fabric industry are upholstery for vehicles, coverings for luggage, engine, and equipment covers, baby carriages, casings for typewriters, yard goods sold by mail-order houses and department stores, shoe materials, furniture upholstery materials, shower curtains, wall coverings, surgical tape, ribbons, and other applications. Major producers in the industry include rubber and chemical companies that specialize in organic and polymer chemistry and a large number of smaller producers who purchase their resin in bulk from a major supplier and concentrate their efforts on the production process of coating fabrics at the lowest possible cost.

Buyers want their color, finish, and durability needs met carefully. Successful selling depends also on preconsultation with designers about the various fabrics needed in the customer's line. Frequently a Wardwell salesperson works for several days, at various intervals, with a customer's designer. A supplier is also expected to furnish samples rapidly—even of new materials—when new items are being considered for a customer's line.

Automobile manufacturers and the consumer divisions of the rubber companies, which do not necessarily buy from producing divisions of the same firm, generally place large orders. Furniture, shoe, and luggage manufacturers tend to place small orders and to repeat them frequently if sales of the item for which the coated fabric is used catch on. A customer's pressure for a low price is related to the number of yards of coated fabric bought and to the ultimate price line at which the product— be it baby carriages or washable wall covering—is offered to the great consuming public.

Harleton Rowe said that Wardwell succeeds by marketing a high-quality product to a large number of customers who desire fast and accurate service. Individual orders are often small, but they are repeated eight to ten times a year.

Manufacturing

Wardwell coats the cloth it purchases from textile producers with a resinous liquid. The mixture can be sprayed on, as is common practice in the industry, but Wardwell uses a calendering process to control the amount of liquid applied, its spread-rate, and its penetration.

Fabric is bleached, stretched, and then run between calenders (large steel rollers) to dry it and smooth it before coating. Vinyl resin, in combination with color pigments and solvents, is applied on the coating machine as the cloth is pulled through to a drying oven at the end of the coater. Coated cloth is later finished by stamping or by rolling it on embossing machines to impart a grain, a raised surface (such as pigskin texture), or any other finish desired. Until recently, each of these three processes—bleaching and smoothing, coating, and then finishing—has been done in batches on separate pieces of equipment.

Coating is the crucial production department. Resin ingredients are prepared and applied under closely controlled conditions. Tensile strength of the resin has to be related closely to the speed of coating machines. Both temperature and the concentration of chemicals have to be held within exact tolerances. Stains left by the rollers or rips in the fabric cause spoilage losses or reduce fabric quality. Close attention by the plant workers to the fabric belt as it is calendered and rolled is required for a satisfactory product.

The process is dangerous to unskilled or careless employees. Machinery is heavy and runs at high speeds. Chemical odors are strong and cannot all be removed in the present building even by the best of ventilating and solvent extraction processes. While the equipment is kept in the best of repair, the rest of the plant is old and facilities are rundown.

Worker turnover is high. Experienced workers can be hired from the glass factories or the chemical plants near the city. When absolutely necessary, new workers are taken on from the large pool of migrants from the hill country and are trained at some cost in lost productivity or rapid turnover.

Last year a Teamster's Union local was voted in to replace an AFL craft union. After one month, the company settled a strike for higher wages for 85% of the union's demand.

Leon Torbit, the plant manager, rose through the ranks. He knows the process and the equipment and he demands careful attention to plant activities by his supervisors who spend most of their time closely overseeing production runs to minimize spoilage and waste. Leon Torbit also spends at least half of his time touring the plant, checking on the status of individual orders and questioning various machine operators. He knows most of the two hundred plant employees by sight, but few by name. Hiring, firing, and discipline are entirely the responsibility of the various supervisors—subject to negotiation on some disciplinary matters with union stewards.

Chemical Research and Development

Chemical research and development is directed by John Minton who earned an advanced degree in organic chemistry years ago and has since followed the old tradition of experimentation. He has six assistants with university training in chemistry, but they basically "engineer" his suggestions. Professional conflicts arise occasionally because John diverges in some instances from currently accepted laboratory and analysis techniques, but his methods are often quite ingenious. Chemical research at Wardwell is really "mixing and brewing" and relies but little on modern quantitative polymer theory. John Minton firmly believes in using "art" and experience in his formulations. However, if manufacturing difficulties arise, he will modify his processes, and he constantly checks the application of his new product ideas to make sure they work out in the plant.

The present vinyl resin resulted from "rational" trial and error that converged on the successful mixture. Knowing the desired properties of the finished compound and the characteristics of the component chemicals, John Minton exhausted many combinations of reactants, allowing for fine differences among different brands of the same product. The result is Wardwell's vinyl resin which has advantages over its competitors' products. The coating is less likely to crack, has better tensile strength, absorbs dye more easily, and can be applied at lower temperatures. It is a quality product demanded for more expensive applications, yet its production cost is not much higher than that of common vinyls.

John Minton has also adapted other processes to vinyl manufacturing. For example, the dyeing process used at Wardwell came from an industrial magazine article about coloring fabrics in the garment industry.

John has over thirty years of experience in working with vinyl and finding a replacement for him will be difficult, but nevertheless he plans to retire within the next year. "I'll be seventy years old soon, and threescore and ten is enough for anyone." Any replacement as director would probably be accustomed to using more sophisticated equipment; new methods might be incompatible with the existing staff of technical people, who must then be retrained. The greatest incompatibility to a modern researcher would be the responsibility for watching after the production process: any new person may be surprised with the autonomy given in order to perform the development activities.

Engineering

Process development, that is, the improvement of equipment used in manufacturing, is carried on by Spencer Wardwell, the president's cousin and a mechanical engineer trained at California Institute of Technology. Spencer joined the company to carry out some recommendations by his consulting firm. He devotes his time to machine design, to some outside consulting work, and to a complete factory redesign now in process. The goal of this change is a factory that will produce fewer defects while utilizing much less labor.

On Spencer's recommendation, a wall was knocked out and the factory floor space was extended by about a third. The result was a longer, more efficient linear series of rollers that made each run easier to mount, process, and finish. This improvement was beneficial since Wardwell depends on a manufacturing process that has little down-time and that can handle orders in a very short time. Increases in roller speed have reduced the crucial turnaround time, but on the very oldest equipment, they have also led to increased defects as tension overcomes the fabric's tensile strength. Workers cannot follow the process at very high speeds. Even at lower rates a marred roller that leaves a mark with each revolution is difficult to detect. Now a pilot model of a new coating machine is under test to prove out its design characteristics of a 50% reduction in labor hours and a 10% increase in fabric output. Discretionary settings have been reduced substantially, mechanical handling has been substituted for manual, and tension controlling devices have been added to reduce tearing.

Engineers seldom stay with the company more than three years. As one said, "I learned a great deal from Spencer about both mechanical engineering and consulting and put up with him to get this knowledge. In a weak moment he once told me that company policy was to kick the worker when he didn't produce and to reward him as little as possible when he did. Of course, that was only Spencer's idea of it. I don't know how Torbit carries out company policy."

Spencer Wardwell said: "We have efficient competitors. Although their manufacturing cost is, as a percent of sales, about the same as ours, their average length of run is 48,000 yards, while ours is more like 12,000. The number of items they carry in inventory is one-fourth our number. But dollar totals are about the same. If we used their methods we could drop our manufacturing cost to 55 percent of sales. Then we could really afford to drop our prices somewhat, undercut them, and shoot up the volume. This would give us a hefty return on the new equipment we need.

"For a near term investment of $12,000,000 over two and one-half years, I calculate that we can cut our labor force by 30 percent and thus reduce our labor cost by

$1,400,000 annually. After that, another investment of $3,000,000 per year for five years will eventually allow us to cut our labor force to 50 percent of what it is now and save another $800,000 per year. This is investment in machinery only—the only kind we really need.

"We need to do this because the Teamsters are now really at our throat. The last contract we signed jumped wage costs 25 percent over two years. They are surely going to ask for more next time. The only way to fight them is to get them out of the plant.

"Our policy should be to triple the length of each run, cut the setup and changeover time by two-thirds, reduce the number of employees and pay them enough so that they won't quit to work at Union Carbide. Just give me seven years and twenty-five million dollars."

General Management

Beckley Wardwell believes in getting expert outside advice. One consulting firm recommended the recent plant expansion. Another firm recommended increased coordination among the managerial group and attempts at cooperation through dinner meetings and general discussion. Dinners were held for awhile and then discontinued when Spencer Wardwell had to be out of town. Meetings led by Leon Torbit for the plant supervisors were discontinued when the bleaching, coating, and finishing supervisors argued at length over technical matters.

Beckley Wardwell spends 20% of his time with two customers and, at times, assists individual salespersons with difficult relationships with other customers or accompanies them on visits to celebrate unusually large orders. But the balance of his work is mainly on financial matters. He analyzes cash balances and cash flows each day with the treasurer. He looks at actual and predicted budget comparisons for previous and succeeding months. He, the treasurer, and the purchasing agent check the investment in inventory each month—both in total dollars and by reviewing summary tally sheets prepared from the detailed records.

With the purchasing agent, Roy Ascoli, Beckley Wardwell reviews individual purchase orders amounting to more than $2,000 and analyzes alternative sources of supply for new items. Beckley Wardwell says: "Clay Weston, the treasurer, and Ascoli are perfectly competent executives. They can perform all the duties asked of them, and do careful work. I spend time with them to keep myself informed. I need the data to press for increased revenues and decreased costs. In my view, a chief executive's major role is to establish the rate of return on investment and the rate of sales growth that he wants and then to push continuously for these. Secondly, I need it to keep the family happy.

"Spencer Wardwell is the only family member in the firm. I was lucky to attract him away from his full-time consulting business with the help of a special stock option arrangement. No one member or one branch of the family has a controlling stock interest, but they all have a personal interest. One or two of them are in the investment business and are convinced they know as much about coated fabrics as anyone else. A few of the others I would call professional Monday morning quarterbacks; this is not something I have not told them directly.

"While a few nephews, cousins, uncles, and aunts have asked for jobs here, I have refused to hire them—except for Spencer. I can't see that they would be any more competent than the people we already have, and none of them seems to want to start in the coating room.

"Judge our managerial methods by our results. Sales are now $45,000,000 a year, whereas they were $9,000,000 ten years ago. Our manufacturing cost is 65% of sales —4 percentage points lower over the same period. We now spend 7% rather than 9% of sales on our total marketing effort. Research and engineering cost us 9% of sales. That compares well with any of the big chemical companies. After taxes, we net out 9% of sales, which is even better than General Motors. A dividend payout ratio of 60% takes better than adequate care of the three branches of the family.

"Look at our balance sheet (Exhibit 1) and I think you will have to agree that I can begin to satisfy all those impulses I have had toward politics in recent years. I'll give up my sales work and that will free up a lot of time. Harleton Rowe can handle all our marketing effort. School board membership, chairman of local welfare organizations, and two terms in the state legislature has not been enough. I've traveled this state—and the country—widely over the past two decades, and have gotten to know a fair number of people. I think I can contribute politically."

Exhibit 1
Wardwell Vinyl Coatings, Inc.
Current Balance Sheet
(In Thousands of Dollars)

Cash	$ 4,800	Accounts Payable	$ 2,500
Receivables, Net	7,500	Accruals	2,000
Inventory	7,200	Long-Term Debt*	2,000
Marketable Securities	4,000	Common Stock and Retained	
		Earnings	27,500
Plant and Equipment, Net	10,500		
Total Assets	$34,000	Total Liabilities & Equity	$34,000

*Debt due in equal amounts over a five-year period. Current amount carried as an accrued item.

New Opportunity

A month ago Harleton Rowe learned that a European manufacturer was looking for U.S. firms to produce and sell a poromeric leather that the European manufacturer has developed and introduced successfully in some regions of the European Common Market. Beckley Wardwell in his characteristic manner encouraged Harleton Rowe to "follow up on any idea that looks promising."

The following information has been assembled by Harleton Rowe, and he now feels ready to report back to Beckley Wardwell.

The European manufacturer is seeking two U.S. licensees for its product. To date, this artificial leather has been used primarily for shoe uppers and to a lesser extent for lightweight shoe innersoles. It can be given the appearance of any kind of leather; it is more durable, and it has some of the same "breathing" characteristics of leather.

Poromeric leather (of which du Pont's Corfam was the first sold on any scale in the U.S.) is not an animal product but a synthetic leather made by coating a non-woven substrate with either a polyurethane or vinyl finish. In the case of Corfam, the substrate had three layers, including one of a woven polyester. When sales did not reach the expected volume, du Pont sold its process and remaining inventory to a Polish company.

The proposal by the Common Market firm is that each licensee should manufacture the substrate (one layer of nonwoven material) and coat it with polyurethane in its own plants and then sell the product primarily to shoe manufacturers, using a specialized salesforce. The European company wants the U.S. affiliate to carry out the entire process for both quality control and process security reasons.

The European developer seeks two U.S. licensees because a tariff of $.12 per pound plus 15% ad valorem effectively rules out at present exports to the U.S. from Western European and Eastern European manufacturers. European technology is widely thought to be 2 to 3 years ahead of U.S. technology in its development stage. The European firm expects to continue its development work and would keep U.S. licensees fully advised of any process and product advances as a part of the licensing agreement. The license fee would average about 1% of net sales.

Current U.S. efforts to manufacture an acceptable leather substitute have failed on the three desirable properties of the substrate (strength, absorbability, breathability). The European firm claims that it has exported one million square yards of its substrate to U.S. coating firms and has had good acceptance from them. Preliminary checks by Harleton Rowe with three of his present competitors (the coating firms) have substantiated this claim.

Several market studies by the European manufacturer indicate the information shown in Exhibit 2.

The market study was carried out using an assumed U.S. price of $23.50 per square yard as contrasted with the shoe upper leather price of $47.50 per square yard.

Exhibit 2
U.S. Sales and Potential Sales of Leather
and Leather Substitutes for Shoe Uppers
and Innersoles
(millions of square yards)

Product	Current year	5 years hence	10 years hence
Leather shoe uppers	75	58	35
Non-leather shoe uppers	5	20	35
Leather shoe innersoles	75	n.a.	n.a.
Non-leather shoe innersoles	1	15	20

Harleton Rowe is enthusiastic about seeking a license. His arguments are: (a) the firm would have an early entry into a rapidly expanding market and thus could capture a major market share; (b) the proposed selling price makes the synthetic leather highly competitive; (c) neither du Pont nor Monsanto Chemical is now interested in the product (du Pont's plant for making Corfam had been built to produce 100 million square yards annually, but its total sales in two years were only 35 million square yards); and (d) the proposed product would have only two layers and thus would tend to stretch and adapt itself to the wearer's foot, whereas Corfam did not.

In a short conversation Rowe had with Spencer Wardwell about the proposal, Spencer Wardwell said, "It's not worth serious attention. I'm having enough difficulty getting money for the new plant, so why bother with something in addition? We don't have the extra $20,000,000 for the initial poromeric leather investment."

Clay Weston said, "Well, we can probably finance the investment by borrowing since, based on preliminary figures, it promises a rate of return close to what we are now earning. But what is the risk? What will the competition be? Will sales of our present products be affected? If sales turn out to be half the amount predicted, will the fixed overhead bankrupt the rest of the company, since the pattern of costs of this venture will be about average for the industry?"

Questions

(1) What has been Wardwell Vinyl's strategy in the vinyl-coating business? Has it been successful? Explain.

(2) Do you recommend that the offer of the poromeric leather license be accepted? Explain. What changes will be necessary for Wardwell if it takes up the license? Explain.

(3) Do you agree with Spencer Wardwell's idea to further automate the plant? Explain.

(4) Would you recommend to Beckley Wardwell that he now pursue the path he has indicated for his political ambitions? Explain.

(5) Assume that your father was a cousin of Beckley Wardwell; he recently died and left you 8% of the common stock in Wardwell Vinyl Coatings, Inc. Prior to this event you had not taken any special interest in the company.

Beckley Wardwell invited you, as a new stockholder, to look over the company. "Naturally, I'd be glad to have any suggestions for improvement. Don't give me a laundry list. As you will discover, we are making changes and improvements all the time—as the profit record shows. Just tell me what you would focus on if you were a member of the board of directors." Your investigation revealed the information in the written case.

FINANCIAL POLICY—
ALLOCATING CAPITAL

Need for Capital

Capital, like personnel, is an essential resource for every enterprise. Equipment must be obtained, materials purchased, employees paid, sales and administrative expenses met—all before goods are available for sale. Then a month or more may elapse before customers pay for purchases. Even a law firm selling only services will incur payroll expenses and have accounts receivable. Capital fills the gap between the time outlays are made and revenues flow back in.

In formulating policy regarding uses and sources of capital, *cash flows* require primary attention. Capital already invested in fixed assets or debts already incurred become active when they affect the inflow or the outflow of cash. Occasionally direct exchanges are made of, say, company stock for land, but these are exceptional shortcuts. Most pressing problems relate to (a) getting capital in the form of cash and (b) allocating cash (liquid capital) to the most propitious uses.[1]

In this chapter we discuss central management's guidance of capital allocation for fixed assets and current assets, the use of cash for dividends, and the related issue of calculation of profits. Then the obtaining of new capital is examined in the following chapter.

---

[1] Remember that accounting profit or loss does not refer to cash. A profitable company may be short of cash when expanding sales call for additional inventory and accounts receivable; likewise it is quite possible for a losing company to liquidate assets (turn them into cash) at a faster rate than losses occur and thereby increase its cash position. Of course, profits should sooner or later generate cash; the question for financial management is when this cash will be available and whether the flow is large enough to meet cash requirements.

Relation of Strategy to Capital Allocation

In a sense, financial policy concerning the use of capital does not stipulate the *specific* uses of capital; these are determined by other management decisions. Plans for sales—such as products to be sold, sales appeals to be stressed, plans for production and purchasing, decisions to "make" rather than "buy," heavy use of automation, and other comparable plans—dictate the uses of capital. Nevertheless, capital plays an essential supporting, facilitating role.

Strategy lays out the positive direction a company will take. Executives throughout the company then create plans for carrying out their respective parts of strategy. And from these plans come specific requests for capital and other resources. Specific allocations of capital can be made only after the creative planning process has generated alternative proposals.

In a well-managed company, however, planning is not done in isolated bits. Instead, tentative ideas are passed back and forth among departments, alternatives are suggested, rough estimates are provided, and objections are raised while plans are still being formed. A vital part of this give-and-take process is checking on the availability of capital and other resources that each alternative would need. And as we have already seen, often a resource —people, plant capacity, vendors' cooperation, capital—can be provided only if certain conditions are met. Bargaining and trade-offs occur. Eventually out of this discussion specific requests for capital emerge.

Financial considerations enter into this planning process in two highly important ways: (1) Financial policies are set that provide guidelines in advance on how capital may or may not be used and how recurring needs will typically be met. The availability of such guidelines expedites the planning process described in the previous paragraph. (2) Targets for financial results are one dimension of company strategy (see pages 103–105). These targets and subgoals derived from them serve as standards to evaluate various proposals.

REGULATING INVESTMENT IN FIXED ASSETS

General Restrictions

In every active enterprise, from landscape gardening to generating electricity, all sorts of proposals are made for additions to facilities. Executives concerned with a particular operation naturally think of new equipment that would enable them to do their job better or at lower operating expense. One way to regulate such proposals is to set forth general areas where investment will or will not be made, or criteria that must be met.

Consistency with long-range plans. Company strategy often stipulates the markets to be sought or the production technology to be used. Such aspects of strategy can be translated into more specific policy guides.

A paper company with a mill in northern United States, for example, became concerned about the increasing costs of its pulpwood. Careful study showed that on many of the types of paper it was making, southern mills using southern pine enjoyed a cost advantage. While shifting to specialty papers was a possibility, the company concluded that the best strategy was to move closer to large raw material sources.

Consequently, a policy of making no major investment in fixed assets in its northern mill was adopted. Only the purchase of miscellaneous equipment necessary to operate existing machines would be permitted, and installation of new machines or substantial expenditures on the existing building would be postponed at least until the outlook for a northern mill improved.

Another firm adopted a similar policy because the probable shift in demand for its product would make its present plant somewhat obsolete. If new processes had to be adopted, then the firm wanted to move into a new building in a suburban location. In the meantime it chose to keep itself in a flexible position and made only essential investments in fixed assets.

A policy that places definite limits on the use of capital for fixed assets must be administered with discretion. A change in technology may necessitate installing new equipment if a company is to continue to compete in a particular industry. If the concern wishes to render distinctive service to its customers, investments in fixed assets may be essential. Nevertheless, investment policies should be disregarded only in unusual circumstances.

"Hurdle" rate of return. The policy just illustrated stipulates a type of fixed asset to be avoided or encouraged. A different kind of investment guide is a minimum rate of return that must be anticipated if capital is to be assigned to a proposal. For example, the policy might be that any new investment in fixed assets must earn at least 15% annually on the initial investment after provision for depreciation and taxes. Then, a proposal to buy an accounting machine costing $10,000 that was expected to result in an average net saving of $1,200 per year during its life would be rejected because the 12% return falls below the acceptable minimum.

For such a policy to be useful, the method of calculating the rate of return should be defined. Depreciation, taxes, interest, net investment, and several other items can be treated in different ways. So, to avoid ambiguity, the policy should indicate the formula that was assumed when the minimum was set.[2]

---

[2]For most situations the estimated rate of return in a typical year or average year is as precise as the underlying data warrant. However, for proposals involving long time periods in which the cash outflows and cash inflows will occur at sharply different and irregular dates, the estimated rate of return should be made by the discounted cash flow method.

Theoretically, the minimum permissible rate of return should be the average cost of capital to the company (a weighted average of the company's long-term borrowing rate and the price/earnings ratio of the company's common stock). In practice, desire for expansion, willingness to sell more stock, funds already available, judgment about future risks, and similar considerations affect management's choice of the minimum rate. Since most executives who propose new investment in fixed assets tend to be optimistic in predicting the benefit of the action, central management of many companies counter by setting the "hurdle" rate higher than the theoretical minimum.

Risk classifications. Many investments are so risky that they should have an expected return higher than the basic hurdle rate. Uncertainty surrounds every investment. The activity made possible by the investment may not work as predicted; workers may like the change or they may sabotage it; materials and energy inputs may cost more than expected or be unavailable; customers' tastes may shift; competitors may react vigorously; pollution controls may be more severe than predicted. Since one investment often is subject to many more such uncertainties than another investment, we cannot compare them without making an adjustment for differences in risk.

One way to deal with differences in risk is to place proposals into classifications reflecting the odds for success. The following table is a simple example:

Risk class	Extra discount factor for risk	Representative investment
High risk	0.2 or more	Exploratory oil well
Medium risk	0.5	R&D development of disposable oil can
Low risk	0.8	Expansion of frozen food display cases
Minimum risk	1.0	Replacement of 40-year old elevators

A company can either set a minimum acceptable return for each risk class, or the predicted result of an investment can be multiplied by the appropriate discount factor to obtain an "expected return." If the classification and the discount factor are accurate, the "expected returns" for all investments have been adjusted for risk and can be compared with one another.

In theory, discounting for risk can be greatly elaborated. A whole array of possible outcomes with probabilities for each can be projected. Successive contingencies can be recognized in a "decision-tree" computation. Risk discounts can be combined with time (interest) discounts. Rarely in practice do the underlying data warrant actual computations of this sort, but the concepts may help clarify the degree of risk involved. More significant and subtle is the absorption of risk by people making various estimates. Central managers should know how much allowance for risk their subordinates have already made in the figures submitted before they do their own classifying or discounting.

The simplest way to use risk classifications is to establish a hurdle rate for investments in each class—say, 15% for minimum risk investments and 30% for medium risk investments. The "expected return" computations give synthetic figures which are best suited to capital budgeting.

Capital Budgeting

Frequently, a company has many more possible investments in fixed assets than it can prudently finance. The issue then becomes which projects to endorse and which to reject. *Capital budgeting* is a method for making this selection.

First, all major proposals for additions to fixed assets are described and analyzed and predictions are made of the amount of the investment and the resulting benefits of each proposal. Obviously, this analysis and prediction must be carefully done because the soundness of all subsequent steps can be no better than the data fed into the process. The whole task will be simplified by promptly screening out all proposals not consistent with marketing, production, purchasing, and personnel policies and with the general investment policy just discussed.

Next, the predicted investment and results of each proposal should be expressed in dollars insofar as possible. The figures that are pertinent are *additional outlays* the company will make if the project is undertaken and *additional receipts* (or reduced expenditures) that will result from the project. (If outlays are widely separated in time from receipts, they can be made comparable by reducing each to its "present value.") Intangibles should also be recognized, both intangible costs and intangible benefits; for example, flexibility or strategic advantage of entering a new market. These intangibles must be listed because the budgeting process deals only with dollar figures and time; it tends to de-emphasize intangibles and strategic considerations.[3]

---

[3]Theoretically the dollar estimates can include contributions to strategic moves or detractions from them. In practice, these broader effects are difficult to estimate (and may not be fully understood by people making the specific proposal), so they are normally treated as "intangibles."

The scope of each proposal determines which intangible factors should be weighed. If the proposal deals only with, say, replacing autos used by sales representatives, we disregard many intangibles because all alternatives assume the same people doing the same work. However, if closing a branch or dropping a product line is at issue then many questions about employee morale, competitors' reaction, and the like must be included. (continued on page 295)

Then, proposals should be ranked, with those showing the highest rate of return to outlay at the top and those with the lowest return at the bottom.

Finally, management can proceed down the ranked projects until (a) the capital available is exhausted, assuming overriding reasons exist for keeping the total within a fixed amount, or (b) the rate of return falls below the minimum acceptable rate. Before projects below the cutoff point are completely rejected, intangible benefits should be appraised to decide whether the added advantages are important enough to move a project up into the acceptable list. Similarly, intangible cost of projects above the cutoff point should be assessed with an eye for projects that might be dropped.

Investment Mix

Every firm makes some high-risk investments and some low-risk investments. The proportions, however, among high-, medium-, and low-risk commitments can vary a lot. Just as the "marketing mix" (see Chapter 8) used by a company should be adapted to its strategy, so also should the "investment mix." All high-risk investments make a company too unstable; all minimum risk forces liquidation. A healthy arrangement is some mixture, like a healthy human diet provides a mixture of nutrients and energy.

Risk profile of a small firm.   Alain Ribout, the owner-manager of a successful motel in the Laurentian mountain region of Canada, faces several attractive propositions: enlarge and improve his present kitchen and parking facilities, add a large wing to his present building, build a new motel 30 miles away at the site of a proposed new ski lift, and invest in the new ski lift. Both the uncertainty and the potential rate of return rise in the order in which the four alternatives are listed.

Selection of any one investment will affect Ribout's interest in making the other investments. For instance, commitments to both the new motel and the ski lift, Ribout feels, would be risking too much on the success of one development. Likewise, if he embarks on a new wing expansion, he hesitates to also be starting a second motel. But he does want to share in the growth of the area. So to keep his overall risk exposure in balance, Ribout is now inclined to make two moves: (1) ensure continuation of his present success by improving the kitchen and parking, and (2) take a high risk by investing in the ski lift.

Note that the rate of return based on incremental results and incremental investment differs from the overall average. For instance, assuming we stay in business, the incremental value of a telephone vs. no telephone will be very high. One of the major reasons for prior screening of capital proposals against strategy criteria, suggested above, is to clarify the assumptions and to narrow down the factors to be weighed for a particular proposal.

A Missouri farmer, to cite another case, is being encouraged by a poultry processor to double his capacity to raise broilers from chicks. This would involve a $100,000 investment in highly mechanized facilities, which could be recovered in four to five years *if* the demand for broilers continues to grow. The farmer actually spends most of his time raising corn, but with present equipment this is not profitable. A shift to large-scale mechanized methods for raising corn would require changing fences and fields and buying at least $85,000 of new equipment. An alternative is to use the fields for grazing beef cattle and to take a job that will provide cash income for current expenses. Since the family can easily muster the small additional labor to care for the expanded broiler activity, the farmer could handle both the broiler and the new corn venture. But he hesitates to take both risks at once. He prefers a choice between (1) the new corn operation plus present broiler activity or (2) expanded broiler activity plus cattle grazing and cash income from an outside job.

A mixture of high-risk and low-risk investments with an eye on dependable cash flow is needed in both of these examples. Since a choice of any one alternative modifies the attractiveness of the others, a policy dealing with the total mix is desirable.

The concept of investment mix has application beyond the particular examples for small and large firms just cited. Single-product firms face questions of acquiring raw material sources or mechanization: an art museum must select the kinds of art and the kinds of services it will provide, and even universities venture forth in some directions and hold back in others. The investment policy on such matters is midway between broad strategic directions and specific projects. It identifies, for all persons involved, areas where investments will be encouraged and other areas where investments will rarely be made. Clearly, the investment mix approach is less mechanistic and more sophisticated than capital budgeting.

An additional risk arises from investment intensity. Data on many businesses analyzed by the Strategic Planning Institute show clearly that heavy investment in mechanization and in inventory and accounts receivable tend to reduce profitability. More capital tied up per dollar of sales increases the risk of low profits. (See the following chart.) The risk is especially great for companies with low market shares.

Summarizing. Policy guiding the use of capital in fixed assets takes several forms. First, we set up general restrictions that screen out many proposals. These restrictions often state the kind of activity that will, or will not, be supported—based on company strategy. Also, hurdle rates-of-return, perhaps refined for different risk classifications, narrow the projects that receive serious consideration. Then, to select among remaining proposals we can either employ capital budgeting or seek a balanced mixture of high- and low-risk ventures.

AS INVESTMENT RELATIVE TO SALES RISES PROFITABILITY DECLINES

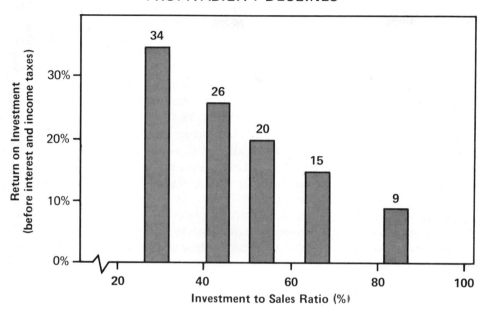

Source: Strategic Planning Institute.
"Investment" is fixed assets at book value plus working capital. The sharp drop in profitability is largely due to two very different reasons: (a) arithmetic—investment intensity enlarges the denominator of ROI; (b) intensity of competition—high investments and fixed costs produce anxiousness to obtain sales.

Leasing Versus Purchase of Fixed Assets

Analysis of investment proposals may reveal more attractive opportunities than can be absorbed by a company's normal financial structure. When this occurs, long-term leasing instead of buying the fixed assets should be considered.

Of course, reasons other than financing may make leasing attractive. The outlook may be so uncertain that owning your own building is imprudent, or prospects of rapid expansion and relocation may suggest flexibility in asset commitments. However, in the present discussion we are concerned with leasing as a way of reducing the need for tying up capital in fixed assets. Here is the way it works. An investor, perhaps an estate or an insurance company, with funds for long-term investment buys a building we want to use and at the same time leases it to us for a long period. The rental payments are high enough to cover real estate taxes, depreciation, and repairs, as well as interest on the capital tied up. Note that these are all expenses we would have to pay if we owned the building.

If the asset to be leased has to be constructed for our own peculiar requirements, we may actually build and equip the structure and then *sell and lease back.* Also, we may have an option to buy the asset when the lease expires, 10 or 20 years hence, at a depreciated value. Both these provisions make leasing even more like owning. The investor, in turn, is in much the same position as a mortgage holder as the investor relies on our contract for interest and the return of the investment. (In some circumstances, the investor may be able to postpone paying income tax.)

A few companies have a *policy* to lease rather than to buy certain types of assets. For example, oil companies and retail chain stores may regularly use such an arrangement for their many retail outlets. Most firms resort to leasing only occasionally for some large asset. Whatever the frequency, the operating cost and the tax implication should be carefully studied because a long-term lease obligation is just as binding as mortgage or debenture bond obligations even though it does not so appear on typical financial statements.

Since a long-term lease creates a continuing financial burden in many respects comparable to owning fixed assets, it must not be used promiscuously. The general policy of a company regarding its investment in fixed assets and capital budgeting comparisons of alternative uses of company resources should normally apply to property leased for a long term as well as property that is purchased.

POLICY RESTRAINTS ON CURRENT ASSETS

Operating Needs for Inventory

The size and the composition of inventory should be determined primarily by operating needs. As explained in Chapter 11, the following factors should be considered: minimum inventory necessary for uninterrupted operations, economical size of purchase orders and of production runs, production for inventory to stabilize employment, advance purchases to get seasonal discounts, and anticipation of price changes and shortages of supply. Inventory policy blending all these considerations is one of the main issues in wise procurement. Financial limitations are a different and additional constraint.

Budgetary Limits on Inventory

Inventory absorbs capital. The cash spent for finished goods, work in process, and raw materials is not available for other uses as long as these stocks remain on hand. Consequently, financial policy dealing with the allocation of capital to competing uses frequently places an overall limit on the size of inventories.

A common way to limit inventory is to budget the total size month by month. Each time the budget is revised, the use of capital for inventory is weighed against other needs. This establishes a mechanism for seeking the optimum use of capital throughout the company. Of course, since inventory serves as a buffer between purchasing, production, and sales, the actual inventory may deviate from the budgeted amount, but the guide to desired inventory levels is clear.

Budgetary control of inventories is particularly well suited to companies that have wide seasonal fluctuations. In the automobile industry, for example, cutting-back of production and disposing of inventory of one model while scheduling startup on production of next year's model is a tactical problem of considerable significance. Similarly, the buildup and disposition of Christmas merchandise and agricultural supplies calls for short-run adjustments.

Policy on Inventory Turnover

A second way to limit inventory is in terms of turnover ratios. Thus, a retail shop may aim for an inventory in relation to sales of 25%, or 4 turns per year. The turnover standard creates pressure to dispose of slow-moving, obsolete stock; accumulation of such stock is likely to lead to future losses. Moreover, high inventory relative to sales increases the company's exposure to price fluctuations. And, since inventory turnover is frequently used by outside credit analysts, a company's credit standing can be improved by fast inventory turnover in relation to industry averages.

For internal administration, separate turnover ratios for raw materials and for finished goods, perhaps broken down by type of product, are more useful than a total composite figure. Often the turnover will be stated in terms of months of supply to avoid arguments about values to be used. A primary purpose of this kind of policy is to induce inventory managers to decide what kind of stock is worth holding and to clean out past mistakes.

Note that as inventory policy becomes more specific, it shifts from a general financial guide to an operating control. This fuzzy dividing line between finance and operations is characteristic of many financial issues and unless adroitly handled becomes a source of jurisdictional dispute.

Investment in Accounts Receivable

Central management's concern with accounts receivable is similar to inventory. First, the company credit policy should aid the execution of strategy. This means that liberalness in granting credit to customers and in making collections should be consistent with stress placed on credit as a sales appeal. Defining the function (service) that it is to perform is primary. Second, budgetary limits may then be set for the total capital allocated to accounts receivable. These limits will arise from the capital-allocating process and will reflect a balancing of alternative uses of capital. And third, turnover ratios can be set to check the soundness of accounts and to avoid future losses from an accumulation of uncollectible accounts. As with inventory, even more detailed constraints, such as "aging" the accounts receivable (that is, listing those 30 days overdue, 60 days overdue, etc.), move from general financial limitations into operations. The basic task of central management in the area of accounts receivable, then, is to set policy regarding (1) purpose, (2) allocation of capital among competing uses, and (3) maintenance of the quality of the asset.

A special issue is the *use of outside financial institutions*—banks, credit companies, and factors—to provide customer credit. Outside firms will be glad to extend installment credit because this is profitable business by itself. For help in carrying regular commercial accounts receivable, the company must pay a fee, the size of the fee depending on who makes the credit investigation, who collects the accounts when due, and who bears the risk of bad accounts. The basic question that central management must resolve is whether to reduce capital needs for accounts receivable by turning to outside firms. The answer hinges on two factors: (1) How important to the company is close customer contact and integration of credit with other services provided to the customer? (2) How does the cost of outside service (the fee paid or the installment profit foregone) compare with income that can be earned by using the capital saved for other purposes?

CALCULATION OF PROFITS

Allocating capital among fixed and current assets, the problem we have just been discussing, is part of a broader task of guiding the flow of capital in, around, and out of the company. Clearly the allocation of cash for dividends is another part, and we explore that question at the end of this chapter. Before doing so, we need to look at a subtle issue that bears on dividends and a whole array of financial matters—policy affecting the calculation of profit.

Management has significant discretion in how profit is calculated. And, more than protection against unwarranted dividends is at stake. Income taxes, reputation in the financial community and hence ability to raise new capital, perhaps executive bonuses—all are affected by this calculation. The three main areas where policy guidance is needed on this matter in a going concern are:

1. Accounting reserves.
2. Capitalization of disbursements.
3. Inventory valuation.

Accounting Reserves

The extent to which accounting reserves are set up may affect company profits significantly. The issue is what expenses to anticipate in accounting reserves and what decline in asset value to show in such reserves.

Expenses that involve an immediate outlay of cash or those for which there is written evidence, such as a bill from a vendor of raw materials, are easily recognized. On the other hand, expenses that require no immediate outlay of cash but that must be met eventually are subject to greater error or manipulation. Depreciation of equipment and buildings, provision for uncollectible accounts, and anticipated expenses such as unassessed taxes or contingent losses are examples of this latter type. Often the amount of the expense is not known accurately, and opinion as to how much should be charged against the operations of a particular year may differ.

The customary way of handling such items is to make a reasonable estimate of the amount to be charged against operations each year, and then to include this figure along with other expenses as a deduction from gross income in the calculation of net profit. At the same time a so-called "reserve" is set up on the accounting books in anticipation of the time when the cash payment or the discarding of assets will take place. It should be remembered that this reserve is not a special cash fund put aside to meet an anticipated cash payment. Such an account does, however, perform an important function in preventing the overstatement of profits.

A conservative policy is to create large reserves even though this cuts stated earnings. Conversely, a company wanting to show immediate profits may build accounting reserves slowly. For example, a steel company may depreciate equipment that will not wear out with 20 years of continuous use at the rate of 10% a year because improved methods of operation will probably make this equipment obsolete in 10 years' time. In contrast, a large resort hotel depreciated its equipment at an average rate that would have taken 50 years to cover the original cost, even though this hotel catered to high-class customers who expected up-to-date service and modern equipment.

Capitalization of Disbursements

A similar issue arises in the treatment of product development expenses and improvements of fixed assets. Here the cash has been paid out, but the question is whether to treat the disbursement as an expense in the current year, and thereby reduce profits, or to *capitalize* it.

The treatment of patents illustrates the problem. If a company buys a patent, it clearly has an asset the cost of which should be charged as an expense, not all at once, but year-by-year during the life of the patent. But when a patent comes out of the company's research laboratory, the situation is not so clear. How much research cost should be attached to that patent, treated as an asset, and written off year-by-year? The more cost that is capitalized as an asset, the higher the profits in the current year.

Likewise, when a wooden floor in the plant is replaced with a concrete one, should the cost be treated as a repair expense or should at least part of the outlay be shown as an asset? Disbursements for intangibles like training or advertising a new product are regularly treated as expenses, but what of the cost of an elaborate demonstration motel built for a World's Fair though to be used for several additional years?

Inventory Valuation

Still another fuzzy area in the computation of profits is valuing inventory. Judgment has to be exercised in deciding what is obsolete, damaged beyond its point of usefulness, or missing an essential bearing. Value depends on future demand as well as on physical condition of the inventory; but future need in the company for repair parts, or demand by customers, often is uncertain. Someone has to say that a specific item is still a good asset or that it should be written off (or down). Here, again, the higher the value attached to inventory carried as an asset, the higher the current profit.

Inflation adds further questions on inventory valuation. If inflation causes a specific item to rise in value while it is held in inventory, the company can sell that item at attractive nominal profit. But the cost of replacing the item has also risen; so much or all of the nominal profit is used up just getting the physical inventory back to the starting size. Real profits have been overstated in such a situation. One way to reduce such a misleading statement of profits is to compute costs on a LIFO (last-in-first-out) basis. Here the price of the most recently purchased item (during inflation this will be the highest priced item) is used to compute profits; the remaining inventory is valued at the earlier and lower prices. Thus the use of LIFO helps to cut down overstating of profits during inflation, but inventory will probably be undervalued in terms of current price levels.

Many companies now use LIFO, and then report in a footnote on their balance sheets how much their inventories are undervalued in terms of current prices.

Policy Issues in Profit Determination

Limitations surround the size of reserves, the capitalization of costs, and the valuation of inventories. The public accounting profession has devoted much effort to establishing "acceptable practice" in these and related areas. Federal tax regulations of what may be treated as an expense on income tax returns (and hence not taxed) are comprehensive and complex. Securities and Exchange Commission stipulations stress full disclosure in annual financial reports. Nevertheless, a substantial latitude for management action in these areas remains.

Central management does not, of course, deal with the numerous specific entries involved in profit computation. Instead, it should set general policy indicating the degree of conservatism to be followed throughout the company. When room for judgment is present, should it be resolved in favor of low value of assets, large reserves, and, to the extent that these entries are acceptable to the Internal Revenue Service, low taxes? Or will the policy be to show as high a profit as is legitimate within the area of judgment?

A related policy issue is *when* guides for profit computation should be changed. If a given method for computing profits is followed consistently year after year, the effect of the method chosen tends to balance out. Profits postponed from last year show up this year and largely offset this year's potential profits that have been deferred until next year. However, if a conservative policy is followed one year and then a liberal policy the next, the effect on results reported for any one year can be much greater. Consequently, many prudently run companies stress *consistency* fully as much as the particular valuation methods employed. Other companies have a policy to postpone and *minimize income taxes* in any legitimate way, including a shift in treatment of matters of judgment if such should be propitious.

Like so many other policy problems we have examined, calculation of profits is interrelated with several aspects of central management. Protection of capital calls for conservative estimation of profits; but income taxes, executive incentives, and ease in raising new capital also should be considered. In addition to these explicit factors, the policy should reflect the kind of company envisaged in its strategy. A risk-taking, fast-growth, volatile firm needs a public image quite different from a dependable, steady-growth, stable enterprise.

DISTRIBUTION OF EARNINGS

Net profits of a company after income taxes belong to the stockholders. This does not mean that stockholders will receive a cash dividend equal to their share of the profits, because the board of directors may decide that part or all of the profits should be kept in the company. Policy regarding the disposition of profits varies widely.

Plowing Back Profits

A very common practice in American business is to use profits as a source of additional capital. Profitable enterprises typically are growing concerns, and additional capital is required to finance this expansion. Rather than distribute profits in the form of dividends and then seek new capital from other sources, many managements believe that it is wiser to use their earnings to meet this need.

One prominent company manufacturing office equipment has relied exclusively on profits to finance its expansion. The founder of this company had an idea but no capital. A loan from a bank was therefore sought to launch this enterprise. The unsympathetic treatment that the founder received at the hands of the bankers made him resolve never to seek their aid again. Finally a partnership was formed with a person who had some capital. The partnership soon became successful enough to finance further expansion from its earnings. This meant, however, that the original partners could not withdraw any profits from the business and that the use of this single source for additional capital would not permit a rapid expansion or exploitation of the market. On the other hand, it did permit a healthy growth of the company, which now enjoys freedom from any long-term financial obligations.

The process of plowing earnings back into the business rather than distributing them in the form of dividends has proved to be such a desirable practice in the past that some authorities advocate a standard policy of distributing no more than half of the profits to the owners in the form of dividends. Such a policy certainly contributes to the financial strength of a company, but it may lead to the accumulation of unnecessary capital if the company is not expanding the scope of its operations. One small company, for example, kept about 20% more capital than it needed for over 10 years simply because the board of directors thought it was "sound" to plow back half of the earnings.

Inflation and Dividends

Except in special circumstances, traditional attitude frowns upon the payment of dividends in excess of current earnings. For instance, one company seeking the aid of investment bankers in the public sale of a large block of its stock was required to make a detailed explanation of its dividend policy because it had paid out more money in dividends during the preceding year than it had earned. Without a good explanation, this was regarded as a blot on the record of the company and a handicap to the sale of its securities.

This tie between current earnings and dividends is especially sensitive during inflation. Inflation leads to an overstatement of earnings because:

1. The cost of materials taken out of inventory is usually understated relative to replacement costs—as explained above in connection with LIFO.
2. The cost of fixed assets (depreciation) is likewise understated. In fact, because the fixed assets often have been purchased a long time ago, the difference between original cost and replacement cost may be large indeed.

These overstated earnings are insidious for three reasons. They give a false guide to the real profitability of the business. They are subject to income tax, and thus a drain of capital out of the company. And they mislead management in pricing and other competitive moves. The combined result is likely to be a shortage of cash simply to maintain the productive capability of the business.

Consequently, during inflation it is particularly important to consider whether current earnings are adequate to warrant paying dividends, or whether an even higher than usual percentage of stated earnings should be plowed back into the business.

Stable Dividends

Another dividend policy, and one that is sometimes contradictory to the idea of plowing back at least part of the profits, is the payment to stockholders of a regular amount of dividends each year. Of course, the payment of regular dividends on cumulative preferred stock is not uncommon, because companies wish to avoid large accumulations of back dividends that must be paid before any dividends can be paid to common stockholders. Common stock and preferred stock on which dividends are paid regularly tend to have a better market and are more likely to be regarded by purchasers as an investment rather than a speculation.

To maintain a stable dividend rate, it is often necessary to retain part of the profits earned in prosperous years, irrespective of the present need of the company for additional capital, so that dividends in less prosperous years can be assured. Thus, a company might pay dividends of $2 a year over a 10-year period rather than pay dividends of $4 a year for the first 5 years and no dividends for the next 5 years. This policy, however, is likely to lead to the payment of dividends in excess of earnings during depression years. If it is clear that a company has refrained from paying large dividends in prosperous years in order to be in a position to continue the stable dividend rate in lean years, then payment of dividends in excess of earnings need not be condemned. On the other hand, if profits are retained in order to provide needed capital, then the payment of dividends in excess of earnings may lead to an inadequacy of circulating capital.

Inflation also bears on dividend policy. The issue is whether the profits that companies report are partly fictitious, and as a result whether dividends based on such profits are actually cutting into capital which should be retained in the business. Here is the argument: If a company depreciates its fixed assets on historical cost (not replacement costs), it is failing to recoup its real costs. Such low costs lead to high stated profits and high dividends. Then, when the company must replace worn-out assets there is insufficient capital to pay the inflated prices of new equipment. This line of reasoning suggests that dividend policy should always be tied to "real" profits.

Need for Adequate Retained Earnings

Net profits left within a company are generally shown in a surplus account, which is more aptly called "earnings retained in the business."[4] It is illegal to pay dividends that wipe out the retained earnings account and create a capital deficit; in fact, most companies prefer to show a surplus that is much larger than current dividend payments. A relatively large retained

---

[4]Surplus may, of course, be created in other ways, such as by purchasing bonds at less than par value and retiring them or by reducing the par or stated value of stock.

earnings account is desired because any operating losses or dividends in excess of profits may be charged against this account without impairing the original capital invested.

Before leaving this topic, one distinction should be made clear. The condition of the retained earnings account may be a restraining factor on the payment of dividends if the account is not as large as the management believes it should be. On the other hand, a large retained earnings account does not mean that the company is in a position to pay dividends. The capital represented by this account may be tied up in buildings or inventories, and dividends are paid in cash—not bricks or commodities. In addition to adequate retained earnings, there must be adequate cash in order to pay dividends. This goes back to the need for additional capital that has already been discussed in connection with plowing back earnings.

Conclusion Regarding Dividend Policy

Major factors to be considered in the distribution of profits are:

1. Present cash position and need for additional capital, especially during inflation.
2. Desire to maintain a stable rate of return to stockholders.
3. Adequacy of the retained earnings account to meet present and future reductions due to dividends and losses.

In establishing a dividend policy, the attitudes of people outside the company should be considered as well as those inside. A stable dividend payment, for instance, will affect not only the income of present stockholders but also the marketability of stock to new holders. Likewise, care to maintain a strong cash and retained earnings position will influence the credit rating of a company and its ability to borrow long-term capital. In addition, the effect of high income taxes on large individual stockholders should be kept in mind when the dividend policy is set.

SUMMARY

Policy guiding allocation of capital cuts across and intertwines with almost all other policy of the enterprise. (a) Restrictions on inventory are directly involved in the coordination of procurement and sales. (b) Credit limitations tie in with customer service policy. (c) Fixed asset controls will affect, to some extent, almost all divisions of the business.

Financial policy should not attempt to stipulate the *specific* uses of capital, as this would extend the financial arm too far into the responsibilities of other departments. Instead, policy on use of capital is primarily concerned with general soundness, total size, and balance between various types of assets.

Capital allocation is not a mechanistic activity based on numerical estimates alone. Instead, allocations are made within the boundaries of service aims specified in company strategy. Judgment about acceptable degrees of risk are introduced either by varying the hurdle rate-of-return or by reducing estimated income to an "expected value." Moreover, the total risk exposure—and the prospective drain on cash—is brought into balance through policy on the investment mix.

The use of cash for dividends should be done on a policy basis because stockholders and creditors develop expectations as to a high but fluctuating payout, a stable rate, or a 100% plowback for future growth. The dividend policy combined with announced strategy enables investors to characterize the company in terms of growth rate, capital gains, current income, and so forth.

Related to this whole cash flow picture is the calculation of profits. Management can emphasize current earnings versus future earnings by the policy it follows on accounting reserves, capitalization of disbursements, and inventory valuation. The result has bearing on earnings available for dividends and also on the company's ability to attract new capital—a major consideration that is discussed in the next chapter.

QUESTIONS FOR CLASS DISCUSSION

1. Tandy Corporation, owner of the Radio Shack and Tandy Leather chains, increased its sales to over $1.1 billion per year during the 1970's. Its profits increased even more rapidly. However, Tandy paid no dividends. Instead, it repurchased substantial blocks of its outstanding common stock. As profits increased and outstanding stock decreased, its rate of return on equity rose to over 35%. (a) How did Tandy stockholders gain from these changes? (b) Under what conditions would you recommend that a company repurchase its common stock rather than pay dividends?

2. Bill Norris, the new treasurer of the Norris Paper Company and nephew of the chairperson of the board, hoped to quickly put to work the theories and ideas he had learned from studying corporation finance at his university. An inventory turn of 4 times and 30 days outstanding for accounts receivable were goals that he was convinced were both useful and desirable. When he pushed the credit manager to tighten up on terms and the purchasing manager to cut back purchases, he was surprised to find that they resisted firmly. A complaint to his uncle only drew the response that this Chicago-based wholesaler and distributor of coarse and fine papers and folding boxes had done well for years with 60 to 90 days outstanding receivables and an inventory turn that, at times, dropped below 2. "But," said Bill to his sales manager cousin, "if we cut

receivables outstanding to 30 days and increase the inventory turn, we will have enough assets to support a sales increase of at least 20 percent. Don't you want that?" "No," said the cousin, "sales are hard enough to make against my competition without requiring that the bakers, grocers, and stationery stores pay cash. If you want to get cash out of the receivables, sell them to Atlantic Factors. We have done this before. They will buy 80 percent of the receivables right away." As Bill Norris, (a) what is your response? (b) What are suitable goals for and constraints over investment in receivables and inventory?

3. A furniture retailer, who features imports from Scandinavia, reports: "With our sales climbing steadily and our profit margins holding up, the net profit figures look great. Ten years ago I wouldn't have believed such figures were possible. The catch is that each year we go further into debt, and a sales downturn right now could throw us into bankruptcy. Last year we made $120,-000 after taxes, and that should give me at least a week on the beach. Not so. Inventory is up $200,000, we're selling every account receivable to the bank, and there's not enough cash to buy new tires for the trucks." What do you suspect is the source of the trouble? What can be done about it?

4. Assume that Alain Ribout sold his motel to an aggressive, financially strong motel chain and that he is now a district manager for that company. (a) How should he decide which of the investment alternatives listed on page 295 to recommend to his new employer? (b) If you think he should recommend more investment than he would have made as owner, do you conclude that big firms do and should take more risks than small firms?

5. The Nelson Construction Company, which specializes in building highways, has a clear policy of selling its bulldozers, cranes, heavy trucks, cement mixers, and other equipment as soon as a major job is completed. What reasons do you think account for this policy regarding fixed assets? What effect does it have on capital requirements and on operating costs?

6. According to economic theory, managers and others with capital to invest will (should?) seek out the maximum rate of return—with due allowance for risk. This theory implies that capital allocations to foreign vs. domestic purposes will be determined by a financial calculation of future incremental return and risk. In this chapter several financial policies have been suggested which may encourage or discourage foreign investment. (a) List and briefly explain examples of such policies. (b) How do you reconcile each item in your list with the economic theory noted above?

7. (a) Would you, as a stockholder, prefer the distribution of a large or a small percentage of net profits in the form of dividends? (b) If you were a member of the board of directors and had shared responsibility for deciding what dividends to pay, would your answer be the same? (c) Finally, if you were an executive of the company, interested in building up the financial strength of the company so as to ensure continuation of your job, would your answer still be the same?

8. A professional football team, the Black Knights, finished last season in the middle of its league. Most of its players will be available to play again next season if you want them. Assume you are asked to prepare an "investment policy" for the payment of bonuses to college stars for contracting to play with the Black Knights. Bonuses annually range from $10,000 to $200,000, depending on a player's demonstrated ability and position. The total you have to invest

in new talent is $600,000. On the average, fewer than a third of college stars who try professional football become regular players, and the odds for becoming a professional star are lower. How do you recommend the $600,000 investment be allocated (number of new players, size of bonuses, and positions)? (To simplify matters, assume trading of players between teams is not permitted.)

9. The directors of General and Standard Machines, Inc. have decided to imitate the General Electric Company and move into the domain of natural resources (see text, page 403). The first proposal that has come to them is an opportunity to buy shares (35% of the total) in a newly-formed Australian firm that owns proven reserves of zinc, copper, molybdenum, gold and silver ores. This proposal carries with it a predicted return on the investment of 24% before U.S. income taxes and an explanation that this rate will hold for at least twenty years because "ore does not get out of date as does machinery, the mines are easy to shut down and re-open because the costs are mainly variable, and the world's need for metals will increase." The board's long-standing "hurdle rate" for capital investments abroad has been a pre-tax return of 30% on the investment. The board has been assured that the Belgian part-owner will proceed no matter what but that the Japanese group will not put up its third of the money unless the Americans do. As a director, would you accept the lower "hurdle rate"? Explain.

10. A successful fertilizer manufacturer says: "We are definitely pushing foreign production and sales because our industry can serve a great need in many areas of the world. At the same time, our policy is to invest no more dollars abroad than we have to." (a) What reasons do you think lie behind the policy to keep foreign investments low? (b) How can a company such as this avoid tying up U.S. dollars? (c) Should the amount of hunger in different countries be a factor in selecting countries in which to invest?

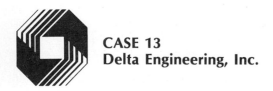

CASE 13
Delta Engineering, Inc.

Delta Engineering, Inc. is one of the thousands of firms in the so-called "military-industrial complex." Founded eleven years ago by three electronic engineers, the firm continues to work on the frontier of rapidly changing technology. However, being a very small part of the vast defense hardware industry is both risky and strenuous, and the three owners of Delta Engineering are wondering how to utilize their currently strong financial position to aid future stability and growth.

Delta Engineering got its start in military electronic-countermeasure-systems (ECM's). ECM's are used to defend against electronic systems of the enemy. For example, if an enemy radar "locks-on" to an aircraft, the aircraft's ECM devices will cause false indicators of its range and azimuth (i.e., distance and direction) for the purpose of confusing and deceiving the enemy radar operators. Of course, other designers will work to incorporate counter-countermeasures into their radars which will reject the false indications. This, in turn, triggers a second round where the ECM schemers must now overcome the improved radar, and so on. The equipment incorporated into ECM's is complex and on the outer fringe of the scientific state-of-the-art.

Broadly, three types of companies are engaged in the technical defense business: (1) Large prime contractors who supply the military services with total systems. (2) Numerous and often small equipment manufacturers who make components for the prime contractors (just as separate manufacturers make antenna, speakers, turntables, record-changers, and the like for hi-fi systems used in homes). (3) Materials and parts producers who make wire, transistors, metal boxes, insulation, circuit boards, etc., for the component manufacturers. Delta Engineering has always been in the second category—a manufacturer of specialized components.

The particular niche of Delta Engineering is amplifiers, mixers, microwave relay links, and closely related equipment. These devices must be very precise and must withstand wide temperature ranges, shocks, salt air, and other adverse operating conditions. Improvements in design are frequent. For instance, over a ten-year period successive steps have resulted in the following improvements in the logarithmic, intermediate-frequency amplifiers:

	Early Units	**Current Units**
Models Available	2	40
Center Frequencies	to 60 MHz	to 200 MHz
Bandwidths	to 10 MHz	to 100 MHz
Risetime	200 nanosec.	10 nanosec.
Dynamic Range	50–70 db	80–90 db
Accuracy	± 2.0 dd	± 0.25 db
DC Response	No	Yes
Temperature Stabilized	No	Yes
DC Input Power	25 watts	1.5 watts

Products originally developed for military use are also sold to universities and industrial laboratories engaged in advanced electronic design. Sixty-five percent of Delta Engineering sales are to 250 customers, including many of the largest and most discriminating users in the world. Customer engineers are very sophisticated, so selling is done on exact specifications. Technical catalogs are widely distributed, and manufacturers' agents "bird-dog" new prospects.

Actually only a third of Delta Engineering sales are previously designed catalog items. Two thirds of the dollar sales are special orders ranging from minor variations on catalog items to original engineered subsystems. Delta Engineering's competitive strength lies in its ability to couple advanced engineering with quality production and to make deliveries when promised. Its 50 employees are accustomed to this highly technical, special-order business, and all senior people are skilled engineers. Last year the company processed about 700 orders ranging in value from $300 to $100,000.

The company has grown in volume and profits, as indicated in the table showing operating results. Variations in recent years primarily reflect fluctuations in military purchases of specialized equipment (Delta Engineering is not prepared to make large runs of standardized items). All growth has been financed through retained earnings. No dividends have been paid on common stock. Internal growth also applies to personnel; relationships are informal, and everyone from president to secretary may join in a special effort to complete a rush order. The profit-sharing plan applies to all employees (32) with more than 2 years of service.

Operating Results
(dollar figures in thousands)

| | Sales | Net Profits | |
	(Shipments)	Amount	% of Sales
Last year	$2,286	$141	6.2
Previous year.	1,863	49	2.6
" "	2,041	87	4.3
" "	1,979	110	5.6
" "	1,864	107	5.7
" "	1,713	95	5.5
" "	1,116	45	4.0
" "	897	39	4.3
" "	522	24	4.6
" "	288	8	2.8
First Year	36	− 3	−8.3

Earnings Statement
(Last Year)

Sales		$2,286,000
Cost of sales:		
Opening inventory	$ 120,000	
Materials purchased	735,000	
Direct labor	319,000	
Factory overhead	497,000	
Total.	$1,671,000	
Closing inventory.	156,000	
Cost of goods sold		1,515,000
Gross profit on sales.		$ 771,000
General & administrative expenses (net)		487,000
Operating profit.		$ 284,000
Provision for federal & state income taxes		143,000
Net profit		$ 141,000

The balance sheet shows a very liquid position, with cash in excess of all liabilities. However, possible uses of available capital being considered by executives far exceed what is currently available. The various alternatives are briefly as follows.

(1) New product development.   To date, Delta Engineering has combined product development with engineering design of special orders. When a growing need—within company competence—is identified, the marketing people seek out and aggressively bid on jobs that include the new product. Although the price may be low and the specifications tight, the hope is that experience with the order will provide the knowledge necessary to quickly design a new product that can be added to the catalog.

The above practice works well for extensions of the existing line. Attempts to get really new lines by this route, however, have been unrewarding. Often a great deal of engineering effort goes into a difficult order that proves to be unique.

An alternative is to assign one or more creative engineers, with technical assistants, exclusively to R&D work. They would seek new catalog products to sell to existing customers. This would require hiring more engineers, either to relieve persons already in the company or to do the work themselves. To achieve momentum and a "critical mass," at least $100,000 per year should be budgeted, not counting the time of marketing and production people who would be frequently consulted. The outcome of such work is uncertain, of course, but the present executives and staff are so busy on existing business that moves into really new lines are unlikely to occur without the concentrated attention that typified the early history of the company.

(2) Promote microwave relay links to TV broadcasters.   Two years ago Delta Engineering launched an effort to reduce its dependence on military purchasing. The company bid successfully on a solid-state microwave relay to transmi. television signals from a downtown studio to the broadcast tower. Recent developments in microwave equipment make it more dependable than telephone lines for such purposes, and Delta's customer is highly satisfied with the performance of the new installation.

Selling the relay link to other TV stations has proved to be difficult. Station engineers don't buy on technical specifications but on demonstrated performance, and they are rightly concerned about very prompt repair service. Consequently, if Delta Engineering is to sell its relay link to any significant portion of 800 potential TV customers, it must (a) acquire agents who are familiar with this industry, (b) stock demonstrator units that can be temporarily installed in TV stations and towers, and (c) establish (or tie in with) a reliable service organization.[1]

Private microwave systems are also being installed for data transmission, for example by Western Union, and by railroads and pipeline companies. Competition from large manufacturers of electronic equipment is keen.

(3) Manufacture circuit boards.   Producers of small lots or individual units of electronic equipment, such as Delta Engineering, now buy transistor chips and affix them to ceramic circuit boards. (Assemblers who put the parts together use high-powered binocular microscopes and vacuum tweezers to handle the parts, which are

---

[1]Each set of broadcast and receiving units costs between $10,000 and $15,000.

extremely small.) Large-scale electronic production, in contrast, can utilize a more integrated process.

Because the demand for ceramic boards from large manufacturers has dropped off, almost all independent suppliers of this material have discontinued their production. This leaves companies such as Delta Engineering with a difficult supply problem. One solution is for Delta Engineering to integrate backward and make its own ceramic boards.

Balance Sheets—as of December 31
(000 omitted)

Assets	Last year	Previous year
Current assets:		
Cash or equivalent	$ 322	$188
Accounts receivable	362	267
Inventory	156	120
Total current assets	$ 840	$575
Fixed and other assets:		
Machinery and equipment	$ 247	$230
Furniture and fixtures	26	26
Autos	24	21
	$ 297	$277
Less Depreciation	128	107
	$ 169	$170
Prepaid expenses	12	11
Cash surrender value—		
officers' life insurance	46	35
Total fixed and other assets	$ 227	216
Total assets	$1,067	$791
Liabilities and equity		
Current liabilities:		
Accounts payable	$ 81	$ 56
Accrued items	68	45
Due to profit sharing	76	59
Income taxes payable	80	10
Total current liabilities	$ 305	$170
Equity:		
Common stock	$ 60	$ 60
Undistributed earnings	702	561
Total equity	$ 762	$621
Total liabilities and equity	$1,067	$791

These ceramic boards are coated with layers of chromium, nickel, and gold and must be carefully made. If Delta Engineering establishes a plant, it will sell boards to other firms like itself. Possibly a joint venture and/or an acquisition of existing facilities can be arranged. Between $250,000 to $500,000 minimum capital will be required.

(4) Buy its own building.   Delta Engineering has always occupied rented space. Presently it has a 10-year lease on a newly constructed building in a good location in Southern California where all its activities are carried on. Space is ample, and about a quarter of the building is sublet to another concern for a branch office and warehouse.

The lease has 4 years to run. However, Delta Engineering has an option to buy the land and the building for $400,000, which because of inflation is about 40% below current replacement costs. The building could easily be mortgaged for $300,000. If the building is purchased, the carrying charges (including interest on the mortgage) will almost equal rental charges; current net earnings would be increased by only $6,000 per year. Nevertheless, the company would immediately have a potential capital gain, and it would gain from further appreciation of these fixed assets.

(5) Dividends.   Mr. Arnold Beame, Delta Engineering's president, says: "Of course we should also consider substantial dividends to the stockholders. Bob Morganthau, Ron Javitz, and I are so deeply involved in making the company go we rarely take an objective look. Defense expenditures have stabilized and may go down. The big companies are likely to do more of their own subsystem work 'in-house' to keep their own people busy. So if further investments involve the kind of chances we took when we founded the company, maybe we should start drawing out capital. There is no precise way to measure which direction to go. We try to forecast where there is an opportunity for us and then assume we are smart enough to make money doing it. The record is not bad."

Question

What uses of capital do you recommend for Delta Engineering, Inc.?

FINANCIAL POLICY—
SOURCES OF CAPITAL

The cultivation of adequate sources of capital is of prime concern to central management. Other aspects of company operations may be just as crucial to success, but none is more relentless in insisting on proper attention. For small and medium-sized firms especially, the supply of capital is frequently a restraint on the successful execution of their preferred strategy.

The principal sources of capital available to most companies are:

1. Owners.
2. Long-term creditors.
3. Short-term creditors.

We shall first review the typical ways capital is obtained from each of these sources and shall then consider how a management can combine the use of various sources to form a financial structure suited to the strengths and the needs of its specific enterprise.

INSTRUMENTS USED TO OBTAIN CAPITAL

Owners

Some cash for investment is generated within a company, if it is at least breaking even financially. Much of this results from a bookkeeping reduction in the value of assets, called depreciation, which is an "expense" but involves no disbursement of cash. Sooner or later, however, cash from such depreciation charges will be needed just to maintain existing capacity.

The second internal source of cash is *retained earnings*. As noted in our discussion of dividend policy, owners normally leave a large portion of the company profits in the enterprise to finance expansion. This flow of funds depends upon the profitability of the company. A dramatic example occurred in Japan during its boom in the early 1970's, as the following table indicates. The companies with high market share and correspondingly high earnings were able to finance almost three-fourths of their rapid growth from retained earnings and reserves. During the period they actually reduced their debt-to-equity ratio. In contrast, the less profitable companies could not finance their somewhat more modest growth from earnings and had to rely heavily on increased debt. Their debt-to-equity ratio increased sharply, leaving them vulnerable to a downturn in business.

Relative Importance of Various Sources of Growth Capital in Leading Japanese Companies

	High Market Share Companies	Low Market Share Companies
Retained Earnings	60%	18%
Reserves	14	9
Equity	3	2
Debt	23	71
Total	100%	100%
Annual sales growth	17.2%	11.2%
Annual return on equity	14.4%	9.3%

Source: Boston Consulting Group.
          Data cover growth period 1970–1975 for two prominent companies in each of thirteen industries, one company with high market share and one with low market share.

The amount of additional direct contributions from owners will depend upon the legal form of organization and the particular rights granted to each class of owner. In a sole proprietorship the amount of capital is limited by the personal resources of the individual who has complete control of the business. Partnerships expand the potential resources, but the lack of stability of partnerships limits their usefulness. So, as soon as capital needs of an enterprise exceed the wealth of one or two persons, a corporation usually is created. Then, raising ownership capital becomes a matter of selling stock.

Common stock. A share of common stock is simply a small percentage of the residual ownership of a company. If 100,000 shares are outstanding, each share represents 1/100,000 of the owner's claim on profits, and on assets if the corporation is liquidated. When additional shares are sold, profits have to be divided into more pieces, which the original shareholders will not like unless the total earnings increase faster than the number of shares; they get a smaller portion of what they hope will be a bigger pie. The new stockholders pay in capital primarily for the right to a piece of this bigger pie, usually expressed as "earnings per share."

If the common stock is *split* (several new shares issued to holders of each old share), of course the earnings per share go down. The individual shareholders retain their percentage claim on the total, however, since they now own more shares.

Preferred stock. Some investors are willing to buy stock having a limit on the dividend they will receive if they also get assurance that special effort will be made to pay such dividends. More specifically, if a company issues $7 preferred stock, a $7 dividend must be paid on each share before any dividend can be paid on common stock. In addition, preferred stock dividends are usually cumulative. Thus, if no dividends were paid on the preferred stock just mentioned for two years, $14 for back dividends and $7 for current dividends would have to be paid on each share of preferred stock in the third year before any dividend could be declared on common stock. Less significant, a preferred stock typically also has prior claim on, say, $100 of assets if liquidation should occur.

Normally, after the preferred dividend has been paid on preferred stock, all remaining dividends are divided among common stockholders. In exceptional situations the preferred stock *can* be made "participating," which means that both the preferred stock and the common stock will share in dividends after a stipulated amount has been paid on each type of security. Participating preferred stock may be issued, for example, to some stockholders who are reluctant to approve an expansion program; they get preferred treatment if any dividends are paid at all, and if the expansion proves successful they also share in the profits from growth.

Frequent use of stock to raise capital. The sale of additional stock is often used to raise money for expansion. To attract particular types of investors, the rights of an issue may be specially tailored. Different issues of preferred stock will have priority in rank and often will vary in the amount of the preferred dividend; voting rights will vary; occasionally preferred stock will be convertible into common stock; and so forth. A package of preferred and common may be sold as a unit. Sometimes *warrants* entitling the bearer to purchase common stock at a stated price are included with a share of preferred stock or common stock, thus giving the holder of the warrant an opportunity to benefit from a price rise. Or, to assure that a new issue of common stock will be sold, existing stockholders may be given *rights* to buy stock at slightly less than the prevailing market price. These special provisions, however, do not modify the basic transaction of securing additional capital through the sale of additional shares of ownership.

Long-Term Creditors

In addition to investments by owners, capital may also be secured by borrowing it from long-term or short-term creditors. Let us look first at reasons why a company may seek funds through long-term borrowing.

Trading on the equity. The advantages and the disadvantages of obtaining capital from long-term creditors are illustrated in the situation facing the Red River Power Company. This local electric company, with assets of about $40 million, wished to finance an expansion program that would cost $9 million. The new expansion might have been financed by the sale of additional stock. The present common stockholders, however, did not wish to use this source of capital because (a) high income taxes make earning of net profits more difficult than earning bond interest, and (b) all profits would have to be shared with the new stockholders.

Interest on borrowed capital is an expense deducted from income *before* income tax is computed. Profits available for stockholders are net income *after* income tax has been paid. Consequently, a corporation in the 48% income tax bracket has to earn almost $2 for each dollar available to stockholders. If capital is borrowed, less earnings are needed to pay for the use of the capital because the tax collector has not yet taken a toll.

The effect of these factors on the Red River Power Company can be seen by comparing the disposition of operating profits (before paying bond interest) under bond and stock financing. The Red River Company already had outstanding $14,000,000 of 9¾% bonds, $9,000,000 of 10% preferred stock, and $9,000,000 of common stock. It was estimated that an average annual operating profit of $5,500,000 would be earned when the expansion was completed. The effect of borrowing the necessary $9,000,000 at 9¾% or selling common stock at par would have been:

	Borrowing $9,000,000 at 9-¾%	Selling $9,000,000 of Common Stock
Estimated annual operating profit	$5,500,000	$5,500,000
Less bond interest	2,242,500	1,365,000
Net profit before income tax	$3,257,500	$4,135,000
Income tax @ 48%	1,563,600	1,984,800
Net profit	$1,693,900	$2,150,200
Less preferred stock dividends	900,000	900,000
Available for common stockholders	$793,900	$1,250,200
Rate of return on par value of common stock outstanding	8.8%	6.9%

The present stockholders would profit by borrowing because a larger rate of return would be earned on capital than would be required for interest. If for some unforeseen reason, however, the operating profit of the company should fall to $4,700,000 or $3,900,000, the earnings on common stock would have been:

**Rate of Return on Common
Stock Outstanding**

Annual Operating Profit	Borrowing $9,000,000 at 9-¾%	Selling $9,000,000 of Common Stock
$5,500,000	8.8%	6.9%
4,700,000	4.2	4.6
3,900,000	−.4	2.3

Thus, by borrowing, the common stockholders increase their possibilities for profits but also incur a greater risk of loss. Such use of bonds for raising capital is referred to as *trading on the equity*.

Instruments for long-term borrowing. Trading on the equity may be accomplished through the use of any of the following instruments:

Mortgages. To attract long-term capital, a mortgage on real estate or other assets may be given as security. If the interest and the principal of the loan are not paid on schedule, the lender may force the sale of the mortgaged property and use the proceeds to repay the debt. If the proceeds do not cover the entire debt, the borrower is still liable for the remaining balance.

Bonds. To borrow large amounts, the total can be divided into a series of identical bonds that can be sold to as many lenders as necessary to secure the sum desired. The bonds may be *secured* by a mortgage or other pledged asset, or they may be *debentures* that rely only on the financial strength of the borrower. Typically, the borrower must continue to meet stipulated requirements such as minimum working capital, no senior debt, conservative dividends, and the like. Also, most bonds either call for *serial* repayment year by year or have a *sinking fund* in which money to repay the debt is accumulated. Bonds usually are *callable* by the borrower if he or she is willing to pay a premium. These provisions are stated in the *bond indenture* and are administered by a trustee.

Long-term notes. Increasingly, large sums can be borrowed from a single financial institution like a life insurance company or a trust company. Here, dividing the loan into bonds is unnecessary. Instead, 10-, 15-, or 20-year promissory notes are used. There is, however, an agreement similar to a bond indenture stipulating various protective measures and the repayment schedule. Such *private placements* avoid underwriting costs. Their use depends largely on the total to be borrowed and the comparative interest expense.

Variations. As with preferred stock, numerous variations are used to tailor long-term securities to attract particular groups of lenders. In addition to the interest rate, maturity dates, and protective features mentioned above, some loans are *convertible* into common stock. If the stock price rises above the specified conversion rate, the lender has the option to switch to an equity security at a low cost. Thus, convertible bonds give the investor the security of fixed debt plus the possibility of benefiting from a rise in stock prices. Another variation is to issue warrants along with bonds. In tight money markets, offering a security that appeals to special classes of lenders can reduce interest expense significantly.

Anyone who lends money for a long term is concerned about the continuing ability of the borrower to meet obligations. Hence, new companies lacking a record of demonstrated ability and companies in risky industries may be unable to borrow for long terms. In contrast, loans will be easier to obtain by an established firm that over the previous ten years has earned at least twice the interest on proposed new debt and in no year has failed to at least equal the fixed payments. Although future earnings are what really matter, past earnings are often used to decide a company's credit worthiness.

Short-Term Creditors

The sources of capital discussed thus far provide capital for a long period. Short-term creditors, however, are better adapted to supply funds for seasonal requirements or other temporary needs. The most common short-term creditors are (1) commercial banks and (2) merchandise vendors.

Commercial banks. The most desirable way to borrow from a commercial bank is to establish a *credit line*. Under this arrangement, the company anticipates its needs for temporary cash and works out an understanding with the bank; prior to the time the cash is required, that credit up to a certain maximum will be available. This gives the bank ample time to make its customary credit investigation, and it also enables the company to plan on the bank as a temporary source of capital. The bank wants to feel confident that the company will pay off the loan within a year; consequently, it checks the character of the people running the company, the nature of its existing assets, use to be made of the money borrowed, obligations already incurred, and the earning record of the company. The bank is also interested in the company's budget of monthly cash receipts and disbursements during the coming year. The aim of the bank is to avoid embarrassing bad debt problems by not making dubious loans in the first place.

For some types of business a commercial bank makes loans that are secured by collateral. For example, an investment house pledges stocks and bonds as security for its bank loans, and a dealer in commodities backs up its loans by means of warehouse receipts or bills of lading. When such security is provided, the preliminary investigation by the bank is less rigorous.

Commercial banks do also make some mortgage loans and buy marketable bonds, but this is not a primary service they render to business firms.

Merchandise creditors. Companies normally purchase products and services "on account"; that is, they make payment thirty to sixty days after products are shipped. With a continuing flow of purchases, some bills will always be unpaid. In effect, the vendors are supplying part of the capital needed to carry on operations. If a company is slow in paying its bills, it may have accounts payable equal to two months of its purchases.

Extensive use of such trade credit is usually unwise. Vendors often offer substantial discounts for prompt payment of bills, which means that this is an expensive source of capital. Furthermore, a company with a reputation for slow payment will not receive favorable treatment from vendors when there is a shortage of merchandise or when closeouts are being offered at low prices.

It will be recognized, of course, that buying on trade credit is but a counterpart of the use of capital to finance accounts receivable from customers.

Other short-term credit. Selling on the installment plan clearly increases a company's need for working capital. As we noted in the preceding chapter, special arrangements can be made with finance companies either to take over or to lend money on such accounts receivable.

Postponing payment of taxes, installment payments on machinery, loans against inventory placed in a bonded warehouse, and even advance payments by customers can be resorted to in periods of stringency. Few companies care to have a continuing policy of obtaining short-term capital from such sources.

With this summary view of possible sources of capital in mind, we can now turn to this issue of how to combine their use in a sound financial structure.

FINANCIAL STRUCTURE
Meaning of Financial Structure *Discussed*

The various sources of capital used by a company make up its financial structure. In establishing policy for obtaining capital, the overall general structure must be considered because the relative importance of one source will affect the desirability of others.

The size of the company, the nature of its assets, the amount and the stability of its earnings, and the condition existing in the financial market at the time the capital is raised—all have an influence on the sources of capital used by the company. From time to time changes will be made, either because capital can be secured more advantageously from another source or because some lender decides to withdraw its capital. Expansion or contraction of the total amount of capital used also will affect the relative importance of the various sources.

At any given time the right-hand side of the balance sheet of a company will reflect its financial structure. So, to review the policy followed by three different companies, we will examine briefly their condensed balance sheets.

Financial Structure of Schultz Electronic Controls, Inc.

The balance sheet of Schultz Electronic Controls, Inc. shown below is typical of many comparatively small manufacturing companies.

Almost three-fourths of the total capital of $2,685,000 was supplied by owners of this company. Par value of preferred and common stock is $1,-600,000, and earnings retained in the business have increased the stockholders' investment by another third of a million dollars. Limited use of long-term notes is shown. These notes are only about one-third of the depreciated value of fixed assets and thus appear to be protected by an ample margin of assets. The serial feature provides for a regular reduction in the amount of the long-term debt.

Schultz Electronic Controls, Inc.
Balance Sheet
December 31, 19—

Assets		Liabilities and Stockholders' Equity	
Cash......................	$140,000	Accounts payable........	$117,000
Accounts receivable (net).....	410,000	Accrued liabilities........	84,000
Finished inventory...........	196,000	Long-term serial notes	550,000
Materials and in-process		Preferred stock, 8%......	600,000
inventory	439,000	Common stock..........	1,000,000
Fixed assets (net)............	1,500,000	Earnings retained in	
		business..............	334,000
		Total liabilities and	
Total assets	$2,685,000	stockholders' equity	$2,685,000

The short-term debt of the company at the time of this balance sheet was comparatively small, the accounts payable to trade creditors being only a fraction of the total assets and actually less than the cash on hand. The company did, however, have a bank line and normally used bank credit to finance a seasonal peak in inventories and receivables from March through August.

Financial Structure of the Red River Power Company

The sources of capital used by the Red River Power Company reflect the difference in the nature of operations of an electric utility company compared with a manufacturing company such as Schultz Electronic Controls, Inc. The balance sheet below shows the financial condition of Red River Power Company after its expansion program was completed.

Red River Power Company
Balance Sheet
December 31, 19

Assets		Liabilities and Stockholders' Equity	
Cash.....................	$ 600,000	Accounts payable........	$ 600,000
Other current assets	400,000	Accrued taxes, etc........	200,000
Fixed assets ... $55,100,000		Mortgage bonds, 9¾% ...	23,000,000
Less allow-		Preferred stock, 10%.....	9,000,000
ance for de-		Common stock	9,000,000
preciation ... 7,600,000	47,500,000	Retained earnings........	6,700,000
		Total liabilities and stock-	
Total assets	$48,500,000	holders' equity	$48,500,000

Perhaps the most striking feature of the financial structure of this company is the large bond issue that represents almost 50% of the total assets. This company could obtain such a large bond issue at favorable rates because of the stable earning records of operating utility companies and also because of the large amount of fixed assets that the company could pledge under a mortgage issue. This company has also issued both common and preferred stock. Earnings retained in the business instead of being paid out as dividends amount to about 27% of its total proprietorship.

Inasmuch as there is no such thing as inventories of finished goods in a utility company and accounts receivable can be collected from customers promptly, the assets of this company are virtually all in the form of fixed assets. The company has used bank loans to finance temporarily the expansion of its facilities.

Financial Structure of The Long-Shot Printing Company

The balance sheet of a company financed on the proverbial shoestring offers an interesting contrast to those already considered. At the end of its first year of operation, the financial condition of The Long-Shot Printing Company is shown on the next page.

The owners of this company have actually contributed less than 22% of the total capital and are relying heavily on both long-term and short-term creditors. Machinery, which is the principal fixed asset of the company, was purchased on time payments; and the vendor, in order to protect its claim, still holds a first mortgage on the machinery amounting to almost two-thirds

The Long-Shot Printing Company
Balance Sheet
December 31, 19—

Assets		Liabilities and Stockholders' Equity	
Cash.....................	$5,200	Trade accounts payable	$61,600
Accounts receivable—net.....	28,400	Notes payable	18,000
Inventories.................	52,500	Accrued liabilities	7,600
Total current assets..........	$86,100	Total current liabilities.......	$87,200
Deferred charges............	3,000	Mortgage on equipment	72,500
Machinery and other fixed		Common stock	40,000
assets—net...............	115,300	Retained earnings	4,700
		Total liabilities and stock-	
Total assets	$204,400	holders' equity...........	$204,400

of its book value. It is doubtful, however, whether even the book value could be realized if it became necessary to sell the machinery at a forced sale. Credit from material suppliers has been used to a point where it exceeds the value of the inventory actually on hand. This means that the vendors are not only financing the entire inventory of the company but other assets as well.

Fortunately, the notes payable are due to an affiliate company that will probably not force their collection at maturity but will accept new short-term promissory notes in exchange for the old ones. Nevertheless, the current ratio is approximately 1 to 1, and any shrinkage in the value of current assets would probably cause immediate financial complications. The company has no bank loan and has been unsuccessful in securing a line of bank credit that it may use in an emergency. It is doubtful if new capital can be attracted to correct the existing weak cash position, with the possible exception that the company might offer a new investor the speculative possibility of sharing in future profits if they are earned. Under such a plan, however, the present management would probably be required to give up part of its control over affairs of the company.

In this situation the company must adopt a strategy of improving short-term earnings with existing assets—a very different strategy from that of Red River Power Company where physical expansion financed by debt with a fixed interest cost was the strategic direction to higher earnings per share. In fact, The Long-Shot Printing Company decided to operate on a three-shift basis, cutting its prices close to incremental cost if necessary to keep the plant busy.

The close interrelation between overall strategy and financial structure is evident in all three of these examples.

SELECTING CAPITAL SOURCES

Industry Patterns

Typical financial structures of companies in its industry will give management a lead on what the financial community will accept as satisfactory. More often than not, however, wide variations in assets, in earnings, and in existing capital structures, in addition to the differences in management, make reliance upon typical industry patterns both unsatisfactory and even dangerous. The policy adopted should suit a particular company and the conditions existing at the time plans for the financial structure are made. Important factors to consider are:

1. Use to be made of the capital.
2. Cost of this capital.
3. Rights granted to persons or concerns from whom capital is secured.

Use of Capital

Funds to finance seasonal peaks or other temporary needs can probably best be obtained from short-term creditors, such as commercial banks. This is a comparatively inexpensive way of raising capital and permits an immediate reduction in the total amount owed after the peak requirements are over. On the other hand, capital for fixed assets or for circulating capital that will be permanently retained in the business calls for a different solution. Because the company cannot expect to have cash to return to the lender for several years, owners or long-term creditors present a more logical source for such funds.

The use of capital will also affect the ability of the company to offer the lender some special security for its loan. As an effective guarantee that a loan will be repaid, a company may pledge as security one or more of the following assets: inventories that can be readily sold on the market, machinery that is standard in design and that can be easily moved from one plant to another, buildings located and designed so that they are suitable for use by other companies, or marketable securities. If valuable collateral can be given to the lender, borrowing will be much easier. If the funds are to be used for purposes that cannot be made to yield cash readily, the raising of capital from owners is indicated.

Cost of Capital

To ascertain the cost of capital, consideration should be given to the original cost of obtaining it and also to the compensation to be paid for its use. In sole proprietorships and partnerships, capital is usually secured by negotiations between the owners and those with whom they are intimately acquainted. Other persons or concerns not personally acquainted with the owners are unlikely to provide capital to such organizations. The cost of procuring such capital, if it can be obtained at all, will therefore usually be nominal.

Underwriting and registration. In the case of a corporation, securing capital by issuing bonds or selling stock to the public often involves a considerable expenditure. Frequently these securities are sold through an investment banker who is equipped to reach prospective purchasers of securities, and in most instances substantial commissions must be paid to the investment bankers for these services. Also, complicated legal requirements must be complied with before such securities can be sold. Federal legislation requires the registration of all widely distributed securities with the Securities and Exchange Commission, and the expense involved in preparing the detailed statements required for registration is quite large. In fact, the minimum cost of registration is so large that it makes the public offering of less than $1,000,000 of securities uneconomical.

Private placement of bonds and long-term notes also entails legal and accounting fees and perhaps a fee to a consultant who helps arrange the loan, but the total expense of procuring capital in this manner is normally less than half the expense of a public sale.

Use of rights. Some companies are able to sell securities directly to present stockholders. This applies particularly to the sale of additional stock similar to that already outstanding. The charters of many corporations require that when additional stock is to be sold, it must first be offered to the present stockholders; and if the new stock is offered for sale at a price somewhat lower than the current market price, the present stockholders will probably exercise their right to buy the new issue. When this procedure is possible, the cost of securing additional capital may be reduced substantially. If, however, there is any doubt about stockholders exercising all of their rights, it may be necessary to employ an investment banker to underwrite the issue, in which case many of the expenses incident to an initial public sale of securities must be incurred.

Adjusting sources to prevailing interest rates. The compensation, or interest, that must be paid for the use of capital not only varies according to the use to be made of the capital, but also is often affected materially by the state of the financial market. To note an extreme case, during the 1940's the rate of return on call loans fell as low as a fraction of 1%; by 1979 it had risen to 15%. Although the interest rate on other types of loans will not fluctuate over such a wide range, it does vary; and if a long-term loan is being negotiated, the fluctuation in the interest rate will affect the cost of capital for a period of many years. Changes in corporate financing costs in recent years are shown in the following chart:

CHANGES IN CORPORATE FINANCING COSTS

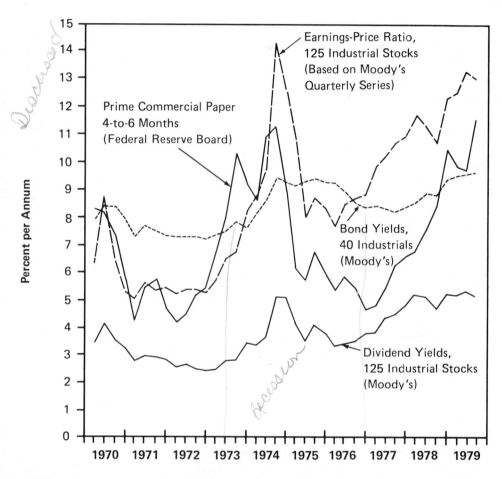

When interest rates are high, a company may choose short-term obligations, with the expectation that these can be paid off from the proceeds of long-term bonds that will be sold at a later date when interest rates are lower. The success of such a plan depends, of course, upon the accuracy with which movement in interest rates is forecast. There is always the danger that the interest rate on the long-term obligation will be even higher when the short-term notes mature, or other changes may occur that will make it difficult for the company to sell its long-term obligations as planned. Income taxes play such an important part in corporate profits that the timing of changes in capital structure may be based on an attempt to get the most favorable tax status.

Return paid on new stock. When common stock is sold to obtain additional capital, the company does not agree to pay a specific amount of interest for the use of the new capital. Nevertheless, the new stockholders will share in any dividends paid, which will reduce the amount of dividends available to the former stockholders. This sharing of dividends is a cost of capital so far as the former stockholders are concerned.

Many companies prefer to secure capital from the sale of stock, even though it is anticipated that earnings necessary to support this stock will exceed the interest that would have to be paid on bonds. Their willingness to pay this larger cost lies in the fact that dividends do not have to be paid when there is not a sufficient amount of earnings or cash to justify their declaration. Conversely, interest on bonds must be paid regardless of the amount of earnings and the cash on hand. If this interest is not paid on time, the stockholders run the risk of losing control of their company and perhaps their investment in it.

We have assumed that capital can be secured from any source at any time provided the compensation offered for its use is high enough. As a practical matter, the sale of bonds or stock becomes so difficult in some phases of the business cycle that new capital is virtually unobtainable from these sources.

Rights Granted with New Securities

A final factor to be considered in selecting the source from which capital should be secured is the authority exercised by the different contributors of capital.

Rights granted to creditors. If capital is obtained from short-term creditors, they usually have no control over the affairs of the company. Of course, if the obligations of these creditors are not paid at maturity, they have the right to bring legal action against the company to enforce their claims.

Likewise, long-term creditors ordinarily have no voice in the current operations of the company, although a bond indenture may impose certain restrictions on the management. For example, the indenture may restrict the amount that the company can invest in fixed assets, it may restrict the future debts that the company can incur, or it may require that the ratio of current assets to current liabilities be not less than 2 to 1.

The loan agreement may also restrict the freedom of the company to pay dividends. Some agreements provide that dividends cannot be paid if the ratio between various types of assets is below the standards established or if there is any default in the payment of interest or principal on the long-term obligations. If any of these requirements are not met or if any interest or principal payments on the bonds are not made, the company may be declared in default. In case of default, the bond trustee has the right to take legal action against the company in order to enforce the payment of the *total* amount of the bonds. These restrictions may become so burdensome that the management prefers to seek capital from other sources.

Rights granted to stockholders. If capital is secured by the sale of stock, the new stockholders have certain rights with reference to the company. The new stockholders frequently have full voting rights, and they thus become participants in the future management and control of the corporation. Sometimes present stockholders wish to retain a balance of control of the company and do not care to grant participation to others outside their group. The possibility that the sale of stock will change the balance of power in the board of directors depends, of course, on the relative size of the new issue as compared with the stock already outstanding, the amount of stock held by those already in power, and the extent to which the present stockholders exercise their right to purchase the new issue.

Preferred stockholders normally do not exercise control over company operations. They usually, though not always, have the right to vote for directors just as do the common stockholders. The par value of a share of preferred stock, however, is typically higher than that of common stock (often $100 and $10 respectively), so a given investment in preferred stock gives considerably fewer votes than an equal investment in common stock. The common stockholder usually runs a risk of losing control to preferred stockholders only if preferred dividends are unpaid for several years and if the charter provides that voting powers of the preferred stockholders are increased under such circumstances.

SUMMARY

An important task of central management is to see that capital necessary to execute the company strategy is provided at a reasonable cost and with a minimum of risk. Short-term creditors, such as commercial banks and suppliers of materials, can be used to cover seasonal needs or other temporary requirements. It is risky, however, to place too much reliance on short-term loans because the capital might be withdrawn when business conditions become unsettled. If used to the maximum for continuing needs, short-term credit will be unavailable for temporary rises in capital requirements.

Long-term loans in the form of bonds or long-term notes are a natural source of capital for companies with relatively stable income. Since the credit is extended for a period of years, various types of protection may have to be granted to the lender, such as mortgage liens, regular reduction of the debt, and limits on additional debts. The greater the stability of a company's earnings and the greater the protections offered, the easier long-term loans will be to obtain and the lower the interest rate. Conversely, unless a company can meet these conditions, few, if any, lenders will extend long-term credit. And, from the viewpoint of the company, heavy fixed interest and debt retirement charges may cause financial disaster for concerns with volatile earnings.

Owners' contributions of capital may take the form of either preferred or common stock. The special provisions of preferred stock, like those of bonds, should be tailored in terms of conditions prevailing at the time of issue. Moreover, the total owners' contribution should be a large enough part of the whole financial structure to be able to absorb shocks and losses of bad times. Typically, the owners' capital is increased by retention of earnings as a company grows, as discussed in the last chapter.

Company strategy influences many of the factors that shape financial policy; for example, movement into risky ventures, building new plants to cut production costs, emphasis on keeping a steady flow of standard business, or limiting research and development expense to enhance current earnings. These kinds of decisions affect the earning base, the kind of assets available for security, and the degree of uncertainty around which a financial structure must be designed. And because of this interdependence of strategy and financial policy, a major change in strategy usually necessitates an adjustment in company financing.

CONCLUSION TO PART 2

A brief re-emphasis of the role of policy in the total management process is desirable here at the close of Part 2, "Defining Major Policy." Three basic points should be kept in mind.

A. Policy amplifies and clarifies strategy. We have seen this in our exploration of product lines, customers, pricing, and product mix in the marketing area; in research and development, production, and procurement in the service creating area; in selection, development, compensation, and industrial relations in the personnel area; and in capital allocation and capital sources in the financial area. In these—and other areas not discussed —a variety of questions keep bobbing up that should be answered in a way that reinforces company strategy. Policy provides these needed guidelines and the bridge back to strategy.

Strategy quite appropriately stresses major directions and criteria. Its strength arises partly from its selectivity in emphasis. To specify all the ramifications would becloud the central theme. Instead, strategy leaves this amplification to policy. What is the implication here? What should be done there? How does strategy limit action in this field? What priorities are implied? These are legitimate questions that management should answer, and it does so largely through policy.

B. Establishing policy, in fact, is more complex and disorderly than we have implied. By stressing the way policy grows out of strategy, we inevitably give an impression that policy formulation is a neat, deductive process. "First pick the strategy, then figure out the necessary policy" is the implied formula. To a substantial degree this is what should be done. But it is an oversimplification. Three important elaborations help to round out the process:

1.   *Not all policy is deduced from strategy.* Policy may arise from at least two other sources. First, managers and the decision-makers respond directly to pressures from the environment. For instance, employing more blacks, reducing oil imports from the Middle East, posting interest charges made on installment accounts—all are probably direct reactions to external events rather than interpretations of strategy. Second, a series of similar actions in specific situations may become a custom, and then this custom becomes so established that it is treated as a policy. Overtime work or customer discounts may be guided by policy that arose in this way. It is hoped that these policies originating in the field of action are compatible with company strategy even though they were not initiated to execute strategy.

2.   *To some extent existing policy influences future strategy, rather than the reverse.* Strategy, we have said, is designed to take advantage of company strengths and to minimize the effect of company weaknesses. In other words, when mapping out a new strategy, the company is treated as an established institution with recognized characteristics. And one of the elements that gives a company its "strengths" and "weaknesses" is its policy. The existing policy may be so ingrained that it is treated as fixed when new strategy is drawn up.

3.   *Most important, revisions and restructuring of policy occur frequently.* Change—in the company environment, in the action of competitors, and in the company's own size and resources—requires adaptation. As time marches on, the strategy may be revised, policies may be modified, organization may be restructured, resources may be shifted, and systems of motivation and control may be revamped. If we were to take an annual picture of the total management structure, each year would differ from the preceding one. Just as an automobile company is designing a new model before this year's model reaches the market, so central management is continuously predicting and responding to change. The dynamic company, like a growing city, seems always to be under construction. So, forming policy is a never-ending process responding to influences in addition to strategy.

C. This untidiness in policy formulation increases the value of a conceptual framework. In a situation where pressures push in opposite directions and where people differ on priorities and values, a mental framework that puts facts and ideas into some kind of order is a great help. Granted that the convenient sequence of industry analysis ⟶ company strengths ⟶ strategy ⟶ policy ⟶ organization ⟶ execution does not always work in just that order. Nevertheless, the model does enable us (1) to sort out and arrange the pieces into familiar categories, and (2) to have a set of logical relationships between the categories that suggests priorities and dependencies. The power of the model is its contribution to both orderly and comprehensive thinking in bewildering, complex situations.

QUESTIONS FOR CLASS DISCUSSION

1. "Long-term leases on fixed assets provide another way to trade-on-the-equity." Do you agree? Explain.
2. McGregor and Casey own a successful filling station which does a relatively large service and repair business as well as gasoline business. McGregor, age 50, is an excellent auto mechanic and runs the repair business; Casey, age 35, takes care of financial matters, gasoline sales, public relations, etc. Currently they have a 50–50 partnership. Casey believes large stations will have a competitive advantage in the future, and he wants to almost double the size of the present station with self-service pumps and a larger line of tires and accessories. McGregor likes things the way they are, and he doesn't like big debts with which Casey proposes to finance the expansion. So Casey suggests that they form a corporation with various kinds of stocks and/or bonds that could be tailored to fit the respective preferences of the two persons.

   Assume the total assets of the enlarged station will be $375,000, with a long-term mortgage of $125,000 and short-term liabilities of $50,000. Recommend a financial structure for the remaining $200,000 which could be allocated between McGregor and Casey in a way that reflects their respective preferences.
3. "It's the source of the money that counts," said the chairperson as the directors of the Files Company, Inc. tried to decide which of two acquisition offers for the company's common stock they should accept. A West German company has offered $28 per share in cash and notes for Files' one million shares of common stock. Payment to the minority holders (25%) will be all cash and the Files family trust, which owns the balance of the common stock, will receive half cash and half ten-year term notes. The second offer is for $31 per share—all in cash. It was made by a well-established U.S. manufacturer of office equipment.

   The Files Company makes and distributes specialized filing equipment in North America and Europe. A subsidiary of the West German firm has, for one year, distributed and sold the Files line in France and Spain. Other subsidiaries make and sell a wide line of office supplies. "We have to compare the two balance sheets," said the chairperson. In summary, these data have been presented: (a) For the West German firm—sales: $300,000,000; net earnings: $16,000,000; depreciation: $8,000,000; cash: $16,000,000; current ratio: 2.7/1; no long-term debt; total equity: $90,000,000; dividends: $8,000,000. (b) For the potential U.S. purchaser—sales: $120,000,000; net earnings: $6,600,000; dividends: $3,300,000; depreciation: $6,000,000; cash: $12,000,000; current ratio: 2.6/1; long-term debt: $32,000,000; total equity: $36,000,000; 8% preferred stock: $10,000,000. (c) For the Files Company—sales: $60,000,000; current ratio: 3.5/1; cash: $3,500,000; net earnings: $3,000,000; net worth: $25,000,000; current market price of the common stock: $20 per share. If you were a director of Files, which offer would you recommend that the company accept?

4. You are one of five officer-owners of a company pioneering in the design and manufacture of atomic-powered pacers. The company has recently received final approval from government authorities to sell its compact, long-lasting pacer for use by humans. Because of the product's superiority over battery pacers, a rapid increase in sales is anticipated. Financing such an increase in operations will require as estimated $5,000,000. The present owners have already paid in $500,000 for common stock; this is all the capital they have, so outside financing must be obtained. A very wealthy Saudi Arabian is seeking equity investments in the United States and has offered to invest $5,000,000 for two-thirds of the common stock of your company. A New York investment banker explains that venture capital is very scarce, but he thinks he could sell $5,000,000 of common stock to about 100 investors. The banker would expect a 10% commission. Also the banker suggests that the existing equity be treated as worth $2,000,000. What action do you recommend the company take?

5. Bob Palmer and Arnold Jones have developed a profitable landscaping business in the seven years since they got out of the Navy and took over the business from Bob's father. Primarily they have secured contracts to take care of lawns in several prosperous suburbs. By hard work, use of labor-saving equipment, and employment of high school dropouts whom they carefully train and supervise, their gross income is approaching $100,000 annually. To cut labor costs they have a wide variety of power-driven equipment, four trucks, and a trailer. All this equipment is either bought on installments with the maximum time period or financed with a term bank loan. Bob and Arnold have growing families, need cash, and say they believe in trading on the equity. (a) Do you think they are wise to go into debt in this way? (b) What will happen to the landscaping business if Arnold accepts his father-in-law's invitation to join him in the contracting business?

6. Look up the current interest rates on bank loans and on high-grade bonds and the dividend yields on utility company stocks. On the basis of this information and your forecast for the future, how do you recommend that Red River Power Company raise $4,000,000 which it needs for transmission lines to tie into a multistate power grid? Assume the existing financial structure of Red River Power Company is as shown on page 323, that it can obtain funds at generally prevailing rates, and that the transmission line must be built to maintain service (estimates show a 12% return on the investment after income taxes).

7. The balance sheet of a strong regional trucking company, whose ton-miles of freight carried had grown more rapidly than the national average but that had still seen some cyclical variations, showed long-term debt amounting to 40% of total liabilities and stockholders' equity. Since this was well above the industry average of about 20%, it had been suggested that the treasurer "clean up" the balance sheet by a sale and leaseback of company-owned terminals to reduce the debt ratio to 25%. The treasurer, too, was worried since current liabilities amounted to 38% of total liabilities and the

equity base thus seemed very thin. Should the treasurer pursue the suggestion?

8. "Pollution controls are killing us," says Gerald Cox, the owner of a small iron foundry. Sales have been dropping and a new government requirement for a $40,000 exhaust control would add only expense and no income. Joe and Dawn Sandusky, a husband-wife team, have a growing precision alloy casting business and need a larger building. Cox's building is very well suited to their requirements, so Cox proposes to sell out to the Sanduskys. Cox wants $120,000 for his total business—plant, equipment, accounts receivable, inventory. The Sanduskys can scrape up only $20,000 cash; they already have $30,000 in their business. An insurance company is willing to buy the plant for $85,000 and lease it to the Sanduskys. If the Sanduskys gradually liquidate the iron casting inventory and receivables, they might realize $65,000; and a quick sale of these assets would yield only $15,000. But they would have to install the exhaust control if they continue to run the iron foundry. Cox recommends that the Sanduskys continue both businesses and indicates that he will accept one-fifth of the stock in such a venture in place of $35,000 of his sales price. The supplier of the exhaust control equipment will take 25% down and a 5-year installment mortgage note for the balance. What do you recommend the Sanduskys do?

9. Multinational corporations face special problems in financing operations in various countries. Debts contracted in a foreign currency may be easy or difficult to repay, depending on shifts in the exchange rate. (a) Assume, for example, that you are treasurer of a corporation that wants to expand operations in Brazil financed by a five-year loan. Would you prefer to borrow the funds in the U.S. at 10% per annum and convert the dollars into cruzeiros, or borrow the cruzeiros in Brazil at 30% per annum? (b) How about financing a German expansion locally at 10% per annum?

10. (a) What is the relation between the rate of inflation and interest rates? Explain this. (b) What do you forecast will be the average rate of inflation over the next twenty years? What is the implication of this forecast for interest rates over the same period? (c) In light of your answer to (b), do you think a company should issue today as many twenty-year, 12% bonds as the financial markets will accept? Explain.

11. Fast-growing, boiler-making, High Tempo, Inc. is doing good business around the world in the energy equipment and chemical process plants field. Stockholders will be asked at the next meeting to authorize a four-for-one stock split and a tripling of the number of common shares from 10 million to 30 million. Current earnings are $27 million, or $2.99 per share outstanding. The company has no preferred stock. A split is estimated by some to increase the number of registered shareholders by 24 percent. Directors doubled the total amount of dividends paid over the past year to a 60% payout ratio. High Tempo has heavily publicized its order backlog of $1.7 billion and its recent increases in market share. Can you explain why the directors have approved and put through these undertakings?

CASE 14
DEC Financing

Digital Equipment Corporation (DEC) is the world's leading producer of small computers. Although small compared with IBM, DEC has been very successful in its particular niche. Starting with mini-computers for scientific research, the company products are now used in medical analysis, industrial process control, data communications, accounting, education, and many other applications. Thirty-eight percent of sales now are made abroad, and this segment of the business is growing faster than U.S. sales.

The dramatic overall growth of DEC during the 1970's is indicated in the accompanying financial tables. This case, written as of March 1980, is concerned with how DEC should finance its continuing growth in the 1980's.

The mini-computer field is filled with competitors. Large-scale computer manufacturers, including Burroughs and IBM, are moving in with smaller size machines. Technological developments in micro-computers pose increasing threats. And new companies are filling specialized needs, just as DEC did when its present management started in the late 1950's. DEC is responding to this competition with aggressive pricing (reflecting lower costs because of its "experience"), new products and software, and an enlarged field service organization.

But, the rapid growth and need to remain competitive require large inputs of capital. Roughly, each additional dollar in sales has to be supported by another dollar in assets. The first and major sources of capital DEC has used in the past is its own earnings. No dividends have ever been paid; every dollar earned has been plowed back into the business.

The second capital source has been the sale of additional common stock. DEC is popular with investors. The New York Stock Exchange price of its common stock has ranged up to fifty times earnings. Even at twenty times earnings, sale of new stock looks attractive compared with borrowing at 10% interest or more. So during the 1960's and 1970's DEC made several public offerings of common stock. Also, a relatively small stream of capital has come from employees exercising stock options. By June 30, 1979, 39% of stockholders' equity ($1,120 million) came from stockholder investment and 61% from retained earnings.

Historically, long-term debt has been a minor source of capital for DEC. The company had virtually no long-term debt until 1975 when $75 million of debenture bonds were sold (interest @ 9-⅜%, due 2000). A major exception occurred in September 1977 when $250 million of subordinated, convertible debentures were sold. These bonds were convertible at the owner's option into common stock at $57 per share, and had an interest rate of only 4½%. However, DEC had the privilege of redeeming the bonds by paying a premium of one year's interest. When DEC announced its

Balance Sheets
(in 1,000,000's)

	June 30, 1979	June 27, 1970
Cash	$ 433	$ 7
Accounts Receivable, net	475	42
Inventories	514	43
Other Current Assets	42	3
	1,464	95
Investments		
Fixed Assets, net	399	20
Total Assets	$1,863	$ 115
Loans & Accounts Payable	$ 99	$ 24
Accrued Wages and Taxes	199	11
Customer Advances, etc.	89	4
	387	39
Deferred Income Tax	15	
Long-Term Debt	341	
Total Liabilities	743	39
Paid-in Capital	439	37
Retained Earnings	681	39
Total Equity	1,120	76
Total Liabilities & Equity	$1,863	$ 115

Income Data
(Operating revenue and net income in 1,000,000's)

Fiscal Year ending about June 30th	Total Operating Revenues	Net Income	Net Income per Share*	Average Price/Earnings Ratio**
1979	$1,804	$ 178	$ 4.10	12
1978	1,437	142	3.40	13
1977	1,059	108	2.78	18
1976	736	73	1.98	24
1975	534	46	1.28	21
1974	422	44	1.27	27
1973	265	23	.72	41
1972	188	15	.50	53
1971	147	11	.35	64
1970	135	14	.50	57
1965	15	1	.03	n.a.

* Adjusted for 3 for 1 stock split in November 1976.
**Value Line figures for calendar years.

intention of redeeming the bonds in January, 1980, the bond holders converted into common stock because at that time the stock could be sold on the N.Y.S.E. for about $70 compared with the conversion price of $57. The net effect, then, is that what started out as $250 million of long-term debt has now become about 4.38 million shares of common stock. This shift is reflected in the following figures:

(in millions)

	June 30, 1979	February 23, 1980
Long-term debt		
Debenture bonds	$ 75	$ 75
Long-term leases, etc.	16	15
Subordinated convertible		
debenture bonds	250	—
	341	90
*Stockholders' equity**		
Common stock @ $1 per share	41	46
Additional paid-in capital	398	658
Retained earnings	681	780
	1,120	1,484
Total long-term debt and		
stockholders' equity	$1,461	$1,574

*In addition to the bond conversion, equity was increased by $99 million of new retained earnings (for the first half of the fiscal year) and $15 million stock purchases via employee stock options.

In the spring of 1980 DEC is again in need of capital. An eighteen-month capital expenditure program calls for $350 million. Accounts receivable and inventories are expected to rise at least $200 million during the coming year. Retained earnings will cover only part of these projected needs. So, if DEC is to continue its present rate of expansion, $400 million outside capital should be obtained.

Unfortunately, the spring of 1980 is a poor time to raise outside capital, especially in the magnitude desired by DEC. The U.S. government is pursuing monetary measures to check inflation. Interest rates are soaring, with the prime rate in the 20% range, and bond prices are depressed. Prices in the stockmarket are relatively low, partly because of the high interest rates and partly because of an anticipated depression. Worldwide inflation and political tensions are undermining confidence generally.

Among the alternatives being considered by DEC's central management are the following:

1. Rely on retained earnings only. This would involve a planned slowdown in growth. Probably attention would focus on full utilization of existing facilities and sharp reduction of capital expenditures. Vigorous expansion could be renewed as soon as economic conditions and financial markets become normal.

2. Arrange short-term loans. Interest cost of such loans would currently be about 20% per annum. However, this rate would vary, falling (or rising) with the "prime rate." As with the preceding alternative, DEC would retain high flexibility about the amount of loans outstanding and shifting to other sources if and when that became attractive.

3. Sell long-term bonds. DEC's present balance sheet and earnings record could easily support $400 million more in long-term debts. High grade 20-year industrial bonds of such companies as Texas Instruments and General Motors Acceptance Corporation are currently yielding around 13½% per annum. DEC would have difficulty getting this rate, especially on a large issue, but 14% is a reasonable possibility.

4. Sell long-term convertible debenture bonds with conversion and redemption provisions similar to the bonds redeemed in January. Because the convertible feature gives the owner a chance to make a capital gain, the yield on such bonds would be lower than ordinary bonds. Probably a conversion option into DEC common stock at $72 per share would be appealing in view of DEC's sustained growth record. (Currently DEC stock is selling at $62 per share; its price has ranged between $82 and $51 during the preceding year.) This probably would reduce the interest rate to 9% per annum.

5. Sell common stock. DEC's sustained growth record and its strong financial position give its stock a much higher price/earnings ratio than most stocks. However, in the current market stocks which pay no dividend are unpopular. Also, the total amount is large for a speculative issue. These latter factors require that DEC's offering price for the new share be below the present market price so as to attract about a 15% increase in common stock ownership. An offering price of $59 per share, $3 below the present market, might induce the sale of 6.8 million shares for $4.01 million.

Questions

(1) Which one of the alternatives listed do you recommend DEC adopt to raise capital? Explain why you made that choice.

(2) Do you have a better plan than any alternative listed? Explain.

INTEGRATING CASES

Strategy and Financing

POWDERED METALS, INC.

"During our first eight years we had to take large risks," said Mr. Hubler, president of Powdered Metals, Inc. "Bankruptcy was always a threat, but we had no choice. We simply proceeded on faith that our small company would master the art of making high-precision parts out of powdered metal, and then the leading companies of the nation would be glad to do business with us. Now, we have mastered the art, at least to some extent, and we are doing business with the Xerox's and the IBM's. But the risk problem has become tougher because we now have choices. We can use our profits to pay off debts and remove the threat of bankruptcy—or we can seize the opportunity we worked so hard to create and help push powdered metal parts into every sophisticated machine that's made—or we can decide to do something in between."

Product/Market Target

The company makes an array of specially shaped gears, bearings, and other machine parts. Instead of starting with the usual casting or forging process, the new metallurgy injects a finely powdered form of iron, steel, or other alloy into a mold and packs the powder together under high pressure. The "raw" part is then placed in a furnace where high temperature unites the fine particles into a solid form.

It is the combination of (a) high-pressure molding in very precise molds with (b) heat treatment ("sintering") that makes the company products distinctive. The molding process enables the company to make oddly shaped parts that are difficult or impossible to produce by ordinary machining. And the sintering process imparts strength and hardness matching or exceeding conventionally formed metal parts. Moreover, the process significantly reduces unit costs, virtually eliminates waste and scrap, and can be used for rapid mass production.

Actually, the technique of producing metal parts by compacting powders has been in use for many years. Early applications were limited to small, relatively crude parts not subjected to heavy bearing or shock loads. The process gained acceptance by providing lower costs than were available through conventional machining or forging methods and by providing unique compositions not readily obtained through conventional melt-alloying methods.

As powder compacting techniques were refined and improved, the competitive advantage broadened dramatically. It is common practice today for engineers to

339

design components specifically for production by the powdered metal process. Load-bearing characteristics, density, dimensional and shape conformity, and ease of machining can now meet a wide range of requirements once considered available only from wrought materials.

The powdered metal industry is generally expected to continue to expand at its current rapid rate because the competitive capability of the process is gaining wider acceptance in all sorts of uses. The largest *tonnage* consumer is and will continue to be the automotive industry: bearings, gears, oil pump vanes, etc. However, the largest *number* of parts, requiring a high degree of precision, are being consumed in home appliances, business machines, recreational products, and the electrical and electronics industries. It is to this latter segment of the market that Powdered Metals, Inc. has directed its efforts.

Some of the more intricate precision parts made by this latter segment of the industry cannot be directly compacted to exact finished dimensions and contours and thus require secondary or finishing operations, generally by machining. Powdered Metals, Inc. has a unique capability in this area, shared with only four or five other of the 90 noncaptive powdered metal parts-makers in the country. The success it has attained in becoming a primary vendor to IBM and Xerox is testimony of Powdered Metals, Inc.'s competence in the high-value-added portion of the market. The company has the "know-how" to continue to penetrate premium markets where its proven competence and highest-grade tools and equipment are demanded.

Four years ago total industry sales of powdered metal parts was $108 million. By last year the sales had risen to $217 million, more than doubling in three years' time. About $120 million of last year's total went to the automotive industry, the balance to the more specialized markets. And this second part of the industry grew somewhat faster than the total, almost 30% per year. This rate of growth may not be maintained, but industry speakers predict an average increase over the next decade of 20% to 25% per annum.

Powdered Metals, Inc. hopes to increase the number of different customers it serves; it is now somewhat vulnerable because two large firms account for over half of its business. However, because of the cost of making precision molds, reorders of specific parts are likely to be placed with the company that produces the original run. An industry rule-of-thumb is that, on the average, a machine part will continue to be used by a customer in making new machines for seven years. Powdered Metals, Inc. has not yet had much experience with such reorders.

The company is well equipped to seek orders for complex parts. It has a very good machine shop where molds are made, its compacting presses and sintering furnaces are new, and it has equipment for secondary machining if this is required. Both Mr. Hubler and Mr. Chang, the chief engineer, are recognized for their specialized knowledge, and the company has established a reputation for high-quality output.

Progress to Date

Mr. A. B. Hubler dropped out of engineering school, became a machinist in the Navy, and later worked at this trade while completing his engineering training at nights. He was a partner in several small firms, and in one of these he hired a bright young engineer, J. K. Chang. These two men soon developed the idea of a new firm in the powdered metals field. Four years later Mr. Hubler had assembled the initial capital and Mr. Chang had studied the latest technological developments. The new firm was launched in a suburb of Columbus, Ohio.

The early years proved to be even more difficult than anticipated. Learning how to get dependable quality from new equipment, training personnel, obtaining test orders from customers and waiting while they evaluated the products in their own shops—all took time and money. But now, eight years later, Powdered Metals, Inc. is a profitable business.

The plant is running on a two-shift basis. The margin between prices and costs is improving, reflecting both an ability to get more attractive orders and improved efficiency in the plant. And the company has a four-month backlog of orders. Exhibit 1 shows the improvement in income over the last five years, from a staggering deficit to a 19% return on the book value of stockholders' equity.

Exhibit 1
Income Statement
(in 1,000's)

	Last year	2 years ago	3 years ago	4 years ago	5 years ago
Net sales	$3,732	$3,019	$1,778	$ 821	$ 316
Cost of sales	2,631	2,262	1,325	644	530
Gross profit	$1,101	$ 757	$ 453	$ 177	$ −214
Selling, general & administrative expenses . .	797	484	386	294	189
Net income	$ 304*	$ 273*	$ 67	$ −117	$ −403

*No income tax has been paid because of loss carryovers for preceding years. At the beginning of the present year the remaining loss carryover was $370,000.

Present Financing

Obtaining the capital necessary to finance Powdered Metals, Inc. has been a strain. During its early years the company relied on equity investments by Mr. Hubler and his friends. Equipment, especially compacting presses obtained from a Japanese manufacturer, was usually purchased at least in part with chattel mortgages, and other loans were secured.

About three years ago the company was successful in a significant recapitalization: (a) 50,000 shares of common stock were sold to the public at $10 per share by a local investment banker; (b) the Buckeye SBIC made a $2,000,000 mortgage loan to the company[1]; (c) debts outstanding at that time were either paid off or converted to common stock. The Buckeye SBIC loan runs for 10 years with $50,000 maturing

---

[1]SBIC's (Small Business Investment Corporations) are private lending organizations that are granted federal tax advantages because they concentrate on lending money to small firms that are having difficulty obtaining long-term capital.

quarterly ($200,000 per year); the interest rate is 8½% per annum. As part of the deal, Buckeye received warrants (rights to buy) for 50,000 shares at $8 per share, which can be exercised any time during the ten years that the loan is outstanding.

This injection of capital, helpful though it was, has not been adequate to support expanding production. New equipment to expand capacity has been financed with chattel mortgages; $300,000 of such mortgages were outstanding a year ago, and an additional $600,000 were issued during the past year. These chattel mortgages mature at the rate of $100,000 per year and bear 10% interest. Incidentally, the Buckeye SBIC was willing to subordinate its claim on this new equipment because the added capacity increases the chance that its warrants will become valuable.

The present financial structure of the company, reflecting these capital inputs, is shown in Exhibit 2.

Future Opportunities

"At long last," Mr. Hubler observes, "we have the opportunity to have a balance sheet look the way the bankers like it. Assuming earnings just stay steady, our cash gain from operations each year will be:

Net income	$304,000
Depreciation.	216,000
Available	$520,000

"With that amount of cash we can make our annual debt repayments of $300,000 and still increase current assets $220,000. In two years our current ratio would be 2:1 and our long-term debt would be only 82% of stockholders' equity. For anyone who has been squeezed for capital for eight years, that kind of a picture has much attraction. And maybe the equipment people would stop insisting on my personal guarantee of those mortgage notes.

"But we didn't enter the powdered metal business to stay even. We believe the industry will continue to grow rapidly, and naturally we'd like to benefit from that growth. The future is never certain, of course; too many competitors may enter the business or some new technique may replace powdered metals. But powdered metals have grown much faster than the industries we serve—business machines, electronics, home appliances, and the like—and Powdered Metals, Inc. has been growing faster than its competitors. So I feel that 20% increase per year for us is very conservative. We should be able to do that and at the same time be more choosy about the orders we take, which will help our profit margin. Of course, if a real recession descends on us, it's a new ball game.

"The main catch is that fast growth takes more capital—capital we do not have. With an additional $500,000 in equipment we could produce a volume of $5,000,000 in sales. The building is big enough to handle $7,000,000—with a bit of squeezing. But as we move beyond $5,000,000, all kinds of machinery will be needed, on the average of 80¢ per every additional dollar of sales or $1,600,000 of new equipment for the expansion from $5,000,000 to $7,000,000.

"In addition, more sales require more working capital. Inventory, accounts receivable, accounts payable, and accrued items all go up. My rough estimate is that the net increase in working capital would be about one sixth of the annual sales. Where

Exhibit 2
Balance Sheet—End of Year
(in 1,000's)

	Last Year	Preceding Year
Assets		
Current assets:		
Cash..............................	$ 199	$ 89
Accounts receivable, net................	650	651
Inventories.........................	637	308
Prepaid and deferred items	89	61
Total current assets	$1,375	$1,109
Plant and equipment:		
Land and buildings	$ 941	$ 909
Machinery and equipment	2,853	2,244
Furniture and fixtures	260	230
	$4,054	$3,383
Less depreciation reserve	−747	−531
Net plant and equipment	3,307	2,852
Research and deferred charges	74	83
Total assets	$4,956	$4,044
Liabilities		
Current liabilities:		
Current portion of long-term debt	$ 300	$ 200
Accounts payable	517	345
Accrued liabilities	109	73
Total current liabilities................	$ 926	$ 618
Long-term debt:		
Long-term loan	$1,600	$1,800
Equipment mortgages	800	300
Total debt due after 1 year............	2,400	2,100
Stockholders' equity:		
200,000 shares outstanding, par value $1..	$ 200	$ 200
Capital in excess of par value	1,800	1,800
Retained earnings (deficit)...............	(370)	(674)
Total equity	1,630	1,326
Total liabilities and equity.............	$4,956	$4,044

is all that money coming from? Retained earnings will help, but in any one year during the growth period the profit on the added volume (say, 9%) doesn't provide necessary working capital (17%).

"I've asked our treasurer, P. L. Jablonski, to explore all the different ways we might finance the business that I'm sure we can get during the next four years. With all those alternatives before us, we can sit down and figure out whether it is wise to go plunging ahead."

Alternative Sources of Capital

Ms. Jablonski summarized the various potential ways Powdered Metals, Inc. might finance its growth as follows:

1. The company's commercial bank suggests no growth this year and cutting inventories $100,000. These actions would allow the company to significantly improve its working capital position. Then the bank would make a short-term loan of $500,000 (perhaps requiring the pledging of accounts receivable if the inventory reduction was not feasible). The interest cost would be prime rate plus 1½% and maintenance of a bank balance of 20% of the loan.[2]
2. The investment banker who helped sell company stock three years ago thinks that improved company performance would create an interest in an additional issue, in spite of the present depressed condition of stocks generally. However, the selling price to the public would be only $7.50 per share, and after underwriting charges and other costs the company would receive $6.70 per share. Thus an issue of 75,000 shares would yield $502,000. Such an issue would improve debt/equity ratios. It would be "expensive" for present stockholders; for example, after such an issue, the people who invested $500,000 three years ago when risks were greater would hold only 18% of the total equity whereas the new stockholders would have 27% of the total equity.
3. An investment broker, recommended by the commercial bank, suggests a "sale and leaseback" of the company's land and buildings (for $800,000) plus the new equipment (costing $500,000). The $800,000 would be used to pay off existing chattel mortgages on equipment. The company would pay an annual rental equivalent to 9½% on money advanced (a total initially of $1,300,000) plus 5% depreciation on the building and equipment. The lease would run for 20 years, at which time the company would have an option to repurchase the land, buildings, and equipment at 20% of the total $1,-300,000 advanced.[3]
4. Mr. Bender, a Cleveland financier and president of Empire Investment Co., proposes a merger with another small firm that he controls. The firm, a

---

[2]The minimum balance requirement, a customary banking practice, means that the company would get only $400,000 for other uses. Assuming an 8% prime rate, the interest cost would be 9½% of $500,000, or $47,500 per year. On $400,000 this is equivalent to almost 12% per annum.

[3]The company would continue to pay real estate and property taxes and insurance just as though it owned the property. The interest portion of the rent would drop as the depreciation portion retired the loan. Broadly speaking, the company would be getting a 20-year loan at 9½%, except that it would have to pay 20% to retrieve its property at the end of the period. There also would be a book loss on the land and buildings at the time of the transaction ($941,000 minus $800,000), but this is not a real loss since the property could eventually be recovered on the basis of the $800,000 figure. Presently, depreciation on the buildings is about $25,000 per year. It is anticipated that Buckeye SBIC will waive its mortgage lien on the land and buildings because it will obtain a first lien on equipment when the $800,000 chattel mortgages are paid off and because its warrants become more attractive.

profitable truck-leasing operation, would be merged into Powdered Metals, Inc. so that the profits from the trucking operation would be offset by the tax loss carryforward of Powdered Metals, Inc. Empire Investment Co. owns the trucking firm and would get 75% of the shares of the merged companies. Mr. Bender says he can always find capital for profitable investments, and he would be able to devise some scheme to provide whatever capital the powdered metal activities can use effectively.

5. Buckeye SBIC is willing to advance more capital if the total debt structure is improved. It proposes a combined package: (a) a $500,000 loan for the new equipment on the same terms as its present loan, plus (b) purchase of 80,000 shares of stock at $6 per share. The $480,000 from the stock sale, $100,000 from reduction of inventories, and current earnings are to be used to retire the equipment mortgages.

Ms. Jablonski notes, "All five of the proposals focus primarily on raising $500,000 to expand production facilities. This will enable Powdered Metals, Inc. to increase its sales to $5,000,000. At the projected rise in sales, that takes care of us for only about eighteen months. Consequently, any plan adopted must also consider the ability of the company at that time to raise further growth capital."

Questions

(1) Do you recommend that Powdered Metals, Inc. buy the $500,000 worth of new equipment at this time? If so, how should the expansion be financed?

(2) Assuming that your recommendation is accepted and that you have $5,000 available for investment, what price per share would you be willing to pay for Powdered Metals, Inc. common stock?

Magna Electric Company (A)

Early in September, John Thorson, President of the International Group of Magna Electric Company, received plans for the coming year from two subsidiaries, Custom Cabinets (Pty.), Ltd. and Magna-Vaal Radio Co. (Pty.), Ltd., both of Johannesburg, South Africa. Since he saw fundamental differences in the two plans (summarized in Exhibits 1 and 2), Mr. Thorson immediately sent copies to Magna Electric Company's President, Eric Hausen, and called a meeting of the Plans Review Board to decide what to do.

Two days later members of the Board trooped into their sparkling meeting room fifty floors above Lake Michigan's shore. Some contemplated the views of the steel mills of South Chicago and the stockyards; others ruminated on what they knew about the South African subsidiaries and studied their copies of Exhibits 1 and 2, selected operating data (Exhibit 3), and comments on the economic outlook for South Africa (Exhibit 4).

Magna Electric Company had bought a 60% interest in the stock of each of the two companies from a South African investment company several years ago. Mr. Rosenberg, Managing Director of Magna-Vaal Radio Co. (Pty.), Ltd., and Mr. Jones, Managing Director of Custom Cabinets (Pty.), Ltd., each own 15% of the common shares of his local company. They have directed the firms for over a decade.

Exhibit 1

Plans Summary for the Coming Year
Custom Cabinets (Pty.), Ltd.

To: Plans Review Board

About: Your concurrence with our operating and capital plans for next year

1. Operations. We plan for sales revenue next year of $1,250,000 (U.S.)
—a 10% increase over the present. This is justified by our forecasts of a 10% increase in radio sales in South Africa next year and a stable market share for our largest customer —Magna-Vaal Radio. No major changes are planned for the plant. Wage rates will increase 3% according to the union contract that will be in force throughout the entire year. Lumber prices will be stable through the year. Our plans for costs are: materials, $530,000; factory wages, $260,000; depreciation charges, $20,000; additional overhead, $200,000; factory profit, $240,000; selling, general, and administrative expense, $150,000.

2. Capital. We plan three items:
   (a) Additions to woodlot and drying kiln, 5,000 square feet at $8 per square foot. This will alleviate an existing bottleneck and allow for an expansion 20% above next year's needs. Construction period, nine months including equipment order lead-time. Return on investment planned, 45%.
   (b) A medium-size tenoner, $25,000 (U.S.). This will bring tenoning machine capacity into balance with moulding and gluing equipment. This fourth tenoner will fit into space currently available between the moulding and the sanding departments. Return on investment planned, 25%.
   (c) Injection moulding machine for forming thermoplastics, $45,000 (U.S.) for an in-line reciprocating screw machine. This equipment is needed not for immediate production but for development and pilot work on plastics that will, we predict, eventually replace carved mouldings and other intricately machined wooden parts. Successful plastic mouldings promise to cut costs to 50% of the cost of carved wood. The savings will be both in materials and in the cost of hand labor.

Exhibit 2

Plans Summary for the Coming Year
Magna-Vaal Radio Co. (Pty.), Ltd.

To: Plans Review Board

About: Your concurrence with our operating and capital plans for next year

1. Operations. We plan sales revenue next year to be $3,675,000 (U.S.).
This is 5% below the current year and reflects our expectation of a recession in the Republic of South Africa's economy. Our own prediction has been reinforced by that of our consulting economist. The recession is not expected to last more than fifteen to eighteen months. In line with this prediction we will shortly take steps to reduce the labour force and diminish stocks (primarily of finished goods). Our plans for costs are: cost of manufacturing, $2,950,000 (U.S.); selling, advertising, and administrative expense, $400,000; special employee benefits, $105,000; provision for depreciation, $57,500; income before taxes, $162,500.

2. Capital. No plans for any nonroutine projects.

Exhibit 3

Selected Information on the Results of Operations of Custom Cabinets (Pty.), Ltd. and Magna-Vaal Radio Co. (Pty.), Ltd.

	Custom Cabinets				Magna-Vaal Radio			
	Sales (in South African Rands)	Units Produced	Net Profits Before Income Tax (Rands)	Pre-Tax Return on Shareholders Equity[1]	Sales (in South African Rands)	Units Produced	Net Profits Before Income Tax (Rands)	Pre-Tax Return on Shareholders Equity[1]
Present Year (est.)	R810,000	125,000	R43,750	18%	R2,790,000	56,250	R150,000	18%
Previous "	630,000	95,000	13,200	7%	2,500,000	53,750	150,000	20%
" "	517,500	77,500	4,650	3%	2,365,000	52,500	156,000	22%
" "	405,000	52,500	25,500	21%	2,260,000	52,500	102,000	15%
" "	415,000	57,500	36,000	29%	2,465,000	57,500	178,000	24%

[1]The effective income tax rate for these companies in the Republic of South Africa is 40%. There is no restriction on the remittance of dividends to the United States.

Exhibit 4

Comments by Vice-President for Economic and Market Research of Magna Electric Co., Inc.

---

1.   This responds to your inquiry yesterday about the future course of the economy of the Republic of South Africa.

2.   The consulting economist to Magna-Vaal Radio Co. (Ltd.), Dr. Jan Tinbergen, is a highly respected economist with an international reputation for his econometric and statistical studies. Of course, there are other economists who will differ with any particular forecast he may make.

3.   A thorough study to enable us to make a reliable prediction about the future of the South African economy and its radio receiver market will require six months, hiring two consulting firms, and the attention of one of our staff. Given funds from the International Group's appropriation, we shall be glad to undertake the study.

Custom Cabinets (Pty.), Ltd., under the previous ownership, sold cabinets only to the radio manufacturing company. However, executives of Magna Electric Company encouraged Mr. Jones to seek other customers. In the past few years he has increased sales until the radio company now buys only 50% of the cabinet company's output. Mr. Jones believes that his previous problem of increasing sales of wooden cabinets for better radios was eased in the Republic of South Africa by the government's then existing ban on television.

The cabinet plant runs efficiently, uses the most modern machinery obtainable, and is staffed by highly trained European craftsmen who are organized into the European Labour Union. It, like the radio receiver plant, is located in a suburb about ten miles from the center of Johannesburg and similarly distant from low-priced housing.

The assembly department of the radio factory operates on a batch process. Demand for radio receivers is not large enough in the Republic of South Africa to set up an assembly line for each class of radio made. Therefore, while the shop has several lines, each line has to be shut down at times for minor adjustments to jigs and fixtures. Restarting requires a certain amount of training time for employees to adjust to the different parts and the slightly modified assembly procedure. Plant workers are mainly unskilled "coloureds" (persons of mixed blood) who learn on the job. Federal law forbids their joining unions.

An act of the South African Parliament requires that certain industries (radios, automobile assembly, etc.) incorporate from 55% to 90% of locally manufactured and assembled parts in the final product. Magna-Vaal Radio therefore has a components manufacturing department as well as an assembly department.

Magna-Vaal sells radio receivers in the medium- to high-priced segment of the South African market. It has a large share of the present receiver market.

One director said: "This orange smoke from the steel mills and the blue water remind me of homecoming at Urbana. But what shall we do about those outfits in South Africa? It looks to me as if it all adds up to whom we are going to believe."

Another director straightened his spine a fraction further and snorted: "When we run into problems like this, the whole thing is just not worthwhile. Look at the difficulties in South Africa. The Davis Cup. People picketing Engelhard Minerals and Eastman Kodak because they have plants there. Those wild-eyed militants pressuring banks on the West Coast not to invest in Johannesburg. I don't want any bleeding-hearts at our doors."

A third director said: "To get back to the issue—it's not whom we believe but whom will we trust? Which managing director do we want to put our money on?"

Question

What decisions should the Plans Review Board make?

Magna Electric Company (B)

The Plans Review Board decided to seek additional information before concurring with plans for the coming year presented by Custom Cabinets (Pty.), Ltd. and Magna-Vaal Radio Company (Pty.) Ltd. In two weeks Mr. Thorson flew to Johannesburg.

In their first conversation, Mr. Rosenberg said: "I've decided that we should lay off 25% of the assembly workers while keeping the testing crews, stock workers, office, and shipping and receiving crews intact. We will keep all the supervisors. Costs will not go down as much as I would like, but it will be easier to resume high-level operations later.

"When I instructed Mr. Klaus, factory manager, to put through the reductions in force, he demurred, saying that business would not drop off, he thought, and that the staff would be needed for the orders on hand or about to come in. When I found, two weeks ago, that he still had not carried out my order, I appointed him as line foreman in charge of manufacturing components and promoted the head assembly factory foreman, Mr. van der Merwe, to be factory manager. He is now going through the factory personnel list and will shortly drop every fourth person.

"You will see that I was correct about the decrease in demand. Our production and shipments are already 10% below last year's rate for the past 10 days.

"When the labour force reaches the planned size and production drops, we can then undertake a rearrangement of the assembly department—knock out a few walls, that kind of thing—which will increase our efficiency. . . ."

Mr. Jones, Managing Director of Custom Cabinets (Pty.) Ltd., said to Mr. Thorson: "Mr. Smit, our factory manager, and I have decided not to lay off any workers. We do not believe in a recession in our economy—the sales rate is as good now as at any time in the past—and layoffs will probably result in wildcat strikes.

"One of the secrets of our profitability is a common trust between our craftsmen and management. I am not going to disrupt this by unwarranted firings. . . .

"If you talk to Klaus, over at the radio factory, you will find that receiver sales are holding up, too. There is a little trouble there with production. Van der Merwe is going to have his hands full. . . ."

Questions

(1) Should Mr. Thorson give any instructions to Mr. Rosenberg or to Mr. Jones while in Johannesburg?

(2) On the basis of data you have, what recommendations do you think Mr. Thorson should make to the Plans Review Board when he returns to Chicago?

Part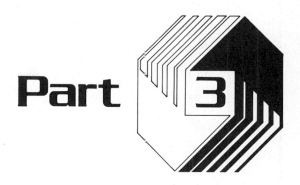

COMBINING BUSINESS-UNITS IN A DIVERSIFIED CORPORATION

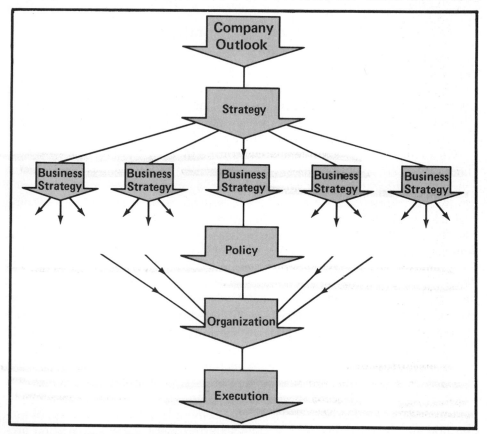

STRATEGY FOR A DIVERSIFIED CORPORATION

Business-Unit Versus Corporate Strategy

Strategy and policy for a *single business-unit* has been our focus thus far, in both Parts 1 and 2. These single product line, self-contained "companies" are the dynamic building blocks of our economic society. Each requires individualized attention. Our prime attention on the creation of strong business-units is more than a convenient analytical approach; it reflects the cardinal importance of these units.

Nevertheless, successful business-units often outgrow their original mission. Their market may have matured; they may have strengths that can be applied to related businesses. Or, a broader base may be needed to match competition or spread risk; assurance of supplies may become critical; perhaps an irresistible deal may present itself. For such reasons as these, many companies find themselves engaged in several different businesses.

Sooner or later the benefits of combining the collection of business-units within a corporation must be assessed. Potentially, the federation of units will be stronger than the sum of each business operating independently. But this does not happen automatically. We need a "corporate strategy" which focuses on the selection and the interrelation of units that will, in fact, yield the benefits of union.

Corporate strategy, in contrast to business-unit strategy, applies to a different level of organization and it differs in content. It is primarily concerned with building an effective collection of business-units. This requires thoughtful investment (allocation) of resources. Some units will be built up, others liquidated; perhaps new units will be acquired. Because this allocation process is similar to that of a financial investment manager changing the composition of securities in his or her portfolio, the term "portfolio problem" is widely used to identify the distinctive aspects of managing a diversified corporation.

A basic approach to formulating corporate strategy is indicated in the following chart. A careful appraisal of the business-units presently owned is the first step. For each unit, the results to date, the standing relative to competitors, threats and opportunities in its environment, and projected future results based on existing plans should be studied. Moreover, the projections for all business-units should be combined into a consolidated picture of what the corporation will be and do if the status quo is maintained.

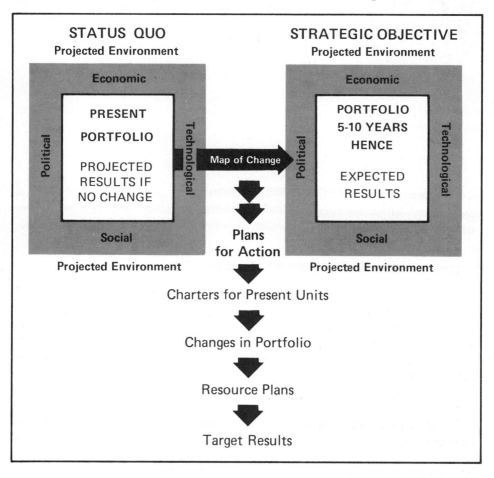

If this combined picture is not entirely satisfactory then the second broad step is to decide what doable changes, executed within the projected environment, would put the corporation in the best balanced position. This becomes the strategic objective. It stipulates the desired portfolio of business-units five-to-ten years hence, their relative competitive positions, the individual unit results, and the combined results for the corporation as a whole.

To move from the status quo to the strategic objective will require some supporting changes along the way. The main features of these planned changes, which become part of the corporate strategy, deal with charters for present units (domains, expectations, constraints), changes in the portfolio, resource plans including sources and allocation of capital, and target results at intervals along the course.

The main elements in a corporate strategy, then, include:

1. The desired portfolio of business-units five-to-ten years hence.
2. Major moves (thrusts) to get from present situation to the holdings pictured in (1):
   (a) charters for business-units to be retained;
   (b) additions or deletions of business-units, including desired acquisitions;
   (c) consolidated resource mobilization and allocation plans.
3. Target results.

The chief issues and hurdles in developing such a corporate strategy are discussed in this chapter, except for the process of acquiring a new firm which is considered in Chapter 16.

PORTFOLIO DESIGN

A good portfolio has several dimensions. Four are always significant: (1) growth and profitability of the business-units considered separately, (2) synergy among the units, (3) risk and profit balance, and (4) cash-flow balance.

1st Ingredient: Attractive Business-Units

The business-units within any diversified corporation will naturally vary in attractiveness. Industry growth rates change, competitors expand capacity, risks assumed turn out well or poorly, and so forth. So an initial step in reviewing portfolio strategy is to compare the relative attractiveness of present units, especially in terms of their *future* prospects for growth and profitability. Corporation resources will be limited, with respect to central management time and perhaps also capital. Consequently, guidance is needed on where to place the "bets."

A useful way to highlight such a comparison of business-units is on an evaluation matrix. One such matrix, adapted from layouts used by General Electric and Royal Dutch Shell, is shown on the following page.[1] Here each business-unit is evaluated on the basis of its industry attractiveness and its competitive position in that industry.

Placing a business-unit on such a matrix involves many subjective judgments. Both the sub-factors to be included and the outlook for each factor have to be decided. Among the sub-factors which determine an industry's attractiveness are: market growth rate, stability of demand, availability of resources, product and process volatility, number of customers and suppliers

---

[1]This matrix is a significant refinement of the more familiar 2×2 matrix stressed by The Boston Consulting Group. The earlier B.C.G. version focused only on cash flow, and simply looked at industry growth versus company market position. The resulting four boxes were designated: 1:1 stars, 1:2 wildcats or problem children, 2:1 cash cows, and 2:2 dogs.

and the ease of entry, governmental support/regulation, gross and net margins, inflation vulnerability. A similar set of sub-factors bear on the competitive position of a business-unit. These include: relative market share, product/service quality and reputation, favorable access to resources, R&D strength, relative productivity and costs, community and government relations. (See Chapter 3 for discussion of industry and business-unit sub-factors.)

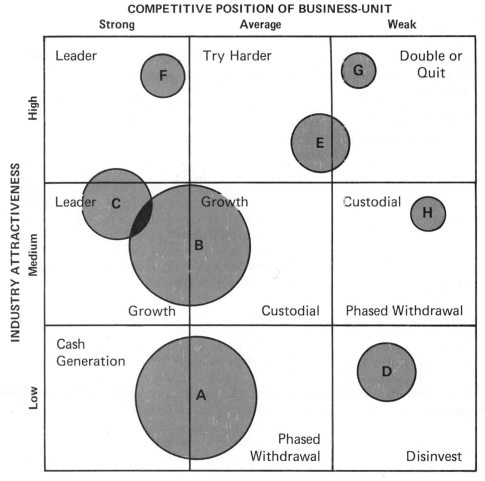

EVALUATION MATRIX
Area within circles indicates relative size of business-units

The matrix is designed to provoke strategic thinking. For instance, in the example shown, business-unit D clearly should be divested, and A, the corporation's original business, has such poor prospects that it should be used to generate cash as it is phased out. In contrast, units E and G may warrant significant resource inputs because they are in attractive industries.

This sizing up of the business-units separately, of course, builds upon the thorough strategic planning done within the respective units. Each business-unit should have its own plans which, if successful, may change its present location on the evaluation matrix. At the corporate level harsher judgments about their *relative* prospects are needed as a basis for allocating scarce resources.

2nd Ingredient: Synergy Among Businesses

A good portfolio is more than a collection of attractive business-units. The fact that the units are associated under a single central management should add extra value. Often a unit when viewed separately has only medium appeal, but when combined with other holdings it may add unusual strength. Synergy and balance are both involved.

Four potential sources of synergy deserve attention. (1) First is the ability of corporate executives to manage (serve as "outside director") various kinds of businesses with acumen. Historical data show that the more successful diversified companies stick to "related" businesses. Thus, Federated Department Stores in its diversification stays with retailing because its central managers understand that type of activity. In contrast, Teledyne in its initial growth phase concentrated on new high-technology businesses. The rationale is that the experience gained and the competence needed in guiding one part of the portfolio will be especially valuable to *other business-units* in related fields.[2]

By no means rare are companies with managements that dislike decisive action. The president of a medical supply company had placed close friends in charge of branch operations and was unwilling to replace these executives in spite of submarginal performance. Nevertheless, this company was attractive for merger because the elimination of two losing units and the change of one additional executive made the remaining activities a successful venture. Quite clearly, managers with an objective viewpoint, introduced following the merger, were all that was needed.

(2) Synergy may be possible from the broader use of a particular strength of one of the business-units. The Campbell Soup Company provides a well-known example. Over the years this company has built up a strong national selling organization for its soups. When it acquired Pepperidge Farm, an East Coast producer of specialty breads, cookies, etc., it used its marketing strength to give Pepperidge Farm products national distribution.

In another case, the R&D capability of a production systems company helped a machine tool business develop electronic controls for its equipment. Similarly, the national repair service organization of a printing press company is a great boost to the sale of Swiss-made auxiliary equipment.

---

[2]This argument also has negative connotations. As we shall see, considerations of balance may suggest that unrelated businesses be assembled, but if this is done part of the cost will be added complexity in management.

(3) Vertical integration is another potential source of synergy. For instance, an assured supply of paper periodically becomes critical for magazine publishers. Time, Inc. has its own paper subsidiaries which provide supply protection. At the same time, Time's paper mills are assured of a large steady customer with a minimum of selling effort.

(4) When business-units are relatively small, the parent may be able to provide a centralized resource more efficiently than the units could obtain that resource independently. The prime example, of course, is raising capital in major financial markets on terms which separate units could not command alone. But there are many other possibilities. Small commercial banks, when they are combined into one group, find substantial economies in electronic processing of checks, deposits, billings, etc. (The local unit is also able to make larger loans because the total capital which sets size limits is larger.) The central room reservation service which hotel and motel chains provide is a significant advantage to local units in maintaining occupancy.

Care must be exercised in seeking synergies. Some possibilities run into antitrust barriers. Also, obtaining a synergistic benefit clearly implies that two or more business-units will operate within certain constraints; and over time that requirement may become a serious drag. Many vertical integration schemes, for instance, tend to limit flexibility, as rubber companies tied to obsolete national rubber plantations discovered.

Nevertheless, the prospect of synergistic benefits may influence decisions of which business-units to retain—or add—in a total portfolio. The potential impact of ability to manage, use of special strengths, vertical integration, and central resource pools should be at least considered.

3rd Ingredient: Risk and Profit Balance

A third consideration in portfolio strategy is the degree of risk and the resulting fluctuation in profits that is acceptable. The mix of businesses selected clearly affects the overall uncertainty about the stability and size of sales and profits.

An issue here is whether to reduce risk by diversifying even with some sacrifice of profits, or to support risky ventures with potentially high profits. Similarly, there may be a trade-off between liquidation with a known payout versus continuing in business with an uncertain future.

Prevailing norms provide two portfolio guides. (a) Companies in mature businesses are expected to shift investment to new lines of business in order to provide continuity even though the new businesses are more risky than the present ones. For example, Handy & Harman's traditional activity of processing silver and gold is "mature," because major new uses of these venerable metals are unlikely, and rising metal prices dampen much increase in the physical volume of present uses. So Handy & Harman has adopted a long-run objective of deriving half its future profits outside the precious metal area. It is steadily adding business-units in other high-value-added industrial processes. This is an explicit strategy of reducing the risk associated with remaining in its primary field.

(b) Another indication of the importance attached to survival is the concept that a corporation should not bet its existence on a single, risky venture. No publicly owned firm relies entirely upon the success of drilling a particular off-shore oil well; it gets other investors to share the risk on that well, and then it "diversifies" to part ownership in other wells, probably in other geographical areas.

Hedging against cyclical risks is often proposed. If you are in the construction business, the idea is to also enter a business that goes up when construction goes down. In practice, cyclical hedges are very difficult to find. A corporation supplying auto manufacturers, for example, may enter the replacement-parts market because this has a much more steady demand; but the replacement-parts industry is at most stable, not contra-cyclical, so the combined result is only a dampening of the auto production fluctuations. To return to the Handy & Harman example, that corporation does have a large refinery for secondary recovery of precious metals, so when metal prices rise, the refinery is busy even though the processing mill is slack.

In a shorter term view, some revenue stabilization can be achieved by balancing *seasonal* products. The old nostalgic "coal and ice" business is now reflected in Head's production of skis and tennis rackets, of ski clothing and shorts.

In each of the above examples, one specific risk is offset (to some extent) by another with counterbalancing characteristics. The aim is greater stability of revenue and profits, even though the average result may be lower than the "expected" returns from one of the ventures alone. Carried to the extreme, this averaging of risks leads to a conglomerate where a catch-all collection of businesses is assembled with no special effort to match one against another. (Full diversification gives a corporation an average growth about the same as the GNP, a growth rate unacceptable to many managers and investors.) However, even the high-flying conglomerates rarely admit to such indiscriminate averaging. Instead, some other rationale dominates portfolio selection—such as synergy—and risk balancing is a constraint to bring total exposure down to a level acceptable to major stakeholders.

4th Ingredient: Cash Flow Balance

Growing businesses typically absorb cash—for working capital as well as for plant and equipment—even when they are highly profitable. In fact, companies do fail because their cash resources cannot support a very successful "take-off" of their product. Mature and declining businesses, in contrast, often generate cash, as assets are gradually being liquidated. Such net investment flows vary widely by kind of business, having a high early peak in mining, for example, and the reverse in magazine publishing where consumers pay in advance for subscriptions.

One additional dimension in building a portfolio, then, is balancing cash flows. *Internal* generation of needed cash is the aim. Of course, this is not the only potential source of cash; new equity and loans can be secured for profitable ventures, and declining ventures rarely need or justify new infusions. Nevertheless, our tax system makes internal generation of cash a significant advantage. Cash paid to stockholders as dividends is subject to personal income tax; even if the stockholders are willing to reinvest it in the corporation, they have much less—maybe only 50%—to so invest. However, if the corporation itself makes the reinvestment directly, the personal income tax bite is avoided. (Underwriting expenses are also avoided.) Moreover, if a new business-unit is showing a loss which can be offset against a profit of some other unit, then to that extent (and temporarily we hope), the corporate income tax can also be avoided until the loss-carry-over is used up.

Since internally generated cash is a comparatively inexpensive and convenient way to finance growing business-units, one or more "cash-cows," as cash generating units are often called, are attractive segments in a portfolio even when their long-run prospects are poor. This ability to shift cash flows from cash-cows to stars and wildcats can provide a corporation with immortality—Ponce de Leon's fountain of youth!

Summarizing: The design of a desired portfolio considers several different factors, including: attractiveness of the business-units separately, synergy, balanced risk and profits, and cash flow. The weight attached to each factor depends upon the strengths that the corporation already possesses, environmental opportunities, and personal values of its key executives.

MAJOR MOVES TO ATTAIN DESIRED PORTFOLIO

Charters for Present Business-Units

The portfolio strategy for a diversified corporation blends several different considerations, as we have just seen. The long-run strength and direction of the consolidated group is the dominant criterion. The various business-units are assigned roles in terms of what is good for the *family as a whole*.

In this composite plan, some business-units are destined to grow rapidly; others have to modify their emphasis, overcome particular weaknesses, or demonstrate improved capability before they will be strongly supported; a few may be encouraged to take high risks because the potential gains are great; several have the role of cash-cows; one or two may be retained largely for the protection or strength they give one of the "stars"; and so on.

With this overall concept in mind, it is possible to negotiate a "charter" for each existing business-unit. This charter will be an agreement between corporate executives and the senior management of the business-unit regarding:

1. The *domain*—the product/service/market scope—in which the business-unit will operate.
2. The *expected results,* including sales growth, competitive position, productivity, profitability after interest and taxes, cash generation, R&D output, community leadership, and perhaps other objectives. Some of these will be numerical and sharp, others may be intangible and "soft."
3. *Constraints* regarding expected interaction with other business-units of the company, external behavior norms, required management systems, and the like. These, too, may be quantitative or qualitative.
4. *Resources* which will be made available from the corporation and those which the unit is free to acquire itself.

Such charters are the bridges, the connecting links, between corporate strategy and the strategies of the various business-units. They define the mission of each unit insofar as that mission is shaped by corporation-wide considerations. As with all strategy, the content is selective, focusing on vital issues while deliberately excluding procedural and personal relationships. For each business-unit, its charter sets the scope and broad objectives of its activities. And for the corporate office, each charter provides the major guidelines for approving or disapproving various proposals for specific actions.

We should note that business-unit charters are not holy words passed down from omniscient corporate officials. Rather, they emerge from recurring give-and-take discussions between executives at the corporate and business-unit levels. Business-unit executives must be active participants because they know most about possibilities and problems of the business, and because they must psychologically accept the challenge that the charter provides. At the same time, a location within a family of business-units inherently creates needs which must be fitted into the more specific strategies of the respective units.

Changes in the Portfolio

In addition to providing a basis for charters for existing business-units, corporate portfolio analysis flags the need for additions and deletions in the portfolio. Which of the present units are irrelevant and a drag? What gaps need to be filled with split-offs or acquisitions? And if acquisitions are called for, what characteristics should they have?

Opportunities for new synergy or improved balance may stand out during the careful portfolio analysis outlined above. *Or* proposals from internal entrepreneurs or outsiders may call attention to ways the overall portfolio could be strengthened. Once recognized, such potential additions become "opportunity gaps" for strategic planning.

The next question is whether to try to fill the opportunity gaps by *internal growth or acquisitions.* Sometimes there is little choice. For example, when Pan Am recognized that its international bookings were being jeopardized by the lack of coordinated domestic flights, merger with an existing domestic airline was the only realistic alternative. To start its own domestic flights was neither economic nor legally feasible. So a tie-up with someone like National Airlines was the direction in which to move.

In other circumstances, gap-filling by acquisition is impractical. Proctor & Gamble learned that antitrust barriers prevented it from getting a running start in the bleach business through an acquisition of Clorox. Clearly, for legal reasons the bigger the parent company, the more it will have to rely on internal growth in new businesses which are closely related to its existing businesses. Moreover, in a brand new industry acquisition candidates may not exist. When Western Union moved into satellite communications, for example, the necessary satellites were not yet in orbit.

Between these extremes, however, a choice often exists. In many states, for example, commercial banks can increase their geographic coverage either by opening new branches or by acquiring existing banks in the desired location. Acquisitions provide faster entry and perhaps some resources (such as people, market position, trademarks, or patents) that would be difficult to assemble. On the other hand, acquisitions often bring with them unwanted assets or traditions; they may foreclose taking other attractive steps; they may be more difficult to meld into the family; and/or they may be expensive.

During the late 'sixties and early 'seventies, many corporate planners fell in love with acquisitions. Corporate strategy and acquisition plans were treated almost as synonymous. Now a more balanced view prevails. A total portfolio strategy is developed, as outlined in this chapter, and acquisition criteria and opportunities grow out of this broader picture. Acquisitions often are a significant facet of corporate strategy, but they are only a part.

Divestments are the other side of the coin, hence also a part of strategy. The matrix analysis suggested at the beginning of the chapter identifies business-units which both now and in the future make little contribution to corporate goals. Further study of synergy and of risk and cash flow balance refine this diagnosis. In any turbulent environment some business-units will become either a continuing drain on resources or at least a drag on energies that could be better directed elsewhere.

In practice, divestments are usually made too slowly. Even outstanding companies are reluctant to get rid of—in Boston Consulting Group language —their "dogs." RCA held on to its venture in computers until losses were in the hundreds of millions; General Foods dabbled first in gourmet delicacies, then in the fast-food business well beyond the point of no return; Johnson & Johnson kept TEK brushes long after that unit failed to serve the evolving corporate strategy. Such tardiness is explained partly by waiting for a propitious opportunity to sell or liquidate the unit. The primary cause, however, is personal. There is no inside champion for disposal, as typically will be present for an acquisition; some people will lose their jobs; and senior executives are reluctant to admit that they cannot make a success of anything they direct.

Without clear strategic direction, these normal pressures for inaction are likely to dominate. To avoid the high cost of inaction, both corporate strategy and effective execution are needed.

Resource Plans and Target Results

A well conceived corporate strategy provides several kinds of guides. It leads to coordinated charters for existing business-units, and also to plans for additions to and deletions from the present line-up, as we have just seen. In addition, two other forms of guidance should be developed.

The projected courses for various business-units will generally call for *resources* from the central corporate pool, notably capital and perhaps executives or central services. To help assure that these resources will be available when needed, a summary program of the expected flows to and from the business-units should be prepared. Such a program will (a) alert corporate officials of any prospective need for obtaining new resources. A revision in capital structure may be involved, and if so, groundwork for the issuance of new securities should be laid. Contingency plans reflecting shifts in capital markets may be advisable.

Also, (b) the resource plans will show in approximate numbers how much will be allocated annually to each business-unit for what purposes, at least as future developments are now conceived. These allocations will probably be revised as wants unfold. Nevertheless, the strategy provides guideposts, and any major deviation in resources needed will call for a review of the continuing wisdom of the strategy. Meanwhile, the various business-units can proceed with their planning on the working assumption that the projected resource allocations will be made available to them over the next several years.

A final set of guides tied in with the strategy are the *target results*. Every strategy is designed to reach certain goals by given dates. These are the expected consequences of the stipulated actions. Some of these target results will be *financial;* perhaps sales, profits, return on investment, or earnings per share. Other targets may be more *qualitative:* market position in selected industries, community endorsement, product leadership, resource base, and the like. Such targets are good for keeping on course, motivation, and control, as we shall see in Part 5.

MODIFICATIONS DURING EXECUTION

Corporate strategy as described in the preceding pages is a powerful tool. It pulls together the actions of the various business-units into a balanced, synergistic program; it channels scarce resources; it endorses missions for operating managers, and sets targets for overall results. But it is a difficult tool to use.

The Lure of Exceptions

Cynics say that most corporate portfolio "strategy" is merely a high-sounding rationalization of acquisitions already made. Somehow, the argument runs, between risk balance, cash flows, and synergy you can justify any combination. And it is true that many promoters who are guided by little or no consistent strategy do dress up their actions with the language of strategic management. However, the possibility of such chicanery does not reduce the strength of strategic management for those who sincerely use it as a way of harnessing their own behavior. We don't forego medical treatment just because a few quacks exist.

The real difficulties in practice are more subtle. A common problem is the temptation of "a good deal." For example, a proposed acquisition may offer attractive short-run financial benefits. One company may have a large tax loss carryover, and if a profitable unit can be merged into that company the taxes that the profitable unit would otherwise have to pay can be avoided.

Acquisition of companies for far less than their replacement cost is also tempting, even though replacement would be a serious mistake.

Or, mergers may be suggested solely because of differences in price-earnings ratios. Suppose the stock of the Apple Company is selling at twenty times its earnings per share and the stock of the less glamorous Orange Company at ten times its earnings. Then if Apple acquires Orange and its price-earnings ratio stays at twenty, the capitalized (market) value of Orange's earnings has doubled.

The acquisition of privately held businesses may be focused primarily on inheritance and estate taxes. Or, a proposal may pivot around the predilections of a few key individuals. Indeed, the resourcefulness of match-makers is an impressive display of human ingenuity.

"Good deals" are fine *provided* they also are compatible with corporate strategy. The danger is that managerial energies and other resources will be side-tracked into ventures that are alluring at the moment but do not contribute to a strong, balanced portfolio. In contrast, if a corporation has thought through its strategy, then it already has a screening mechanism to quickly decide which proposed deals warrant further attention. Too often the strategy is fuzzy and the "good deal" is embraced as an exception.

The reverse also occurs. Actions that should be taken are postponed—as exceptions. Here the common examples are sick business-units where drastic action is unpleasant. A *Fortune* 500 corporation turned down an opportunity to sell (at a loss) one of its oldest business-units which was clearly in a declining industry; because of its long affiliation, an exception to the recognized strategy was made. Losses increased and three years later the division was liquidated because no buyer could be found. In another corporation, an ailing division with dim prospects was nursed along for seven years, as a "special case." The serious cost in this instance was the required time and attention of senior management which could have been much more productive if it had been spent on growing businesses.

Because exceptions to beautifully designed plans are sometimes warranted, the tough judgment is what special benefits are great enough to justify intentionally going off course. Our observation is that exceptions too often win the day.

Baffling Uncertainties

In designing corporate strategy, many uncertainties must be resolved. Somehow, through some combination of facts, expert opinion, and intuition, forecasts of business conditions, industry outlooks, and business-unit success must be made. Of course, revisions and contingency plans may be included. But without agreed-upon forecasts a full-blown strategy cannot be formulated.

Many forecasts can be made with reasonable confidence, at least within the time-span and tolerance limits necessary for strategic planning. Other factors such as international political developments or finding a cure for cancer are baffling. And when several key factors are interdependent, scenario forecasting is often the best we can do. For example, the attractiveness of a company planning to produce manganese from modules lying deep on the ocean floor depends upon technological advances, world price of manganese, and international agreements on a law of the sea—to name only three related uncertainties. Forecasting in such areas is hazardous. And when a parent corporation is largely dependent upon a naturally biased business-unit for assessment data, the evaluation becomes even tougher.

Two dimensions which are increasingly frustrating for international investment are rates of inflation and foreign exchange rates. Inflation is pushing long-range planning away from profits based on conventional accounting to annual cash flows. Then the cash flow estimates have varying value due to shifts in exchange rates, if we assume that transfer of the money will be permitted. The cumulative uncertainty in such computations may well exceed the tolerance of practical planning.

In such circumstances, some parts of a corporate strategic plan may have to retreat to "prepared opportunism." The future is seen too dimly to lay out market positions and other expected results. Yet a conviction remains that truly attractive opportunities will develop, and those firms ready to serve such opportunities will benefit from an early start. So the corporate strategy seeks to position one or more business-units where they can move promptly as the prospects become clearer. Such a strategic position may involve frontier technology, local marketing and distribution systems staffed with indigenous personnel, transportation facilities, skill and favorable reputation in managing joint enterprises, ties to world markets, or access to raw materials.

Under prepared opportunism a particular business-unit may be encouraged—its charter may provide—to develop along certain lines which the unit acting alone would shun. Within the parent corporation's total portfolio may be several such business-units, each building strength on a particular front. Then as events unfold, those strengths that prove to be valuable can be forged into a more specific plan. Rarely will all the specially directed units find a significant role in the final program, and to this extent effort and investment will have to be discarded. The hope, of course, is that the strengths actually used will be sufficiently valuable to offset losses on the others.

Such a strategy lacks the completeness, neatness, and efficiency of a fully developed plan. However, it does have the virtue of feasibility in the face of baffling uncertainties.

Workability Test

No strategy is well conceived until its workability is weighed. If the chances of it being carried out are remote or the cost of doing so are very high, then the strategy itself should be at least reassessed.

Two implementation issues are directly created by corporate portfolio choices which we have been exploring in this chapter. Since they can be serious enough to lead to a modification of portfolio strategy, they should be noted here.

Sometimes corporate strategy makes demands of a business-unit which are inconsistent with the strategy that the unit would follow if it were independent. For example, the business-unit may wish to expand whereas the corporate strategy wants it to be a "cash-cow." It is natural for unit executives to feel that they should be permitted to use the cash they generate to strengthen their own position, instead of denying themselves for the benefit of a small upstart activity.

In other cases, business-units are asked to incur risks (or avoid risks) because doing so helps corporate balance. Synergy may require that a business-unit refrain from developing its own raw materials. Or prepared opportunism may call for a form of expansion that is very expensive from the unit viewpoint. Such corporate demands seem especially onerous to managers of a business-unit when they arise unexpectedly because of some other activities of the corporation and the cause is unrelated to their own situation.

Now, in a decentralized corporation the commitment of local executives to their strategy is very important for successful results. If the business-unit executives think that the corporate guides "don't make sense," foot-dragging or misleading information or other maneuvering is likely to occur. A conviction of unit executives that a corporate-imposed strategy "will never work" can very easily become a self-fulfilling prophecy! The basic point is that there is a practical limit to which the business-units can be "pushed around." And this limit is a constraint on what corporate strategy is workable.

Portfolio strategy may create a second kind of workability strain. Each business-unit strategy calls for a managerial system (planning, organizing, leadership, and controlling) which is suited to that strategy. A large "cash-cow" unit needs a different management system than a unit experimenting with coal gasification. The desirable management system for a commercial bank differs from that for an aircraft manufacturer. The more diverse the units within a portfolio, the more heterogeneous will be their management systems.

Few corporation managements have the capability of understanding, melding, and skillfully directing widely diverse management systems. Such diversity raises temperamental and management style issues as well as difficulties of intellectual grasp. "We just don't know how to run that kind of business" is a frank and perceptive comment often heard.

Here again is a practical constraint on corporate portfolios. Cash flows and risk balance may appear desirable, but not beyond the point where effectively administering the diversity of units is no longer feasible.

SUMMARY

This chapter shifts attention from business-units, which have been the focus up to this point, to the assembly of such units by a diversified corporation.

At the corporate level prime consideration goes to developing a strategic "portfolio" of business-units to be in the total family. Four criteria are important in this portfolio design: (1) attractive business-units each considered separately in terms of its industry and its competitive position; (2) synergy that will arise from having a particular mix of business-units within a single corporate group; (3) the combined balance of risk and of short- and long-term profitability; and (4) the prospects of internal generation of cash by some business-units that will help finance projected expansion of other business-units.

Several types of additional strategic plans should be derived from the portfolio design. (a) For each business-unit which is to be retained, a "charter" can be negotiated covering domain, expected results, constraints, and resource support from the corporate pool. (b) Desirable acquisitions, spin-offs, and divestments of business-units will be indicated. (c) The total financial, critical personnel, and other corporate resource pools required can be estimated; then plans can be laid for mobilizing and allocating these resources. (d) Consolidated results targets can be set for intermediate and longer-range periods. Such supporting plans, coupled with the portfolio design, constitute the corporate strategy package.

Carrying out such a corporate strategy calls for unusual persistence. In addition to the array of unexpected events affecting the several business-units, alluring opportunities to make acquisitions which deviate from the portfolio design may arise. Also, the business-units cannot be treated like pawns on a chess board; the morale and responsiveness of managers within the business-units may significantly affect what can be done with those units. Consequently, compromises and adjustments in corporate strategy are likely. Nevertheless, some integrated and consistent direction is far better than mere opportunism or passive drift.

QUESTIONS FOR CLASS DISCUSSION

1. IC Industries was for years the Illinois Central Railroad, and half of its $3 billion assets are still related to transportation. Recently the corporation has been diversifying. It acquired Abex, a prominent manufacturer of railroad brake shoes and wheels, castings, automotive parts, etc.; Midas with its chain of muffler and related auto repair shops; Pet (milk) which has a line of nationally advertised grocery products; several soft-drink bottling companies; and other companies. It is also active in real estate development. Now 41% of its operating profits come from commercial products, 44% from consumer products, 14% from real estate, and only 1% from transportation. (a) In terms of portfolio strategy, what role do you think the railroad company is assigned? Where would you place the railroad on the "evaluation matrix"? (b) What rationale do you think explains the corporation's choice of diversification moves? Do you think the apparent portfolio strategy is wise?

2. In the medical field, both hospitals and nursing homes are trying to find the optimum scope of their services. (a) What advantages do you see in a merger of a community hospital with one or more nearby nursing homes? What disadvantages? (b) What guidelines for mergers of other kinds of enterprises does this analysis suggest?

3. "General Foods Drops Burger Chef" said a headline in the *Wall Street Journal*. General Foods Corporation is a large and successful food manufacturer and distributor. Its many lines include Maxwell House coffee, Birdseye Frozen Foods, Jell-O, Post Cereals, and Kool-Aid. Burger Chef is a chain of 900 fast-food outlets catering to the same market as McDonald's and Burger King. General Foods acquired Burger Chef when it was already established and growing, and expanded the chain even more. During General Foods' ownership, Burger Chef lost money; however, if this loss just reflected wrong management personnel, General Foods had resources to hire new management to turn the business around. From a *portfolio* point of view, do you think General Foods should have kept Burger Chef?

4. Individuals vary widely in the way they balance risk and potential profit. A few endure great hardship and risk their lives for a chance to discover gold. Others take an operating job in their home town with the telephone company and put their savings into government guaranteed savings accounts. (a) Assume *you* just inherited $100,000 with the proviso that you invest it in any of four places in any proportion you choose: residential real estate, U.S. government short-term bonds, exploratory drilling for oil in northern Canada, your own business. How would you allocate the $100,000? (b) Assume you inherited $1,000,000 with the same conditions; how would you allocate it? (c) Assume a corporation has $10,000,000 cash not needed for present operations; how should it decide what to do with the cash?

5. Apollo, Inc. has been unusually successful with the development and sale of its solar energy equipment for homes. Its stock is selling for 17 times earnings on the San Francisco Exchange. Apollo has already acquired a water-heater company, and it is now considering a larger acquisition of Thor Cement Company. Thor is a medium-sized manufacturer of cement located for many years in central California. Its earnings have followed the industry pattern, but it is losing market position. Over-the-counter, its stock sells for 6 to 8 times its earnings. An investment banker proposes that Apollo simply issue 200,000 new shares of its stock and exchange these for the 200,000 shares of Thor stock. The banker presents these figures:

	Shares Outstanding	Annual Earnings	Book Value	Earnings Per Share	P/E Ratio	Market Value per Share
Apollo	600,000	$1,200,000	$10,000,000	$2.00	17	34.00
Thor	200,000	800,000	7,000,000	4.00	7¼	29.00
Combined	800,000	2,000,000	17,000,000	2.50	17	42.50

    (a) Do you recommend that Apollo proceed with the acquisition?

    (b) Should Thor accept? Explain your answers.

6. Several of the large oil companies have made substantial investments in coal mining. (a) From the viewpoint of portfolio strategy, do you think this is a good move for the oil companies?

    (b) Several Congressional representatives have criticized oil companies for this kind of diversification and have introduced bills to stop it. What is the public policy objection to oil companies entering the coal business? Do you think the possibility that such legislation might be passed should deter oil companies from buying coal deposits now?

7. What are the chief differences in scope and content of a business-unit strategy as described in Chapter 5 and a "charter" described in this chapter for a business-unit which is part of a diversified corporation? What *reasons* lead to these differences?

8. Assume that you are the business manager for a monthly magazine, *World Health*. The magazine carries news and semiprofessional articles on new pharmaceuticals, instruments and equipment, new laws, public health experiments, and the like. Readers are people in the health field who either sell products or services worldwide or who want to know what is happening abroad for ideas applicable at home. *World Health* was started in the U.S. and four-fifths of its subscribers are in the U.S. Most of its advertising revenue comes from companies active in the U.S. However, a few years ago the magazine was purchased by a large European publishing corporation. The new owner used its mailing list to help build subscriptions abroad, but otherwise gave the editor and you a free hand. Both of you are enthusiastic about building circulation over the next five years. However, a few months ago the owner has requested that you "concentrate on getting a positive cash flow. We need cash for other promising investments. The value of the dollar is down; your paper and

distribution costs have skyrocketed; and at the home office we see little of the progress that you say you are making." (a) How energetically are you going to push increasing the cash flow to the home office? (b) Under what circumstances do you think the home office is warranted in trying to turn *World Health* into a cash-cow?

9. The research department of Merrill Lynch, Pierce, Fenner & Smith, Inc. studied the most recent wave of merger activity and concluded that corporations were not engaged in a bargain hunt for "cheap" assets as many investors believed. The ratio of tender price to book value was far enough above one which indicates that acquisitions were being made at about replacement cost. So it is not "cheaper to buy them rather than build them." Strong and sound companies bought other financially strong companies. Most acquisitions were made in the same or related business sectors. Acquired companies had an average debt-to-equity ratio of 45%. Buying companies accepted a fairly large dilution of their own shares by paying a premium above market price that pushed the acquired company's price/earnings ratio above that of the buyer. Companies being acquired were above the average of the stocks in Standard & Poor's 500-stock index in their earnings growth and their generation of cash flow. If acquiring companies were *not* buying cheap assets and were also *not* trying to realize an immediate gain in the market price of their stock, what were they doing?

10. The president of the consulting subsidiary of a major New York City bank said: "Premiums above the existing market price paid by corporate acquirers merely for the purpose of diversification are equivalent to charitable contributions to random passersby. They may even subtract from the value of the shares of the buyer. For shareholders, the inescapable conclusion is that true diversification is almost always a bad deal. The shareholder can gain the same diversification by buying the potential seller's shares on the stockmarket at only the going price. The shareholder need not pay the premium." Why, then, do companies diversify? How can the shareholder gain?

CASE 15
Singer Portfolio

Singer is one of the great names in world business. Except for Coca-Cola, Singer Sewing Machines are perhaps the most widely known products in history. They have been sold to fashion designers in Paris and to natives in remote jungles. For over a century, Singer products have traveled on rivers, over mountains, and across deserts to virtually all parts of the globe. Yet in the 1980's, central managers of the Singer Company must decide how small a portion of their total assets should be devoted to sewing machines.

Since 1851, Singer Sewing Machines have been sold directly to users, usually through company stores or agencies. Installment credit and a quality product have been major sales appeals. Production in large plants in the U.S. and England has been supplemented by partial fabrication and assembly in less industrialized countries. By 1958, sales had reached $600 million. A centralized organization in New York perpetuated management practices which up to the late 1940's enabled the company to produce two out of every three sewing machines sold in the world.

The first marked change in company mission occurred in the late 1950's and early 1960's under the leadership of Donald P. Kircher. By this time it was clear that the market for sewing machines in the U.S. and Europe was maturing. More serious, Japanese competition provided severe price competition and was making serious inroads into market share. Management was stodgy.

Kircher set out to rejuvenate the sewing machine business by cutting costs, decentralizing, and focusing on higher-priced models. He also diversified. Early acquisitions were in businesses related to Singer's expertise in making machine production precise and in demonstrating products to customers, but additions soon became more loosely coupled to the traditional business. Twenty-two acquisitions between 1958 and 1963 helped sales to double and profits to triple. By the end of the 1960's, Singer had significant investments in power hand tools (Craftsman line), knitting and carpet tufting machinery, furniture, graphic systems, traffic controls, mail order, consumer credit, housing, heat pumps, home entertainment, business machines, aerospace products, weapon control systems, air-conditioning, gas meters, electronic controls, audio-visual training equipment, etc.

Unfortunately, several of these diversification moves ran into serious trouble. And the 1974 downturn in general business put Singer in a profit-credit squeeze. Its business machines were especially troublesome. Although first in the market with a workable electronic cash register system, the line had to be dropped and several hundred million dollars of loss absorbed. A heavy billion dollar debt accumulated during the expansion period increased the pressure. And at this juncture Donald Kircher, who had guided company growth for seventeen years, became seriously ill. At the end of 1975, Joseph Flavin was brought in from Xerox (and IBM World Trade before that) to become Singer's new C.E.O.

Flavin first gave much of his attention to eliminating losses and reviving Singer's credit standing. From the latter part of 1975 through 1977, a variety of its businesses were liquidated or sold. These included: electromechanical billing and accounting machines, European electrical refrigerator and appliance manufacturing, German mail-order, water resources, graphic systems, business machines, mailing equipment, knitting and tufting equipment, traffic control, and housing. While $158 million was recovered, the net loss on liquidating these assets came to $332 million. And during the liquidation period, these businesses incurred operating losses of an additional $81 million.

The impact of these shifts in Singer's portfolio of businesses is reflected in Exhibits I and II.

By the beginning of 1978, Flavin felt that the house-cleaning was over, and a five-year program for Singer's "development period" was adopted. Targets for the development period are: (a) revenue growth of 10% or more per year, (b) operating income as a percent of sales to increase to 10%, (c) debt/equity ratio to be reduced to 0.6 to 1, (d) an "A" credit rating for the company's funded debt by the early 1980's.

Exhibit I

Total Company Income Data—1961–1978
(in millions, except per share data)

	Net Sales	Income from Continuing Operations	Less Charges for Discontinued Operations	Net Income	Per Share Net Income	Common Stock Dividends
1961	$ 1,037	$ 38	—	$ 38	$ 2.26	$ 1.30
1966	1,644	66	—	66	3.94	2.20
1971	2,054	77	$ – 5	72	3.87	2.40
1972	2,174	90	– 2	88	4.82	2.40
1973	2,489	102	– 8	94	5.32	2.45
1974	2,617	29	–39	–10	– .89	2.45
1975	1,980	–38	–414	–451	–27.68	.30
1976	2,115	59	15*	74	3.98	.10
1977	2,285	75	19*	94	5.11	.25
1978	2,469	60	3*	63**	3.33	.75

*Predominantly tax loss credits.
**The difference between $161 million operating income shown on Exhibit III and the $63 million net income is due to deductions of $59 million for interest and $49 million net for income taxes, plus $10 million net for other adjustments.

Exhibit II

Balance Sheets, December 31, 1978 and 1974
(in millions)

Assets	1978	1974
Cash	$ 89	$ 87
Accounts receivable (net)	385	357
Inventories	483	546
Prepaid expenses, etc.	12	13
Current assets of discontinued operations	—	375
Total current assets	969	1,377
Investments	120	151
Plant, equipment, and property	281	331
Deferred charges and goodwill	66	65
Non-current assets of discontinued operations	—	110
Total assets	$1,435	$2,034
Liabilities and Equity		
Notes and loans payable	$ 112	$ 356
Accounts payable	177	
Accrued expenses	213	459
Other current liabilities	40	
Total current liabilities	542	815
Long-term debt	327	405
Other long-term liabilities	64	45
Total liabilities	933	1,265
Common and preferred stock outstanding	228	179
Retained earnings	274	590
Total equity	502	769
Total liabilities and equity	$1,435	$2,034

In his report to stockholders, Flavin states: "We are confident that these objectives are reasonable and obtainable. We fully recognize the seriousness of our mature market conditions for sewing. However, we believe our corrective action programs will improve our results. We see continued strength in the developing world for sewing and for our non-sewing products. Other products manufactured for consumers show excellent potential, and our products and services for government remains stable with growing profits. . . . Each individual line of business will pursue new opportunities to expand its activities, develop new operating philosophies, suggest investments for future efficiencies in manufacturing and marketing, and find new levels of cooperation between product areas."

Nine lines of business were retained. The sales volume and operating profit of each of these lines for the five years 1974 through 1978 are shown in Exhibit III. The 1978 investment in each line is stated in Exhibit IV. Supplementing this financial data,

Exhibit III

Sales and Operating Income by Lines of Business, 1974–1978
(in millions)

Net Sales	1978	1977	1976	1975	1974
Sewing Products:					
Consumer Sewing Machines	$1,160	$1,112	$1,074	$1,058	$ 963
Industrial Sewing Machines	136	123	133	114	135
	1,296	1,235	1,207	1,172	1,098
Products Manufactured for the Consumer:					
Power Tools and Floor Care	169	169	116	89	77
Furniture	154	142	125	102	178
Control Products	125	134	116	87	98
Air-Conditioning and Heating	123	102	88	79	112
Meter Products	74	63	55	52	57
	645	610	500	409	522
Products and Services for Government:					
Aerospace and Marine Systems	462	379	353	342	352
Education	66	61	55	57	59
	528	440	408	399	411
Company Total	$2,469	$2,285	$2,115	$1,980	$2,031

Operating Income (Loss)

Sewing Products:					
Consumer Sewing Machines	$ 78	$ 95	$ 91	$ 78	$ 70
Industrial Sewing Machines	(9)	(4)	9	(9)	16
	69	91	100	69	86
Products Manufactured for the Consumer:					
Power Tools and Floor Care	25	26	19	15	10
Furniture	24	18	8	(6)	12
Control Products	13	17	13	2	6
Air-Conditioning and Heating	5	2	(3)	(11)	(2)
Meter Products	9	7	7	8	11
	76	70	44	8	37
Products and Services for Government:					
Aerospace and Marine Systems	31	27	24	19	19
Education	5	6	5	7	8
	36	33	29	26	27
Operating Income before Corporate Expenses	181	194	173	103	150
Less: General Corporate Expenses	20	20	21	16	12
Operating Income for Company	$ 161	$ 174	$ 152	$ 87	$ 138

Exhibit IV

Investment by Lines of Business—1978
(In millions. Assets at end of year.)

	Assets	Depreciation	Capital Expenditures
Sewing Products:			
Consumer Sewing Machines	$ 632	$ 26	$ 24
Industrial Sewing Machines	115	2	2
	747	28	26
Products Manufactured for the Consumer:			
Power Tools and Floor Care	63	2	7
Furniture	69	4	4
Control Products	48	4	5
Air-Conditioning and Heating	50	1	1
Meter Products	31	1	1
	261	12	18
Products and Services for Government:			
Aerospace and Marine Systems	203	8	12
Education	19	2	1
	222	10	13
Total applicable to product lines	1,230	50	57
Amounts applicable to corporate	205	3	7
Total Company	$1,435	$ 53	$ 64

the following paragraphs briefly summarize the nature and competition for each line.

Consumer Sewing Machines

Singer manufactures and sells a broad range of consumer sewing machines. In the U.S., Canada, and Europe, emphasis is on the deluxe and upper-middle-price range, including the world's first electronic home sewing machines. Singer and Sears Roebuck & Co. are the leading retailers in the U.S. However, these markets are mature and unit sales are declining.

In Latin America, Africa, and Asia, unit and dollar sales are still growing. As a result of the Singer retail-shop network and availability of installment sales plans, the company has a leading position in many of these countries.

The company operates over 3,000 retail outlets where soft goods and related appliances and services supplement sewing machine sales. (900 in U.S., 1,400 in Western Europe and Canada, 900 in rest of the world.) Sales are divided: 27% in U.S., 35% in Europe and Canada, 38% in Latin America and elsewhere. In all markets, price competition from machines produced in the Far East is very keen.

Industrial Sewing Machines

Singer also manufactures and sells a wide variety of industrial sewing machines through a worldwide network of dealers. Competitors are numerous, and demand is affected by the cyclical nature of the garment industry. A new line of electronic machines introduced in 1976 encountered start-up production difficulties. Also labor problems have arisen in connection with the restructuring of production at Clydebank, Scotland. Nevertheless, the modular design of the new line is being well received by users. In a departure from previous policy, Singer is supplementing the primary machines with specialty machines manufactured by other companies.

Power Tools and Floor Care

For forty years Singer has made portable electric power tools (drills, saws, routers, hedge trimmers, chain-saws, etc.) for Sears' top-quality Craftsman line. Sears is the only customer, so volume depends upon Sears' sales. Singer also produces vacuum cleaners, which are sold through Singer retail stores, dealers, and to major retailers such as Sears under private labels. However, Singer is a relatively small producer of vacuum cleaners compared with its position among the top five for the various types of power tools it makes.

Furniture

Singer is one of the leaders among the many producers of bedroom and dining room furniture in the U.S. It makes a range of medium-priced bedroom and dining room suites as well as a medium-high-priced collection of colonial and "country styled" furniture. These products are marketed through an extensive retailing network in the U.S., consisting of large national accounts, mass merchandisers such as Sears, and department stores, as well as independent furniture dealers. The furniture industry is highly competitive, and demand is affected by levels of residential construction and consumer spending trends. Singer furniture plants also produce cabinets for Singer's consumer sewing machines.

Control Products

Major products in this line include electronic programmers, switches, components and valves for automatic washing machines and dishwashers, electrical switches for automobiles, and valves and thermostats for automobile air-conditioners. Production is highly automated, and the division is a high-volume supplier to mass-production oriented manufacturers. It competes with a number of other large producers in its various product areas. Demand for control products is significantly dependent upon economic conditions in the automobile and home appliance industries.

Air-conditioning and Heating

This division produces various lines of furnaces and air-conditioning equipment for residences, unitary heating and cooling equipment for stores and other commercial establishments, packaged terminal air-conditioners and heat pumps for hotels and office buildings, and electric heat for residences and commercial establishments. Commercial products are marketed directly to installing contractors through manufacturers' representatives, and residential products are sold through distributors to installing dealers. The manufacture and sale of air-conditioning and heating equipment is intensely competitive and volume is significantly influenced by economic conditions in the housing and construction industries. Although not a top producer, Singer is innovative in product design and has been improving its relative position in the segments of industry in which it operates.

Meter Products

This division has served the gas utility industry since 1836. Its principal products are household gas meters and related items for U.S. residential installation. It also tests, repairs, and replaces gas meters for certain utility customers. Only a few large companies, such as Singer, compete in this rather mature market. Growth will depend on increased supplies of natural gas for residential use. New potential markets are arising in those developing countries which have ample natural gas resources. Singer also makes gas meters and flow controls for industrial purposes.

Aerospace and Marine Systems

Singer develops and sells a broad line of navigation systems for aircraft, spacecraft, and marine vessels; anti-submarine warfare systems; aircraft, spacecraft, marine, and industrial simulators; and related systems and products.

Advanced technology is involved in all this work. For instance, as a leader in controlling weapons for anti-submarine warfare, Singer is now developing acoustic systems to counter and/or confuse the weapons of enemy ships. Simulators for training purposes are being designed for the space shuttle program and for the F16 fighter planes. For the General Abrams (XM-1) tank, a gyro-stabilized fire control is being developed that permits the gunner to maintain aim on a target while the vehicle travels at high speed over rough terrain. As these examples suggest, development rather than large-volume production is typical.

Most of this business is for the U.S. government (though often as a subcontract). It is subject to intense competition from other companies, many of which have a much larger "defense business" than does Singer. Risks relate to the size and nature of government spending, renegotiation of prices, timing of interrelated programs, and technological shifts. Nevertheless, Singer's rate of profit has been normal for the industry.

Education

Singer is a relatively small competitor in the manufacture and sale of audiovisual equipment and film strips for educational users. The company also operates Job Corps centers (vocational training) for the U.S. Department of Labor, an activity which accounts for almost half of its education sales.

Singer's development plan described above received a severe blow in October, 1979, when Flavin announced a sharp cutback in sewing machine production. The plant at Clydebank, Scotland, is to be closed, permanently discharging 3,000 employees, nearly a third of Singer's workforce in sewing machine plants; the number of company-owned retail stores in Europe and North America (the backbone of Singer's sewing machine distribution system) also are to be reduced. To cover losses on the total restructuring of the sewing machine business, a $130 million reserve has been created. Additional operating charges up to $50 million are likely during the next few years.

Underlying this retrenchment is a marked drop in the demand for domestic sewing machines. A recent market analysis shows that fewer Americans are interested in sewing. Probably a similar trend is occurring in Europe. Even if Singer can hold its thirty percent share of the market against severe price competition (a machine costing $123 at Clydebank can be made in Taiwan for $65), volume will fall.

Percent U.S. Women Owning Sewing Machines		
	1970	1985 forecast
16 to 24 years of age	46	18
25 to 29 years of age	79	31

In developing countries, however, sales have been increasing about 10% per year since 1972. Margins are higher, and in 1978 Singer earned $73 million operating profit on sales of $460 million. So the weakness lies in the economically advanced countries.

Questions

(1) If Joseph Flavin had asked you, at the end of 1978, for your assessment of Singer's portfolio of businesses, what would you have told him? What changes, if any, would you have recommended?

(2) Now add the news about trouble in the sewing machine area. How would your assessment and recommendations change?

MERGERS AND ACQUISITIONS

Mergers are exciting. They make headlines; new thrusts into growth areas are foreshadowed; realignments of supply are imminent; the status, security, and social relationships of many people are affected; large blocks of capital are involved; government agencies gird for action.

For managers of a specific enterprise, however, the excitement of a merger is incidental since a merger with another company is a major event in the life of an enterprise; it may be the key to success or failure. And like the marriage of a man and a woman, it has deep emotional as well as economic effects. Consequently, mergers should be approached with care.

Corporate strategy, discussed in the previous chapter, indicates the kind of new business-units desired. Now we turn to three related issues:

1. Should the new unit be developed within the corporation or be an acquisition of an existing outside company?
2. If it is to be acquired, how should it be financed?
3. What steps need to be taken to assure that the anticipated benefits will be realized after the merger takes place?

These questions apply to both mergers and acquisitions. Formerly, the term "merger" applied to the consolidation of two companies about equal in size, whereas "acquisition" involved a larger firm taking over a smaller one. Since this distinction is no longer consistently observed and is not significant to our analysis here, we use the words interchangeably.

ACQUISITION VERSUS INTERNAL DEVELOPMENT

Why Look Outside?

Every merger involves complicated financial negotiations, revamping organizations, career readjustments, perhaps physical moves, and other changes. A central manager could avoid most of these burdens by expanding from within instead of merging with a stranger. Consequently, a merger must offer strong advantages over internal expansion. Typically, a sound merger must provide major benefits in terms of (1) time, (2) expense, or (3) physical possibility.

The mergers of local banks to take advantage of new technology, mentioned previously, provide the needed volume of activity quickly; slower internal growth would postpone the use of new methods for years. Similarly, when Du Pont Laboratories was successful in discovering several new drugs, a marketing organization capable of contacting doctors throughout the country was needed immediately. Building such an organization from scratch would have taken a long time, so Du Pont acquired Endo Laboratories with its established marketing know-how and contacts in the ethical pharmaceutical field. Incidentally, this was the first exception in twenty-four years to Du Pont's general policy of expansion from within rather than via mergers.

Expense as well as time is often critical. Creating a new "going concern," especially in a field already keenly competitive, can be costly in terms of initial investment and losses during the buildup period. In the insurance industry, for example, finding a significant number of new policy holders requires a substantial input of time and expense. So if a corporation wishes to have an insurance division—and many do because of the cash flow advantages—acquiring an existing firm is much simpler.

Likewise, if rare assets are needed, say a Coca-Cola franchise in Miami, or the talent of an outstanding entrepreneur, a merger may be the only feasible way to obtain the resource.

Antitrust Restrictions

Many potential mergers that would improve productivity are illegal! So before management spends much time exploring a possible acquisition, it should "see its lawyer."

To protect the free enterprise system, the United States government has a battery of antitrust laws and regulations. Unfortunately, much uncertainty and disagreement exists regarding the application of these laws; each new U.S. Attorney General brings a different viewpoint, and court decisions provide no clear-cut guidelines.

It is helpful to recognize the basic premise of antitrust effort—broadly, that competition is best protected by having many small, viable, locally owned competitors in each industry. Of course, competitors cannot be created by the passage of a law; instead, the antitrust laws try to prevent actions that reduce the number of effective competitors.

More specifically, the Antitrust Division is likely to challenge the acquisition of a competitor (a horizontal merger) if (1) only a few companies already dominate the relevant market, (2) either of the merging companies already serves over 20% of the market, (3) the merger decreases the number of companies in an expanding market, or (4) the merger makes entry of other companies quite difficult. So, except for very small firms, horizontal mergers are forbidden. The chief ambiguity arises in defining "industry" and "market." For instance, are skis just a small part of the sporting goods industry or an industry of their own? Is a major milk distributor in Los Angeles within or outside its market if it acquires a milk distributor in San Francisco? On such questions as these, see your lawyer.

A vertical merger (acquisition of a supplier or a customer) gets into trouble when a new supplier would have difficulty entering the market or a new customer would have difficulty obtaining supplies, because the merger forecloses part of the market. Here again, the bigger the company, the more likely the objection. Recently, further uncertainty was added when the wording of the Clayton Act was amended to cover mergers that *may* substantially lessen competition or *tend* to create monopoly. Under this revision, the effects of a merger on potential, as well as on existing, competition must be considered.

These expanding legal constraints, which are vigorously enforced, have forced many companies to sharply alter their merger policy. Especially the larger companies are placing increasing reliance for growth on their own research and development because antitrust considerations virtually preclude expansion within their existing industries via mergers. Except for sharp diversification, mergers must be a highly selective aspect of corporate strategy.

FINANCING THE MERGER

Once a potential merger is identified that seems to be the best available way to move ahead with the corporate strategy, the second major question is, "What financial arrangements will be attractive to both companies?"

Every merger has its unique features, and the financial arrangements must reflect these. Nevertheless, we can suggest an approach to the main issues that arise in most mergers. Think of a merger as a swap. The company being acquired is trading a business for cash or securities of the surviving company. Involved in this trade are two packages of assets and two sets of owners; *each* set of owners attaches its own value to the assets it is giving up and to the assets it receives. The crux of negotiating the swap is to devise an arrangement that leaves each set of owners with a new package of assets that it prefers over the assets it has parted with.

To apply this approach, we must understand (1) the value both parties attach to the business being traded and (2) the value to both parties of the payments to be made. The following illustration indicates the main elements involved in a merger and the value assigned to these elements by each party.

Value of Business Traded

In valuing the business being traded, agreement must be reached on what is to be traded and the value to be attached to it.

What is included. A company may be acquired either by taking over ownership of the corporation stock or by purchasing the assets. When stock ownership is the mechanism, the entire legal entity with its intangible assets and liabilities is acquired. Later the corporation may be dissolved and a complete melding may occur, but at the time of the merger we think in terms of the complete enterprise. (If minority blocks of stock remain outstanding, clearly only a percentage of the ownership is traded, but it is still a percentage of the total concern.)

Main Elements in Negotiating a Merger

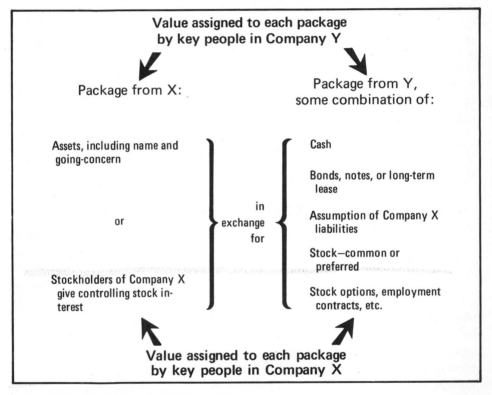

Value assigned to each package
by key people in Company Y

Package from X:

Package from Y,
some combination of:

Assets, including name and
going-concern

or

in
exchange
for

Cash

Bonds, notes, or long-term
lease

Assumption of Company X
liabilities

Stock—common or
preferred

Stockholders of Company X
give controlling stock interest

Stock options, employment
contracts, etc.

Value assigned to each package
by key people in Company X

Sometimes a corporation owns assets that the acquiring firm does not want, for example, a large tract of land or a company store. Or there may be serious disagreement over the values attached to a separable asset or liability. In such cases, the tangible and intangible assets along with current liabilities and mortgages are transferred. This leaves the old corporation still with the same set of stockholders, but the corporation now holds the cash or the securities received in the trade instead of its former operating business, plus assets excluded from the trade.

Basis of evaluation. With agreement on what is to be traded, attention shifts to the subjective values each party attaches to its business. Obviously, subjective values differ. People and companies vary in their needs, opportunities, and resources. So, no bookkeeping figures or a simple formula can produce a value acceptable to everyone. Historical costs, book value, and market price (if the stock does have a market price) may influence the evaluation, but usually each individual feels that a particular package of assets is worth more, or less, than these conventional measures show.

A rational basis for setting a value is to estimate the incomes that the company (or its assets) will provide over a period of years, including the disposition of the assets at the end of the period; to adjust these annual estimates of income for uncertainty (for example, cut the figure in half if there is only a 50-50 chance that the estimated net income will arise in the specified year); and finally to reduce each of the adjusted or "expected" incomes to present values by allowing for alternative uses of the resources that are being committed to the venture in question. This gives a discounted present value of future incomes.[2]

But note that present owners and the acquiring company will come out with quite different answers even if they use the same "rational" approach. The acquiring company will manage the assets differently and it expects to obtain synergistic benefits from the consolidation; consequently, its estimated incomes, uncertainties, and alternatives are unlike those of present owners if the merger is not consummated. In any economically sound merger the minimum the owners will accept (their value of the property if the merger is not completed) should be well below the maximum the acquiring company might pay (the present value of all incomes including the expected benefits arising from the merger). The spread between these two figures leaves a wide margin for bargaining. These outer limits are rarely revealed in the negotiations because both parties seek a substantial part of the margin and because they also attach different values to the payment package.

Other Considerations

Present value of future company income, just discussed, is not a complete picture, especially to the owner of a family business. People who have devoted their lives to building an enterprise normally have deep concern about perpetuating the company name and reputation; their interest is in the future welfare of their employees; they want the company to continue to give support to the community in which they live. Also, in selling the company, these individuals may be sacrificing an attractive salary and a prestigious position.

The acquiring company has no such emotional attachments to the firm being absorbed, but it does know that such considerations cannot be ignored.

---

[2]We have deliberately used more general wording here than is found in the typical "discounted cash flow" procedure because company owners usually have personal values that are broader than the strictly financial figures commonly used in cash flow analysis.

To a large extent, the combined company can meet the social obligations to the community; in fact, it may make substantially larger community contributions than would be made if the companies continued separate existences. Brand names and perhaps company names are often continued because of the goodwill attached to them. Employment may actually increase, although some individuals will suffer. The acquiring company may have a more liberal pension plan (and if past-service credits are large, the final merger arrangement may be adjusted to cover them). Often key executives are given an employment contract for three to five years, and the senior executive may be elected to the board of directors of the combined company.

Unless the executives of the company to be absorbed feel that these "other considerations" will be reasonably met, serious negotiations may never start.

Value of Payment to Be Made

The second half of a merger trade is a package of cash or securities exchanged for the acquired business. This *quid pro quo* must be attractive to the buyer and at the same time must not involve too high a sacrifice for the seller. Here, again, we must consider what is being traded and the value each party attaches to that package.

Form of payment. The most common type of payment in mergers is stock of the surviving corporation. For instance, Radio Corporation of America gave 3,450,000 shares of its common stock for the F. M. Stamper Company, a privately held frozen food concern. RCA stock with a quoted market value was attractive to Stamper stockholders; on the other hand, it was newly issued stock, so existing RCA operations were not hampered by the acquisition.

Payment in the form of common stock is especially likely when that stock has a high price-earnings ratio. Thus, electronics Company A with a price-earnings ratio of 20 would find it advantageous to use its stock to acquire Company B having a price-earnings ratio of only 8. In the simplified illustration below, the market value of the shares of the combined company has increased $6 million as a result of using Company A's price-earnings ratio on Company B's earnings. In the example, two-thirds of this increase goes to Company A stockholders and one-third to Company B stockholders.

Cash is, of course, the simplest form of payment. It is used when the acquiring company is highly liquid and sellers are not confronted with high capital gains taxes.

Many other forms of payment are used to meet particular circumstances. Preferred stock gives the sellers greater assurance of dividends. Debenture bonds or notes provide even greater security but are less favorable from a tax standpoint. Bonds or preferred stock may be made more attractive by having them convertible into common stock. Or stock options (rights to

Illustration of
Effect of Price -Earning Ratios
(Assume one share of A is exchanged for two shares of B, and
A's price-earnings ratio remains constant)

	Shares Outstanding	Total Earnings	Earnings per Share	Market Price per share	Imputed Total Market Value
			Before Merger		
Company A	1,000,000	$1,000,000	$1	$20	$20,000,000
Company B	500,000	500,000	$1	$ 8	4,000,000
					$24,000,000
			After Merger		
Company A	1,250,000	$1,500,000	$1.20	$24	$30,000,000
Former owners of Company B	—	—	—	$\dfrac{(\$24 = \$12)}{2}$	($ 6,000,000)

purchase common stock at a fixed price) may be used to give the seller an opportunity to benefit from company growth.

Frequently, a combination of several forms of payment is used. The Ingram Company, for example, received cash for its net current assets, 20-year mortgage bonds for its fixed assets, and a large block of stock options that gave it an opportunity to share in any synergistic gains that might grow out of merged operations.

Tax on payment. Sellers are concerned about the income tax they will have to pay on the package of cash and/or securities they receive. If they get only voting stock in the surviving company, as in the RCA example on page 383, the transaction is tax-free. The stockholders are merely exchanging one form of equity for another; no capital gains have been realized, and hence there is no basis for levying an income tax. (Of course, if stockholders subsequently sell their stock, any appreciation over their original cost is taxable.)

In contrast, payment in the form of cash or bonds that have a fixed value does establish a capital gain that is taxable. And some stockholders may find such a tax quite onerous. One way to avoid the tax pressure on stockholders is the sale of assets by the corporation. If a corporation exchanges its assets for cash and/or bonds, *it* will be subject to capital gains tax on any appreciation over its "cost," but the stockholders incur no tax obligation since they simply continue to hold the same stock in the same corporation.

Market liquidity. In addition to tax implications, the response of a seller will be influenced by liquidity. Stockholders of corporations whose stock is closely held often have difficulty selling their stock quickly. Family-held companies are the prime example, especially when cash is needed to pay inheritance tax. So, in appraising any merger proposal, the stockholders will be concerned about the salability of the securities they receive. Stock in a large corporation that is actively traded on a major stock exchange is attractive because it is liquid. Of course, the significance attached to liquidity, or to a tax-free exchange, depends upon the specific financial position of each stockholder.

Financial structure of acquiring company. The acquiring company, likewise, evaluates the alternative forms of payment in terms of its particular situation. Cash may be readily available or extremely scarce. Long-term debt of the company may already be so high that the issuance of additional bonds would be imprudent. Of course, if the assets acquired can support more debt, then a loan from a third party may supply cash to use in partial payment to the seller. (A sale-and-leaseback of the fixed assets can be used in the same way.) But normally the acquiring company must guarantee repayment of the loan, and this becomes a contingent liability even though it does not show on the balance sheet.

Perhaps convertible preferred stock will appeal to the owners of the prospective acquisition, but a relatively small issue of an additional form of stock would interfere with larger financing by the surviving company in the future. In other words, both debt and equity payments should be appraised in terms of their effect on the total financial structure of the acquiring company.

Loss of control. When common stock is used for a large acquisition, one or two of the new stockholders may become the largest owners of stock in the surviving corporation. They are then in a strategic position to gain control. Perhaps this prospect will be unattractive to the executives currently in charge of the acquiring corporation.

Dilution. Stockholders of an acquiring company will also be concerned about "dilution." Usually dilution refers to a reduction in earnings per share. For example, assume that Company A with 100,000 shares of stock outstanding gives an additional 10,000 shares to acquire Company B. If Company A's previous earnings of $500,000 are increased to only $535,000 when A and B are combined, then Company A's stockholders will see their earnings per share drop from $5.00 to $4.86. Although the management of Company A can enthusiastically report increased sales and higher total profits, the picture on a per-share basis is the reverse. Presumably such dilution is only temporary; a sound merger should help increase earnings proportionately more than the increase in shares outstanding. Nevertheless, any merger proposal that shows short-run dilution will require strong justification.

Negotiating a "Good" Merger

Clearly, a variety of considerations enter into a good merger. We start with a potential combination of businesses that will generate productivity gains and perhaps also strictly financial benefits. Our task then turns to devising and winning acceptance of a trade that is attractive to the management and the stockholders of both the acquiring firm and the acquired firm. The following brief case illustrates the adaptation that may be necessary.

The Enid Corporation of Ohio was highly successful in manufacturing and selling indoor-outdoor acrylic carpeting in Midwest and Eastern United States. It had annual sales of over $50,000,000 and profits of around $3,-500,000, or $1.75 per share of common stock. The stock was listed on the American Stock Exchange and had been selling in the $26–$35 range. West Coast sales, however, had declined for four years following the death of Enid's original representative in Los Angeles. To correct this situation, Enid wished to acquire Thomas & Son, an aggressive wholesale floorcovering distributor in San Francisco. This firm had been earning after taxes about $200,000 per year and the senior Mr. Thomas was ready to retire. Executives of both Enid and Thomas thought a merger "made good sense."

Enid first suggested a simple exchange of stock, mentioning 100,000 shares of its stock, then selling at $30 per share. This would have given Thomas a price of 15 times its earnings while avoiding a dilution of Enid's earnings. Thomas felt the price was low because its earnings did not reflect two pieces of undeveloped land that Thomas believed could be sold for as much as a million dollars. Also, the debt position of Thomas & Son was complicated by the financing of this and other real estate.

The discussion then shifted to the purchase of all assets except real estate, which would remove the threat of a capital gains tax on stockholders. Thomas then said the corporation would rather have cash than stock. Enid next proposed a package consisting of: $500,000 cash; $1,800,000 in 6% notes, maturing $100,000 per year over 18 years; a "consulting" contract with Mr. Thomas, Sr., of $35,000 per year for 10 years; and an employment contract with Mr. Thomas, Jr. for $30,000 per year (his present salary) for 10 years. Later, to recognize goodwill and growth potential, Enid added stock options giving Thomas & Son the option to buy 100,000 shares of Enid common stock at $33 per share any time during the next 5 years. And on these terms the deal was made.

Both sides were happy. Mr. Thomas, Sr., said: "We keep all our real estate, get a steady flow of cash into the corporation, I'm on a liberal pension, and Tom has a good job. All these incomes add up to $2,950,000 or about Enid's original offer. Then top it off with an option that should be worth another million in five years."

Enid's president was equally pleased. He reasoned: "Our major gain is strong distribution on the West Coast, with young Thomas committed to stay on the job. Mr. Thomas, Sr., has been drawing big bonuses, so much of his pension can come out of a reduction in executive compensation. Any way we figure it, the $400,000 pre-tax earnings will more than cover the interest, capital cost, and other charges. So we expect to get an immediate improvement in net profit. True, the book value of the assets we acquired is a bit under the $2,300,000 we paid, but within a few years our profit from West Coast operations should be at least $500,000."

Note that each executive used different criteria to place a value on the business being transferred and the package of payments being received. Both packages of assets had been tailored to fit the particular situation. The swap was good. Nevertheless, the long-run soundness of the merger remains to be demonstrated in the profitable growth of Enid's West Coast business.

MAKING MERGERS SUCCESSFUL

Many mergers fail. Often the anticipated benefits do not develop, at least to the degree predicted, and unforeseen problems arise. Some of these failures are due to poorly conceived combinations—the marriages of convenience that never were thought through. Others are high-risk ventures that turn up in the losing column. Rarely can managerial skill save such ill-fated mergers.

More disturbing are the well-conceived matches that do not work out. Such results usually can be avoided by proper managerial action. Experience with successful mergers suggests a twofold approach: (1) perceptive, careful management and (2) special attention to communication and motivation.

Perceptive Management

The first step in making mergers successful is a *specific program* to bring about the projected results. This requires spelling out the necessary changes and the resources—new engineering, new equipment, hiring and training people, advertising, etc.—and then setting a timetable. Probably the program will need adjustment, but this adaptation will be easier if the various moves have been delineated in advance. In addition, changes needed to reconcile the policies and the procedures of the merged companies should be identified and scheduled. Such programming demands a lot of time and thought by key people (one of the reasons it is often neglected), but it pays off because in the merger process individuals who have never worked together before are expected to do new work.

A second step is realignment of and staffing the *organization* needed to execute the program. Every merger upsets the subtle understandings of status and power in the two companies; the jockeying for new positions is inevitable. Although the situations may be too fluid to define detailed relationships, placing responsibility and providing a prompt means for resolving differences of opinion are essential for positive action. The new mixture of personalities in every merger makes this reorganizing a very delicate task.

Installing dependable *controls* is a third essential element. Cash controls and accounting reports usually are quickly adapted to a format familiar to central executives. However, meaningful cost data and information on market development, research and development effort, management development, and other intangibles are rare. Many a merger has foundered because executives lack a means of knowing what was really happening in their new operation.

Communication and Motivation

Cutting across the more explicit management actions just described is a critical need for communication and motivation. A merger signals change. Just what will be changed is unknown, so anxiety builds up in many people whose jobs might be affected. Rumors substitute for facts and spread rapidly.

In such circumstances, key executives should make their plans known just as soon as possible. If some matters are unsettled, they can at least indicate how and when these will be resolved. The communication should be two-way, giving employees an opportunity to ask questions and to hear frank answers. New executives have low *credibility* in the early stages of a merger, and they need to explain what will be done and then see that it happens. Suspicion of motives is apt to flare up at any time during the first year or two, and executives need to be available to make personal explanations of actions they take.

An aspect of communication is when to discuss problems and with whom. One successful pattern is to explore what changes are necessary and how merged operations will be organized *before* the agreement is final. Usually these discussions include all key executives who will have to work together. If a marriage does take place after such a frank exchange, its chances of success are high. The chief drawback is that airing of problems may cause one party to withdraw. But if the courtship cannot survive frank recognition of what living together involves, then major personnel and morale difficulties should be anticipated.

Coupled with as full communication as possible should be positive reinforcement—tangible or intangible rewards—of desired behavior. By emphasizing the achievements of a merger and rewarding them, management builds a new morale. Employee attention shifts from concern with the past to interest in the future.

We shall examine programming, organizing, communicating, and controlling more fully in later parts of this book. As indicated, mergers generate some especially difficult tasks of execution. Unless these receive their full share of attention, the entire merger effort may be futile.

MERGER VIA TAKEOVER

The vast majority of mergers are "friendly," that is, they are recommended by the directors of both companies. But recently the business world has been dazzled by a rash of "takeovers" in which the acquiring company gains control of another concern without the cooperation of its existing management. Here the "raider" gets control of the majority of the stock, ousts the existing management, and then arranges a favorable merger.

Use of Tender Offers

A raider may gain control of the desired merger partner in several ways: (1) by joining forces with key stockholders not supporting the management (for example, Hilton acquired the Statler Hotel chain in this manner); (2) by acquiring stock on the open market (for example, James Hill's classic fight for the Burlington Railroad); and (3) by soliciting proxies of stockholders (Young used this route to gain control of the New York Central Railroad). Today, these methods are either unavailable or becoming very expensive.

Currently, the popular path to control is a "tender offer." Here the raider makes a public offer to buy or exchange stock. The terms may be any one of the alternatives we have already discussed under friendly mergers—cash, common stock, convertible preferred stock, and so forth. However, the offer has a value well above the prevailing price of the stock being sought, typically 25% to 30% higher than the market price under the old management. In other words, the raider bypasses company management and appeals directly to stockholders.

Prior to the passage of new laws regulating tenders, this was a cloak-and-dagger game. Surprise offers, secret deals, extra commissions to brokers, counterattacks, splitting stock, and legal injunctions were all employed in a manner reminiscent of the battles between the industrial barons of the 19th century. Slowly the process is becoming more open and orderly.

Who Is Vulnerable?

No company will attempt a takeover unless it sees an opportunity to substantially improve the return to its stockholders by better management and/or by synergistic benefits of a merger. Consequently, a firm is vulnerable to takeover: (1) when it shows poor performance relative to other firms in its industry, and especially when its dividends are declining more than those of its competitors; (2) when it has surplus liquid assets or large unused borrowing capacity; (3) when it holds assets that could be sold for more than their market value; or (4) when potential synergistic benefits are being disregarded.

The best defense against a takeover is, of course, managing the company so that its assets are wisely deployed, its earnings record creates a good price for its stock, and synergistic benefits are aggressively exploited. Under these conditions, a stockholder gains little or nothing by transferring the stock to a raider.

Such a sound defense against a takeover takes time. If a company is really vulnerable and finds itself being raided before it has time to put its house in order, the management can, and often does, seek a friendly merger with some other company on terms as attractive as those of the tender. Management casualties are usually lower in a friendly merger!

Economic Effects

The immediate effects on a company of a takeover are costly. Anxiety is at a peak, personal hostilities are generated, and none of the perceptive management steps discussed in the previous section can occur in advance. Nevertheless, a takeover does serve as one way of deposing a stodgy management. More important, the possibility of a takeover lurking in the background serves as a spur to management. No longer can executives be complacent just because company stock is dispersed among so many stockholders that no one can make a significant complaint.

From the point of view of society and of a stockholder, then, the potential threat of a takeover stimulates good management. All parties—stockholders, society, *and* management—will be better off if the company is administered so that the costly process of takeover is impractical.

SUMMARY

Merging with another company can be a major step in carrying out a desired strategy. The acquired company may provide a much needed resource, give access to a new market, extend company operations back into earlier stages of production, provide a scale of operation that will support improved technology, or improve company services and productivity.

Not all mergers are so well conceived. Some are opportunistic, taking advantage of short-run financial gain. Ideal, of course, is a partner that both pushes us forward on basic strategy and is financially advantageous.

Whatever the fit, the "price" paid must also be weighed. A heavy debt burden, troublesome stock options, and exhaustion of cash reserves can result, and this unhealthy financial condition can seriously deter execution of other facets of company strategy. Or the package given to owners of the acquired company, say common stock, may create no strain. Since we know that a strong financial structure is closely related to future growth, both the *quid* and the *quo* of the merger deal require close scrutiny in terms of their impact on the master strategic plan.

Even soundly conceived mergers fail if the two institutions are not melded by good follow-up action. Numerous internal adjustments in both companies need careful planning, organizing, and controlling; new motivations and communication flows have to be established. These are problems that we examine more fully in the next two parts of this book.

 QUESTIONS FOR CLASS DISCUSSION

1. In a widely publicized case, American Express threatened to take over McGraw-Hill Book Company, a leading publisher of books and trade magazines and owner of several business-related services. American Express's basic reason for wanting McGraw-Hill was an opportunity to correct "stodgy family management." Harold McGraw, president, responded (a) that Roger Morely, president of American Express, was making unethical use of information he obtained as a member of McGraw-Hill's board of directors; (b) that the integrity of a credit-rating service owned by McGraw-Hill would be questioned if

American Express owned it; and (c) that the company was being well run as a comparison of its sales and earnings with other publishers clearly showed. Other third-generation members of the McGraw family finally rallied in support of the president and American Express withdrew its offer. American Express proposed to pay $40 per share for McGraw-Hill stock. Prior to the take-over move McGraw-Hill stock was selling on the New York Stock Exchange for $26; a few weeks after the offer was withdrawn, it was selling for $24. (a) What effect do you think the American Express offer will have on the morale and actions of McGraw-Hill management? (b) Do you believe that family members who own less than 25% of the outstanding stock were justified in declining an offer of $40 per share, 54% above the previous market price?

2. Not long ago the chairperson of the Securities and Exchange Commission warned board directors, lawyers, and accountants of unfortunate results from continuing emphasis on acquisitions and mergers. "Unfortunately . . . most discussions of tender offers seem to center on . . . various devices to comply with or avoid the application of the federal securities laws and the state antitake-over requirements . . . The most unsettling aspect . . . is the legitimacy which hostile tender offers have come to enjoy. It has become acceptable to treat corporations as the sum of their properties and to assume that corporate control may change hands with no greater concerns of the consequences than accompanies an exchange of property deeds in a game of Monopoly." The chairperson also took issue with the speculators, arbitrageurs, and lawyers who benefit from the takeovers and can then easily walk away once the transaction is completed. "The corporation is more than the aggregate of its tangible assets. . . ." (a) What did the chairperson mean by the phrase "the most unsettling aspects"? (b) What might the corporation be other than the sum of its assets? (c) Why might the lawyers and accountants be especially interested in devices to avoid the application of various laws? (d) Is this social responsibility on the part of the specialists?

3. (a) Companies that stress long-range planning often become involved in mergers. This is especially so when the long-range planning focuses on strategy rather than on budgeting. How do you explain this tendency? (b) Review the key elements of strategy outlined in Chapter 5 and identify the areas where a merger is likely to be an attractive way to proceed.

4. In The Enid-Thomas merger described on pages 386–387, *assume* that the following difficulties arose after the merger was completed: (a) anxiety and communication difficulties during the first year reduced the effectiveness of the Thomas employees; (b) the Thomas product line needed trimming and more emphasis placed on Enid products—a switch that was not readily accepted by the Thomas group; and (c) Thomas, Jr. wanted to take independent action on a variety of matters and was "too rich to be motivated from Ohio" so he resigned after three years. What action might Enid executives have taken to minimize or forestall these difficulties?

5. Many "developing countries" now want companies located and operating within their boundaries to be at least 51% owned by local citizens. Assume that you, as international manager for Scripto, Inc. wish to acquire an office supply firm in such a country for the purpose of setting up a local assembly plant. Would you agree to the acquisition if you can obtain only 49% of stock ownership? Is there any alternative that you think might be acceptable to you, the

local government, and the manager of the local firm? Aside from ownership, are there other conditions related to the acquisition which you believe are especially important?

6. Consider the possibility of merging the college you are now attending with the nearest comparable college. Would there be significant benefits? To whom? What do you think would be the most difficult obstacles to such a merger?

7. "Takeovers should be encouraged because they protect stockholders against an 'in-group' of managers who may be protecting their own jobs." "The only successful takeovers are those that give the stockholders a better deal than they have had or expect to get." "The takeover is a raider's device. Usually it wants to liquidate or milk the company for immediate financial gain without regard to its social responsibilities to employees, customers, and the community. Consequently, takeover bids should have to go through the same advance warning, full-disclosure process with the SEC as a new financial offering." With which quotation do you agree? Do you have any other suggestion for regulating this kind of activity?

8. The reverse of a merger is a "spin-off"—the separation of a single company into two or more independent concerns. In practice relatively few spin-offs or divestments occur, and most of these arise from antitrust activity of the federal government. (a) How do you account for the much larger number of mergers than spin-offs? Are the economic advantages predominantly in favor of increased size? What of other social considerations? (b) Assume that you as president concluded that dividing up your company made good sense. What problems do you foresee in accomplishing the split-up? (c) Do your answers to (a) and (b) apply to profit decentralization; that is, establishing semiautonomous self-contained divisions?

9. Directors of Clark Oil and Refining Co., of West Allis, Wisconsin, were actively considering making a tender offer for some of the five and a half million odd shares of the company that were outstanding (exclusive of the 1,654,574 shares owned by Mr. E.T. Clark, chairperson). The stock had been trading at about $32 per share on the New York Stock Exchange. Clark Oil's cash position had sharply improved after the $91 million sale of some gas properties. Then the chairperson said that he had been approached by another company interested in acquiring Clark Oil stock at a price "substantially" exceeding the current market price. In two days of trading the price of the stock increased by $16 per share. As a director, what seems feasible to you now?

10. Once upon a time, according to a business school professor and a consultant, $2 + 2 = 5$ in the world of investment. "Synergy" was the explanation and companies pursued active diversification strategies. Then something changed. For example, Kaiser Industries, a holding company, was split into half a dozen firms—the operating companies it held; stockholders then got $21 for shares that previously sold at $12. Also, UV Industries then went out of business and distributed the proceeds; liquidation left shareholders with about $45 per share —more than the share price of about $17 before dismemberment. Other companies followed, and W.R. Grace thought of dividing itself into as many as seven publicly-held companies. The professor and the consultant *now* say that further dismemberment "would be a shame." "Short-term financial rewards would prevent sustained value creation for the future. . . . Over the long-run future, a properly managed diversification strategy really can make $2 + 2 =$

5. Under dismemberment, $2 + 2$ will only equal 4." Why do the consultant and the professor say this?

11. Financial policy seeks a good adjustment of the company to suppliers of capital; personnel policy, a good adjustment to suppliers of labor; purchasing policy, a good adjustment to suppliers of things; marketing policy, a good adjustment to suppliers of outlets. And the list can be extended to other important resource groups. (a) How does social responsibility fit into this array of policy? (b) Does the answer to the previous question differ for small vs. large companies?

CASE 16
Brunswig Corporation

"Well, Martin, that's the twenty-sixth offer we've had to buy us out in five years. Why do we listen to all these people? I'm not sure this one is as sound as the last one from Allied Machinery Products Corporation. What do you think?"

"I'm surprised. Schneider Transmissions, Inc. must have heard about the Allied offer and cooked this deal up in a hurry. Even though they are just across town, they have never given us a hint before that they were interested in an acquisition. Well, let's think about it. The first thing I want to do is to check with some of our people. Those who have worked at Schneider might have a few clues."

Martin Brunswig, Chairman of the Board and President of Brunswig Corporation, and Walter Brunswig, Executive Vice-President and Chairman of the Finance Committee, left the University Club—one for the main plant and the other for a family council at the Brunswig Country Club. This new, and unexpected, merger offer promised to delay the process of persuading 92 other family members to accept the brothers' opinion—that it would be only sensible to sell out to Allied Machinery Products Corporation.

Brunswig Corporation's principal business is the manufacture and the sale of a wide range of types and sizes of gears, gear drives, and shaft couplings for transmitting power in ranges of 1 to 30,000 horsepower or more. Brunswig's gears are found on tilting drives for basic oxygen steel furnaces, kiln drives for cement processing, paper machine drives, oil refinery compressors, as reduction gears for river towboats, mixer drives for penicillin manufacturing, and as equipment for satellite tracking and radar installations.

Brunswig produces a wide line of standard gear drives and speed reducers as well as special gears and shaft couplings made to order in sizes from 1 inch to 24 feet in diameter and from 1 pound to over 40 tons in weight. It sells directly through its own salesforce working out of 39 district sales offices in the principal industrial markets of the United States as well as through more than 250 distributors. Brunswig products are basic components of industrial machinery, do not have a seasonal sales pattern, and are not dependent on any one industry or industry grouping; but sales volume is affected by the general level of industrial activity.

The company's sales and distribution organization is widely recognized as among the most effective and efficient such networks in U.S. industry.

Brunswig is a leading producer in its lines. It has substantial competition for shaft couplings and smaller gears but very limited competition in the sale of large gears and very large couplings. Market share is as high as 40% to 60% in some lines. To maintain its position, Brunswig engages in sales engineering, applied product engineering, and testing, together with some development work on methods of mechanical power transmissions. It has 100 engineers and machinery designers engaged principally in these programs on which it spent $2,500,000 last year. The firm has secured some patents, but it does not depend for its business on any one or a group of such patents.

About 2,800 employees work in three plants in the same southern Ohio city. None are represented by unions, and there has been no strike in the hundred-year history of the company. Hourly and salaried employees share in a trusteed, noncontributory, incentive profit-sharing retirement plan to which Brunswig contributes a share of net income. Salaried employees also have a contributory pension plan.

Brunswig owns the three plants of varying ages and of cement and steel construction. Its buildings and machinery are well maintained and adequate for the presently anticipated volume of business.

Family members own a majority of Brunswig common stock and have administrative control over the corporation. Martin and Walter own 35,000 and 40,000 shares, respectively. Other directors who are family members own 50,000 shares amongst them. The over-the-counter price is currently $31 bid and $33 asked. The price range last year was $22–$30 and the year before was $26–$36. Pertinent financial data for Brunswig Corporation are given on the next page.

Schneider Transmissions' offer, in general terms, is to merge Brunswig Corporation into Schneider Transmissions, Inc. through Schneider's purchase of up to 49% of the outstanding shares of Brunswig common stock for $60 per share in cash and the exchange of 1.54 shares of Schneider Transmissions common stock for each share of Brunswig common for the balance of the outstanding shares. The most recent closing price of Schneider common on the New York Stock Exchange was $40 per share. The stock is ranked A by Standard & Poor's.

Schneider Transmissions has three product groups:

1. Mechanical components such as chains, sprockets, flexible couplings, gears, speed reducers, clutch plates, and pumps.
2. Engineered systems, such as bulk materials handling equipment for mines, lumber and steel mills, and power plants, and equipment for the biological and mechanical treatment of sewage, refuse, and waste water.
3. Construction machinery such as concrete mixers, highway pavers, and maintenance equipment.

Schneider Transmissions sells in the United States and Canada through company offices and local distributors. It has regional distribution centers in 11 cities. Abroad, the company has 11 sales offices as well as manufacturing and warehousing operations in Argentina, Australia, Brazil, England, France, Italy, Germany, and Japan. The main manufacturing facilities are in various southern Ohio cities.

Development engineering and sales engineering are the responsibility of each product group. The company spent about $4 million last year on this work.

Acquisitions in the past three years include two major manufacturers of quick-opening fasteners, a specialized gear manufacturer, a valve manufacturer, two

Brunswig Corporation
Statement of Income
(000's omitted)

	5 Years Ago	Preceding Year	Preceding Year	Last Year	Current Year
Net Sales	$48,494	$58,837	66,753	$63,621	$58,405
Cost of Goods Sold.	33,013	38,671	43,251	41,294	38,300
Depreciation	1,850	2,093	2,213	2,609	1,943
Selling & Administrative					
Expense	8,455	9,724	10,978	11,101	10,766
Interest Expense	326	366	200	283	414
Net Income after Taxes	2,399	3,906	5,069	4,372	3,396
Per Share of Common Stock:					
Net Income	$2.47	$3.90	$4.88	$4.13	$3.18
Cash Dividends Paid.	.825	1.05	1.20	1.25	1.40

Brunswig Corporation
Balance Sheets
(000's omitted)

	Last Year	Current Year
Current Assets	$29,397	$29,099
Investments	1,669	1,704
Net Property & Plants.	19,380	19,946
Other Assets	4,751	4,595
Total Assets	$55,197	$55,344
Current Liabilities	$ 9,617	$ 8,683
Deferred Liabilities	2,509	2,644
Long-Term Debt	7,472	7,456
Common Stock		
(authorized, 2,500,000 shares;		
issued 1,077,000 shares)	2,692	2,692
Additional Contributed Capital.	4,611	4,621
Retained Earnings	28,296	29,248
Total Stockholders' Equity.	$35,599	$36,561
Total Liabilities and Equity	$55,197	$55,344

sewage disposal manufacturers, and recently, a medium-sized company that makes gears, speed reducers, clutch plates, and couplings. This latest acquisition, when combined with the firm's other gear manufacturing facilities, has allowed Schneider Transmissions to become a significant—but by no means the most important—factor in gear and coupling manufacturing. As it consolidates its organization in these lines and, above all, when it combines the sales work and develops a tested marketing capability, the company will be a very strong competitor in the mechanical power transmission industry. Market share in the gear and coupling lines may well increase to 15%–18% if the marketing work is done effectively.

Selected financial data for Schneider Transmissions, Inc. are as follows:

Schneider Transmissions, Inc.
Selected Financial Data

Year	Net Sales	Net Income	Times Interest and Preferred Dividends Earned	Dividend per Share of Common Stock	Price Range of Common Stock on NYSE
	(000's omitted)				
Current	$217,000	$ 9,610	3.36 times	$1.50	$44–$40
Preceding	191,200	8,928	4.14 "	1.50	52– 34
"	185,000	8,463	n.a.	1.50	55– 30
"	165,400	10,843	n.a.	1.50	36– 25
"	159,600	8,020	n.a.	1.20	36– 24

Schneider Transmissions, Inc.
Balance Sheets
(000's omitted)

	Current Year	Last Year
Cash and Marketable Securities	$ 5,600	$ 7,000
Accounts Receivable.	41,100	37,000
Inventories.	54,300	43,700
Total Current Assets	$101,000	$ 87,700
Net Property	41,300	36,200
Other Assets	7,700	5,500
Total Assets	$150,000	$129,400
Total Current Liabilities.	$ 35,900	$ 19,300
Long-Term Debt	14,800	14,500
$2.50 Cumulative Preferred Stock		
(570,000 shares outstanding)	11,480	11,420
Common Stock (2,992,000 shares)	29,992	29,453
Capital Surplus.	11,473	12,502
Retained Earnings	46,355	42,225
Total Liabilities and Equity	$150,000	$129,400

Allied Machinery Products Corporation proposes that substantially all of the Brunswig assets and business be transferred to a wholly owned subsidiary (to be organized by Allied) in exchange for Allied preferred stock and common stock and the assumption by the subsidiary of substantially all the liabilities of Brunswig. Employees of Brunswig will become employees of the new subsidiary, which will continue to conduct Brunswig's business with Brunswig's name after the closing. The present Brunswig Corporation will be dissolved.

Allied's plan is to distribute 0.4921 of a share of Allied voting $3.50 cumulative convertible preferred stock and 0.32 of a share of Allied common for each share of Brunswig common stock.

Allied makes proprietary hydromechanical and electromechanical systems and components and proprietary machining systems. Its principal offices and plants are in a city about a hundred miles distant from the plants of Brunswig.

The proprietary systems and the components are parts sold as original equipment to the aircraft and aerospace industries, the mobile equipment industry, the oil heating industry, and the petrochemical processing industry. These components account for about 82% of sales, while the balance is made up of machine tools and total machining systems sold to the general metalworking industry. Both the machine tools and the component parts require a high degree of research, development, engineering, and manufacturing competence. For all products, Allied has patents or some special processes and trade secrets that give it special property rights.

The components sold as original equipment include hydraulic pumps and motors, pneumatic starters, underwater power plants, hydrostatic transmissions, and constant speed drives that convert variable input speed from a jet or turbine engine to constant output speed to drive alternating current electrical generators. They also include electronic controls and instruments, oil burner fuel units, lubrication pumps, condensers, and evaporators for use in air-conditioning and refrigeration systems.

The numerically-controlled or direct-computer-controlled multi-operational machining systems perform a variety of metal-cutting operations and can change from one operation to another without interrupting the manufacturing process. The machines are highly accurate and are best suited for low-volume metalworking operations such as the production of prototypes and small-lot runs.

Allied exports from its own plants and has licensed other firms in all the major industrial countries in the world to produce its components and machining systems. It has three plants abroad in Sweden, Switzerland, and France.

A technically-trained salesforce and independent distributors sell the Allied line. Field engineers provide technical services to support sales effort. Other firms compete with Allied on one or more products, but none duplicates more than a small portion of its business.

Allied owns a large number of patents that are important in the aggregate to the conduct of its business. About 700 graduate engineers and engineering employees work on a wide range of applied research and product development programs that are conducted in addition to the regular product adaptation and testing work of the sales engineering group. Company policy is to spend about 5% of net sales on research and development work.

During the past two years, Allied has acquired eight small to medium-sized manufacturing firms that produce electronic systems and special alloy castings. For these it paid, in the aggregate, $6,400,000 in cash plus 612,000 newly issued shares of common stock and 252,400 shares of $3.50 cumulative convertible preferred stock. Selected financial data for Allied Machinery Products Corporation can be found on the next page.

Allied employs about 11,000 people, of whom 6,700 are production and maintenance employees. About 2,500 of these workers closed down two plants for 40 days and 40 nights earlier in the year as part of an effort to win a new 3-year contract. They succeeded. The company has various retirement plans, including pension, profit-sharing, and money purchase plans covering most of the employees.

A week after the surprise visit and presentation by Schneider Transmissions executives, the Brunswigs—Martin and Walter—sat at lunch. Martin said to his brother:

"I believe what the Allied people told us. Their goal is to increase earnings per share of stock by increasing their market share, expanding their balance sheet leverage, and developing improved products to increase profits. They are clearly organized for action on mergers and, on the other hand, they are determined to avoid a takeover of their own company by making it too expensive. Their policy is to strive for a consistent improvement in earnings and, through this, to influence a high valuation of their stock by analysts as well as the general public.

"They have also defined their basic characteristics as being a 'mechanical engineering company' with interests in special market segments that have a relatively high growth potential. Of course, we know their special skills and advanced competence in aircraft and aerospace components and machine tools.

"But, in talking with them, I am impressed as much by their knowing all the financial moves—straight-line depreciation rather than sum-of-the-digits, smoothing profits through the development cost account, having high debt-leverage so that a raider can't buy you with your own money, diversifying to give a raider potential antitrust trouble, LIFO inventory, not amortizing goodwill, etc.—as by their knowing that our gears can be coupled with their hydrostatic equipment to develop a continuous speed device using an electric motor. This will expand the range of any electric motor well beyond the limited number of r.p.m.'s that it was originally built for. You and I know that our product lines are complementary and that there are many mutual development opportunities.

"How are we going to persuade the rest of the family? The yield on Allied common stock is very small (see Exhibit A), but the use of both preferred and common stock will get dividends to them. And the preferred is not callable for the first five years. The exchange of stock with Allied is tax-free at present, and a capital gains tax would only have to be paid if the stock were sold some time in the future. But the Schneider proposal is nontaxable now only on the common stock part. Anyone who holds some of our original shares might have to pay capital gains on the cash portion. The maximum this would be per share would be $13.17 (25% of $60—$7.313).

"Allied management knows how to run a diversified company. Look at their proposal for a separate subsidiary. No one will be hurt by that move.

"And there is a final reason that I may have to pass up in public discussion. It will be a real pleasure to deal with stockholders who understand technically what this company is all about and to work with a technically-oriented management in a similar line of business.

"But what are the arguments in favor of Schneider Transmissions that we may have to meet? Schneider is local. We know the people and can trust them. And those

Allied Machinery Products Corporation
Selected Financial Data

Year	Net Sales (000's omitted)	Net Income	Times Interest and Preferred Dividends Earned	Dividend per Share of Common Stock	Price Range of $3.50 Preferred Stock NYSE	Price Range of Common Stock* NYSE
Current	$242,000	$14,300	4.3 times	$.80	$95–75	$91–64
Preceding	215,000	11,246	3.6 times	.80	83–71	87–29
"	152,000	8,020	n.a.	.60		30–18
"	122,000	5,253		.50		37–20
"	109,000	4,095		.50		24–18
"	108,000	2,581		.50		28–19

*This stock is ranked B+ by Standard & Poor's.

Allied Machinery Products Corporation
Balance Sheets
(000's omitted)

	Current Year	Last Year
Cash and Marketable Securities	$ 4,657	$ 5,904
Accounts Receivable.	45,600	41,246
Inventories	91,023	87,690
Total Current Assets	$141,280	$134,840
Net Property	80,087	74,339
Other Assets	5,007	4,702
Total Assets	$226,374	$213,881
Total Current Liabilities	$ 61,855	$ 84,270
Long-Term Debt	70,648	65,730
$3.50 Cumulative Convertible Preferred Stock (3,000,000 shares authorized)	200	197
Common Stock, par value $1, (15,000,000 shares authorized)	4,853	4,124
Additional Contributed Capital	46,139	21,492
Retained Earnings	42,679	38,068
Total Liabilities and Stockholders' Equity	$226,374	$213,881

whom we can't we can keep a good eye on. Their asset size is closer to ours so we will be a more important part of the merged operation. Schneider is expanding, but not so rapidly as to destroy any sense of where we have been and where we are going. The people there are not trying to play any go-go conglomerate role. The money looks good. And certainly the products match. Schneider has no labor or union troubles. Why turn elsewhere for a partner when you've got the fellow down the street?

"Well, we'll have to persuade the others and then set up a special stockholders' meeting soon. It looks as if the Allied common stock will be close to $65 a share for awhile and the price of the preferred will be about $77 a share."

Exhibit A
Comparative Per-Share Data

	Preceding Year	Last Year	Current Year	Net Book Equity
(1) To Brunswig Shareholders:				
(a) Net Earnings:				
Actual......................	$4.88	$4.13	$3.18	$34
Pro Forma, assuming merger with Allied Machinery:				
Common Stock	.79	.87	.90	
Preferred Stock.............	1.72	1.72	1.72	
Total......................	$2.51	$2.59	$2.62	$48
(b) Cash Dividends:				
Actual......................	$1.20	$1.25	$1.40	
Pro Forma, assuming merger with Allied Machinery:				
Common Stock	.19	.26	.26	
Preferred Stock.............	1.72	1.72	1.72	
Total......................	$1.91	$1.98	$1.98	
(2) To Allied Shareholders:				
(a) Earnings Applicable to Common Stock:				
Actual......................	$1.84	$2.38	$2.72	$16
Pro Forma, assuming merger	2.46	2.72	2.84	$12
(b) Cash Dividends:				
Common Stock	.60	.80	.80	
Preferred Stock	3.50	3.50	3.50	

Questions

(1) What alternatives do you see for the Brunswig Corporation shareholders and management?

(2) As a member of the Board of Directors of Brunswig Corporation, what would be your vote on the various alternatives? Explain.

INTEGRATING CASE

Strategy and Diversification

GENERAL ELECTRIC–UTAH INTERNATIONAL MERGER

The merging of the General Electric Company and Utah International, Inc. raises a variety of issues. What benefits arise from combining two dissimilar giants? Where is the synergy? Will traditional U.S. doctrines of competition be violated? Will General Electric's outstanding managerial savvy suit mining ventures? How does one finance a $2 billion acquisition? Who will reap resulting financial gains—and personal glory?

To help answer these questions, the scope of each company's activities is briefly sketched and the key financial data summarized. Then a more detailed analysis of this landmark event, as seen by *Fortune,* is presented.

The General Electric Company has become one of the largest manufacturing concerns in the world. The contributions in 1976 of its major categories of operations to sales and net income were:

	Sales (millions)	share	Net Income (millions)	share
Aerospace	$ 2,099	14%	$ 95	13%
Consumer goods	3,307	22	198	26
Industrial components and systems	4,787	32	266	35
Industrial power equipment	3,074	21	72	10
International	4,024	28	196	26
General Electric Credit Corporation	—	—	59	8
Corporate eliminations	−2,595	−17	−136	−18
Total company (before Utah)	$14,696	100%	$ 750	100%

In recent years, almost all of General Electric's growth and diversification has come from its own initiative; it is not a conglomerate built via acquisitions. A significant part of its success arises from sophisticated management processes.

Utah International is not a manufacturing enterprise like General Electric had always been. Instead it focuses on mining. Its major venture is mining of coking coal in Australia. In addition, it mines steam coal, notably in the Four Corners area in New Mexico; iron ore, primarily in Brazil; uranium, and copper. To support the foreign mining, Utah International also is in ocean shipping. These mining and related activities account for 95% of its sales and earnings; the remainder comes mostly from oil and gas production. Eighty-three percent of its sales and 86% of its earnings in 1976 originated outside the United States.

The growth of Utah International and of General Electric prior to the merger is reflected in the financial data in Table 1, and the financial structure of the two companies is shown in Table 2, at the end of this case.

A few months after the merger of these two companies was completed, Louis Kraar of *Fortune* wrote an article on the courting and marriage process. Mr. Kraar's description of these events is as follows.[1]

The combination of these great enterprises created the largest corporate merger in U.S. history. More than anything else, the merger served to fulfill the needs and ambitions of the two men who conceived it—Reginald Jones, Chairman of General Electric, and Edmund Littlefield, Chairman of Utah International.

Utah, though highly profitable, was also very risky—90 percent of its earnings came from a single commodity in a single country, metallurgical coal from Australia. Littlefield, now approaching retirement, was eager to obtain greater security for Utah's shareholders and was willing to trade off some of his company's fantastic growth to get it. The most prominent of all those stockholders was Littlefield himself; when his talks with Jones began, he, his wife, and their children held shares worth about $50 million.

For his part, Jones wanted to make a lasting imprint on his corporation by providing a new source of earnings growth and creating what he likes to call "the new G.E." Utah provided him with a means to make that concept credible. When the opportunity arose, he relied not on his hallowed planning staff, but rather seized the chance to personally lead his company into its biggest move in many years.

Littlefield, a director of G.E. for the past dozen years, and Jones were on friendly terms. Both served on the Business Council, and espoused a conservative political philosophy. The possibility of a merger was broached by Littlefield in an informal conversation late one evening in May 1975.

Victimized by Good Fortune

As they talked, Jones complimented Littlefield on the great job he had done with Utah. The G.E. chairman, who constantly refers to "the bottom line," was well aware of Utah's spectacular earnings growth, then 24 percent a year, compounded, for the prior decade, compared with 5 percent for his own corporation. Jones' recent experience with rising prices had made him keenly aware of the value of raw materials, for they seemed to be the best hedge. But he most admired the way Littlefield prudently minimized his own risks by signing up customers for coal, iron ore, and uranium to long-term contracts (with escalation clauses) before developing a new mine.

---

[1]Louis Kraar, "General Electric's Very Personal Merger," *Fortune* (August 1977). Reprinted by permission. Copyright by Time, Inc.

Though Jones had no way of knowing it at the time, Littlefield had been waiting for just such a moment as this. He eagerly told Jones the tale of a company that was being "victimized by our own good fortune." While Utah's mineral interests were highly varied, its disproportionately large investment in Australia greatly concentrated the risks. To make the situation worse, Utah's continued growth required plunging more capital into Australia to expand both its metallurgical-coal and its iron-ore operations.

Littlefield urgently wanted to diversify. His yearning to spread the risks was heightened because Utah's iron mine in Peru was about to be expropriated, which, he says, "drove home to me what a big blow that could be." Even in Australia, where similar risks seemed remote, he had grown wary. The Labor government worried investors by increasing taxes and talking up economic nationalism.

Secondarily, Littlefield was concerned about capital. Utah had plenty of its own, but he felt it would be comforting to have access to a great deal more. The company's significant stakes in everything from steam coal in the U.S. to iron ore in Brazil would require substantial funds to exploit in the years ahead.

The Utah chairman carried a much heavier burden than most C.E.O.'s because he was tied to the company by blood. He belongs to one of "the families," the innumerable descendants of Utah International's founders, who still owned collectively 40 percent of the stock.

For nearly half a century, Utah was a heavy-construction company, first a leading builder of railroads in the West, then a major contractor for such dams as Hoover, Bonneville, and Grand Coulee. By the end of World War II, though, the company had lost much of its early vigor—until Littlefield came along.

Littlefield had avoided employment in the construction business because of feuding among the families. But in 1951, the chairman, Marriner Eccles, prevailed upon him to come in as vice-president and treasurer. He accepted the job only on the condition that he did not have to hire anyone's relations. Soon he was running the corporation in ways that yielded the profit record which Jones so admired.

Littlefield had his own game plan for the construction business, which was then unprofitable. By carefully selecting its work, he put that part of the company into the black and then sold it to Fluor Corp. in 1969.[2]

Littlefield poured Utah's capital completely into mining. The company's able geologists located valuable minerals in the U.S., Canada, and ultimately Australia. Utah became one of the first American mining companies to anticipate and feed Japan's hunger for raw materials, and Littlefield took care to develop a mutually beneficial two-way trade. To control the cost of transportation, Utah's biggest single operating expense, the company ordered large ore-carrying vessels from Japan, which was then desperate for foreign exchange and sold them at relatively low prices. Thus Littlefield helped cultivate an early relationship with the Japanese trading companies and steel mills that proved to be of enormous, continuing benefit. By the time he sat telling his "troubles" to Jones, a decade of steady expansion had increased sales eight times, to $686 million, and multiplied the share price fourteenfold.

For several years, Littlefield explained to the G.E. chairman, he had hoped to diversify by acquisition. But Utah's lean management team, superb as it was at

---

[2]This was a major divestment. At the time, construction activities accounted for 60% of Utah's gross revenues and 69% of its employees.

mining, knew practically nothing about other industries. Much of the business world was equally ignorant of Utah, which had never bothered with advertising or public relations. Littlefield had meager means for evaluating possible acquisitions and the executives who would come with them. Utah's assets totaled about $1 billion, and he figured he would have to buy $1 billion more "to get the risks down to 50 percent, which I thought was tolerable." As he recalls with characteristic modesty: "Frankly, I didn't think I was that good."

Consequently, he decided to look for a company that would acquire Utah. For months prior to his New York trip, he sat alone in his office poring over Moody's *Handbook of Common Stocks* in search of an appropriate corporation. It had to be one that offered broad diversification, could afford the $2 billion he was thinking about asking for Utah, and could get by the Justice Department's antitrust monitors. That last prerequisite, he felt, ruled out the major oil companies.

After turning many pages, he chose three corporations "that we could seriously look at." And G.E. was one of these.

The Boss Liquidates Empires

Jones had his own reasons for liking what he heard. He felt that his company had "fumbled around and missed the computer industry" after a costly, abortive effort. His well-reasoned arguments for abandoning that business, in fact, had helped propel him from financial vice-president to the chairmanship in December, 1972. Though he rarely said so, Jones believed that G.E. had also made other "terrible mistakes." During the rapid inflation of the early Seventies, for instance, the company got caught selling power-generation and transmission equipment under long-term contracts with inadequate escalation provisions. Now he wanted to make his own batting average better than those of his predecessors by expanding G.E. into faster-growing fields while doing everything he could "to limit downside risk."

Until Utah came along, Jones had carefully selected businesses inside the company that seemed to offer exceptional potential, feeding them capital while relentlessly weeding out the losers. Quite naturally, as Jones puts it, "no one wanted to liquidate his empire," so he simply told the managers of fading products: "You have no money to continue." Gradually, G.E. stopped making vacuum cleaners, fans, phonographs, heart pacemakers, an industrial X-ray system, and numerous other products that failed to deliver the returns that Jones demanded.

These executions were far more visible than the birth of exciting new ventures. G.E.'s hottest prospects were such businesses as engineering plastics, carbide cutting tools, apparatus service shops, and the company's financial subsidiary, General Electric Credit Corp. Indeed, synthetic materials and various services were becoming the fast-growth standouts in a corporation long known for its mastery of electrical products.

The traditional mainstays no longer provided a dynamic expansion of earnings. Sales of equipment to the public utilities had fallen off as these companies came under financial pressure, and Jones figured that they were unlikely ever to regain their relative importance for G.E. Nuclear power plants, one of his great hopes, were losing money causing a drain that was sure to continue for some years. Even G.E.'s more solid position in jet engines partly hinged on the uncertain fate of military programs, such as the controversial B-1 bomber. Plainly, G.E. needed something more.

As Jones listened to Littlefield's proposition, he recalled some of the basic economic trends that his planners had spotted. Manufacturing, G.E.'s main activity, seemed to be declining in its importance to the economy. Thinking in his usual broad-gauged manner, Jones saw himself "fighting to gain a diminishing share of G.N.P." The rapid rise in prices of raw materials had encouraged him to consider finding assured supplies and perhaps integrating backward. The light-bulb managers, for instance, toyed with the notion of mining tungsten. But nothing much had happened yet. Because of its sheer size, G.E. tends to move at a deliberate pace.

As an important part of his concept for "the new G.E.," Jones wanted to beef up the company's position overseas. Its share of most foreign markets was still quite small, less than 5% for most products. In "the G.E. culture," some managers still tended to think in terms of domestic product lines, rather than of the opportunities awaiting around the world. To shake domestic executives out of their provincial mind-sets, Jones had gone so far as to team them up in internal joint ventures with G.E.'s international units. As Littlefield described a corporation that sold mainly abroad, Jones sensed a fresh means for G.E. to become the "worldwide company" he envisioned.

Before mentioning the idea to anyone, however, Jones and Littlefield decided to continue exploratory conversations in private, which they did through the next six and a half months. Littlefield wanted what he calls "maximum understanding before proceeding," and he refrained from drawing in his only confidant, Utah's financial vice-president, James Curry, until late October. Jones did confide in only one person, Alva Way, his own successor as chief financial officer. All these individuals went to great lengths to camouflage the purpose of their investigations and meetings.

Disturbing the Ostriches and Emus

While the figures looked great to Jones, he realized that their validity depended heavily on Australia's economic climate. To get a better feel for the country and Utah's operations, he and Way flew out there in November. In the Bowen Basin of Western Australia, he saw that Utah's situation was indeed fabulous. Most of the company's coking-coal reserves lie close to the surface of this flat, sparsely populated area. The ecological problems are minimal, largely because the Australians are relatively relaxed about the impact a few miners have on a vast frontier. As Jones toured the area, he mused: "Here, you only disturb ostriches, emus, wallabies, and kangaroos."

Utah's facilities are so highly mechanized that each of its four mines is run by only 500 people, including clerks. Huge draglines take off a hundred feet or so of overburden to reveal a seam of what Jones calls "pure black gold." "My God," Jones exclaimed when he saw it, "you just scoop it out." In an around-the-clock operation, the coal is crushed and cleaned, then loaded on five 140-car trains to be hauled to the sea for shipment to Japan and Europe.

Over the Thanksgiving weekend, Jones dispatched Way to Brazil, where Utah owns 49 percent of the Samarco iron mine. Carved out of the brush, the mine has reserves of at least 300 million metric tons. Its output travels 246 miles through a slurry pipeline—the longest iron-ore line in the world—to the Atlantic coast, where it is pelletized and loaded aboard ships. The pipeline assures many years of relatively stable transportation costs from mine to seaport. And Utah has negotiated long-term contracts to deliver the pellets to steel mills in the U.S. and Europe.

Their firsthand impressions convinced Jones and Way that the risks were quite manageable. Clearly, Utah was an efficient, low-cost producer. And from their talks with Australian businesspersons and government officials, they anticipated a new conservative government that would be more hospitable to foreign investment.

Finally, Jones was ready to act. In early December when he and Littlefield were in Washington for a Business Council meeting, they reached the terms that would go to their boards. G.E. would issue 41 million new shares to purchase the company, but Utah's ample earnings would more than compensate for the dilution, allowing Jones to promise that the merger would increase G.E.'s earnings per share "from the very first day." Littlefield's stockholders would get a premium, 1.3 shares of G.E. (worth $68.74 on the closing day) for each Utah share (worth $47 when the deal was announced).[3] Just two days before the boards met, Australia elected a conservative government, and everything seemed to be going well.

Enter the Department of Justice

Then the scene turned to Washington. As Jones put it, the marriage arrangements stipulated that "we had better be damned sure that the deal would not present substantial problems on the antitrust front." In a letter that G.E. hand-delivered to the Justice Department, Jones asked for a business advisory clearance, basically a review of the merger and assurance that the government did not plan to fight it. He also decided against lobbying Congress or the executive branch, reasoning that any signs of an attempt to influence Washington would only cause trouble.

He hoped to complete the merger in about five months, by May, 1976, but as things turned out, Robert Morse, the attorney who headed the Justice Department investigation, was ready to give it quite a bit more of his time. Morse felt that he was playing a role in a drama—"the most important merger ever"—whose denouement could affect the future of the nation's energy supplies.

Initially, Morse examined three areas that seemed to have some antitrust potential. Utah mines copper, and G.E. is one of the largest American users of that metal, a circumstance that prompted fears that the merger might foreclose other copper suppliers from selling to G.E. Steam coal posed other questions for Morse: "Who buys steam coal? Utilities. Who sells to utilities? G.E." His concern here was whether G.E. could use Utah's steam coal to unduly influence equipment-purchasing decisions of the utilities. Finally, he investigated whether G.E. might be able to force its suppliers of steel to make reciprocal purchases of Utah's coking coal. Ultimately, none of these issues provided grounds for a challenge.

---

[3]During 1976, the market price of General Electric stock ranged from $46 to $59¼. The dividend payout was also attractive to Utah International's stockholders. In fiscal 1976, Utah International paid $1.15 per share. General Electric was then paying $1.80 on each of its shares, which if continued on the 1.3 shares exchange for each Utah International share would yield $2.34—more than double what Littlefield's shareholders had been receiving.

A Reaction to Uranium

What caused more concern was Utah's uranium business. Westinghouse had promised to supply uranium to the purchasers of its reactors, but ran into trouble when it couldn't lay its hands on enough to cover its contracts. If G.E. controlled a uranium producer, it would have a captive supply and could gain an insurmountable competitive advantage. Thus Justice's initial antitrust review came out opposed to the merger. Soon G.E. lawyers were phoning Morse to ask how they could modify the deal to make it acceptable. He replied: "You have enough high-priced attorneys to come up with an idea."

Eventually, they worked out a new arrangement. G.E. and Utah relinquished control of the uranium assets until the year 2000. The subsidiary, Lucky Mc (named for the amateur prospector, Neil McNeice, who found its first lode in Wyoming), has been spun off into a separate company run by an independent board of trustees. G.E. retains ownership and will get most of the profits, but has agreed not to buy Lucky Mc's uranium and cannot influence its choice of customers.

Finally, on October 1st, after some prodding by Jones, Justice announced that it did not "presently intend to bring action to enjoin the proposed merger." The way was now clear. In December stockholders of both companies approved the fusion, and the joining together was consummated on December 20th.

Avoiding the Heavy Hand

But the marriage was just beginning. The surprise announcement had shocked and disappointed many of Utah's employees. "We dropped a bomb on them," Jones now acknowledges. The mining company's managers had come up together within Utah, like one another, and relished the informality and opportunities available in a lean, fast-growing corporation. Some of Utah's 5,500 employees worried about being submerged in G.E.'s 380,000. Even as well placed an executive as Keith Wallace, a senior vice-president of Utah, concedes he had felt "some concern" about suddenly being "in a big company, where your future is not as certain."

The last thing that Jones wanted was a disruption of Utah's management team or an overlay of bureaucracy that would impair its ability to make quick decisions. He reassured Utah's management that G.E. would be a gentle mate. The mining company kept its own board, which includes five descendants of the founders; G.E. simply added Jones, Way, Vice Chairman Jack Parker, and Utah's financial vice-president, Curry. And, in what he calls "a signal to both companies," Jones made it plain that no one in his organization may so much as approach Utah's management without going through Jones, Way, or Parker—who have largely left Utah alone.

Preserving relative independence seems important to Utah's continued vitality, though how long this freedom will last remains to be seen. G.E. prides itself on strong financial controls and conformity to its own culture. But it does not know the mining business, so Littlefield expects Utah to remain autonomous "as long as it gives a good account of itself." Under G.E.'s rules, Littlefield will have to retire as Utah's chairman within two years, but he can remain on the board for yet another six, until his seventy-first birthday. He still acts in the interests of "the families," which now own about 5 percent of G.E.—more than any single institutional investor or individual.

Just as Jones had promised, the merger pumped up G.E's earnings (by 7 cents a share last year), but it has also stirred more imaginative visions. Among other things, Jones claims that Utah's business relationships in Australia, Brazil, and Japan will increase "customer acceptance" of G.E.'s other products in those markets. But neither he nor any of his senior executives can clearly explain how a Japanese steel mill that buys Australian coal, for instance, will be made more receptive to the purchase of G.E. equipment. To be sure, the business relationship will help open doors. But the Japanese buy from Utah's mines because the prices are attractive, and for the same reason they purchase most of their capital equipment at home rather than getting it from suppliers in the U.S. In short, it's difficult to see G.E.'s selling job getting any easier.

As the Justice Department learned, G.E. does not actually "control" Utah's raw materials, for most of them are committed under long-term contracts. But the company still gains a degree of price protection from Utah's natural resources. Eventually, of course, Utah could develop fresh sources of copper, tungsten, and other minerals for G.E.'s own use. In addition, G.E. might one day be able to market a coal-gasification system along with steam coal from Utah's mines. But any push too far, too fast toward such tie-ins could well provoke antitrust action. For the foreseeable future, Utah's output will go mainly to its usual customers, mostly abroad.

On balance, the arrangement wrought by the two chairmen has given each essentially what he wanted. Jones has made an indelible mark on his corporation, which now looks more like "a new G.E.," with its completely fresh source of earnings. Littlefield has given the Utah families and other owners a greater sense of security with a tax-free exchange of stock. He also did very well for himself. The Littlefields' recently acquired G.E. holdings are now worth $19 million more than the Utah International shares they held when the merger was first announced.

Questions

(1) Do you believe that the General Electric-Utah International merger is desirable from a broad social viewpoint?

(2) (a) Aside from the personal interest of Jones, is the merger wise for General Electric in the long run? Explain. (b) Aside from the personal interest of Littlefield, is the merger wise for Utah International in the long run? Explain.

(3) In view of General Electric's acclaimed management skills, do you recommend continuation of the "hands-off" relations between General Electric's headquarters and Utah International?

Table 1

Growth of the Two Companies in Financial Terms
(in millions, except per share data)

Utah International, Inc. year ends October 31.
General Electric Company year ends December 31.

	Sales	Net Income	Net Income per Share	Total Assets	Equity
Utah International, Inc.					
1976	$ 944	$ 179	$ 5.67	$1,263	$ 684
1975	686	112	3.54	1,046	541
1974	501	98	3.11	909	455
1973	332	62	1.99	827	386
1972	226	44	1.42	700	333
1971	118	38	1.23	618	298
1970	101	32	1.05	437	260
1965	89	11	.37	133	75
1960	69	9	.30	94	38
General Electric Company					
1976*	$15,697	$ 931	$ 4.12	$12,050	$5,253
1975	13,399	581	3.17	9,764	4,069
1974	13,413	608	3.34	9,369	3,704
1973	11,575	585	3.21	8,324	3,372
1972	10,240	530	2.91	7,402	3,085
1971	9,425	472	2.59	6,888	2,812
1970	8,727	328	1.80	6,199	2,554
1965	6,214	355	1.96	4,300	2,107
1960	4,383	219	1.25	2,939	1,569

*General Electric Company 1976 data include *both* its former activities and Utah International, Inc.

Table 2

Utah International, Inc.

Consolidated Balance Sheet—Oct. 31, 1976
(in millions)

Assets		Liabilities & Equity	
Cash	$ 37	Current liabilities	$ 237
Accounts & notes receivable	80	Long-term liabilities	223
		Other liabilities	119
Inventories	113		
Other current assets	11		
Total current assets	241	Total liabilities	579
Investments	302	Common stock, @$2 share	63
Property, plant & equipment, net	720	Additional paid-in capital	91
		Retained earnings	529
		Total equity	684
	$1,263		$1,263

General Electric Company

Balance Sheet—Dec. 31, 1976 and 1975
(in millions)

Assets

	1976 (Includes Utah)	1975 (Excludes Utah)
Cash	$ 1,613	$ 853
Current receivables	2,717	2,597
Inventories	2,355	2,115
Total current assets	6,685	5,565
Investments	1,286	1,050
Property, plant & equipment, net	3,357	2,562
Other assets	722	586
	$12,050	$ 9,763

Liabilities & Equity

	1976 (Includes Utah)	1975 (Excludes Utah)
Current liabilities	$ 4,605	$ 3,964
Long-term liabilities	2,073	1,646
Total liabilities	6,678	5,610
Minority interests	119	84
Common stock, @$2.50 shr.	576	469
Additional paid-in cap.	618	483
Retained earnings	4,251	3,288
Less: treasury stock	-192	-171
Total equity	5,253	4,069
	$12,050	$ 9,763

Part 4

ORGANIZING THE ENTERPRISE

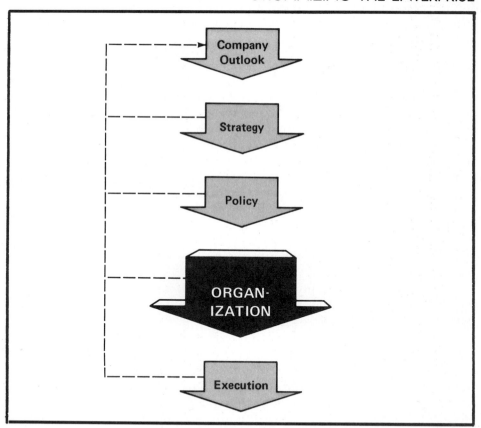

MATCHING ORGANIZATION WITH STRATEGY

Organizing for Growth

A change in a company's strategy and policy usually leads to realignment of its organization. Some activities will be expanded, others curtailed; new priorities will determine which divisions report directly to senior executives. Unless these adjustments are in tune with the shift in objectives, the anticipated growth may never materialize.

In designing an organization we are concerned with the way the myriad of activities required to operate any firm are assigned to people. To be effective, each person has to focus on particular segments of the total task. At the same time, each person's work must be coordinated with the work of others. All sorts of grouping of activities and of interconnecting links are possible—just as letters of the alphabet can be combined in numerous ways —but the particular combination into subgroups and these subgroups into larger divisions has a profound impact on the successful execution of any strategy.

Central management must frequently review the interaction between strategy/policy and organization structure. This matching of strategy and structure shows up most dramatically as a firm moves through different stages of growth. So this chapter deals especially with issues arising in the shift from one stage to another. Chapter 18 then examines the way staff, services, and other divisions provide connective tissue between the basic divisions that we discuss in this chapter. Two further issues—the organization of central management itself and the staffing of positions created in the organization design—become the foci of the following chapters.

Need for Activity Analysis

Just as the selected strategy and its implementation policy are unique for each enterprise, so too is the organization design: organizing calls for perception of subtle differences, imagination in devising special combinations, judgment in balancing benefits and drawbacks, and human understanding in turning an intellectual concept into a social reality. Although common patterns exist, we can't jump from a particular strategy to a predetermined form of organization.

The link between strategy and organization design is activity analysis. What work—planning, operating, controlling, and so forth—must be performed to execute a specific strategy and its associated policy? We need this transformation into work or activities because at least the formal aspects of organization deal with who does what work.

When the J. C. Penney Company, for example, gave up its long-standing "cash sales only" policy and started to grant credit, an array of new activities arose in the accounting, customer credit, and financial control sections of each store as well as in the home office. Likewise, Dole Pineapple Company's decision to make rather than buy its tin cans in Hawaii added activities ranging from purchase of tinplate to running a conveyor from the can shop to the warehouse. It is these new activities that are the grist for any organizational change that may be needed.

When thinking about organizing a large department or an entire company, as central managers must do, a comprehensive review of *all* activities necessary for successful operations is desirable. To examine only a part—the "squeaky wheel"—is likely to lead to a remedy that creates as many new problems as it removes old ones.

The degree of detail to which this analysis should be carried depends upon the scope of organization being considered. When an executive is studying broad, overall organization structure, a listing of major activities is usually adequate. However, when the organization of individual jobs is the aim, listing of minute details may be useful. In either case a lot more detail is analyzed in the design process than appears in the final conclusions because (1) the organizer must be sure to have a complete and realistic grasp of the work involved, and (2) novel and strategic combinations of duties are apt to be missed if the organizer thinks only in terms of large customary groups of work. Also, greater detail should be considered in those areas that are new, that are especially crucial to success, or that have been sources of trouble.

With the activities in mind, our next step is to decide how they can best be grouped together into manageable divisions, departments, sections, or other units. In management circles, this grouping is called *departmentation* even though the final units are not necessarily named departments.

STAGE 1—ONE DOMINANT INDIVIDUAL

The simplest form of organization is one key individual with a group of helpers. The central figure is aware of the details of what is happening and personally gives instructions to the helpers as to what they should do. Of course, the helpers learn the routines of repetitive activities and can proceed with minimum guidance. And they may become specialized in their normal assignments; for example, accounting, dealing with customers, or making repairs. But changes from customary patterns and initiative in moving in new directions rest with the boss.

DISTINGUISHING CHARACTERISTICS OF STAGE I ORGANIZATION

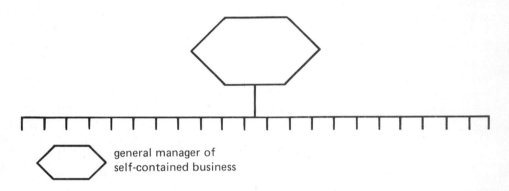

general manager of
self-contained business

Many small businesses (dress shops, drugstores, filling stations, etc.) are operated in this fashion, often with remarkable success. The key individual normally has high energy and skill, doing part of the work as necessary. Even though the business may be legally a corporation, action pivots around the moving spirit. One such self-made businessperson, for instance, was excused from a budget discussion at a directors' meeting to help repair a broken air-compressor that had brought the shop to a standstill.

Organizations dominated by one individual can change strategy quickly *if* the change is within the capacity and the interests of the central person. A lawyer can easily decide to enter the real estate business, or the TV repair shop can add home alarm systems to its line. A few more helpers with technical knowledge will suffice. The key uncertainty is the central person. Thus, an expansion of a Canadian motel, described briefly in Chapter 13, depended on whether Alain Ribout was prepared to supervise the building and running of a nearby unit. Too often the necessary adjustment in managerial organization is overlooked; an energetic entrepreneur pushes ahead on an attractive expansion without analyzing the nature and the volume of new activities and then discovers the difference in Stage I and Stage II organizations.

STAGE II—FUNCTIONAL DEPARTMENTS

Dividing the Managerial Load

Functional departments become necessary when the entrepreneur alone can no longer keep track of all of the operating activities. As the business expands, there are just too many people to be seen, quotations to check, letters to answer, inventory to watch, even for the most energetic manager. Especially when the business involves non-routine activities and frequent emergencies, the manager must be free of normal day-to-day operations. Otherwise mistakes are made, opportunities are passed by, and the work of helpers is slowed down waiting to see the boss.

The normal remedy is to appoint functional managers—one for selling, another for accounting, a third for production, and so on. These people (or *their* helpers) answer most of the questions that bubble up from activities; they check on progress and expedite lagging action. Being specialists, they are likely to be more expert in their particular field than the general manager. And because they focus on a narrower array of work they become more sensitive to its particular needs and opportunities.

DISTINGUISHING CHARACTERISTICS OF STAGE II ORGANIZATION

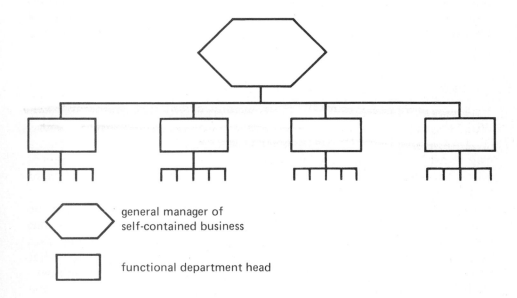

general manager of
self-contained business

functional department head

With such help, the behavior of the general manager should differ sharply from that of the dominant individual in a Stage I organization. The general manager has to be willing to delegate. This means no longer knowing just what is happening day-by-day and accepting decisions that are not quite the way the general manager would have made them. A cardinal purpose of creating functional departments is to give the general manager time to focus on interdepartmental coordination and on policy and strategy issues. Many executives whose success as Stage I managers makes possible a Stage II organization find this required change in their personal behavior very difficult and sometimes impossible.

An organization made up of functional departments is well suited for companies which have only a single "business-unit." For example, firms concentrating on automobile insurance typically have departments for sales-underwriting, claims, finance, investment-treasury, and legal matters. Similarly, a hi-fi equipment manufacturer will probably have R&D, production, marketing, and finance as basic departments. With only a single line, coordination between departments can be handled through procedures, scheduled meetings, and mediation by the general manager. Each department continues to render the same kind of service, so neglect of parts of the business is unlikely. And a general manager concentrates on maintaining effective teamwork.

A strategy of a "full line" of services to a single set of customers also matches a functional setup reasonably well. In "one-stop banking," for instance, a customer contact (branch office) department will be aided by headquarters departments dealing with checking accounts, small loans, commercial loans, safe deposit, trust, and other services. Here the relationships overlap more and competition may arise for the concentrated attention of the customer contact personnel, but customer service provides the mediating objective.

Defining the Scope of a "Function"

The use of functional departments creates some problems of its own: (a) What constitutes a function—how shall the boundaries be set? (b) How should activities within a function be organized? Until we have at least a way to approach these questions, the concept of a Stage II organization is difficult to apply to enterprises ranging from aviation and banking to yacht building and zoo-keeping.

Functions singled out for separate status as a department often reflect the differential advantage emphasized in the strategy. A department store that places great reliance on advertising, for instance, treats advertising as a major function and not as a subordinate part of marketing. Companies that rely on leadership in product design will treat R&D as a major department. Perhaps purchasing will be separated from other operations to give it strong emphasis.

In addition to such strategic functions, every firm has a variety of activities that do not neatly fit into a limited number of major departments. Two general guides are helpful in this respect:

1. Place in the same department those activities that have the same immediate objectives. For example, activities as diverse as running a cafeteria, performing medical service, and administering a pension plan may be placed in the personnel department because all of these contribute to the objective of building an efficient work force. In the same manner, the management of salespeople and of advertising may be placed under the sales manager, because the objectives of both these activities is the same—to procure sales orders.

2. Place in the same department activities that require a similar type of ability and experience for their efficient management. For example, in pharmaceutical companies quality control is often placed in the research department. Control of the quality of pharmaceuticals requires someone who is objective, analytical, and expert in laboratory techniques. These similarities with research seem to warrant combined supervision even though the mission of the two activities differs significantly. Budgeting and finance might be placed in the same department for similar reasons.

Advantages of functional departments depend partly upon the integrating theme for the particular unit. Expertness with a similar type of problem, adequate attention to an activity that otherwise might be given hurried treatment, consistent action in such matters as price concessions, and easy coordination of activities having a common purpose are among the benefits often secured.

Except in unusual circumstances, the number of major functional departments (not counting staff and services) in a Stage II organization should not exceed about six.

Organizational Options within Departments

Although a small functional department can be organized on the one-dominant-individual basis, its own size and the need for systematic relations with other departments soon call for orderly grouping of internal activities. One form is, of course, further assignment of work by subfunctions. There are other options. Among the common bases for further subdivision are:

Products. For many years in the typical department store the buyer was king. There would be separate buyers for hosiery, jewelry, gloves, shoes, millinery, and dozens of other products. Normally, each buyer was responsible for the purchase of the merchandise, its pricing and display, and its sale. Of course, there were storewide departments for such activities as building operations, delivery, finance, accounting, advertising, and personnel. Nevertheless, the very crucial trading function remained the domain of the respective product buyers. This provided close coordination of buying and selling each product, and it aided control by localizing responsibility.

With the recent substantial expansion of suburban branches, the role of the department store buyer has been changing. Because of the distance factor, buyers cannot directly supervise the people selling their products in the several outlets and they have difficulty maintaining their former close observation of display and proper maintenance of stocks. Buyers are becoming primarily providers of merchandise and sales promotion planners. Nevertheless, divisions by product line remain very important.

Product subunits are also often introduced in engineering and production. And as we shall see, building around products is a key feature of Stage III organizations.

Processes. Manufacturers—and government offices—often perform several distinct processes that may serve as the basis for organizational units. For example, in steel production typically we find separate shops for coke ovens, blast furnaces, open-hearth furnaces, hot-rolling mills, cold-rolling mills, and the like. Each process is performed in a separate location and involves a distinct technology. Even if the company shifts its basic technology from blast furnaces to oxygen converters, the plant will be divided organizationally into process units.

Libraries, to cite another field, normally divide their work into units dealing with book acquisitions, cataloging, circulation, and reference. There may also be separation by type of "customer" such as children, schools, and adults.

The grouping of activities by process tends to promote efficiency through specialization. All the key people in each department become expert in dealing with their particular phase of the business. On the other hand, process classification increases problems of coordination; scheduling the movement of work from department to department on each order becomes somewhat complex. Also, since no department has full responsibility for the order, a department may not be as diligent in meeting time requirements and other specifications as a group of people who think in terms of the total finished product and their customers.

The organization issue just posed—product versus process grouping—has additional ramifications. It ties in with the desirability of subcontracting, extent of mechanization, and of course the characteristics of executives needed.

The conflict between the desire to increase skill in performance through specialization and mechanization, and the need for coordination to secure balanced efforts recurs time and again in organization studies. Insurance companies, hospitals, and even consulting firms face the same issue.

Territories. Companies with sales representatives who travel over a large area almost always use territorial organization. Large companies will have several regions, each subdivided into districts, with a further breakdown of territories for individual sales representatives. Airlines, finance companies with local offices, and motel chains all by their very nature have widely dispersed activities and consequently use territorial organization to some degree.

The primary issues with territorial organization are three:

1. What related activity should be physically dispersed along with those which by their nature are local? For example, should a company with a national salesforce also have local warehousing, local assembling, local advertising, local credit and accounting, and local personnel? And how far should the dispersion occur—to the regional level or to the district level? Typically, whenever such related activities are dispersed, they are all combined into a territorial organization unit.
2. How much authority to make decisions should be decentralized to these various territorial units? In other words, how much of the planning and control work should go along with the actual performance?
3. What will be the relations between the home office service and staff units and these various territorial divisions?

We will discuss these last two issues in the next chapter, but it is important to recognize that they must be satisfactorily resolved if territorial units are established.

The major advantage of territorial organization is that it provides supervision near the point of performance. Local conditions vary and emergencies do arise. Persons located a long distance away will have difficulty grasping the true nature of the situation, and valuable time is often lost before an adjustment can be made. Consequently, when adjustment to local conditions and quick decisions are important, territorial organization is desirable. On the other hand, if a lot of local units are established, some of the benefits of large-scale operation may be lost. The local unit will probably be comparatively small, and consequently the degree of specialization and mechanization will be correspondingly limited.

Customers. A company that sells to customers of distinctly different types may establish a separate unit of organization for selling and servicing each. A manufacturer of men's shoes, for instance, sells to both independent retail stores and chain stores. The chain-store buyers are very sophisticated and may prepare their own specifications; consequently, any salespeople calling on them must have an intimate knowledge of shoe construction and of the capacity of their company's plant. In contrast, sales representatives who call on retailers must be able to think in terms of retailing problems and be able to show how their products will fit into the customer's business. Few sales representatives can work effectively with both large chain-store and independent retail customers; consequently, the shoe manufacturer has a separate division in sales organization for each group.

Commercial banks, to cite another example, often have different vice-presidents for types of customers—airlines, manufacturing concerns, stockbrokers, consumer loans, and the like. These people recognize the needs of their particular group of customers and they also are in a good position to appraise the credit worthiness.

Ordinarily, customer groups include only selling and direct service activities. Anyone who has been shunted around to five or six offices trying to get an adjustment on a bill or a promise on a delivery will appreciate the satisfaction of dealing with a single individual who understands the problem and knows how to get action within the company. On the other hand, this form of organization may be expensive, and a customer-oriented employee may commit the company to actions that other departments find hard to carry out.

Summary. This short review of product, process, territory, and customer departmentation indicates the many variations that are possible in organizing within a major department. A full analysis of the various options would go beyond our main focus on central management. However, even this brief discussion does indicate the necessity of clearly relating central organization to basic operations "where the real work is done." Also a by-product of this review is to mention alternatives to functional departments. In special circumstances we may decide that, say, an international department or a government contract department fits a company strategy better than a functional department.

This necessary elaboration of a Stage II organization does not change its basic features. We start with a sharply focused domain and differential advantage mission, and then we establish specialized departments each of which has a different though important contribution to make to that mission. The work of these departments is interdependent, so the entire operation has to be managed as an integrated whole. The role of the general manager of such an organization is to find department managers who will be responsible for day-to-day operations while the general manager concentrates on integration and longer-run strategy and policy issues.[1]

STAGE III—SELF-CONTAINED PRODUCT OR REGIONAL DIVISIONS

Successful enterprises outgrow a Stage II organization. They become too large or too diversified. As a Stage II company grows from less than a hundred to over a thousand employees, communications become more formal, standard procedures prevent quick adjustments, the convenience of each department receives more consideration than company goals, and people feel insignificant in terms of total results. Careful management can diminish these tendencies, but sooner or later sheer size saps vigor and effectiveness.

In addition, successful companies take advantage of opportunities to diversify product lines, to develop new sources of materials, and to provide new

---

[1]The department managers should participate in strategy and policy formulation, as will be pointed out in Chapter 19. Their primary duty, however, and the viewpoint they are expected to bring to central management deliberations, is that of running a specialized department very well.

services in response to changing social needs. This adds complexity. But large functional departments often give secondary attention to such opportunities; they are busy doing their established tasks well. So the new developments fail to receive the attention and the coordinated effort they deserve.

Unless a company makes a deliberate strategic decision to stay relatively small and clearly focused on a particular mission—a strategic option few U.S. companies elect—a shift in organization becomes necessary.

Concept of Semi-Independent Divisions

The basic remedy for oversize is to split up into several Stage I or Stage II divisions. A series of separate business-units is created within the larger corporation.

Establishing manageable "businesses." Ordinarily these divisions are built around product lines. That part of marketing dealing with a particular product is transferred from the marketing department to the product division. And likewise with production, engineering, and perhaps other functions. Ideally each division has within it all the key activities necessary to run independently—it is *self-sufficient*. Moreover, the management of the newly created division is given a high degree of authority, making the division *semiautonomous*. The general manager of such a division then has virtually the same resources and freedom of action as the president of an independent company and is expected to take whatever steps are necessary to make the "little business" successful.

Even when it is practical to place within a division all of its own marketing and production activities, some central services are retained. Obtaining capital, exploratory research, and staff assistance on labor relations, law, and market research, for example, usually can be performed more economically in one place for all divisions of the corporation. Such central assistance gives operating divisions an advantage over fully independent companies.

Typically, self-contained divisions are built around product lines. A company may have anywhere from two to (for General Electric Company) a hundred such product divisions. The same idea, however, has been applied by department store chains on a territorial basis. And large metal fabricators place their mining and transportation activities ("process" units) in self-contained divisions.

Advantages. Breaking a large firm into several self-sufficient, semiautonomous divisions has several managerial advantages:

1. Morale is improved because people see the results of their own efforts and feel the importance of their action.
2. Communication is faster, often face-to-face, and the significance of information is easier to recognize.
3. Adequate attention can be given to individual customers, product adjustments, and other matters that may be brushed over in a larger organization.

DISTINGUISHING CHARACTERISTICS OF STAGE III ORGANIZATION

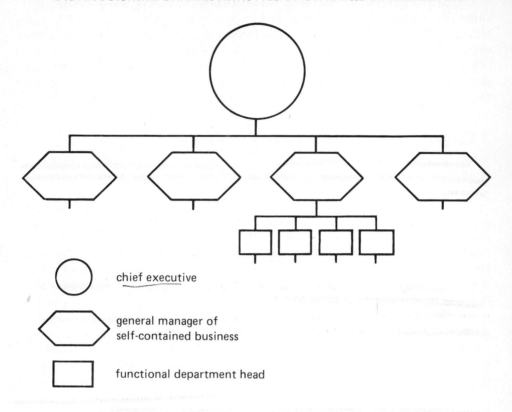

chief executive

general manager of
self-contained business

functional department head

4. Coordination of production with sales, costs with income, personnel training with needs, and other interfunctional adjustments are improved.
5. Control can be exercised more promptly and with fuller appreciation of the total circumstances.

With more manageable and sharply focused divisions, changes in strategy can be put into effect more rapidly.

Difficulties with Optimum Size

In applying the concept of small, self-contained divisions we soon discover that functional departments often cannot be neatly divided. Technology and other forces dictate an *optimum size* for various activities. For instance, an oil refinery to serve Spokane, Washington, alone would be much too small to be efficient. On the other hand, the task of increasing employment of minorities can readily be divided and assigned to separate divisions.

The optimum size issue is complicated because optimum volume is not the same for each function. A men's clothing firm, for instance, found that plants with two to three hundred employees could achieve virtually all economies of scale in production and that larger plants generated more personnel problems. However, the output of one such plant would be far too small for marketing purposes. National advertising and promotion were the key to the firm's marketing success, and the sales volume needed to support national distribution was six times the output of a single plant.

The optimum size of an elementary school, to cite a very different industry, would be small if we think of travel time for pupils, and quite large if we focus on the cost of heating and maintaining the buildings. Professionals in the key function—education—have still a third view of optimum size; they want classes of about twenty-five. Assuming the main criterion is quality of education, then the optimum size of a school will be the number of grades times twenty-five. (A change in educational "technology" to the ungraded system would probably lead to a different answer.)

These differences in optimum size affect the number of self-contained divisions we establish. In a steel company, for instance, marketing considerations call for twenty or thirty separate divisions, each focused on a product/market target. Production technology, however, dictates that almost all the end-products come out of a few large plants. These plants can't be split up by product lines. So twenty or thirty self-sufficient product divisions are impractical. The best we can do is break out a few products, such as oil-field pipe or barbed wire, that have separate plants for their final stages of manufacture. In fact, a review of self-contained divisions in a wide variety of industries indicates that most of them have a volume of work that is below the optimum size for one or two functions and above the optimum size for other functions. The aim, of course, is to build divisions that are *optimum in size for critically important functions,* even though this results in some diseconomies in other areas.

Compromise Arrangements

Companies often try to get most of the benefits of self-contained divisions and also keep functional operations at optimum levels. For instance, one paper company leaves production in a single functional department, but it breaks product engineering and marketing down into strong product divisions. The division managers are expected to act like "independent businesspersons" except that they must contract for their supply of products from the production division.

A comparable arrangement is used by a food processor, except that in this instance it is selling rather than production that is centralized in one department. Each product division does its own product design, engineering, buying, production, merchandising, and pricing, but it utilizes the sales department to contact customers. The rationale here is that a single field organization can cover the country more effectively for all divisions than they could do separately.

Whenever a product division has to rely on an outside department for a key activity, problems of adequate attention, coordination, and control become more difficult. Occasions for bickering jump dramatically. Central management has to judge whether the harm done by restricting the self-sufficiency idea is offset by the benefits of the larger-scale activities in the functional department.

All sorts of compromise arrangements are found in practice. Sometimes the product division has the option to buy services from outside companies instead of using the inside department if it can obtain better service at less cost. This clearly puts pressure on the central department to be responsive to the needs of the divisions. In other cases the centralized department merely notifies the divisions what capacity it has available, and the divisions must live within this limit. Understandings are needed on the planning horizon, transfer prices, emergency changes, quality of service, risky experiments, and the like. Basically such issues should be resolved in terms of what contributes most to company strategy, and this interpretation usually must be made by central management.

The compromises just discussed all presume self-contained product or regional divisions will be the primary organizational form of the corporation with an exception being made for some one functional department. Two other kinds of modifications, midway between Stage II and Stage III formats, are also used. One leaves the functional departments intact and merely establishes a so-called "product manager"—really a staff person who keeps track of his products in the various departments and attempts to negotiate adjustments that will aid his line. As with any staff (see the next chapter), the strength of a "product manager's" influence can range from merely raising questions to suggestions that carry the weight of commands. The second kind of variation, found in the space industry, construction companies, and consulting firms, is "project management" (sometimes called matrix organization). Here competent individuals are temporarily assigned by the functional departments to a project team. This team, usually with its own manager, runs the project somewhat like a product division might; but when the project is completed, members of the team return to their functional base.

Organizing for Strategic Benefits

The difficulties of achieving a smoothly running set of self-contained operating divisions, just discussed, naturally raise the question of when a shift from a Stage II to a Stage III organization is worth the effort.

Recently, more and more attention is being focused on business-unit strategy and policy, as discussed in Parts 1 and 2 of this book. This emphasis encourages the use of a Stage III organization. Ideally, whenever a distinct business-unit strategy is warranted, we would create an organization division to match the strategy in its scope. Then a set of division executives can easily combine strategic planning with execution of that plan.

However, as already noted in our discussion of optimum size, the business-unit needs a minimum volume of activity to support its own marketing organization, its own production, and so forth. Until the volume reaches this level some kind of compromise arrangement may be necessary.

If central managers feel confident that a business-unit will attain in a year or two sufficient volume to support its own organization, they may create the organization immediately. High expenses will not be covered by income during the start-up period. But the expectation is that these initial losses will be offset by the benefits of an aggressive strategic thrust.

A conservative alternative is to delay splitting off the activities covered by the strategy. Instead, these activities are left in functional departments, or in a division with a different strategic mission. The managers of these multiple-mission operations—perhaps with the aid of a product manager—will have to cooperate in getting the fledgling business-unit started. They test the market; they experiment with production; they watch responses of competitors; they feel their way. And only after these initial probes signal promising results will a separate division dedicated to the strategic domain be created. Of course, a danger in this conservative approach is that the managers who are involved with several different strategies will not provide the energetic, coordinated effort required to make each of these strategies successful.

An aviation equipment manufacturer, for example, wanted more Air Force business and concluded that greater flexibility in meeting technical requirements would help toward this goal. Central management set up a separate "government-business" division, even though it entailed more overhead and some resistance in functional departments, primarily to gain the desired flexibility in meeting technical requirements. Similarly, a women's shoe company decided to integrate forward into selected retail outlets. This marketing thrust might have been assigned to the existing sales department. However, management decided on a separate retail division because analysis showed that adjusting store inventory to local tastes was vital; a separate division was expected to be more objective and to act more quickly in this critical area.

A decision *not* to set up a separate carton division was reached by a paper company. Here investigation revealed that this segment of the industry was already mature and that low cost was crucial to success. So the company strategy was to operate only its most efficient plants as near capacity as possible. Although a separate carton division would have provided more intensive marketing effort, it would have contributed little toward cost reduction. Consequently, the proposal to form a self-contained carton division separated from the larger container branch was turned down.

We see in these examples that organization changes are intimately connected with the strategy selected.

STAGE IV—CONGLOMERATE ORGANIZATION

Conglomerate organization differs from a Stage III organization of self-contained divisions primarily in the absence at headquarters of service and staff units and the limited attempt to secure synergistic benefits among its components. Typically, conglomerates are built from previously independent companies, each with its own traditions and a full complement of central services. Moreover, these companies are not expected to contribute to each other's business. So there is little to be gained from "coordination" and from overall service units. A conglomerate truly is a collection of disassociated businesses.[2]

Primary Attention to Investment Portfolio

The main benefits of conglomerates are financial. Operating companies are brought into the corporate structure mainly to diversify risks or to provide cash flow balance, as outlined in Chapter 15. "Corporate planning" in the majority of conglomerates consists entirely of looking for attractive acquisitions and does not deal with businesses already in the fold. The presumption is that each operating unit will do its own strategic planning, except for major questions on sources and uses of capital.

Since the interactions between the central office and the operating companies in a conglomerate are largely limited to finance, the basic organization structure can be simple. The chief executive in each operating company reports to the president or a group vice-president in the central office. In addition, there will be the usual transfer of funds and upward flow of financial reports. That is all that's needed.

Of course, each operating company has its own organization; this may be a Stage I, II, or III organization or any variation that best suits the needs of the particular company. Incidentally, the legal status of the operating company is not significant from the viewpoint of managerial organization. Each operating unit will be treated as a separate company even though its corporate identity may be washed out for financial reasons.

Role as "Outside" Member of Board of Directors

Although the organization may be simple, the role that the supervising executive from the central office plays in the management of an operating company can be extremely valuable. This executive should be an ideal "outside director."

---

[2]A conglomerate differs sharply from a mutual fund. The conglomerate owns all of or a controlling interest in its companies and accepts final responsibility for their overall management. A mutual fund owns only a small fraction of the stock, takes no responsibility for management, and simply sells its stock if it is dissatisfied with company results.

DISTINGUISHING CHARACTERISTICS OF STAGE IV ORGANIZATION

Conglomerate all

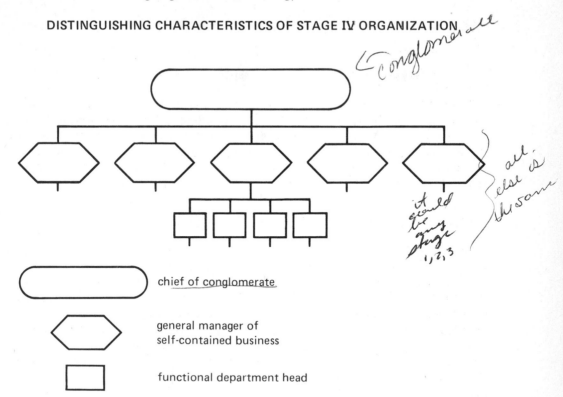

it could be any stage 1, 2, 3

all. else is the same

chief of conglomerate

general manager of
self-contained business

functional department head

Every company needs objective senior counsel to its chief executives, as explained in Chapter 19. Presumably this independent counseling is the main job of an outside member of the board of directors. Unfortunately, all corporations face severe difficulties in attracting to their boards of directors individuals who are (a) wise, courageous, and well informed, and also (b) sufficiently concerned to devote energy and initiative to the affairs of that particular company. Obtaining good outside directors is a chronic and serious problem.

A conglomerate, however, can overcome this difficulty. It has sufficient stake in the success of its operating companies to locate and employ individuals who are fully qualified to be good "outside directors." Such a person should devote full time to serving as a member or head of the board of, perhaps, half a dozen operating companies. By assuring that major decisions are wisely made, insisting that unpleasant action be taken promptly, and counseling on future possibilities (as explained in Chapter 19), a strong director can stimulate operating executives.

By aiding with finance and by providing able outside directors, then, conglomerates help make their operating companies strong. Most of the central management functions, however, should be left to fully staffed operating companies.

SUMMARY

Company strategy and policy set directions, limits, and goals. But these broad plans must be matched by a corresponding managerial organization to carry out the implied array of activities. In this first chapter of Part 4 we have focused on basic structure. Two themes keep reappearing: (1) structure depends upon size and complexity, and (2) structure should reinforce strategy.

As a company succeeds and grows, it must change its organization. Four quite distinct stages are clear. Stage I represents the small, budding enterprise in which *one dominant individual* does both long-range planning and day-to-day managing. Sooner or later the business exceeds the capacity of even the most energetic single manager, and a shift must be made to Stage II in which day-to-day operations are delegated to *functional departments*. Then as the firm expands and diversifies, the functional departments become too large and bureaucratic, so a further shift is necessary to a Stage III organization composed of *self-contained product or regional divisions*. Finally, though not necessarily, a collection of independent companies may be combined into a Stage IV *conglomerate organization*.

Many variations and compromises are essential to fit the organization to the specific technology, optimum size, resources, and other features of a specific firm. A cardinal aim in making such variations should be to strengthen the company in those areas it has chosen to build strategic distinction. In this way the organization gives potency to the unique services the company wants to provide.

Every organization consists of more than the primary operating divisions —the topic of this chapter. Questions of decentralization, the placing of staff and services, communications systems, the organization for central management itself, and providing people to fill the proposed positions—all call for careful attention. These issues are discussed in the following three chapters.

 QUESTIONS FOR CLASS DISCUSSION

1. Sr. Gomez, president and part-owner of Tubora, S.A., is concerned and decidedly unhappy because his company, a manufacturer of tubes and plastic bottles used to contain cosmetics, seems to be on a profit plateau. Sales are up nicely; profits are not. He explains: "So that I could concentrate on our rapidly

growing sales and on my general responsibility to hold the company together, I brought in a production manager, a chief mechanic, an accountant, and a personnel manager. But our profits show the added expense of all these managers. I still have to walk through the plant several times each day to check on quality and on the settings of the machines. The slightest deviation can throw off the colors and the printing. Then I like to come in early and leave late so that I can talk with the second-shift supervisor and see the results of the night's work. The personnel manager hasn't yet shown that she can get the people on the line to stop talking and work harder. I really should spend almost all of my time out of the office making sales. But troubles with machine settings and arguments between the operators and mechanics seem to come to me for settlement. And the new accountant has not helped us to cut costs. What can I do with an organization like this one?"

2. Prepare a list of not more than eight key factors which often arise in departmentation problems. These factors which are mentioned frequently in this chapter as an advantage or disadvantage of a particular arrangement, are likely to be involved in both high-level and low-level design choices and in any stage. (Suggestion: look at the advantages of functional departments briefly listed on page 421, and at the advantages listed for self-sufficient units listed on pages 425–426. Then check whether the same kind of issues arise in other situations, and add other factors if necessary.)

3. Jean Stevens is the owner-manager of a very successful restaurant. Located on a main highway in an attractive setting about 20 miles outside of Atlanta, it is a favorite place to have "a really good dinner" for both people in the area and from the city. There are tables for 200 people in addition to the bar and a large terrace. The restaurant reflects Ms. Stevens' personality and ability, and it has grown as a Stage I organization. (a) Now Ms. Stevens wants less burden of day-to-day operations. Do you recommend a Stage II organization? If so, define the functional departments. (b) What problems would arise if Ms. Stevens, or new owners, tried to expand to several other locations? Would you recommend a Stage II or a Stage III organization for the expanded operations?

4. The Mercedes Bicycle Company is doing a flourishing business with its "Syncro-Shift" and "Mountain King" models, and it now has some international as well as national sales. Contributing to its success is the engineering design and quality control in its Indianapolis plant. Assume that your uncle is president of the company and seeks your advice, as a student of management, on organization. To date, organization has been based on expediency, but your uncle feels "the time has come to build our organization around some consistent principle." Assuming a Stage II organization, what basis would you recommend be used for organizing within the production department? Within the marketing department?

5. A successful TV set manufacturer with a Stage II organization has just completed arrangements to take over a small electronics plant in England as a first move in international expansion. The English plant will become a production base for the British market. A major anticipated gain will be use of U.S. engineering and production know-how in the newly acquired plant. Should the manager of the British plant report to the production vice-president in the home office? If so, what happens to marketing and finance of the British operation?

6. By concentrating first on lightweight models, Honda has become the leading producer of motorcycles in the world. Now Honda is pursuing a similar strategy in automobiles. All engineering and most production is done in Japan but, of course, marketing activities are widely dispersed. (a) In its organization, to what extent should motorcycle and automobile activities be combined together or separated? Consider both (i) each major function, and (ii) as an example of its marketing structure, Honda activities in the United States. (b) What synergies should Honda try to obtain from having both lines of products?

7. Expansion into the total packaging field has created organizational problems for a successful producer of tin cans. For years the company had plants located throughout the country. Strong functional departments in sales, production, and finance maintained close watch on sales to specific customers, costs, and full utilization of investment in equipment. The executives knew the can business thoroughly and "ran a tight ship." The recent expansion includes acquisitions of companies producing plastic, paper, and glass containers for food and many other consumer products. The new strategy is to provide a complete packaging service adapted to improved technology and changing consumer requirements. Each segment of the packaging industry involves mass production, and price competition is keen. What kind of organization structure do you recommend to match the new strategy? Make clear which units are to be primary operating departments and what relationships service divisions (if any) are to have with the operating departments.

8. (a) Many executives regard acquisition of their company by a conglomerate with fear. The idea of being "taken over" comes as a great psychological blow. How do you account for this feeling? (b) Do executives have more, or less, opportunity if the company they work for becomes part of a conglomerate? (c) Is there any reason to presume that the conglomerate executives will push for actions contrary to healthy growth and good service of the operating unit?

9. In preparation for a well-predicted downturn in general business (which company executives expect to be a major recession), the L and J Company of Midwood, Indiana, sold off the three least profitable subsidiaries of its Leisure Products Division, cut in half the predicted sales of its ARV (replacement parts for automobiles and recreational vehicles) Division, stopped all capital expenditure in its Consumer Products Division and Small-Motor Division, and made no changes in plans for its Financial Services Division (loans to customers and consumers to finance purchases of L and J equipment). These actions (a) changed Leisure Products to a one-plant division with regional sales of hunting and fishing equipment, (b) shut down half of one plant of the ARV Division and changed the products of the other plant to much less expensive replacement parts for recreational vehicles, (c) anticipated a 25% drop-off in sales of compressors and of small-motors, and (d) called for a reduction of 30% in the salesforce of the door-to-door sales Consumer Products Division. Then the president began to consider slimming down the organization. Why not get out of Leisure Products Division altogether by putting its production in the ARV plant, combine the ARV and Small-Motor Divisions (they both sell mainly to manufacturers) and have only three divisions which operate in somewhat different markets? This action would save some expense of administrative overhead. Or why not go further and return to a Stage II organization which might have three different salesforces but would need fewer manufacturing plants, fewer

control systems, and an easier life for the central executives? Do these proposed changes in the organizational structure seem wise to you? Explain.

10. (a) A university could be organized so that each course ran as a separate, self-contained unit (the students would sign up, use equipment, and pay for each course just like they do for private airplane flying lessons). Or each department might be so organized; or each division. What are the key factors that determine what separations, if any, of this type should be made? (b) Should any of the following be seen as self-sufficient divisions: dormitories; bookstore; intercollegiate athletics; eating halls? Should they be expected to at least break even financially?

11. The Dotman Company purchased all of the cocoa powder and half of the coffee beans used in its food products from brokers in New York. It bought the other half of its coffee bean requirements in Africa and South America. The coffee beans were purchased, roasted, processed, and sold by the coffee division of this food-products company. The cocoa powder was purchased by the candy division but also used as a raw material by several other divisions, including baked-goods and beverages. The treasurer has put in a strong plea to centralize these two activities for several reasons. One, the dollar amounts of the purchases were 50% or more of the materials costs of two of the using divisions; two, the special skills needed had little to do with the activities of the balance of the baked-goods and beverage divisions; three, the treasurer could then control more carefully the dollars invested in inventory, foreign exchange, and the forward-purchase commitments of the company. What do you think? Should an international purchasing division be established analogous to the company's international exports division?

CASE 17
Western Nadir Markets, Inc. (R)

Everyone agrees, since the recent expansion of operations and the opening of new stores, that the organization structure of Western Nadir Markets, Inc., a locally owned chain of retail grocery stores, is no longer adequate for a firm of its size and complexity of operations. Frederick Engels, assistant to the president, has undertaken a special project whose objective is to determine what jobs are necessary, what departments are advisable, and how many executives are needed for an effective formal organization.

Western Nadir Markets has operated 20 conventional supermarkets in West Coast City for some years and has gained a solid reputation as a sound grocery firm, based in part on its excellent merchandising of meats and in part on the design and location of its stores. These all serve the wealthier areas of West Coast City and are attractively laid out with wide aisles, paneling on interior walls, and occasional art exhibits by local artists. Exterior decor ranges from psuedo-Colonial to modern and varies by location. Each store has a special-order meat-cutting service and an arrangement for direct consultation between customer and butcher. The procedure for meats follows the policy on perishables explained by the president, Mr. Calhoun Marks, as: "Perishable products are over half of the customer's regular food purchases. Quality can vary substantially and is hard to judge. Consider that a customer's reputation as a cook can change with the succulence of the roast beef or the tenderness of the steak served. Here at Western Nadir the customer has learned to have absolute confidence in our perishables. We have succeeded by specializing and by differing somewhat from the average."

In addition to the well-established stores, Western Nadir Markets has recently opened and now operates two discount supermarkets in West Coast City and four discount supermarkets in Pacific City. One more discount supermarket is past the planning stage in West Coast City. Ground is about to be broken. The two cities are 110 miles apart. Air service between them operates from airports on the fringes of each city. Further plans are to close out three nonprofit conventional supermarkets in West Coast City and to open two in the right locations in Pacific City. Beyond this, Mr. Marks believes firmly in the future of discount markets.

Discount supermarkets are distinguished from conventional stores by having larger sales volume and lower gross margins on the various product lines. Typical sales are $300,000 per week in a discount market and $115,000 per week in a conventional market. On the average, net profit as a percent of sales is the same in the two kinds of stores if they are equally well managed. Last year's total sales for the company were $215,000,000. Post-tax profit was 0.7% of sales, while the industry average was 1.2% and Western Nadir's average over the previous ten years was 1.4%.

Discount supermarkets typically have modern decor, somewhat less luxurious appointments than the ordinary Western Nadir market, meat-processing in an area not open to the public, parcel pickup systems (no carryout service), long hours, night stocking of shelves, tray-packing, and cut-case display.[1]

Exhibit 1 on the next page shows the number of employees typically required by Western Nadir in both discount supermarkets and conventional supermarkets. Exhibit 2 presents departmental statistics for both types of operations.

Meat and produce section managers in all stores report to the head buyers for meats and for produce at company headquarters in West Coast City. One person has the title of store manager in each discount supermarket, and has responsibility for groceries, frozen foods, and other items but not for meats and produce. The store security operative in the conventional supermarkets ordinarily assists the grocery section assistant manager.

The headquarters organization currently consists of Calhoun Marks, president; head buyers for meat, for produce, and for all other items; a merchandise and operations manager (who has been mainly busy with planning for new stores); an assistant to the president; a warehouse manager; a personnel manager; a chief engineer; and a controller. The discount supermarket store managers report to the president, as do the grocery section assistant managers of the conventional stores.

---

[1]Goods are displayed in the original cartons with the top end part of the sides of the carton cut away to expose the contents.

This practice is believed by many to have contributed to the low profit results, since Mr. Marks, although acknowledged as a highly capable store executive, has spent his time with new store planning, with financial matters, and with supervising the operations of the discount supermarkets.

There have been troubles with the newer discount markets. The company has not had experienced managers to move to them and has found the transition from the ordinary Western Nadir operation quite difficult for its executive force.

The headquarters executive organization is commonly recognized to be a thin management. The size of the force is also a reason for the success of the firm since executive and administrative salaries are $375,000 per year less than the industry average for comparable chains.

Exhibit 1
Typical Staffing Tables

	Discount Supermarket	Conventional Supermarket
Store Manager..............	1	—
Grocery Section		
Assistant Manager...........	1	1
Cashiers...................	10	5
Stock Clerks..............	11	6
Meat Section		
Manager..................	1	1
Butchers..................	5	2
Produce Section		
Manager..................	1	1
Helpers	2	1
Stock Room		
Supervisor	1	1
Store Security	2	1

Source: Company records.

In working on his project, Mr. Engels collected some ideas that seemed to him to have merit and that, when analyzed and related to the information he already had, would provide the basis for his report.

Several assistant managers of the conventional supermarkets said: "We no longer have access to the president, controller, and chief engineer as we once did. This is fine for us, since we now decide problems on our own; but it causes troubles in the five stores that face severe and above-average competition from the big chains. Two of those stores are about to be closed down because the people who run them can't keep their heads above water on their own."

The meat and produce buyers said: "We are now too busy to adequately supervise our sections as we once did. This is important since gross margins are much higher in our sections than in others. Remember, we are the big profit contributors in this company. The problem can readily be alleviated by creating two merchandise

Exhibit 2
Departmental Statistics

	Nadir Conventional Markets			Pacific City Discount Supermarkets		
	Percentage Space Allocation	Sales per Worker-Hour	Gross Profit as % of Sales	Percentage Space Allocation	Sales per Worker-hour	Gross Profit as % of Sales
Grocery	47%	$ 90.25	17.0%	53%	$120.50	12.5%
Meats	18	146.70	23.2	8	137.38	16.0
Produce	12	105.25	28.2	10	105.25	27.3
Dairy	5	—	31.5	5	—	25.1
Frozen Foods	10	—	25.0	4	—	18.0
Bakery	5	—	31.5	5	—	25.1
Nonfoods	3	—	31.5	15	—	25.1

manager positions reporting to the president. We could then hire new buyers and spend much more of our time in the field working with the store section managers. If Mr. Tung (the merchandise and operations manager) would redirect his attention to grocery and frozen food operations, then the operating organization would be complete."

The controller, R. A. Peyton Broz, member of the board and of the founding family, said: "I remarked once before that I used to burn the candle at both ends and that now I have lighted the middle too. That still goes. Tomorrow, however, if the board approves, we hire a new controller and I become treasurer and financial vice-president. The way to maintain effective control over this organization and to allow for adequate planning is to define responsibility by the kind of installation. By this I mean that each store should have a manager responsible for all its costs and profits and that we should have two operating divisions. The conventional supermarkets and the discount stores differ in their work—look at the way they handle meats as just one example, and you can think of others—their costs are different, and the standards by which we should judge them differ. Return on investment for discount markets should be 50% more than that for conventional markets. That's what it is in the average well-managed firm in the industry. Mingling responsibility for them in any way will destroy our chances for adequate control and effective planning."

The warehouse manager said: "I have to hire a second warehouse supervisor for the new installation in Pacific City. Operating in two cities means that there has to be a local supervisor in each. I can't be an effective executive while spending a lot of time traveling back and forth. We need an overall supervisor for each installation —like the manager in the new stores—and a person above him who is also local if there are more than five or six different facilities in each city. Graicuna's work on span-of-control and the studies by psychologists on perception that came up with the 'rule-of-seven as a limit on perceived variables' show this clearly. Local attention without time wasted in travel means effective operation."

Question

Write Mr. Engels' report. Include: (a) impact of growth and change in strategy, (b) a chart showing the new structure that you recommend with all key jobs, and (c) reasons supporting your proposals.

BUILDING AN INTEGRATED STRUCTURE

The grouping together of major activities discussed in the preceding chapter does not complete the organization structure. All but the smallest firms need a variety of auxiliary units. And the relationships of these units to the basic operating divisions must be clarified. To achieve a total, integrated organization design, attention must be given to:

1. Location of service units.
2. Decentralization within functional departments.
3. Roles assigned to staff.
4. Use of committees.
5. Management information systems.

These aspects of organization are important in welding the several parts into a coordinated, overall structure.

SERVICE UNITS

Most operating activities belong in the departments and divisions described in the previous chapter. Nevertheless, some auxiliary operations can be performed better in separate units.

Nature of Service Units

The distinction between operating departments and service units has been very helpful in one of the large rubber companies. After careful study, this company decided to establish separate organizational groups dealing with the following activities:

1. Tires
2. Footwear
3. Mechanical
4. Chemicals
5. Crude rubber
6. International
7. Advertising
8. Industrial relations
9. Public relations
10. Engineering
11. Research and development
12. Purchasing
13. Traffic
14. Legal

This is an imposing list, and if all groups were treated alike, the president would have a difficult task in securing coordination. To overcome this difficulty, the company has identified the first six units as "operating divisions." These are the units in which the basic consumer services are created. Each is large enough to have its own production and selling units, and each is responsible for showing tangible operating results. Thus, the basic structure is a Stage III organization.

All the other groups in the foregoing list are called "service units." Each of these units has relatively few employees compared with the operating divisions. There is a clear understanding throughout the company that the purpose of these auxiliary units is to help the operating divisions do their jobs better. Only in this way can the existence of the service units be justified. In this particular company, finance and accounts are treated as a third category and report directly to the board of directors; most other companies with large product divisions, however, consider these functions as services.

While this example emphasizes units serving the entire company, the same general idea is often found in the organization within a large department. Production departments, for instance, often have their own production scheduling, toolroom, stockroom, quality control, and other auxiliary units that serve the production shop. Similarly, large sales offices have units dealing with travel, customers' correspondence, display material, and the like.

Service units simply perform certain work for the benefit of the operating departments. This is usually work that the department itself would have to perform if it had not been assigned to the specialized service unit. For example, a filing section may relieve the sales department of the bother of keeping all records pertaining to each of its many customers; a computer center may do mathematical work for engineering and other departments; and a warehouse may relieve the sales supervisor of all problems connected with the physical handling of goods.

In situations such as these, the relationships between the service units and the operating departments are relatively simple. There should be a clear understanding of (1) just what services are to be performed, including questions of speed and quality of work, and (2) how the service unit is to be notified as to what is needed. Of course, supervision will be necessary to make sure the work flows as planned, but the organization is simple and clear cut.

Benefits and Drawbacks of Separate Service Units

The facilitating, supporting role of service units should never be overlooked. There is a tendency, particularly on the part of people in the service units, to recommend the transfer of more and more duties and control to the service unit. Up to a point, this may be quite desirable. Members of the service unit may have *special skills and knowledge* about such matters as traffic, real estate, or engineering. Moreover, they will not be so involved with operating details and will be able to give *adequate attention* to these functions. However, the activities are not ends in themselves. Any increase in the size of a division must continually meet the test: "Is this work adding to the overall effectiveness of the company, and can it be done better by separating it from operating activities?"

The chief reasons, then, for setting up service units are to get the benefits of specialization and adequate attention. The drawbacks of service units should not be forgotten, however. Most obvious is additional overhead expense. Salaries of specialists in the service units must be paid, and usually offices and equipment must be set aside for their use. Unless the service unit can create significant economies in operations, these overhead expenses may absorb all the benefits from a separate unit.

Less tangible but often more important is the added complexity that service units create. More units are involved in day-to-day operations, more relationships must work smoothly, and the task of coordination may be complicated. Sometimes members of a service unit become so interested in their particular activities that they lose sight of overall company goals. Consequently, we should guard against the assumption that separate service units are always desirable.

Location of Service Units

If agreement exists that a service activity should be separated from operation, further questions arise as to how many such units are needed and when to place them in the total structure. The chief considerations are economies of single unit versus coordination of the service with basic operations.

A single service unit is often able to secure the maximum economy, particularly in a medium-size or small firm, through concentrated attention, standardization of routine, specialized technical knowledge, and distinctive skill of the central unit. Moreover, the volume of work may warrant only the employment of a single set of experts in, say, insurance or traffic, or a single installation of expensive equipment such as a computer.

Single units, however, increase coordination difficulties. The farther removed—physically and organizationally—the service unit is from the operations it serves, the greater are the problems of coordination. Communication is more difficult and the service unit is less responsive to the needs of local people. Since the aim of the unit is to facilitate operations, ease of coordination weighs heavily.

The main alternative locations for service units are shown in the chart on the following page.

ALTERNATIVE LOCATIONS OF SERVICE UNITS
(Shaded Areas Indicate Service Activity)

(A) Organization with no service unit; each operating
section performs its own auxiliary activities.

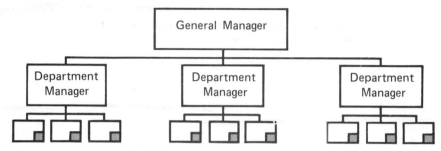

(B) Organization with service units in each operating department.

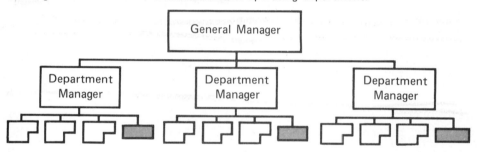

(C) Organization with separate service unit.

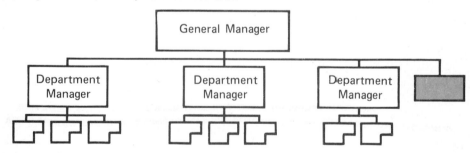

(D) Organization with multiple service units.

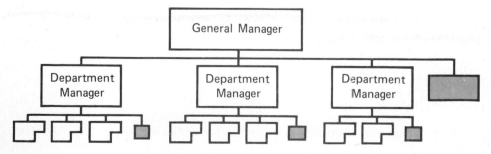

DECENTRALIZATION

Grouping activities into operating companies, divisions, departments, and service units is the most easily recognized aspect of organization. A second essential aspect, which does not appear on the organization chart, is deciding the level at which decisions should be made. Decentralization is concerned with who in a vertical hierarchy really "calls the shots."

Decentralizing to Match Stage of Growth

The four stages of growth discussed in the preceding chapter clearly imply different patterns of decentralization. In Stage I, primary authority remains centralized in the one dominant individual. Of course, subordinates decide whether a particular request or condition fits the normal way work is done. They may be highly skilled people, and the boss may get their advice about plans in their field of specialty. But the dominant individual chooses new directions of effort, allocates resources, keeps track of progress in diverse areas, approves subordinates' proposals, initiates changes when necessary. Often relationships are informal, and subordinates learn from experience what is desired behavior. Significant exceptions to the normal patterns, however, are first checked with the central figure.

Growth forces decentralization, at least from the top person to the department heads. The manager of a charter airplane service in Alaska faced this change suddenly when oil was discovered on the Arctic coast. Prior to the oil boom the company had six planes; the manager, with the advice of the pilots, decided on what business to accept, which planes to use, when to do maintenance work, how to pay for planes, and the like; flying and landing the planes was left to the pilots. With the intense oil activity, business of the company mushroomed; a traffic manager, a flight supervisor, a maintenance engineer, and a treasurer were quickly added to the headquarters. And who should decide what had to be clarified? Stage II had arrived.

While in a Stage II organization, authority and supervision of regular operations shift from the general manager to the functional department heads, the degree of further decentralization within the various departments depends upon the size and the kinds of work. We will suggest guides for shaping these intradepartment relationships in the next section.

Each division in a Stage III organization has within it all of the delegation issues of the Stage II setup (or of Stage I if the division is that small). In addition, since such divisions must be semiautonomous to obtain the desired benefits of adaptability to special opportunities, substantial decentralization should prevail between the chief executive and the division general managers. Communication is a prime consideration here. This became apparent to the president of an advertising agency that expanded from its consumer product business to financial institutions. The ideas and the problems of the personnel working with the new type of client did not reach the president in their original form. After passing through a couple of layers of supervisors, an idea was likely to be modified, warped, and misinterpreted. Even if the basic idea was retained, a considerable period of time elapsed before a meeting of minds could be achieved. In this case the president finally recognized the need to delegate a high degree of freedom to a vice-president to run the new type of business according to the latter's best judgment.

Because conglomerates, in Stage IV, typically arise from merging previously independent companies, high decentralization between the chief executive and the general managers of the operating companies is normal. In fact, the typical issue is how central management can participate in company planning more rather than less. The relationship suggested in the previous chapter is that of an active outside board member. Such an arrangement leaves operating decisions and the initiative for broad planning with the general managers, but it ensures compulsory consultation before major decisions become final.

Decentralization within Functional Departments

Just as the grouping of activities *within* functional departments varies widely (see pages 421–424), so does the degree of decentralization. In departments such as research, projects can proceed on their unpredictable course quite independently. By contrast, high automation of an oil refinery leaves limited degrees of freedom to local operators.

The usual situation calls for a mixture, some topics being decided by the department head and others decentralized well down the line. Consider, for example, a Midwest grocery chain. The functional departments in this case included buying, warehousing and transporting, finance, public relations, locating and constructing new stores, and "store operations." A major issue arose over discretion to be allowed each store manager compared with regional branch offices. After much study the company concluded:

1. Some of the functions obviously have to be placed under the jurisdiction of local store managers. This includes authority over the following activities:
   (a) Arranging displays and maintaining the store so that it will be attractive to customers.
   (b) Selling merchandise to customers. All stores have cashiers, stockclerks, and salesclerks, and the responsibility of selling includes selection, training, and general supervision of these employees.
   (c) Under certain conditions, buying a few products, such as butter and eggs, from their customers. Also, paying incidental expenses.
   (d) Keeping some simplified records of sales, stock, cash receipts, and cash disbursements.
2. The responsibilities of the branch office are considerably greater than those granted to the individual stores. In addition to supervising the operation of stores, the branch office has authority over:
   (a) Selecting the merchandise from that supplied by the central purchasing department that the local stores will carry in stock.

(b) Determining the price at which each article of merchandise should be sold, and making such adjustments to the price as current competitive conditions and the size of inventory necessitate.

(c) Directing the advertising for all stores of the branch, and working out plans of sales promotion to be followed by the store manager.

(d) Compiling and analyzing accounting and statistical information regarding the operations in the branch area, which will aid the branch manager in appraising the results of past activities and in making decisions regarding future activities.

Each department in a company should be given separate attention. And as external and internal conditions change, the decentralization of particular types of problems may have to be increased or decreased. The optimum setup can usually be determined by carefully weighing the following:

1. What factors must be considered in making the decisions, and at what point in the organization it is easiest to get current information about these factors.
2. The ability of the members of the organization to whom the authority is to be delegated.
3. The need for speedy "on the spot" decisions.
4. The importance of the decision to successful operations.
5. The need for consistent and coordinated action by several divisions of the company.

Delegation of Authority and the Task of Control

The separation of planning and making of decisions on specific problems from the place where performance occurs inevitably creates control difficulties. Thus, a sales manager sitting in the home office who decides to solicit sales in a new territory also needs a control mechanism to insure proper execution of the plan. Or, if authority as well as performance is decentralized (for example, the sales representative is given authority to decide which customers to solicit), a different control mechanism is required. In the first situation, a means of making sure the sales representatives did an effective job of calling on the specified customers is needed; in the second case, a measure of how wisely the sales representative selects customers also would be helpful.

ROLES ASSIGNED TO STAFF

The rounding out of an organization design should consider, in addition to service units and decentralization, possible uses of staff.

Numerous criss-crossing of influence and communication is an essential part of every organization design. Procedures establish normal, routine paths for passing information, and many other lateral contacts are incorporated into systems for planning and control. Moreover, advisory or "staff" relationships play an increasingly important role as a company grows and engages in more complex activities.

In practice, the scope of a staff assignment may vary widely—from office flunky to a key member of central management. Consequently, care is needed in figuring out just what staff relationships will aid in the execution of a new strategy in an existing organization.

General Staff Assistants

In its simple form, the idea of staff is used when a busy executive appoints an assistant to help do the work. At first, an assistant may be primarily a *fact finder,* gathering and analyzing information for use by the executive in resolving troublesome problems. As the assistant gains experience, the executive may ask for *recommendations;* in fact, the assistant may prepare written instructions so that the executive receives recommendations and papers needing only the executive's signature to put the proposal into effect. This kind of help enables an executive to deal with problems in a relatively short period of time; in fact, a more careful study of the problem may have been made than if the busy executive tried to do it alone.

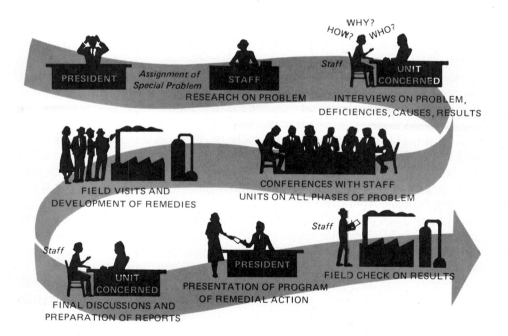

Good staff assistants also work with other subordinates of the senior executive and with people outside the department and the company. They must, of course, contact such people in the process of gathering information. In addition, they normally discuss possible solutions to a problem with all people concerned. It sometimes happens that in this examination and exchange of ideas, the problem resolves itself. The staff assistant has served in the capacity of a *catalyst* or a *mediator* and therefore needs only report to the senior executive that the problem is solved.

On other problems that require centralized decision, the staff assistants may play an important role in *explaining* and *interpreting* the plan of action. Their detailed knowledge about the problem and intimate association with the senior executive put them in a good position to explain what is wanted. This interpretative function of a staff assistant again saves the time of a busy executive and improves mutual understanding throughout the enterprise.

In still other situations, the busy executive may ask the staff assistant to keep an eye on some particular aspect of operations, such as expense ratios, governmental regulations, or inventory turnover. Then, if there is need for executive action, the assistant takes the initiative in preparing a recommendation and calling the whole matter to the superior's attention. In this way the staff assistant serves as *eyes* and *ears* for the boss.

Specialized Staff

The general staff assistant, such as has just been described, typically carries the title of *Assistant to* the sales manager, the president, or whoever the senior may be. These assistants may be asked to help with any or all of the activities of the executive.

The staff concept also may be applied to assistants who concentrate on some one function, or aspect, of operations. For instance, one staff specialist may concentrate on legal problems, while another works on public relations. Perhaps enough engineering problems arise so the executive needs personal help in this area. The chief executive of a large company may have a specialist on organization planning, another for expense control, and still a third working on executive personnel.

Although such people may be specialists in some one area, the nature of their relationship with the senior executive and with other employees is like that of the general staff assistant. They investigate, recommend, interpret, and follow up on problems in their particular sphere. Being specialists, it is quite likely that they possess technical knowledge that may be superior to that of anyone else in the organization. Through the staff arrangement, this technical knowledge is put at the disposal of the senior executive and all subordinates who come in contact with staff personnel.

The work assigned to a staff specialist may become so heavy that additional personnel are needed to help with the work. Consequently, there may develop a small organization unit on public relations, expense control, or other fields. This group may be called an "office" or a "service division." Size and title, however, do not change the nature of the relationship.

Essential Factors in Good Staff Relationships

The preceding illustrations of staff have assumed that it always is a full-time job. While this is often true in larger companies, full time is not a necessary feature of the staff concept. The important thing is the relationship, and it is entirely possible for an executive to devote part time to staff work.

The staff relationship implies that the individual is working on behalf of an executive; is doing things the executive would do if time permitted; has no authority to issue orders, but may pass along instructions or interpretations in the name of the senior executive.

Staff relationships may be used in any department of a business enterprise. Most of the examples already cited have been of staff work directly under a chief executive, but the idea has many other applications. The sales promotion director in the sales department, the industrial engineer in the production department, the cost analyst in the accounting department, the economist in the purchasing department, and the safety director in the personnel department are all positions where a considerable amount of staff relationship typically is found.

Use of Functional Authority

Occasionally a staff person may be given functional authority with respect to certain types of problems and may work in an advisory capacity over a much wider area. Functional authority is permission to issue directions to people not under your line supervision; such directions deal only with specified activities or certain aspects of those activities. Except for their source of issuance, these directions are to be treated as though they came from the senior executive.

The use of functional authority is illustrated in a manufacturing firm that has a general office in Chicago and plants in Kansas City, St. Louis, and Cleveland. Each plant manager "runs" a plant and has line authority over all employees at the plant, including local accountants. On the other hand, the chief accountant at the central office is responsible for maintaining accounting records for the entire company, and has functional authority over *how* the records are kept at each branch.

The reason for granting functional authority in this instance is fairly clear. The weekly sales report of the company might be misleading if one branch accountant reported orders received as sales, whereas another unit of the company did not report goods as sold until they had actually been shipped. Likewise, one branch accountant might charge depreciation on machinery at one plant at a much lower rate than was used by another branch, with the result that the combined figures for the company as a whole would lack the consistency needed for comparisons and for income tax returns.

A large part of the authority of several important departments is functional. For example, an industrial engineering unit in a factory often selects equipment and prescribes the tools and the methods to be used in production operations. The sales promotion departments of some companies stipulate the methods for presenting new products and the time the products will be introduced.

In all these examples, the executive with functional authority does part of the planning of the activity. The functional executive may prescribe policy, set up methods, or determine the time when activities are to be undertaken, thus saying how the activity is to be performed. The line executive, on the other hand, is responsible for seeing that the instructions issued by those with functional authority, as well as instructions "coming down the line," are carried out.

Functional authority is a useful concept in the proper situations; but like many good things, if used in excess or at the wrong time, it can cause trouble. Among the dangers and the disadvantages of functional authority are:

1. If several different people exercise functional authority over a given operating executive, that individual may be swamped with specialized instructions.
2. The effectiveness of line supervisors may be weakened by heavy use of functional authority. As more and more instructions come from the functional specialists, the status of the line boss may be undermined.
3. Functional authority sometimes leads to autocratic and inflexible administration. Functional specialists may become narrow in their viewpoint and insist that their plans be followed even though they are not well suited to a specific local situation.

For these reasons functional authority should be granted only when it is clearly desirable, and provision should be made to see that it is not used arbitrarily. Functional authority works best when (a) only a minor aspect of the total operating job is covered, (b) technical knowledge of a type not possessed by the operating executives is needed, and (c) consistency of action in several departments is important.

Composite Relations

A single executive often has a variety of relationships, depending upon the subject and who the other person is. A controller, for instance, normally will (a) have line authority over employees in the department who keep company books and prepare reports, (b) have functional authority throughout the company over accounting systems, and (c) act in a purely staff capacity when suggesting how expenses may be cut. Similarly, a personnel director is likely to (a) have line authority over the employment office, cafeteria, and other employee service operations; (b) exercise functional authority with respect to compensation ranges, length of vacations, dismissal procedures, and the like, and (c) provide much constructive advice regarding training, promotion, motivation, etc., in an advisory capacity.

These illustrations show that designating a person as "line" or "staff" is at best vague. For a real grasp of relationships, the authority or the influence of each executive should be defined for each subject dealt with and for various groups contacted. *Customary* roles help clarify such definitions, but we should guard against oversimplification.

USE OF COMMITTEES

Management organization is primarily concerned with the duties and the relationships of individual people. This concentration on the individual as the basic operating unit is necessary for efficiency in action and for purposes of control.

There are situations, however, when several individuals acting as a group can do a particular task better than a single person. When a management task has been assigned to a group, rather than parceled up among several individuals, a *committee* has been formed.

When to Use Committees

Use of committees is a widespread practice; in fact some astute students of administration believe that committees are so widely used that they become a serious drawback to efficient operation. Executives may use committees to avoid making difficult decisions; whenever they are in a tough spot, they "appoint a committee." All too often the committee is "a group of people who keep minutes and waste hours." Consequently, we should be careful just how and where committees are fitted into the organization.

Situations in which committees have been found to be helpful include the following:

1. Management committee composed of all department heads and the general manager in a Stage II organization. Weekly meetings of such a committee provide an occasion for *exchange of information* and a clearing-house for interdepartmental troubles.
2. Salary committee composed of a personnel staff representative, department head, and immediate supervisor. To avoid charges of favoritism, such a group must approve any changes in salaries. This adds *safety and acceptability* to the decisions.
3. Community Chest campaign committees composed of representatives from each section in the organization. Here the main benefit is to *secure cooperation.*

Committees may be useful in many other situations. The foregoing cases merely illustrate how committees may be helpful in promoting coordination, providing integrated group judgment, and securing cooperation in the execution of plans. Committees can also be effective training devices. Through participation on committees, executives become aware of major company objectives and of effective ways of achieving these objectives. Training, however, is a secondary benefit because rarely is it practical to set up a committee primarily for the purpose of training its junior members.

Situations Where Committees Are Ineffective

One drawback of committees is that they are often *slow* in reaching a decision. This was well illustrated by a pricing committee in a metal cabinet manufacturing company. Just after a competitor announced a price increase, one committee member—the marketing manager—left on a sales trip. Before the manager returned, a second member—the controller—started vacation. Thus, the committee seriously delayed the response to the competitor's move.

Another company drastically modified its use of committees after the board of directors found it almost impossible to place responsibility for some poor investments. The decision to make these investments had been made by a committee. When the decision turned out to be unwise, the members of the committee each said that they had not really been in favor of the action but had simply gone along with the others. The net effect was that *no single person could be held accountable* for the action that was taken.

When decisive action is important, committees are often of little help. The balanced, tempered decision that presumably comes from committee consideration may, in fact, be simply a *compromise* that is neither "fish nor fowl." The management committee of a medical supply company, for instance, could not agree on how much to spend for advertising. After long discussion, they decided on about half of the amount originally requested by the sales manager. Unfortunately, this drastic cut made the advertising campaign ineffective. It would have been better either to have cut the advertising expenditure to a nominal figure or to have undertaken a campaign large enough to impress hospital buyers.

Committees are a relatively *expensive* way of arriving at a decision. If half a dozen people spend from 9:00 A.M. to 10:20 A.M. in a committee meeting, a whole executive-day of time has been used up. Outside preparation time and the effect of interrupting other work add substantially to the time actually spent in meeting.

Benefits and Limitations of Committees

No standard answer can be given to the question of the nature and the number of committees a particular company should have. The most common advantages and disadvantages are summarized briefly in the diagram below.

In addition, before establishing a committee, thought should be given to the social setting in which it will work. This will include such things as the availability of competent members, the prevailing attitude toward committees, and the techniques of supervision normally used. It is safe to conclude that the appointment of committees should *not* be the standard answer to difficult problems, nor a standard device to cover over weaknesses in management.

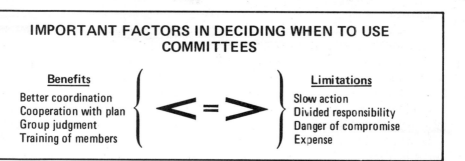

> ## IMPORTANT FACTORS IN DECIDING WHEN TO USE COMMITTEES
>
> **Benefits**   **Limitations**
>
> Better coordination   Slow action
> Cooperation with plan $<\ =\ >$ Divided responsibility
> Group judgment   Danger of compromise
> Training of members   Expense

MANAGEMENT INFORMATION SYSTEM

Both staff and committees supplement the elementary structure of divisions, departments, and sections in an organization. In performing their assigned tasks they help tie together the various parts. More important, however, in assuring smooth relationships and integrating action is the management information system.

The management information system consists of designated communication channels for various kinds of information related to company activities. Formal instructions follow the chain of command, but information must flow more widely and quickly. Three essential elements of every information system are the (1) data base, (2) report flow, and (3) communication of intangibles.

Data Base

Operating procedures. The most obvious part of any information system is the flow of business papers from section to section. A sales order, for instance, conveys vital information from customer to sales representatives to sales headquarters to warehouse (and if a special order, to engineering and plant) to shipping to credit control to billing. Similar procedures exist for purchasing, employment, capital expenditures, and a host of other normal transactions that are repeated time after time. These procedures are crucial for effective day-to-day operations, and they interlace all segments of the organization.

In passing, note that operating procedures spell out organizational duties. Each step in a procedure is part of a bundle of duties assigned to someone; it stipulates from whom information (usually on a piece of paper) will be received, what action that person will perform, and to whom the processed information should be sent. Thus, clarifying procedures is one way to clarify an organization. Of course not all duties are parts of procedures, but a large segment of total company activity can be viewed in this manner.

Information systems use these operating procedures in two ways: (1) The procedures themselves contain a lot of instructions on who tells whom what. (2) Summaries of work flowing through one or more steps in a procedure can be used as measures of what is happening—for instance, a monthly summary of new orders received, of export shipments, or of the number of employees added to the payroll will be significant pieces of information to several managers.

Accounting records. A second major data source is accounting records. Financial accounting's first obligation is to give outsiders—stockholders, bankers, vendors, and others—a consistent digest of the total company status. But the financial records typically are expanded to gather a wealth of data useful for internal management. In fact, a good internal accounting system classifies financial data according to organizational units.

Accounting data always constitutes a major input to the information system; in small companies it may be almost the only formal input. Because of wide use, much debate occurs about the way expenses and income are allocated and summarized. Part of the art of designing internal accounting systems is to provide information in a form that will be most useful to management.

Other sources. Many companies regularly compile data on industry prices, market position, employee absences, and a variety of other subjects, but there is no common practice on what to include. Also, the company control system—which will be discussed in Chapter 23—frequently calls for systematic observation of selected control points.[1] Here again, selective identification of data that will be truly valuable to a company decision-maker is needed.

Report Flows

Fully as important as deciding what information to compile is determining to whom the data will be communicated. This question quickly gets us back to departmentation and decentralization because company design of these matters determines who can make use of particular batches of information on a recurring basis. Also, the effectiveness of staff personnel depends on their receiving current information as the basis of their advice. So

---

[1] Some executives who stress control consider the information system to be a subsidiary part of the control function. We prefer separate treatment of the information system because it nourishes planning as well as control and because it has a marked effect on the interpersonal relationships within an organization.

we establish a standard pattern specifying what information goes to each executive.

On the other hand, sending reports to people who find the data irrelevant to their work simply clutters up and confuses their assignments.

Keeping such an information flow in tune with changes in organization and strategy is no easy task. When a company adds a product line, decides to make rather than buy materials, or otherwise modifies its strategy, shifts occur in the kinds of data needed. When the organization is reshuffled—as is often desirable to match the new strategy—executives needing particular reports change.

Communicating Intangibles

The information system we have been discussing deals with recorded "facts," most of them conveniently expressed in numbers. Significant as such data are, they give only part of the picture. Missing are reasons why, feelings about the facts, guesses on how other people will respond to the same data, new ideas, and a variety of other more subjective types of data. And communication of this kind of information is as essential as communicating hard facts.

Information about intangibles is typically transferred orally. The information system should deal with these personal communications just as it does with written reports, indicating the kinds of data that are to go to designated people. Job descriptions often include paragraphs stating "Keep (service manager) advised of . . ." for this purpose.

Unfortunately, this part of the system is more difficult to operate. Face-to-face meetings with individuals are hard to arrange, especially if they are very busy, and there is no objective way to keep track of what information passed between them. Physical proximity of offices, field trips, review sessions, intercom equipment, and closed circuit TV are all devices that aid desired communication flow; but chief reliance must rest upon customary behavior and expected roles. As we round out an information system, then, we move from routine, mechanistic reports to highly personalized communication of subjective impressions. And when we want to modify an information system to fit a new strategy, it is the latter behavioral features that are most difficult to readjust.

Use of Computers

Computers, and even more the peripheral communicating equipment, are useful in classifying and speeding up the flow of standardized information. For example, a dress buyer for a national chain of women's ready-to-wear shops can have on hand in the morning a complete analysis of yesterday's sales throughout the country, and for high-style merchandise such information is very valuable. The elements of the information system—identifying useful basic data, deciding how to classify and summarize them, picking people who should receive the information, and getting it to them—have not changed; but with computers, once the system is designed it can work automatically and rapidly. In fact, many executives find they are now receiving too much rather than not enough of such mechanically processed information; this criticism, however, is really a matter of refining the system.

Computers are of little help with subjective data, and they have no way of knowing what different kinds of data might be useful in dealing with unique situations. So a major task in redesigning information flows to take full advantage of computer capabilities is to preserve a balance. The intangibles have always been the more troublesome part of a total information system, and with a plethora of computer sheets waiting to be studied, the danger increases of skipping lightly over key intangibles.

SUMMARY

Organization design should begin with the major structure of operating activities—discussed in the preceding chapter. Much elaboration is necessary, however, to achieve a balanced, integrated pattern of behavior. And a good design yesterday may be outmoded today.

When a company changes its strategy and policy, then the whole fabric of relationships that ties the work of employees together may need readjustment. For instance, when a petroleum company decides to move into petro-chemicals, it faces new markets, rapidly changing technology, and large investments; decentralization of this segment of the company soon becomes a necessity. At the same time, the benefits of nationwide advertising and marketing of gasoline are creating a centralizing pull in the gasoline end of the business; here enlarging the influence of the central marketing staff, including greater use of functional authority, makes sense.

Five ways to refine an organizational design have been discussed in this chapter.

1. Distinguishing between operating and service units helps to clarify the structure. It aids in defining relationships and also is useful in allocating human resources and in resolving jurisdictional conflicts. Fundamentally, a service unit exists only to facilitate the work of operating departments, and its performance may be judged in these terms.

2. Decentralization of decision-making by chief executives and general managers is broadly set by the "stage" format they select. Within departments, however, wide variation in the degree of decentralization is possible. Strategy and policy indicate the relative weight to be assigned to flexibility, efficiency, etc., and these considerations determine the level at which specific types of issues can best be decided.

3. Although adding complexity, staff assistants can provide relief to an overburdened manager. Also, staff specialists can provide technical advice

that otherwise would not be available within the company. For carefully defined subjects, staff may be given functional authority that expedites the handling of matters of secondary importance.

4. Committees can supplement and strengthen individual effort. In the right situations, they aid in securing coordination, cooperation, and group judgment on important problems. As a management tool, however, they are expensive and slow; responsibility is diffused and hence control is more difficult. For these reasons, care should be exercised in using committees to strengthen the organization structure.

5. Finally, the management information system builds essential links between the many specialized activities. Each time a change is made in strategy or policy, or in the organization design, provision should be made for getting new kinds of information to selected people, and for weeding out information flows that no longer serve a useful purpose.

In our dynamic world every enterprise is continually adjusting to new opportunities and problems. The organization structure that is designed to help meet these challenges should also change. It can and should be a responsive tool of central management.

QUESTIONS FOR CLASS DISCUSSION

1. To assure that the strategy of a business-unit is kept abreast of current changes in competition, markets, technology, government actions, and other external influences, what role would you assign to staff instead of line personnel? Use a specific industry or company to illustrate your answer.
2. (a) A stockbrokerage firm with one main office is considering "contracting-out" (having an outside company do the work) all its computer work rather than enlarging its own computer service unit. Assuming the cost is the same, what difference, if any, will this choice make to the operating people using the output of the computer? (b) The firm is also considering contracting-out its janitor work. What difference, if any, will this make to operating people? (c) How would your answers to (a) and (b) be affected by the firm's having ten offices instead of one?
3. (a) Assume you are a sales representative for a company that builds and equips outdoor swimming pools at private residences. How much authority to decide on the following would you want: Which potential customers to call on? What pool designs to offer? What price to quote? What payment terms to grant? What delivery date to set? What guarantees to make? (b) You have just been promoted to regional sales manager. Now, how much authority should each sales representative have? (c) If you were president, where would you locate decision-making authority for each subject?

4. (a) Assume that you are a staff assistant to the president of Kellogg Company, manufacturers of well-known breakfast cereals. The president is concerned about the impact that the scarcity of energy is having on the company, both on costs and interference with operations. He asks you to look into the matter and recommend what action, if any, he should take. What will you do?

   (b) The president is also concerned about public criticism of children's TV programs (sponsored by Kellogg) "that shape personalities and create unhealthy demands." Again, he asks you to look into the matter and recommend what action, if any, he should take. What will you do?

5. What authority do you recommend be delegated to the manager of a company-owned McDonald's Hamburger shop? What about decentralization to the district supervisor of, say, twenty such shops? Who should have functional authority over either or both of these managers—with respect to what subjects? Give reasons for your answers. (Consider here only company-owned shops, not franchised shops.)

6. Assume that you are designing an organization structure for a multinational food corporation (like General Foods) which has subsidiaries in Canada, England, Germany, Italy, Australia, and Brazil. Each subsidiary has its own production plant and markets that output in its own country and some surrounding countries. U.S. products are shipped worldwide, except where subsidiaries are able to serve the market more economically. Inevitably questions of decentralization arise. Do you recommend a *higher degree of decentralization* (freedom to make decisions) (a) in production than in marketing? (b) in personnel than in production? (c) in marketing than in personnel? Explain why.

7. Do you recommend the use of committees to interpret or respond to the external data referred to in question 1? If so, who should serve on such committees and what would each committee do?

8. (a) Do you think every major department of a company is entitled to a representative on each standing committee? (b) Would you consider the same factors in deciding on the size of and in selecting members for a (1) budget committee, (2) shop grievance committee, (3) salary committee, and (4) safety committee?

9. When a firm decides to expand from domestic to international operations, the difficulties of effective communication increase. (a) Illustrate this proposition in terms of expansion to any specific foreign country with which you are familiar. Consider all aspects of a management information system identified in this chapter. (b) What can central management do to minimize these difficulties?

10. (a) What contributions should an internal management information system make to the total data needed to formulate company strategy? You may wish to review Part 1 to identify data needed. If you believe the industry affects the internal data that will be relevant, select an industry or a company to make your answer more specific. (b) Where will the additional data needed come from? Who should collect it?

11. In addition to marketing in the U.S., Volkswagen is opening assembly plants and doing some purchasing of components here. (a) Which staff units in the German headquarters should be concerned with U.S. activities? (b) For each of these staff units, what should be the relationship to U.S. managers?

CASE 18
Mercy Hospitals of Adelbourne

Sister Marguerite Perry, Sister Administrator of the Mercy Hospitals complex in Adelbourne, the capital city of an Australian state, has before her a second consultant's report on what the consulting group sees as the administrative and organizational difficulties of the hospitals and its recommendation for action. Should she accept the report and pass it on to the Board of Counsel with her recommendation for the Board's approval?

There are four Mercy Hospitals in Adelbourne—Mothers' Hospital, Children's Hospital, Heart and Chest Disease Hospital, and St. Nicholas Hospital of Mercy—each in a separate building but all on the same site and connected with each other and with the central services of pathology, radiology, induction training, general administration, and staff housing. The hospitals were founded by and are, in a sense, still owned by a Catholic order, the Order of Sisters for Apostolic Service. The Order had been formed to do apostolic witness, and the hospitals are one of its activities. Others include a school, an orphanage, and several halfway houses.

Sister Perry, in her duty as administrator, is responsible to the Board of Counsel of the Mercy Hospitals and to the President of that Board, Sister Anna Reardon, who is also President of the Advisory Board of several of the other institutions. Both nuns are members of the Order of Sisters for Apostolic Service. The Mother Superior of the Order is also resident in Adelbourne.

Of the four hospitals, St. Nicholas Hospital of Mercy is unique in that its capital funding comes from the federal government in Canberra and its operating funds are supplied almost entirely by the city of Adelbourne through payments for hospital services supplied to those qualifying for city support under the level-of-income criterion. This means that the City Auditor is involved in the analysis of costs and services. Funds for the other hospitals come from public appeals, from payments by the national health insurance plans, and from private payments.

Exhibit A indicates the existing formal organization structure of the Mercy Hospitals.

Members of the Board of Counsel, in addition to Sister Anna Reardon, President, are the Director of Medical Services, the Matrons of Mothers', Children's, and Heart and Chest Disease Hospitals (all Sisters of the Order), the legal counsel to the Order, the Chairman of the Adelbourne Ecumenical Council, and three medical consultants who are also professors at the Medical School of the University of Adelbourne. The membership of the Board of Counsel had been established at the time of formation of the three older hospitals and well before Mercy Hospitals became large enough and with a sufficient medical staff to be teaching hospitals for the Medical School.

Sister Marguerite Perry, the Sister Administrator, had come to her position in Adelbourne from a smaller hospital in another capital city. Within two months after

EXHIBIT A

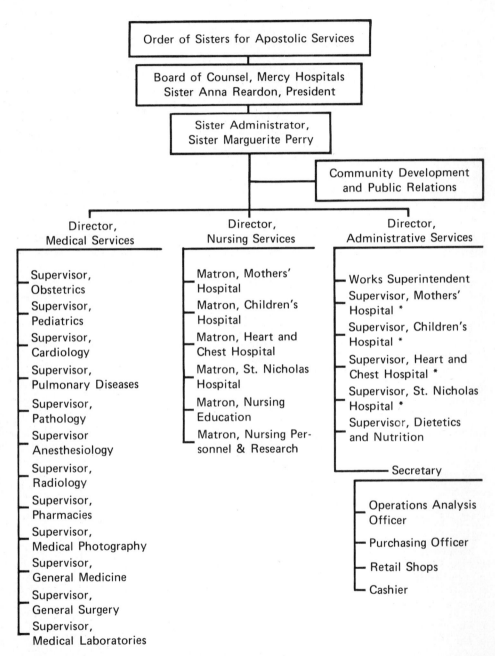

| Order of Sisters for Apostolic Services |

| Board of Counsel, Mercy Hospitals Sister Anna Reardon, President |

| Sister Administrator, Sister Marguerite Perry |

| Community Development and Public Relations |

Director, Medical Services

- Supervisor, Obstetrics
- Supervisor, Pediatrics
- Supervisor, Cardiology
- Supervisor, Pulmonary Diseases
- Supervisor, Pathology
- Supervisor Anesthesiology
- Supervisor, Radiology
- Supervisor, Pharmacies
- Supervisor, Medical Photography
- Supervisor, General Medicine
- Supervisor, General Surgery
- Supervisor, Medical Laboratories

Director, Nursing Services

- Matron, Mothers' Hospital
- Matron, Children's Hospital
- Matron, Heart and Chest Hospital
- Matron, St. Nicholas Hospital
- Matron, Nursing Education
- Matron, Nursing Personnel & Research

Director, Administrative Services

- Works Superintendent
- Supervisor, Mothers' Hospital *
- Supervisor, Children's Hospital *
- Supervisor, Heart and Chest Hospital *
- Supervisor, St. Nicholas Hospital *
- Supervisor, Dietetics and Nutrition
- Secretary
- Operations Analysis Officer
- Purchasing Officer
- Retail Shops
- Cashier

* Each Hospital Supervisor had reporting to him a Personnel Officer, a Medical Records Section, a Maintenance Officer, a Chief Ward Worker, a Receiving and Billing Officer, and a Budget Officer.

her arrival she had noted what she believed to be serious administrative problems and had persuaded the Board of Counsel to engage a well-known Australian management consulting group to survey these problems for her. The preliminary report of this group did not recognize nor analyze three of what Sister Perry regarded as major problems for Mercy Hospitals: (1) strong representations from the Medical School of the University that the education of its clinical students and of the interns was not being adequately coordinated, planned, and controlled; (2) reports from the City Auditor that Mercy Hospitals' costs for patients when expressed in dollars per bed, per patient, per patient-day, and per square foot were all higher than the same costs in Royal Brisbane, Royal Perth, and Royal Adelaide Hospitals—which had about the same number of beds and staff members as Mercy Hospitals and which were also teaching hospitals; and (3) information about patients in the wards was incomplete for other operative subunits also treating the patient, and feedback to ward records was also incomplete. Record forms varied from hospital to hospital.

Sister Perry then dismissed the group and hired another consulting organization. The main points of the analysis and recommendations of the second group are summarized in the following paragraphs.

All staff consider themselves highly trained, with a high level of education, and thus expect to be brought into the decision-making process and to have their opinions sought and considered before major decisions are made. The Residents Staff Association, the Nurses Staff Association, the Technicians Staff Association, and the Interns Staff Association[1] have all been formed to make representations on these matters to Sister Reardon, Sister Perry, the three directors, the various supervisors, and the Board of Counsel. Usually the staff associations cannot act until various decisions have been made and the information is available to the members of the associations; then they may react forcefully.

The nuns who serve as paramedics, nurses, and matrons (about 7% of the Hospitals' personnel are Sisters of the Order) do, as a natural aspect of their community, discuss and bring common problems to the Mother Superior. If she believes that the issue is serious enough, the Mother Superior instructs the Sister Administrator in a way to alleviate the problems of the nuns. As one example, the Sisters receive special time off to attend retreats and do apostolic work in the community that is unrelated to their work as technicians or nurses. Lay personnel have, of course, standard time allowances for sickleave and holidays.

Many of the nuns, particularly the younger ones, believe that their hospital work is routine and mundane and can be better carried out by lay staff. They believe that their apostolic role is often submerged and thus feel frustrated and unfulfilled in their work.

The matrons have inherited special status from the days when the patient care offered was less complex and when the hospital was non-teaching. They tend to follow an old British tradition of rigid status differentiation and of control by the matrons over the nurses, the ward workers, and the interns. Their position on the Board of Counsel reinforces this. The Board, as a result of its composition, is primarily concerned with medical problems and its decisions are medical in nature. For example, one question before the Board is whether to spend $100,000 on some new equipment for the care of premature babies or to use the same funds for the intensive-care

---

[1]Analogous to local unions in U.S. terminology.

cardiac unit. Sister Perry had resolved this issue, she thought, after discussion with the three directors, but later she noticed it as an agenda item before the Board.

The Board of Counsel has considered for years the question of adding a geriatrics unit to St. Nicholas Hospital but has never reached a conclusion even though the Chair of the Adelbourne Ecumenical Council and the legal counsel believe that geriatric medicine is a serious issue for the state.

There are some problems of communication among the staff members. Two prominent examples, mentioned by both parties, are communications between the Works Superintendent and the various medical and surgical supervisors. Issues of equipment, laboratory design, and operating theater design are often hard to resolve. The directors of Administrative Services and of Medical Services delegate these issues to their subordinates since the issues are highly technical. Doctors are not trained in the necessary negotiating and discussion skills; instead they are accustomed to acting as experts in a one-to-one relationship.

As their approach to dealing with these issues, the second consulting group made five major recommendations:

(1) Revision of the membership of the Board of Counsel.
(2) Establishment of an Executive Management Board.
(3) Functional Committees modeled on Likert's "linking-pin" theory of administration.
(4) A new approach to measuring the Hospitals' major objective of providing competent patient care.
(5) Committees on Medical Education.

The Board of Counsel is to remain advisory to the Order of Sisters for Apostolic Service. Its revised membership should include a President nominated by the Order, the Hospital Administrator, the three Directors, one representative of the State Health Department, and four lay members nominated and appointed from the public at large. These members should be qualified and professionally able lay people in any field of endeavor.

To implement policy and to have responsibility for the operations of the hospitals, the Executive Management Board should consist of the Hospital Administrator, the three Directors of Services, the Secretary, and one other member nominated and appointed by the Hospital Administrator.

Functional Committees (three in number), chaired by the respective Directors and including either the Director or a Supervisor from each of the other two service areas, are to discuss, review, and report to the Hospital Administrator once per month on all important matters involving each Service. It is expected that each Service will form further Functional Committees to be concerned with the major departments of each Service and to include representatives from other Services.

The consulting group was unable to determine how the comparative costs of service cited by the City Auditor were determined and the Auditor would not reveal the cost-determination process used, so the consultants took the problem of measuring patient care to the Nursing Personnel and Research Department. After lengthy consideration by discussion groups at all levels, the major points to be appraised in judging the quality of patient care were divided into two categories—Direct Care and Indirect Care (see Appendix A for the complete document). The proposed standard is 85%. A percentage result above that would be characterized as Very Good.

The Committees on Medical Education are to be chaired by the supervisors of the various medical services and are to include the chief resident for that service, a

APPENDIX A
PATIENT CARE ASSESSMENT

	M	T	W	T	F	S	S

WARD:

WEEK COMMENCING: TIME:

DEPENDENCY CATEGORY:

DIRECT CARE   POSSIBLE SCORE

A. PATIENT
   1. Position   10
   2. Safety   10
   3. Hygiene   10
   4. Nutrition   10
   5. Bed Unit   10
   6. Privacy   10

B. TECHNICAL SKILL, NURSING
   KNOWLEDGE AND JUDGEMENT
   1. Drug Administration   10
   2. Charts and Observations   10
   3. Protective measures   10
   4. Appliances and special equipment   10
   5. Physiotherapy   10
   6. Wounds   10
   7. Pain Relief   10

C. PRE/POST OPERATIVE OR PRE/POST
   INVESTIGATION
   (DIAGNOSTIC PROCEDURES AND TESTS)
   1. Patient Knowledge   10
   2. Preparation/specific treatment   10

D. PSYCHO-SOCIAL
   1. Emotional
   2. Social   10

E. REHABILITATION
   1. Involvement of outside agencies
   2. Involvement of patient & relatives   10

INDIRECT CARE

F. ENVIRONMENT
   1. Immediate
   2. General   10
   3. Noise

G. WARD ADMINISTRATION
   1. Hospital Policies & Procedures
   2. Equipment and stores   10

DAILY TOTALS:

GRAND TOTAL FOR WEEK: FINAL _____

NB.   MARK N/A IF ANY POINT NOT APPLICABLE.

     POINT ALLOCATION —   EVERYTHING SATISFACTORY   = 10
                        A FEW THINGS WRONG   = 5
                        MORE THAN A FEW THINGS WRONG = 0

representative chosen by the Medical School of the University of Adelbourne, two interns, a block matron or a ward charge sister, and a representative from Administrative Services chosen by the Secretary or one of the hospital supervisors.

Interestingly, the first and strongest objection to the idea in the consultant's report (which Sister Perry discussed with all the senior administrators and the presidents of the various staff associations) came from the Director of Medical Services. He stated that his work schedule was already overfull and that adding committee meetings—even meetings of the proposed Functional Committee—would completely overload his position.

Questions

(1) List the problems seen by Sister Perry and the consultants. Explain, to the extent you can, how the recommendations will help to resolve the problems.

(2) Do you see any further problems or consequences that the consultants do not deal with?

(3) Would you, as Hospital Administrator, pass on the recommendations to the Board of Counsel?

GOVERNING THE ENTERPRISE

Vital to the success of every enterprise is the organization for central management itself. We have just examined major issues that central management should consider in organizing the total enterprise, but we touched only briefly on arrangements for the small group of key people who decide on such matters as company strategy, policy, and organization structure. The need for a workable understanding of "who is to do what" is fully as important for activities of senior executives and board members as it is for people in a laboratory or a branch office.

More than internal organization is involved. Just who wields power in modern society is also at stake. Currently the debate focuses on boards of directors, but inevitably the relation between boards and senior managers is also questioned. The primary issues—from the viewpoint of making business enterprises more effective—include:

1. How can the board of directors be maintained as an independent, strong check on senior managers?
2. Should the board be composed of representatives of special interest groups, or should it be dedicated to the well-being of the enterprise?
3. How should the full-time senior managers be organized to assure that central management tasks are done well?
4. How should those in power be ousted if they are doing a poor job? (Discussed in Chapter 20.)

INDEPENDENT CHECK ON SENIOR MANAGEMENT

Within a company we can easily trace formal authority up to the "chief executive officer." But where does the C.E.O. get power, and who checks up on performance?

Legal Theory

Stockholders of a corporation are not expected to perform management functions, and typically they are even more passive than they need be.

Except for rare insurrections, stockholders do little more than vote for directors, approve recommendations submitted by management, and hopefully collect dividends. Normally they simply sell their stock if they do not like the way the corporation is run.

A large stockholder may be active, to be sure, but this is almost always done as a director or perhaps as an officer of the corporation. Once in a while, when a corporation is badly mismanaged, a group of dissident stockholders will wrest control from the existing management. However, they too pass management responsibility to a "new" board of directors. So, the stockholders *per se* do not provide central management.

According to legal documents, the board of directors establishes objectives, sets policy, selects officers, approves major contracts, and performs many other functions. Unquestionably the board has authority to do these things. The practical question is: Can we expect the board to perform these functions well or should most of the initiative and activity be delegated to executives of the corporation?

An Inactive Board

The activities performed by boards of directors vary widely. Until recently, most boards left the entire administration of the firm to executives.

The rationale for such an arrangement was that operating problems can be settled best by people who have an intimate acquaintance and long years of association with the company. These people can dispose of problems in their normal daily contacts without bothering with a meeting of the directors. The directors then confine their attention to formal action on dividends; to the election of officers; to the approval of any public reports; and to decisions on various minor matters, such as the approval of a given bank to be used as depository for company funds or the granting of a power of attorney to some trusted employee. Most of these actions are taken upon recommendation of the senior executives, and consequently the meetings of the board of directors have been perfunctory affairs.

However, a sharp change is taking place. Especially for corporations whose stock is owned by many people, boards of directors are becoming much more active. Underlying this switch are: (a) a restiveness about "the establishment" and a general challenge to anyone in a position of power; and (b) a series of social reform movements dealing with ecology, women's rights, consumer protection, aid to developing nations, human rights, questionable payments, nuclear power, and the like—all of which put pressure on the conduct of business. Organizations such as the New York Stock Exchange are sensitive to these social attitudes, and they are insisting on reforms in the way companies are governed.

Incidentally, this challenge to the way corporations have been run is worldwide. In Europe and many developing countries, numerous efforts are being made to enlarge participation in board activities.

Far from clear, however, is just what these reactivated boards should do. A closely related question is who should be board members.

Inside Versus Outside Boards

An inside board. In the past, a board of directors often consisted largely, if not entirely, of executives of the company. Such directors are well informed about internal operations, the success of the company is of great importance to them, and they are readily available for discussion when critical issues arise.

Unfortunately, operating executives have difficulty taking a long-run objective view of their company. They are inevitably immersed in day-to-day problems and they are emotionally committed to making certain programs succeed. Moreover, they cannot disassociate themselves from social pressure of their colleagues and particularly of their bosses; they are naturally concerned with maintaining the goodwill of these persons who can make life easy or hard for them. To assume that these operating executives can change their perspective and their loyalties when they walk into an occasional board meeting is unrealistic.

Rarely can an inside board develop unaided an objective, independent, and tough-minded view of the company as a whole.

An outside board. As the name implies, an outside board of directors is composed of people whose principal interest is in some other company or profession. A banker, a prominent attorney, and senior executives of companies in other industries are commonly used as outside directors.

The advantages and disadvantages of outside directors are just the opposite of those for inside directors. The persons coming from the outside have independence of judgment and objectivity; they can see the company from a different point of view, and they are not wrapped up in short-run problems. On the other hand, they lack an intimate knowledge of the company operations and its relations with outside groups. More serious, they lack time to become fully informed; having major commitments in their principal line of activity, they cannot be expected to devote more than a few hours a month for the nominal directors' fee that is customarily paid. All too often people accept a directorship for the prestige attached or as a friendly gesture. They are willing to give advice, but they cannot be expected to exercise initiative in seeking directions for the company to expand or in weighing the likely consequences of proposed changes in company policy.

Since the aim is to secure an objective appraisal and independent check on senior managers, widespread opinion now favors a *majority* of outside directors. And an increasing number of publicly owned corporations are moving toward at least two-thirds outside directors. A recent survey of about 1,000 *large* corporations by the American Association of Corporate Secretaries found that almost 80% had at least a majority of outsiders.

These figures apply to corporations in which management and ownership are already clearly separated. In closely held corporations, however, a tight association of a few owners-directors-managers continues mostly in the traditional pattern. There is little basis for assuming that larger corporations need objective review more than smaller ones. So, the contrast in board membership reflects sensitivity to external pressures rather than need for guidance.

Extent of Board Participation

Election of outside board members only sets the stage. What are such directors expected to do? Their independence also means that they lack knowledge and time to deal with day-to-day operations. And their interference with supervisory relationships would certainly lead to internal confusion. To cite an analogy, a U.S. senator should not try to steer a battleship.

Who takes the lead? Furthermore, it is doubtful that outside boards—acting as a group (or committee)—can be expected to exercise active leadership. Again, limitations on knowledge, time, and the process of arriving at decisions stand in the way. In unusual circumstances the board may grasp the initiative. But most of the time the creative proposals and well designed programs will come from the full-time executives. The primary role of the board will be to make sure that senior managers do, in fact, provide the active leadership. Board members can prod, help, evaluate, occasionally veto, stimulate, or request action—all of which are aids to central management.

Realistic role for board of directors. A feasible assignment for a board of directors, then, would normally include at least the following duties:

1. *Approve major changes in strategy, policy, organization structure, and large commitments.* This assumes that carefully prepared recommendations on such matters will flow up from the senior executives. Even if the board approves a large majority of the recommendations made, the necessity for developing a thoughtful justification of the proposals stimulates executives to think through such changes from all angles. This careful preparation of a recommendation by executives may be as valuable as the combined judgment of the board of directors.
2. *Select top executives, approve promotions of key personnel, and set salaries for this top group of executives.* This assignment is both delicate and highly important. It requires independent and yet informed judgments. The board of directors is in a better position to perform this task than anyone else.
3. *Share predictions of future developments, crucial factors, and responses to possible actions.* Here the board is contributing to planning in the formulative stage. The benefits of the broad experience and the diverse points of view are made available to the executive group. Outside members of the board can provide this sort of counsel without unrealistic demands on their time.

4. *Evaluate results and ask discerning questions.* The board should appraise operating results both for prudent control and to obtain background information. This evaluation process should include the asking of a variety of penetrating questions. Most of these questions will be readily answered, but a few may set off a line of thought previously overlooked. Both directors and executives should recognize that the prime purpose here is to see problems from new and useful angles.

5. *Provide personal advice informally.* Already familiar with the company, a director may be an excellent source of advice to executives. The treasurer may call a banker-director about a recent change in the money market, or the marketing vice-president may call another company executive about a new advertising agency. Or the president may want to test out an idea before a formal recommendation is presented to the board as a whole. The informality of these contacts encourages a free exchange of tentative ideas and intuitive feelings.

A board performing the functions just described is particularly valuable because such a check and an independent viewpoint can rarely be developed within the executive group. This is a facilitating role, however. It assumes a harmony of values and objectives which, as we shall see later, may not exist.

Maintaining Independence

In the role just outlined for a board of directors, the initiative on most matters is assigned to the chief executive officer. There is danger that this full-time manager may choose to consult the board only in a perfunctory manner. Perhaps the outside board members just do not "get into the act" until after important decisions are already made.

Several devices are available to help assure that outside board members do take an active part in at least two or three areas. The board may appoint standing committees composed of a majority, if not all, outside board members. The increase in this practice in just three years is indicated on the accompanying chart. Subjects most often covered are:

1. *Audit.* This committee reviews directly with the outside auditor both the auditing process and the findings. Ninety-seven percent of the large companies surveyed by the ASCS had such a committee. Of these, 93% were composed entirely of outside directors and 99% had a majority of outside directors.

2. *Senior management compensation.* Both salaries and bonuses for officers and other senior executives are approved by this committee. About five-sixths of the large companies surveyed by ASCS had such a committee. Of these, 69% were composed entirely of outside directors and 96% had a majority of outside directors.

3. *Nomination of new board members and senior executives.* This committee focuses on management succession; it transfers the power of picking successors from the chief executive officer to a more broadly based group. About a third of the large companies surveyed by the ASCS had such a committee. Of these, less than a half were composed entirely of outside directors but 96% had a majority of outside directors.

A more potent possibility, though not yet widely used, is an agenda committee. This device enables outside directors to select the subjects to which they will give most attention. Thus, trouble is more difficult to "brush under the rug," and new opportunities can be assured of full study.

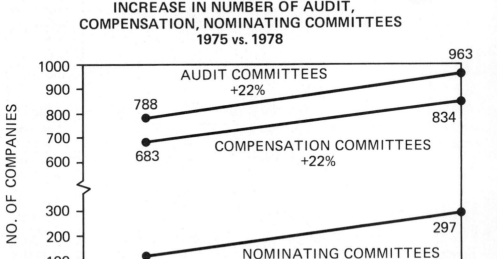

INCREASE IN NUMBER OF AUDIT, COMPENSATION, NOMINATING COMMITTEES 1975 vs. 1978

Source: Survey by the American Society of Corporate Secretaries, Inc.
The 993 respondents were predominantly large, publicly-owned corporations.

Since many smaller companies and not-for-profit enterprises are organized as corporations, they, too, face the question of just what their boards of directors should do. Managers of not-for-profit hospitals and smaller organizations often look to their boards for money-raising and a minimum of interference with running the institution. Nevertheless, the issue of basic responsibility for direction of the institution is, at least legally, within the scope of the board. But how they carry out this assignment is unclear.

DEDICATED VERSUS WATCH-DOG BOARD

Who should the outside directors be? This question is closely linked with the duties assigned to the board. For instance, if a director is to help set the monthly agenda, then a resident of Saudi Arabia would be an unsatisfactory choice, no matter how much stock the person owned.

Interest Group Representation

One proposal repeatedly heard is that various interest groups should be represented on the board. According to this thesis each major resource contributor (see resource converter model in Chapter 1) might expect to designate a representative. Indeed, for years it was customary to invite an investment banker or commercial banker whose firm helped finance the company to "sit on the board." Another example is the co-determination movement in Europe which provides for labor representatives to be board members.

Community representatives or a consumer representative are often proposed, but their selection and relation to their constituency has no traditional pattern. Even more ambiguous as to representation status is "a woman on the board" or "a black on the board." Nevertheless, pressure is mounting for selections based on such criteria.

The advantage of having interest group representatives as directors is also its weakness. The chances of continuing cooperation from the resource represented are improved. To some extent the resource has been "co-opted." But the very fact that such directors are obligated to promote the interests of their particular groups undermines their loyalty and objectivity toward the company itself. A major customer, for instance, can advise regarding the market and may be inclined to buy from the company of which he is a director; however, his inside knowledge of the company will also put him in an advantageous bargaining position. And when a choice has to be made, his first loyalty is to his major employer.

Of course, having two or more related jobs is not unusual, and an individual may be scrupulously careful to withdraw from one or both roles when a conflict of interest arises. Most professional bankers feel that they conduct themselves in this manner. On the other hand, open and frank discussion is unlikely among persons who may find themselves on opposite sides of the table tomorrow.

If a board of directors consists largely of interest representatives—like a little United Nations—the potential usefulness of the board shifts. It might become a forum in which commitments to a program are developed. The boards of some not-for-profit institutions function in this way. For business corporations, however, much more flexible and extensive negotiations for resources are needed (as the key actor analysis described in Chapter 4 implies). Moreover, if the necessary corporations were joined together in a single board, the antitrust prosecutors would raise a storm.

Alternatively, if the board is to perform as suggested in the preceding section of this chapter, then watch-dog directors are inappropriate. Instead, directors unquestionably committed to the company are required. Such directors may well have diverse backgrounds. But each is selected, like a Supreme Court Justice, for his or her capability rather than as a representative of an interest group.

Conflicting Interests

When John Doe sells a large block of land to a company of which he is a director we say there is a potential conflict of interest. The danger is that Doe will use his internal influence to promote a deal which is not optimum for the company but is very beneficial to him personally. There are other sorts of conflicts of interest, as with a group representative discussed above, but it is the personal gain problem that rears its ugly head most often.

The dividing line is fuzzy. A director may recommend the employment of a neighbor's son, but if that son is married to the director's daughter, the qualifications of the young man better be outstanding. The head of a very large corporation almost lost his job because by some coincidence his nephew was writing much of the company's casualty insurance. The eminent president of a large life insurance company did resign when there was public criticism about a long-term loan by the company to a firm in which the president was a significant stockholder.

It is unfair to condemn all such relationships. The normal protection is (1) to make one's connections clearly known, and (2) to insist that an objective, independent assessment is made of the benefits to the company of any transaction. However, the mores of what is an unethical divided interest have been changing over time, and vary from country to country.

On the borderline now is the question whether a company's investment banker or a partner in its outside legal counsel should serve on the board of directors. These have been two traditional sources of well informed outside directors, and there has been virtually no scandal associated with the practice. Nevertheless, the presence of such individuals on the board probably does affect where the company does its banking and where it turns for legal advice.

Obtaining Good Directors

Good directors will be increasingly hard to recruit. We have already presented a case for (a) increasing the number of outside directors, and (b) significantly raising the work they will be expected to do. On the other hand, we have (c) cautioned against using "watch-dogs," and (d) even raised question about the propriety of directors who may gain personally from their part-time association. Where, then, are suitable directors to be found?

As in the past, some senior executives of leading companies will serve on each other's boards. Prestige, useful contacts, and some general knowledge come from such posts. But as the workload gets heavier and the legal constraints more annoying, this will not be an expanding source of outside directors. Professional outside directors probably will increase, though slowly. These are usually people with broad experience, either as former executives or as consultants, who devote a significant amount of time to any directorship they accept. In return, they are paid a fee—often $6,000 to

$15,000 per year. University presidents and business school deans will continue to be a source.

In addition, companies will probably move down a status level to tap a larger pool of talent. Top vice-presidents of other companies are often very well qualified. They (and their main employers) probably would welcome the exposure to another corporation. Likewise, some professors may supplement administrators as an academic source. A few lawyers and financiers may find a directorship intriguing even though there is an understanding that it will not lead directly to professional engagements. Even with these additional sources many companies will have to search to find a full complement of good directors.

Because good directors will be scarce, the development of boards as strong independent arms of corporate government may be slow.

"Outside Directors" within Diversified Corporations

Each business-unit within a diversified corporation needs the same kind of independent check on its activities as we have been advocating for separate companies. Someone outside the unit itself should approve major changes in strategy and organization, select top executives and set their compensation, share vital forecasts, evaluate results, insist that unpleasant problems be confronted, provide personal counsel. This is the "outside director" role.

A unique strength of a diversified corporation (using a Stage III or Stage IV organization) is its ability to provide people to act as "outside director" for each self-contained business. At least one corporate executive should be so designated for each business-unit. The dilemma, noted above, of obtaining good outside directors is thereby avoided. The person appointed can be given the time and resources necessary to be well informed and to be concerned about the unit as a total undertaking. Contacts with other units and with external developments give the individual broad perspective; at the same time, he or she is not protecting a particular department within the business-unit, nor is beholden to the general manager for his or her job.

Because the parent corporation has such a large stake in each business-unit, it can afford to recruit and pay able individuals to fill this role—typically one person will serve, say, half a dozen units. Along with finance, this "outside director" service is a primary contribution that parent corporations can make to strong operating divisions.

ORGANIZING FOR CENTRAL MANAGEMENT

Although the board of directors has an essential role, the major burden of central management must be carried by full-time senior executives.

They are the persons who must work out operational definitions of strategy and policy based on a careful appraisal of trends, company strengths, obstacles to be overcome, impact on the rest of the company, and the like. The executives, with rare exceptions, negotiate major agreements for the company. They are the ones who represent the firm to congressional committees. A review of the annual budget with an understanding of its implications is an assignment senior executives are best able to perform.

An active, outside board does not reduce the demands on the time of senior executives. Instead, preparing presentations for the board and responding to their questions adds another dimension in getting plans approved. The decisions should be wiser, but participation by an independent board complicates rather than simplifies the process.

Legal Titles

Officers of a corporation—president, vice-presidents, treasurer, secretary, etc.—are formally elected by the board of directors in accordance with provisions of the company's bylaws. Occasionally, the bylaws also contain a realistic job description for these officers; but typically the bylaws simply make some sweeping statements about the duties of the president and the treasurer and say little or nothing about other officers. Often a senior executive such as a general manager is not a legal officer at all, whereas an individual performing perfunctory duties in the secretary's office may be formally elected by the board. Common practice is to leave the legal authorization quite general, because this is difficult to change; instead, the actual working relationships are developed orally, by exchange of memoranda, or possibly in a company organization manual. Legal titles, then, give us only vague clues about how a top management actually functions.

A quick review of the distinctive tasks of central management presented in the beginning of this chapter will reveal that much of the work must be performed by full-time, thoroughly informed company executives. If the company is to be strong, these senior executives must provide initiative and leadership. Others may help, but in a typical enterprise the senior executives must provide the dynamic force.

Of course, senior executives may also be owners and directors; but as we have seen, they are not in an optimum position to provide strong leadership in those capacities.

The Chief Executive

Normally, the chief operating executive also serves as the focal point for central management. This individual usually holds the title of "president" but for diplomatic reasons may be named chairperson of the board, executive vice-president, or perhaps general manager. Ideally, this individual has vision; lays plans for 5, 10, or 20 years ahead; is a master of strategy and a negotiator; has the ability to pick able personnel; stimulates and leads both immediate subordinates and employees throughout the company; is a popular and effective leader in civic and industry affairs; expects high standards of achievement by subordinates; and courageously takes remedial action when all is not well.

Again, realism forces us to admit that no single person can excel in all these respects; and even if one had the ability, that individual would not have the time to do all these things personally. Consequently, wise chief executives try to see that important activities they cannot perform themselves are done by someone else in the company. This conclusion leads us to the question of how the chief executive's "office" can be organized.

A "President's Office"

Dual executive. The most common way to relieve the central management burden on the president is to share the job with another senior executive. Various combinations of titles are used: chairperson of the board and president, president and executive vice-president, or president and general manager are examples. Whatever the titles, the two individuals have to develop their own unique way of splitting the total task. The division is likely to reflect the particular interests and abilities of the two individuals. One person may handle most external relations, while the other works with executives within the company. One may focus on long-range development, and the second may deal with current problems. Sometimes the division is along functional or product lines. Perhaps no continuing pattern exists; each works on whatever seems most pressing at the moment. Regardless of how the work is shared, an intimate and frequent interchange is desirable so that the two individuals function as a closely integrated partnership.

Occasionally, three people work together as peers, but the integration of their thoughts and activities into a single president's office view is difficult.

The dual executive arrangement works better in the top job than in other executive positions—probably because a higher proportion of the total work involves planning and deliberation and less time is involved in supervising daily activities. Nevertheless, it is a delicate arrangement and depends on getting the right combination of personalities.

Group vice presidents. Diversified corporations with a Stage III or Stage IV organization often extend the "president's office" in another way. Group vice-presidents are added to take over relationships with clusters of business-units. These senior executives share frequently and informally in the thinking and planning for the entire corporation. However, they are designated as the main contact for typically four to eight business-units, and they keep track of these units more closely than is possible for other senior executives. These are the people who perform the "outside director" role for their assigned units.

Group vice-presidents usually have no staff of their own. Instead, they rely on staff which serves the entire "president's office." Like the dual executive, they are members of a partnership right at the peak of the executive pyramid.

Management Committee

A further sharing device is the management committee, perhaps called policy committee or planning committee. Here all top level managers serve on a committee that deals with several central management tasks. Establishing strategy and policy, building long-range programs, appraising capital expenditures, and reviewing annual budgets are typical activities.

A top management committee has all the inherent advantages and limitations of any committee, as discussed in the preceding chapter. It clearly is a good coordinating mechanism; but if it is just an added assignment for executives who are already fully occupied with managing their respective departments, not much creative central management work will be accomplished in committee meetings. The firms with best success with a genuine central management committee have deliberately relieved their members of a significant part of their supervisory burdens, often by placing a single deputy under each member. The members are then expected to devote a quarter to half their total time to central management problems assigned to them by the president.

Central Management Staff

Another well-recognized way to assist the chief executive with central management tasks is the use of a staff. Several leading companies, for instance, have a staff group working on *long-range planning*. These people study future trends, explore possible additions to the product line, project requirements for buildings and for training personnel, and prepare similar data and recommendations for consideration by the president. The organization for long-range planning is a special problem in itself because central staff should tap the ideas of thinking people throughout the company. A few firms rotate young executives in and out of the long-range planning group for this purpose. Decentralized companies may select a long-range planning person in each operating division; the ideas of these persons are then funneled up to a coordinating staff, the chief executive, or to the management committee if one exists.

The use of an *organization planning* staff reporting to the president is becoming more common. Such a unit assists in adapting the company organization structure to changing needs. A related task sometimes combined with organization planning is *executive personnel development*. Executive development may simply be part of the training activity of the company; but in some cases the personnel staff advisor to the president shares in the selection, development, and compensation planning for senior executives.

The role of the *business economist* is often confined to making cyclical forecasts of volume and prices in the industry; however, in a few instances the business economist has become an active participant in central management discussions. Similarly, *financial analysts* occasionally become advisors on central management issues.

These are merely illustrations of the kinds of problems the top staff may handle. Such people do more than assemble information specifically requested by the president, helpful though this may be. To be a really significant member of the team that assures that central management tasks are performed well, a staff member must be a respected, intimate advisor of the senior executive. Such staff members are hard to find, and not all chief executives know how to use staff effectively on difficult, intangible problems.

The particular combination of staff, multiple executives in the president's office, or committees obviously must be fitted to the needs of each company and to the personalities holding top positions. But whatever the design, provision for getting the central management tasks done well is crucial.

Socially Responsible Governance

Central management of corporations can be considered from at least two viewpoints. The managerial view, which we take in this book, assumes that we are working from the inside of the enterprise trying to make it more effective. The viewpoint of society in general is different. Here results and impact on society are all that matter. From this outside viewpoint, if corporations serve society well, they should be encouraged. If they do not, then the institution should be modified or even abolished.

As corporations become larger and more powerful, their impact comes under closer scrutiny. Also as our society becomes more interdependent and sensitive to the health of each part, more people are deeply concerned about the behavior of each wheel in the complex machine. For these reasons, corporations are now in the limelight. The very success of our business enterprises makes them the target for investigation and criticism.

With a lot of people wishing the world were different, any institution as powerful as our business enterprise system is sure to get a share of the blame. Inevitably, suggestions for altering the system will be advocated.

A popular point of attack is the board of directors. The board is presumed to have the ability to change the behavior of the corporation. Therefore, reformers propose changes in the composition of the board, or in the legal liability of board members, or in the way a board operates. The shift to more outside directors, discussed above, and pressure for special interest representation on boards reflects in part this public concern. Business corporations (and powerful not-for-profit corporations) can disregard this challenge to past board practices only at their peril.

Basically, the response proposed in this chapter is (1) that corporations should indeed make sure that they strengthen their boards and use them for a continuing objective check on the direction and results. But (2) each board should be committed to serve its company with an undivided interest.

As a general scheme, we do not expect the board to be the place where agreements with various resource contributors are negotiated. If the board becomes a meeting place for special interest groups, or a device to induce cooperation, then it cannot effectively serve the function of constructive, objective "advice and consent."

In a pluralistic society with many different enterprises, each looking for new niches to serve, competition for resources and customers determines who will survive and grow. Each enterprise—"resource converter" in the language of Chapter 1—is continually looking for new and more acceptable relationships with key actors. And an important function of the board of directors is to see that this process of dynamic interaction with the changing environment is wisely pursued. However, the board should not be turned into a town meeting for interest representatives. Instead, each board has the important task of assuring that its enterprise is an alert, responsive, effective participant in the competitive system.

Each board should do its utmost to create a strong, virile company, a company which performs its particular mission with distinction. Society is served by such effective "resource converters."

QUESTIONS FOR CLASS DISCUSSION

1. Courtney C. Brown argues that the board of directors of a large corporation should have its own staff people to gather information—anywhere inside or outside the corporation—for use of the board and to otherwise assist the board in its objective governing of the corporation. (a) What advantages do you see in such an arrangement? (b) What disadvantages? (c) Are there better ways to provide adequate assistance to outside board members?

2. The president and chairperson of the board of Koch Electronics, Inc. has proposed to the other members that the board be increased to nine members from seven and that three outside members be elected to fill the new positions and one now vacant. This will give the board a majority of outside members and will add a well-known inventor of electrical and electronic products, a top-level executive of a diversified Japanese producer of electronic subassemblies, defense, and industrial products, and the president of an insurance company. Koch Electronics of Hartford, Connecticut, assembles parts and subassemblies bought elsewhere into a specialized line of electrical and electronic office equipment. "I am not suggesting that we add interest-group representatives but, rather, specialists who can give us expert advice on trends and technology in our field and on risk-management, especially about our product liabilities.

These three have helped us before, informally." Four executives of the firm, an investment banker whose company floated both stock and bond issues for Koch Electronics and an individual owner of 10% of the common stock are the other board members. (The largest single stockholder—16% of the shares—is the president.) As the second largest stockholder, what is your position? Explain.

3. (a) Does a Stage I enterprise—one dominant individual—face the kinds of problems described in this chapter? (b) To what extent does such an enterprise need a separate check on the chief executive to perform at least the duties listed on pages 468–469? (c) How do you recommend that a small, privately owned enterprise obtain the kind of guidance you suggested in answering (a) and (b)?

4. (a) "Students should select at least one of their numbers, and preferably two or three, to serve on the Board of Trustees of their university." Do you agree? Why? (b) Should employees of a university have a representative on the Board of Trustees? Why? (c) Would your answer be the same for customers and employees of (1) an airline, and (2) a telephone company? Why?

5. (a) Do you recommend that corporations make special effort to find women to appoint as directors? Should they give preference to women over men in such appointments? (b) Answer the same questions with regard to blacks. (c) Answer the same question with regard to American Indians.

6. In April, members of the audit committee of California Life Corporation's board learned that last year's financial report—due two weeks earlier—had not been filed with the S.E.C. The company and its independent accounting firm were at odds in a bitter accounting dispute. The annual report, when filed, would have to show a loss of $3.2 million dollars despite earlier, widely-made predictions of a profit of $2.6 million and despite the then president's exhortation to company officers to "be creative." The audit committee's new and inexperienced chairperson had assembled a committee twice during the previous twelve months. "Who has the supreme wisdom to say he's smarter than the people who are in there every day?" an audit-committee member asked. Another said: "There's a limited amount of time and a lot of ground to cover. The whole atmosphere and protocol of a board meeting make it difficult to play the role of critic as the S.E.C. envisions." There is an element of trust among directors. Said a third director: "Without a full-time staff for audit-committee members, it's impossible for an outside director to get into the bowels of the company. An insider said: "Anyone who assumes an outside directorship these days is taking a substantial risk. Why you should do it, I don't know." Do you agree? Explain.

7. Wise company strategy is concerned with keeping company activities in tune with its changing environment, as discussed in Part 1. What organizational provisions can be made to assure (a) sensitivity to and preferably anticipation of significant changes in the environment, and (b) prompt adjustment to such changes? Who perceives and who initiates?

8. Several research studies have identified one of the key tasks of central management to be coordination of the functional departments or operating divisions of a company. Should this task of coordination be assigned to a management committee or an executive committee, or should it better remain the responsibility of the president or the chief executive officer? What kinds of issues can a single executive resolve that a group could not?

9. According to recent law in West Germany, a corporation with more than 2,000 employees has one-half of its board of directors elected by its employees; the other half are elected by stockholders, as in the U.S. The theory underlying this "co-determination" is that employees have as vital an interest in company operations as do stockholders. (a) What effect do you think such co-determination is likely to have on (i) the way the board functions, (ii) the decisions the board makes on strategy, policy, etc., and (iii) the long-run strength of the company? (b) Why has the co-determination concept received little support thus far in the United States?

10. Almost all not-for-profit enterprises are governed by a *board* of directors (or trustees). This applies to hospitals, universities, museums, professional orchestras, unions, co-ops, etc. As in profit-seeking companies, the boards typically appoint full-time executives to actually manage the enterprise. (a) How do you explain such widespread use of boards (instead of an individual) to be the top governing management? (b) Who should select the boards of hospitals? universities? orchestras? mutual insurance companies? Why? (c) If a board is inactive and its enterprise declines, who if anyone should initiate corrective action?

CASE 19
Columbia Bell Telephone Co.[1]

"Maybe I should resign," thought Gene Williams. "We don't agree on what the board of directors should do and I'm not interested in being merely a show-piece director." Williams, a political science professor at the state university, has been active in the civil rights movement and is an articulate spokesperson for the black community. Six months ago he was elected a director of Columbia Bell—the first college professor and first black to serve on that board.

The monthly board meetings which Williams has attended have all been well planned, friendly sessions. Routine legal actions—approval to file documents, signature authorizations, bank loan agreements, and the like—take up some time. Operating results and short-term projections are reviewed. At this stage, board members typically exchange views on the economic and political outlook. Then a vice-president or department head makes a brief presentation of current problems and plans for his or her division of the company. These presentations are intended to inform the board, not seek its advice. By this time, several directors have to leave for other appointments, and the meeting is adjourned.

---

[1]Columbia Bell Telephone Co. operates as a regulated utility in two large states. Although it is a subsidiary of A.T. & T., it has an impressive outside board of directors and is fully responsible for operations in its territory. The present organization of the company is indicated in the accompanying table. Its assets are over $3 billion and it has almost 30,000 employees.

At the close of the last meeting Williams asked, "Does Columbia Bell have any basic problems which the board should be digging into?" Another director responded, "That's what we pay the management to do."

The president took the question more seriously. "We have lots of problems and want all the help we can get. Perhaps you are thinking of our 'equal opportunity' posture, and I'd be grateful if you had the time to take a thorough look at what we are doing on that front. Or if there is any other area which concerns you, I'll be glad to arrange for you to talk with our people."

Williams did find the time to visit with nine Columbia Bell executives and staff people, and came to two conclusions. (1) The company is actively pushing equal opportunity for blacks and for women. In fact, to increase its percentage of black and women employees in areas where they are under-represented, reverse discrimination occurs. The number of blacks and women in middle management is still low, and almost non-existent in upper management. However, there is strong evidence that time is needed for minorities to gain experience and for vacancies to occur. Conclusion: just keep the pressure on.

(2) The chief problem confronting Columbia Bell is labeled "marketing" but is even more fundamental. Williams has sorted his notes into three piles (see attached): (a) Threats, (b) Inertia, (c) Possible Actions. This is where the board of directors should be active, Williams believes.

Williams has talked on the phone with several other outside directors about the importance of "marketing" to the future of Columbia Bell, and has received a cool response. One said, "Our job is to keep the company financially sound, like it now is. The utility commissions will never accept extra marketing expense as a necessary outlay, so we can't recover the expense in income. It would simply cut net earnings." Another commented, "Let's let A.T. & T. worry about future competition. They ought to do something to earn their overhead charge." A third said, "As directors we should not interfere with internal organization. That is a managerial job. We can't know enough about the specifics to tell the president how to run the shop. We come from a wide range of companies and are appointed to assure that the stockholders and customers both get fair treatment, also the employees."

Questions

(1) To what extent and in what ways should the board of directors of Columbia Bell involve themselves in the "marketing" issue?

(2) How do you recommend Columbia Bell be organized to deal with future competition and "marketing"? Should other steps, in addition to organization, be taken?

Notes Based on Interviews

Threats

1. Columbia Bell now must permit customers to hook up their *own* equipment to company lines. Many new competitors sell phones, PBX equipment (in-house exchanges), etc. to customers. Columbia Bell must now sell, as well as lease, such equipment to meet competition. We have some advantage in repair service. But field is now open to computer companies and many others.

2. Cable TV may move into interacting systems. Customers will then shop, buy, pay bills, select news on their initiative. Meter reading in customers' houses—electricity, water, gas—is also a possibility. Columbia Bell would merely lease lines—maybe glass fiber optics—to customer's home or business; routine, low-profit end of business. Millions in revenue at stake.

3. Other big companies have headstart in satellite communications. Already used for TV and radio. Large future market for national business hook-ups—computer data, picture-phone and conferences (compete with airplane business travel), instant photocopies of documents and drawings. IBM and Xerox getting into this, including software. Mostly competes with Long Lines.* Maybe will use Columbia Bell's local connections, but as routine service—see #2 and #1. Again, multi-millions involved.

4. Competitors will design, sell or lease, train, and maintain entire communication systems for major users—including software. Customer-oriented systems vs. hardware which Columbia Bell stresses.

5. Small satellite receiving—and maybe transmitting—stations at plants and company headquarters are being engineered. These would bypass the Bell system entirely. We would not get even routine business.

Inertia

---

1. Columbia Bell, like rest of A.T. & T., very *service* oriented. Pride in being best telephone system in world. Feel like stewards, *not entrepreneurs.*

2. Bell Labs and Western Electric (subsidiaries of A.T. & T.) generate new products. Excellent engineering. Technically, not customer, oriented. Think in terms of products. Columbia Bell relies on them for new sources of income.

3. Engineering and Operations are dominant departments in Columbia Bell. They produce the good service. Have most influence on budget allocations. Commercial Department "necessary"—second-class citizen. Local push for new services is weak.

4. Promotion from within very common. Heavy internal training; therefore executives rise through ranks. Believe in present company values.

5. State Public Utility Commissions regulate service, approve rates. Must serve all customers, so Columbia Bell may be saddled with uneconomic customers (like Postal Service). Good service helps rate increase. Expenses must be in line to get reasonable return on investment. So, more attention to expense control than profits. Commissions indifferent to *who* provides future services.

Possible Actions

---

1. Add staff to the Commercial Department. Specialize by type of business—chain stores, banks, interstate trucking companies, stockbrokers, etc. Each group design

---

*Long Lines is a separate division of A.T. & T., operating the long-distance connections between regional companies like Columbia Bell.

and promote communications systems suited to its business. Work with departments to give each business what it needs.

2. Reorganize Commercial Department along industry and business lines, not geography unless industry section needs local reps. Rename Marketing. Do staff job in
   #1 plus. Act like competitors whose survival depends on creating better total
   communication systems suited to new technology. Maybe transfer some installation and maintenance from Operations Department to new industry sections. Rate
   setting?

3. Bring in experienced marketing executives. Put in key spots, maybe next president.

4. Tie all approval of capital expenditure projects to new kind of service listed in #2.
   Use ROI standards by kind of business.

5. Reward "entrepreneurs" with bonuses; never done in Columbia Bell.

6. Call in A.T. & T. industry experts. Maybe hire management consultants.

7. Possibly organize national companies to give full service to particular industries.
   Use regional companies like Columbia Bell for local operations only. Bypass state
   utility commissions. Meet competitors head-on.

Supplement to Organization Chart
Main Functions of Each Department

Engineering (design of facilities): customer equipment; outside plant; switching equipment; transmission.

Plant (installation and maintenance of facilities): construction, installation,
and maintenance of local switching, trunk lines, outside plant, etc.; connections to network; response to trouble reports.

Traffic (running the plant): operators—toll calls, number assistance, etc.; assign lines and numbers; supervise use of circuits and trunk lines; service evaluation, future usage.

Commercial (interface with residential and other small customers): sales,
negotiation and coordination of service for small customers; coin service; an-
noyance call bureau; teller and cashier service; community relations.

Accounting: customer billing; payroll processing; supplier payment; corporate accounting; banking activities; financial planning.

Directory: directory compilation and production; sale of Yellow Page advertising and special listing; directory delivery.

Sales: planning, negotiation, and administration of sales to large business
customers and sales of data (non-oral) communications; special services.

ORGANIZATION OF OPERATING ACTIVITIES

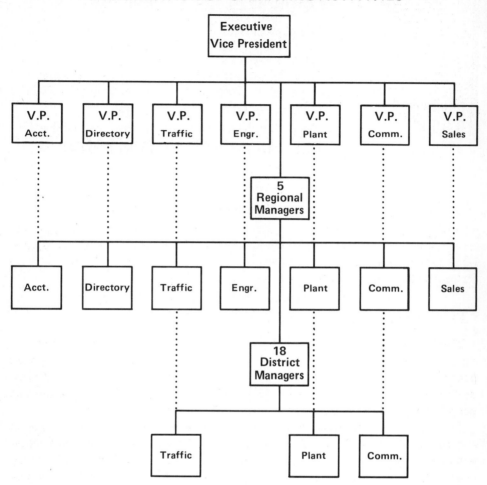

EXECUTIVE PERSONNEL

Without suitable executive personnel in a company, sound strategy, effective policy, and a clear organization plan soon become unrealistic aspirations; with good executive personnel, they provide the guidance and the structure for purposeful enterprise.

Developing Executive Personnel

The development of a competent group of immediate subordinates is a duty that can never be fully delegated. Larger companies may have a service unit that provides assistance in dealing with executive personnel problems, but each executive still carries primary responsibility for having competent people in key positions under his or her direction.

The typical manager is concerned with only a relatively few executives and other key personnel. These are likely to be people he or she has worked with over a period of years; they may well include many close friends. An executive is expected to see that they perform today's tasks effectively and also develop so that they can assume the larger responsibilities of tomorrow. This development involves habits, attitudes, and skills that may take years. Except for filling unexpected vacancies arising from death or resignation, executive personnel is a long-run problem. Because of these *personal, intangible,* and *long-run* characteristics of executive personnel development, general policy is inadequate to deal with specific situations. In addition to using policy, the manager should give personal attention to the delicate and highly personal situations in the company or department.

Wide variation in company practice

Since executive personnel involves personal relationships, considerable difference occurs in the way executive selection and development is handled in various companies.

A president who evaded responsibility. In one relatively small company with eight key executives, the president had been for many years the key figure in coordinating operations. The subordinates were given considerable latitude within their own departments, but they were expected to concentrate their attention in their own areas. The executives were very friendly with one another, and the president had a personal interest in and a deep loyalty to each of the members of the group. There was a general understanding that the sales manager would probably be the next president, and beyond that the matter of executive succession was given little thought.

The cold facts of the situation were that the sales manager was an excellent salesperson but not an effective executive. The manager was indecisive and preferred not to assume administrative responsibility. As long as the president was active, these traits were not a serious handicap to the company. The sales representatives were experienced individuals who were glad to accept the kindly suggestions of the sales manager and who were able to proceed with a minimum of supervision.

When the president died and was succeeded by the sales manager, the latter's lack of executive ability created an acute problem. Other executives found it difficult to get positive decisions from the new president, who in an effort to please everyone, was likely to reverse decisions. Coordination, or lack of it, was largely a result of the voluntary contacts between the several executives. The new president could not adjust to the new responsibilities of the job and suffered a nervous breakdown within three years. The person who was next appointed as president had considerably more ability but had been given virtually no training for the job as chief executive. Six to eight years elapsed before the company really recovered from the shock of the death of a president who failed to provide adequately for a replacement.

Note also that the president made no provision for change in the scope of company activities.

Looking back on this case, one wonders why a successful president for so many years failed to anticipate the difficulties upon his withdrawal from the company. Perhaps he never faced the question squarely. More likely, he recognized the limitations of the sales manager but could not bring himself to take the drastic action that would have been involved in the selection and training of another executive to be his successor. This would have created strain and upset personal friendship. Since no immediate action was necessary, he probably evaded the issue and hoped it would work out all right somehow. Had he taken the necessary action when he was still president, the company would certainly have been better off and the sales manager spared a nervous breakdown. This would have taken considerable courage, however, because there was no assurance that all the people concerned would have recognized the need for the action.

Informal development program. More thought is given executive development in many companies than appears on the surface. Frequently these concerns have no announced program or procedure but do give the matter of executive personnel regular attention. One company, for example, has a "little green seedbox" that contains a card for each key person who is a present or potential manager of one of the concern's principal operations. Each year the work of these people is reviewed by a senior executive along with the individual's supervisor, and when a person is assigned to a new position his or her performance is watched closely. Then, as opportunities open, people are moved into positions of increasing executive importance. If it is decided, after watching a person for several years, that the individual has reached maximum, his or her card will be removed from the file.

Wide variations exist in this type of approach. Typically, the cards or the pages in a loose-leaf notebook contain little information other than a record of the positions a person has held, the salary, and perhaps notations on any outside civic or educational work done. If the president or a senior vice-president is the one who directs the activity and makes sure that each person's performance is reviewed at least once a year (though not necessarily in a formal review session), then it is likely that considerable executive development work will take place and that the selection of people for promotion will be based on a broad view of the person's experience.

Where the activity is treated more casually or where the reviews are sponsored by an individual who lacks prestige with other executives, the attention given to executive development will probably be substantially less. In any event, the kind of training on the job that occurs depends almost entirely upon the interest and the ability of the supervising executive. Given the proper company tradition, backed by the necessary inspiration and guidance of the chief executive, such informal plans for executive development have worked remarkably well in some companies.

Essential Elements in a Sound Program

The informal approaches to executive development just illustrated have two basic weaknesses: (1) little thought is given to preparing for growth or major changes in strategy, and (2) executive development receives low priority in the plans of most executives. To overcome these limitations, highly formalized programs of executive appraisal and replacement schedules have been created, especially in multinational concerns where lack of qualified executives may be a major restraint on expansion.

Even though substantial disagreement exists on how formalized executive development should be, we can identify several basic elements that every manager should keep in mind when dealing with executive personnel problems. Whatever the forms and the procedures used, the manager's thinking should embrace the following steps:

1. A prediction of the types and number of executives the company (or department) will need for successful operations in the future.
2. A review, or inventory, of the executive talent now available.
3. A tentative promotion schedule, based on the two preceding steps, that provides for filling each of the positions in the anticipated organization and,

insofar as possible, for a potential replacement for each of the key executives.

4. A plan for the individual development of each person slated for promotion,
   so that each may be fully qualified for the responsibilities.

5. Compensation arrangements that will attract and hold the executives covered in the foregoing program and provide incentives for them to put forth
   their best efforts.

The significance and the nature of each of these steps will be considered
in the following sections. A detailed analysis of techniques, however, is
beyond the scope of this book.

ANTICIPATING EXECUTIVE REQUIREMENTS

The basis for any long-range planning for executive personnel is a prediction of the kind of people that will be needed. Surprisingly, this obvious first
step is sometimes overlooked. In one company, for example, the top administrator held the view that "we always have room for good people around
here," and on several occasions had hired competent people with no clear-cut
idea of what they were to do. These individuals either got bored waiting for
a significant assignment or created friction by interfering with activities of
other executives.

A more common failure is to assume that a title provides an adequate
guide to the kind of person needed. A hard-driving, enthusiastic sales supervisor is quite a different individual than an analytical and imaginative
planner of merchandising campaigns, and yet either of these persons might
have the identical title of product sales manager. Before sound executive
development can be done, a clear understanding is needed of (1) the jobs to
be filled and (2) the characteristics of the persons needed for these jobs.

Jobs to Be Filled

A study of strategy and future organization, along the lines indicated
earlier in this book, will result in a long-range organization plan with descriptions of each key position needed. These position descriptions are not
necessarily put in writing, but there must be an understanding of the duties
and the relationships of each executive position. If plans for the future
administrative organization have not already been clarified, then organization analysis becomes a first step in the executive personnel program.[1]

Position descriptions prepared for organizational purposes differ in emphasis from those used in an executive development program. The more

---

[1] We clearly are recommending that organization design *precede* executive selection. Of
course, in the short run a company must be managed by the executive talent available, and
since the available executives may not fully match the ideal organization, the only practical
action is to adjust the organization so that optimum results will be obtained. Executive development, however, should continue to be aimed toward the best future organization we can realistically expect to achieve.

ticklish aspects of organization involve defining the borderline between the various units and spelling out interrelationships when activities must closely coordinate. Such divisions of responsibility are not so important for executive development purposes. Here, interest centers on the major duties to be performed, the degree of decentralization and hence the judgment that must be exercised by people at different levels in the organization, the importance of initiative and enthusiasm, and similar matters. In other words, we need to sense the role the person in the executive position will play in the operation of the enterprise.

Characteristics of Persons Needed for These Jobs

The second phase of this analysis of executive requirements is to translate the duties into *person specifications,* that is, the personal qualities an individual needs to fill a given position effectively. We can describe the duties of a football quarterback or a plant superintendent, but it is another matter to set up a list of qualifications that a person should have to fill such a position successfully.

These person specifications may be stated in terms of knowledge, supervisory skill, emotional stability, judgment, dependability, ability to deal with outsiders, social attitudes, and the like. Unfortunately, it is difficult to define requirements for positions in such terms because experience shows that people with quite different makeups may be successful in the same kind of a job. Another way to draw up person specifications is to list the principal things they will be expected to do, such as build customer goodwill, control expenses, plan for future expansion, or stimulate and develop their subordinates. This kind of a list is easier to prepare but is not entirely adequate when an individual is being selected for work that is quite different than he or she has already done. For instance, it is hard to appraise the ability of a crack salesperson to be a sales supervisor because there has been no opportunity to observe the individual doing the kind of activity that is required of the sales supervisor.

In the establishment of person specifications, then, we find one of the first reasons why executive development cannot be reduced to fixed procedure. Specifications for the end product are not exact. Nevertheless, if there is to be any careful planning, it is necessary to build up reasonably accurate and useful descriptions of the kind of executives that will be needed to fill the organization.

One additional point should be emphasized. Much executive development work cannot be expected to show results in less than three to five years and some of it may take much longer. Consequently, the organization structure five years hence is more important than the present one.

The outlook and the strategy for the company must be studied to forecast the volume and the nature of activities. These will throw light on the organization structure that will be needed and hence on the requirements for executive personnel. Moreover, the existing organization may be far from ideal. A logical time to realign duties and to correct organizational weaknesses is when executive personnel are being shifted. If this is to be done, plans for executive development should, of course, be based on the new, rather than the old, organization structure.

INVENTORY OF EXECUTIVE TALENT

The second basic step in planning an executive personnel program is appraising the executives already in the organization. The organization and position analysis just discussed predicts what executive talent will be needed; the appraisal of executives, considered in this section, shows what talent is available to meet these requirements.

Generally an inventory of executive talent is taken to discover weak spots in the normal flow of executives through the promotion channel. It indicates where additional development work is needed to assure that satisfactory replacements are available when necessary.

A good inventory will also bring to light the competent executives who are not being used to their fullest capacity. For example, the president of a pharmaceutical company was shocked when his nephew resigned, along with two key salespeople, and established a competing firm. Evidence clearly indicated that these people had not been assigned to challenging positions and they considered their prospects for promotion so remote that they preferred to take the risk of establishing a new enterprise. A good plan of executive appraisal would have shown the president that these people were prepared for additional responsibilities. He should then have tried to find positions that would more fully utilize their ability, and if this was not possible, he should at least have openly examined the situation with each individual. In other words, an executive inventory would have been useful even though there was no immediate need for replacing key personnel.

Different Uses of Executive Appraisals

Executive appraisals may be used in several different ways, and their value will be improved if these uses are recognized at the outset.

1. The primary purpose of executive review may be to *select* a person for an existing or anticipated vacancy. For this purpose an objective appraisal of the person's future potential is needed.
2. Executive appraisal may point to the need for development when abilities of executives are matched against the person specifications for a given position. Individual *development programs* can then be built around deficiencies. When the emphasis is on personal development, the appraiser can identify much more closely with the individual being reviewed and together they can seek out opportunities for improvement.
3. Executive appraisal may be used to establish bonuses and to pay increases or other forms of *compensation.* Here attention centers on past

achievements rather than future potentials. Objectivity is needed here, as it is when considering individuals for promotion.

When a company uses its executive appraisal for several different purposes, as is usually true for those companies that have a well-rounded executive development program, it is important to maintain a balanced point of view. Objectivity is vital, while at the same time a sympathetic interest in the individual is needed for planning for individual growth.

Informal Appraisal of Executives

No systematic appraisal, or inventory taking, of executive ability is made in many companies. Nevertheless, considerable informal appraisal typically takes place. This was the method followed in a financial company, for example, that had 32 senior and junior officers and approximately 85 first-line supervisors and other key employees. The size of the company permitted each senior officer to know personally all of the executives as well as some of the outstanding operating persons.

The president and the senior vice-president made it a practice to "keep their eyes on the staff." They asked questions and otherwise followed the work of the various executives closely enough to have a clear impression of what most of the people were doing. In addition, they occasionally talked with the individual officers about the people under their supervision and what might be done to assist in their development. The officers felt that more formal ways of inventorying executive talent were unnecessary in their situation.

Informal executive appraisal, such as that just described, is a natural and continuing process that should be used by everyone in a managerial position. The more formal appraisal techniques, discussed in the next paragraphs, supplement rather than substitute for this type of evaluation. The informal appraisal is done at convenient times, in connection with other work; consequently, it creates no special burden on executives.

Limitations of this method are: (1) some executives who are primarily interested in technical problems may fail to size up the persons with whom they come in contact; (2) the appraisals may be incomplete, with emphasis on past performance and little attention on future potential; and (3) in larger concerns where no one executive can know personally all of the present and potential managers, it is extremely difficult to compare candidates in one department with those in another and to exercise any measure of guidance and control over an executive development program.

Systematic Evaluation of Executives

To overcome the limitations of informal executive appraisals, several companies have definite procedures for executive personnel reviews. In their simplest form these evaluations consist of only an annual memorandum written by the supervisor of each executive outlining the person's outstanding accomplishments and weaknesses, the steps taken for development, and future potential.

At the other extreme are rather elaborate evaluation forms that record an overall appraisal of the person's work during the past year, a rating of personal qualities, promotion possibilities, and plans for individual development. The Armed Services use a similar technique; in fact, the file of fitness reports is the primary basis on which Navy officers are selected for promotion.

These formal evaluation plans build up a record covering each executive, which is very helpful when he or she is being considered for transfer or promotion. Usually several different people have submitted appraisals and the total record is not dominated by some single event, as may happen when sole reliance is placed upon informal appraisal. Moreover, the formal procedure tends to make the evaluation more thorough and consistent.

On the other hand, standard forms and procedures by no means insure that appraisals will be made carefully and honestly. Unless the executives making the appraisal believe that the whole process is worthwhile, they may fill in the form hastily and with answers that they think will lead to the promotions and transfers they would like to see made. Evaluation procedures do, of course, use time of busy executives, and they add a formality to highly personalized relations among executives.

In some manner suitable to the enterprise, a review or inventory of executive talent should be made. This knowledge of the capacity and the weaknesses of the executives is essential for building a sound executive development program. The formality of the approach depends on the size of the company, its rate of change, and traditions regarding attention to personnel matters.

PLANS FOR FILLING EXECUTIVE POSITIONS

Development of executive personnel, as already noted, is largely a long-run problem. Individuals need time to develop the knowledge, skills, and judgment required in most executive posts.

Need for Planned Executive Progression

The treasurer of a medium-sized company wished to retire within a year and recently told the president. In the discussion at the next meeting of the board of directors, two facts emerged: (1) the assistant to the treasurer, specially selected two years earlier, had displayed more energy than judgment and clearly was not qualified to replace the treasurer, and (2) there was wide misunderstanding about how vital a role the new treasurer should play in overall company operations (some board members wanted a senior executive, whereas the president thought in terms of a cashier). Two years elapsed before a satisfactory, strong person could be found.

Having the right person in the right position at the right time is of supreme importance, especially when expanding or shifting into a new field. Here is an area, then, where long-range planning is of vital importance— even though human behavior is hard to measure and to predict, and results may not turn out just as planned.

Staffing-Plan Approach

Transfer and promotion of executives is a normal occurrence in a typical business concern. Deaths, retirements, and resignations create vacancies. New positions, resulting from expansion, have a similar effect. If these positions are filled by promotions, additional vacancies are created in the lower ranks. In fact, one vacancy at the vice-president level may result in shifts of half a dozen people at lower levels. The problem is how a company can plan to meet such changes.

The staffing-plan approach rests on three ideas we have already discussed. The first is anticipating executive requirements in terms of positions to be filled and the person specifications of executives needed in such positions. The second is a policy of promotion from within. The third, assuming promotion from within, is the inventory of executive talent discussed in the preceding section, which provides the personnel data needed for concrete planning. Staffing tables are simply a device for weaving this information into a tentative plan.

Staffing plans, such as the one on the next page, show for each executive position (and anticipated position) one or more persons who might be moved into that spot. The preparation of such plans requires that the person specifications for each position be used to select the best candidate available within the company. Some companies distinguish between candidates who are already qualified and those who need a year or more training before they would be prepared to take on the new duties. To be useful, such a chart should be realistic. Thus, if some contemplated positions are now vacant, they should be shown in this way. If there are no real candidates for a given position, this too should be frankly revealed. Of course, one individual may be considered as a candidate for two or more positions.

Ideally, every senior post in the company should have one or more potential replacements listed. Some people contend that there should be a replacement for every executive throughout the organization. Such an ideal is often very difficult to achieve in practice, and there is serious question as to how much money and effort a company should spend training a replacement for a person who, in all probability, will stay in the present position for ten or more years. On the other hand, having replacements for executives who are likely to retire or to be promoted to other positions is highly important. Some

JOB NO.	JOB TITLE	JOB INCUMBENT	AGE	SENIOR CANDIDATE	JOB NO.	AGE	JUNIOR CANDIDATE	JOB NO.	AGE
MANAGEMENT LEVEL GROUP "A"									
2C21	Service Manager	K. L. Foster	47				G. E. George C	5C64	38
							A. A. Day C+	3C23	35
2C52	Sales Engineer	B. C. Johnson	65	C. D. Dewey C	3C24	42	L. M. Mason D+	5A28	38
2C77	Const. Manager	E. E. Bryant	49	No Senior			E. F. Burnes C+	6B16	37
2C12	Accountant	F. G. Bray	55	No Senior			No Junior		
	"B" Office Managers								
3C22	Loc.	G. H. Miller	63	)			)E. D. Hill C	6F41	42
3C23	Loc.	A. A. Day	35	)G. E. George C	5C64	38	)M. N. Johns C+	7B18	35
3C24	Loc.	C. D. Dewey	42	)L. M. Mason D+	5A28	38	)W. X. Hobbs C	4A72	33
	Local Service Mgrs. "A" & "B" Offices								
5C31	"A" Office	R. R. Colby	62	)					
5C64	Loc.	G. E. George	38	)M. N. Johns C+	7F21	35	X. Y. Bell C+	6A57	37
5C65	Loc.	R. S. Williams	41	)W. X. Hobbs C	4A72	33	E. D. Hill C	6F41	42
5C66	Loc.	S. T. Fuller	57	)					
4C12	Zone Maint. Prom.	T. U. Webster	51				R. S. Williams D+	5C65	41
							X. Y. Bell C+	6A57	37
9C31	Zone Modern. Prom.	"Vacancy"		No Senior			T. V. Dodge D+	7D41	32
9C46	Zone Maint. Super.	V. W. Gary	58	F. E. Hyde C+	7F46	39	No Junior		
9C18	Zone Field Eng.	P. T. Monroe	39				T. U. Olson D+	7A81	48
							U. V. Larsen C	4B29	41

Staffing Plan

Sample sheet from staffing plan of Otis Elevator Company. "Senior candidates" are qualified to take over position without further training other than normal job indoctrination; "junior candidates" need one to five years more training. Letters after names tie in to annual executive appraisals. Note that some individuals, such as Hobbs and George, are listed as candidates for more than one position.

staffing plans attempt to show this timing; but more often the likelihood of a shift, and consequently the need for a fully prepared replacement, is left to the judgment of the people reviewing the plan.

Such staffing plans are subject to frequent revision. Unexpected changes in company operations or in the personal lives of executives may shift requirements. Some people will develop faster and others slower than anticipated; in fact, as time progresses, some persons will be added and others will be dropped as candidates for particular positions. Not infrequently, an understudy is moved to still another position and a new understudy must be found. Nevertheless, preparation of staffing plans serves a very useful purpose in pointing up where available replacements or candidates for new positions are lacking. Moreover, it forces realistic review of the persons who are likely to be promoted; if they need further development, immediate steps may be taken to start the necessary training.

Staffing plans are, of course, confidential documents because they reflect highly tentative promotion plans that may have to be revised later. For this reason, some executives prefer never to put their ideas down in writing. For smaller companies or for a single department this may be satisfactory, *provided* the same basic thinking takes place. The chart is merely a device to help an executive think through a very "iffy" subject. It is the systematic analysis of executive placement, rather than the particular pieces of paper, that is important.

Methods of Selection

Planned placement of executives modifies, but by no means eliminates, the need for wise selection of individuals to fill executive positions. Possible candidates must first be identified; later, one of these may be designated as an understudy; and when the vacancy occurs, the final selection must be made. This sifting process should improve the selection because judgments are made at different times, often several years apart, and this provides opportunity to reconsider earlier impressions. In addition, there will, of course, be unexpected vacancies for which final selections must be made quickly.

The use of periodic appraisals to provide data on individuals and the matching of such data against position descriptions and person specifications have already been recommended. The surprising thing is how often these basic steps in selection are disregarded. Many executives are inclined to substitute their intuitive likes and dislikes of individuals for the analytical approach suggested.

Selection will also be improved generally if *group judgment* is used. The appraisal of individuals involves so many intangibles and personal bias is so difficult to remove that the views of at least two or three people should be considered in making executive decisions. The final decision usually rests with the immediate supervisor, subject to approval by the boss. In addition, the views of other executives who have worked with the candidate, and of the central personnel advisor who has studied all available candidates, should be considered. Often the views of all these people will confirm the wisdom of the proposed selection. If there is a difference of opinion, then a warning has been raised and further observation on the points in question can be made. Probably in no other phase of business administration is group judgment more valuable than in executive selection.

When tentative selections of one or more candidates for a position are made several years before the actual vacancies occur, *trial on the job* may be possible. A candidate may pinch-hit in the job when the present incumbent is off on vacation or on special assignment. This is not an adequate test because usually the interval is too short for the candidate to exercise much initiative, but it may throw some light on that person's capabilities.

A more likely arrangement is to assign the candidates to work in a department or a branch where they can demonstrate ability to do certain phases of the work. Such assignments typically serve the purpose of both training and selection. If time permits, people may be tried out in several different positions. What people have done in the past is no definite assurance of what they will do in the future, but it is probably the best evidence we can obtain.

No mention has been made of psychological tests for selecting executives. When a quick selection has to be made from individuals outside the company, test data may be a useful supplement to other sources of information. However, when careful appraisals of people already in the company are possible and group judgment and trial on a series of different jobs can be utilized, psychological tests in their present state of development rarely add much that is useful.

Removing Ineffective Executives

Strong performance in each executive position is vital to company effectiveness. More than salary expense is at stake. A weak incumbent blocks the possibility for a more capable person to do that job well.

Removing ineffective executives is always painful. Recently, legal complications have been added. A company must be wary of charges of discrimination based on race, religion, or sex. Now, even the use of a normal retirement *age* may be illegal. Instead, clear evidence of inadequate performance is necessary to remove an executive who wishes to stay in the job. No longer can the boss simply say, "You're fired."

This need for clear evidence will force companies to maintain more elaborate, explicit (and expensive) performance evaluations—and evaluation of future usefulness. Instead of merely treating old Bill kindly until he finally reaches compulsory retirement age, records which he sees will have to spell out bluntly how obsolete he has become.

These evaluations should have a future focus, covering among other things:

1. ability to contribute to projected new activities of the company—for example, willingness to move, capacity to learn new technology or language, health and energy;
2. commitment to the company versus outside interests, and tendency to take jobs with competitors;
3. effectiveness in securing cooperation of people in other departments and outside the company.

Unless senior managers have the courage to make unpleasant personnel decisions, and also develop the tools which enable them to act wisely, their company can become choked with mediocre performers.

DEVELOPMENT OF EXECUTIVE TALENT

Executive training cannot be accomplished well *en masse*. As already noted, executive training deals with a relatively few individuals, each of whom is typically in a different stage of development and is preparing for a different job. Consequently, executive training should be approached on an individual basis.

Plans Center on Individuals

The planning for executive progression, already described, points to the areas where each individual needs further development. Any gap between the specifications for a position and the abilities already possessed by the candidate should receive attention in the development plan. Likewise, if a person's performance on the present job does not measure up to what is desired, these weaknesses should be corrected.

One company asks the following questions in designing a development program for each executive:[2]

Designing an Executive Development Program

1. WHAT IS THE PERSON? What are the candidate's executive qualifications, strengths, and weaknesses?
2. WHAT MAY THE PERSON BECOME? What are the candidate's possibilities and growth potential?
3. WHAT DOES THE PERSON NEED TO GET THERE? What experience does the candidate still need for the position aspired to?
4. WHAT PLANNED COURSE OF ACTION SHOULD BE TAKEN? What action is needed to fill the gaps in the candidate's experience?

One aspect of individual development plans deserves emphasis. Most of the initiative and the work must come from the individuals themselves. To be sure, the company has a vital stake in the matter and typically does a number of things to assist in the process. Nevertheless, good executives cannot be developed unless the persons do a large share of the work. Since in this chapter we are concerned with company action, our discussion necessarily focuses on what managers can do to guide and aid the process.

Training on the Job

By far the most important and lasting training an executive receives is on-the-job training. In all types of work there is no adequate substitute for actually doing the operation; this applies to executive planning, direction, and control fully as much as it does to selling or operating a machine.

Supervisors or other executives close to operations can make work experience much more valuable if they will *coach* the people being trained. Just as athletic coaches make suggestions, watch performance, point out weaknesses, and encourage athletes to do better, so may executives help their subordinates to learn on the job. Good coaches need to understand the emotional as well as the intellectual makeup of their proteges and to use discretion in the time and the manner in which they make suggestions. They need to cultivate mutual respect and a desire for improvement. Conceived

---

[2]Formulated by George B. Corless, Exxon Corporation.

in this manner, the combination of work experience plus coaching can become a powerful tool for executive development.

When an individual is a candidate for the position of an immediate boss, the *understudy* method may be employed. The younger person takes every available opportunity to think through what action he or she would take if given responsibility and put in the boss's situation. The senior, in turn, welcomes suggestions and wherever practical, permits the understudy to participate in action or even to carry out particular projects on his or her own responsibility.

Often an executive cannot get all the needed training on a single job. For example, in preparing for the position of sales manager, the person may spend several years as a sales representative, two or three years in the sales promotion division, perhaps five years as a branch manager, and at least three or four years as an assistant sales manager. Many companies make a regular practice of such *job rotation* for purposes of executive training. The staffing plans described previously may provide for transfers that do not immediately put the best person available in each vacancy; instead they use some of these vacancies as training spots for individuals who are thought to have high executive potentials.

Job rotation for executive development normally assumes that a person will fill a given position for a few years and will show the ability to handle that job well before being moved on to the next position.

Training off the Job

A variety of activities are useful supplements to training on the job. The following list, while by no means complete, indicates some of the possibilities.

Committees. Committees are rarely established solely for the purpose of training. Nevertheless, they often do provide fine opportunity to sense the viewpoints of other departments and to become acquainted with problems outside the normal scope of one's position. Consequently, people may be assigned to committees partly for the training they will get from participation.

Company conferences and courses. When a company undertakes a new activity or a new approach to some function, such as operations research or management-by-results, conferences or perhaps even a whole course on that subject may be desirable. The difficulty of finding a subject and a time when enough executives can attend such courses places a definite limit on how far this type of training can be carried.

Industry contacts. Literally thousands of trade associations hold meetings and make studies on various problems relating to their particular industries. Work with such trade associations, or with professional associations, provides a range of new ideas and an opportunity to explore problems with persons who are not indoctrinated with the same company approach. Trips to other offices or plants often have the same broadening effect.

University courses. Universities are giving increasing attention to executive education and often provide a variety of courses on business subjects. Many companies encourage their executives to take courses in areas where they have limited background. Also, several universities are offering intensive 4- to 12-week courses in top-management problems; these are particularly valuable for persons who are moving from departmental positions to jobs demanding wider perspective.

Individual reading. Few executives have the time or the energy, after a busy day, to study long and difficult books. They often do gain much information, however, from regular reading of trade periodicals and professional journals. Also, if they are assigned some special project, they may do considerable outside reading.

Adaptation of off-the-job training to individual needs is particularly important because the executive has only limited time to devote to such purposes. The executive has a major job to perform and, in trying to get the maximum benefit from on-the-job training, does not want to slight this major assignment. Consequently, the off-the-job training should have real significance for the individual to justify the additional effort it entails.

EXECUTIVE COMPENSATION

Plans for executive selection, promotion, and development will lead to limited success unless the executives believe that their compensation is reasonable. To round out the picture, then, we need to take a brief look at such issues as base salaries and pensions, executive bonuses, stock options, and nonfinancial compensation for executives.

Base Salaries and Pensions

Basically, setting salaries for executives may be approached in the same way as pay for lower-level employees.

1. The different positions are compared with one another in order to establish a reasonable internal alignment. Usually salary grades are not necessary, but the several positions should be at least ranked and some means used to determine the approximate spread between the different positions.
2. Executive salaries are related to outside compensation. This is difficult, because comparable jobs in different companies are hard to find. Usually it is possible, however, to set the president's salary in some reasonable relationship to companies of similar size in the same industry. Also, salaries of junior executives frequently tie into, or overlap, those established under the

employees' salary administration plan. With both ends of the "salary curve" established, a general curve for the entire group can be drawn.

3. Allowances for individual differences are made by establishing a range from starting salary to maximum for each position.

This approach to executive salaries is far from exact. The relative importance of positions is hard to measure and is likely to be colored by the efficiency or the inefficiency of the particular incumbent. Nevertheless, a decision as to salary has to be made, and this approach is as fair as anything yet devised.

Because of the uncertainty in evaluating individual positions, and also because there can be a wide difference in the individual performance of persons holding the same position, a wide salary range often with a 50% spread from the minimum to the maximum for a given job is customary. For example, it might be determined that the president should be paid somewhere between $65,000 and $100,000 per year, whereas the sales manager should be paid between $40,000 and $60,000 per year. This still leaves room for considerable judgment regarding the specific salaries, but there are at least some general guides from which to work.

Executive Bonuses

Many companies use bonuses for their executives. In fact, one recent study shows that approximately 50% of all companies use this method of compensation in one form or another. Bonuses enable the company to vary executive compensation in good and bad times, and they serve as an important incentive.

The use of a bonus plan is illustrated by a lumbering concern that recently received stockholder approval for an executive bonus fund. A 6% return on the total stockholder investment is first set aside from net profit; then 20% of any profit in excess of this amount is put into the executive bonus fund. The division of the fund among the several executives is determined by the board of directors. Actually, percentage shares amounting to approximately three-fourths of the total fund are assigned at the beginning of the year, at the same time that base pay for the executives is set. The remainder of the fund is kept in a "kitty" and is used to reward special performance during the year.

Variations on this general pattern can be made with respect to the size of the total fund and also the division of the fund among the several executives. But the general idea of a fund somehow related to profits is fairly common practice. Of course, many special bonus arrangements are designed to meet particular situations. For example, a sales manager may receive a bonus on total sales volume. Whenever such special arrangements are made, care must be taken to make sure the executive works as a member of the total management team, even though the bonus is determined by only one or two factors.

When executives have an opportunity to earn a large bonus, the size of their base salaries is usually cut. In general, the base salary plus the average bonus that will be earned over a period of years should about equal the total amount that would have to be paid a comparable executive earning salary alone.

Stock Options

Executives may be given an opportunity to buy stock in their company for several reasons. Some people believe that stock ownership will significantly increase an executive's interest in company welfare. In other cases the company may not be able to pay executives a cash salary and bonus large enough to retain their services, and some form of stock bonus or stock option is used to supplement the cash compensation. By no means the least important reason for using stock options and similar schemes is an attempt to help executives meet their personal income tax problems.

Since income taxes rise sharply as the amount of the annual income increases, many executives find that a large portion of their bonus has to be paid to Uncle Sam. Consequently, executives would prefer to have their income relatively stable, rather than large in some years and small in others. Even better, they would like some arrangement to have their financial returns from the company classified as a capital gain on which the income tax is substantially less than on current income. Stock option plans, which give an employee the privilege of purchasing the company stock at some stipulated figure, may help an executive meet these personal income tax problems.

The laws and rulings on such matters are highly technical, but in general they provide that if executives buy stock below the current market value, they have to consider the difference between their purchase price and the market value as current income. Under special circumstances, they may be given an option to buy stock at close to the market price prevailing when the option is granted, then wait for the price rise before exercising the option, and still count their profit as capital gains. If executives hold their stock over a period of years and the market value rises in the meantime, they can, of course, sell the stock at the higher price and treat the rise in value as a capital gain. In general, then, stock options do not enable executives to avoid personal income tax. They may, however, give them more flexibility in adjusting the time when the income is considered to be earned, and possibly the income from a stock option may be treated as a capital gain.

Nonfinancial Compensation

In thinking about executive compensation, we should recognize that virtually all managers are motivated by nonfinancial considerations as well as the cash payment for their services. In fact, after salaries enable them to live comfortably, the nonfinancial factors become increasingly important. For example, some persons respond to the urge for power, others desire social prestige, and some will sacrifice additional income for security. Improving the company's position in its industry or otherwise "winning the game" is often a strong spur, and the desire to create something and to render social service is a more common motive than is generally realized.

The ability of a company to provide such nonfinancial compensations usually is not a matter of deliberate decision by the board of directors; nevertheless, they are vital forces in enabling the company to attract and retain competent executives, and they should be recognized when decisions are being made regarding financial compensation.

SUMMARY

An able corps of executives is crucial for the execution of any strategy. The selection and the development of executive talent often is given inadequate attention, however, because problems are not diagnosed far enough in advance and because personal relationships may make an administrator reluctant to take the necessary action.

A systematic approach to building the needed corps of executives includes: (1) anticipating executive requirements through advance organization planning and forecasts of the positions to be filled along with specifications for persons needed to fill them; (2) taking an inventory of executive talent available within the company; (3) developing tentative plans for using the available talent to fill the anticipated positions, and noting needs for further training or additions; (4) helping individuals to meet their current and planned responsibilities through on-the-job and off-the-job training, and (5) providing compensation that will attract the quality of executives required and keep their morale high.

Larger companies may find printed forms and standardized procedures helpful, whereas the central managers in smaller firms may use the same method of attack with no formal paper work. In fact, there is always danger that the use of forms will become a substitute, rather than an aid, for the careful thought that development of good executive personnel demands.

Flexibility in the use of this systematic approach is necessary to adapt it to individuals. Executive development is always a personalized matter, and no standard approach will fit all situations exactly. Application to a particular group of persons, or to a single department within a company, calls for ingenuity, especially in preparation for major changes.

QUESTIONS FOR CLASS DISCUSSION

1. Many more women and members of minority groups are currently being trained for managerial positions which for years have been filled almost entirely by men. (Women now make up over forty percent of the labor force, and in many business schools about the same percentage.) What effects do you foresee of this enlarged pool of talent on (a) competition for managerial positions, (b) managerial compensation, (c) selection and training policies of companies?

2. "Our policy is to search out retirees or semi-retirees whom we think can help the bank," said the personnel director, a vice-president of a growing and successful medium-sized bank in a very large urban area. "Earnings last year were excellent because net income increased substantially, because expense was controlled rigidly and because effective income tax rates decreased. . . . Other operating expense (which includes all personnel costs) as a percent of average total resources decreased to 2.93%. . . . Another measure of efficiency in which we take great pride is total resources per staff member which was $1.49 million at the year end." Do you think that age when hired leads to efficiency? Explain.

3. How do executive personnel problems and the practical ways of dealing with such problems differ in Stage I, Stage II, Stage III, and Stage IV companies (described in Chapter 17)?

4. How should the concept of "equal opportunity" be incorporated into the executive personnel practices examined in this chapter? Should preference in selection be given to any categories of candidates—such as blacks, women, native-born, mature, agnostic, etc.—which at present have disproportionately low representation in a tier or level of management jobs?

5. Multinational corporations increasingly are using local citizens of a country in managerial positions of operations in such countries. And, several developing countries have laws requiring the use of their citizens in managerial positions of subsidiaries located in their country. (a) Do you think this strong emphasis on the use of local "nationals" is desirable? Explain the pros and cons. (b) If foreigners are permitted to hold only one or two positions in upper management of a subsidiary, which positions should the multi-national parent fill with outsiders? (c) If a foreigner is placed in a subsidiary, should he or she be paid the same salary that a "national" would receive in that position? (d) From what countries should a multinational corporation recruit its regional and headquarters managers? How should such managers gain adequate understanding of conditions in the several countries that they supervise?

6. "The economic mission of some companies permits a lot of individual initiative and freedom of action, but many other firms such as public utilities and mass production operations require steady dependability to create the services people need. No organizational arrangement can change these basic requirements.

Consequently, most of the younger generation that defies regulated behavior would be misfits in the latter type of business and should not be hired." Do you agree with this statement? Should organizations be modified to accommodate rebellious youth, and if so, how?

7. (a) When should executives be brought in from other companies? (b) How can this be done with the least disruption of morale to individuals already working for the company? (c) Does such action indicate a failure on someone's part in executive development duties? (d) How does the concept of a dynamic strategy, emphasized earlier in this book, relate to the preceding questions?

8. How do executive recruitment, development, and compensation differ in a fast-growing company and a company with stable volume?

9. If a diversified corporation decides to use a particular division as a "cash cow" (see Chapter 15), what can it do to retain and motivate highly competent executives?

10. A professor of nursing and family life at a local university has approached you, the training director, to sell you a series of 10 weekly lunch-hour seminars for working parents called "Balancing Work and Family Life." Your firm, the largest in the area, holds many training sessions for all levels of employees, but the training is ordinarily technical in nature and deals with the special tasks of particular jobs. You have references from the professor and have called several friends in the training business around town. One said that such issues had not surfaced as an employee concern. Another said "highly popular with a small, self-selected group but the Friday sessions always ran overtime—1 and a ½ to 2 hours." A third said: "We bought it but it seemed to be only pregnant women who were interested." Your staff psychologist prefers individual counseling rather than group discussions. In view of the high and growing percentages of working women and single parents in the labor force, would you select such a seminar for your company?

CASE 20
Scott-Davis Corporation (R)[1]

Scott-Davis is one of the top five producers of food and household products. Starting with several food lines, it grew steadily primarily because of its effectiveness in marketing. Household products, which could also be sold through retail grocery outlets, added to volume and profits. Then growth slowed down, and failures of two new products raised doubt about the mystique surrounding the company's marketing

---

[1]Adapted from J.E. Schnee, *Study Guide and Casebook* for Newman and Warren, *The Process of Management*, 4th ed. (Englewood Cliffs: Prentice-Hall, Inc., 1977), pp. 65–69. Reproduced by permission.

skills. Five years ago Martin Richmond replaced an aging Chairman and Walter McGill moved into his former position as President of the Food Products Division.

Both Richmond and McGill have moved vigorously to revitalize Scott-Davis. McGill has sought to "build a fire under the sales organization." As he explained to a consultant brought in to assist in the process:

"Under the Marketing Director (in addition to our strong field sales organization), we now have a product group manager who supervises the work of anywhere from three to seven product management teams. Product management teams are charged with developing programs for advertising, promotion, packaging, and pricing which they feel represents sound marketing programs for the one or more specific products to which they are assigned. (See Chart.)

"This arrangement, while it caused certain problems initially, has worked out very well. Our biggest difficulty, recently, has been to recruit and keep top-flight people in the field sales organization. We have always tried to promote from within but in the last five years, we have had increasing difficulty in this respect. Nowadays the people coming out of school don't seem interested in sales as most of us were when I joined the organization over thirty years ago. Even our company, where sales has always been the center of attraction, is having more trouble getting the kind of people we want.

"For several years now, our customers, chains, supermarkets, and drygoods stores have gotten larger and tended to centralize more of their purchasing. This demands that we develop an even more professional field sales organization. Our sales people must not only stock shelves and work with store managers on displays and deals but must understand the structure and politics of buying decisions. In this way we can match our sales efforts with customer buying frameworks and build a proprietary relationship between ourselves and our customers. Thus positions in our sales organization should have infinitely more challenge and respectability than in the old days when we laughingly referred to ourselves as 'peddlers.' "

McGill went on to describe the company's efforts to attract and develop college and graduate school business students:

"In the last four years, the company has hired over one hundred graduates and put them into our sales training program. We overpay them in order to get them and move them into management positions, even before they are ready, in order to keep them. Yet over this period, we lost almost 50 percent of these cadets. If they move into good district and regional posts, they can earn as much or more (counting commissions and bonuses) as their counterparts in product management posts, but they won't stand still. About one-quarter of the group we 'lose' stays with the company in staff or product groups but we really don't need them there as much as in sales management.

"When you talk to them about why they are leaving, you get the same answers: 'too much travel,' 'I don't like selling,' or things like 'I can't identify with the products.' I'm beginning to wonder what kinds of crazy ideas they get in college these days."

McGill asked the consultant to work with Dick Stahlings, head of the management planning group in the Personnel Office, to develop ways for improving the national sales organization. The two have observed field operations and, at McGill's suggestion, later held a three-day conference.

For instance, the consultant attended a salary review meeting in which National Sales Manager, Phil Abel, was reviewing a Regional Sales Manager's evaluations and recommendations for his District Managers. Stahlings normally joined in such discussions, and the consultant went along. At one point, R. Sanger the Regional Sales Manager, said:

"I wish we could do something for Carter (a District Manager). He is very loyal to Scott-Davis, and I can always depend on him to carry out instructions with great care. He has been getting only token raises for several years because he is already at the 'good' level in his salary range. In fact, his raises have not kept up with inflation so actually he has had a decrease in salary."

Abel interrupted, "But you agree his performance never has been, and never will be, 'superior.' It takes more than just loyalty to go to the top of the range. If he needs more money, and he probably does, encourage him to push for a larger bonus."

"I'd sure like to see Chris Borg in that spot," said Stahlings. "Within two years as product manager she has really put our dried soups on the map. You'd see some action in any district she managed." Sanger winced, knowing Borg's reputation for aggressiveness, and observed, "I'm sure we would, but we already have a long-time career person in that job. Let's look at some of my other people."

Stahlings arranged the three-day conference at a nearby resort for all the marketing executives, including the regional managers and marketing executives from other divisions of the company. Several senior executives agreed to serve as a panel on the last afternoon to hear and respond to issues developed earlier.

Many issues were discussed at this meeting, with high turnover in the sales management training program being but one of five main topics which Stahlings placed on the agenda. The consultant, who attended this meeting as an observer, noted that despite Stahlings' efforts to dig into the causes of the high turnover, there apparently was little real interest.

Each time Stahlings sought to steer the group into a deeper analysis of causes by introducing specific cases, the discussion tended to drift back to generalizations and then to other issues on the agenda.

The national sales manager, Phil Abel, virtually cut off the discussion by saying, "Look, Dick (Stahlings), let's stop worrying about high turnover in the 'jet program.' Perhaps, if we had a little higher turnover at the district levels, we wouldn't have this problem. We have a certain number of district managers who were promoted as a reward for good sales efforts rather than because they had high management potential. Others did a good job as district managers for a while but may have burned themselves out or become 'fat cats'. Most of the time, when I suggest we move someone who I feel is in one of these categories, the regional manager leaps in defense or tells me there isn't a better person ready. If we get some of this dead wood out of the road, we wouldn't lose so many of our 'jets'."

The consultant was surprised at the tense silence which followed this statement. Finally a regional sales manager, Peter Moore, asked, "Are you sure about those 'dead wood' or 'fat cat' labels? Have we got people who are not doing a better job than their replacements could do or are we allowing their . . . (district managers') . . . lack of potential for regional management jobs to color our appraisal of how they carry out their district jobs?"

Some discussion followed and then the meeting broke for cocktails and dinner. The consultant sat with a group of three regional managers which included Peter Moore. He asked Moore to elaborate on his earlier comment and Moore laughed and said, "No thanks! I'm probably already in the doghouse. It's fine for them . . . (national executives) . . . to talk about 'dead wood' and 'fat cats' but I'll be damned if I'm going to sacrifice a lot of good D.M.s . . . (district managers) . . . just to give their charm school graduates a managerial position. It takes time for a district or regional manager to get to know the structure and politics of the buying organizations that must be dealt with. Good sales managers need the charm and drive of the old peddlers plus the instincts of good lobbyists. These are not things you learn in school or practice behind a desk writing reports. Most of these kids lack the background and experience to move as fast as they want whether they realize it or not. Besides, many take a D.M. job merely as a stepping stone either into product management or to another company."

After dinner, the consultant took a stroll with Peter Moore and tried again to draw him out. After some evasiveness, Moore made the following statement:

"The real problem here is not with regional and district management. It's at division and corporate level. When they created these product management teams, field sales suddenly became a bunch of second class citizens. Product management has all the glamour, good money, and like the senator in a book I just read, 'unencumbered by responsibility they act with great authority'.

"We have a lot of good men in district and regional management jobs—and don't be mistaken, when Abel . . . (national sales manager) . . . was sounding off about 'dead wood road blocks', he was talking to us as well as about D.M.s. Is a person automatically dead wood or a fat cat just because he or she doesn't want to move up to national sales or higher? There are lots of regional and district managers who have gone as high or higher than they want. I'm not complacent! I have one of the best regions, in terms of results, in the company. I want to make it still better but do I have to aspire to becoming president to convince them I'm not complacent? How can I take good D.M.s and move them aside or back to smaller districts just because they don't want a regional manager's headache? How can I tell them that they are road-blocks; that merely doing a good job isn't enough; that we need their spot as a stepping stone for some climber who will be gone in less than two years?"

Later that evening, at the bar, the consultant found from "off the record" comments that several of the regional sales managers seemed to share Peter Moore's sentiments but most avoided making direct comments on the subject. One regional manager, Gil Green, however, disagreed:

"You guys can talk all you want about how unfair it is, but the fact of the matter is we can't afford to keep people in key districts or regions unless they have real upward ambition and potential. Those jobs must be filled by persons who use them to train themselves for the top. We can't afford the luxury of filling these positions with people who are content to do a 'good job' there for the next twenty years."

A heated debate between Moore and Green followed. Several regional managers who previously had agreed with Moore either left or remained quiet. At the end, Green chuckled and said, "What are we getting so hot for? I don't know why we're arguing about district and region jobs anyway. Our real problem is to attract and keep more trainees at the lower level, isn't it?"

Questions

(1) What are the primary issues raised in this case and what is causing them?

(2) If you were the consultant, what would you recommend to President McGill?

PARTIAL ORGANIZATION CHART

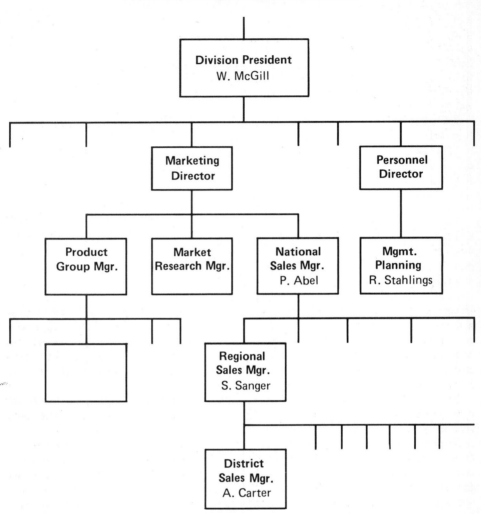

INTEGRATING CASES

Strategy and Organization Structure

Solartron Electronics[1]

With its new ownership, Solartron again faces questions of basic organization design. Its impressive history has created both strengths and weaknesses which must be weighed in making these design decisions.

Original Mission of the Company

The company was founded in southern England by two engineers, first to repair but soon to manufacture laboratory instruments. Oscilloscopes, amplifiers, and a variety of testing equipment were developed during this early period. Within two years, funds were badly needed for expansion. Mr. John Bolton then joined the firm providing capital and becoming managing director. He continues to be the leading personality in overall management.

Bolton quickly observed that customers expected Solartron to carry inventory for prompt shipment and to grant credit. This tied up capital. And since the company sold only in the British Isles, inventory turnover tended to be slow.

Electronic systems, which were just becoming popular at that time, offered attractive diversification. By building systems only on customers' orders, inventory turnover could be increased. Moreover, the potential growth was high, and opportunities for creative innovation were great. At this early stage, Solartron chose a strategy of focusing on electronic systems for customers who had relatively little sophistication about the equipment. Thus, Solartron would perform a service in system design as well as equipment manufacture.

From that time to date, laboratory instruments have been the bread-and-butter line (the cash cow) while electronic systems have provided the excitement and the high growth prospects.

Solartron works on several different kinds of systems. Among the more important are (a) radar simulators, used by several governments to train air pilots; (b) electronic cash registers, to be used by a chain of drugstores—Boots—to compile data for prompt sales analysis and for perpetual inventory control; (c) high-speed

---

[1]This case is based on three much longer cases prepared by Mr. Peter Brengel under the supervision of Professor Kenneth R. Andrews for l'Institut des Methodes de Direction de l'Enterprise (IMEDE), Lausanne, Switzerland.

checkweighers, to be used in packaging of consumer products at speeds of up to 120 per minute; (d) cybernetic teaching machines, to be used to train punch-card operators to prepare cards accurately; (e) X-ray spectrometers, to be used to make quantitative analyses of metals and chemicals; (f) other state-of-the-art research done on contract for potential customers.

Organization to Achieve the Mission

Bolton had a conviction that the best organization to carry out Solartron's strategy would be a series of highly decentralized, democratic operating divisions. "To the extent possible, managers at all levels will be given the opportunity to discharge their responsibilities as they think best within the broad framework of agreed-upon plans."

He conceived of each product line being run by a small company with a potential maximum of about 500 people. This was to facilitate face-to-face communication and informal coordination. The organization was to be "flat" with a minimum of supervisory levels and very limited staff at headquarters. Bolton explained, " 'Peaky' organizations and the 'great man' approach to management fail to reap the full potential of human ingenuity. Really, managerial needs are, like vacuums, abhorred in nature. They will ultimately be filled of their own accord—especially when competent people are readily at hand to fill them."

Actually eight separate operating companies were incorporated, with Solartron Electronics becoming a "Group." Consistent with this pattern, central research was set up as a separate company as was a production division. These latter two divisions could take on subcontracts from the product divisions, and they could (and did) accept contracts from outside the Group. The service units at headquarters were few and small—accounting, finance, personnel, and overseas sales.

With respect to people, a company document states, "Our emergent philosophy of life lays great stress not only on the importance of the individual as a person, but on the essential need to devise a 'permissive' system in which individual initiative is nurtured and encouraged to make its maximum possible contribution to the whole. . . ." Status was minimized. No executive parking places and a common lunchroom symbolized the shirt-sleeve atmosphere. However, the large number of companies created a lot of board of director positions (highly respected in British circles), so engineers at Solartron could move into prestigious jobs at a much lower age than was possible in most other companies.

The atmosphere was heady. A variety of interesting new systems to work on, welcome to innovative ideas, open discussion with anyone in the company, prestigious titles—all helped. Bolton generated enthusiasm, and made speeches on modern management to distinguished groups. Solartron was recognized as a great place for a young engineer to work. And, in fact, Solartron attracted an unusually able group of scientifically educated people.

Company stock was made available to managers and key employees. This process continued so that Bolton held 40%, other executives 40%, and outsiders only 20%.

The results from a financial viewpoint were less impressive. During the years when overall employment grew from about 400 to 1,500, Solartron was barely able to break even. And this was possible only by capitalizing a lot of research and development expense. Several difficulties emerged in trying to make the organization design work effectively:

1. Bolton explained to stockholders that designing and building systems for a diverse group of unsophisticated customers was turning out to be much more time-consuming and expensive than anticipated. Solartron has been trying to master a lot of different businesses all at the same time.
2. The volume of work in each product line has been too small and irregular to permit the product divisions to build up their own engineering and production capacity. Each division can afford specialists only for market research, general system design, and customer relations. When it receives an order, it must subcontract most of the work to the research division for detailed design and to the production division for actual fabrication. The consequence of (1) and (2) has been very high overhead for the volume of shipments.
3. With demand coming unpredictably from several product divisions, scheduling and coordination in the research and production divisions has been poor. Frequent design changes after work was started have made the situation worse. The results are slow deliveries, high costs, and very weak accountability.
4. The personnel attracted to Solartron lack production and profit orientation. And the internal procedures of the company (its deliberate informality) provide no controls to keep its high-flying engineers in line. In other words, Solartron failed to match its decentralized structure with informal and formal controls which are necessary to get work completed on time.
5. The instrument division maintained its market position during this period but it was handicapped by being treated in much the same way as the divisions focusing on new systems. The nature of its marketing and its production call for more conventional planning, organizing, and controlling.

Strategy Revision and its Consequences

During the growth phase, described above, Solartron developed an impressive public image and a variety of system-product lines in various stages of marketability. But the cash drain could not be sustained. The accumulated deficit, after eliminating capitalized R&D, was equivalent to about $2 million, and the net book value of stockholders' equity was cut to $1.25 million.

Three interrelated changes have been made: (a) emphasis is switched from seeking new system-products to making existing lines profitable; (b) the organization is centralized and streamlined; (c) overhead is sharply reduced.

Operating activities are now in only two divisions, instruments and systems. The instrument division is virtually self-contained with its own engineering, production, and marketing—all located in a separate building. For systems, the old product line divisions have been disbanded. Now there are single, consolidated departments for R&D, production, and marketing. The two service units at headquarters are administration (accounting, finance, etc.) and personnel. Decisions for each division are made by a small group of department heads and corporate officers.

Bolton remarks, "In some respects, especially concerning our organization, we appear to have made a complete reversal, but I suppose that is all part of the process of organic growth. It appears to me that a period of decentralization of initiative and authority is necessarily followed by a period of centralization. . . . Each phase brings its benefits and its counteracting problems."

The manager of the Instruments Division is pleased with the change in his set-up. For the first time in about eight years he knows where he stands, and is free to adjust all his operations to best suit the instrument business.

The new systems division is facing more problems of adjustment. There are morale problems with people who are no longer active "directors" of a company and with others who relished the atmosphere and promise of the former structure. There is now reserved parking for executives. Some managers have resigned, but those remaining are an unusually talented group.

A longer-run difficulty is that the functional departments within the Systems Division include no people with overall product responsibility. Product-line coordination—from the cultivation of a prospective customer to the delivery of a system tailored to the customer's needs—is thrust upon a busy group of senior executives.

The transition to the new organization is still in process. The hope, of course, is that the change can be made without losing too many of the past strengths. Thus far, most of the changes have been in formal organization. Revised planning and control procedures are still being worked out. Slowing that task is the fact that most of the young managers have little experience in a systematized operation.

A recent financial projection anticipates that at least a year will be required to get the combined operations on a break-even basis. However, by the third year the hope is that volume will be up 35% and profits at a reasonable level.

New Corporate Governance

In a move to help Solartron gain access to long-term capital, its stockholders recently sold 57% of the outstanding shares to Schlumberger Limited for the equivalent of $4.6 million. Schlumberger is a large worldwide concern which makes geophysical studies for oil and mining companies. It pioneered in the use of seismographs, and has since expanded its services to the oil industry. Long a user of electronic equipment, Schlumberger has recently acquired several equipment manufacturing firms in Europe and U.S.A. This diversification, however, is quite small relative to Schlumberger's primary activities.

In commenting upon the new ownership Bolton said, "As part of the worldwide network of electronic companies that Schlumberger is building up, Solartron can benefit from the marketing, research and development, and possibly production activities of its sister companies; at the same time Solartron represents their major electronic interest in the U.K."

Bolton continued, "I thought it was very important to take advantage of the experience and ability of our parent company's top people. For this reason I asked Mr. Jean Riboud of Schlumberger to sit as chairperson of the Solartron Board, and our request has been accepted. Two other European executives of the Schlumberger organization will also serve on the Board. . . . These men will contribute significantly, and not impede my freedom of action as Managing Director of Solartron."

Prior to the sale of the large block of stock, Solartron's Board consisted of six of its executives and two merchant bankers, with Bolton as chairman. Bolton used board meetings primarily to explore new ideas since operating decisions were made more frequently by the executives concerned.

Mr. Schneersohn, a director of Schlumberger European who negotiated the stock purchase, has these observations: "I wish to emphasize that money is the least important qualification that we offer. Schlumberger's primary attraction is their ability to contribute administrative management and technical skill, probably in that order of importance. . . . In return, we are looking for a company with a good product produced in relatively small quantities, a good organization and, most important, (a company) with one or two really good management people. Solartron seems to be a company that will fit well into the group structure that I have in mind. . . . Looking critically, I would say that Solartron has been run a bit loosely in the past and stands in need of more effective management control. Solartron has always stressed growth. This is no longer as important a requirement as in the past. . . . Overall, we are very pleased to have Solartron as a member of our European electronics group."

Question

What changes, if any, in (a) organization and (b) other managerial arrangements should Schlumberger make in Solartron Electronics?

EARLY ORGANIZATION CONCEPT

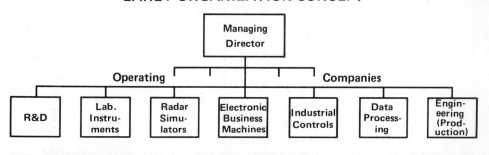

REVISED ORGANIZATION

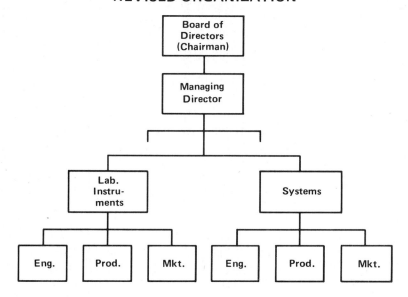

THE HANCOCK COMPANY[1]

The Hancock Company is a chemical manufacturer primarily making drug chemicals such as vitamin preparations, sulfa drugs, antibiotics, hormones, and reagents. Its products are used by pharmaceutical and drug manufacturing concerns; veterinary products manufacturers; food and beverage manufacturing houses; educational, commercial, and industrial laboratories; industrial establishments; and ultimate consumers to whom the products are dispensed by hospitals or physicians or on physician's prescription through retail drugstores.

Sales of the company have grown very rapidly, as shown by the following record:

Year	Sales	Year	Sales
25 years ago	$ 8,100,000	5 years ago	$ 81,100,000
20 years ago	8,370,000	3 years ago	93,200,000
15 years ago	15,660,000	2 years ago	108,500,000
10 years ago	37,350,000	Last year	111,700,000

Company profits have grown with sales, and its ratio of net profits to sales is about average for the large firms in the pharmaceutical industry.

No small part of this great expansion of sales has been the fruit of the extensive program of research that the company began in the early thirties and has continued to the present time. This department contains units specializing in organic and biochemical research, microbiological research, and physical and inorganic chemical research, plus a development unit specializing in chemical technology and production.

Since new products are frequently introduced into the line and the methods of use of the company products are constantly changing, the relative importance of different product groups in the sales pattern is constantly shifting. From time to time, new products or modifications of old products are introduced that do not fit exactly into existing product groups but overlap almost any product grouping that may be set up in either their research, production, or sales characteristics.

For example, the following table shows the shifts in the percentage of total company sales volume experienced by a number of product groups, which for obvious reasons cannot be named specifically, during a period of 20 years.

These shifts in product line and sales volume naturally create planning and coordination problems, and this case is primarily concerned with the dynamic nature of the company's business. First the general organization will be briefly described; then measures taken to date for guiding individual products will be explained.

---

[1]This case was written primarily by Professor Ralph S. Alexander for The Executive Program in Business Administration, Graduate School of Business, Columbia University. Reproduced by permission.

**Percent of Total
Company Sales Volume**

Product group	25 years ago	15 years ago	5 years ago
A	11.3	10	5
B	9.6	8	5
C	7.7	2	—
D	7.3	5	1
E	7.0	12	0.5
F	6.9	3	2
G	3.9	4	3
H	3.9	2	0.3
I	3.8	4	1
J	—	15	27
K	—	7	6
L	—	—	15
M	—	—	12
N	—	—	9
Others	38.7	28	13.2

General Organization

The general organization structure is indicated on the following chart. Naturally the size and range of activities of each section varies, as is indicated in the following discussion.

Plant	Location	Employees	Products
Main	Baltimore, Md.	4000	antibiotics, vitamin preparations, hormones, general drugs
Seneca	Oswego, N.Y.	1200	antibiotics, sulfa drugs, reagents, laboratory chemicals
Sawmill	Three Rivers, Mich.	1500	vitamins, hormones, antibiotics, general chemicals
Beacon	Beacon, N.Y.	550	specialty products for retail sale under Hancock label

Production. Production is carried on in four plants, each of which has a manager, manufacturing manager, plant engineer, personnel manager, purchasing clerk, and financial services manager.

In the Production Division there is a central Manufacturing Planning Department that (1) determines production requirements for all products and subdivisions consistent with production capacity, inventory levels, minimum costs, and related factors; (2) schedules all manufacturing, packaging, and quality testing operations; (3) establishes inventory levels for all goods and materials in accordance with established policies; (4) requisitions materials and containers; (5) maintains stock records for all types of goods and materials; and (6) collects and informs other divisions about production schedules, deliveries, inventories, batches, costs, charging rates, yields, raw material factors, and all other production matters.

Marketing. The Manager of Special Sales handles all sales to competing or complementary firms and to all other house accounts. The Manager of Distributive Branches has charge of physical distribution of the products of the company through its four branch warehouses located at San Francisco, Chicago, St. Louis, and New York, and from the Baltimore plant. The Manager of Sales Service handles complaints and adjustments and plans and supervises the handling of the paperwork order routine. All advertising and sales promotion work is directed by the Manager of Advertising and Sales Promotion.

The General Sales Manager directs the activities of the field sales force through 20 district sales managers, each of whom supervises about 10 sales representatives who call on wholesalers and pharmaceutical and veterinary manufacturers to make sales, on retailers to do missionary work, and on physicians and hospitals to do general promotional work. The Manager of Sales to Pharmaceutical and Veterinary Manufacturers and the Manager of Sales to Distributor Accounts develop policies, prepare plans, and generally supervise contact with the groups of customers they serve, working through the General Sales Manager in so doing. Neither of them has any direct official authority over sales representatives. The Manager of Sales to Industrial Accounts directs a force of 25 sales representatives; they have no necessary contact with the district sales offices beyond occasionally calling on those offices for desk space and secretarial service.

Research. All medical, biological, and biochemical research either is done in the laboratories in Baltimore or is closely administered from there. The Development Section, which assists in the development and improvement of production processes and in the solution of production problems in the various plants, has representatives stationed in each of the several factories.

Also in the Research Division is the important Quality Control Section, which is responsible for directing the establishment of quality standards and methods of testing. Purchased materials cannot be used in any plant until released by Quality Control; finished goods cannot be shipped until released by this section; and all wording on labels and advertising concerning quality must be approved.

Engineering. The Engineering Division is divided into three departments. The Design and Construction Department has charge of planning, construction, and installation of new equipment and facilities including buildings. The Industrial

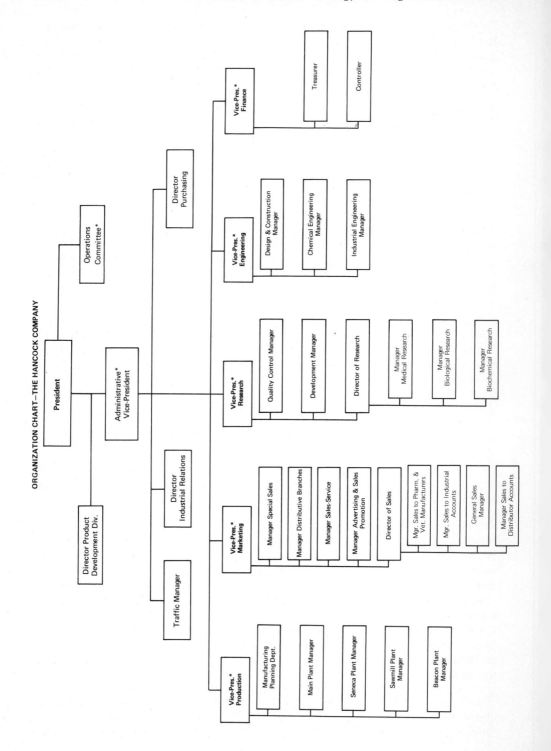

ORGANIZATION CHART—THE HANCOCK COMPANY

Engineering Department devotes its efforts to setting standards through time and motion studies and statistical analysis. It also studies operating methods and develops and plans improvements in equipment. The Chemical Engineering Department deals mainly with planning, development, and improvement of processes, including pilot plant operations on new products.

Records and finance. The activities of the Controller's Division and the Treasurer's Division are centralized in Baltimore, where a fairly complete battery of IBM machines is maintained. Customer billing is done there, and branch plant and warehouse payrolls are handled there. These divisions perform the normal accounting, tax, and financial functions, but they do not take an active part in the interpretation of financial data in terms of management problems.

Traffic. The Traffic Department handles all traffic operating procedures, selection of carriers, tariff work, schedules, and requests for rate revisions. Branch plants and sales branches comply with traffic instructions issued at Baltimore.

Purchasing. The work of the Purchasing Division is somewhat more decentralized. The purchasing clerks in each plant are authorized to write purchase orders up to $500 for any one order. In all other cases they requisition the central Purchasing Division in Baltimore.

Industrial relations. The Industrial Relations Division develops and administers employee relations programs to maintain high quality personnel and desirable employee attitudes. These programs include: personnel research, placement and education of employees, collective bargaining, wage and salary administration, employee services, security, health, and safety.

Special Arrangements for Products

The organization of The Hancock Company just described represents an expansion of the structure the company has had for many years. With the increase in dollar volume and number of products, however, a number of difficulties have arisen. To overcome these difficulties, a Product Development Division has been set up. The history of this division illustrates the character of the internal strains facing the company.

Product development. New products are typically discovered or at least developed in the Research Division. After a useful product has been found and the production processes have been worked out in the laboratory, it is then passed on to the Engineering Division for pilot-plant operation, planning of new equipment, and carrying through to the factory floor until the product is ready to be produced as a full-fledged member of the line.

Unfortunately, this arrangement for the technical aspects of new product work fails to solve all the problems connected with it. When a new article is ready for production and commercial use, it still has to be tested and released for distribution by the Food and Drug Administration and has to be worked into the sales line. If this work were left until the test-tube and pilot-plant stages were completed, the ultimate results from a profit standpoint might prove to be far from satisfactory. The commercial aspects of a new product need to be explored concurrently with its technical features. Stories are current in the industry of a firm that spent half a million dollars developing a new product only to find that its total possible sales were about $50,000 a year. The sales department was too heavily burdened with the day-to-day crises that attend the work of capturing and holding customers to do much with the task of exploring the market possibilities of a new product let alone that of appraising its probable effect on the cost and profit structure of the firm.

For many years top executives of The Hancock Company personally gave attention to this work, but as the company grew they had less and less time for it. After several make-shift arrangements, top management decided, five years ago, that a separate Product Development Department was needed. Mr. Paul Stanton was appointed head of this new unit, and he set out to explore the areas within which his unit might operate to the profit of the company.

Mr. Stanton soon felt himself handicapped by what seemed to him a lack of product policy on the part of the company. For example, there seemed to be no clear-cut determination as to the extent to which the company should sell products, such as insecticides, that were somewhat outside the drug field. There also seemed to be some confusion whether the company should develop a line of products to be sold over the retail drug counter under the Hancock label.

Exhibit A

(Statement for Organization Manual prepared by Mr. Stanton shortly after his appointment as Director of the newly created Product Development Department.)

Director, Product Development Department

Reports to: The President.

In carrying out his responsibilities he:

1. Correlates and directs all matters related to the establishment of new products by the company.
2. Surveys and analyzes the sales and market possibilities for present and new products in existing and new fields.
3. Determines sales potentials for products in development or suggested for development.
4. On the basis of market surveys and analyses, recommends development or production of new products.
5. Estimates actual sales of new products to guide the planning of necessary production and sales facilities.
6. Coordinates the company's efforts in developing new products, including the recommending of manufacturing capacity, sales programs, and distribution plans.
7. When necessary, carries out initial sales of new products prior to turning them over to the Marketing Division.
8. Studies and reports on the probable effects of the introduction of new products on the financial, cost, and profit structure of the company.

During the next three years, Mr. Stanton attempted to build up the organization of the Product Development Department and to expand its activities. (A statement of duties that Mr. Stanton prepared for inclusion in the company organization manual is given in Exhibit A.) In the process of doing so he engendered antagonism among several of the operating divisions to such a point that neither he nor his assistants were able to obtain the cooperation that was so vitally necessary to the proper performance of the department's functions. For example, he urged that the Product Development Department should employ a small force of specialty salespersons to conduct pilot marketing programs in the course of introducing new products to the market, and that most new products should not be turned over to the Marketing Division until the bugs had been worked out of the system of distributing them as well as producing them. This did not exactly endear his department to the members of the Marketing Division. Finally, Mr. Stanton made a connection elsewhere and left the company. His place was taken by Mr. John Boyle, a very able young man with excellent technical and business training, pleasing personality, and great vigor and drive, who previously had been an executive of a smaller company.

Marketing research. About this same time, at the suggestion of the Administrative Vice-President, careful study was given to the establishment of a Marketing Research Department. This step was finally decided upon when Mr. Boyle assumed direction of the Product Development Department (now elevated in the organization hierarchy to the status of a "division") and the new department was made a part of the enlarged division. Since Mr. Boyle was not able immediately to dissipate the lack of sympathy between his division and the sales groups and since the tasks of sales analysis and making sales estimates still remained in the Marketing Division, the work of the Marketing Research Department has been confined mainly to explorations of the market for new products and to economic studies for top management.

Product managers. The large number of products made by the company and their diversified nature caused other complications. Each product, or at least each group of them, possessed problems of its own with respect to its improvement, the control of its quality, its production, and its marketing. For example, the problems involved in handling narcotics are especially unique in the rigid control required because of government regulations and the socially dangerous nature of the products themselves. Several years ago, the management decided that these problems required special attention. A product manager was appointed to devote attention to the narcotics line. Later, other persons were assigned to this type of work, each specializing in the problems of a separate group of products.

The responsibilities of a product manager are described in the organization manual of the company as follows: The product manager is responsible for assisting general management and operating executives in improving the profit contribution of the products that are assigned. Acting in a staff capacity, the manager is responsible for continuous analysis, evaluation, and coordination of all company activities affecting these products, including sales, production, scientific, purchasing, engineering, financial, and related matters. Serving as a focal point in the company for information about the products, he or she makes recommendations, after close collaboration with interested operating departments, on policies and programs designed to strengthen their competitive position and increase their profits. The product manager is responsible for assisting in the management of contracts affecting the products and for maintaining outside contacts and relationships as assigned.

The results are not always happy. The operating executives sometimes complain that the product managers get in their way. For example, a product manager often feels the need of visiting members of customer trades in order to get a more realistic idea of the market conditions for the assigned products than can be obtained from a desk in Baltimore. This is resented by the Marketing Division executives who feel that relations with a customer are a delicate matter and should not be disturbed by other representatives of the company whose questions might raise embarrassing doubts in the minds of the customers visited.

Likewise the sales executives are sometimes embarrassed by the estimate of sales possibilities issued by product managers. In estimating the sales of a product, the latter usually deal in terms of sales potentials, the volume that Hancock would get if it got all the sales of the product. When the sales executives submit their estimates of what they actually expect to sell during a coming budgetary period, general management sometimes fails to distinguish between the differing bases upon which the estimates are made, to the chagrin of the marketing group.

Initially, the product managers were to focus on *existing* products, serving as staff directly to the Operations Committee, whereas the Product Development Department was to concentrate on *new* products. However, the distinction between modification of existing products and new products was hard to draw in practice. Also, individuals who became familiar with a new product had a background that could be valuable in watching its market position, profits, changing costs, and other warnings of trouble ahead. For these reasons the product managers have been merged into the Product Development Division. The personnel picture (excluding secretarial help) under the merged setup is as follows:

Product or Activity Group	Personnel	Salaries
General Administration	1	$ 54,000
Miscellaneous Products	1	36,000
Industrial Products	1	30,000
Narcotics and Vitamins	3	68,000
Veterinary Products	1	32,000
Pharmaceutical Products	2	62,000
Specialties	1	20,000
Antibiotics	2	52,000
Laboratory Chemicals	1	30,000
Inorganic Chemicals	1	30,000
Total	14	$414,000

Examples of Current Issues

Typical of the problems that arise almost daily at The Hancock Company are the following:

Proposal A. At a recent meeting of the Pharmaceutical Manufacturers Association, Hancock's chief engineer picked up the information that Upjohn is about to patent a new process for the production of cortisone (used in the treatment of arthritis) that presumably will reduce the manufacturing costs to a tenth of present costs. Further, Upjohn is willing to license one or possibly two other manufacturers to use the new process. The license fee would be a flat sum to cover most of Upjohn's research cost on this project, plus a royalty on production of about 25% of the new manufacturing cost.

Hancock's Process Development Section has also been seeking a way to reduce cortisone costs. The researcher in charge of the project says they have several interesting possibilities, any one of which might "break" in a few months. Of course, the output of any new process would have to be subjected to clinical tests, pilot plant operation, and FDA approval.

Proposal B. An assistant to the Manager of Sales to Pharmaceutical and Veterinary Manufacturers proposes that Hancock's product "L" be promoted to veterinary suppliers. "L" is a hormone product that under some circumstances aids human female fertility, and it has achieved a recognized position in the ethical drug field. Recently a veterinarian who works with fox farmers reported that "L" apparently had beneficial effects in breeding foxes. (Most foxes will breed only once in the spring of the year. If a female does not conceive, as often happens, she will have to be maintained for another year with no pups.)

The veterinary sales group in Hancock is always alert to possible animal use of drugs that have proven helpful to humans. The conversion of antibiotics to animal use, for example, has been a profitable development for Hancock. So, the Manager of Sales has forwarded the "L" proposal to the Veterinary Product Manager in the Product Development Division with a note: "This looks like a good prospect. Can Manufacturing supply us with the large quantities needed for our market at reasonable prices?"

The Veterinary Product Manager has, to date, made two telephone calls. The Director of Medical Research said that the person who knew most about "L" was now deeply involved in "the new pill" project and should not be distracted because of the high priority potential of this project. The Sawmill Plant Manager, where "L" is now manufactured, said that any large increase in output would require new facilities; he further commented, "I'd prefer to keep veterinary production out of our plant. It upsets quality control. To get costs down you cut corners, and the people are likely to carry this attitude over to other products."

QUESTIONS

(1) What changes in organization do you recommend to enable The Hancock Company to administer both existing and new products more effectively?

(2) Are other changes, in addition to those you propose for the organization, needed?

(3) Explain how Proposal A would be handled in your setup. Be specific about who will provide ideas, information, judgments, coordination, and binding decisions, and indicate the sequence and timing of decisions.

(4) Do the same for Proposal B.

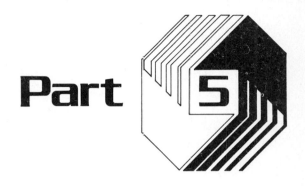

Part 5

GUIDING THE EXECUTION

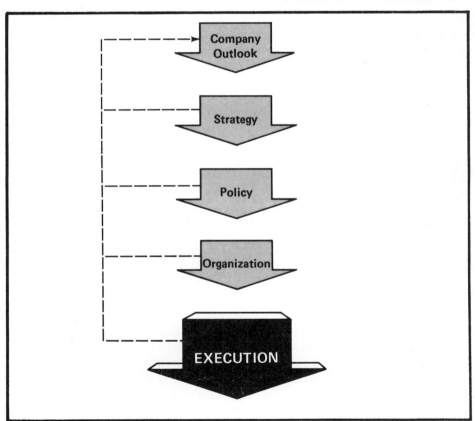

SHORT-RANGE AND LONG-RANGE PROGRAMMING

14

Establishing strategy and policy, building organization, and developing executives are all vital to the management of any enterprise. However, there is still another group of activities that requires executive attention if the company is to achieve its goals. Steps must be taken to "get things done." This group of managerial duties we shall call *execution,* and the term is used here to cover:

I. *Short-range and long-range programming,* which deals with what actions are to be taken when.
II. *Activating,* which is concerned with direction and motivation.
III. *Controlling,* which seeks to assure that the results actually accomplished correspond with plans.

Steps in Execution

A large part of the time of junior executives is devoted to execution, that is, detailed programming, motivating, coordinating, and controlling. Central managers also must give a significant portion of their energy to getting things done. Policy formulation and organization planning set the stage, but no services are rendered and no profits are earned until action by first-line operators actually takes place.

Again, a word of warning about these three steps in execution is appropriate. In practice, they are not watertight compartments that take place in just the order listed. Management is a continuing and complex activity in which the various phases are often mixed up. A program for putting a major policy change into effect may cut across minor policies, organization, and control procedures. Data developed in day-to-day control often are used in preparing short-range and long-range programs. Nevertheless, for purposes of understanding management, the division of execution into phases is essential, and the outline puts these various parts into logical relationship and perspective.

Nature of Programming

Our preceding discussion of managerial tasks has put primary emphasis on *what* should be done and has given little attention to deciding *how much* and *when.* Programs add this element of sequencing and timing.

Once an objective or "mission" has been established, the executive making the program first decides what principal steps are necessary to accomplish the objective and then sets an approximate time for each. When an entirely new activity is involved, the program may also indicate who is to undertake each of the steps.

While central management can delegate most detailed scheduling work, it should take an active part in shaping broader programs. Key issues faced in this important task will be examined in terms of:

1. Short-range programming.
2. Critical path analysis.
3. Long-range programming.

SHORT-RANGE PROGRAMMING

Programs for Special Purposes

Numerous short-range programs are drawn up and carried out in each department of a company. These programs deal with activities ranging from launching a sales campaign to installing air-pollution control in a power plant. Normally, central management delegates this kind of programming to department executives. However, when several departments are involved, a large amount of capital is committed, or when delicate external relations are at stake, central management takes an active part. Often for such situations the program is not neat and simple, as the following examples reveal.

Expansion program. The operators of the hotel facilities at the Grand Canyon wished to develop an expansion program that would enable them to give better service to the many people who want to visit this scenic spot. Investigation revealed that two types of changes were needed in the physical facilities—betterments that would improve the service in the existing plant and major expansion of room and restaurant facilities. Any significant addition to total capacity, however, would have required more water; additional water could be secured only by investing $1,500,000 to run a pipeline to a spring several miles up the canyon. Pumping water from the bottom of the canyon to the brim would require additional electric power. This would probably mean bringing in a new power line. Moreover, a new sewage line would have to be laid in a ditch blasted out of rock.

The investment in these new facilities would not have been justified if they were to be used only two or three months of the year. Consequently, serious attention had to be given to attracting visitors to the canyon in the spring and the fall when, in fact, the weather is more desirable than in the summer.

There were additional factors involved, but enough have been listed to indicate the need for some kind of a program that would divide the total problem of expansion into logical *parts* and indicate a *sequence* in which these parts should be attacked.

In this case, a time schedule probably could be established only for the first two or three steps, but the program did indicate all the steps involved and a sequence for dealing with them. Thus the program laid out a systematic approach to a very complex problem. Since the desirability of expanding facilities depended so largely on extending the tourist season and building other off-season business, changes in facilities were restricted to betterments until the practicality of the promotion program was tested.

Tax revision program. The desirability of a special purpose program also became apparent to a company that sought to reduce the federal excise tax on its products. The company quickly recognized that the chances of success would be materially improved if the industry as a whole presented its case rather than each manufacturer operating independently. Clearly, the newly formed industry association should make contacts with all of the influential congressional representatives and senators. To be most effective, however, the pleas of the manufacturers needed to be backed up by significant pressure on the part of local constituents. This meant that the retailers, and to the extent possible the consumers, should be enlisted in the overall campaign.

If the efforts of all these people were to be most effective, there was need for a common program in which the role of each group could be clarified and some attention could be given to the timing of the several efforts. In a situation such as this, involving many independent enterprises and people, a detailed program and schedule covering an extended period probably would be of little value; but at least a general program was essential to get coordinated effort. Since the program basically concerned public opinion, there was great need for personal leadership and flexibility as the work proceeded.

Programs for special purposes, such as the two just discussed, are often difficult to project very far into the future. Forecasts of future needs and of operating conditions may be unreliable because the activity is so new and different. This unreliability of forecasts makes it hard to set dates and to estimate volume of work. Moreover, strategy in meeting competition or winning support of people often plays a key part in such programs, and it is difficult to decide on strategy very long in advance.

Basic Steps in Programming

The examples of programming given in preceding pages indicate that skill is needed in fitting the general concept to specific situations. Nevertheless, six elements or steps are found in the majority of instances. Managers will do a better job of programming if they are fully aware of the nature and the importance of each of these steps.

1. Divide the total operations necessary to achieve the objective into parts. The division of an operation into parts is useful for planning, organization, and control. Planning is improved because concentrated attention can be given to one part at a time. Organization is facilitated because these parts or projects can be assigned to separate individuals, if this will give speedier or more efficient action. Such division also aids control because the executive can watch each part and determine whether progress is satisfactory as the work is carried on without waiting for final results.

If the division into parts or projects is to be most effective, the purpose of each step should be clearly defined. The kind of work, the quality, and the quantity should all be indicated.

Often a single part of a large program is itself again subdivided; in fact, this process of subdivision may be continued for three or four stages. For example, an anniversary program of a department store may include as one of its parts a sale of men's suits. This sale in turn may be divided into buying, advertising, displaying, selling, etc. The advertising project may be divided up into selection of merchandise to be featured, writing the copy, preparing illustrations, scheduling the days and the newspapers in which the ad will appear, and integrating the suit sale ads with other advertisements of the store. Thus the concept of programming is applicable to situations ranging from large operations down to the work of a single individual.

2. Note the necessary sequence and the relationship between each of these parts. Usually the parts of a program are quite dependent on each other. The amount of work, the specifications, and the time of action of one step often affect the ease or the difficulty of performing the next step. Unless these relationships are recognized and watched closely, the very process of subdividing the work may cause more inefficiency than it corrects.

Any necessary sequences are particularly significant. For example, a motel chain had to complete refinancing its debt before embarking on a West Coast expansion. These necessary sequences have an important bearing upon scheduling. They tend to lengthen the overall time required for the operation, and since a shorter cycle gives a company more flexibility, the necessity of delaying one action until another is completed should be carefully checked.

3. Decide who is to be responsible for doing each part. If the operation being programmed is a normal activity for the company, the assignment of responsibility may already be covered by the existing organization. In an airline, for instance, the opening of a new route involves sales promotion, personnel, traffic, air operations, maintenance, and finance; but assignment of each of these activities is already set by the established structure. However, if the program covers a new operation, then careful attention should be given to the question of who is responsible for each part. These special assignments do not necessarily follow regular organization relationships and create only a temporary set of authorizations and obligations. In a very real sense, a special team is formed to carry out the program.

4. Decide how each part will be done and the resources that will be needed. The amount of attention that must be given to each step in setting up a program will depend upon the circumstances. Sometimes standing methods and standing procedures will cover almost all of the activities (as is true of military programming), and in other situations questions of "how" will be fully delegated to the persons responsible for each part. Nevertheless, the executive building the program must have enough understanding of how each part will be performed to appreciate the difficulties in the assignment and the obstacles that may be encountered. In particular, the executive needs some understanding of the *resources* that will be necessary to carry out each part of the program.

For realistic programming the need for (a) materials and supplies, (b) facilities, and (c) people must be recognized. Then the availability of these necessary resources should be appraised. If any one of them is not available, another project to obtain the resource should be set up; this may be treated either as an additional part of the original program or as a subdivision of the project needing the resource. For example, if necessary personnel are unavailable, then plans should be made for hiring and training new employees. Many programs break down because the executive preparing them does not have a practical understanding of how each part will be carried out and the resources that will be needed.

5. Estimate the time required for each part. This step is, of course, closely related with Steps 3 and 4 above and really involves two aspects: (a) the date or the hour when the part can begin, and (b) the time required to complete the operation once it is started. Possible starting time will depend upon the availability of the necessary resources. The time when key personnel can be transferred to a new assignment, the possibility of getting delivery of materials from suppliers, and the seasons when customers are normally in the market all have a bearing on when it is possible to begin any given part of a program.

The processing time once the activity is begun is typically estimated on the basis of past experience. For detailed scheduling of production operations, time-study data may permit a tight scheduling of activities. For a great many activities more time is consumed in conveying instructions and getting people actually to work than is required for the actual work itself. Unless this "nonproductive time" can be eliminated, however, it should be included as part of the estimated time.

6. Assign definite dates (hours) when each part is to take place. This overall schedule is, of course, based on the sequences as noted under Step

2 and the timing information assembled under Step 5. The resulting schedule should show both the starting dates and the completion dates for each part of the program.

Sometimes considerable adjustment and fitting is necessary to make the final schedule realistic. A useful procedure is to work backward and forward from some fixed date that is considered to be controlling. In promoting a new dress fabric, for example, the importance of the selling season may be so great that the retail season is taken as fixed and the schedule is extended back from these dates. In other situations the availability of materials or of facilities may be the controlling time around which the rest of the schedule is adjusted. It is, of course, necessary to dovetail any given program with other commitments the company may have.

Another important qualification is to make some allowances for delay. It is not desirable as a general practice to have such allowances all along the line as this may tend to create inefficient performance, but there should be safety allowances at various stages so that an unavoidable delay at one place will not throw off the entire schedule.

Programs may have to be revised, of course, to take account of unexpected opportunities or difficulties. If each of the six steps just outlined has been well done, however, these revisions usually can be merely adjustments of the initial planning.

Strategic Thrusts

Thrusts were identified in Chapter 5 as one of the key parts of a company strategy. These are the clear-cut moves to be started in the near term as steps toward a longer-range goal. Opening a plant in Taiwan, or building a salesforce to contact retailers directly instead of relying on wholesalers are examples.

Short-range programming is an excellent device to assure that these thrusts receive adequate attention. The normal pressure of continuing day-to-day activities tends to push unusual work into "tomorrow." Also there may be simple resistance to change. Consequently, if a desired thrust is merely added to a list of things-to-be-done, it is likely to develop slowly and may get buried. In contrast, if a program including the features just outlined is prepared, action should result.

Contingency Programs

A "fire emergency plan" is a classic example of a contingency program. If the event occurs, a whole series of predetermined actions by assigned persons are to take place, and a special set of rules guide the behavior of all other people. The event is likely to be so serious that interruption of normal operations is warranted. And the need for prompt action justifies a standard response even though the precise location and size of the fire cannot be predicted in advance.

Most contingencies, however, do not warrant such an elaborate standby program. By far the most usual way to deal with new situations is to *revise* prevailing programs. As outlined in Chapter 23, actual (and predicted) progress is frequently compared with the program; then whenever significant deviations are spotted, a revision of the program is at least considered. The revision technique has several advantages over contingency planning: It avoids the costly effort of preparing many plans which are never used. And the revision can be fitted much more closely to the specifics of the new situation than is possible when a plan is devised far in advance.

Contingency programs may be desirable for critical events such as a labor strike, a sudden influx in orders from customers, a major break in foreign exchange rates, or the like. The factors which justify contingency programs include: (a) the need for prompt action before the revision process can take place, (b) the seriousness that the contingency will occur about as predicted. In a company that has a well-developed planning and control system, not many contingencies meet these tests.

A secondary benefit of preparing contingency programs is training to deal with changes. Even though an alternative program is never used, the managers who prepared it are more aware of where adjustments may be necessary and whom to consult. Psychologically, they are more receptive to change. Actually, most of this training benefit can also be obtained from fully exploring alternatives when the master program is adopted.[1] When planning skill is developed in decision analysis, the training benefit of contingency programs is reduced.

Think in abstract terms

CRITICAL PATH ANALYSIS

Development of PERT

Critical path analysis is a special technique for studying and controlling complex programs. It was developed in its more elaborate form as an aid in the design and the production of Polaris missiles, and it has been used for virtually all subsequent space age projects. The particular technique applied to the Polaris program was called PERT (Program Evaluation and Review Technique); many variations of the basic ideas have been used before and since PERT received wide publicity. The technique is of interest to us here because the central concepts of critical path analysis can be helpful in many programming problems.

---

[1]The term "contingency planning" is sometimes used in decision analysis. When the future is uncertain and two or more "states of nature" have to be considered, we may plan what we would do under each "contingency." Usually such projections are only concerned with estimating possible results, and they are not a commitment to a course of action, as in programming.

The design and the production of Polaris missiles involved a staggering number of steps. Specifications for thousands of minute parts had to be prepared, the parts had to be manufactured to exact tolerances, and then the entire system had to be assembled into a successful operating weapon. And, *time* was of the essence. The basic steps in programming, just discussed in the preceding pages, were applicable; but the complexity of the project (and the fact that many different subcontractors were involved) called for significant elaborations in the programs.

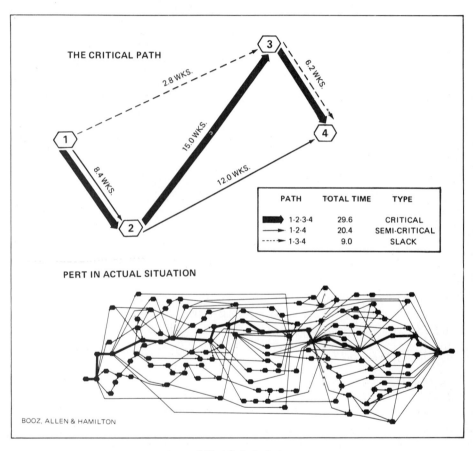

Critical Path Analysis

The upper chart shows, for a very small segment of the total network, how the critical path is computed. The lower chart indicates how complex the networks may be.

Major Features of Critical Path Analysis

The basic ideas involved in this refined programming technique are:

1. All steps and their necessary sequences are placed on a diagram (see the following charts) so that the total *network* is explicitly set forth.
2. The estimated *time* required to complete each step after the preceding step has been finished is recorded.
3. Then by adding the required times for each step in any necessary sequence —or path—the path having the longest time can be identified. This is the *critical path.*
4. If desired, the difference between the total required times of the critical path and other paths can also be computed. Such differences are *slack times* or margins in which delays would not hold up the final completion.

Now, having identified the critical path, management can focus its attention on either reducing the time of steps in this path or at least watching closely for any delays. Also, management knows from slack time data where high pressure to meet estimated processing times may be unwarranted.

The calculation of the critical path should, of course, be repeated as work progresses because some steps will be completed faster than anticipated and others will be delayed. These new data will certainly change slack time estimates, and a different critical path may arise.

With careful thought, the total network of steps and sequences can usually be prepared with reasonable reliability—at least for programs dealing with physical products. Time estimates prove to be less reliable, especially for new and unique activities. To deal with this uncertainty regarding time, often three estimates are obtained from the persons who will be doing the work: optimistic, most likely, and pessimistic. Then a weighted average of these three elapsed-time estimates is used.

In critical path analyses of complex programs, such as Polaris, computations are sufficiently involved to make use of an electronic computer very helpful. In simpler programming situations, such as building construction, a computer is by no means essential.

General Applicability

The main features of critical path analysis have application to many programs that are not sufficiently complex to warrant the complete PERT treatment. Often just the preparation of a network chart of sequences of steps will clarify the interconnections between actions taken by various departments. The launching of an additional magazine by a publishing firm, for example, was aided by such a chart.

Moreover, the concept of a critical path can be used in many programming problems even though an entire network is not charted. In a company making nationally advertised men's shirts, for instance, the critical path runs from line-building through sales promotion to plant scheduling and on to order filling. Acquiring grey goods, training personnel, and similar steps have to be done, but they are not "critical" from a timing viewpoint because of the early leads necessary in sales promotion. Programming in other companies may be geared to the erection of new facilities or perhaps the training of personnel. In all these situations, a recognition of what steps are part of the critical path will direct management efforts in "getting things done" to the crucial spots.

A word of caution is in order. Critical path analysis focuses on time, and few companies have data that enable them also to fit costs into the same framework. We would like to know how much speeding up or slowing down each step will change costs. Usually such cost estimates—even rough ones —are prepared only after critical steps are identified and an executive is trying to decide whether to make a change in plans. Similarly, critical path analysis does not deal with alternative ways of reaching a goal. The network is presumed to be settled. Of course, if the analysis identifies a serious bottleneck, then management may resort to a different method and may establish a new network.

Nevertheless, for many programming problems, timing is the major consideration. And for such programming problems, critical path analysis can be a valuable refinement.

LONG-RANGE PROGRAMMING   *x power plants*

Nature of Long-Range Programming

Programming increases in difficulty as the time-span covered is extended, yet such extension is well worth the trouble in some circumstances. We have been discussing program cycles ranging from a few months to perhaps 2 years. Long-range programming seeks to extend the period covered to, say, 5 to 10 years.

Underlying any long-range program should be a well-defined strategy. The strategy establishes the basic directions and the criteria for which the program is developed. Policy, considered in Chapters 6 through 14, provides the guides and the limitations within which action is to fall. Establishing these is, of course, part of the total process of long-range planning. The *program* introduces a time schedule—the how much and when aspects—and thereby sets the intermediate objectives (which in turn become the targets for more specific and detailed short-range programs).

Applications

One of the classic examples of long-range programming is the conversion of the Bell System to dial telephones. Forecasts of telephone usage—based on population growth, higher gross national product (GNP), and telephoning habits—indicated that manual switching could not handle the load. Besides, automatic dialing would improve service and hopefully cut costs. So the goal was clear, but the magnitude of the task was tremendous. Design of equipment had to be refined for recording calls, relaying long-distance calls, tieing in with independent companies, and the like. Completely new exchanges had to be built, millions of dollars of switching equipment had to be manufactured, and millions of consumer units had to be produced. Before any of this physical equipment could be installed, people—engineers, installers, and operators—had to be trained. Incidentally, company policy dictated that the transition was to be made with only seconds of interruption in service and no layoffs of regular employees. The public had to be prepared for the switch and educated to use the new equipment; utility commissions had to be kept advised. And the multimillion dollar investment had to be financed.

This incomplete list suggests the range of elements in the program. Many of the preliminary steps were taken ten years before the conversion in that area was finished. And with new developments in technology and markets, the process is still going on.

The Bell System example is enlightening because (a) a whole series of interrelated steps were programmed years in advance, and (b) the programming was done in terms of several elements—markets, engineering, facilities, personnel, and finance—not for just a single element such as finance.

The magnitude and the predictability of the Bell System is unique, of course. Nevertheless, quite different companies can use a similar approach. The Suburban Fuel Company, for instance, did long-range programming even though it was a small-town firm with net worth of only $100,000. For many years the family owning Suburban Fuel had been in the retail coal business. When fuel oil began replacing coal, the company also became a fuel oil distributor. Finally, when the grandson of the founder became president, he decided to withdraw from coal altogether and he set up a long-range program to do so. The program involved: (1) gradual disposition of coal facilities—no new equipment, sale of some trucks, and sale of the coal yard as a plant site in 5 years; (2) strengthening the fuel oil distributorship—adding trained burner service workers, leasing more trucks, closer tie-in with sale of oil burners, and more systematic promotion of annual service contracts; and (3) withdrawal of most of the capital invested—the fuel oil distributorship to be "spun off" as a separate company, and liquidation of the original coal company at favorable tax rates. Initially a 5-year program, it actually was completed in 4½ years because a good opportunity to sell the coal yard turned up.

In this example, we again see (a) a series of interrelated steps extending over a period of years and (b) a plan that embraced several different elements. The timing of the various steps was subject to adjustment, as was also true in the telephone conversion, and no attempt was made to spell out detail several years in advance. But the master plan provided a definite guide for actions all along the way.

The preceding examples may be misleading because only a small portion of business firms actually prepare long-range programs in a clear-cut fashion. The main reason is simple. Most companies cannot, or do not, forecast the nature and the volume of their activities for 3, 4, or 5 years, let alone 10, years ahead. Perhaps they know the direction they would like to go (their objectives); but uncertainties about competition, technical developments, consumers' actions, political changes, economic changes, and the like make timing hard to nail down.

Because of the difficulty of precise long-term forecasting, we need to examine carefully the benefits the typical company can reasonably hope to obtain from long-range programming and problems that must be overcome if it undertakes this management device.

Major Benefits of Long-Range Programming

A central management that embarks on long-range programming usually seeks these advantages:

(1) *Long-cycle actions are started promptly.* An automated plant takes at least 2 or 3 years to design, build, and get in operation. A bright idea for a new product often requires 3 to 5 years for research, development, testing, and process engineering before it is ready to be marketed. Recruiting and training salespeople for electronic computers takes several years, assuming they cannot be hired away from established competitors. Raising a new crop of timber for lumber may consume 25 years.

Long-term programming indicates when such actions should be started. Opportunities will be missed or crises in servicing customers may develop unless a company takes early action. To fail to act is equivalent to a decision to postpone entry into the contemplated operation. Even though predictions of need are uncertain, there may be no feasible alternative to starting down the road.

By preparing the best program that available knowledge will permit, a company increases the probability that it will be aware of when long-cycle actions should be initiated.

(2) *Executives are psychologically prepared for change.* Many actions embraced in a long-range program need not, and should not, be taken immediately. They can await a year or more of actual experience, and by then some modification in the original plan may be desirable.

Nevertheless, even though the program is changed, the process of preparing it aids adjustment to new conditions. As a result of preparing the program, the idea that some kind of change in response to shifts in the environment must take place is already accepted. And probably the nature of the adjustment will have been considered; for example, transfers of personnel, refunding a bond issue, or local production in a foreign country. Then, when conditions are ripe, executives are prepared to move quickly. Good news or bad news may arrive unexpectedly, and the company response may differ from the program; but the ability to recognize the opportunity, to appreciate the range of actions that are necessary, and to get in motion has been sharpened by the mental exercise of preparing (and revising) a program.

The pace of technological and economic change is quickening. Product life cycles are shorter and competitors move into profit opportunities more quickly. Consequently, the ability of a company to adjust promptly to shifts in its environment is crucial to getting ahead and staying ahead in modern competition. So this psychological preparation for change that we have been discussing is more vital to central management today than it was a generation ago.

③ *Actions having long-term impact are coordinated.* Often an action taken to meet an immediate problem also significantly affects future operations of the company. For example, to get quick coverage of the West Coast territory, one firm gave exclusive distribution rights to an agent who also sold related products. The agent was successful in establishing itself as the local representative and the immediate problem was resolved. However, the firm soon expanded and diversified so that it needed a strong national sales organization of its own sales representatives; and the successful independent distributor on the West Coast proved to be very difficult to supplant.

The selection of executives for key posts, the licensing of a company patent, and acceptance of a government subsidy are further examples where short-run solutions may prove troublesome in the future.

Now, if a company has a long-range program, central managers will be able to sense more easily whether current decisions do, or do not, fit into a consistent pattern of long-term development.

Note that in this list of benefits of long-range planning we do not include "a blueprint for future action." Only rarely are prediction and control of conditions several years hence sufficiently accurate to permit close adherence to a 5-year plan. But such a program does help identify actions that should be initiated now, it lays a psychological base for prompt adjustment to opportunities in the future, and it provides a pattern so that action on today's problems can be compatible with long-range plans.

Problems Involved in Long-Range Programming

Preparation of a long-range program of the type we have been discussing needs guidance. Key problems are what topics and period to cover, how revisions will be made, and who will do the work of developing the plans.

Topics covered. Too often so-called "long-range programs" are merely financial estimates conjured up by a bright young analyst in the controller's office. Such estimates take the form of annual profit and loss budgets for perhaps the next 5 years.

For operating purposes, dollar sales estimates have little meaning unless someone has thought in terms of the products that will be sold, the customers who will buy them, the prices obtainable in face of competition, and the selling effort necessary to obtain the orders. Similarly, the projected volume of goods must be conceived in terms of the resources necessary to produce them: plant capacity, trained workers, flow of raw materials, engineering talent, etc.

Therefore, long-range programs should be stated in physical terms. But it is impractical to spell out such plans in full detail; instead, management should identify the crucial factors and build the program in these terms. One of the keys to successful programming is this identifying of topics to be used; omissions of vital factors will make the program unrealistic, whereas too many factors will make it unwieldy.

The long-range program should also be translated into dollar results: revenues, costs, profits, and capital requirements. Dollars are the best common denominator we have, and the financial results are an important aspect of any program. Use constant dollars first; then adjust for inflation. But the main point is that dollar figures alone are not enough.

Period covered. Five years is the most common period covered by long-range programs. There is no magic in this figure, however. Logically, long-range plans should be based on the necessary elapsed time for such important action as product development, resource development, market development, or physical facility development. Three years may be long enough, or perhaps 10 years will be needed.

In fact, the necessary time varies. Resource development may have to be started 8 years before materials will become available, while 2 years may be adequate for market development. To deal with this variation, several companies (a) plan an action *in detail* only when a start is necessary, or (b) prepare a comprehensive program for 3 or 4 years ahead and then extend the period only for those areas requiring longer lead times.

Revisions. As results of first steps become known and new information about external conditions is learned, long-range programs need revision. The typical procedure is an annual review in which near-term actions are planned in greater detail, a new year is added on the end, and adjustments are made in plans for the interim period.

Under this scheme, programs are revised several times before the period to which they apply finally arrives. This provides flexibility in long-range programming. It also entails a lot of work, and executives may become cavalier about plans for 5 years hence since such plans will be revised over and over again. These disadvantages of several revisions are strong reasons for restricting the period covered and making sure the benefits listed previously are actually being obtained.

Who prepares long-range programs? Central managers will certainly participate in long-range programming, as noted in Chapter 19. Equally clear, however, is the fact that they cannot do the job alone. They will need help obtaining ideas and specific data. Moreover, if the programs are to guide current commitments and if there is to be the desired psychological effect on executives throughout the company, <u>all major executives</u> should participate—research directors, plant managers, sales managers, and the like. Since these executives have other pressing duties, they probably will ask a staff assistant to help with long-range planning.

Altogether, then, central managers, operating executives, and their staffs probably will contribute ideas, data, judgment, or approval. A bit complicated, yes, yet necessary if the programs are to be carefully prepared and are to serve their intended purposes.

Long-range planning in small firms. Long-range planning in a small Stage I enterprise is necessarily more informal than in a large company. Executives lack the time to prepare detailed estimates; often basic historical data will never have been recorded. Nevertheless, the basic process as outlined above should be followed, for the small firm has as much to gain by anticipating opportunities as a large one.

One entrepreneur with only 16 employees has a loose-leaf notebook with alternative 5-year programs based on different key assumptions. Perhaps because of his engineering training, he has spelled out steps and resources for different rates of growth in either of three directions. The estimates are his personal, subjective guesses; but when he makes a major investment or signs a long-term contract, he has a clear idea of where the action is likely to lead him.

In addition to pressure on time, small business managers have difficulty thinking objectively about events several years away. Typically they are so immersed in day-to-day activities it is difficult to make a mental switch to a longer horizon. Preparing some estimates to present to a sympathetic board member can be a helpful discipline in this respect.

＊ Small firms should be involved in long-range planning.

SUMMARY

Through programming, a manager formulates an integrated plan covering what, how much, when, and who.

Six basic steps should be taken: (1) divide the total operations necessary to achieve the objective into parts, (2) note the necessary sequences and relationships between each of these parts, (3) decide who is to be responsible for doing each part, (4) decide how each part will be done and the resources needed, (5) estimate the time required for each part, and (6) assign definite dates when each part will commence and end.

When faced with complex programming problems, a manager can use *critical path analysis* to identify those parts of the total activity that must be watched most closely if the final objective is to be met on time.

Long-range programming follows the same steps as any other programming. However, because of the great difficulty in forecasting accurately several years in advance, long-range programs have to be revised several times.

Long-range programming is part of the more inclusive process of long-range planning. establishing strategy and setting policy are also parts; they set directions, criteria and limits. The *program* then introduces a time schedule—the how much and when—and breaks the broad plan into more specific steps.

While long-range programs must not be regarded as fixed, they do help flag actions with long lead times that should be started immediately, prepare executives to act promptly when opportunities or difficulties do arise, and provide a basis for reconciling short-run solutions with long-term plans.

QUESTIONS FOR CLASS DISCUSSION

1. In Latin America and other foreign countries, the cultural attitude toward time differs from that in the U.S. Staying on schedule is more a wish than a commitment, and even in social engagements no one expects people to arrive at the appointed hour. Explain how this attitude toward punctuality affects programming in business. What can be done to retain at least many of the benefits of programming?
2. Assume that your university is under heavy pressure to improve its performance as an equal opportunity employer. Unless it develops an acceptable program for increasing the proportion of women in higher faculty ranks and in higher administrative positions, it may lose its $18,000,000 annual research contracts funded by the federal government. What *program* do you recommend? (Be as concrete as you can—except that you may use "X's" and "Y's" for specific numbers of people.) Does the concept of programming as outlined in this chapter fit this kind of situation? Explain.
3. The president of the Springfield National Bank has decided that the bank should increase its proportion of women employees from supervisor through officers. A conservative institution with 6 branches, the bank has 22 officers and 50 additional "exempt" personnel (supervisors, managers, etc.). Only 10 of these are now women, whereas the president believes the bank will be vulnerable to social and governmental pressures until the proportion reaches 20% to 33%. Turnover in the past has been low, 7% among officers and 10% among other exempt personnel. The proportion of women at the operating level is already high. (a) Outline a program for accomplishing the bank president's goal. (b) Explain whether the programming steps listed on pages 528–531 were relevant to your task in (a).
4. A U.S. auto equipment manufacturer has purchased a European patent for an antismog muffler. To make this new product, the following major steps must be completed:

A. Decision to add product.
B. Engineering work completed.
C. Financing arranged.
D. Material purchase orders placed.

E. Production started.
F. Sales campaign arranged.
G. Initial orders received.
H. Initial orders shipped.

Analysis indicates the following necessary sequences between the above events and the estimated time required to perform the work to advance from one event to the next. (Work cannot move forward until all necessary preceding work is completed.)

Necessary sequence	Estimated time	Necessary sequence	Estimated time
A to B	60 days	C to F	2 days
B to C	20 "	D to E	40 "
B to D	30 "	E to H	45 "
B to E	75 "	F to G	60 "
B to F	30 "	G to E	2 "
C to D	2 "	G to H	10 "

(a) Prepare a PERT diagram showing the network of the above events. (b) Determine the critical path. (c) Explain how your answer to (a) and (b) would be useful in launching the new product.

5. Your boss, the vice-president and controller of Sierra Electric Utility Company, Inc., has just given you, a new member of the Planning and Budgeting staff, these instructions: "We have direct instructions from the chair of the board to prepare a new, 8-year program for changes in the generating plant using an expected growth in peak load requirements of only 1% per year, and lengthening the expected time for the completion of our joint venture in the nuclear power plant two or possibly three additional years. How much new capacity— and of what kind—will we need and when must it come on-stream?"

You have the information on page 543.

Operations at present are at capacity with no reserve. The nuclear plant under construction has been delayed by the Nuclear Regulatory Commission. Chances are 50–50 that our share will be available in the fourth and fifth years, and 95% probable that it will be available in the fifth and sixth years.

The vice-president for customer services stated that he had plans for a new, very low home-heating rate that would soak up idle capacity during the winter and help to meet his plans for a 3% growth rate in annual sales. (Air-conditioning has led to a peak demand in July.) Population increases will provide a very strong push toward meeting his plans.

The operations vice-president stated that Sierra was lucky to be able to meet demand requirements now and that, after this year, there would be no available extra power from tie-lines with other utility companies. He sees brownouts and complaints without new capacity next year. "The extra power from tie-lines (up to 60,000 kilowatts) is contracted for elsewhere next year. I don't see how we could get it back."

Natural-gas fueled plants require a 4-year lead-time and a minimum capacity of 300,000 kilowatts. Gas turbine units can be operating in one to one-and-a-half years after ordering, and each has a minimum capacity of 25,000

Peak Load Requirements in 1,000's of Kilowatts

	Last year actual	Present year	2nd year	3rd year	4th year	5th year	6th year	7th year	8th year
Peak load @ 3% growth	1,830	1,885	1,942	2,000	2,060	2,121	2,185	2,251	2,319
Added each year		55	57	58	60	61	64	66	68
Previously planned new capacity			100[1]	100[1]	50[3]		150[2]	150[2]	
Peak load @1% growth	1,830	1,848	1,866	1,885	1,904	1,923	1,942	1,962	1,981
Added each year		18	18	19	19	19	19	20	19

[1]Sierra's share of a joint-venture nuclear energy plant.
[2]Sierra's new, natural-gas-powered, generating plant.
[3]Gas turbine units.

kilowatts. They are 50% more expensive to operate than are the larger plants; purchased power (even when available) is still another 15% more expensive.

6. The future rate of inflation is difficult to predict. Assume that you are the business manager for a local hospital and are preparing a program to be presented to your board of trustees for the construction of a new wing. How will the inflation rate affect this program? How do you propose to deal with this unknown?

7. Compare the length of period you would recommend for long-range programming of (a) a telephone company, (b) the college or university you are attending, (c) a TV broadcasting station, and (d) a quiz show for TV. What are the reasons for differences in the period covered?

8. Prepare a program to reduce the total number of faculty and staff members of your college or university by 10% to meet the decline in college enrollments expected in the 1980's.

9. Many Stage III companies have created a position entitled "Director of Long-Range Planning" or just "Director of Planning." Often such staff people report to a central corporate executive and have counterparts at the division level. What should a director of long-range planning do? How will his or her work differ from that of his or her counterparts in the various divisions? To whom should each report?

10. Chapter 4 recommends the analysis of key actors as part of the basis for formulating strategy. How can this concept of key-actor analysis be used in making a program for (a) introducing a new product into the market? (b) cutting energy costs for your university?

CASE 21
Apex Internacional

The Apex Equipment Company is embarking on its first venture in foreign manufacturing. Still unsettled is how bold to be in this new thrust.

The company has a successful record in the automobile equipment *replacement* industry. Basically it waits until the major manufacturers of its kind of product produce models which are incorporated into new autos. Then Apex very carefully duplicates each model, and sells these in the replacement market. Auto supply jobbers sell Apex products to the thousands of shops, garages, and filling stations that repair autos and trucks.

Of course, the original equipment manufacturers (OEM's) also sell their products in the replacement market. However, with the passage of time there are a variety of models fitting various cars, and the volume of replacement sales on any one model is small relative to the production runs for new car use. Apex has designed its manufacturing activities to handle short production runs, and is thus able to compete with OEM's in the replacement end of the industry.

Apex has decided not to seek OEM business from the big U.S. auto producers (or foreign producers in their home country). The competitors are too big and entrenched; and such a move would require Apex to do much more R&D than at present. But the situation in developing countries which are getting into automobile production is quite different.

In a country such as Brazil, auto production starts as primarily assembly of imported parts. However, to save foreign exchange and to provide local employment, the governments of such countries push hard to increase the use of locally produced parts. Tax benefits, tariffs, and import quotas are all used. As soon as a part is available locally, barriers to imports are likely to be imposed.

Apex sees an opportunity to be an OEM supplier in Brazil—and later in other such countries. The company has demonstrated its ability to make products that work just as well as the original equipment, and it knows how to produce in relatively small quantities. One Brazilian company is already in the business but its quality is considered to be inferior. A European producer may set up a Brazilian plant. So, if Apex opens a local plant, it can promptly become a leading supplier for local OEM and replacement parts, probably with tariff protection.

Joe Androtti, Apex Production V.P. "The fastest way to get started, and with the least risk now, is to rent a small plant in the Sao Paulo area. Then when we are successful and know our way around—say, in three years—we would have to move, presumably to our own larger plant in Belo Horizonte (Brazil's third largest city, with a vigorous industrial development program). Production space can be rented in Sao Paulo—at a high price. Lead-time on the equipment delivery in the U.S. ranges from four to nine months. Then allow three months for shipping and clearing customs, and two months to get set up. That adds up to a minimum time to get started of fourteen months.

"A second alternative is to build a somewhat larger—though still small—plant in Sao Paulo. We would just postpone deciding what to do when we outgrow such a plant. Planning, approvals, and actual plant construction would probably take two years. But we should be able to have the equipment in and ready to go within that time. Unfortunately, Sao Paulo is crowded and may get worse, the smog is terrible, and the government offers no special incentives to locate there.

"In contrast, Belo is courting new industry. Maude Weaver has figures on the financial picture. It is very difficult to rent in Belo, and if we start there we would at least lay out a larger operation from the beginning. No future moves would be anticipated. The entire physical setup at Belo is more attractive than in Sao Paulo, but since more government approvals are involved we should figure on two and a half years to get started there."

Maude Weaver, Apex Treasurer. "If we located in Belo we can, in effect, get our new building at half-cost, have no real estate taxes for five years, and also receive a subsidy for training new workers. I know Brazilians have a reputation for being slow in taking official action, but two other U.S. firms told me that they had no major trouble. Their advice is to ask for your full needs while you are at it.

"My figures on our capital requirements boil down to this: Renting in Sao Paulo gives the lowest investment, but with rent expense figured in the production, costs per unit would be at least as high as those in our owned plant in Sao Paulo, and we would have to move in a couple of years.

"If we go to Belo immediately, we could hold back on some of the equipment until we needed it. Of course, working capital is (or should be) a function of actual volume rather than capacity. So our capital investment when sales are running $6,000,000 would not be much higher at Belo than at Sao Paulo—about $3,000,000 total. Production costs per unit should also be about the same. When volume moves above $6,000,000 the advantages of the larger plant at Belo would really show up.

	Sales at Capacity	Investment in Plant & Equipment	Net Working Capital
Rental plant in Sao Paulo	$ 3,000,000	$ 300,000	$ 750,000
Small owned plant in Sao Paulo	6,000,000	1,200,000	1,500,000
Full-scale plant in Belo	12,000,000	1,800,000	3,000,000

"Incidentally, Brazil has high inflation which confuses the picture a bit. But in Brazil almost everything is 'indexed', including the amount you must repay on a loan. So we are making our estimates in constant dollars.

"Now the catch is—where do we get the $1,050,000 or the $3,000,000? Our domestic business is growing and with inflation it soaks up most of the cash it generates. We can borrow $1,000,000 from the banks on short-term loans. Above that, and certainly for $3,000,000 (which is almost 25% of our present assets and 50% of stockholder's equity), we must negotiate a long-term loan. The negotiating should start six months before we need the cash."

Paul Nichols, Apex President. "Key personnel will be our bottleneck in this Brazilian venture, in my opinion. Our present agent in Sao Paulo, Salvador Silvana, has done an excellent job of importing and selling our products. And he is promoting the expansion. However, like many Latin American businessmen he has several other projects and does not want to devote his full time to Apex Internacional. He does want to handle all local sales. So, we will need a Brazilian general manager and a Brazilian production manager. I wish we had a Portugese-speaking financial person to send down, but we don't.

"From a personnel angle, a modest start where we can test and train executives would be preferable. It is particularly difficult to select executives in a foreign country where you don't know the subtleties. I'd feel better about going the Belo route if I had full confidence in the general manager.

"The general manager should know the business backwards and forwards, preferably with technical background. Maybe the general manager should work for Salvador for a while as well as here in the U.S., and help plan and negotiate. It may be difficult to attract and hold a good person for two and a half years, however. I guess we should start looking and be ready to act. Who runs the project in the meantime? Production is a bit easier because we can send a couple of engineers to Brazil during the start-up period.

"Another consideration is our organization here at headquarters. We have only an Export Manager who concentrates entirely on foreign sales. I'm not sure how involved our key department managers should or will get in far-off Brazil. Maybe we should be thinking in terms of an international division."

Howard Schaller, Apex Export Manager. "It is always difficult to know how hard to push in a foreign situation. There are at least two reasons for moving fast in Brazil. First, if we are going to stake out a major position we should get there before others do. There is room for only a couple of manufacturers in Brazil. If we move aggressively maybe we can discourage others from entering. Second, the government attitude about foreign investments might change quickly. I don't think it will in Brazil, but other countries have had sudden shifts in governments and in economic policy. If we are already set up inside the country our position is much more secure.

"Once our production capability is established, then the more support for local production there is the more we will benefit. Silvana believes we can develop a $12,000,000 volume in our line of business within four or five years. It may be optimistic, but the potential is there. With profit margins fifty percent higher than in the U.S., this should be a real moneymaker. Meanwhile, Silvana should do everything he can to build Apex's reputation for quality."

Question

Outline a five-year program that you recommend for Apex's entry as a producer in Brazil.

ACTIVATING

The wisest strategy, policy, organization, and programs come to naught until they are put into action. This need to translate ideas into action has been a recurring theme throughout our discussion, but it warrants further recognition in a separate chapter. Central management plays an important role in activating an enterprise by:

1. Creating a *focused climate*.
2. *Managing* major changes.
3. Making *MBO-type evaluations* of key executives.
4. Using *incentives* in a demanding way.

Controlling is also necessary in achieving results and will be explored in the next chapter.

*CREATING A FOCUSED CLIMATE   ᵇʰᵉʳʷⁱⁿ ʷⁱˡˡⁱᵃᵐˢ

Every established organization has its own climate, or culture. There are traditional values about customer service, spending money, accepting risks, beating competitors, dealing with Communist countries, taking the initiative, and many other matters. This climate obviously affects the ease or difficulty of carrying out a specific program. The prevailing values may make that program popular (or unpopular), and they shape local interpretations.

Careful Use of Executive Influence   ᵖʳᵉᵛᵃⁱˡⁱⁿᵍ ᵛᵃˡᵘᵉˢ.

Executives, and especially senior executives, help form the climate within their bailiwick. They cannot escape being public figures. Their behavior is closely watched for cues. The vice-president who jokingly said, "Guess I'll walk through the office in my shirt sleeves just to start a rumor," was well aware that many people would try to infer meaning from even his casual actions.

Because they are inevitably in the local spotlight, central managers should behave in a way that creates a climate favorable to the execution of company strategy. And it is actions and decisions, more than words, which convey the message. The president who is lavish with his personal expense account will have difficulty securing strong support for a cost reduction program. Likewise, the promotion of a product manager who uncovered a new market for a product will send signals throughout the organization. Specific decisions are magnified because they help generate widespread feelings and attitudes.

The importance of climate is highlighted in a recent study by McKinsey and Company. These management consultants carefully compared the central management practices in a set of companies with excellent performance records against a comparable set of companies whose performance has been "not outstanding." Differences in climate is closely associated with differences in results. Among their findings are the following.

Stress Selected, Simple Goals

The excellent companies all had a few well-recognized goals or themes. "Our company is built around customer service . . ." "Growth is essential. We expect to be the largest company in our industry within five years . . ." "Pioneers in banking . . ." Such terse statements as these illustrate an overriding goal. Usually the less successful companies did not have clear-cut, integrating concepts of mission.

To an outsider these goals seem almost naive. However, they have taken on real meaning within the companies which use them, and somewhat like a religious creed, they call forth emotional commitment.

Obviously, these overriding goal statements should be linked to company strategy. Strategy (as used in this book) has more facets; but often a tersely stated mission does capture the essence of the strategy.

A second type of goal typically found in the successful companies is more immediate short-run objectives. These are the "thrusts" in our definition of strategy; for example, "a mini-size car ready to market in 1985," or "current, error-free, computerized subscription lists by the end of the year." At any one time a successful company singles out only a few such themes for prime attention. Usually they are simple to understand, achievable, and have a strong action focus.

Of course, the thrusts or themes change as old ones are achieved and new ones are added. The more successful climate is one that avoids a complex array of themes with varying priorities. Instead, the normal pattern is focus on a few carefully selected thrusts. The evidence suggests that the excellent companies somehow sift through a great diversity of influences and alternatives, and select for emphasis in operations a simplified set of goals. On major issues, at least, a clear-cut value system replaces uncertainty and ambiguity.

Build Acceptance Through Symbolic Behavior

These goals and thrusts become powerful values in the company climate only when they are strongly supported by the central managers. The McKinsey study shows that the chief executive can set the tone. The way the executive allocates time and attention tells what he or she considers important. But because the C.E.O. cannot be in many places at once and personally participate in many decisions, the more effective C.E.O. takes actions which become symbols of the values he or she is advocating. Here are four kinds of useful symbols.

1. *"Hands-on" participation* by the key executive. Calling on customers to get their reaction to products and service, attending the closing of an important sale, personal review of affirmative action moves, participation in new product meetings, conducting discussions or having dinner with executive trainees are examples. Perhaps the C.E.O. gets involved only on a sampling basis, to avoid being a bottleneck, but there is no doubt about genuine concern.

2. *Positive reinforcement* of actions which are consistent with the overriding goal or selected thrusts. This includes field visits to locations where positive action has occurred, with praise to participating workers; special awards for outstanding performance; on-the-spot granting of additional assistance to people already moving in approved directions. Some executives give such reinforcement again and again over a sustained period to drive home the central message.

3. Pointing out *"role models"* of desired behavior. An example of successful performance makes a goal seem real and doable. Just as the four-minute mile is no longer a fantasy, so can a pilot's on-time record or branch manager's inventory turnover be singled out for others to follow.

⚹4. Support of *myths*. Every company has its stories of exceptional actions: the president who personally delivered a bicycle on Christmas Eve so as not to disappoint a customer; the power-line repairer who kept electricity flowing to a hospital during an ice storm; Samuel Bronfman who dumped an entire batch of whiskey down the drain because the taste was not up to quality standards; the manager who was fired the day it was discovered that he had lied to a Congressional committee; and so on. Over time the details of the stories may get distorted, but they are part of the company lore. Such stories which support the overriding goal can be repeated to help establish the mystique of the company.

Through such well-worn methods as these, the central managers of excellent performing companies make clear the selected company values. And by creating such a climate, people throughout the organization are more likely to execute their various assignments correctly and enthusiastically.

This repeated emphasis on a few selected themes builds focused behavior. By clarifying priorities, it improves performance. However, the analysis and testing which precedes the execution stage may be complex, prolonged, and sophisticated. Part of the skill in creating an effective, uncluttered climate is being most careful in selecting those goals and thrusts which are paramount.

MANAGING MAJOR CHANGES

Activating often involves change. The focused climate just described may become outdated by new opportunities. Or, within its general scope, a new product, energy-saving technology, or a new organization may be necessary. Central managers especially must be active in bringing these changes about.

A change in strategy always involves a difficult transition. Relations with suppliers and customers will be altered, people will have new jobs, priorities and power will be shifted. As the following chart suggests, years not days typically are required.

FIVE- TO NINE-YEAR CYCLE OF STRATEGIC TRANSITION

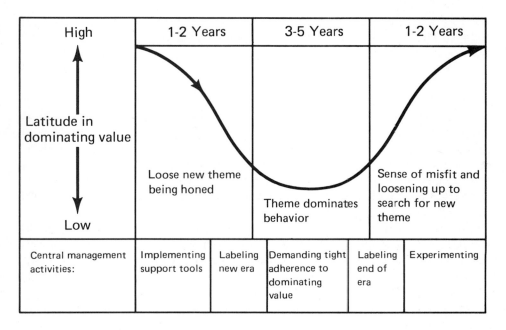

High	1-2 Years	3-5 Years	1-2 Years
Latitude in dominating value — Low	Loose new theme being honed	Theme dominates behavior	Sense of misfit and loosening up to search for new theme
Central management activities:	Implementing support tools	Labeling new era	Demanding tight adherence to dominating value	Labeling end of era	Experimenting

Source: T. J. Peters, "Symbols, Patterns, and Settings: An Optimistic Case for Getting Things Done," *Organizational Dynamics* (Autumn 1978), p. 21.

During the early stage, the new strategy and the accompanying policy and programs are still being worked out. Some people will be involved in this new planning, and through this participation they will understand and probably endorse the change in direction. Other people will necessarily be "minding the store" because previous activities must be continued to maintain company momentum while modified activities are being planned and tested. (The 1983 model automobiles must be made and sold while the 1984 and 1985 models are being developed.) Then comes a phasing-out of the old and building support for the new. It is during this transition and throughout middle stage that central managers build acceptance through symbolic behavior, as described above. Finally, pressure builds for another tack, and central managers must start preparing people psychologically for fresh leaps forward.

The transition from an old strategy to a new one creates special problems in activating. Behavior previously endorsed now has to be modified. And experience clearly demonstrates that the momentum of a going concern is not redirected merely by giving an order. Central management can aid in the transition by:

1. Relieving anxiety promptly.
2. Identifying areas where modifications in individual and group behavior are needed.
3. Providing time to learn new behaviors.
4. Giving positive reinforcement to desired behavior.

Relieve Anxiety Promptly

Rumors about changes that might upset cherished relationships spread rapidly. Once the status quo is shattered, employees give attention to all sorts of idle speculation. For instance, just an announcement that the company has bought a new computer can generate stories about closing down an office, firing half the people in the accounting department, or transferring the engineering staff to San Diego. Anxiety builds up, each minor statement or action of central management is interpreted many ways, efficiency drops, and employees begin looking for other jobs.

Much of the anxiety comes from uncertainty—not knowing what is going to happen. To be sure, some anxiety also arises because people are unsure how well they will fit into a new position or under a new boss. Only actual experience in the new setup can remove the latter insecurity, but anxiety from the unknown can be reduced by management.

Prompt communication is vital. Even though specific answers of precisely what will happen often cannot be given because plans have not yet been developed in detail, full discussion of known facts is helpful. Publicly recognizing employee concern, presenting a positive feeling about the future, and scuttling a variety of mistaken rumors all relieve uneasiness. If decisions are not yet made, then a statement of when they will be made and how they will be communicated is much better than no news at all.

An especially sensitive period is when negotiations for, say, a merger are still in the confidential stage. Then the most that can be done is to check false rumors and to assure employees that they will be informed early of any action that will affect them. Confidence in management's credibility is important at this stage.

Identify Behavior Changes

Supplementing every formally planned organization is a host of customary though unspecified relations. Pat Lee knows whom to contact about payroll deductions, passes along advance information on big orders to the production scheduler, picks up hints on the boss's temper from his secretary, and in other ways fits into an intricate social structure. Now, when a major change in organization and activities occurs, the old social structure breaks down and for a time no one is sure (1) where to get and give bits of information, (2) who has influence in the revised power structure, and (3) whose "suggestions" to consider seriously. During this period of flux, work gets done very slowly.

By identifying the principal areas of disruption, central management can anticipate where trouble is likely to occur. Also, by supporting selected people in disputes, by feeding information through particular channels, and by weighing and if possible accepting recommendations coming from staff or line, central management helps shape the new social structure.

Individual values and habits have to be modified, as well as the social interaction just discussed. For example, for years Tom Novello has worked closely with six southern wholesalers; he knows their buyers personally, and their goodwill has been considered a real asset. Now a decision to sell direct makes these wholesalers insignificant customers. Novello has to stop giving them special attention; the priority goes elsewhere. Since in this instance, as is frequently the case, friendships are involved as well as personal skills or knowledge that gave the possessor a distinctive worth, the new policy is tough to accept. Because emotions and habits are involved, the implications of a major change may lead Novello to unconsciously reject the general idea even when he gives verbal acceptance to it.

Provide Time to Learn New Behavior

Adjustments in behavior take time. When we first do any new task—riding a motorcycle or instructing a computer—we are clumsy and unsure how to interpret cues. The same is true of executive action. And when we *change* behavior, we may have to unlearn old habits and attitudes before picking up the new ones. Social interaction also has to be "learned"; here two or more people are involved, and they have to respond to each other as well as to their own motivations.

Management should recognize the need for this learning period. Even when employees have no reluctance to adopt the new objectives, the early operations will be hard and slow. Practice is needed, and minor adjustments often have to be made. Also, in the kind of strategy changes we have been discussing in this book, some jockeying for position by energetic executives is sure to occur. Time for a "shakedown cruise" is clearly necessary; the tough question of judgment is how long to allow.

Give Positive Reinforcement

Learning the new behaviors will occur faster if management notices new actions that are along desired lines and gives these strong encouragement. This is the period to build acceptance through symbolic behavior, as already described. Usually the new behavior will require extra effort, and special recognition will help sustain that effort during the learning period.

Such recognition of desired behavior also helps relieve anxiety built up during the transition. People are unclear as to just what should be done in the new situation and they will welcome reassurance when they are on the right track. Some doubt is likely to exist about the feasibility of the new direction, so every opportunity to point out where it is succeeding should be used to build confidence in the plan. Role models of desired behavior should be identified.

Activating a new strategy or reorganization, then, calls for keen perception by central management of the modifications in customary behavior that will be necessary to make the revised plan succeed. By following closely the way people are responding, managers can spot the desired behavior and can encourage people to follow that course. Such positive management will reduce the learning time and will relieve anxiety.

MBO AT THE EXECUTIVE LEVEL

The activating methods discussed so far apply to everyone in the company or department involved. They create a general setting or climate for actions by individuals. Valuable as such a climate is, managers must do more. Specific direction and motivation for each subordinate is also necessary.

MBO—Management by Objectives—is an activating technique that can be easily adapted to executives at the highest level of a company. The underlying concepts of MBO are simple, and may be known by other names, such as "management by results," which is a more accurate term. Nevertheless, the use of MBO in the executive suite calls for diligence and skill.

Basic Steps

The process begins with a manager (of any rank) agreeing with an executive about the results she or he is expected to achieve during an ensuing period—three months, six months, or perhaps a year. Such an agreement on results expected should be based on a mutual understanding about several things: (1) the sphere of activities the manager is concerned with, that is, the organization; (2) the desired goals for these activities, both long-run and short-run; (3) how achievement of these goals will be measured and the level of achievement expected by the end of the period planned; (4) the help the manager may expect from the executive and others; and (5) the freedom and the restraints on how the manager pursues the goal.

Then at the end of the period the executive and the subordinate again sit down to review what actually was accomplished, to determine why deviations (both good and bad) from goals occurred, and then to agree on a new set of goals for the next period.

At each review there is grist for a new discussion because a new set of results is available for appraisal and a new set of targets and priorities needs to be agreed upon. As the process proceeds, the executive has repeated opportunities for counseling the individual and for relating individual performance to company strategy, policy, organization, and programs. Hopefully, these discussions will be carried out objectively and frankly. As a minimum, the manager should know what is expected and how his or her performance will be measured.

One of the advantages of this form of MBO is that it sets the stage for frequent interchange about goals and their achievement. In fact, when people work on distinct projects, the review may occur at the close of one project and the beginning of another. In other instances the reviews and new goal-setting sessions become a part of programming discussed in the preceding chapter. So, if a person's total job and total performance are covered in such a project or programming discussions, an additional period appraisal serves little purpose. Often, however, these discussions are sharply focused on a particular end result, and an annual examination of overall performance picks up loose ends and gives balanced direction. Whatever the timing, the important thing is that open communication take place between each manager and the direct supervisor on the five factors listed above.

Benefits Sought

Several benefits should arise from such regular goalsetting/results review sessions.

1. Attention is focused on *achieving results,* not just being active. And these results are promptly compared to company goals. Of course, activities will be necessary to achieve the results, and much of the discussion and the resource allocation will be tied to such activities. Nevertheless, if the activities are not leading to desired results—because of either internal or external events—the manager is expected to initiate revised action that will lead to the specified goal(s). In other words, the MBO system assumes considerable decentralization to and initiative by subordinates. And if results are not turning out as hoped, the person who has accepted the responsibility should be doing something about it.

✳ 2. *Personal commitment* to carry out the agreed-upon mission is more likely. The opportunity to discuss the assignment and the help needed to get it done, usually leads to a feeling by the junior manager that the task is doable. Also, the goal has been endorsed by the boss as being wise and in the interests of the company. In psychological lingo, the aim is to have the goal internalized and legitimized. And if the subordinate has made the stated results a personal aim, both effort and resourcefulness are increased.

3. *Balanced goals* can be agreed upon. Especially at the upper management levels, several competing goals are almost always present. The marketing vice president, for instance, is concerned with advertising, pricing in specific markets, new products, sales training, and branch offices, just to mention a few subjects that might arise in a single week. Some results like direct costs are easily measured, while others like community service are intangible. Typically, short run results steal attention from longer-run objectives even though the latter may be more significant. Senior executives are vitally concerned that goals and results are kept in an optimum balance. MBO reviews provide a forum where these balancing issues can be considered in concrete action terms.

4. *Dual accountability* can be enforced. As business operations become more complex, we often have two or more people cooperating to achieve a single result. For instance, both personnel staff and the district manager may be responsible for training recently recruited M.B.A.'s. An engineer, plant manager, and accountant may be accountable for cutting the cost of product X by 15%. A good way to handle such joint projects is to hold *each* person accountable for the *total* result; this places a premium on cooperation to get best results. The MBO process is flexible enough to use this dual accountability concept.

5. *Interrelated support* can be provided. Meeting an air pollution regulation, for example, may call for changes in product specifications, modified manufacturing processes, some new equipment, a revised cost standard, and retraining. In an MBO review the plant manager who takes on the goal of meeting this regulation can spell out to the boss the help that will have to come from other departments. Or—as we have repeatedly stressed—strategy, policy, programs, organization, and control are interdependent; a change in one is likely to require adjustment in others. So, for example, when expansion into Mexico is undertaken, a variety of adjustments will be necessary. Ideally, these supporting adjustments will be fitted into the expansion plans from the beginning. But MBO planning and review sessions provide another occasion when the "total package" concept can be explored.

6. The MBO process is particularly well suited for activating managers of *decentralized operating units* and of units located some distance from the central office. Opportunities for casual contacts and informal coaching are fewer the greater the distance between the central office and the operating unit. Also when a shift in strategy has occurred, central managers need a mechanism that gives them a chance (1) to examine the interpretation of the

new directions being made by subordinates, and (2) to reinterpret their intent. MBO reviews do provide such opportunities to explore the implementation of new strategy.

This list of potential benefits of MBO indicates important phases of activating individual managers. If for some reason the MBO procedure is not used, other methods of accomplishing each of the six phases should be found. Adroit use of incentives, still another dimension of activating, is discussed in the next section.

DEMANDING USE OF INCENTIVES

Important as climate and individualized goals are in activating, central management still has to create a situation in which key employees get deep personal satisfaction from achieving tough company goals. These key people —managers, top staff persons, and outstanding performers in engineering, sales, etc.—are a select group; they have ability and drive, as already indicated by the positions they hold. The challenge is to keep their vigorous efforts channeled toward the strategy that the company is pursuing.

Broadly speaking, central management can influence this eagerness to cooperate through:

1. Identifying factors that motivate these persons.
2. Recognizing the inherent limitations on management's capacity to use such incentives.
3. Applying incentives wisely and courageously.

Executive Motivations

The influences that spur people to exert themselves are not obvious and clearcut. Also, individuals differ in their responses. Nevertheless, we can identify several factors that are likely to motivate the kind of persons who reach key positions.

Financial rewards. Overemphasized though it is, in our society money does matter. It is a crude symbol of success, but it is a means of achieving other ends such as security, living comforts, independence, and the like.

We have already discussed the setting of executive salary levels in Chapter 20. The desirability of keeping pay scales (1) in line with rates being paid by other companies and (2) in equitable internal alignment was stressed. Such a salary structure enables a company to attract and to retain competent executives. But note that the base pay tends to be stable and tied to other salaries. Central management is not free to jockey the pay up and down.

The variable pay elements are merit increases, bonuses, and perhaps stock options. These are the incentives that can and should be used courageously as rewards for outstanding work toward achievement of a strategy.

Sense of achievement. Executives, like other people, take pride in the results of their efforts. Real satisfaction arises from knowing that telephone calls go through, homes are heated, news is timely, or test equipment improves quality. And there is satisfaction in being a good competitor in business just as there is in sports.

More subtle is an inner sense of achievement, of having a challenging assignment and doing it well. Here we are concerned with an important aspect of what the psychologists call "self-realization."

A sense of achievement is a personal matter; it depends on one's own aspirations and values. Central management cannot grant it. Instead, central management tries to create conditions in which key persons feel that they are achieving. Toward this end, winning a strong commitment to company strategy is a primary requirement. Then placing individuals in jobs matched to their abilities and aspirations is a second requirement. When both requisites are met, a strong drive toward company objectives arises.

Social status and recognition. Typical executives like recognition of their accomplishments. This can come partly from their supervisors and other respected individuals who are familiar with their work. In addition, the estimation of one's friends and the community at large carries considerable weight. Since people outside the company have no direct knowledge of what a person does, they rely on titles, nature of an office, and other perquisites —and spending patterns that presumably reflect salary. The "symbols of office," then, can provide strong motivation.

Part of our heritage is the idea that people can raise their social status. Most of our ancestors migrated poor and uneducated; the children and their children after them improved their station in society. Success in business has been one of the major ways of improving one's social status. So, central management can use the prospect of a promotion or assignment to a key job as an incentive.

Power and influence. History records extreme cases of lust for power, but this motivation need not be pushed that far. There is a thrill that comes with making large purchases, watching a plant operate partly as a result of one's own guidance, seeing a new product that includes one's own choice of design, or supervising a pension plan that one piloted through to final adoption. This kind of exercise of power or influence is quite legitimate—in fact, essential. We observe it especially in government and charitable enterprises where the financial rewards are low. For some individuals it is a strong motivator.

when you give out titles you've got to be careful on what it will do to the rest of the org.

Restraints on Use of Motivators

Awareness of motivators is only a start. Using them requires insight and skill. For example, an action intended as an incentive usually has other effects too. Thus, W. J. McGill might respond favorably to more power, but the assignment of authority to McGill will involve an array of organization issues—scope of duties, decentralization, and the like. The same is true to a lesser extent for the use of titles to give McGill status. Perhaps maintaining a sound organization is more important than the incentive effect of a special concession to please McGill. So the use of most motivators has to be dovetailed with related considerations.

Perceived fairness poses another limitation. The feeling that any reward should be fairly won is very strong in the United States. A suspicion that favoritism or casualness has been involved in a promotion or a granting of power can cause a lot of hard feeling. Therefore, central managers try to have everyone who knows about a reward feel that it was fairly granted. This need for known reasons supporting a move cannot always be met, and central management then faces a dilemma of either withholding an incentive or antagonizing a number of people who will not understand why the action was taken. (A misunderstood reward can have far-reaching effects. If a belief arises among employees that promotions, bonuses, and the like are made on a capricious basis—and not for supporting official strategy—then a widespread attitude of "why bother to try" may develop.)

"Calling the Shots" Courageously

Also delicate is motivating particular individuals without upsetting group cooperation and morale. Incentives frequently single out one or two persons for distinctive treatment, and this inevitably creates disappointments if not hard feelings among those not so chosen. Clearly, when people are promoted or given more power, their status relative to their associates rises. When several individuals aspire to the same job, say vice-presidents hoping for the presidency, the disappointment of being passed by can be acute. Good people may resign, others may lose heart and stagnate. However, such costs probably are inevitable; and the loss that would arise from delay or compromise would be far larger.

Going outside the organization to fill an attractive post has the same discouraging effect on those passed over. However, the message is clear. The people making the appointment will not settle for just average performance. They expect distinctive results, and are willing to make an unpopular move to get them.

Demotion or discharge of an executive is hard to do because more often than not the person has been a personal friend for several years. Procrastination is expensive, however. The main cost of a weak executive is that his or her occupancy of a key position prevents a more able person from doing that work well. A baseball team cannot afford a rightfielder who bats only .100. In addition, *if* the person's weakness is recognized by other executives, failure to clean out "dead wood" from an organization tends to undermine the determination of other people to exert themselves. A wise and courageous practice is to remove ineffective individuals from key posts; if the company has an obligation to them, they can be given early retirement or jobs better suited to their abilities.

The opposite kind of a move is pleasant all around. Moving a person who is widely recognized as able into a key spot motivates the person and colleagues as well. Individual justice and the good of the organization coincide.

Concluding this brief discussion of motivating, which is one aspect of the broader managerial function of activating, central managers have a never-ending task of sensing what impels their key people. Within the limits of their powers and without undermining other aspects of administration, they seek to tie these motivations to company strategy. At the same time they must watch the impact of rewards going to one person on the whole executive group.

SUMMARY

Central managers play a dual role in activating an enterprise, that is, "putting the show on the road." They must work with their immediate subordinates just as all other executives must initiate and stimulate action of people assigned to them. In addition, central managers strongly influence the activating process throughout the enterprise, partly by the examples they set and partly by establishing certain practices as standard procedures that all executives are expected to observe.

Important elements in this activating process are: (1) creating a focused climate by selecting overriding goal(s) and major thrusts, and then repeatedly stressing the importance of these key themes; (2) managing changes in strategy and in the focused climate; (3) within this general setting, carefully guiding and evaluating the performance of each subordinate, using a form of MBO adapted to high-level executives; and (4) assessing the incentives which are important to the key people in the organization, and then within constraints, courageously exercising power via those incentives.

This discussion has concentrated on activating by central managers. Although the emphasis will differ, most of the concepts presented can also be used by lower-level managers. The emphasis on developing a clear sense of purpose, and then persistently keeping individual efforts directed toward that purpose, can be applied to even the smallest section of an organization.

 QUESTIONS FOR CLASS DISCUSSION

1. Lesley Pond (53) has just been named to replace G.G. McCarthy, long-time national sales vice-president of a large consumers products company, who is

retiring. Pond is one of four long-service regional managers. The other three regional managers are much younger, recent appointees. Pond must decide what to do with another long-service regional manager, Alvin Dart (61). "I don't know why McCarthy put up with Dart so long. Dart hasn't had a new idea in ten years. His volume is not even keeping up with inflation, and most of his sales force have been in their jobs longer than Dart has been in his in Atlanta. I must admit his expense ratio is low, but there is no reason to hope Al will really push the new line. The company would go down the drain if we were all like Al. Maybe I can find him a government job, or cut his salary so that he will quit." What do you recommend that Pond do about leadership in Atlanta?

2. (a) The development of a company climate—as described in this chapter—calls for continuing, vigorous, enthusiastic effort. Do you think that the kind of personality who will do this task well is likely *also* to be a good, objective, rational planner? (b) Among your classmates, which ones do you predict will be: (i) sharp, objective, analytical planners? (ii) effective climate builders? (iii) tough makers of unpleasant decisions? Now considering yourself, do you believe that you will be good in all three of the dimensions just listed?

3. Contrast the president's task of activating in a Stage I company and in a Stage II company—using the description of these two types of enterprises given in Chapter 17.

4. What part, if any, should a person with staff duties (as defined in Chapter 18) play in the different steps in activating? If you wish, in your answer assume that the staff person is concerned with sales promotion or with production scheduling and that we are interested in the activating of salespeople or of plant supervisors.

5. Chapter 4 outlines a way to analyze competitors and other key actors in a company's environment. To what extent is a comparable approach useful in activating key actors within a company?

6. The MBO approach for activating individual managers suits line executives whose results can be clearly identified and cleanly measured. (a) Give examples of how this approach can be applied to an advertising manager, an employee training director, and an air pollution engineer. What difficulties, if any, do you foresee in adequately covering the work of such positions? (b) Explain how the concept of dual accountability, explained on page 556, might be applied to these positions. Does dual accountability help resolve some of the difficulties you identified in response to (a) above?

7. A management consultant says: "In my observations, senior managers do a better job of communicating with and motivating their good subordinates than their weaker subordinates." What may account for this behavior, and what effect is it likely to have where it occurs?

8. Assume that you have a good job with a small but growing and successful competitor of Xerox. Your responsibilities have grown with the company; two years ago you transferred to the West Coast division and bought a house; the outlook is rosy. Two weeks ago the newspaper reported a rumor that your company was being acquired by Burroughs Corporation and would be fitted into their computer and office equipment department. Your boss says he knows nothing about the rumor; he did fly to headquarters for a two-day conference last week; and he did ask you to update your three-year sales estimate. (a) How do you feel? (b) What do you say to the people working for you?

9. A major oil company has just decided to close down its Kentucky refinery two
   years hence; local crude oil is running out and the refinery does not have
   modern, efficient equipment. Many of the employees have 10 to 20 years of
   service in this refinery, which is on the Ohio River 20 miles from a minor
   industrial center. If you were in charge of the refinery, what steps would you
   take in anticipation of the closing?
10. The culture and business traditions of a country influence the way managers
   deal with their subordinates. To what extent do you think the proposals for
   activating outlined in this chapter would be effective in: (a) Japan—where
   duties of individuals are not sharply defined, and much more emphasis is
   placed on group (section, division, department, etc.) responsibility. Also in
   Japan managers have lifetime employment with one company, and pay is
   based largely on seniority. (b) Germany—where authority is normally highly
   centralized in a small top-management group, and expense and other controls
   tend to be detailed.

CASE 22
Southeast Textiles[1]

The Southeast Textiles company is a medium-sized manufacturer of heavy-duty
clothing. Although 80% of its sales come from overalls, work pants and shirts, and
work gloves, the company also sells semifinished heavy-duty fabric to other textile
and manufacturing companies for conversion into industrial packaging material and
for camping equipment. As a regional producer of a relatively specialized product
line, Southeast has enjoyed more than 35 years of fairly stable profit and growth. In
the past 5 years, however, increased competition both from larger domestic firms and
from imports have shrunk Southeast's sales and profit margins, and last year the
company suffered its first operating loss in two decades.

In an effort to increase efficiency in the company's major mill in Allison, North
Carolina, where 90% of its products are produced, an intensive modernization program was undertaken. New equipment was purchased, new procedures were introduced, and the work force was cut from 800 to 690 hourly workers. A team of
consultants was used to advise the company's management during the study that
produced the program, and one member of the team, Norman Dean, was hired to
become staff assistant to the plant manager, Roger Headrick.

Dean works closely with Headrick on the many problems associated with the
modernization program and spends one to two days a week with the company's
president, Oliver Hall, and the corporate treasurer, James Davis, advising them on

[1]From J. E. Schnee, *Study Guide* for Newman, Summer and Warren, *The Process of Management,* 3rd ed. (Prentice-Hall, Inc.), © 1972. Reproduced by permission.

the use of a newly acquired computer system. Hall had been the driving force behind the modernization and was the one who recommended that Headrick hire Dean. Headrick recognized that Dean had a fine background in industrial engineering and was a real "whiz" on computers and modern scientific management techniques. He had reservations, however, about taking him on as his assistant.

"Once we get the new methods and equipment functioning smoothly," Headrick said, "I'm not sure I'll know what to do with him. Despite all of his book knowledge, he still doesn't know many of the tricks of our business, and he has, on more than one occasion, rubbed my people the wrong way by trying to jam his ideas down their throats. Basically he is a pleasant young man, but he is trying hard to justify this program and the faith Hall has in him, and so he can be awfully pushy. But the president has quite a high opinion of him, and right now he is a big help in the transition."

Hall indeed does have a high opinion of Dean. "This is one of the brightest young men I have met," Hall said. "He knows his stuff and he won't be held back by any 'We have never done it that way' arguments. Rog Headrick is a first-rate man with a good solid background in the practical problems of our business. With Dean to keep him informed about more modern management techniques, we have a first-rate team in the mill.

"In addition, Dean is working with Jim Davis and me to get our overall management information-system modernized and to help us use that fancy new computer system we bought to do more than highly specialized clerical work. We had a tough time getting him away from his former firm and had to pay him a very fancy salary, but we think he will earn every penny of it."

One of the areas in which savings were expected from the modernization program was the production control department. James Rose, manager of production control, has been with the company for 12 years and in his present position for almost 5 years. He reports to Headrick and is responsible for scheduling the flow both of raw materials and of finished product as well as actual production planning. He works closely with the plant's purchasing agent and warehouse manager, Everett Sims, and the other members of Headrick's staff (see Exhibit 1).

Prior to the modernization program, Rose had 21 clerks, 3 expediters, and 4 supervisors in his department. With the completion of the plan for the new program, Dean recommended that Rose's department be reduced to 12 clerks, 2 expediters, and 2 supervisors. This was to be accomplished through new methods and through greater use of the company's computer located in the administrative offices adjacent to the Allison mill. The shift in production control required not only a reduction in work force but also a change in the nature of most of the scheduling clerks' jobs, requiring somewhat different and higher levels of skills. Rose, after studying the plan, recommended that the company implement it over a six-month period. This would allow him more time to reduce his work force by means of attrition and transfers and more time to retrain the clerks who would remain. Headrick was sympathetic to this approach but agreed with Dean that it would be too slow and costly. The transition was to take place in one month and on Davis' recommendation the existing work group was given three weeks' notice and the opportunity to begin retraining on their own.

During this period, 8 of the original 21 clerks quit, and 4, at their own expense, had begun taking courses offered in a nearby technical institute. Three of the original group of clerks and 2 supervisors were transferred to other jobs. At the end of the

Exhibit 1
PARTIAL ORGANIZATION CHART,
SOUTHEAST TEXTILES

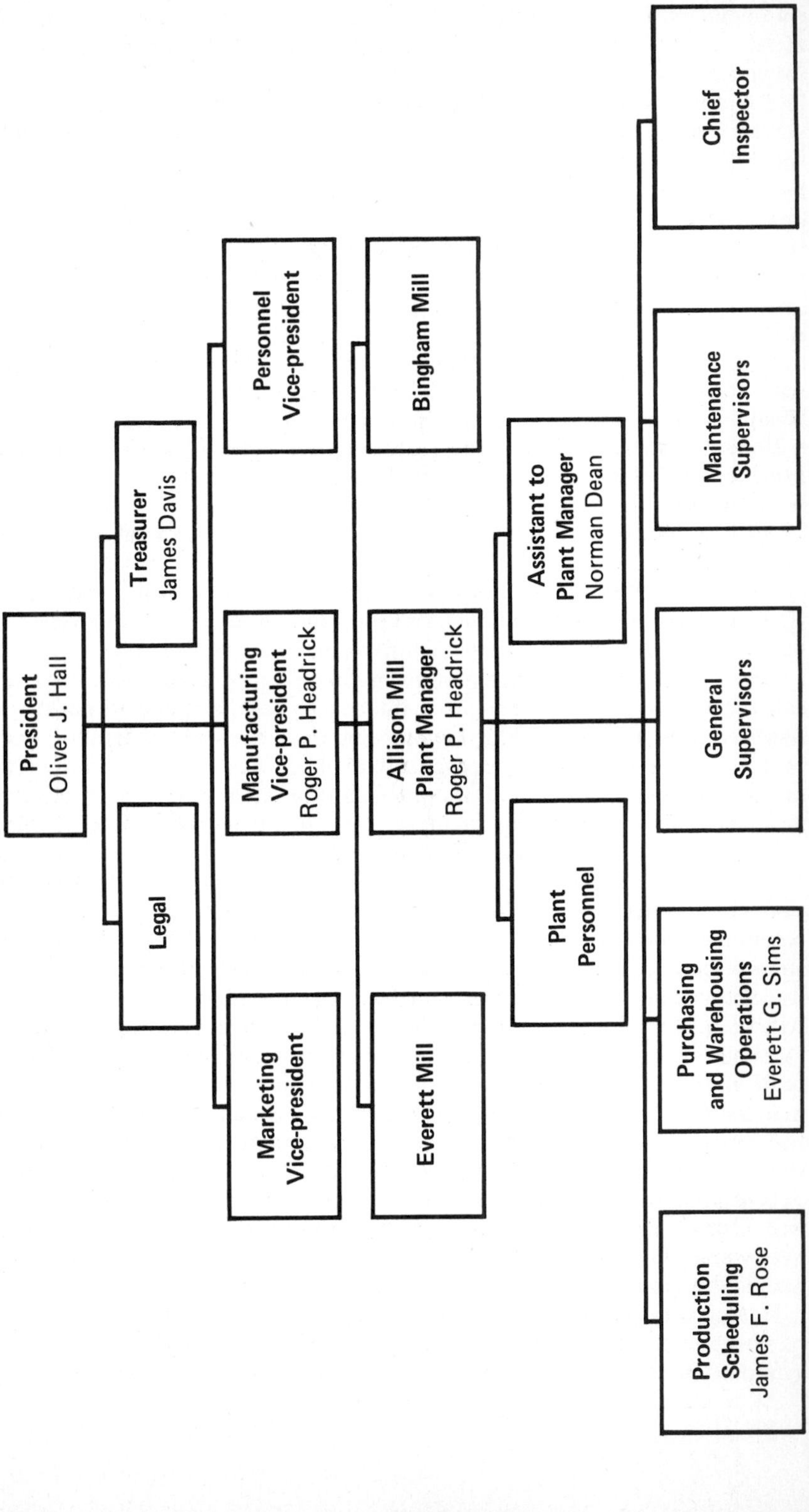

President
Oliver J. Hall

Treasurer
James Davis

Legal

Marketing
Vice-president

Manufacturing
Vice-president
Roger P. Headrick

Personnel
Vice-president

Everett Mill

Allison Mill
Plant Manager
Roger P. Headrick

Bingham Mill

Plant
Personnel

Assistant to
Plant Manager
Norman Dean

Production
Scheduling
James F. Rose

Purchasing
and Warehousing
Operations
Everett G. Sims

General
Supervisors

Maintenance
Supervisors

Chief
Inspector

month, 10 clerks, including one of the 4 attending classes, 1 expediter, and 2 supervisors were let go. Nine new clerks and 2 new supervisors were hired and the new system was formally introduced. Wage rates for the clerks were increased by 8%, and for the supervisors, by 10%.

The next eight weeks were extremely hectic ones throughout the mill where similar changes were taking place. In production scheduling, 2 clerks and 1 supervisor resigned and were replaced. During this period, Rose and Dean were almost constantly in conflict over how to resolve the numerous crises that arose. After several more months, things settled down, the work force stabilized, and it appeared that the program might at last begin to produce the savings that had been promised. At this point, costs were still running higher than Dean had originally estimated but lower than before the new program was instituted. Dean had worked long hours and had supplemented Rose's limited knowledge in certain aspects of the new system. He had at first recommended transferring Rose to another position and replacing him with someone more familiar with the new approach, but Headrick vetoed his proposal.

Because new equipment and layout costs throughout the mill had been high, the president was constantly checking with Headrick and Dean on when the economies would start to show up. Headrick was quick to admit that Rose had been of great help in curbing the president's desire to see more dramatic and more immediate cost reductions.

The three men who had been in Rose's department prior to the changeover seemed to adjust to the new system and to the newer employees, and the department's effectiveness increased. Headrick gave Rose much of the credit for the relatively smooth transition within the production control department because of Rose's skillful handling of his personnel. Many of the other departments had had a much rougher time maintaining morale in the face of the changes that took place. Rumors persist that production workers are being joined by many of the men and women doing technical, clerical, and low-level white-collar tasks in an attempt to bring in a union. So far, no formal request for representation elections have been made.

The president praised Headrick and Dean for their work, but warned them to keep an eye out for union trouble. Hall said: "We have too much invested in this new program to see it thwarted by having to work with a union. One of the reasons I moved the company down here in 1946 was to get away from the fetters a union can place on you. We may have to make a lot more changes before we are through and I don't want to have to bargain every change in wage-rates and work-rules with a union. So keep an eye out for trouble and try not to push your people any harder than you have to. Try to recognize and reward the good ones and get rid of the troublemakers."

Although operations continued more or less smoothly, a major problem arose in the production scheduling department on a certain Friday. As a result of a breakdown in the computer on Thursday afternoon, much of the data required for completion of production schedules for the next two weeks was not available. As a result, at 8:30 on Friday morning, Rose suggested to Headrick that they revert to procedures that were followed prior to the new program to complete the work which would be needed by Monday morning.

Headrick called Dean in and the three men discussed the problem. Dean listened to Rose's suggestion and said: "No good, Jim! If you go back to those methods with only 12 people, you'll never finish on time and we'll start the week in a real hole.

Most of your people don't even know the old system. I think we had better just wait until they de-bug the "monster" [computer]. If they get it going by eleven o'clock, we can still finish up by giving your people a couple of hours of overtime."

Rose asked: "What happens if they don't get it fixed on time? If I start now, we can get the job finished with the old system even if we need a couple of hours tonight and a half-day on Saturday. The overtime costs will be a fraction of what it will cost us on downtime in the mill if we don't have the schedules by Monday morning."

Dean countered by saying he was sure they would get the computer problem traced in time to avoid the extra cost of bringing the people in on Saturday. "Besides, if worse comes to worst and they don't get us the data we need till this afternoon, then we can bring them in Saturday."

Headrick decided somewhat reluctantly to go along with Dean. By twelve o'clock on Friday the problem with the computer had been traced to the failure of a component in its central logic system. A replacement was promised by one o'clock. Work was at a standstill in his department and Rose again requested that he be authorized to get started on the old system. This time, both Dean and Headrick firmly agreed it was probably too late and that with the problem diagnosed they would get the data they needed by two o'clock. Rose was told to ask his people to put in 3 hours of overtime Friday night and a half-day on Saturday.

Unfortunately, the component needed in the computer was not delivered and installed until two o'clock, and when a test was run on the system, a more serious problem, hitherto undetected, was found. The computer serviceworkers indicated that now, even working through the night, they could not complete repair and testing in less than 24 hours. When Headrick was informed of the bad news by Dean, he called Rose and told him to get busy with the old system. Rose protested: "Look, Roger, it's almost three o'clock. It's just too late now. When I explained the situation to my people earlier, I had a tough time getting some of them to agree to stay late tonight and an even tougher time getting them to agree to come in on Saturday if we needed them. Those with families want to get home, and the single ones have dates. I had to pull out all stops and virtually plead with several to come in tomorrow. All but one agreed to come if we needed them, but it was reluctantly. How can I go back now and tell them we do need them, when they'll find out, as the oldtimers know, the work simply can't be done even with a full day on Saturday?"

Dean's response was: "Plead? For heaven's sake, why should you have to plead? Don't those people have any loyalty to the company? Once in a rare while we really need to have them give a little extra and you have to plead? Perhaps if you didn't pamper them so, they would recognize that they have an obligation to the firm."

Rose answered angrily: "The firm has an obligation to them, too. If we keep 12 people late tonight and foul up their weekend plans, it should be for a darn good reason. If I get started now, we still won't finish until ten or eleven o'clock on Monday morning even if they work till eight o'clock tonight and all day Saturday. If we start fresh on Monday and I ask them to come in an hour earlier, we'll finish by noon if the computer is fixed this weekend. We are going to lose half a day in the mill on Monday any way we do it now and I don't see any point in making matters worse by asking my people to ruin their weekends."

Dean was equally adamant and insisted that Rose at least try to get the work done by Saturday. Headrick ended the discussion by saying: "Look, Jim, we've got a bad situation now no matter what we do. If I lose a half-day in the mill at this time of the year, it's not going to be good and the president won't listen to any excuses blaming the computer. He will want to know why we couldn't work around it. You know how touchy he is about his new brainchild. Get started right now, keep the workers until eight o'clock tonight and as long tomorrow as necessary, but get those schedules done."

When Rose left, Dean shook his head and commented: "I don't want to put all the blame on Jim, but if he knew more about the new system he would have been a day and a half earlier in requesting the data we need from the computer. The system was designed to protect against machine failure by giving us a day or so slack at the end of the month. I can't help but feel that this might have been avoided if we had someone in production control who was more familiar with the new system than Jim."

After leaving, Rose announced the decision to his supervisors and then joined them to tell the scheduling clerks. They reluctantly agreed to stay, and the three who had worked under the old system were told to assist Rose in instructing the others.

One of the three, Ken King, asked to speak with Rose privately. He explained that he had planned on asking for the afternoon off so that he and his wife could get to the rehearsal for their son's wedding. The wedding was to be held in a town four hours' drive from their home. "When you asked us to stay late tonight, I almost died," he said. "If I have to stay, I will; but we'll miss the rehearsal and won't get in before midnight for the wedding tomorrow. No matter what you say about this afternoon, I can't come in tomorrow."

Rose thought a moment and then advised King to tell the company nurse that he had a severe headache and wanted to go home immediately. "I'll okay it when she calls me," Rose said. "I'd like to give you the time, but under the kind of pressure we are facing, I can't."

King thanked him, left, and did as he suggested. By eight o'clock, it was apparent to Rose that the department could not finish the work on Saturday and he called Headrick at home to ask what he should do. Headrick indicated that whether they finished or not, he wanted them to try and insisted that if they worked harder they might still make it. Nine of the 12 clerks reported for work on Saturday and worked until five o'clock, but the schedules were not completed until almost noon on Monday. Because King was one of the three who knew the old system, his absence had slowed things down, but Rose was certain they could not have finished much earlier even with King. He was surprised, in fact, that they had done as well as they had.

The mill worked on certain stock items Monday morning and did not get into the new schedules until almost two o'clock. As a result, a considerable increase over standard costs was anticipated.

On Monday morning, Dean learned informally of what had happened to Ken King. He confronted Headrick with what he had heard and suggested that the time had come to replace Rose.

Questions

(1) If you were in Headrick's position on that Monday, what disciplinary action, if any, would you take with respect to Rose?

(2) What reaction up and down the organization would you anticipate to your action?

(3) What other actions do you recommend that Headrick and/or Hall take to establish a leadership tone that would aid in implementing changes in the company?

CONTROLLING OPERATIONS

Inspired strategy, wise policy, ingenious organization, and perceptive programming and activating all may fail to create an outstanding company unless the final phase in the management cycle—controlling—is also done well. Management control involves watching what is actually happening, evaluating this performance, taking corrective action if necessary, and developing a data base for the next round of planning. The primary aim of control is to assure, insofar as possible, that plans are actually carried out.

Numerous controls are used in every well-managed company. Central management obviously cannot, and should not, try to follow all these detailed measurements and evaluations that occur daily. Instead central management should focus on:

1. The design of the company control structure.
2. Exercising control of overall results and of unusually crucial activities.
3. Utilizing control data to help formulate new strategy, policy, and programs.

First we need to examine the nature and the variety of applications of the basic control process.

NATURE OF THE CONTROL PROCESS

Three elements will be found in every control system:

1. Standards of acceptable performance are established.
2. Actual (or predicted) performance is appraised in terms of these standards.
3. When performance is found to be unsatisfactory, or unusually good, appropriate managerial action is initiated.

Many problems arise in the application of this simple sequence: what should be covered by the standards and how tough they should be; who will do the measuring of performance and how this information will get transmitted to the people who evaluate it; and what types of corrective action will lead to improved performance in the future. Often a choice must be made between post-action control, yes-no control, or steering control. Let us look at a few illustrations.

Representative Control Systems

The following examples differ not only in the activity being controlled, but also in the character of the controls being used. They show ways to adapt controls to each specific situation.

Control of sales volume. For many years a chemical company had kept track of its sales in terms of dollars and physical units for each major line of products. Trends in these figures were the cause of rejoicing or dismay, but a new sales manager felt that they did not enable him to pinpoint difficulties and to take specific corrective action. Consequently, he expanded the sales control system in two ways. First, he kept track of sales results in much greater detail; all orders were analyzed in terms of sales representatives, type of customers, geographical areas, and products, and cross-classifications of each category were charted. Second, he tried to develop some criteria for what sales should be in each category. For this purpose, he developed an index of activity for types of customers (consumer industries), geographical regions, and long-term trends for products. From this information and data on past sales, he developed quotas for subdivisions of the sales analysis. These quotas were adjusted up or down as changes occurred in the market.

These two steps generated a mass of statistics. However, with the aid of a sales analyst, the sales manager could identify particular areas or industries where orders were falling behind quota. Often the sales representatives concerned had a good explanation for the deviation, but in other instances remedial action was obviously called for. The sales representatives grumbled about spending a great deal of their time with the new statistics. The sales manager, on the other hand, was convinced that the expanded controls brought to light difficulties that might have remained buried in the large totals formerly used. Experience also indicated that the sales representatives, who received the control data as soon as the sales manager, became more diligent about covering each part of their assigned territory.

This example raises the question of how detailed controls should be. The previous controls of the chemical company were too general to be useful for operating purposes. On the other hand, if the company had pursued the pattern of control to very small territories and fine industry divisions, the mass of statistics would have been overwhelming and the variations of doubtful significance.

Another notable feature of the system was a variable standard. If industrial activity in a particular territory was booming, the sales representative was expected to secure higher sales; but a decline in the market being served was also taken into account in appraising the sales representative's results.

The assumption here is that the factors causing the expansion or the contraction in the market were beyond the sales representative's influence.

Inventory control. One way to achieve control in considerable detail and
still not swamp executives with masses of information is to have measuring
and corrective action taken by the people who are performing the operation
—or perhaps done automatically. This possibility is illustrated by the inventory control system of a cash register manufacturer. This firm has to keep
on hand 65,000 different parts so that finished machines can be assembled
rapidly as customers' orders are received.

Briefly, the control system involves: (1) Establishing the minimum stock
for each part (the *standard*). Whenever the supply on hand falls below this
minimum, a standard order for additional stock is placed. (2) Maintaining
a perpetual inventory record of each item and comparing this with the
minimum standard. Formerly, this record and its examination *(appraisal)*
was done by stockclerks on tags attached to the front of the bin containing
each part. More recently, maintenance of the inventory record and comparison with the ordering point has been assigned to an electronic computer. (3)
Whenever the stock on hand falls below the minimum standard, a requisi-
tion for additional materials is issued *(corrective action)*. Of course, as demand and technology change, the standards have to be adjusted, and periodically a physical inventory is taken to make sure that the records are
accurate.

This rather conventional inventory control system suggests two possibilities for many other controls. Once a clear-cut control is designed, it often can
be operated by people close to the operation, perhaps the operators themselves. Upper management then can limit its attention to design of the
system and checking to be sure that it is being properly utilized. And, in the
extreme, when both the standards and the corrective action are clear-cut
and current performance can be measured in quantitative terms, the entire
control process can be automated.

Control of large capital expenditures. Typically, large capital expenditures must be approved by the board of directors before they can be advanced
beyond the planning stage. Often all projects contemplated for a year are
assembled together in a capital expenditures budget, as explained in Chapter 13, and specific approval is given for those projects the board considers
most desirable. Once approved, the project description becomes the control
standard, and subsequent steps are checked against this standard.

In terms of the basic control process, this procedure differs significantly
from the two controls we just examined. In the previous examples, as in
many controls, measurement takes place after action is completed. So these
controls fall into the broad class of "post-action" controls. In contrast, the
directors' review of capital expenditures occurs during the process—after
the plan is completed but before commitments are made. This control, like

many in-process quality controls, is a "yes-no" control. Action may not proceed until approval is given. The board of directors reserves the function of comparing specific proposals against its standards before any damage can be done. This holding a tight rein is in sharp contrast to a control system that operates routinely, if not automatically.

Executives maintain control over some activities by withholding permission to act until they give their approval to the specific acts. Appointment of key personnel, signing large contracts, selling fixed assets, and starting a sales campaign are often treated in this manner. Progress is slowed, but the executives feel the particular subjects are of such importance that they are unwilling to rely upon such standards as they can define with appraisal after the action is completed. Obviously only a limited number of activities may be treated in this slow manner in a large, vigorous enterprise.

Strategy control. In addition to post-action controls and yes-no controls, a third class is steering-controls. Control of a spacecraft headed for the moon, for instance, takes place days before the flight is finished. As soon as the craft leaves the earth, a forecast is made of where it is headed; corrective action is taken immediately based on the forecast. Post-action control, after the craft either hit or missed the moon, obviously would be too late.

Company strategy is like the flight of the spacecraft. We can't afford to wait for completed results before exercising control. Instead, we rely primarily on updated forecasts. (a) We monitor key assumptions about consumer tastes, governmental action, interest rates, competitors' actions, and the like. If new information indicates that operating conditions will differ from the original assumptions, corrective actions may be taken at once. (b) At major "milestones"—for instance, when market tests are completed or just before making a large investment—the entire strategy is reviewed, using all new information available, and a new forecast of results is made. The forecasted result is compared with company objectives, and a decision is made whether to continue on the present course or to modify it.

Steering-controls are far from precise, but they have the great advantage of prompting an adjustment while an array of possibilities is still open. Also, people being controlled feel that steering-controls are devices to help them reach objectives rather than a judgment of past success or failure.

Budgetary control. The best *comprehensive* control system is based on financial budgets. Here the already existing accounting structure is the base; the budgets are simply a prediction, or plan, of what various accounting figures should be at some future date. Income and expense accounts for, say, the next year are estimated and are summarized into a budgeted profit and loss statement. At the same time, changes in assets, liabilities, and equity are estimated and are summarized into a budgeted balance sheet for the end of the period.

For control purposes, the budgeted figures become the standards. Then when the normal accounting data come in, they are considered a measurement of actual performance and are easily compared with the budget standard. Of course this procedure can be followed for departments as well as the total company and for monthly, annual, or any other periods for which regular accounting figures are compiled.

Financial budgets have several outstanding advantages: (1) The measuring process is already well established and requires no additional expense. (2) All parts of the company are covered with the same comprehensiveness of official financial reports. (3) The use of dollars as a common language permits coordination and consolidation of plans for different parts of the business. (4) The control mechanism is directly related to one or more typical company objectives; for example, earnings per share, return on investment, or sales growth.

Being so closely tied to conventional accounting, financial budgets also have limitations: (1) Accounting figures do not promptly reflect intangibles such as customer goodwill, employee morale, executive development, research and product and process development, equipment maintenance, or market position. (2) The annual accounting period may not match the physical production or marketing cycle, so that expenses are hard to relate to resulting income and arguments arise over allocations. (3) Early warning of trouble is usually buried; also the accuracy desirable for financial reports delays budget comparisons. These drawbacks strongly suggest that budgetary control should be accompanied by other types of control in order to achieve a balanced control structure.

In actual operations the primary problem with financial budgets is how they are used by executives. If budgets are merely predictions by staff personnel or the central accounting office instead of carefully conceived plans by line managers, they will not be accepted as reasonable standards. And when the standard is not respected, the whole budgetary process is regarded as an annoying distraction. Also budgetary control has to be supported by central management, by its insistence that deviations be acted upon and by requesting revisions of budgets when changes in strategy and programs are made.

Control of executive development. The examples of control discussed thus far have all dealt primarily with objective data. Many important aspects of business operation are not so clear-cut. Nevertheless, control of these intangibles may be even more crucial to long-run success than things that are easily observed and measured. Executive development falls into this intangible category.

One well-managed company measures its progress in executive development in two ways. Annually, its key executives must report executive development activities undertaken by people in their departments. The reports cover special training assignments, appraisal reviews, training meetings, civic and trade association activities, and the like. The company recognizes that such reports omit perhaps the most important training that takes place on the job. It also recognizes that the activities reported may not have resulted in any significant executive development. However, the hope is that emphasis on training activities will encourage executives and operators alike to give attention to the basic process.

The second measure of executive development used by this company is the number of people considered to be ready for promotion. Data for this purpose are assembled from an executive inventory, such as the one described in Chapter 20. Again the unreliability of the data is recognized, but they are used simply as the best information available.

Two control techniques are illustrated in the case just cited. One is the use of activities rather than end results. This is done because the company cannot afford to wait until the end of the process (5, 10, or 20 years in the case of executive development). Moreover, actual measurement of progress is difficult if not impossible. Basic research, legal work, and public relations are further examples of business functions posing this sort of measurement problem.

The case also again illustrates the use of steering-control. If the number of people classified as promotable is inadequate to meet projected requirements, a danger signal has clearly appeared. In fact, more promotable people may be present than the inventory shows, or conversely, the estimates of employees' capacity to take on added responsibilities may be over-optimistic. Nevertheless, the warning is sufficiently serious so that more careful consideration and probably corrective action is called for. Every good control system makes wide use of steering-controls because they help to identify trouble in the early stages.

The attempts to control executive development just described also point to a danger. Executives can become so absorbed in making the measures look good—for example, lots of training meetings and high evaluations of subordinates—that they fail to accomplish the underlying objective. In other words, because the controls do not deal specifically with desired end-results, they may misdirect effort.

Standards of Performance

The cases just discussed illustrate various kinds of controls. Now, let us turn to a more general review of the three basic steps in the control process —setting standards, appraising results, and corrective action.

Some standard or guide is essential in any form of control. Even informal control requires that executives have some plan or standard in mind by which to appraise the activities they are supervising. These standards should come directly from the strategy, policy, deadlines, specifications, and other goals established in earlier stages of the management cycle.

Satisfactory performance, of course, has many aspects, and it is impractical to set control standards for all of these points. Instead, *strategic control spots* are picked out for regular observation. Important considerations in picking these strategic points are: (1) catching important deviations in time to take corrective action; (2) practicality and economy in making observations; (3) providing some comprehensive controls that consolidate and summarize large blocks of detailed activities; and (4) securing a balance in control so that some aspects of the work, such as developing executives, will not be slighted because of close controls on other phases. What to watch is vital in every simple and effective control system.

"How good is good" is the next question. For each control point, an *acceptable level of performance* must be set. How many sales orders per month do we expect Jean Jones to obtain? What level of absenteeism is considered dangerous? Is a labor cost of $13.95 per unit satisfactory for our deluxe model? The answers to such questions become the accepted norms—the par for the course. One of the best ways of providing flexibility in a control system is to devise acceptable and prompt ways of adjusting these norms.

Appraising Performance

Some comparison of actual performance with control standards may be done by a manager. A sales manager, for example, may occasionally travel with sales representatives to observe their performance and the attitudes of customers. Typically, however, *control observations* are made by someone other than the executive—an inspector, a cost analyst, a market research person, and the like. Also, some control data are derived as a by-product of other record keeping. Expense data, for instance, may come from payroll records and inventory records; sales data may be gleaned from a file of customers' orders.

Such separations of measuring performance from its evaluation and corrective action necessitates *control reports*. The information must be communicated from person to person, and this raises a host of questions: What form should be used? How much detail should they contain? To whom should they be sent? How often should they go? Can reports be simplified by dealing only with exceptions to standards?

The effectiveness of a control is usually increased by *prompt reporting*. If some undesirable practice is going on, it should be corrected quickly. Moreover, the cause of trouble can be learned better if people have not had several weeks to forget the circumstances. Also, employees, knowing that a prompt check on deviations from standards will be made, are more likely to be careful in their daily work. Consequently, the sooner a control report reaches a manager, the better the control will be.

Another practical issue in appraisal is whether *sampling* will provide adequate information. Perhaps refined statistical techniques, such as statistical quality control, can be used to decide the size of the sample and the inferences that can be drawn from it. In some operations—aircraft manufacturing, for example—100% observation is essential. And, we have already noted that for certain key actions—capital expenditures and executive appointments are typical—a manger may insist on giving personal approval before performance continues.

For activities which take a long time from start to finish, such as launching a new product or counteracting a competitor's invasion into our home market, *updated predictions* of future results may be vital. Such revised projections—based on results to-date and external changes—become the basis for steering control.

The engineering term "measuring and feedback" provides another way of describing this appraisal step in the control process.

Corrective Action

Real control goes beyond checking on work performed. Unless corrective action is taken when standards are not met or when new opportunities appear, the process amounts to little more than a historical record.

As soon as a deviation from standard is detected, the causes of the variation should be investigated. If the deviation is unfavorable, perhaps the difficulty will be due to a lack of supplies, a breakdown of machinery, a strike in a customer's plant, or other hindrance in *operating conditions.* In such situations, the executive will take immediate steps possible to remove any obstructions.

At other times, the difficulty will be personal in nature. Perhaps there is a simple *misunderstanding,* a failure in human communication; this may be quickly corrected. More troublesome is *inadequate training* of persons assigned to do the work. As a rule in such cases, help is provided until the person has received the training needed. Of course, if investigation reveals that the person simply does not have the necessary *basic ability* and never should have been selected for the job, transfer of the work or a replacement of the individual may be the only satisfactory remedy. All too often, the gap between performance and standard reflects a lack of effort. The person may be able to do the work and may understand what is wanted, the operating situation may be satisfactory, but the needed *incentive* is lacking. This, then, calls for additional motivation by the manager.

Corrective action sometimes leads to a *revision of plans.* The check on operating conditions and on selection, training, direction, and motivation of the operators may reveal that the standards themselves are unrealistic. If control is to have any meaning in the future, such standards should be revised. Also, the delay in work may have been so serious that schedules need to be rearranged, budgets revised, or customers notified. These changes in plans should give operators and executives a new set of standards that are reasonable criteria for future actions. Or the controls may have flagged results much better than predicted, and if such results can be expected to continue, new standards should be set.

CENTRAL MANAGEMENT CONTROL TASKS

What is central management's role in all this controlling activity indicated in the preceding discussion? The answer lies in three areas: (1) design of a balanced control structure for the total company, (2) actually exercising control at selected spots, and (3) using control data to help shape new strategy and programs.

Company Control Structure

The control structure of a company is more than the simple aggregate of the various controls used by different executives. These controls should be examined to be sure that no important considerations are missing; balance and emphasis should be checked to be sure they are in harmony with basic company objectives; and the compatibility of the controls with company planning, organization, and supervision should be assured.

Assuring adequate coverage. The table on page 577 suggests a way to examine a company control structure. In the left-hand column should be listed all those result areas that central management believes should be controlled by someone in the enterprise. The areas listed in the table are merely suggestive. In practice, the management of any single company will undoubtedly want to be much more specific on some points and to omit others.

With the result areas identified, senior executives can discover a great deal about control in their company by filling in the rest of the table. Usually a company will have very good controls in some areas and only vague and informal systems in others. This may be due to historical custom or to the relative ease of obtaining certain kinds of data. As a result of the analysis, central management will know where to try to devise additional controls that will fill in the missing gaps.

Relation of controls to decentralization. In thinking about who should set specific norms, appraise current performance, and take corrective action, organization structure should be related to control structure. The greater the decentralization of authority to make decisions, the further down the hierarchy should be the short-run control activity. It is simply inconsistent to give a manager freedom to run a division or a department and then to have some outside person make frequent detailed checks of just what is being done and suggest corrective action. In fact, control of routine activities is often performed further down the line than decision-making.

On the other hand, the manager who makes a delegation needs some reassurance that the authorization is being wisely used. Consequently, summary reports of results are submitted monthly or quarterly to senior executives. Also, senior executives may wish to watch a limited number of "danger signals" both for control and as a basis for future planning.

In addition, senior executives may want to be sure that adequate controls are being used by their subordinates, even though none of the reports come

Approach to Company Control Structure

Result Area to be Controlled	System Design		Exercising Controls		
	Control Points	Form of Measurement (Indexes)	Set Specific Norms (Pars)	Appraise and Report	Take Corrective Action
General Management					
Profitability	————	————	Who?	Who?	Who?
Market Position	————	————	"	"	"
Productivity	————	————	"	"	"
Technical					
Research	————	————	"	"	"
Personnel Dev.	————	————	"	"	"
Employee					
Relations	————	————	"	"	"
Public Attitudes	————	————	"	"	"
Sales:					
Output	————	————	"	"	"
————	————	————	"	"	"
————	————	————	"	"	"
Expenses	————	————	"	"	"
————	————	————	"	"	"
————	————	————	"	"	"
Resources used	————	————	"	"	"
————	————	————	"	"	"
————	————	————	"	"	"
Other	————	————	"	"	"
Production:					
Output	————	————	"	"	"
————	————	————	"	"	"
————	————	————	"	"	"
Expenses	————	————	"	"	"
————	————	————	"	"	"
————	————	————	"	"	"
Resourses used	————	————	"	"	"
————	————	————	"	"	"
————	————	————	"	"	"
Other	————	————	"	"	"
Research & Eng.:					
Output	————	————	"	"	"
————	————	————	"	"	"
————	————	————	"	"	"
Expenses	————	————	"	"	"
————	————	————	"	"	"
————	————	————	"	"	"
Resources used	————	————	"	"	"
————	————	————	"	"	"
Other	————	————	"	"	"

to them. A simple example is insistence on tight controls on cash disbursements in a branch office with no further attention (except the annual financial audit) being given by the supervising executive. Quality controls and production controls are frequently handled on the same basis. In effect, a pattern of control is stipulated when the subordinate manger is appointed, but exercise of this control is a part of the delegation made to this manager.

Integrated data processing. A total view of the control structure for a company emphasizes the large number of control reports that must pass through the organization. Original data have to be compiled and then analyzed, and reports must be sent to the operator, the boss, and perhaps a staff group. In addition, summaries or reports of exceptions probably go to a senior executive. The total of these reports in a large company is staggering.

Electronic data processing equipment can speed up the analysis and the distribution of this control information—*if* it is in numerical form. Perhaps such equipment can also cut the expense of report preparation, though the usual result is a substantial increase in the number of reports (better control) for hopefully the same expense. However, to achieve this speedier, elaborated flow, the procedures for handling data have to be revised. Potentially, all original data will be fed into the computer, and there they become available for planning as well as control purposes. We then have integrated data processing.

This new speed and ready availability of data should be utilized in the company control structure. They may make certain controls in headquarters, *or* in the field, more feasible. At the same time, a danger should be recognized—a plethora of numerical reports will increase the tendency to overemphasize those factors that can be expressed numerically. Consequently, integrated data processing should be regarded as an aid and not as a determining factor in the design of a company control structure.

Relation of controls to other phases of managing. In stressing the desirability of having central management carefully shape the company control structure, we are not suggesting that a lot of controls be superimposed on other management activities. For example, the target dates set in programming of normal operations or elaborated in a PERT schedule automatically become norms in the control process; quality control standards are simply the logical extension of product policy dealing with quality; and so on. Controls are the means for assuring that such plans are fulfilled.

Similarly, goal-centered performance reviews include agreeing on personal goals for the next six months or a year and then comparing accomplishments with the goals at the end of the period. Many of the goals thus established will simply be norms for factors already included in the control structure, and control reports will be used in the discussion of results. Of course, additional unique goals may be agreed upon and a temporary control cycle set up. But if the company control structure deals with crucial areas, a factual basis will already exist for much of the performance appraisal discussion.

Controls Exercised by Central Management

Design of an effective control structure is a major central management task. But even an ideal structure will not relieve central management from exercising some controls itself. Several attempts have been made to identify a limited number of key result areas that central management should watch. The most suggestive of these is a list used by the General Electric Company. According to this approach, the effectiveness of overall management can be appraised in terms of:

1. Profitability, in both percent of sales and return on investment.
2. Market position.
3. Productivity, which means improving costs as well as sales.
4. Leadership in technological research.
5. Development of future key people, both technical and managerial.
6. Employee attitudes and relations.
7. Public attitudes.
8. Balance of long- and short-range objectives.

Note that this list places considerable emphasis on strength for future growth as well as on current profitability.

In addition, the General Electric Company and others expect senior executives to single out crucial problems in their particular industry or function and to watch these closely. Incidentally, what is crucial shifts from time to time—union relations may be especially sensitive at one time, foreign competition at another. So, the attention of top management shifts, leaving for subordinates the task of continuing vigilance.

As emphasized in Chapter 19, central management has a particular responsibility to be alert to *new* developments that may create opportunities or obstacles. Consequently, much of the data examined by central management is not for routine control but a source of possible cues to future changes.

Using Control Data for Future Planning

Business provides a continuing flow of services. In the same day, managers are checking on final "delivery" to today's customers and also preparing for next year. Control contributes to this never-ending preparation for the future by feeding in appraisals of current successes and difficulties. For central management, inevitably removed from day-to-day action, this building for the future is certainly the most exciting facet of control.

The *replanning* that is prompted by control reports may be short-run. Often a program for raising capital or launching a new product has to be speeded up or slowed down because of success—or lack of it—in pilot plant tests. Or, a rise in production costs may precipitate a withdrawal from a marginal market or an adjustment in prices.

Likewise, control reports provide one of the main considerations in deciding what to aim for in the *next planning period*. The quality achieved, the rate of output, the expenses, and the consumer acceptance in the past period are guides to what may be expected in the next round. Care must be exercised in merely projecting the future on the basis of past experience, because conditions change and improvements are possible. Nevertheless, to disregard past performance is even greater folly. And it is control reports that provide the most readily available data on past performance.

Central management also uses control data in designing *new strategy*. Targets, we noted in Chapter 5, are one dimension of strategy; they identify the criteria by which success will be measured and indicate levels of achievement expected. So in considering strategy, one of the first steps management takes is to see how close to such targets actual performance has been. As with short-range planning, this past performance is a significant input in deciding where to set future targets.

More significant, however, are the reasons why targets have been exceeded or not achieved. Market potentials may have changed, international trade barriers may have been lowered, competitors may have exploited a new technology, or the company may have lost its distinctiveness in key personnel. Such factors as these may show that a new operational strategy is needed. We do not mean that control reports will be the only stimulus to revising strategy; environment, industry, and key actor analyses (recommended in Chapters 2, 3, and 4) should also flag future opportunities and problems. But in a going concern, the take-off point is a careful reading of how well we are doing relative to what we set out to do. In this manner, central management uses the control system as a springboard in deciding future strategy.

SUMMARY

Strategy, policy, and organization provide the broad guides and the framework for the activities of a company. Planning is then extended to detailed methods and procedures, and on to programs and schedules. The managers turn all this preparatory work into action as they issue operating instructions and motivate people to execute the plans. Even then, the task of managing is not complete; there remains the vital step of control.

Control is necessary to insure that actual performance conforms to plans. The specific measures for control should, of course, be adapted to the particular activity. Nevertheless, three basic steps must always be present: (1) Standards of satisfactory performance should be set up at strategic points —points that will provide timely, economical, comprehensive, and balanced checks—and, for each point, a norm or level of achievement should be agreed upon. (2) Actual performance should be compared with these standards by sampling, 100% inspection, or perhaps required confirmation, and appraisal reports should be sent to all persons directly involved. (3) When significant deviations are detected, corrective action is necessary; that is, adjusting operating conditions, improving competence of assigned operators, motivating, or perhaps modifying plans.

Central management becomes involved in controlling in three main ways: (1) It reviews the numerous controls that operate within the company to make sure that all key points are adequately covered and that the net emphasis of the controls is in harmony with company objectives. This is a matter of design of the total control structure. (2) Central management itself exercises control on overall company results and on a few selected activities that are especially crucial to long-run results. (3) Even more important, central management utilizes data from control reports to assess how well company strategy is being achieved. This analysis provides an important base for setting new targets and perhaps reshaping the operating strategy. Thus the controls serve as a feedback into company planning, and the management cycle of planning, organizing, activating, and controlling starts anew.

 QUESTIONS FOR CLASS DISCUSSION

1. Transnational, Inc., of Houston, Texas, is concerned about controlling "questionable payments" which might be made by executives of its foreign subsidiaries. Both "grease" (payments to do promptly what receiver is supposed to do) and "bribes" (payments to do what receiver is not supposed to do) are involved. Also, either local government officials or local business executives may be receivers. Control is complicated because local custom in some but not all countries where Transnational operates condones such payments. In contrast, U.S. law prohibits payments to government officials even where local practice endorses it. What ways do you suggest Transnational use to control questionable payments?

2. Pioneer Life Insurance Co. knows that several of its competitors have sold large quantities of insurance to doctors by actively soliciting and providing special service to pre-med students while they are still in school. These early associations lead to large policies after professional success is attained. Pioneer wishes to apply this same approach to MBA candidates, and has appointed John Bunyon vice-president in charge of the new program. Bunyon in the home office can get a specially designed though standard type of policy approved, devise sales approaches, prepare promotional material, and the like. However, the use

of such aids depends on individual salespeople who are located throughout the United States. Salespeople work under General Agents, and are paid a commission on their sales. They have wide latitude in seeking clients and selecting suitable policies for each client. How do you recommend that Bunyon try to control the MBA program?

3. The Cardiz Construction Company—builders of shopping centers, offices, schools, and churches—is concerned about its public relations. Complaints about noise, dirt, upsetting ecology, workers' disregard of community customs, etc. are becoming increasingly troublesome. "We talk to our people over and over," Mr. Cardiz says, "and they correct the specific complaint. But two weeks later a group of mothers are picketing around 'the old oak tree' or a town clerk wants us to sweep up some dust in front of the mayor's house." Like other construction firms, Cardiz gets its business through competitive bidding for contracts that normally have a fixed price and penalty clauses for late completions. Each project manager is measured on how well actual performance stacks up against contract provisions. The project manager's job is complicated by the use of subcontractors for many parts of the work. How do you recommend that Mr. Cardiz get better control of public relations?

4. You are the proprietor and manager of a small, specialty restaurant near a college campus that sells high-quality Greek food, wines, and beer. Hours are 11:30 A.M. to 8:30 P.M. six days each week. Revenue is satisfactory overall, although quite erratic, but profits are well below your hopes and desires and nowhere near your wildest dreams. What should you do to gain control? Think about steering-control, yes-no control, post-action control, control of an activity rather than results, sampling, adjustment of norms, and corrective action. How might you apply these ideas?

5. Mr. Paul Ingram, owner-manager of a successful company making automatic scales and proportioning equipment for the feed, glass, rubber, coal, and other industries, is going to retire. For years he kept in close touch with all activities; but now, serving only as board chairperson, he will need different controls. At present the main formalized controls are: (a) a thorough final test and inspection of all outgoing equipment to assure quality; (b) job cost estimates coupled with actual job costs, used primarily to assure that prices used in bidding for new work are in line with actual costs; (c) a daily report on cash in the bank; (d) monthly profit and loss estimates; (e) semiannual balance sheet and income statement prepared by an outside auditor, who also prepares the income tax returns. Financial budgets have never been attempted; however, annual sales estimates are used to set quotas for the six regional sales representatives, and annual estimates of factory and administrative overhead are used to set overhead rates in the job costing system. Mr. Ingram says, "I know from talking with sales personnel about bids and orders what is happening in the market, and the number of people around (106 total, currently) determines most of the expenses. Our people know their jobs and do them well. But how to be sure that Walter Perez (the new general manager) is running a tight ship while I'm in Florida is another matter. Unfortunately, accounting reports don't tell whether your engineering is good enough to beat competitors on the

new jobs that will keep the plant busy next year." What kind of a control structure should Mr. Ingram insist on, what reports should he receive personally, and what kinds of decisions should he reserve for his own yes-no control?

6. (a) What effect does inflation have on managerial controls? (b) What can be done to maintain effective control in periods of double-digit inflation?

7. Scientific management devotes much attention to motion and time study, production scheduling, selection and training of workers, preventive maintenance, materials specifications, and other features of shop management. What bearing, if any, does each of these facets of scientific management have on the job of a plant superintendent in controlling operations in the plant? Should the president be concerned about the use of such techniques in designing the company control structure?

8. Many department stores that have opened suburban branches consider each branch simply as an additional opportunity to contact customers; the buying, advertising, credit, accounting, and most other activities are performed at one location by centralized divisions. In contrast, Race Brothers has branches in separate communities up to 150 miles from the state capital where its main store is located. Because of this dispersion, each branch is a fully integrated unit with its own buying, credit, accounting, delivery, etc. The main store does provide a variety of services for all branches, but each branch is expected to operate as an independent unit. Discuss the differences in control systems you would recommend for a company with suburban branches and for Race Brothers.

9. Assume that the President of the United States placed you in charge of gasoline rationing. One aspect of your total program is assuring that actual sales of gasoline conform to your regulations. How would you try to achieve such control? (Make any reasonable assumptions about the nature of your program, and then describe a control system that is compatible with such a program.)

10. A liquor company, specializing in gin, cordials, and a very light Scotch whiskey, and selling internationally in six countries, has long stated that its corporate goals are an annual rate of growth of 10 percent for revenues and a 15 percent per year return to each stockholder from a combination of dividends and capital gains in the stockmarket. These goals have been achieved for at least 15 years through the administrations of three different presidents. The company has, however, reached what its executives believe to be its maximum achievable market share. Thus they predict that revenue will continue to grow with the market growth of about 4 percent per year and that the return on investment to shareholders will also decline. To meet the growth target, it has been proposed that the firm buy the assets of a regional brewing company making a locally well-known beer. After the purchase, even though beer drinkers differ from hard-liquor drinkers, total sales for at least the first year will grow by 25 percent and, since the assets are offered at a significant saving below replacement cost and at a 10 percent discount below market price. the 15 percent target for shareholders will probably be met easily. (a) What is your appraisal of this company's definition of its strategy? (b) How do the growth and

rate-of-return percentages meet the need for overall control standards? (c) What controls will be needed for the beer-making subsidiary?

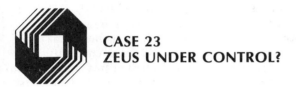

CASE 23
ZEUS UNDER CONTROL?

Zeus Corporation has eight divisions (legally wholly-owned subsidiaries). Most divisions are manufacturing businesses related in some way to electronics. They have had varying degrees of success, but overall Zeus has been quite profitable.

Help from Headquarters

Senior managers at Zeus believe that a significant part of their success is due to their planning and control system. *Longer-run planning* focuses on developing new lines of business; it consists of (a) selecting a domain that looks promising; (b) deciding how to attack that domain, under the guidance of a Design Review Committee; and (c) preparing thrust plans and budgets, under the guidance of Project Teams. The Design Review Committees and Project Teams are drawn for these temporary assignments from anywhere in the corporation, and they are expected to cover a stipulated sequence of steps.

Annual planning for ongoing business in each division starts in September with corporate approval of the division's general plan for the following year. Then more specific plans spelling out departmental activities are prepared in October and November. These are expressed in operating budgets and capital expenditure budgets, which are approved by corporate staff and executives by the end of November. The corporate staff people feel that "making a good sales forecast is usually the heart of good annual planning."

Once its annual budgets are approved, each division is given wide latitude in carrying them out. Headquarters *control* consists largely of comparing actual performance against the budget. For capital expenditures, divisions are free to invest within the overall limit; if a division finds that it needs more funds, it requests an upward revision in the total—a process that typically takes four or more weeks.

C.D.C. Mission

One division of Zeus, the Credit Data Company (C.D.C.), provides credit information from a central data bank to lenders. Rapid information about a consumer who wants credit on a new car or wants to open a charge account anywhere in the nation is a distinctive aspect of this service.

C.D.C. offers (1) to install a "total system" in its customer's credit office, including a small computer and full procedures for using this machine to tap the huge memory of large computers at C.D.C.'s headquarters, and (2) 24-hour on-line availability of currently updated credit information on many consumers. "We can tell the lender —our customer—almost immediately whether a prospective borrower does or does not pay his or her bills. It's as simple as that." Other information is often available. The bulk of its business relates to consumer credit, although recently C.D.C. has embarked on providing a similar service regarding business credit.

C.D.C. has enjoyed rapid growth, ranging from 20% to 50% per year. Its central computer center has capacity to store 60 billion bites of data. These files have information on 90 million consumers throughout the United States. Each month about 100 million updates are posted, and the system can handle 100,000 requests for data in a peak hour. There are already 8,000 service terminals located throughout the country.

Feud Regarding Controls

Zeus managers are naturally pleased with C.D.C.'s success, but the corporate staff is unhappy with the way the control system is working.

Part of the difficulty stems from C.D.C.'s conservatism in estimating its future sales. Repeatedly C.D.C. has underestimated its actual growth, and central staff says that this shows an inability to plan. C.D.C. managers point out that their growth plans have always been ambitious, and to promise more would have a low probability of achievement. (The use of budget fulfillment as the main criterion for annual bonuses may have some influence on this debate.) And C.D.C. managers find that explaining profits above budget is easier than profits below budget.

The squabble about "pars" for annual sales has laid the basis for difficulty regarding capital expenditures. Because sales growth has exceeded the annual budgets, C.D.C. has repeatedly sought additional funds for facilities to handle this unplanned volume. This behavior corporate staff views as "lack of control."

Last year corporate staff made an analysis of why C.D.C. was so far off in its capital expenditure budgets. Over half of all capital outlays were found to be for computers, so attention now centers around computer purchases. "To get on top of this situation, we now have a separate capital budget for computers. Moreover, before a computer order can be sent to a supplier, it must be okayed by us (corporate staff) to be sure that it comes within the budgeted total. If it does not, C.D.C. must submit and get approval of an upward revision in its capital investment plan for computers."

Within the finance and purchasing departments of C.D.C., there is no mystery about what had been taking place. Two kinds of computers were being purchased— very large ones for central processing of data, and many small ones which were resold or leased to customers as part of the system package. The small computers are standard "shelf" models which can normally be obtained within a week. In effect, they are raw materials, and their purchase fluctuates with the number of new customers obtained.

In contrast, the large computers are indeed capital equipment which provides capacity in the central data bank to store more information and respond to more inquiries. These large computers must be ordered eighteen to twenty-four months in advance. To be sure that it would not have to turn down new business because of lack of capacity, C.D.C. management has been placing orders on the assumption that business would grow fifty percent per year. Annual budgets typically anticipated twenty percent growth. The difference between the optimistic and conservative assumptions is considered by C.D.C. management as a safety factor or "contingency plan." When actual growth is less than fifty percent, C.D.C. slows down delivery of the large computers—often with a penalty fee—and it may temporarily accept excess capacity which will be filled up by subsequent growth.

Until recently this ordering of large computers has not been reflected in the annual budgets. Only actual receipts of equipment are picked up in the capital expenditure account. Under the circumstances, it is not surprising that C.D.C. might be requesting an increase in its annual capital expenditure budget to pay for computers which in fact had been committed for in the previous fiscal year! When discovered, corporate staff concluded that C.D.C.'s capital expenditures were "out of control." On the other hand, C.D.C. management contends that it has been acting prudently so as to assure optimum growth, which Zeus executives urge C.D.C. to obtain.

Under the new system of a separate budget for computers, corporate staff is having difficulty reconciling orders and deliveries for all kinds of computers with the current year's profit and loss budget and with next year's budget which has not yet been approved. And C.D.C. management is not inclined to simplify the confusion.

One undesirable effect of the wrangling is that toward the end of the fiscal year, C.D.C. must get approval of an upward revision of the computer budget before orders for small computers are official. This causes delays of over four weeks. Meanwhile C.D.C. is failing to provide the *prompt service* which it has been telling new customers is a hallmark of a relationship with C.D.C.

Question

Assume that you are an outside consultant. (a) What capital expenditure control system do you recommend that Zeus Corporation use for C.D.C.? (b) Are there any changes outside your recommendation for (a) which are needed to make your proposal work effectively?

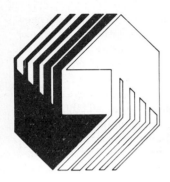

INTEGRATING CASES

Strategy and Execution

LOS RANCHOS DE PARAGUAY

"On the last Thursday in December, much to my surprise, I found myself on the plane from Brussels to Asunción reversing a journey I had made six months earlier when I came to Europe as an assistant to the managing director of La Société d'Aliment[1] to continue my year of executive training with this European manufacturer and distributor of food products. Although I had learned, during my four months at the meat-packing plant in Paraguay, that the sales and profit performance of Los Ranchos de Paraguay (a wholly-owned subsidiary of La Société d'Aliment) had been steadily deteriorating, neither I nor anyone else in the Brussels headquarters had suspected how bad the situation would become until the September floods resulted in the loss of about 10,000 head of cattle and the subsequent resignation of the managing director in Paraguay.

"On Tuesday, two days before my plane trip, the managing director in Brussels called me into a meeting during which he and the other chief executives explained what they knew of the situation at Los Ranchos and then asked me if I would be willing to take over as managing director there.

"Since this would be my first central management assignment (at age 32), I told them, 'Provided you don't expect miracles, I'll give it a go.' We agreed then to have a formal review after I had been in Paraguay a year to see whether or not it would be worthwhile for me to continue my efforts there. Since Los Ranchos was the company's only cattle-raising and primary manufacturing operation, there had always been some question as to whether or not it was wise for La Société d'Aliment to be as fully integrated as to own a ranching and meat-packing company. La Société was diversifying steadily by adding new retail products sold in old and new geographical regions of Europe."

Malcolm Littleton, the teller of this tale, had grown up on a sheep station in New Zealand and had attended a technical institute to study animal husbandry. But then, after graduation, he had chosen to work for the Shell Oil Company. After ten years with Shell—most of which he spent in South America in various sales and personnel jobs—he left to join La Société d'Aliment.

"Our quick review and the briefing in Brussels showed me that the situation in Paraguay had rapidly worsened. Annual losses had mounted steadily over the past

---

[1]Literally, in English, "The Food Company."

four years from $150,000 to $1,800,000. The effects of the disastrous flood had been increased enormously by a three-day delay in getting a fleet together for a rescue attempt while waiting in the hope that good news would come down the Rio Paraguay. In addition to the 8,000 cattle lost directly in the flood, about 4,000 others (cows in calf and some weakened by disease) died.

"The packing plant had operated for only three months in each of the two previous years, rather than the normal five months, and had slaughtered 46,000 head in contrast with a killing capacity of 100,000 head over a six- to eight-month season under the best conditions. As a trainee I had realized that morale was low. The work for the people on the killing floor had been cut back to a total of 50 days. They had an uninterested, surly way of working that differed markedly from their actions of shouting, whistling, and joking when things were going well. They made up a unified gang. One was either in it or out because of the kind of work. A meat plant is a pretty bloody sort of a place with the animals hanging to be drained, the red and raw meat lying on tables, the gruesome-looking machines extruding fat and an unpleasant, dominant smell to the place. It took me at least four days to recognize that this was just a production process and that the people were rough, tough workers because of the kind of work.

"The plant workers seemed to walk off their jobs for nothing. In the warm climate of Paraguay it is pretty tough when 30 half-skinned carcasses are left on the line. All the managers then had to pitch to and work for six hours just to clear up the one line.

"I also remembered from my time as a trainee that the department heads had seemed careless about their responsibilities and that they argued and fought amongst themselves in a way I had never seen at Shell. Also, there appeared to be much friction between the ranchers and the plant management. Most of the ranchers thought of themselves as in the cattle-raising and cattle-tending business. They cared little or nothing about the beef potential of the cattle or the fat-to-lean ratio of the meat. Some of them remembered times when cattle were slaughtered for their hides and tallow and the carcasses were left to rot.

"Los Ranchos owned and leased 1,800,000 acres in various locations on both sides of the Rio Paraguay north of Concepción. On these it ran 90,000 head with an annual take-off of about 10%; that is, about 9,000 cattle were selected for slaughtering each year. Turnover[2] was $7,500,000 of canned, frozen, and processed meat from the packing plant. Most of the beef extract and corned beef was packed in our largest-sized cans for eventual sale to institutional buyers in Europe, Africa, and North America. The frozen beef was shipped in bulk to La Société d'Aliment plants in Europe for further processing.

"As on all the large ranches in Paraguay, our cattle count was never certain and the animals were mainly of poor quality. Low-yielding breeds, poor grass, and an unfavorable terrain and climate in the Gran Chaco contributed to this. Paraguayans seldom, if ever, got the 20% annual take-off that was common in Argentina.

"Local butchers bought up the best quality cattle from the Paraguayan ranches and left about 150,000 to 200,000 head to be slaughtered by the four packing plants that exported beef.

---

[2]"Turnover" is the European term for annual sales.

"The first task that I had to plunge into immediately upon arriving in Paraguay was to buy cattle forward for the slaughtering season that began in March. We had to make almost immediate purchases of cattle to be delivered later from April through August. The chief buyer was young and inexperienced and had just been appointed the year before. Never having done so, I did not know how to set up and organize a buying operation. We were going to learn through experience, a disproportionately time-consuming process. Also we did not understand at first that even the largest sellers were ranchers and not economists. They were prepared to wait for a price they thought was just. They knew little of the procedures for maximum weight gain. My chief buyer did not clearly understand that the cheapest cattle did not result in the cheapest beef.

"That season we bought outside and brought in from our own ranches 76,000 head, the highest number processed since Los Ranchos had been purchased ten years before by La Société. When we found ourselves paying the highest prices at the end of the buying season for the wrong cattle with an insufficient yield analysis, we realized that purchasing would have to be planned by regions, that delivery deadlines would need to be set with the ranchers, and that the cost of walking, trucking, or barging the cattle to the plant would have to be balanced with the weight loss associated with the transportation.

"My two major objectives for the trial year were to reduce the loss by 50% and to increase plant volume substantially. Reducing the loss would mean, in part, tighter control on our own ranches to see that half of the 10,000 new head newly brought in from Argentina were not lost to rustlers, as had happened the year before. It also meant travel by small plane to the ranches to improve communications with the ranch managers who were often hard to find. (Small plane travel was dangerous because of terrain conditions, frequent storms, incomplete instrumentation, and understaffed weather advisory services). Increased plant volume was necessary to give our people work to see how the operating system responded under pressure, to cut overhead charges per pound of beef packed, and to provide employment in a country that badly needed jobs. About 1,500 people worked in the plant and 600 on the company-owned ranches, and there were 150 staff administrators.

"My first view of the managing director's job was that it was going to be a lonely kind of position. I could not get extensively involved with the people in the company for two reasons: (1) Doing so might well bias my opinions of them and my judgment as to whether or not the operation should be continued in the long run. (2) I could not forecast what I was going to find out about the managers during the first year. I even had to tell my wife to be careful about incurring social obligations to families or charitable groups.

"Three very early actions were intended to be symbolic. They affected the management only. We traded in the Buicks, Fords, and Chevrolets owned by Los Ranchos for Volkswagens and Fiats. We made the managers pay for milk. It was no longer free to their families. We reassigned the gardeners so that they no longer kept up the staff compounds around the plant. I would say that these actions were understood, although they were not liked.

"Two major administrators left. The administrative manager (age 56) had expected to move into the managing director's job. He quit when his gardeners were taken away. The controller, a 30-year-old Argentinian who was very dynamic, moved into the administrative job. Then the factory manager resigned at the end of the packing season. We went to three shifts for making cans for six months to build up stock and slaughtered 10 hours each day for five months. The factory manager told me this meant that his workload was 16 hours per day for the first four months of the season and that the work pace was too heavy for him.

"It was risky to build a stock of 2 million cans because they had to be made in advance of the selling season. If I guessed the wrong sizes, we could not move the product. If the cans were improperly made, the canned meat would go bad during the two months we held it at the plant and the cans would blow. Actually, we canned in two shifts for two months rather than by the former practice of one shift for as long as needed for the pack that year. By going to two shifts we packed in 7- to 12-oz. cans rather than in 4-lb. butcher cans. The meat then sold for a higher price per pound and gross revenues went up an extra 10%.

"During the first year we cut overhead from $1,650,000 to $1,200,000 and reduced our total loss to $911,000. Cutting overhead was not easy. We cut out the legal department entirely, cut teletype expenditures from $30,000 to $15,000, decreased our interest rates with the local banks from 13% to 10%, and reduced our compensating balances when I found that the banks were charging us standard commercial rates despite the fact that our loans were guaranteed from Brussels and Zurich. Since we were 1,500 miles up river from Buenos Aires, we had to carry a minimum two-month inventory of both supplies and meat; but we reduced to this from a four-month average. Also we cut our loans receivable from ranchers from $900,000 to $180,000. We could pre-finance them for their operations, but many of them were not rolling over the loan at the year's end. We tightened up on the promissory notes and made the ranchers agree to two signatures or a mortgage if they wanted pre-financing. Then also we insisted that the cattle being grazed for us would be stamped with our brand in advance of any financing.

"By the time these things were done, the end of the first year was approaching. I was eager to talk with the people in Brussels since I wanted them to give me help through advice and to recognize that there was no easy road ahead. Before the year's end they sent out an agricultural consultant for an independent view.

"I explained to him what had happened and then listed the following short- and long-range tasks that lay ahead without putting them in any order of priority:

"(1) Budgetary meetings have been pushed down to the plant department level for more participation, but each department budget still contains overhead and equipment account allocations. There is no direct-cost budget system as yet. Reports still come out 30 days after the month's end.

"(2) Benchmark controls such as daily cattle costs, the number of cattle processed per week, inventory investment before the packing season, and so on, have not yet been introduced.

"(3) Each department (16 in total) is still run by a manager and an assistant manager when, in my opinion, only one is needed. What procedure can we introduce or use to be fair to the people who have to be let go? Some are Paraguayans, some European. The labor law requires two to three years' severance pay for long-service employees. How can we help in locating jobs?

"(4) I am about to hire an able young Argentinian as a replacement for the plant manager.

"(5) The tax per head slaughtered is renegotiated each year with the Paraguayan government. Would it be useful to work with the three other foreign-owned companies in tax negotiations?

"(6) The Swiss (Nestlé, Maggi, and Knorr) have formed a buying group and are successfully playing off the producers of meat extract one against the other to drive down prices. How can we best operate?

"(7) The ranching side of the business has no managerial accounting system. Can one be installed that would do more than report historical costs?

"(8) Although money was spent in the first year to repair fences, clean out water tanks, rebuild, repaint, and clean the workers' sleeping huts, improve the dipping facilities, and sow some of the dryland in the Gran Chaco with Lehmann's lovegrass from South Africa and with blue gramma, there are still innumerable improvements possible on the ranching side.

"(9) I need some feedback from Brussels as to whether Paraguay is going to be an integral part of the supply situation in the future so that I shall not go ahead with putting up projects in the dark.

"(10) The company-owned ranches could be cut to 900,000 acres and still the stocking could be increased to 146,000 animal units.

"The consultant listened and left. One month later we met in Buenos Aires—the managing director from Brussels, the consultant, the director of production in France, the head of the legal staff, and I. I told them what I had told the consultant. They had the figures. The consultant said he had learned only one point that I had not covered—I was regarded by the management group in Paraguay as distant and cold, a little frightening to some, and there was a certain level of anxiety because they were not all getting to know me. He also had a recommendation. The company should sell off Los Ranchos de Paraguay. Even with the best efforts, it would not be more than a break-even operation.

"My view, as expressed, was that enough could be done to cut costs, raise prices, improve pasturage and cattle breeds, change the product mix, and improve the control system so that Los Ranchos would break even within another year and turn a handsome profit within two years. But profit and return on investment were not the question. Did operating a ranch and primary manufacturing facilities on a continent and in a country 7,000 miles from Brussels make any sense as part of a European secondary manufacturer and distributor of food products? What could Los Ranchos de Paraguay do for La Société that the market could not? Would I be shutting myself off from advancement in Europe by staying in Concepción to continue the turnaround of Los Ranchos? My assignment the year before had had all the earmarks of improvisation and I could see no point to continued improvisation in planning for Paraguay or for my future."

QUESTIONS

(1) How would you answer Malcolm Littleton's questions in the preceding paragraph?

(2) What programs appear to need to be planned for and with what priority if Los Ranchos is not sold?

MANAGEMENT OF CONVAIR[1]

The Corporation

By 1960 General Dynamics had become one of the great corporations of the country. Its sales were around two billion dollars and it produced, profitably, some of the most complex equipment known to man. Its major operating divisions were:

Astronautic (Atlas missiles)
Electric Boat (submarines)
Fort Worth (B58 bombers)
General Atomic (nuclear development)
Liquid Carbonic (liquefied gas)
Electrodynamics (electric motors)
Pomona (electronics plus Terrier missiles)
Stromberg-Carlson (telephones, electronics)
General Aircraft (leases or sells planes traded-in for jets)
Canadair (aircraft)
Convair

This case focuses on one product of one division, but the issues raised are basic to the entire scope of General Dynamics and to many other companies. The division—Convair—was by far the largest component brought into General Dynamics (in 1954); and the product—the 880 and 990 passenger jets—rolled up the largest loss ever achieved by a nongovernment enterprise on a single venture, around $425 million.

General Dynamics was founded by John Jay Hopkins. Under his inspiration net earnings, $600,000 on sales of $31 million in 1947, rose to $56 million on sales of $1.7 billion in 1957, the year of Hopkins' death. Hopkins was a man of great energy who kept posted on each division of this expanding empire largely by direct and unannounced visits. In 1953 he did bring in Frank Pace as executive vice-president "to have someone in the office to answer the phone" and especially to maintain Washington's confidence in the company. Pace had served as Director of the Budget, and during the Korean crisis as Secretary of the Army.

Aside from golf, the law, and the high order of intelligence, Pace and Hopkins were complete opposites: Pace temperate in all things, oratorical, deliberate, anxious to be liked, a product of the federal staff system, prone to rely on his second-in-command in the making of decisions; Hopkins volatile, creative, earthy, intuitive, ingrown, willing to listen but unwilling to share the making of decisions with anybody, a loner more likely to give the world the back of his hand than to extend the palm of it. In 1957 cancer caught up with Hopkins. His hand-picked board of directors decided (over Hopkins' strong objections) that Pace should be president. Hopkins died three days later.

Pace described the task of managing the enterprise he inherited in these terms: "When you have a company, employing 106,000 people, made up of eleven different divisions, each a corporation really in its own right, most of which were separate

---

[1]For a fuller discussion of this period in General Dynamics history, see "How A Great Corporation Got Out of Control," by Richard Austin Smith in *Fortune,* January and February, 1962. The present case is composed of excerpts from these two articles. Reprinted by special permission; © 1962, by Time, Inc.

enterprises before they joined the organization, and headed by men who were presidents of corporations, with their own separate legal staffs, financial staffs, etc., all of these highly competent men—the only way to succeed is to operate on a decentralized basis. Our total central office in New York City was something like 200 people, including stenographers. This group can only lay out broad policy. Your capacity to know specifically what is happening in each division just cannot exist. If you did try to know everything that was happening and controlled your men that tightly, they would leave or would lose the initiative that made them effective."

Convair's Move into Commercial Jets

The Convair division was headed up in 1955 by General Joseph T. McNarney with John V. Naish as executive vice-president. Tough-minded Joe McNarney, ex-chief of U.S. forces in Europe, had always been pretty much of a law unto himself, while Jack Naish wore his fifteen years' experience in the airframe industry like Killarney green on St. Patrick's Day. The division had already pulled off a successful commercial-transport program; the propeller-driven 240's, 340's, and 440's were world-famous. But what prompted Convair to consider making the formidable move into jet transports was a suggestion by Howard Hughes.

Hughes wanted jets for TWA; but before Hughes and Convair could agree on a design, Boeing and Douglas came out with long-range jet transports (the 707 and the DC-8) which scooped the market. Still determined to get into jets, Convair turned to the medium-range market. For this plan, Hughes proposed to buy 30 planes. After considerable engineering work, the executive committee of General Dynamics' board, headed by Hopkins, unanimously approved McNarney's program based on the assumption it would make money after 68 planes were sold, that potential sales of 257 aircraft could be realized, and that the maximum possible loss was only $30 million to $50 million.

By this time three airlines—TWA, Delta, and KLM—had already taken options to buy the 880. Now the committee instructed Convair to go ahead and get letters of intent from them within the next fortnight. The committee laid down only three conditions in authorizing the program: first, that GE guarantee the 880's engine; second, that the ability of the airlines to pay for the jets be investigated by an *ad hoc* committee of Pace, Naish, and Financial Vice-President Lambert Gross; third, that management was not to go ahead without orders in hand for 60% of the estimated 68-plane breakeven point.

The last provision proved to be quite flexible. The breakeven point on the 880 had been understated: after closer figuring, Convair raised it to 74 planes in May, up 6 planes in two months. When KLM did not pick up its option, the executive committee indulgently dropped its 60% condition, allowing Convair to go ahead with only 50% of the breakeven point assured. The new figure was made to fit the fact that by now Convair had only 40 firm orders (10 from Delta and 30 from Hughes).

A Doubting Thomas

Both Convair assistant division manager, Allen Morgan, and B. F. Coggan, the division manager, had informed management back in 1956, at the time 30 planes were sold to Howard Hughes, that the 880 was underpriced. Their conclusions were ignored then because of the difficulty of substantiating their cost estimates at so early a date. But now a year had elapsed, the 880's design was frozen, and components had been ordered preparatory to starting up the production line. So the cost of the aircraft could be figured with precision; it was an amalgam of money that *had* been spent on research and development and money that *would* be spent on materials, fabrication, and assembly. Usually about 70% of the material costs of an aircraft is represented by items bought from outside suppliers—the engines, pods, stabilizers, ailerons, rudders, landing gear, autopilots, instruments, and so on—with only 30% of the total material costs being allocated to the airframe manufacturer himself. The 880 ratios followed this general pattern. But when an engineer in Convair's purchasing division began totaling up the various subcontracted components, he came to a startling conclusion: outlays for the vendor-supplied components of each 880 totaled more than the plane was being sold for (average price: $4,250,000). He took his figures up the line, pointing out that when research and development costs of the aircraft (they totaled some $75 million) were added in, along with the 25 to 30% of the material costs allocated to Convair itself, nothing could be expected of the 880 program but steadily mounting losses. He recommended that Convair abandon the whole venture, even though the loss, according to his estimates, would be about $50 million.

Whether the engineer's recommendation and his supporting data ever reached New York headquarters is something of a mystery. In any event, when the engineer persisted with his analyses, Convair decided he was a crank and fired him—he was reinstated two years later after time had confirmed the accuracy of his judgments.

Target No. 1: United Air Lines

The sales problems that confronted Convair in 1957, however, were something that couldn't be sloughed off with the firing of a critic. At the start of the 880 program in March, 1956, the potential market had been estimated at 257 planes. By June of that year Convair had raised the figure to 342, but in September it was down to 150 after an on-the-spot appraisal had let the air out of the sales estimates for European airlines. These gyrations gave substance to an industry rumor that the division undertook a thoroughgoing market analysis only *after* commitment to the 880 program, but at least one point was clear about the "final" forecast of 150. The bulk of that number, as General Joseph McNarney, Convair's president, said at the time, had to be sold before July 1, 1957, or the 880's production line could not be economically maintained. The trouble was that an understanding with Howard Hughes had kept Convair from selling the 880 to anybody but TWA and Delta for a whole year. This had already caused the loss of customers who preferred a 707 or DC-8 in the hand to an 880 twelve months down the road. So in the spring of 1957, when Convair was at last free of the commitment, it had still sold no more than the forty 880's (to TWA and Delta) that started off the program. The success of that program, with only a few months to go before McNarney's July 1 deadline, now hinged on selling the remaining major airlines, American and United.

Convair's first target was United, which it had listed as a prospect for 30 aircraft. For a time things seemed to be going Convair's way in its pursuit of this critical $120-million sale. Boeing, Douglas, and Convair were all in competition for the United contract, but Convair had the edge with its 880, for it was then the only true medium-to-long-range jet aircraft being offered. All Boeing could offer was essentially the long-range 707, too big and, for its seating capacity, 50,000 pounds too heavy to suit United. The size could be reduced, of course, and some of the weight chopped out, but not 50,000 pounds unless Pratt & Whitney could substantially lighten the engines, the JT3C-6's used on the 707 aircraft. With Pratt & Whitney unwilling to make this effort, United's board decided in favor of the 880 on September 27, 1957, subject to a final going-over by United's engineers.

Soon thereafter, United's President William Patterson called General Dynamics' Executive Vice-President Earl Johnson, whom Pace had put in overall charge of the jet program, out of a board meeting to tell him Convair was "in." But perhaps the most consequential call was one Pratt & Whitney's Chairman H. Mansfield "Jack" Horner then made on Patterson himself. Spurred on by Boeing, Horner had been galvanized into action, and now he wanted to know whether something couldn't be done about getting Boeing back in the competition, if Pratt & Whitney could come up with a lighter engine. Patterson referred him to United's engineers, who made very encouraging noises. They themselves had been pushing Pratt & Whitney for just that. Both Boeing and Pratt & Whitney then went into a crash program, the former to scale down the 707.

Within a few weeks Boeing had come up with a new medium-range aircraft—the 720—45,000 pounds lighter than the 707. United then invited Boeing and Convair to cut their prices and both did, though Convair refused to cut below what Pace recently described as "the bare minimum." In November, United's chief engineer John Herlihy compared Convair's 880 and Boeing's 720 and then strongly recommended the latter. His reasoning: the commercial performance of the GE engine was an unknown quantity, while "we had the Pratt & Whitney engines in our other jets and wanted to regularize our engines if we could"; moreover, the narrower fuselage of the Convair 880 permitted only five-abreast seating, a shortcoming United had vigorously protested back in 1956 when Convair had first solicited its opinion of the 880 design; the Boeing 720, on the other hand, was wide enough for six-abreast seating, a difference of as many as 25 passengers at full load in the tourist section of a combination first-class/tourist airliner. This meant, in Herlihy's view, that the 720 with its lower operating costs per passenger-mile was a better buy than the 880 with a $200,000 cheaper price tag. On November 28, 1957, United's board approved purchase of 11 Boeing 720's, with options for 18 more.

"Merely a Modification"

The loss of United meant a sharp reduction in the market potential of the 880, dropping it from 110 to 80 planes. Worse than this, Convair had a powerful new competitor in what had been its private preserve, the medium-range field. That competitor was now going to make it tough for Convair to sign up American Airlines just at the time when Convair expected to sell the airline 30 planes, nearly half of the 880's dwindling market potential. Discussions with American had been going on for some months, though pressure had naturally increased after United chose the Boeing 720 in November. But in January, 1958, American notified Johnson, who was in overall charge of the negotiations, that it too was going to pass up the 880 for twenty-five 720's.

In February, however, Convair was able to reopen discussions with American on the basis of a revolutionary new engine General Electric had just developed. Called a turbo fan-jet, it required 10 to 15% less fuel than a conventional jet to do the same job (under flight conditions) and provided 40% more power on take-off. The aircraft that Convair intended to use with these new engines, later designated the 990, was billed as "merely a modification" of the 880. It was a modification to end all modifications. The 990 had a bigger wing area than the 880 and a fuselage 10½ feet longer; weighed over 50,000 pounds more; required an enlarged empennage, a beefed-up landing gear, greater fuel capacity, and stronger structural members; and was supposed to go 20 mph faster.

Many of these changes were imposed by American's hard-bargaining C. R. Smith, whose talent for getting what he wanted out of an airframe manufacturer was already visible in the DC-7. But Smith hadn't stopped with just designing the 990; he designed the contract too, using all the leverage Convair's plight afforded him. In it he demanded that Convair guarantee a low noise level for the plane, finance the 990's inventory of spare parts until American actually used them, and accept, for American's $25-million down payment, twenty-five DC-7's that had been in service on American's routes. The DC-7 was then widely regarded as an uneconomical airplane, 12% less efficient to operate than the DC-6, and, as Convair discovered, it could not be sold for even $500,000 in the open market. When General Dynamics reluctantly accepted this down payment, worth only half its face value, American signed up for twenty-five 990's with an option for twenty-five more.

"We Had to Go Ahead"

Looking back, director Alvord recently commented on the whole affair: "Earl Johnson brought back a contract written to American specifications with an American delivery date, but the plane was not even on paper. It was designed by American and sold to them at a fixed price. There was not even any competitive pricing." What is more, Alvord says, "the 990 was signed, sealed, and delivered without board approval. It was just a *fait accompli*. An announcement was made to the board that there would be a slight modification of the 880." Pace himself believed at the time that the 990 was only a slight modification. He now says, "If we had known at the outset that major changes would be needed, deeper consideration would have been given it."

The decision to go ahead on the 990 was an important turning point in the fortunes of Convair and of General Dynamics itself. The reasoning behind it has been stated by Pace: "When the Boeing 720 took away our sale to United, we found ourselves in competition with a plane just as good as ours. This is just what we wanted to avoid. The 880 seemed doomed. We had to go ahead with the 990 or get out of the jet business. American had not bought any medium-range jets . . . When the fan engine was developed, they told us, 'We will buy your plane if you produce a plane like the 990.' It was absolutely vital for us to follow American's wishes. We had to have another major transcontinental carrier. I thought I was taking less of a gamble then than I did entering the 880 program."

But what this amounted to was that General Dynamics had now committed itself to a double-or-nothing policy, gambling that the success of the 990 (beginning with the American sale) would make up for the failures of the 880. The nature of this gamble is worth specifying, in view of the fiasco that eventuated:

The plane had been sold at a price of approximately $4,700,000. Yet nobody knew how much it would cost because its costs were figured on those of the 880, which were still on the rise and unpredictable.

The number of planes Convair must sell to put its jet-transport program in the black had gone up sharply. The breakeven point on the 880 had been 68 planes at the start (March, 1956), a figure that by 1958 should have seemed impossible of fulfillment. Nothing but dribs and drabs of sales to lesser airlines could be expected of the 880, for the "majors" (TWA, United, and American) had already been sold or refused to buy. Convair's commitment to the 990, which had a breakeven point of its own, meant the division must sell 200 of the 880's and 990's to keep out of the red.

The success of the 990 depended largely on its being the sole plane on the market with a fan-jet engine. When it built the plane around the GE engine, Convair was confident that Pratt & Whitney would not make a fan jet. Barred from making a *rear* fan jet—GE's licensing agreement prevented this—Pratt & Whitney simply built a *front* fan engine. Boeing used this for the 720B, which took away a good deal of the 990's potential market.

The 990 was to be built without a prototype, or advanced model. General Dynamics had "lucked out," to use President Earl Johnson's phrase, on the 880 without testing a prototype. So now the company was again going to gamble that it could take a plane directly from the drawing board into production without any major hitches. Said Rhoades MacBride, by way of fuller explanation: "Our time for debugging the 990 was severely compressed because we wanted to take advantage of being first with the fan-jet engine. If we had built a prototype and flown it, we would have minimized our advantage in having the fan engine before Pratt & Whitney had it. We realized that if everything went right, we would be way ahead. If the 990 didn't fly as stated, we would be in terrific trouble."

"Our Basic Mistake"

Yet if ever a plane needed a prototype and plenty of time for testing, it was the 990. As Earl Johnson himself conceded recently: "Our basic mistake in judgment was that we did not produce a prototype to fly to virtual perfection. From a management standpoint we should have said, 'If you haven't the time to build a prototype, then you shouldn't get into the program.' " The 990 was an extremely fast aircraft, with short-field characteristics and a brand-new engine. The decision to go it without a prototype meant that Convair had committed itself to attaining the very high speed demanded by C. R. Smith—635 mph—the first crack out of the box. As it turned out, a lag of only six minutes in the 990's flying time on a transcontinental run of 2,500 miles was to result in C. R. Smith's canceling his contract because American wouldn't be able to bill the 990 as the "fastest airliner in the world."

"The Furnace Treatment"

Just before Convair undertook the 990 program, General McNarney retired and the division got a new president, hard-driving John Naish. Naish's succession clearly indicated that Convair was still an empire within General Dynamics' empire and would likely remain so. Pace had wanted the Convair job for Earl Johnson, the old Army buddy he'd made his No. 2 man. McNarney wanted Naish; McNarney got Naish. And the new Convair chief had soon made plain his confidence he could handle anything that came along—if left strictly alone. As he said at the time: "The company has a great many people who like to solve their own problems. It believes in the furnace treatment—you throw people in the fire and you can separate the good metal from the dross very quickly."

Naish had already got a taste of the furnace treatment at Convair, for troubles were piling up on all sides. Total orders for the 990 were only 32, while those for the 880 were still stuck at 44. Overhead on the jet venture had risen as production of the Convair-made F-106 dwindled and the Atlas program, which also shared the San Diego facilities, had had to be moved to another plant on orders from the Pentagon. But these were just first-degree burns in comparison to the furnace treatment Convair's new head was about to get from Howard Hughes over the 880.

Hughes's vagaries had already caused Convair plenty of lost sales and missed opportunities. When the 880 got to the production stage, the Hughes group—TWA engineers and executives—had quietly set up shop in an abandoned lumberyard near Convair's San Diego headquarters and for a time Hughes caused more mystification than trouble. As 1959 wore on, however, it became increasingly difficult to get Hughes to commit himself on the final configuration (styling and arrangements) of his 880's and making it certain that overtime would have to be used to meet the tightly scheduled delivery dates of the 990's—they'd been promised to American for the spring of 1961—if their dates could be met at all. As a matter of fact, in September (1959) Sales Vice-President Zevely was already notifying the airlines the 990 would be late.

Convair let more precious months slip by trying to humor Hughes before it came to a shattering conclusion: all his stalling on the final configuration of his 880's had its roots in the fact that he hadn't the money to pay for them on delivery.

Convair chose to pull his 880's off the line and put them out on the field. What made this decision so fantastic was that 13 of the planes were in different stages of completion. Now the economics of an aircraft production line are geared to "a learning curve," which simply means that labor costs go down as each production-line worker becomes familiar with his particular phase of putting the plane together. On the first 880 the learning curve was at its peak with labor costs of roughly $500,000, on the fortieth or fiftieth plane labor costs were designed to drop below $200,000. Thus removing Hughes' thirteen 880's from the line in *different stages* of completion meant that the learning curve for them would have to be begun again at the top—to the cost of Convair, not of Hughes.

"It's Not a Baby Any More"

This disastrous decision was made by Jack Naish, with an OK from Frank Pace and Earl Johnson. But even then New York was far from on top of the situation. Pace maintains he never knew the 880 was in serious trouble until after the Hughes decision: "We knew we had problems, but there were no major difficulties as far as we knew. The information that came to us fiscally, in a routine fashion, through Naish and substantiated by Naish, would not have led us to believe the extent of the losses that were occurring." Earl Johnson is not even sure just when he himself became alarmed over the jet program. "It's difficult to answer that. It's like living with a child—when do you notice it's not a baby any more?"

The sad truth was simply that General Dynamics was still being run as a holding company with no real control from the top. Its headquarters staff had been kept at 200, and this, in Pace's view, "automatically recognizes that it is impossible to police the operation of the divisions." But even if there had been a will, the means of policing seem slender indeed. Pace had established no reporting system that could tell him quickly when a division was in trouble; the key figures were buried in pages of divisional operating statements. General Dynamics' Financial Vice-President Richard Knight is still overhauling the system of auditing the divisional books so as to prevent any doctoring of the figures to make a divisional president look good. In short, millions of dollars of publicly owned money could be on its way down the drain at Convair before New York was aware of it.

In a letter of May 10, 1960, addressed to General Dynamics' stockholders, Pace reported jet-transport charges of $91 million (as of March 31, 1960) but added "[We] have every reason to believe [the program] will be one of our most successful ventures." By mid-August, however, Pace's springtime optimism began to show the signs of an early frost. It will be remembered that from the very beginning the 880 had been grossly underpriced in relation to its material costs; now Convair had virtually given up trying to keep those heavy costs within the budgeted amounts. For almost a year San Diego had been abuzz with rumor that losses on the 880, "the sweet bird of our economy" as local citizens called the 880, might reach $150 million. Some 880 components had overrun their original estimates by as much as 300%.

Four months later (January, 1961) Hughes got his financing and Convair was confronted with the problem of completing his aircraft. And some problem it was. Since no two planes were in exactly the same stage of completion, they couldn't be put back on the production line. They had to be hand-finished on the field, at costs many times those prevailing on the line. Moreover, engineering changes had to be made—some Convair's and some Hughes'.

A $40-Million Discovery

By February of 1961, General Dynamics was beginning to reap the economic consequences of the disastrous Hughes decision. New York "discovered" that Convair had not only failed to write off all jet losses the previous September but had incurred additional ones. These, amounting to $40 million, spelled the end for Jack Naish and for August Esenwein, the executive vice-president Pace had put under Naish to try and control costs. "I felt," said Pace recently, "that if I couldn't get more accurate judgments from Naish than I had gotten, he ought to go." Then he added, "Whether these problems were passed on and not properly interpreted by Esenwein and Naish, I can't tell. There are conflicting points of view now that we go back into the problem. But we in New York didn't know the magnitude of the problem."

Regardless of whether New York knew then or not, the whole business community was shortly to learn how profound was Convair's trouble. The risky decision to build the 990 without a prototype began to bear some even more expensive fruit. Seventeen of American's twenty-five 990's had to be delivered during 1961, the first one in March. A flight test of this particular airplane in late January, 1961, four months later than the date scheduled in a previous announcement of Pace's, disclosed wing flutter and other problems that required rebuilding the landing flaps, the leading edge of the wings, and the outboard pylons. These were not too difficult to correct from an engineering point of view, but as a General Dynamics vice-president sadly remarked, "If you get into production with a plane whose design has to be changed, the magnitude of the troubles you then encounter becomes exponential." Moreover, these corrections now had to be made on overtime because of the tight delivery schedule to American. Ultimately this was to burden General Dynamics with an additional $116-million jet write-off.

The burning question, of course, is why New York *didn't* know the magnitude of the problem. Naish maintains he leaned over backward, because of his initial opposition to the jet program, to clear important decisions with either Johnson or Pace. Last fall a member of General Dynamics' executive committee, still puzzling over why New York had been so much in the dark for so long, pressed Pace on the point. He wanted to know why, even if Naish's information had been suspect, Convair's controller hadn't told Pace of the losses, or why he hadn't learned of them from MacBride, whom Pace had sent out early in 1961 to investigate, or from Earl Johnson, whom Pace had given overall responsibility for the jet program and sent to Convair in late 1958 and early 1959 when the division was plainly in trouble. Pace, at a loss to explain, wondered whether he ought to resign. No, said the director, and Pace needn't make any apologies. After all, he wasn't trained as a businessman. He (the director) made no apologies for not being able to walk into an operating room and perform like a surgeon. So Pace shouldn't feel badly about not being trained as a businessman.

The Wages of Sin

Unhappily for General Dynamics, the departures of Naish and Esenwein did little to lighten the corporation's load of trouble. Nor was Rhoades MacBride, General Dynamics' No. 3 man whom Pace put in as acting president of Convair, able to bring the division under control (after ten months he too was to be washed out of office). There had simply been too many sins of commission and omission to be cured by chopping off heads in San Diego.

General Dynamics ran into trouble with American over the 990. The gamble, mentioned earlier, that Convair's engineers could guess the jet power needed to meet the speed and fuel requirements in the American contract, had failed. In addition, the 990 was already six months late, so in September, 1961, Smith canceled his order. Now the General Dynamics board was confronted by two choices, both bleak. It could turn back the uneconomical DC-7's Smith had induced them to accept in lieu of a $25-million down payment, then with the $25-million cash reimbursement as a cushion, cut the price of the 990 and try to sell it to other carriers; or it could try to get a new contract from Smith. A few audacious directors, including Crown, were for trying choice No. 1, but the opinion of the majority, as epitomized by one member of the board, was: "Now let's not get C. R. mad. Earl Johnson knows him. Let's go and appeal to him."

The upshot was that Pace, Johnson, and Henry Crown paid a call on Smith. There Colonel Crown related a little story about his having let a construction company off the hook even though, legally, he had had every right to hold them to a disastrous contract. Smith made no comment but when Pace and Johnson pursued the same thought he finally said: "I understand your problem, but I have stockholders. You told me, Earl, that the plane would go a certain speed." A new contract was signed with American and it was a tough one. The airline cut its order from 25 to 15 planes, with an option to take 5 more if Convair could get the speed up to 621 mph. Upwards of $300,000 was knocked off the price of each aircraft. With wind-tunnel tests completed, chances are now good that Convair will be able to meet the 621-mph specification.

But even as this article goes to press in mid-January, the end of General Dynamics' jet travail is not in sight. Howard Hughes has just canceled his order for thirteen 990's, an order that, surprisingly enough, Convair had accepted during the period when Hughes couldn't even pay for his 880's. SAS and Swiss Air have cut their original order from nine 990's to seven. Moreover, the market is just about saturated insofar as additional jet sales are concerned, even for a fine plane like the 880. As for the 990, it too has missed its market. To date only sixty-six 880's and twenty-three 990's have been sold, which puts Convair well behind Boeing's 720 sales in the medium-range market. Small wonder that when somebody suggests selling off Convair, a General Dynamics vice-president ruefully remarks: "Would $5 be too much?"

"This Has Hurt Us in Washington"

The failure of General Dynamics' management has had some serious collateral effects. As a member of the executive committee remarked: "The public has lost confidence in us. This has hurt us in Washington. We have to inject people of stature into the management." The company recently lost out on two of the three big defense contracts (the $400-million Apollo space-craft contract went to North American, Boeing got the $300-million Saturn S-1 booster system). Its executive committee has also failed to find a new chief executive officer, "a man forty years old with one hundred years of experience" as John McCone remarked in turning down the job, and this has further delayed General Dynamics' much-needed reorganization.

Though the great losses are now a matter of history, the subject of what went wrong with the company will no doubt be discussed for as long as there is a General Dynamics. "It's a grave question in my mind," said one of the company's senior vice-presidents, "as to whether General Dynamics had the right to risk this kind of money belonging to the stockholders for the potential profit you could get out of it. All management has to take a certain risk for big gains. But I don't think it's right to risk so much for so small a gain."

There are, however, larger questions of management's responsibility for the well-being of the corporation. That responsibility, in the jet age, is to keep management techniques developing at the same pace as the technologies they must control.

Question

What should Frank Pace have done to get better control at General Dynamics?

Part 6

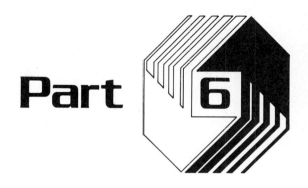

CONCLUSION: ACHIEVING BALANCE

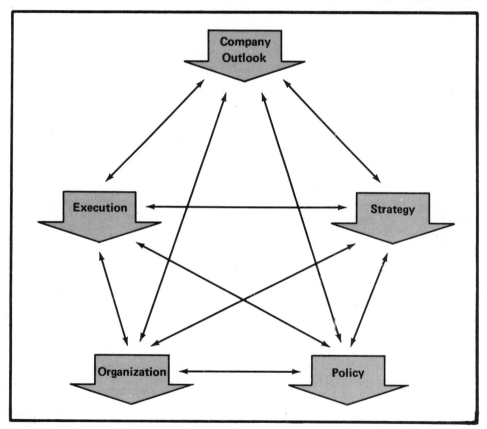

MANAGING MULTINATIONAL ENTERPRISES

The Total Task of Managing

To think sharply about a complex subject like managing, we usually divided the subject into parts for separate analysis. Thus, in this book we have shifted our focus successively from selecting strategy to defining policy, on to designing organization, and finally to guiding execution. This separate treatment helps in analysis, but it also detracts from sensing the interconnection and the complexity of the total task of managing. Central managers necessarily give much attention to achieving a balance of the various actions they sponsor. They must build their company into an integrated whole.

In concluding, then, we want to put the parts back together again. We will do this in two ways, first by reviewing the overall task of managing a multinational company, and second by discussing the integrating role of central managers.

The Attraction of Multinational Operations

"Go abroad, young man!" is the modern paraphrase of Horace Greeley's guide to opportunity. Companies, too, seek growth possibilities in foreign markets.

For years most U.S. firms were preoccupied with the vast free-trade area within our boundaries. In terms of time and communication, Los Angeles was then much farther from Chicago than Paris or Tokyo is today. But, as national markets became more competitive, exports took on added attractions. Also, oil, copper, steel, and other industries needed large supplies of raw materials from abroad. Those pressures led to substantial exports and imports.

Then as foreign markets grew and nationalistic controls hampered trade, business moved to the next and current phase of fully integrated operations —both manufacturing and selling—in offshore locations. For example, over one-third of both sales and net income of Ford Motor, IBM, Colgate-

Palmolive, National Cash Register, H. J. Heinz, and Pfizer arise outside the United States. Many other firms also are multinational in scope.

Such integrated operations abroad are growing rapidly, both for U.S. firms and for firms based in other countries. They create worldwide competition, with resources and know-how seeking opportunities in a highly adaptable fashion not confined to the country of origin. Most "multinational" companies start from a well established domestic operation but seek to optimize both the source and the allocation resources on a worldwide basis. They pose new challenges to our ability to manage.

This chapter deals with the *management* of companies that conduct manufacturing, selling, and related activities in several different countries. We will focus here on the issues that are particularly significant to multinational enterprises. Effective management of local operating units is assumed. This emphasis on "parent" operations serves two purposes: (1) it highlights the distinctive features of multinational companies, and (2) it illustrates the application of the basic analytical framework of the entire book to a different business.

STRATEGY OF MULTINATIONAL FIRMS

Multinational operation requires careful planning of overall strategy in terms of the international nature of the total business. Important issues in formulating multinational strategy are the differential advantage to be obtained, the selection of countries with the greatest long-run growth potential, the balancing of risks, and the timing of expansion.

Differential Advantage Sought

A firm embarking on a multinational course needs synergistic advantage to offset the inherent costs of operating in several different cultures. Many of the policy, organization, and control decisions that a firm adopts tie back to the fundamental question of "why we think we can do it better" than a local national company.

Important among possible rationales for operating abroad are the following:

1. *Technical know-how.* Manufacturing companies may go abroad to make use of the research and engineering already done for domestic operations. Clearly, one of the advantages Caterpillar Tractor has in its worldwide operations is its *engineering design* of heavy earth-moving equipment. *Processing know-how* is more likely a distinctive advantage for chemical and engineering companies. In some instances, as in pharmaceuticals, either the products or the processes are protected by worldwide patents, although even here the progressive updating of technology may be fully as important as the legal protection.

2. *Access to markets.* A worldwide company itself may provide an attractive market. Thus, "Nestles uses so much chocolate in its numerous plants that

it can provide an assured market for a large supply of the raw material—cocoa beans." Or the company may have a widespread marketing organization and be able to dispose of much larger quantities than could any company in the country of origin; for example, Dole has a great advantage in disposing of Philippine pineapple. Perhaps a company has bigger access to markets simply because of its superior marketing—a significant factor in Sears Roebuck's success in Latin America.

3. *Capital.* Especially in developing countries, the capital resources of a multinational company contribute to its relative strength. The ability to make large investments (coupled with technical know-how) has aided companies making everything from fertilizer to flashlights in India.

4. *Managerial skill.* Hard to determine and often overrated, the managerial skills provided by a multinational company often do provide it with a distinctive advantage. Philips' Gloeilampenfabrieken, the giant Netherlands electronics manufacturer, obviously owes part of its success to managerial ability; and the 57 varieties of H. J. Heinz are world-famous for a similar reason. The French writer, Servan-Schreiber, picks managerial ability as the basis for *the American challenge* to the entire European business community. Currently, business analysts are wondering whether Japanese management style will produce unusual results in foreign settings.

If a company bases its international strategy on any one or combination of the factors just discussed, it must be sure that it does in fact have an advantage that is both relevant and continuing. For example, mass marketing techniques that are geared to suburban shopping centers can cause disaster in foreign countries. Production processes based on high labor cost are not necessarily optimum in countries with a large labor supply. Some of the "know-how" advantages are fleeting; local competitors will catch up. So, if a long-run strategy rests upon a technological superiority, the multinational company must be reasonably confident that it can maintain its lead.

Defense rather than offense is sometimes the prime mover in multinational strategy. For years, a company making, say, radios or sewing machines may have exported to a South American or an African country. Then, local production or low-cost Japanese competition makes serious inroads. In this new environment, the company may have to choose between either establishing its own foreign plant or giving up a large segment of the market. But even if the strategy is initiated for defensive reasons, the company should have a clear advantage by which it hopes to keep a distinctive niche in each of the countries in which it operates.

Countries Attractive for Growth

Building a strong subsidiary in a country often takes years, and to obtain a significant industry position after other companies are entrenched is costly. Consequently, the multinational company needs some strategy regarding the kinds of countries that offer the greatest long-run potential. One metal container company, for instance, is setting up plants in developing countries—even though they may merely make bottle caps initially—in order to be established when real growth occurs. Other firms operate only where the per capita purchasing power is high. One rubber company, to cite a different criterion, will have nothing to do with countries affiliated with the Soviet bloc. Many other variations exist.

A useful approach to identifying countries attractive for growth is a careful appraisal of the following factors:

1. Estimate the potential demand for the major services the company expects to provide. This will be tied to industrial and economic development, living conditions, natural resources, population, education, consumption attitudes, and other social and economic influences.
2. Assess the importance in each country of the distinctive strengths of the company. These strengths will include the differential advantages the company hopes to exploit. Also, the strengths of prospective competitors and the likely responses of other key actors must be weighed.
3. Predict the general environment and its associated risk. Important factors to consider in this connection are prospects for:
   Controls on foreign exchange
   Inflation
   Import and export restrictions
   Legislation against foreigners
   Expropriation and nationalization
   Onerous taxation
   Political upheaval
   War
   Deterioration of financial, utility, and other services

Analysis of this sort led a leading manufacturer of control equipment to concentrate its expansion in Western Europe, with secondary attention to Japan. All other parts of the world are to be served by exports from the United States or Europe. On the other hand, a large pharmaceutical manufacturer anticipates increasing pressure to manufacture at least the leading drugs locally. Consequently, it is setting up a large number of small local plants where much of the final fabrication and packaging is done. The company hopes that this localized activity will give it an edge in the importation of new and complex drugs (which carry wide gross profit margins) from the home country.

Building a Balanced Portfolio

A multinational firm must watch its risk and cash flow balance, as explained in Chapter 15. Some European companies, for example, are entering the U.S. market as a hedge against communist takeover of their government. At the same time, U.S. pharmaceutical firms are expanding in Europe partly because of the threats of even more U.S. government regulation of medical affairs. Large Japanese firms, which must import most of their raw materials, are clearly seeking several different sources as a protection against political disruption in any one supplying country.

Similarly, the demands on scarce resources require an overall balance. A well known advertising agency, for instance, announced that it was entering the international arena but soon ran out of experienced executives to send abroad. Consequently, it is now pacing its growth to only northern Europe and Brazil. Capital also is a frequent constraint. Even large companies may be unable to finance vigorous growth in several countries simultaneously. Commitments already started in Australia may prevent a strong push into Japan. So the growth strategy must be kept in balance.

Timing of Expansion

Timing also looms large. Five years often elapse between a decision to manufacture in a given country and the efficient operation of a new plant. Government permits, site acquisition, engineering design, building construction, import of specialized equipment, hiring and training of workers, establishing dependable sources of materials, overcoming start-up difficulties, and shaping a viable social structure all take time. For this reason, many U.S. companies entered the European Common Market early, before trade barriers had been significantly reduced. Not all of these plants proved to be wise investments, but some companies built a strong position because they were ready to produce quality goods when the market opened up.

Multinational service organizations face a similar question of when to enter additional countries. Thus, for years all but two U.S. banks relied on "correspondents" for most of their foreign activities. Then, the growth of the Eurodollar market precipitated a great scramble for offices at least in London. In this instance, as with advertising agencies, multinational service organizations have delayed expansion until worldwide marketing and manufacturing organizations were well established. Industrial engineering and public accounting firms, on the other hand, have built strong positions by being in the vanguard of economic development.

Political instability strongly affects timing strategy. Indonesia presents a classic problem of when multinational companies should enter a strife-torn area. Rich in human and natural resources, yet needing outside capital and know-how, Indonesia attracts investments of oil and other multinational companies. Nevertheless, serious losses have been incurred by companies that have entered the area under political regimes that were later overthrown. Comparable political difficulties have arisen in Central Africa. Here, companies anxious to get a foothold in the large potential market have often discovered that their early association with one political regime becomes a handicap at a later time.

What services to perform, in which countries, with what balance, and at what time, are recurring issues in multinational strategy. Specific situations pose an array of additional angles, but these four issues give a sense of central management's strategy problems.

USE OF POLICY   ~~Pg 424~~   AND 431

The use of policy as a management tool is even more significant in multi-national firms than in Stage III multidivision firms that operate within a single country. In both types of enterprise, the operating divisions have their own policies. However, the multinational enterprise must distinguish clearly between those facets of its activities in which it seeks synergistic benefits—and hence needs centralized policy and coordination—and those activities that should not be governed by central policy. Selectivity is crucial. Possible issues on which multinational guidance may be warranted are illustrated in the following paragraphs.

Standardization of Products

The degree to which products will be the same in various countries calls for policy guidance. The most widely known product throughout the world is Coca-Cola. The Coca-Cola Company has a strict policy that its product is to be uniform, a standard that is difficult to achieve since bottling is done by numerous independent local distributors throughout the world. Product consistency and a worldwide reputation take priority over local tastes. In contrast, Unilever permits its operating companies to adapt their soap and food products to the particular tastes and needs of the countries in which they are operating. This flexibility permits local units to stress, say, margarine versus cooking oils in accordance with national dietary habits.

Equipment manufacturers find standardization among countries difficult to achieve. A U.S. food machinery manufacturer, for example, had to change all dimensions from inches to metric measurement; and to simplify shop operations, it also had to modify the specifications slightly. Electric motors, switches, compressors, and even bolts that were purchased had to be adjusted to what was locally available. Users of the machines wanted to be able to obtain repair parts quickly and they preferred designs with which local workers were familiar. Consequently, the policy of this company is to have separate specifications for Europe and for South America. IBM takes an opposite tack. The parts for its machines are the same throughout the world. Such a policy is feasible because IBM has long stressed providing its own service to customers, which includes assuming the burden of maintaining an inventory of repair parts.

The choice of a product standardization policy, then, is influenced by company size and its volume of sales in each country, the importance of adapting to local needs, and in particular the strategy the company has chosen to make its services distinctive.

Regional Specialization of Production

A multinational company has the possibility of concentrating production of each of its products in one plant and then trading. Theoretically, this permits sale of a full line in Country A, one product being made locally and the rest imported. The same situation prevails in Countries X, Y, and Z. The advantage, of course, is lower cost arising from making a large quantity of a single product in each plant instead of a variety of products only in the volume needed in the local market. In practice, the trades do not balance off neatly, but the central concept of regional specialization can be utilized. Singer Company, for example, partially concentrates production of its industrial, high-quality domestic, and low-quality domestic sewing machines in three different countries.

If the parts going into products are standardized, then regional specialization of parts manufacture is possible. IBM in Europe has made considerable progress in this direction.

Unfortunately, a regional specialization policy is difficult to apply. It relies on inexpensive and uninterrupted movement of goods across national boundaries; it assumes that product standardization and economies of scale are substantial; and it applies only when the production capabilities of the various countries are compatible. Note also that a high degree of central coordination is required.

Transfer Prices

The prices at which raw materials, parts, or finished goods are transferred from one division of a company to another is always a troublesome problem. Transfers across national boundaries create additional difficulties. For instance, a high transfer price increases the profits earned in the exporting country and decreases the profits of the importer; this affects who gets income taxes and which local managements "look good." The transfer price may also influence the choice of long-term investment, selling prices, and local allocation of effort among products. Consequently, a multinational company must have some policy regarding the value attached to goods (and services) moving from one operating unit to another.

Mobil Oil Corporation, for instance, ships crude oil from the Middle East to a refinery in the Netherlands, and then ships the refined product from the Netherlands to Sweden for sale to consumers. The managers of Mobil's affiliates in each of the three countries and the respective national governments all naturally feel that their share of the final sales income should be higher. Where the profit shows up is not a matter of indifference to them.

Virtually all companies transfer at "market price" if such a figure exists for the product at the time and the place the transfer occurs. Beyond that, policies differ sharply. Some firms use a negotiated price, a figure that presumably approximates what a competitive price would be. Others use direct cost plus a markup percentage set up by headquarters. A few use total budgeted cost, including a "fair" return on local investment. In some circumstances, the starting point is a budgeted selling price from which distribution and processing costs are deducted to arrive at the value of the product received.

A guide for multinational managers among this array of possible policies, we suggest, is to focus on the incentive effect of transfer prices. Put the variability—the residual profits—in those units that have the greatest maneuverability to make or lose money. For divisions performing a standard function (for example, pipelines in an integrated petroleum operation), set transfer prices to cover full costs and depend on budgetary control rather than "profit margins" for incentives.

Proportion of Local Ownership

All multinational firms are holding companies. They are parent companies only, investing in local concerns that are organized in conformity with the requirements of the particular country in which they operate. A major policy question in this regard is what share, if any, of each operating company should be owned by local citizens. Billions of dollars of present and potential foreign investment are affected by this issue.

Referring to our discussion of partially owned subsidiaries in Chapter 16, the parent company gains many advantages from 100% ownership—flexibility in assigning functions, freedom in setting transfer prices, avoidance of arguments about fairness to minority interests, simpler decision-making, and by no means least carrying the full risk and receiving all the net profits.

Full ownership, of course, means higher investment. The chief drawback of 100% ownership is the loss of a potential incentive—stock ownership by local employees—but even this can be largely overcome by bonus plans and stock options in the parent company.

Multinational companies face an added dimension. *National pride* and *national economic independence* enter, often with heavy emotional and political overtones. The idea that a foreigner controls even a tiny part of the national gross product or the national employment can rally popular opposition. And if (1) a natural resource is involved and (2) a major sector of the economy is affected—as is true of copper in Chile and Zambia and oil in Libya—then governments can rise or fall on the ownership issue.

The alternative ownership arrangements are numerous. Simple variations start from full ownership by the parent, move to a minority local interest (the typical request of Canadians who want an opportunity to share in profits of local companies), and extend to 51% (controlling) local interest.

Moreover, different kinds of shares with various voting rights can be introduced, and options or contracts to gain control at a later date can be added. The ownership right, itself a social device, can be circumscribed by contracts with individuals or governments.

From this array of possibilities, most multinational enterprises adopt a policy that gives them a consistent stand on this troublesome issue. Firms like IBM wish to use regional specialization and have a special reason for insisting on the flexibility that comes with 100% ownership. Also in this case rapid technological development makes avoidance of bickering over who deserves credit more significant.

In contrast, when the multinational company provides only technical know-how and the local firm carries complete responsibility for organizing production and marketing, a local ownership interest both is fair and generates incentive for local initiative that is essential for success. Who should eventually control the local operation depends on who will make the major *continuing* contribution—a matter hard to measure but at least shifting the discussion from power to a constructive issue.

Exploitation of natural resources generates the most emotion. Here, rising nationalism makes 100% foreign-owned companies politically untenable. An increasingly popular arrangement is to grant the multinational company control during the first twenty years and/or until it has recovered its investment plus, say, 20% profit per annum—and then to transfer majority ownership to local (perhaps governmental) interests.

These examples clearly indicate a close interdependence between a firm's strategy regarding products and countries and its policy on the sharing of ownership with local interests.

Optimizing Exchange Risks

Multinational firms inevitably face foreign exchange problems. Most transactions of each operating company will be in its local currency; but when goods are exported or imported and when dividends from local operations are returned to the parent company, the local money must be converted into foreign currency. Rates of exchange—the value of one currency in terms of another—do change, especially when a local inflation is creating balance-of-payments difficulties.

A common policy followed by smaller firms is to *ignore* exchange fluctuations. Under this approach, each local company seeks to maximize its profit, and transfers to the parent are made when surplus funds are available. Hopefully, exchange rates will be favorable, or at least average out over a period of time. The rationale for ignoring exchange fluctuations is that the firm will be more successful by concentrating on the business it knows than by dabbling where it is not an expert.

An alternative and more sophisticated policy is to *minimize exposure*. This can be done in several ways: (1) Borrow locally to finance local operations so that repayments never get involved in foreign exchange. The catch, of course, is that only part of the total needs of the local unit can be borrowed, and interest rates may be quite high. (2) Rent buildings and other assets, thereby reducing local investment. Again, availability and cost limit the extent to which this can be done. (3) Hedge in forward exchange markets by "selling" a foreign currency to offset fixed obligations (and perhaps investments in assets that will not depreciate) in that currency. For this, as for other methods, there is an expense involved in avoiding the risk.

In fact, firms often adopt a policy of *minimizing interest costs,* even though doing so may add to foreign exchange risks. Money is borrowed where the interest rate is low and is transferred via foreign exchange to countries with high interest rates. When exchange controls hamper such direct movements, the same result can be achieved by either delaying or prepaying a settlement for goods that the multinational firm ships from one country to another. Since high interest rates frequently signal inflation and foreign exchange difficulties, such transfers of funds can increase exchange risks.

A still more daring policy is to deliberately *seek profits* from changes in exchange rates. Rarely will a multinational concern simply speculate in foreign exchange quite unrelated to its other business. However, it may feel that its intimate knowledge of some countries provides such a good basis for predicting rate changes that it is justified in shifting its holdings of these currencies in anticipation of future changes.[1]

The five policy issues discussed—standardization of products, regional specialization of production, transfer pricing, proportion of local ownership, and optimizing exchange risks—by no means exhaust the policy problems facing multinational enterprises. They do demonstrate that the concept of policy formulation can be helpful in dealing with the more unique aspects of multinational operations as well as with the more common problems facing national companies that were examined in Chapters 6 to 14.

ORGANIZING MULTINATIONAL OPERATIONS

Geographic dispersion of the multinational enterprise intensifies most of the organization problems faced by domestic firms. The variety of languages, laws, loyalties, and customs require more adaptation and complicate integrated action. Basically, the problems are the same; the difference is one of degree.

---

[1] Attempting to profit from changes in foreign exchange rates is similar to trying to outguess inflationary price changes. For policy restraint on such risk-taking see pages 291–293.

Worldwide Departmentation

A multinational firm is a Stage III company (as defined in Chapter 17). The primary emphasis, of course, is on geographical divisions rather than product divisions. Normally, all activities in each country are placed under a single executive. Distance, national differences, and especially local political considerations accentuate the need for a coordinated, consistent posture in each country.

But the stress on national divisions leaves unsettled how these units tie into the overall organization.

In many industries where production plants are small, both marketing and at least the final stages of production can be performed economically within each country. So here, the *regional* type of structure remains dominant and the national units report to an overall regional or world office.

For companies dealing with a single line of products that require large-scale operations, such as steel or copper, a basically *functional* structure works well. Each national unit is predominantly either marketing or production, so it can be assigned to an appropriate worldwide functional department.

Recently worldwide *product* divisions reporting directly to the president of the parent corporation have become more common. This arrangement reflects increasing international competition focused on standardized product lines. Success depends on prompt adjustment to changes in supply or demand anywhere in the world. And, improved communication and air travel now permit this sort of coordination.

As in domestic corporations, the choice of a regional, functional, or product structure should reflect the strategic emphasis the firm has selected. However, in multinational corporations the ever-present need for coordination within each country often does lead to mixed or matrix arrangements.

National or Regional Decentralization

Most multinational organizations are highly decentralized in some respects and centralized in others. Activities tied to consumers or operating employees—selling, granting credit, pricing, delivery, customer service, bookkeeping, warehousing, and the like—should be adapted to local conditions, and wide discretion in such matters should be exercised by managers of national units.

The benefits of synergy, on the other hand, usually come with centralized direction. For example, process and product know-how, worldwide quality reputation, and regional specialization of production can be fully utilized when they are centrally designed and controlled. Multinational firms whose strategies stress such concepts are committed to centralization on at least these key strategic weapons. Even a commitment to capitalize on managerial know-how implies that the techniques of planning, organizing, leading, and controlling will be stipulated by central headquarters.

The organizational task, then, is to sort out the kinds of decisions that need to be centralized and those that can be more expeditiously made in local units. And, having defined the dimensions of freedom at various levels, our multinational manager must make sure that the structure is understood by all executives—a substantial endeavor because of the diversity of backgrounds and expectations of the people involved.

Providing Expert Services Where Needed

A perpetual headache in multinational management is obtaining full advantage of the expertise that exists within the company. How can the know-how of executives in the domestic operating divisions and the wisdom of central staff be incorporated into decisions in operating companies dispersed throughout the world?

The difficulty arises from several causes. The experts are busy with their primary assignments, and they give low priority to a request for advice from Calcutta or Copenhagen. Even when they do spare time for foreign matters, they have difficulty in communicating. Language, background, and unfamiliarity with local conditions make it hard for them to perceive the local situation and give advice that is realistic. Moreover, the local executives often lack sufficient training to sift and adapt the ideas they receive.

The most common device for overcoming this barrier is a *liaison staff,* that is, people whose primary role is communicator of pertinent questions to the experts and translator of answers to operating personnel. Such a staff may be attached to the chief executive of international operations and/or to regional managers if they exist. Unfortunately, experience with a staff of this sort is not always favorable. Both General Electric Company and Ford Motor Company have created a large international staff, disbanded it, and recreated it. As with all staff, there is danger that persons far removed from the scene of action will become more bureaucratic than helpful.

An alternative is to try *lowering the communications barrier* itself. This may be done by increasing opportunities for travel, personal contact, and observation. Managers of domestic divisions may be given indirect or even direct "responsibility" for foreign activities similar to their domestic ones. Full-time task teams may be formed to study major problems. Cooperation may be explicitly added to performance appraisal factors. These and other devices are intended to create a "We're all in the same family" feeling.

Few multinational companies are happy with the spotty success they have achieved in getting good advice focused on local problems. Opportunities for improvement are high in this facet of organization.

Coordination Between Countries

Shipping products from one country to another requires careful coordination. The Singer Company, for example, ships sewing machines from England to over thirty countries; the receiving countries want the right model at the right time, and the English plants want a balanced, stable production schedule. Multinational oil companies ship crude oil from half a dozen sources to several different refineries, which in turn ship finished products to a score of consuming nations. Or a company constructing a flour mill in South Africa imports specialized equipment that must fit the building erected on the spot. In each instance, activities in several countries must be closely synchronized.

This coordination task is complicated by its international dimensions. Usually a special organization unit is created to assure that misunderstandings are held to a minimum and that each country acts in a way that optimizes cost-income for the company as a whole. Oil companies often create a major Supply and Distribution Department devoted solely to this task. In other industries, a special scheduling unit is located at each plant, but it has a unique international status. The manager of one such unit observes: "The mechanics are easy once you understand the needs and cost factors of each location; I spend most of my time being an international diplomat."

Again we see—as with departmentation, decentralization, and specialized services—that multinational coordination has its particular difficulties and intensities, but it is basically the same kind of phenomenon faced by managers of domestic firms.

KEY PERSONNEL

Operating units in each country will have their own personnel policy suited to local needs. To realize the potential benefits of their multinational affiliation, however, key technical and executive personnel must somehow acquire the best knowledge and skills available in the total system. Capturing this benefit is crucial to a successful multinational enterprise.

Use of Nationals as Executives

IBM follows a practice of filling all executive positions in the hundred countries in which it operates with local citizens. Two ends are served by this local use of nationals (that is, citizens of the country in which they work). Executives in each country know intimately the language and the customs of their market and their workers. Moreover, nationalistic demands to give jobs to local citizens rather than foreigners are fully met.

But IBM is an exception. Virtually all companies agree that *most* local executives should be nationals, for the reasons stated. Complete adherence, however, restricts promotion opportunities. Under the IBM system, the best person available *in the total company* cannot be shifted into a vacancy unless that person happens to be a national of the country in which the vacancy occurs.

An alternative is to give nationals preference, but when foreigners are clearly better qualified, to place them in the positions. Still another variation used by one large oil company that wishes to "internationalize" its general managers is a clearly stated policy that no nationals will be appointed general managers in any country (1) until they serve a tour of duty in a foreign country and (2) agree to accept a transfer at a later date out of their native land. Because this guide is consistently followed, executives seek foreign assignments since they know this is the path of advancement, and local employees resist fewer general managers who are foreigners because they are not regarded as obstacles to advancement of local people.

A final alternative we should mention is maximum use of nationals *except* in the top *financial* position; the presumption is that a non-national in this job will be freer of local loyalties and more objective in appraising operating results.

Developing Multinational Managers

If nationals are to fill most, if not all, of the key positions in each country, the need for executive training is obvious. In the newer countries, especially, competent and dependable executives are very scarce. And, a core of senior executives qualified to move from one country to another, or to top staff jobs, needs even broader training.

The special requirements for a multinational executive include: (1) language; (2) sensitivity and adaptability to differences in culture, especially with respect to communication and motivation; (3) background in international trade and finance and in the economic problems of the country where assigned; (4) grasp of company procedures, technology, and successful practices; and (5) unusual degree of patience and tact combined with perseverance.

The first three of these special qualifications can be developed off-the-job; the company can assist by making time available and paying expenses of outside courses. Knowledge about the company is normally acquired on-the-job in a series of assignments including work in company headquarters and in key departments. Tact and perseverance, insofar as they can be consciously developed, call for personal counseling. And so a whole array of executive development techniques should be carefully combined to foster the growth of multinational executives.

Compensation of Executives in Foreign Assignments

Both the need to supplement local executive talent and the process of executive development call for assigning people outside their home country. Such working abroad complicates pay rates in two ways.

(1) Salary scales differ from country to country. For instance, using the official exchange rate, U.S. pay is about double the British pay for a similar job. So, should a Yankee working in England be paid by U.S. or British standards? And what of a Britisher in the United States? Of course, living costs, taxes, government benefits, social requirements, and the like do differ substantially, but few executives agree on the extent to which such factors offset the differences in cash salary.

(2) People living abroad want some things that they enjoyed at home but that may be costly in a foreign country. Brazilians in the United States find that domestic servants must be paid what they consider executive salaries, whereas North Americans in Brazil find that frozen vegetables are exorbitant. Few executives—and their spouses—are adaptable enough to quickly give up all of the particular living comforts they are accustomed to.

One large multinational firm meets these pay pressures as follows: (1) Executives' base salaries and their retirement accumulations are tied to what the job they hold would pay in their home country. The assumption is that the executives relate their salaries to standards in their native land and that they plan to retire there. (2) In addition, they receive allowances for moving, extra living and housing cost, children's education, biennial trips home, and—if the location is unpleasant—"hardship."

This arrangement provides a consistent and "fair" pay in terms of a person's home base. However, two individuals from different countries might receive quite different total compensation for the same job, and this can become a source of irritation. (Americans' base salaries may be paid partly in local currency and partly in dollars in the U.S.A., so that their local scale of living will not conspicuously differ from that of their peers.) Also, if allowances are too liberal, the executives have trouble readjusting when they return home and receive only their base pay.

Whatever the particular system of allowances, clearly an executive away from home is a high-priced person. Possibly as international assignments become recognized as valuable steps on the way to the top, instead of an inconvenient way to save a few dollars, the premium paid to our mobile executives can be reduced.

CONTROLLING MULTINATIONAL ACTIVITIES

Distance and diversity of operating conditions also create problems of control within a multinational enterprise. The three dimensions of these control problems, discussed in the following paragraphs, illustrate the special burden a multinational firm undertakes in addition to the normal control tasks in each of the operating units.

Understanding the Concept of Constructive Control

For cultural reasons, the control process is poorly understood in many countries. Often the significance of completing work on time and of maintaining quality is not accepted. Local life proceeds more casually; so when western control standards are imposed, the action appears to local workers as unwarranted and capricious.

Similarly, accounting records in many countries are scanty, inaccurate, and often manipulated to reduce taxes. Naturally, managers do not look to such records as aids to prompt coordination of activities.

In some cultures, business relationships are closely entwined with personal friendship, kinship, reciprocal favors, and *simpatico* feelings. In such situations objective appraisal and tough corrective action are too irritating to be tolerated.

A first step, then, for a multinational manager in securing control is to win acceptance of the concept. Executives in operating units must understand that survival in world business requires realistic objectives, performance standards based on these objectives, regular measurement of performance, prompt feedback of control data to people who can undertake corrective action, overall evaluation, updating of targets, and correlation of incentives with results. Without acceptance of this process, the best-designed control systems will achieve only moderate effects.

Operating Controls that Encourage Optimum Performance

Every multinational firm must have dependable, understandable accounting reports from each country. Due to local variations in bookkeeping practice, already mentioned, the establishment of a worldwide accounting system is no small task. But once in place, it does permit the introduction of annual and five-year budgets, measurement of growth in sales and profits, and other usual financial control devices.

Essential as such financial controls are, reliance on financial reports alone is especially dangerous in a multinational business. The opportunities and the difficulties in each country make necessary more complete and sensitive yardsticks. Criteria such as market share, government relations, quality maintenance, customer service, cultivation of new customers, physical productivity, employee training and turnover, plant maintenance, innovation and modernization, protection of assets from inflation, cooperation with other units of the company—all are control measures that the multinational headquarters should watch in each country in addition to financial reports.

Frequent evaluation is inappropriate. A thorough semiannual review plus prompt evaluation of major changes or deviations from plans serve most multinational companies better than monthly reporting, which is likely to become routine.

Periodic Product-Stream Evaluation

The controls just described help keep each operating unit "on course," but they do not check the continuing desirability of the course itself. This broader evaluation is difficult because most multinational firms sell the same product in different countries, ship materials or parts from one country to another, and in other ways seek synergistic benefits from joint activities. Separate controls in each country do not tell whether the desired overall benefits are being obtained.

Consequently, special studies that consolidate the incomes, costs, and investment from all countries dealing with a *product line* are needed. Since typically several lines are handled, at least when all countries are considered, a lot of unscrambling of assets and joint costs may be necessary. So the analysis becomes involved, too involved for routine periodic reports. Fortunately, a special appraisal, say every two years, is adequate because changes in product line or production strategy can only be made in relatively long time cycles.

With an analysis of how product lines are measuring up to original plans, a reappraisal also of markets, competition, technology, and other external factors is in order. This may lead to significant shifts in company strategy. And so we find ourselves completing the full management cycle of strategy, implementing plans, execution, and control—which provides the basis for a revised strategy and a new cycle.

SUMMARY

Managers in multinational companies face a variety of issues arising from the international climate of the total operation. Balancing these issues calls for unusual skill. Company *strategy* seeks to extend strengths in one country to many other markets; it requires judicious selection of countries where these strengths will be most beneficial; and it lays out the timing of international expansion.

Among the *policy* issues created by worldwide operations are the extent to which products will be adapted to local needs, regionalization of production, allocation of profits to different countries via transfer prices, participation in ownership of operating units by local nationals, and speculating or avoiding foreign exchange risks.

Organization has to be adjusted to the strategy and the geographical dispersion. To capture full synergistic benefits of technological know-how, uniform quality, or reorganization of production, decision-making must be centralized—whereas national differences pull down decisions related to people. Special provision for communicating and coordinating is necessary to assure that the multinational advantages are attained.

Staffing with local nationals is desirable, but this creates a need for multinational training of executives. To provide such training, and in the senior levels to utilize exceptional talent, people must move across national boundaries. Whenever this is done, a prickly problem of salary and cost-of-living adjustments arises.

A multinational scope of operation increases both the need for and the difficulty of *control*. The underlying concept of constructive control has to be developed, reliable measures of tangible and intangible results must be created, and provision must be made for assessing integrated results as well as performance in each country.

Overshadowing these distinctive aspects of multinational management is the demonstration that the broad framework we have used throughout this book to analyze the central management tasks of national companies provides an equally effective means for thinking through the overall management framework of the most complex business enterprise man has yet conceived.

QUESTIONS FOR CLASS DISCUSSION

1. Reflecting rising nationalism, many developing countries have passed laws requiring that business firms be 51% owned by local citizens. (a) What difference is this new legislation likely to make in the way subsidiaries that were previously 100% owned by multinational corporations are managed? (b) How do you recommend that multinational corporations respond to the new requirements?

2. To help forestall U.S. restrictions on importation of foreign autos and to increase its share of the U.S. market, a subsidiary of Toyota Motor Co. Ltd. (Japan) assembles some light trucks in its Long Beach, California, plant and is "considering" assembling passenger cars in the U.S. (a) What unusual management problems do you think Toyota will have manufacturing in the U.S.? (b) Do these problems differ from those a U.S. company such as Ford would have assembling its cars in Japan? (c) Would your answers to (a) and (b) be the same for Volkswagen instead of Toyota?

3. Most multinational enterprises deal with products or raw materials. Recently multinational advertising agencies have had a spurt of growth. (a) Recognizing that advertising must be run in local media, use the local language, and appeal to local viewpoints: what differential advantage does a multinational advertising agency provide? (b) What kinds of policies, organization, and control will a multinational advertising agency need to provide the differential advantage you identified in your answer to (a)?

4. For at least half a decade foreign companies have been steadily and rapidly increasing their investments in Spain while native entrepreneurs and investors have been keeping their money under the mattress. How can this

somewhat puzzling fact be explained? Why would foreign companies see much better opportunities in Spain than do its domestic firms? One Spaniard said, "Multinational companies first compare Spain to the underdeveloped countries, where the political and social uncertainties are even greater and where there is difficulty in getting skilled labor and managers. Then they compare it to the superdeveloped countries where costs are higher and native competition much more intense. And Spain suddenly looks very good." Local business executives see a declining growth rate (less than 1.5 %), inflation at 16% per year, borrowing costs at 18% and higher, unemployment at 10% or more, energy costs up steeply since 1977, more autonomy to local governments, rising street crime and acts of terrorism—all of which mean great political and economic uncertainty. Do these differences in perception and judgment explain the acts of the multinationals?

5. Multinational operations are faced with an additional array of uncertainties such as tariff charges, fluctuating foreign exchange rates and controls, different tax regulations, political upheavals, wars, varying growth rates, and additional sources of competition. Does the existence of these uncertainties mean that long-range programming (see Chapter 21) should not be attempted by multinational companies? If you do recommend use of long-range programming, explain how you would deal with these uncertainties.

6. Assume that you have a good job and a promising future with a bank, a manufacturing company, an advertising agency, or another kind of business that appeals to you. Your company has undertaken international expansion, and the president asks whether you would like a foreign assignment. (a) What inducements would you want before you accepted a 3-year assignment? a 20-year assignment? (b) What effect might the inducements you ask for have on your effectiveness in the foreign post? (c) Do you think nationals of other countries should receive the same kind of treatment that you request?

7. Belmont Fashions sells a wide variety of men's dress shirts and sport shirts featuring some high-style brands and some low-cost brands. In addition to its New York "contract" production, it runs its own plants in Texas and in Hong Kong. Compare the task of central management control of the Texas plant with control of the Hong Kong plant. In your answer consider (a) the criteria used, (b) who does the measuring and how often, (c) the interpretation of results, and (d) the types of corrrective action that are likely to be effective.

8. In a recent year foreign direct investment in the United States (equity holdings of more than 10 percent ownership) rose by 18 percent to about $41 billion. In the same year, U.S. direct investment abroad increased 12 percent to $168 billion. But it was done differently. American firms usually built subsidiaries from scratch, particularly in high-technology industries. By contrast, foreign companies that came to the U.S. more than half the time acquired existing U.S. companies whether or not they brought in advanced technology of their own. (a) Can you explain these differences? (b) What implications for executive development and for control by the owners do these differences have?

9. How do the portfolio issues faced by a diversified U.S. corporation (see Chapter 15) differ from those of a multinational corporation?

10. One of the complications of multinational operations is the difference among countries in norms of ethical behavior and social responsibility. Both the

formal standards (often expressed in law) and the strictness of their observance vary. (For example, wide differences exist with respect to bribery, tax evasion, treatment of workers, and agreements with competitors.) If you were working abroad for an English-based multinational company, which set of standards would you follow? What is the potential business impact of your ethical decisions?

CASE 24
MAINTAINING FINLAND'S POSITION IN METALS

Finland's leading metal company, Outokumpu Oy (called OKO in this case), must decide how it wishes to position itself in the world metal industries during the 1980's. OKO has been an acknowledged leader in mining and refining technology, but currently faces severe financial constraints.

Home Base

Finland is perhaps most widely known for its courageous fight for survival during World War II, and for its ability through neutrality diplomacy to maintain independence ever since. Located on the Baltic Sea, with Russia on its eastern border and Norway and Sweden on its north and west, Finland serves as a buffer between the East and the West.

Geographically, Finland is larger than Great Britain or West Germany. But with a population under 5 million, it qualifies as one of the smaller of the small nations. Although about a third of Finland's length lies above the Arctic Circle, the Gulf Stream and air currents keep it warmer than other countries at the same latitude. Its major ports are open for shipping year-round.

For several decades now, manufacturing has displaced the traditional forestry and agriculture as the leading contributor to the total economy and to employment. Incidentally, Finland's per capita GNP is higher than Japan's and Great Britain's. Companies such as OKO have played a significant role in this development.

As with many small countries, imports and exports are especially important to Finland—close to one-quarter of GNP. Raw materials are the chief imports, and manufactured goods the major exports. Although the Soviet Union is the leading single country in Finland's foreign trade (20% of the total), at least two-thirds of exports and imports are with Western nations.

By U.S. standards, Finland has a lot of government planning and government ownership. However, compared to its immediate neighbors, it places heavy reliance on private ownership and initiative. All the leading companies are expected to be economically viable and earn a reasonable return on invested capital.

Synergistic Diversification

For the first thirty years of its existence, OKO was just a copper company, mining a relatively small deposit at Outokumpu. Since then three interrelated developments have drastically changed the scope of the company.

(1) OKO has greatly expanded the numbers of different metals it mines and refines. In addition to copper, zinc, nickel, cobalt, and pyrite concentrates are major products. Other metals are often associated in ore bearing these major ones, with the result that OKO also produces some chrome, lead, gold, silver, cadmium, and talc. Whenever a metal ore is found in commercial quantities in Finland, OKO will mine it. Moreover, having mined this ore OKO proceeds to refine it into base metals—with only minor exceptions.

(2) For several metals, OKO has integrated forward, adding still more value to the original resource. For instance, copper is converted into tubing, bars, sheets, wire, and other forms. Much of the company's chrome now goes into its stainless steel.

(3) Compared with the major ore deposits of the world, Finland's deposits are neither very large nor very rich (a high percentage of metal). Consequently, throughout its history OKO has had to give much attention to productivity. In both mining (mostly underground) and refining, the most efficient and up-to-date technology is used. Since World War II, OKO has done pioneering R&D in metal refining. So successful has this effort been that OKO is able to license some of its processes and may be hired to construct refining plants in other countries. More than anything else, OKO's "flash smelting" process has made the company world-famous. Over half the world's new copper smelters are licensees of OKO. In addition, an X-ray analyzer of ore slurry is a key element in automated concentrators, and is even more widely used than flash smelting. OKO's "tramp iron detector," initially designed for use on crushers, has been converted into a security device against airport hijacking.

Note that all three of these developments—different metals, forward integration, and advanced technology—have been synergistic, and have enabled OKO to sell most of its products abroad in the face of world competition. In fact, 78% of OKO sales are exports.

Recession: Impact on Financing

The diversification program just outlined enabled OKO to expand substantially in the 1960's and 1970's. In the past decade both sales and assets have grown more than fourfold. Much of this increase reflects inflation, but overall tonnage and employment did rise. The company is now divided into four operating divisions, and the relative importance of each is indicated in the following table.

Unfortunately, profits have been much lower than the estimated net income that was used to justify the investment in new facilities. For example, the most recent major expansion into stainless steel is a technological success, but selling prices have dropped and this new plant is barely breaking even. During the last few years economic activity in Europe especially has been slow, and selling prices for most metals and metal products have not kept pace with rising wage and interest rates. See the accompanying income statement.

Division	Sales (million marks)*	Exports	Number of Employees	Management Comment on Profitability
Mining & Metallurgy	615	85%	5,060	Except for cobalt (prices and profits up dramatically because of turmoil in Zaire), the profitability remains unsatisfactory due to low prices of metals.
Copper & Copper Alloy	476	59%	1,838	Increased productivity has improved profitability, but a satisfactory level has not yet been reached.
Stainless Steel	429	75%	1,141	Profitability remains unsatisfactory due to low price level and continuing start-up expenses.
Technical Export	307	97%	417	Profitability remains favorable. However, this year was unusually high due to large deliveries of smelter equipment to Soviet Union and the Republic of Korea. Preceding year sales were 175 million marks.
Central Management & "Other"	8	94%	669	Includes R&D, which costs 3.2% of sales—primarily for exploration and metallurgical research.
Total	1,835	78%	9,125	

* For quick conversion, assume 4 Finnish marks equal 1 U.S. dollar.

OKO went heavily into debt to finance its diversification. Now that profits have not risen as expected, this debt is a serious burden. In fact, the depreciation and depletion charge is less than necessary to replace capital so the situation is even more strained than the income statement shows. (Depreciation based on replacement values would have been 220 million marks, instead of the 156 million marks used for the income statement.)

Because of this financial squeeze, the present central management has switched to a conservative investment policy during the last three years. In the OKO annual report, management says frankly, "In order to improve the financing situation, major expansion programmes will have to be shelved for the time being." Investments have been made (175 million marks last year) only to complete expansions already started and even more to improve productivity. Perhaps a clearer indication of the policy reversal is the drop in employment from a peak of over 10,000 to 9,100 —a very significant action in a country where increased employment is a major social objective.

Present Options

No one is fully satisfied with OKO's present operations. In physical terms the volume is static, profits are very small, employment is down. So, central management must weigh alternative approaches to the future. The following threefold grouping suggests several possibilities. The various thrusts can, of course, be re-sorted into other combinations.

(1) Continue the present strategy. This includes (a) focusing investments and R&D on improved productivity, (b) seeking to reduce the debt burden and improve the debt-equity ratio, (c) continuing to export products and services to the best markets currently available, and (d) deferring other expansion until metal prices and economic conditions improve and risk is reduced.

(2) Stress growth from Finland's resources. OKO's growth through diversification was based on this approach. It involves (a) finding and mining Finland's mineral resources, (b) refining these ores into base metals by using advanced, sophisticated technology, (c) integrating forward into metal fabrication in selected areas to increase the value added, and (d) exporting products and services to the best markets available.

The copper ore deposits now being mined will be exhausted in about ten years, so intensive exploration will be necessary to maintain local supplies. For years local farmers and explorers have been encouraged to bring in rock samples.

The creativeness of Finnish miners and engineers in taking full advantage of valuable resources has already been described. Note that under this strategy OKO's "domain" is defined by Finland's resources, not by potential world markets. Likewise, the outstanding technology has been developed primarily to improve local productivity; its saleability abroad is a fortunate by-product.

(3) Expand abroad. This strategy would include (a) opening sales branches (in places like Brazil, western U.S., South Africa, Korea) to promote the sale of technology, (b) developing more systematically the marketing of OKO's fabricated products —perhaps through the same sales branches, (c) contracting for long-run supplies of ore or ore-concentrates that can be refined in OKO's plants, and (d) looking for joint

OKO Income Statement
(in million Finnish marks)*

Gross Sales		1,835
Adjustments		79
Net Sales		1,756
Expenses:		
Materials & supplies	625	
Employee expense	523	
Other expenses	321	1,469
Operating margin		287
Deductions:		
Depreciation	156	
Other income & expense (net)	2	
Interest	101	
Foreign exchange losses	17	
Direct taxes	3	279
Net Earnings for the Year		8

OKO Balance Sheet
(in million Finnish marks)*

Assets		*Liabilities & Equity*		
Cash	52	Current Liabilities		831
Receivables	533	Long-term debt:		
Inventories	396	Bank loans	634	
Current assets	981	Loans from pension funds	111	
		Bonds	343	
		Other long-term debt	231	1,219
Fixed assets	1,271			
Other assets	178	Reserves		111
		Stockholders' equity:		
		Share capital	283	
		Reserves	77	
		Retained earnings	9	369
	2,430			2,430

*For quick conversion, assume 4 Finnish marks equal 1 U.S. dollar.

ventures with local foreign companies which can use OKO's know-how and/or products.

In exporting technology, OKO can simply grant licenses, as it has done for its flash smelting process. Or it can *design* an entire plant. Or it can make much of the equipment in its own shops and sell that perhaps as parts of a total plant. Of course, OKO's future ability to sell technology in any of these stages depends on its continuing development of advanced techniques suitable to conditions in the users' country.

Central management has to recognize several influences bearing on its choice of strategic thrusts. For instance, because of the country's history and strict neutrality posture, Finland is wary of becoming very dependent on materials from a single nation. Finland is so small that it does not have much power in the international arena, and prefers not to be in a position where it can be pushed around.

OKO has long been sensitive to the needs of its employees. It stresses safety and has a liberal pension plan. On several occasions it has built up inventory rather than have a layoff. In exchange, there have been relatively few work stoppages.

In such a small country the supply of engineers is naturally limited, and the number of those who speak English or other world languages is even smaller. (Finnish, like Hungarian, has Mongolian antecedents rather than Greek or Latin, and it is hard to learn. The second language in Finland is Swedish.) So there are personnel constraints, as well as financial ones, on the number of different thrusts OKO can undertake.

Relationships between OKO and the Finnish government are close. In fact, in connection with the financing of various expansion projects, different ministries have bought stock, with the result that the government now has voting control. However, government officials rely heavily on the technical judgment of company management. Thus, at present the government is going along with the conservative strategy even though it would like to see an expansion of jobs and exports. On the other hand, if company management presents a new proposal which it believes is economically viable, the government would probably make additional capital contributions.

Question

Outline the future strategy that you recommend OKO pursue, and justify your position.

INTEGRATING ROLE OF CENTRAL MANAGERS

Each of the many managerial issues and tasks discussed in the preceding chapters deserves thoughtful attention. Sooner or later a central manager is likely to face all of them. Their full significance, however, lies in their contribution to a basic approach to managing a total enterprise. Each topic has been included because it fits into a framework for thinking about the challenge of overall, integrated management.

The following brief conclusion reemphasizes the central themes we have been unfolding. Individual chapters necessarily focus on separate facets. And there is always danger that we become so absorbed with these particular parts that the broader structure becomes blurred. To counteract this danger, we stress again the structure of the book as a whole. The selection of subjects and their sequence are significant; they present a mental framework—a way of thinking about a very complex phenomenon.

Three related themes deserve emphasis:

1. A way of moving from broad social-technological-political-economic developments to company programs tuned to these developments.
2. The design of balanced, integrated company programs in which (a) the several parts each contribute to a consistent central mission, and (b) the magnitude and timing of effort is realistically related to company size and resources.
3. Recognition that such programs have long-run viability only when they include a practical reconciliation of diverse social pressures; and that, in fact, managers have a critical and unique role in devising bases for continuing cooperation that give realistic implementation to social reforms.

FRAMEWORK FOR STRATEGY AND PROGRAM FORMULATION

The managers of an enterprise are bombarded with data—from the daily press, television, customers, vendors, trade periodicals, government publications, their own people, their own observations, and many other sources. Some device is needed to screen out what is relevant to the enterprise, and these bits of information have to be related to practical action. Moreover, managers of going concerns are confronted with a host of "what do we do here" questions. And all these "inputs" appear in raw, unlabeled form. Clearly, a way of thinking is needed to bring some kind of order into the situation.

A framework for dealing with companywide problems has been presented in this book. It comes from a "general survey outline" used by a successful management consultant in several hundred companies, and it has also proved to be quite helpful to operating executives. Basically the framework identifies issues, puts them into a logical arrangement so that the normal interactions can be readily seen, and provides a flow of thought leading from external opportunities to concrete company actions. Although the framework is easier to describe as a sequence of steps, in practice we grasp ideas and information as they appear and use the framework more as a sorting and organizing device. Then when opportunities are spotted, the framework guides us to additional angles that should be investigated.

Select Company Strategy

The guiding thrust of all central management action is the company strategy. Strategy defines the mission. It provides the justification for the company's existence as an independent social unit. And being the top statement of purpose, it is the end result in terms of which many other subgoals and activities are weighed.

Viewed from another angle, strategy identifies the key bases for company survival. It should specify (a) the domain; that is, the product/market niches the company seeks to serve, (b) the differential advantages that the company will use to establish an attractive position in this domain, (c) the major thrusts which should be started soon, and (d) the target results to be used in measuring accomplishments. No one of these elements alone is an adequate statement of strategy; each provides a necessary dimension to a meaningful, operational company objective.

To formulate strategy, we urge in Part 1 a three-pronged analysis. First, relevant factors in the whole dynamic environment can be brought into focus by concentrating on the outlook for the industry(s) in which the company functions. Careful review of the demand, supply, and competitive forces will yield a forecast of volume and profitability and will identify crucial factors for success in that industry. Second, an evaluation of the strengths and the weaknesses of the specific company will indicate its ability relative to competitors to take advantage of opportunities uncovered during the industry analysis. Third, the likely response of key actors to company moves is predicted. Then in light of industry prospects, company strengths, and key actor analysis, central management selects propitious market and/ or supply niches as its field for social contribution.

Formulating strategy calls for keen judgment in selecting key factors that warrant emphasis. The strength of strategy is not an elaborate program.

Instead its essence lies in singling out from numerous influences a few critical determinants. Companies will differ in the particular way each seeks distinctiveness. But unless a central management finds (and keeps up-to-date) some unique and attractive combination of the four dimensions listed above, its company will be unable to attract an inflow of resources essential for continued existence.

Diversified corporations control several business-units, *each* of which should establish its own strategy along the lines just summarized. These "companies" are the centers of action; most strategy is formed at their level. However, the parent corporation does need a portfolio strategy to guide the expansion, curtailment, or acquisition of various parts of its empire.

Use Policy to Elaborate Strategy

While strategy is selective in its points of emphasis, policy provides more complete coverage. Through policy we assure that "all the bases are covered." There will be policy guiding relations of the firm with all its main resource groups.

A policy is a standing guide for making decisions on a given subject. Each time a question regarding, say, price increases to match inflation or employment of blacks arises, we turn to policy for the established answer. Policy

**USE <u>POLICY REVIEW</u> TO INTEGRATE
COMPANY STRATEGY WITH OPERATIONS**

Consider impact of strategy on policy for:

MARKETING:

    Product line and customer
    Pricing
    Marketing mix

HUMAN RESOURCES:

    Selection and training
    Compensation and benefits
    Industrial relations

CREATING GOODS AND SERVICES:

    Procurement
    Production
    Research and development

FINANCIAL RESOURCES:

    Sources of capital
    Allocation of capital

provides consistency of action and greatly simplifies the process of management. By establishing policy in all major functions of a company, we can create reinforcing effort throughout the enterprise.

Policy offers an important means for correlating many facets of a business with strategy. The work of each division and department can be reviewed for its compatibility with a new strategy, and policy can be adjusted wherever opportunity is found for strong supporting action.

The array of policy issues, examined in Part 2 and relisted in the chart above, is likely to be affected by a change in strategy. So a good way to begin this reconciliation of strategy and policy is to check each of these issues. Not every one of the topics listed will be significant for a specific company, and others may need to be added to deal with unusual resource groups; but the topics do identify issues encountered by many, many enterprises—profit and nonprofit alike.

Such a policy review for consistency with strategy elaborates the strategy. Occasionally this spelling out of strategy implications will raise problems sufficiently serious to require a readjustment in the strategy itself. More often, it flags the need for updating a traditional pattern of behavior in one or more departments.

Build a Supporting Organization

Strategy and policy must have an organization to carry them out. Both historically and conceptually, organization is a vehicle to execute strategy. So essential is the organization, in fact, that a weak or unsuited structure can nullify the best of plans.

To assure a good linkage between strategy and structure, we propose in Part 4 that the operating activities implied by a strategy and its associated policy be laid out first, and then that an organization be designed which suits these activities. The conclusions of such an exercise must be tempered, however, by the size of company and the available personnel. Size forces us to consider typical stages in corporate growth, and key personnel is a moderating influence on the variety of auxiliary services fitted onto the underlying operating units.

Organization design directly affects the prestige, power, influence, and compensation of key individuals. It has a great impact on their motivation. So part of the skill in effective organization design is to arrange managerial and other positions so that these motivators encourage people to work for success of the strategy—and not for some divergent or bureaucratic ends.

Guide the Execution

In one sense selecting strategy, formulating policy, and designing organization are all preparatory. The action we can observe objectively is the actual activity of shaping and exchanging products, services, and diverse satisfactions. It is the execution of plans that really counts.

Central managers devote a significant portion of their energies to execution—and first-line supervisors an even higher percentage. As outlined in Part 5, execution includes programming the action, providing leadership and motivation, and controlling allocations and results. It is the "make happen" phase of managing.

Two aspects of a central manager's role in execution call for continuing self-discipline. (1) Since central managers personally can be active in only a small part of total transactions, they influence execution largely by setting patterns for others to follow. Through their own behavior they create a leadership tone; they foster control practices and check only occasionally to see that regular use is made of these control devices; and in resolving specific problems they are as much concerned with future precedent as with the case at hand. Every social group has its customary practices and values that govern its behavior. Central managers guide execution primarily by helping to shape the customs and the values followed within their company and in its relations with resource groups.

(2) The external calls on a central manager's time may be heavy. Sometimes the manager can't escape seeing an important customer, arbitrating a personnel dispute, appearing before a Congressional committee, meeting with a Consumers' Protective Committee, negotiating a new stock issue, and a host of other worthy activities. The danger is responding to so many external requests for time that the mission—the strategy—of the enterprise gets shunted aside. One of the main virtues of specific programs and well-designed controls is to keep primary attention focused on primary tasks to be accomplished each day. This means, of course, that we must see that the programs and the controls are regularly adjusted to match any changes in strategy.

Now, with this framework of strategy formulation, policy elaboration, organization, and execution—and the components of each—clearly in mind, we can deal with the disorderly bombardment of data and problems noted at the beginning of this section. The numerous inputs can be quickly placed into a meaningful, operational way of thinking about a complex endeavor. The framework becomes a powerful tool for keeping perspective and making use of the wealth of information and ideas available to us.

NEED FOR INTEGRATED TREATMENT

Reconcile Diverse Changes

The strategy→policy→organization→execution framework has an appealing, logical flow. Unfortunately, management problems cannot always be treated in this convenient sequence. The managers of any dynamic enterprise always face a cluttered, mixed-up situation.

In a normal company several forces contribute to this jumble. (a) Pressure for change may originate anywhere—not just with an opportunity for improved strategy. Perhaps the Urban Redevelopment Corporation offers us a downtown plant, or a salesperson has a great idea for advertising, or a control has failed to signal a shortage, or the government is challenging our fair employment practice, or we have an unexpected opportunity to hire an outstanding scientist. Such events may call for action anywhere in the total system.

(b) Diverse changes occur at the same time. With separate departments responding to their sector of the environment and pushing for their respective goals, one may be courting a foreign distributor while another is offering to increase local employment while a third is seeking a government subsidy.

(c) Moreover, a mixture of old and new often confounds the situation. This year's seniors must be taught while we are also designing new programs for entering freshmen; a new breed of systems analysts is working side by side with our traditional cost accountants.

This sort of bubbling, moving activity is fine *provided* changes in one place do not detract from efforts in another. Obviously, changes that reinforce each other, and thus yield synergistic benefits, are desired. Central management and other coordinating mechanisms have a never-ending task of reconciling the many changes that occur daily in a healthy organization.

One of the major contributions of a well-articulated strategy with its supporting policy, organization, and programs is to serve as the *basis for such reconciliation*. The diversity of the changes makes a central, preeminent rationale especially valuable. Proposed changes can be evaluated in terms of their contribution to the major mission. The very complexity of activities calls for such a synthesizing standard for coping with our environment.

Watch Magnitude and Timing of Changes

In the short run, company resources are always limited. A progressive management sensing new opportunities must be careful not to strain these capacity limits.

Accounting reports and financial budgets typically provide a mechanism for living within the firm's financial ability. More difficult to measure and to predict is the capacity of personnel to handle external pressures and opportunities. Meeting a deadline on new pollution controls, launching a new product-line, and developing a matrix organization all at the same time may be so confusing that important actions are missed. A thinly staffed division may be able to keep a mature operation running as usual but lack capacity to switch production to foreign sources.

A related issue is timing of changes. Clearly an effort to increase the employment of blacks will not mix well with an economy drive and cutting of total personnel. A laboratory already running at capacity and considering a move is not ready for a new government contract.

The changes proposed in all these examples might be highly desirable when considered alone. But when they are combined with other changes, the total burden creates an overload. Here, again, the need for an integrated treatment is clear.

Several of the cases in this book, such as Jodie's Ladies Wear, Los Ranchos de Paraguay, and Early Learning Associates, give the reader some feel for the heterogenous array of issues confronting central management all at the same time. But even these cases contain only selected facts already sorted into categories; reality is much more messy. Central managers of business firms, because of the positions they occupy, face pesky, ambiguous, intractable pressures involving a variety of values not immediately reflected on company balance sheets. Great skill is needed to respond to the topsy-turvy world in ways that reinforce each other and that are within the capacities of the enterprise.

UNIQUE SOCIAL ROLE

A third dimension of the work of central managers, in addition to focusing on the strategy→policy→organization→execution approach and keeping the company moving in an integrated fashion, is contributing to social development. They do this—not as an extra duty on the side—but as an integral part of directing company responses to its changing environment.

In the process of finding workable bases for getting necessary resources, central managers make a unique and valuable contribution to social problems. They help shape many reform proposals and provide practical tests of their feasibility. Of course, many reforms do not directly affect business operations—court reform, integrated education, and urban government are examples. In such areas executives may be concerned citizens, but their positions in a corporation neither qualify them nor obligate them to be leaders. However, where a reform directly influences the conditions on which business is transacted—as in employment conditions, quality guarantees, and environmental protection—central managers and other executives make three kinds of contributions.

1. Managers help create the conditions on which cooperative endeavors take place. Each strategy conceives of a joint undertaking involving services, jobs, markets, taxes, etc. Each policy relating a company to its environment sets conditions on which exchanges will or will not be made. Each program lays out times and quantities when specific flows will occur. These interactions between a company and various interest groups are not incidental or charitable matters. They are necessary to performing a mission and to survival.[1]

As our discussion especially of policy indicated repeatedly, managers want a continuing flow of resource inputs and continuing outlets for services and

---

[1]For expansion of this point see the discussion of the "resource converter" model on pages 3 and 4.

satisfactions that the company generates. Consequently, they give close attention to maintaining markets, building reputations, assuring supply, obtaining permissions, and the like. This kind of concerned behavior lies at the very heart of successful business operations.

Now, if any interest group wants to alter the conditions on which transactions occur—either to satisfy its own aspirations or under outside pressure—thoughtful managers try to devise a way the new conditions can be met without jeopardizing the cooperative venture they direct. All sorts of adjustments in conditions of work, material utilized, information provided to investors, side effects on ecology, and the like are hammered out in the frequent negotiations that take place between providers of resources and a company. Necessity forces some of the changes, while others are invented to attract better resources. Whatever the motivation, clearly the managers benefit from helping to create workable reforms.

Safety, shorter hours, paid vacations, company pensions, and air-conditioned offices illustrate improved working conditions featured by many firms to attract and retain workers. Product quality, often including guarantees, has long been a means of wooing customers. Stable earnings attract investors. These and many other business practices add to "the quality of life." Managers do not provide these conditions as a generous, emotional gesture. Rather, they try to put together a package of satisfactions that will assure a continuing flow of resources.

The tough, practical question is how much of what satisfaction it is possible for a business to offer. Managers are actual participants, along with the beneficiaries of a proposed added satisfaction, in creating specific answers to that question.

2. *Managers serve as mediators for competing reforms.* Worthy reforms often compete with each other. Consider the proposed goals for an electric power company as an example. Clean air, cool water, dependable and cheap electricity, low requirements for foreign exchange, beautiful countrysides, conservation of natural resources—are all commendable social objectives. But if we give unbridled priority to any one, several of the others will suffer. New technology may help, and power company managers have an obligation (and strong incentive, as noted above) to find improved ways to satisfy several of the listed objectives at once. Nevertheless, we know that a balance has to be struck in the degree to which the competing pressures will be met.

Central managers unavoidably serve as mediators in this balancing process. The firm as a resource converter—the power company in the preceding example—is the place where the competing pressures collide. For instance, environmentalists don't negotiate directly with consumers who are insisting on power for their refrigerators. Instead, each group puts pressure on the power company to serve its parochial desires. Managers of the power company would like to keep everybody satisfied, but they are caught in a squeeze.

Consequently, the managers must try to negotiate an agreement with each group that will satisfy some of its desires but not be so burdensome that the company cannot also make peace with other pressure groups.[2]

When managers make proposals to a resource supplier and when they reject other requests, they are acting in effect as mediators.[3] They are exploring how far to go along with the desires of each competing group. This is a hard and unpopular assignment. But managers should accept the role because (a) they know best what impact concessions in one direction will have on the ability of their company to satisfy other pressures, and (b) they have a strong incentive to arrive at a workable understanding (their company shuts down if agreement cannot be reached).

3. Managers can serve as advisors on national priorities and institutional changes. Thus far we have pictured the manager as one who adjusts to new goals—not a person who sets the goals. We believe this emphasis is correct, but we do not intend to rule out a manager's participation in the debate that typically surrounds the establishment of a new social standard. Today setting new standards usually centers on some kind of legislation.

Federal and state governments are playing an increasing role in social change. They make laws that press the laggards into line—on minimum wages, food quality, plant safety, and the like. They also initiate reform in such areas as equal employment, air and water pollution, social security, and financial underwriting. And in spending 38% of our gross national product, they support many causes.

In the arena where priorities get hammered out, business executives have a difficult and often conflicting role. As private citizens they are indeed entitled to voice their preferences on the directions national effort should take. And if their companies participate in filling a need, they will be more knowledgeable on that subject than the average citizen. A farmer, to pick another advocate, can speak from experience on the desirability of farm subsidies. However, a beneficiary such as a farmer can scarcely be expected to be impartial. So we rely on the legislative process to set priorities, and we look to interest groups for expert testimony and advocacy of their cause. The ethical problems involve the manner and the openness of pleading one's special interest.

A typical issue is society's decision as to the kind of environment it wants, with full recognition of the sacrifices necessary to achieve that end. Are consumers willing to pay more for poorer vegetables in a move to eliminate

---

[2]In this example several different quasi-judicial but nonetheless competing government agencies also get into the act. However, the main burden of initiating proposals for resolving competing pressures rests with managers of the power company.

[3]This proposing and rejecting may take place in a formal bargaining process if the interest group is represented by an official body. Or, it may consist of testing the attractiveness of a "package of satisfaction" among customers, suppliers, or workers responding individually.

use of DDT? Should cities be built up rather than out so as to preserve the rural landscape? Do we want airports close to cities for the convenience of passengers or located far away to cut down noise for city dwellers? Resolution of such issues cannot, and should not, be made by business executives alone. They can provide expert testimony about feasibility and costs; but if they have an established position, they may also be admittedly biased advocates. Other interested parties should also be heard. And the social value decisions should be thrashed out in some legislative forum.

We believe that business executives should actively participate in setting social values, even though this joining in the debate makes them a target for those who disagree with the guides which emerge. The social forum needs the inputs which only business managers can provide; and managers are entitled to advocate a course convenient to them just as other interested parties should advocate their preferences.[4] But it is a mistake to think that the primary social responsibility of business is this sharing in the formulation of values—important though that may be.

The first responsibility of business is the generation of goods and services in harmony with the goals of society. When national priorities change, the business system must make a myriad of adjustments in the flow of goods and services. When growth and social attitudes bring particular aspects of our environment to a critical point, business must help find revised methods of producing the services people want while keeping the environment healthy. As the economy becomes more affluent and people's personal desires shift, business must devise ways of providing more opportunities to achieve self-expression, security, and other aspirations. This kind of constructive adaptation is a cardinal task of central management.

From a pragmatic view, managers play a major role in social change. They are not preachers but doers. And this is a task they are uniquely well qualified to perform.

Permeating all three of the themes we have been summarizing—strategy execution, integration, social change—is a strong emphasis on adjusting and adapting to future needs and opportunities. This emphasis makes managing a creative, rewarding endeavor.

---

[4]The concept of participating, but not dominating, in the establishment of social goals is vital. Much past criticism of business arose from unilateral, short-run decisions by business firms that were insensitive to the ramifications of their actions.

Part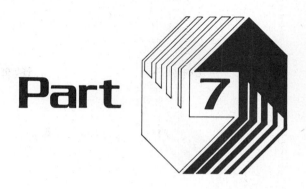

COMPREHENSIVE CASES

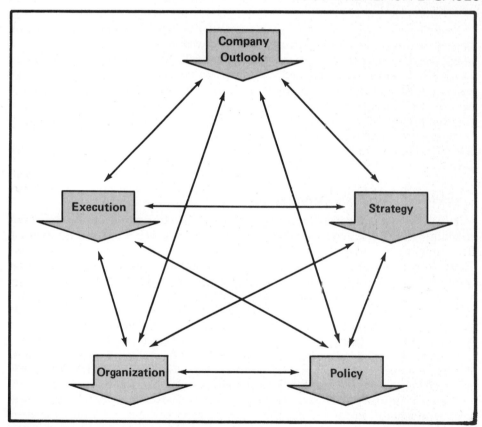

COMPREHENSIVE CASE 1

Reed Shoe Company*

Reed Shoe Company was organized nine years ago to produce and market special-ly-designed and recreational footwear. From first-year sales of $150,000 and a net loss of $55,000, the company progressed to third-year sales of $750,000 and its first profit —$25,000. Growth continued, and two years ago the company was able to enlarge its equity capital base by selling 100,000 shares of common stock with a net realiza-tion to the company of $3.75 per share. Sales topped $5,000,000 last year with post-tax profit of $245,000. Its founder and president, Tom Reed, believes the com-pany has now reached a critical point in its development. He is convinced that he has to make fundamental decisions which will determine the character of the busi-ness for at least the next decade.

LEARNING THE SHOE BUSINESS

Tom Reed joined his family's business, Yankee Shoe Company, immediately after graduating from Dartmouth's Tuck School of Business with a major in marketing. The company was then directed by Tom's father and uncle, Franklin and Nathan Reed, who were the third generation of owner-managers of a New England shoe manufacturing business. Throughout its history, Yankee Shoe Company had concen-trated on a conservatively-styled line of men's shoes that featured comfort and durability. In the years following World War II, when the men's shoe industry began to give greater emphasis to style, Tom's father and uncle refused to follow the trend. In their view, styling introduced a risk that they wished to avoid. They were confi-dent that there would always be an assured, if limited, market for "sensible" shoes that were immediately comfortable when new, were designed and built for long life, and could be resoled and reheeled repeatedly without losing their shape. The result of the undeviating application of this policy was a steady volume of sales year after year with equally steady profits. The company's shareowners, all family members more interested in assured dividends than in growth, were satisfied with this per-formance.

A year after Tom entered the family business his father died, leaving the direction of the company wholly in the hands of his uncle. Tom spent that year and the next

---

*This case was written by Melvin Anshen, Paul Garrett Professor of Public Policy and Business Responsibility, Graduate School of Business, Columbia University.

at the head office in Boston, "learning the business" by sitting in on management meetings, participating in the budget process, analyzing production costs, accompanying salespeople calling on the independent retail shoe stores which carried the Yankee line, and talking with the purchasing agent and the factory manager about their responsibilities and problems. He then became a sales person, first in the Midwest and later in Southern and Mid-Atlantic territories. After five years in the field, he was promoted to the position vacated by the retiring sales manager, with responsibility for supervising the company's twelve sales representatives, and began to participate in the general management of the company under his uncle's leadership.

In this role Tom became increasingly frustrated by Yankee Shoe's commitment to conservatively-styled "comfort" shoes. While he agreed with the judgment that there would always be a profitable market for such shoes, he saw little opportunity for significant growth in sales and profits. He expected style to have growing importance in buying decisions for men's shoes in the years ahead, parallel to the rising interest in style in all men's apparel. He also saw a trend toward special-purpose shoes, constructed and styled for specific uses. One area especially drew his attention: the mounting consumer interest in a variety of athletic and recreational activities in which the old-fashioned, all-purpose "sneaker" was beginning to be displaced by footwear uniquely designed for specific uses: in basketball, tennis, sailing, and in the newly-popular activity of jogging. He believed this whole area held possibilities for rapid growth, with interesting opportunities for those companies that moved in early and established strong brand "images."

Drawing on his experience as a college athlete (varsity basketball and tennis at Dartmouth) and in the shoe business, and working with a friend who was a chemical engineer, Tom developed and patented a process for forming a "sandwich" of honeycomb sponge rubber bonded between flexible, fibrous "breathing" plastic sheets, which would serve as an unusually resilient, supportive, light, and comfortable inner sole for athletic footwear. The material has a unique capacity for retaining its shape when subjected to sudden shocks and repetitive twisting stresses and strains. Tom had a few dozen pairs of canvas-top shoes made up with this innersole material for trial by tennis and squash players of his acquaintance. Their favorable appraisals led him to conclude that indeed he had developed a distinctive material for sport and recreational footwear, at least equal to and probably superior to anything then on the market. He visualized its application to a variety of specialized shoes which, with colorful external styling to accord with the trend in sport and recreational clothing, would meet excellent consumer acceptance.

Tom's discussion of this potential development with his uncle met a stubborn refusal even to consider enlarging the scope of the business. His uncle argued that much of the apparent market was likely to be a "fad" of temporary duration. Further, athletic and recreational footwear used different materials and manufacturing techniques than the company's traditional line and would require substantial investment in new equipment, as well as new manufacturing skills. Also, these types of shoes were usually sold in sporting goods stores, rather than in shoe stores, and would therefore require additional sales representatives and advertising support. "Why take such a risk?" his uncle asked. "We've got a nice, steady, assured business with an established and respected name. Why move into an area that we know nothing about, which isn't even likely to be an enduring market?" Tom's talks with his uncle became increasingly acrimonious, and it became clear to Tom that their basic attitudes were so antagonistic that he would be better off and happier outside the business.

LAUNCHING THE NEW COMPANY

After eleven years with the family firm, Tom decided to resign and organize his own company to manufacture athletic and recreational footwear for men and boys. He negotiated an amicable agreement with his uncle to purchase the Yankee stock he had inherited from his father for $200,000, a sum that he judged sufficient to launch his new business and see it through what he anticipated would be its difficult early period. He decided to focus first on a line of tennis shoes, and then expand to other sport and recreational categories.

Tom employed a part-time styling consultant whose shoe-design studio served several large shoe companies. To minimize his initial investment in fixed assets, he contracted with a small plastics company to produce his bonded rubber-plastic sandwich material. This he shipped to a leading New England manufacturer of a diversified line of athletic shoes with idle factory capacity; the manufacturer contracted to produce the Reed line of tennis shoes with a minimum-quantity guaranteed output.

Tom's next step was to persuade one of the Yankee salespersons to join him in his venture, taking compensation partly in a modest salary and partly in stock in the new company. He budgeted $40,000 for an advertising campaign, using the services of a Boston advertising agency to prepare small-space ads that were placed in the Eastern editions of several general sports and specialty tennis magazines and in regional magazines along the Atlantic seaboard from Boston to Florida. The advertisements featured the unique design characteristics and distinctive styling of Reed "Air-Tread" tennis shoes.

A headquarters office was opened in Boston where Tom installed as office manager, bookkeeper, secretary, and general factotum, his cousin, Phyllis Reed, who had just graduated from Wellesley and was looking for a job in a small business where, as she said, she "could get involved in everything." With all these arrangements in place, Tom and his one sales representative, Joe Ferguson, went "on the road" to sell Reed tennis shoes to specialty tennis shops and general sports equipment retailers in the New England, Mid-Atlantic, and Southern territories.

"The results in the first few months," Tom Reed later reported to a friend, "were better than my worst fears and worse than my best hopes. We had a great product, but nobody knew it. We gave retailers an opportunity to take an attractive 50% mark-up on retail (100% on their cost), selling them styles for nets after cash discount of $9.00, $12.00, and $15.00, with suggested retail prices of $17.95, $23.95, and $29.95. We were telling our story to amateur tennis players by advertising in magazines with good coverage of the amateur tennis market. But there were lots of tennis shoes already in those stores, many with well-known brand names that retailers and tennis nuts were familiar with. You had to believe in the comfort and playability of our shoe to buy it, and you had to wear it to believe in it. It was a tough sell. But Joe and I found a few stores willing to place initial orders with a return guarantee for unsold stock, and we slowly began to get favorable word-of-mouth support. Sales really started to move in the second year. It was a good thing I had that $200,000 nest egg, however, and no money tied up in plant and equipment, because it was a traumatic time financially, with more dollars going out than coming in."

Midway through the second year, when rising sales encouraged confidence that the business was moving ahead, Tom negotiated his first bank loan, purchased a small vacant shoe factory in Haverhill, Massachusetts, leased machinery, employed a crew of experienced workers and a plant supervisor, and became a full-fledged manufacturer of tennis shoes. "It was a high-risk throw of the dice," he later said, "but I felt I had to take the chance. I was getting murdered on that contract manufacturing deal. There was no leverage on volume, no way to make a profit out of growth. I just had to sink money in a fixed asset base.

"We didn't try to produce our own sandwich innersole material—that didn't happen until the following year when we could make another fixed investment—but we did start to build our own shoes. We still lost money, but we pushed sales up to half a million dollars and I thought I could begin to see that famous light at the end of the tunnel.

"I was working myself silly, of course. I was still on the road selling, along with Joe Ferguson and another salesperson I hired. But I was also back at the factory, working with my plant supervisor to organize the machinery and the workflow, and in the office teaching Phyllis how to be a bookkeeper—something she didn't learn at Wellesley, but she's a quick learner—and then teaching her how to be at least a rudimentary treasurer and controller and credit manager and office manager, too. I was also purchasing agent for materials and parts, not to mention personnel manager and advertising manager. I guess I didn't see much of my wife and kids through that year and a half. And I worried a lot about the whole structure collapsing on my head. There were times in there when I thought I was somehow working an eight-day week in seven days."

In the third year, Reed Shoe Company sales pushed above $750,000 and the firm earned its first profit. A development of even greater importance for the business was the growing popularity of jogging, a recreational and health activity that expanded explosively two years later. Tom Reed discovered jogging as a health-enhancing activity for himself at this time. He also discovered that his patented inner sole could be incorporated in a running shoe as advantageously as in a tennis shoe. So the "Air-Tread" jogging shoe was introduced as the company's first significant line extension. By last year, when sales topped $5,000,000, 80% of the sales were generated by the jogging line, the balance coming from tennis shoes. The growth of the jogging line is shown in the following table.

Unit Sales of Reed "Air-Tread" Tennis and Jogging Shoes (000 of pairs)

	Total	Tennis	Jogging
5 years ago	104	83	21
4 " "	190	114	76
3 " "	235	94	141
2 " "	308	93	215
Last year	345	69	276

THE JOGGING SHOE INDUSTRY

Precise data on the jogging population and on their purchase of shoes and clothing are not available. Trade papers frequently estimate that from 20 to 25 million Americans are regular joggers (double the number two years ago). Annual purchases of special jogging shoes and clothing are believed to aggregate almost $500 million. In a market dominated in earlier years by such foreign brands as Adidas and Puma from Germany and Tiger from Japan, U.S. brands such as Nike, Brooks, New Balance, Etonic, and Reed are now active competitors. Nike claims first place with 33% of the total jogging shoe market against second-place (formerly the leader) Adidas with about 20%. In addition to the 25 million joggers, industry analysts believe that another 7 to 10 million Americans find jogging-type shoes so comfortable, and possibly so colorful as well, that they wear them regularly as general-purpose footwear. Although some analysts feel that the figures cited above are as much as 25% high, the market is clearly substantial.

The design and construction of jogging shoes has become a technology of considerable complexity. Competing brands each claim to offer unique advantages derived from such features as aerated, cantilevered, and wedge soles; laced and solid bodies; straight and flared heels; special arch support structures, and other developments. The style aspects of jogging shoes receive as much attention as their construction, with brilliant tones, decorative stripes and swirls, and other colorful trimmings.

Specialty retailers concentrating on running shoes and associated clothing and gear are expanding rapidly, often by the franchise route. One such organization, Athletic Attic Inc., based in Jacksonville, Florida, claims to have 140 outlets, with new franchised units opening at the rate of one per week. Special-focus magazines (*Runner's World, The Runner,* and *Running Times*) provide editorial content of interest to all classes of runners from neighborhood joggers to long-distance racers, including evaluations of footwear and other items, articles on health and medical topics, and related subjects. These publications carry advertising for shoes, clothing, chronographs, and many other items for male and female runners of all ages, all levels of skill and commitment, and all running environments—urban, suburban, and open country, and on- and off-track.

Retail distribution channels for jogging shoes and clothing are not clearly defined, nor is there any agreement among trade sources about the relative volume of merchandise moving through different categories of stores. In addition to outlets specializing in jogging shoes (a growing number of which are adding clothing for joggers), special-line retailers (identified previously as "tennis shops") and general sporting goods stores promote jogging shoes and equipment. Traditional shoe stores feature jogging shoes. Department stores display jogging shoes in their shoe departments, and jogging clothing in other departments (often identified as "recreation" or "leisure" departments), as do such chain organizations as Sears, Montgomery Ward, and J.C. Penney. In all these diverse outlets, jogging shoes are available at prices ranging from about $15 at the low end to as high as $50, and clothing is offered at a comparable price range. Retail mark-ups are in the range from 40% to 50% of selling prices, often reduced to 25% to 30% for special promotions.

Some industry analysts are skeptical about the likelihood of maintaining the recent growth rate in the jogging market. They are optimistic, however, about two other possibilities. One is the application of special construction features, and special styling also, to shoes for other sport and recreational uses. This spring, for example, shoe trade sources report that the exploding popularity of soccer is opening a large new market opportunity. They estimate that as many as four million adults, youths, and children are playing soccer.

Some athletic shoe manufacturers anticipate that the market potential in soccer shoes, assuming continued growth at the existing rate, would compare favorably with that in running shoes. To support their growth forecasts, they cite additional television coverage of North American Soccer League games, expansion of the league from 18 to 24 teams, and the recent growth of youth and adult amateur soccer leagues at a 20% annual rate. They also call attention to the attraction of soccer as a high school competitive sport in a period of severe budgetary constraint for school athletic programs. A high school can field an entire soccer squad for little more than the price of a ball, compared with the $300 required to outfit one football player.

The leading company in the soccer area is Adidas. Its print advertising features well-known professional players. It also has secured the endorsement of NASL for three models of soccer shoes. Eltra Corp.'s Converse division, long established in the athletic shoe business with particular emphasis on basketball shoes, has extended its line to football, baseball, running, and soccer shoes. Its advertising manager defines its primary soccer target as the youth market, players "who for the most part, have not made a commitment to one particular brand." It uses endorsements (secured in return for payments from Converse for every pair of Converse soccer shoes purchased) from the United States Soccer Federation and the American Youth Soccer Organization, with a combined membership of 800,000 in over 100 member soccer leagues.

Two companies whose growth is closely tied to jogging (New Balance Athletic Shoes and BRS Inc. with its Nike line) are believed by trade sources to be planning expansion into soccer shoes. (Nike jogging sales are reported to have grown from $25 million to $150 million in the past five years while its product line expanded from 10 to 72 models.) Brooks Mfg. Co. is reported to be ready to commit $50,000 for print advertising for soccer shoes in the Mid-Atlantic and Northeast markets.

The second broad area for growth is the invasion of the standard shoe market by high-style special-construction shoes which consumers find more comfortable and attractive than slip-on leather "loafers" for all-day wear. "Your basic man's shoe," says one enthusiast, "really hasn't changed for a couple of hundred years, beyond substituting machine for hand production. We have the makings of a footwear revolution in what first appeared to be strictly an engineered shoe for runners. We can put comfort and style together as they have never been joined and we can do it at a price that will permit middle-income people to own half-a-dozen pairs of shoes where they used to think two pairs, one black and one brown, were all they needed."

REED SHOE COMPANY ORGANIZATION

In carrying out his responsibilities as president of Reed Shoe, Tom Reed relies on the advice of three friends he persuaded to join his board of directors when the company added to its equity capital by the sale of 100,000 shares of common stock. Clement Fairweather is a senior vice president of the bank that loans money to help finance the company's current operations. John Beggs is chairman and chief executive officer of a diversified manufacturing company. Hale Allyn has taken early retirement for health reasons from a management consulting firm and occupies himself on a part-time basis by serving as an outside director of several small companies.

"These are wise and experienced men," Tom comments. "They have a knowledge about business operations that adds a valuable dimension to my own abilities. Further, the fact that they are not involved in the pressure cooker of the company's daily operations, as I am, gives them a different sighting on the company's situation and prospects than mine. Our board meets quarterly, usually for half a day. In addition, I talk to them individually between scheduled meetings, whenever something comes up on which I'd like to check my ideas with an independent point of view. They're personal friends of mine, but they tell me frankly what they think, and don't pull their punches when they believe I'm about to make a mistake or haven't evaluated all aspects of a situation.

"Of course, they serve another purpose, too. Their presence on the board impresses some of the stockholders, gives them a little more confidence that we know what we're doing. Don't get me wrong. I'm still the largest stockholder and the ultimate boss of the whole operation. But I can't conceive the circumstance in which I would make an important decision without asking their counsel."

The fifth member of the board is Joe Ferguson. "Joe's a director because he was in on this adventure from the start," Tom said. "But his experience is narrow, wholly in sales, and he doesn't contribute much to board discussions."

The formal organization structure of Reed Shoe Company below the board of directors is shown in Exhibit I. In reality, Tom Reed notes that additional boxes with his name in them should be added above the positions of sales, production, and finance managers because he actively directs each of these functions. "That is one of the problems that makes this a critical point in the development of the business. Up to now I have spent a lot of time with each of these managers and am involved in all significant decisions in each of these areas. While the thought may cross your mind that I am reluctant to delegate responsibility to the three individuals concerned, the truth of the matter is that they are relatively inexperienced in handling the responsibilities attached to their jobs.

"Joe Ferguson is 38 and up to last year when I designated him as sales manager he had spent fifteen years as a shoe salesperson, including his time with Yankee Shoe before he came in with me at the start of Reed Shoe. He's a good sales representative and is totally committed to the company. But he knows very little about being a sales manager, especially in such areas as recruiting, training, supervising, and compensating salespeople. If you appraise him against the broader responsibilities of a marketing manager, you have to conclude that he is lacking in experience in all aspects of profit management, including budgeting and pricing. Moreover, if we move into some of the new kinds of merchandise and retail stores I am considering, he starts as a novice.

"Sam Adams is 45. His education did not go beyond high school. He got a job at Yankee as an apprentice shoemaker and worked up to be a supervisor. He's a good supervisor. But if you put his ability and experience up against a competent production manager, about the best you can say is that he has native intelligence and a desire to learn. He doesn't know much about cost analysis or budgeting. He has no experience in union negotiations. And his knowledge of machine technology is self-taught, derived wholly from working with shoe machinery.

"As for Phyllis—well, she's just a great person, probably far superior to me in general intelligence. But she majored in French at college and never laid eyes on an

Exhibit 1

REED SHOE COMPANY
Organization Chart

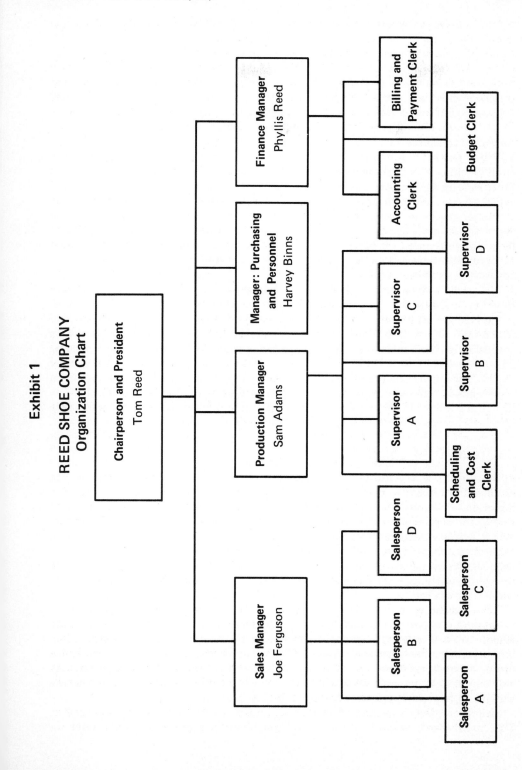

accounting record or a balance sheet until she came to work here. Everything she knows about finance and control she learned from me and from a couple of night-school courses in accounting she has taken at our local community college. She's so smart and learns so fast that I'm confident that in, say, five years she could be a competent treasurer and controller for a business of the size Reed Shoe might be at that time. But she can't do that job right now without me leaning over her shoulder and answering her questions. She can't deal with our banker. She just lacks credibility with him. He likes her all right, but he doesn't have confidence in her as a corporate treasurer.

"Up to now, the business has simply been too small to carry the salaries of fully qualified managers in these three important functions. I've had no choice; in all but routine daily activities it has been necessary for me to function as chief cook and bottle-washer. We are now at a stage in our growth where this situation can't continue. I'm doing too much. I don't have enough time to be an adequate chief executive officer. I don't have time to plan for the future of the business. But that future is right on our doorstep and either I am going to make the critical decisions or circumstances are going to make them for me, possibly in ways that may not be advantageous for the business.

"I'm going to have to recruit fully-qualified, experienced managers for the three functions and superimpose them above Joe Ferguson, Sam Adams, and Phyllis Reed. If the business continues to grow, as I am confident it will, it can carry the burden of the salaries required to attract people of the quality I want. But there is always the risk of making mistakes in hiring. On top of that, it's not going to be a popular move with Joe, Sam, and Phyllis. They think they're doing okay. I doubt that they realize how much of their responsibilities I have shouldered. And I want to keep them as seconds-in-command who may ultimately replace the outsiders I bring into the firm. I'm not confident I know how to explain and justify this move to them in a way they will accept. It's a very delicate matter."

FUTURE POSSIBILITIES

Tom Reed sees the prospects of Reed Shoe in the following terms. "Here we are at $5 million in sales. That's a long way from where we started. But, in the other direction, it's also a long way in the running-shoe business from Nike, Adidas, and Puma, and even some of the smaller companies that are considerably larger than we are. We've begun to get distribution through a fair number of retail outlets, both general sporting goods stores and specialty running shoe retailers. We've got a great product. On its merits, it's at least equal to the best on the market. We're beginning to get consumer recognition in the markets where we have distribution. But so far those markets are limited to the Eastern Seaboard. So where do we go from here?

"One possibility is to reach out for national distribution, either in one big move or region by region. If the latter, then I suppose our next move should be into the Middle West. But even regional expansion would require a major investment in manufacturing capacity—an investment, I judge, of at least a million dollars. We obviously don't have that kind of money. We'd have to go into debt financing; possibly we could sell some more stock, although I know investors are not exactly waiting around to buy the stock of a small operation like ours in an industry like this. Furthermore, the immediate effect of such a move on profits is likely to be negative. Unit production costs would rise in the first phase of expansion, though later we should realize substantial economies of scale. Sales and advertising expense would go up, too. An interruption of the growth of bottom-line earnings would surely make some of our stockholders nervous. I guess it would make me nervous, too.

"When you start to think in these terms, you have to evaluate prospects for the industry. It's been through three years of absolutely phenomenal growth. But there are those who say that practically all the potential joggers in the American population are already out there jogging and the number of new recruits for this truly splendid activity will be limited to what is provided by population growth.

"Of course, there are also those who say that jogging will turn out to be a fad—like bowling—and will tilt down hereafter, maybe falling to half its present volume, possibly even further. If that should happen, it's going to be a real jungle of a business because the big established firms are not going to give up volume without one hell of a fight. I guess it's practically inevitable that that fight would focus on prices and margins, and that would be tough for a business of our size because we don't realize the kind of economies of scale that the big operators enjoy. I figure that for shoes of comparable quality and style, our unit production costs are at least 10% higher than the big firms' costs. If it didn't totally knock us out of the ring, it could at least make us into a not-for-profit business. And that's not the kind of business I want to run. I like profits.

"But there are other possibilities all around. For example, there are a growing number of people buying jogging shoes who never do any jogging. They simply like their comfort and their style. I know men, and some women too, who wear them just about every day strictly because they are light, easy on the feet, and they look great. There's a big potential market that has sort of created itself. Nobody's advertised running shoes for everyday wear. But we could do that. If we got serious about it, it would certainly mean we would have to try for distribution through regular shoe stores. It would be a tricky promotional job, too—telling a persuasive story about general use of what most people think of as a special-use type of shoe. And we couldn't expect to keep this market for ourselves. It's open to every other company in the business. It's open to the regular shoe companies too—companies that have never made a running shoe.

"Then there are other sport and recreational markets. We started out with tennis shoes, picked up running shoes, and now most of our customers are joggers. We could make a bigger effort in the tennis market. It's still growing. We've never tried basketball shoes. All of a sudden soccer is blooming. We could design, produce, and market a line of shoes for some or all of these markets. All it takes is guts, enthusiasm, and, of course, money. Lots of money—exactly how much would depend on whether to try to exploit these possibilities one at a time or all at once.

"I've got some bigger ideas than these. As you have probably observed, joggers like to wear special clothing, especially clothing carrying the same brand name as the shoes they prefer. There is no market-attitude reason why a line of specially-designed clothing under the Reed name would not be received favorably by people who wear or know about Reed running shoes. Whether we could offer some unique or distinctive features, comparable to our patented 'Air-Tread' inner sole and other shoe construction components, is speculative. But we could certainly style our jogging clothing with the best of the competition. Again, as with expansion in our shoe business, this would mean additional investment in production facilities—and we should certainly bear in mind that we come to the clothing business with no experience in manufacturing technology. Of course, we could also contract out our clothing production, retaining responsibility for its styling (for which we would have to employ a specialist) and its promotion and marketing. That would be simpler and within our reach.

"There's at least one other possibility that is worth examining. That is not to do any of these things. Maybe I should have said there are two possibilities, because there are two quite different ways of not doing any of these things. The first way is to abandon all these ambitious notions of continued growth and settle for being the kind of modest-sized business we are right now. Be a small specialty shoe company; don't look for major growth. In fact, be a Yankee Shoe Company in the tennis and jogging shoe business. You could make a nice living out of it and you could really relax and enjoy life. I could turn over full responsibility to Joe and Sam and Phyllis in their areas. They could handle, or learn to handle, without much help from me, what they are now doing in a business of our present size. And I could free up my time for my family and take up golf seriously.

"The business would probably be profitable enough to let me take winter vacations in the Caribbean and all that. My wife would surely vote for this strategy. But I doubt that it would keep me satisfied very long. After all, I got out of Yankee Shoe because it was exactly that kind of company. If I'd stayed there I would have taken over from my uncle in a few more years and lived exactly that kind of life. But I find the idea of a vigorous, growing company stimulating and satisfying. I resist the notion of stagnation.

"The other possibility is to sell out and look around for something else to start. My banker has steered a couple of prospective buyers my way. I could sell this business and let someone else struggle with the problems of growth. And I could put the money into another business that would give me the kind of challenge I seem to respond to. How much could I sell it for? Well, take a look at our recent performance and our balance sheet and make your own judgment. (See Exhibits II and III.) I think my board would go along with just about any reasonable purchase proposal. Speaking of my board, it might be interesting for you to talk to my three outside directors and get their perspective on these matters."

BOARD MEMBERS' VIEWS

Banker Fairweather had the following things to say about Tom Reed and Reed Shoe Company:

"If you want to understand Tom Reed you have to grasp some fundamental things in his make-up. First, he has a good inventory of the kinds of personal resources that are absolutely essential for developing a business from scratch. He's ambitious for success, he has a lot of energy and drive, and he likes to get personally involved in every nook and cranny of operations. And he's capable, by which I mean that he understands what makes a business go, he sees the relationships between income and outgo, and he can motivate people. They like to work for him.

"He's always thinking bigger than where he is at any moment. When this business was barely launched he was thinking of hitting the $5 million sales mark. Now that he's accomplished that goal he's thinking about tripling it. And if he got to that target he'd be busy setting up a still bigger objective. That's a good thing in a manager. It can also be a bad thing, particularly if the problems generated by size and rapid growth begin to strain the management resources of the individual and his organization. And that's exactly where this business is right now.

"As to opportunities for the company, I think it is beginning to attain a size where further success will begin to take a little skin off some of the competition in the running shoe industry. There are some big animals in that industry. And they are not going to like Reed Shoe's taking business away from them, especially if the total market for the industry levels off or even shrinks, as I think there is a good chance of its doing. I'm not saying I think jogging is a fad that will disappear. But I believe there's a fair likelihood that it isn't going to grow much more and that it may well shrink. How far? Who knows? Even the cessation of growth will make the competition a lot stiffer than it has been so far. Shrinkage would really put pressure on the firms in the industry.

"But putting a brake on Tom's enthusiasm isn't easy. Our bank isn't eager about financing that kind of high-risk growth. I doubt that any other sensible banker would be. I've told Tom this, but I'm not sure he hears me because he doesn't want to hear me. I'm getting into a potentially awkward position. As a banker, I don't want to see a good customer like Reed Shoe overextend itself in a chancy market situation. As a director, with responsibility to non-manager stockholders, I'm disposed to urge caution. But as a friend of Tom Reed, I hate to see his ambition and desire constrained, and he probably would not accept such counsel. I can visualize his inviting me off the board if push comes to shove, and it's not clear what my proper course of action should be in such a situation."

John Beggs has a different view of the company's situation and prospects:

"If there is one thing I've learned in my thirty years in business, it's to give encouragement to a capable manager who believes enthusiastically in his own ideas. You mustn't let a conservative banker throw cold water on his plans for growth, for invading new markets, for expanding and diversifying into new product areas. I've had to put up with a certain amount of that kind of restraint in my own operation and I can remember a couple of really glittering opportunities that got away from me as a result. I'd hate to see that happen to Tom. He's a real entrepreneur and he needs to be encouraged, not held back.

"Is the kind of growth he visualizes in the ways he plans to get it possible? Is it feasible? I think a qualified yes is not an unreasonable answer to both questions. The qualification is only partly a reflection of market uncertainties. There always are market uncertainties. The larger consideration in my judgment is Tom's ability to delegate responsibility. He probably talked to you—as he talked to us in board meetings—about bringing in experienced, qualified senior managers. There's no doubt in my mind that he needs such staff reinforcement. But there *is* a doubt about his ability to delegate to them, while retaining top-level control.

"This is where a lot of successful small business people fail. I'm very sensitive to this problem because I faced it myself. Whether Tom can change his style is problematical. But he surely has a chance. I've been talking to him about it. I think he understands what's involved. And I'm in favor of supporting him if he wants to push ahead."

Hale Allyn's comments were in the following vein:

"A common mistake I find among managers—especially among managers of small businesses like Reed Shoe—is to overestimate their competitive resource strengths and underestimate their resource weaknesses. They fall in love with their own products, especially if they invented them. And they're inclined to plan for the future on the assumption that they will make this or that advantageous innovation while competitors will keep on doing just what they have been doing. The result of this kind of thinking is always an attractive projection of successful growth. They don't recognize how critical their implicit assumption may be. And when competitors also innovate, the results turn out to be less cheerful than the anticipation.

"I think Tom is inclined to make both of these mistakes. The Reed running shoe is a very good product. But is it superior to its larger competitors—in the minds of consumers out there in the marketplace? I really doubt that it is. Does the company have the marketing muscle to fight for a growing share of consumer purchases? I doubt it. Are its production costs in line with competitors' costs? Its material costs? Its marketing costs? Here I have no doubt at all—they're not. At Reed's present and even near-future scale of operations they can't be.

"If you accept these judgments, then how explain the company's growth from ground zero to where it is now? Well, the whole market has been exploding in recent years. If you could place a product of even fair quality in a fair number of retail outlets in this kind of expanding market environment your sales would be bound to grow. But if the market stops growing, that situation will change. And that's where a 'me-too' product backed by a company that is relatively weak in promotional and distribution resources and operates at a substantial cost disadvantage starts to suffer. Is this what lies ahead for Reed Shoe? There's a real chance that it is.

"What about building growth on identifying and exploiting new markets, along the lines of Tom's ideas for other specialty-shoe applications, and also invading the market for standard shoes with a more comfortable and stylish substitute? They're interesting ideas all right and there may well be real market opportunities there. But what does Reed Shoe bring to the competitive battle that is superior to the resources the big companies in the running shoe business can commit? They probably see the same opportunities. And they start with existing resource advantages. They've got more money. They've got stronger brand recognition among consumers. They've got more extensive and more intensive retail distribution. They've got management depth. Tom's ideas may well be sound ones. But it's at least speculative whether he has or can acquire the resources to capitalize on them.

"Speaking as an outside director, before I'd be inclined to support Tom's ideas for continued rapid growth in the ways he sees that growth evolving, I'd like to get him to sit down and lay out a real thorough plan—a professional approach, rather than a dream made up of equal parts of hope, inspiration, and courage. I'd like to see a specific, bullet-biting analysis of comparative resource strengths and weaknesses. This he could do with the help of his board. The strategy should be detailed on paper, and an action program, and a financial projection, too (how much money would be required when, and where it will come from in relation to internal cash flow and external supplements). This is a great way to separate dream from harsh reality.

"Tom has the ability to do this kind of planning. Does he have the discipline? He never has stood still long enough to start doing it. He ought to take the risk of delegating responsibility to his present management group to run the existing business 'as is' for at least a few months—they surely won't destroy it; it has good momentum—and focus close to 100% of his attention on some hard, realistic, detailed thinking about the future, with a view to developing just the kind of plan I've been describing. Put it on paper, not just words but numbers, too. Then he should review it with the board, after we've had a chance to study it in advance. From that would come a plan we have confidence in.

"Will he be willing to do this? Look, I've been his friend for a long time, and I honestly don't know. What I do know is that if he doesn't do it, I am one director who is not going to support him, and if this means resigning from his board, I'll resign. In the circumstances, it would be an act of pure friendship to do just that, but of course he might not see it that way."

Questions

(1) What are the future prospects for growth and profits in the jogging shoe industry? What opportunities do you foresee in related lines of business?

(2) How do you explain Reed Shoe Company's success to date? What are its strengths and resources relative to competitors'? Does it have any serious weaknesses or vulnerable spots?

(3) In light of your responses to questions (1) and (2), what domain(s) should Reed Shoe Company focus on during the next five years?

(4) On what differential advantage(s) should Reed Shoe try to build its future in the domain(s) you recommended in answer to question (3)?

(5) Although he does not use the terms, Tom Reed is talking of moving his company from a Stage I to a Stage II organization. How soon should he start, and how rapidly should he try to make the transition? What will be the costs and the benefits?

(6) Based on the limited information that you have, do you think Tom Reed has treated his three key assistants fairly? wisely? Is his proposal to bring in executives over each of these key people wise? Would you take one of those positions if it were offered to you?

(7) (a) How fast can Reed Shoe Company grow if it relies on internal generation of equity capital? State clearly the assumptions you are making about future profitability (and relate this to your answers to questions (1) through (4)), and about future "trading on the equity." (b) Do you recommend that Tom Reed try to bring in new equity capital? When? On what terms? (c) How does the payment of dividends relate to (a) and (b)?

(8) What strategic thrusts should Tom Reed make in the next year? That is, where should he move first, and how fast?

(9) (a) How should Tom Reed's plans for the next year or two, and the next five years, be stated? What topics? In how much detail? In writing—words and/or numbers? (b) What role should the board of directors play in the formulation of such plans? (c) What role should Joe Ferguson, Sam Adams, and Phyllis Reed play in the formulation of such plans?

(10) *Summary Question:* Assume Tom Reed asks you to recommend to him a strategy for Reed Shoe Company. What is your answer?

Exhibit II
REED SHOE COMPANY

End-of-Year Balance Sheets
($000)

Assets	Last year	2 years ago	3 years ago	4 years ago	5 years ago
Current Assets:					
Cash	$ 38	$ 31	$ 48	$ 27	$ 22
Accounts receivable—less reserve	452	382	327	125	53
Inventories—lower of cost or market	1,137	924	672	335	204
Prepayments	58	52	45	22	15
Total current assets	1,685	1,389	1,092	509	294
Fixed assets at cost:					
Building—pledged under mortgage	480	365	290	290	260
Machinery and equipment	230	205	158	112	58
Other	53	38	22	15	12
	763	608	470	417	330
Less accumulated depreciation	176	129	98	58	26
Total fixed assets	587	479	372	359	304
Total Assets	2,272	1,868	1,464	868	598

Liabilities and Equity

Current Liabilities:									
Notes payable	$ 325		$ 210		$ 150		$ 115		$ 50
Current installment of long-term debt	40		30		13		13		13
Accounts payable	276		217		147		107		40
Accrued expenses	323		256		168		114		55
Income taxes payable	155		127		78		45		24
Total current liabilities	1,119		840		556		394		182
Long-term debt:									
Mortgage on building		230		200		149		162	175
Less current installment		40		30		13		13	13
Total Long-term debt		190		170		136		149	162
Stockholders' equity:									
Common stock—par value $1		300		300		300		200	200
Paid-in capital		275		275		275			
Retained earnings		388		283		197		125	54
Total Stockholders' Equity		963		858		772		325	254
Total Liabilities and Stockholders' Equity	2,272		1,868		1,464		868		598

Exhibit III
REED SHOE COMPANY

Operating Statements
($000)

	Last year	2 years ago	3 years ago	4 years ago	5 years ago
Net Sales	$5,185	$4,310	$3,057	$2,298	$1,150
Cost of goods sold	3,630	3,090	2,232	1,632	828
Gross profit	1,555	1,220	825	666	322
Expenses	1,043	828	546	528	248
Selling, administrative and general	931	738	469	463	207
Other	112	90	77	65	41
Income before income taxes	512	392	279	138	74
Federal and state income taxes	267	201	137	67	31
Net income	245	191	142	71	43
Dividends	140	105	70	—	—
Transferred to retained earnings	105	86	72	71	43

COMPREHENSIVE CASE 2

Saturday Review

At the time of this case, both the management of *World* magazine and prospective investors in *World* face a question of future strategy for the magazine. *World* has an opportunity to buy back its erstwhile parent, *Saturday Review,* which has just come to the end of an experiment with profit maximizing.

The industry outlook is far from clear. In the past, three giants—*Saturday Evening Post, Look,* and *Life*—have encountered such staggering deficits that they ceased publication, to the dismay of millions of readers (and advertisers) throughout the nation. Meanwhile, other magazines including *Reader's Digest* and *Playboy* flourish.

To understand the issues involved, an analysis of the distinctive characteristics of the magazine publishing industry and a review of the events leading to *World's* present status are necessary.

OUTLOOK FOR MAGAZINE INDUSTRY

Magazines' Role in Mass Communication

Today the school child in Kyoto, Japan, and the retiree in Red Wing, Minnesota, can watch with only a split-second delay the marriage of a British princess. The technological advances in transportation, telecommunications, and printing have opened up communications—oral, printed, and pictorial—to all corners of the world. At the same time, the volume of new information pyramids. We know vastly more about many things—from heart palpitations to political candidates in an Israeli election. So, more facts and ideas are communicated to literally billions of people.

Magazines play a distinctive part in this whole communication process. Supplementing up-to-the-minute news, they can convey more background and analysis. Also they can be designed to deliver a particular character of message to a select audience. In contrast to books, magazines build up a continuing relationship—from every week to at least every three months—with their clientele. Each year about 5.6 billion copies of magazines go to 63 million U.S. homes and to millions of offices. Readership is rising steadily and is linked to rising incomes and to higher educational attainments.

The size and the growth of the magazine industry are shown in the census data on the following page. The Department of Commerce estimates that industry receipts

Periodicals in the U.S.

	Number of Companies	Value of Shipments (in millions)
1972	n.a.	$3,460
1967	2,430	3,096
1963	2,562	2,296
1958	2,245	1,651
1954	2,012	1,441
1947	2,106	1,060

Source: Census of Manufacturers.

will continue to grow approximately 6% per year in real terms, with the value of receipts reaching over five billion dollars by 1980.

A second way to view magazines is as an advertising medium. This viewpoint is significant because a majority of magazines that are published could not exist without the income they derive from advertising. (Newspapers, radio, and television also depend heavily on advertising.) While academic and religious journals often carry no advertising, many trade publications obtain all their income from advertisers; other magazines fall between these two extremes. For the industry as a whole, advertising provides 62% of total revenues, whereas readers contribute 38% through subscriptions or purchase of individual copies.

Magazines face strong competition for the advertising dollar. As indicated in the following table, only 6% of total advertising expenditures flows to magazines. Newspapers, television, direct mail, and radio each take a larger slice.

Advertising Expenditures

	1972 % Total Advertising	% Gross National Product
Newspapers	30	0.60
Magazines	6	0.13
Radio	7	0.14
TV	18	0.36
Outdoor	1	0.02
Direct Mail	15	0.29
Other	23	0.46
Total	100	2.00

Moreover, magazines are falling behind. During the decade 1963 through 1972 advertising revenues for magazines rose 43%, but total advertising grew 76% and

GNP 95%. Only television maintained a pace equal to the national economy as a whole. (See table on page 660.)

The lackluster performance of advertising revenue for magazines is serious on two counts: (1) It leads to a serious profit squeeze, since costs are rising while incomes flatten. (2) It suggests that readers are spending less time with magazines. Advertisers want their messages where they will receive attention. If magazines cease to capture the interest and the time of their readers, they also cease to be good advertising media. Pushed to its logical conclusion, this argument says that, in the judgment of people who place advertising, magazines generally are doing a poorer job of serving customer needs than other communication channels.

Rise and Fall of Individual Magazines

Industry data inevitably cover up shifts that are occurring within the total. A diversity of trends is especially characteristic of the magazine industry where over 2,400 firms publish more than 9,000 magazines. This wide array can be classified into nine broad groups: homemaking, professional, farm, trade and industry, business, recreational, religious, juvenile (including comics), and general reader. To a large degree, what happens to one group is unrelated to the appeal of another group. Even within groups, performance varies greatly. For instance, within the professional group are the *Journal of the American Medical Association,* which carries more pages of advertising than any other magazine, and also the *Business History Journal,* which has no advertising and struggles for existence.

Since *World* and *Saturday Review* fall in the general reader category, we should look at what is happening there. Three conspicuous deaths highlight the problems facing general reader magazines. In a span of less than four years, three of the most widely read magazines in the nation—*Saturday Evening Post, Look,* and *Life*—were suffering such large losses that their publication was abruptly halted. (See the table on page 662 for the trend in circulation of these and other well-known magazines.)

The first big jolt was the demise of the *Saturday Evening Post* in 1969. For years the *Post* had been *the* leading magazine of the nation, a hallmark of middle-class gentility, a pioneer in marketing research, a very prestigious outlet for the leading short-story writers and novelists of the day, and the most expensive advertising medium per page available. It was as universally respected as Benjamin Franklin whose picture was incorporated into its masthead, and it enjoyed a circulation of over 6 million copies each week. To many of its readers, the collapse of the *Post* was inconceivable.

In fact, the *Post* had been ailing for several years. Basically people got tired of reading it. *Life* and *Look* offered livelier, easier reading material on current topics; television provided entertainment in one's easy chair; paperbacks made good novels readily available. Moreover, the *Post* belonged to an older generation. While the *Post's* circulation stabilized, *Playboy* grew dramatically by providing pornography, satire, and fashion advice for the modern young male. Because the *Post* no longer provided a unique way of contacting the large middle- and upper-class market, advertisers turned to other media. Meanwhile costs of publication rose unremittingly. The drop in advertising income, coupled with higher costs,

Advertising Expenditures and Gross National Product
U.S.A. 1963–1972
(Index 1967 = 100)

Year	Gross National Product ($ Billion)	Index	Advertising Expenditures ($ million) News-papers $	Index	Magazines $	Index	Radio $	Index	TV $	Index	Outdoor $	Index	Direct Mail $	Index	Other $	Index	Total $	Index
1972	1,151.8	145	6,960	141	1,480	116	1,530	148	4,110	141	290	152	3,350	135	5,340	133	23,060	137
1971	1,050.4	132	6,250	126	1,399	109	1,440	140	3,590	123	261	137	3,050	123	4,850	121	20,840	124
1970	976.4	123	5,745	116	1,323	103	1,308	127	3,596	124	234	123	2,766	111	4,628	115	19,600	116
1969	930.3	117	5,753	116	1,376	108	1,264	122	3,585	123	213	112	2,670	107	4,621	115	19,482	116
1968	864.2	109	5,265	107	1,318	103	1,190	115	3,231	111	208	109	2,612	105	4,303	107	18,127	107
1967	793.9	100	4,942	100	1,280	100	1,032	100	2,909	100	191	100	2,488	100	4,024	100	16,866	100
1966	749.9	94	4,895	99	1,291	101	1,010	98	2,823	97	178	93	2,461	99	4,021	100	16,679	99
1965	684.6	86	4,457	90	1,199	94	917	89	2,515	86	180	94	2,324	93	3,663	91	15,255	90
1964	632.4	80	4,148	84	1,108	87	846	82	2,689	92	175	92	2,184	88	3,405	85	14,555	86
1963	590.5	74	3,804	77	1,034	81	789	76	2,032	70	171	90	2,088	84	3,189	79	13,107	78
Increase '63 to '73	95%		83%		43%		94%		102%		70%		60%		67%		76%	

Source: Department of Commerce & McCann-Erickson, Inc.

spelled large deficits. After several frantic attempts to change the magazine's image, the *Post's* management was forced by financial pressures to call a halt.[1]

Look and *Life* were both launched in the latter 1930's to feature photojournalism —full-page, candid shots of dramatic events and pictorial analyses of social issues. Both were very successful. *Look,* a biweekly published by Cowles Communications in Des Moines, Iowa, was initially directed at a slightly lower income level than *Life* and undertook fewer erudite series on such subjects as "Religions of Mankind" and "History of the Middle Ages." *Look* struck a responsive audience, and circulation soared to over 7 million. In 1970 it carried more than $60 million in advertising! Yet its last issue appeared on October 19, 1971.

A magazine like *Look* is expensive to prepare, print, and circulate. And all these costs were rising to swallow up the millions of revenue dollars. Rising costs, however, were only part of the story. Renewals of subscriptions fell sharply, as did newsstand sales. In 1970 newsstand sales at 50¢ a copy were only 3% of the total, and renewals at the basic subscription price of 17 cents to 19 cents per copy for 1 to 3 years fell below 30%. These facts indicated that readers no longer felt that *Look* was worth its price. To bolster circulation (and thereby keep advertising rates up), *Look* under-took heavy promotion for subscriptions at cut prices ranging from 10¢ to 15¢ per copy. Seventy percent of new subscriptions were obtained only by discounting the single copy price up to 80%.

The disenchantment of *Look's* readers became known to advertisers. In the first six months of 1971, ad pages were down 1.4% to 572 in spite of a 100% gain in cigarette ads (due to the newly imposed ban on use of TV). The combination of the drop in advertising and circulation revenue and the rise in costs led to an estimated loss of $4 million for the year. The following year looked even worse, so management dropped the curtain.

Many writers in the trade press speculated about steps that might have been taken to save *Look.* Essential to all these plans was some formula to increase the value of the magazine to its readers. Apparently, the improvements in television news cover-age were sufficient to undermine *Look's* primary appeal. No one found an adequate substitute before the end came.

The withdrawal of the *Post* and *Look* with a combined circulation of almost 15 million left a lot of readers that *Life* (published by Time, Inc.) might have picked up. But trouble in the general reader magazine field proved to run deeper than just competition. Even though subscribers were paying only about 12 cents for a copy of *Life* that cost 41 cents to edit and print, many in 1970–1972 failed to renew. *Life,* unlike *Look,* chose to let circulation drop, hoping that soon only loyal readers who would pay full rates would be left. But the subscriptions kept going down, as did newsstand sales. In addition, advertisers departed when they discovered that televi-sion could deliver the same mass audience at lower cost.

During the last five years of its existence *Life* accumulated a deficit of $35 million. Relief was sought in various ways—trimming the size, using a lower quality of paper, cutting the staff. On the editorial side, special efforts were made to deal with stories that received scant attention in the daily press and newscasts. Nevertheless, the tide kept running out. A final blow was an increase in postal rates that added $13 million

---

[1]Subsequently the name *Saturday Evening Post* was sold to another company, which is trying to find an editorial strategy that will make viable use of the great reputation.

Circulation of Selected Magazines
Circulation in 1,000's
(Index 1960 = 100)

Year	Saturday Review #	Index	Saturday Evening Post #	Index	Look #	Index	Life #	Index	Reader's Digest #	Index
1973	751a	314	b	0	c	0	d	0	18,232	147
1970	615	257	b	0	7,837	126	8,527	127	17,829	144
1965	398	167	6,640	107	7,663	124	7,327	109	15,603	126
1960	239	100	6,226	100	6,202	100	6,727	100	12,369	100
1955	151	63	4,638	74	4,077	66	5,604	83	10,236	83
1950	101	42	4,069	65	3,200	52	5,364	80	6,045	49

Year	New Yorker #	Index	Atlantic #	Index	Harper's #	Index	TV Guide #	Index	Playboy #	Index
1973	477	111	326	118	332	139	18,775	274	6,670	611
1970	456	106	326	118	379	159	15,339	224	5,290	485
1965	469	109	285	103	290	121	10,261	150	2,925	268
1960	431	100	277	100	239	100	6,863	100	1,091	100
1955	396	92	221	80	192	80	2,980	43	228	21
1950	332	77	176	64	159	67	161	2	e	0

(a) As of April, 1973, when *Saturday Review* filed for bankruptcy. (b) Discontinued publication February 8, 1969. (c) Discontinued publication October 19, 1971. (d) Discontinued publication December 29, 1972. (e) Started publication December, 1954.

Source: Ayers' Directory of Publications & Standard Rate and Data Service.

to *Life's* cost each year. Forecasts for 1973 and 1974 showed an additional $30 million loss with no convincing reason to assume a turnaround would then occur. Even for Time, Inc. the burden was too heavy, and publication ceased at the end of 1972.

Life Magazine

	Circulation		Advertising
Year	*Average Paid (in thousands)*	*Pages*	*Gross Revenue (in millions)*
1937	1,195	2,224	$ 4.4
1950	5,340	3,816	80.4
1955	5,604	4,398	121.0
1960	6,746	3,360	138.8
1965	7,368	3,247	163.2
1970	8,518	2,043	132.4
1971	7,111	1,993	111.0
1972	5,637	2,025	91.2

Not all general reader magazines are ailing. The most conspicuous exception is the *Reader's Digest,* with clearly the largest circulation (over 18 million in 1973) and still growing. Its editorial policy aims at general interest, nonpictorial articles for all the family. About half are digests and half are original. Topics covered embrace self-improvement, psychology, ecology, government, community action, health, "unforgettable characters," campus, travel, etc., and a liberal sprinkling of jokes. *Reader's Digest* has not succumbed to the cynicism and naked realism of much modern writing. It gives the reader a feeling that American virtues still have validity.

Also alive and kicking, though not growing, are the venerable monthlies *Harper's* and *Atlantic.* They cater to an audience with intellectual curiosity and concern for national well-being. The *New Yorker* is a flourishing regional magazine, focusing on the trials and the exhilaration of metropolitan living. Its biographies of unusual people are exhaustive, rambling, and threaded through pages of advertising. With guides to plays, concerts, dining out, and art exhibits, it has won an enduring loyalty among sophisticated readers. And there are many other magazines that have found a particular scope or viewpoint that appeals to a segment of general readers.

The *TV Guide* has made a unique record in the entertainment field. Overlaying the basic television programs with not-too-weighty stories on stars and shows, it has an amazing combined circulation of over 18 million.

Commenting on the success and the failure of individual magazines, a leading trade analyst observed: "All successful magazines have one thing in common: They must provide a service to the reader. This service aspect, whether it is construed as entertainment, how-to, information, news, etc., is the underlying assumption of all media. The ability to meet this challenge determines whether a magazine lives or dies."[2]

---

[2]*Media Information Newsletter,* December 14, 1972.

In concluding its analysis of the publishing industry, Standard & Poor's state that in 1973 periodicals specializing in homemaking arts, outdoors and sports, and sex were among those posting the strongest gains.

Revenue and Cost Factors Affecting Survival

While service to readers is the vital core of a magazine, economic factors also determine its ability to survive. Magazines have several distinctive characteristics affecting their (1) revenue, (2) costs, and (3) cash flow.

(1) Revenue, as noted in the preceding discussion, typically comes from two main sources—magazine sales (subscriptions and newsstand sales), called circulation income, and advertising. Briefly:

Circulation income = f (product, price, promotion)
Advertising income = f (circulation, rates, selling effort)

Thus, management faces a dual pricing problem; for example, it can sacrifice circulation income as *Look* did and hope to recover the decrease on advertising income. Quite different approaches are being followed by other magazines. *Harper's* in a letter to its subscribers in the fall of 1973 stressed that it had not raised its subscription price since 1965, whereas virtually all its competitors had. On the other hand, *Esquire* in a full-page ad in the *New York Times* makes a strong point of its raising the subscription price while keeping advertising rates constant.

(2) Cost fluctuations are affected by the almost universal practice in the industry of no vertical integration; paper is purchased, printing is subcontracted, and physical circulation is frequently handled by a contractor. This practice lowers capital investment (and ease of entry) while increasing the proportion of variable costs.

A significant part of most magazines' costs vary with the size of the circulation— postage, paper, distribution, and printing (after 100,000). This variability is especially important when the subscription price is low; some magazines literally lose money on every additional copy they print and sell unless this loss is offset by higher advertising income.

The costs that are not affected much by ups and downs in circulation—at least in the shortrun—include editorial expense, promotion of new subscriptions, company overhead (rent, accounting, top salaries, and the like), and circulation record-keeping. A rise above, say, 10,000 in circulation will not cause these expenses to change. However, such expenses rarely remain "fixed" over any length of time. Typically, management decides to *invest* more, or less, in these inputs with an eye to long-run benefits. A major promotional drive, for example, is an investment this year (even though it appears as an expense on the profit and loss statement) aimed at a continuing higher circulation and at higher advertising income in subsequent years. The payout on such promotional outlays obviously depends on what it costs to get new subscribers and whether they will renew their subscriptions. Editorial outlays, for example a foreign correspondent or a new feature column, have the same investment, delayed response, and uncertainty characteristics.

(3) The cash flow, and therefore the capital requirements, of a magazine publisher are affected by the income and the cost fluctuations just mentioned. Sizable disbursements may be required to build a strong editorial product and to develop market

acceptance for that product. The income, especially when the purchase price of a copy of the magazine does not cover the variable costs, is delayed until the pages of advertising and the advertising rates rise.[3]

A unique offset to this delayed advertising revenue is the advance payments for subscriptions. Subscribers *prepay* for as long as three years. This prepayment generates cash, and also a liability to deliver magazines in the future. The liability aspect arose, for example, when *Life* ceased publication in 1972; a reserve of $7 million was set up to settle prepaid subscriptions that could not be transferred to some other magazine. Conservative financial practice is to segregate advance cash payments (in an investment account) and to make the cash available for operations only as magazines are delivered.

In addition to the "economics" of magazine publishing just discussed, managers must deal with inflation. The most pressing current hurdle is the announced 145% increase in Class II postal rates (to be spread over five years) and a proposal for an additional 38%. The U.S. Postal Service is trying to institute a policy requiring its rates to cover all costs, and magazines—which on a per pound basis have been subsidized for years—will be hard hit. Paper, another major cost, is in short supply. Its price has already gone up sharply and probably will go higher. Wage and salary rates are rising in the entire publishing industry at least as fast as in the general economy.

Importance of Renewals

The *percentage of subscription renewals* is the most sensitive index of a magazine's health. It reflects the success of editorial policy in serving readers—disinterested readers don't renew. Also, cut-price and high-pressure subscription drives usually seduce a lot of subscribers who are far from avid readers, and when the subscription expires they do not renew. Typically, only about 20% of new subscribers who were attracted to a magazine by cut prices ever renew at the regular price. In contrast, 40% of those who subscribe at the full price do renew, and the percentage rises to 60% for readers who subscribe for a third time.

Advertisers are fully aware that renewal percentages indicate the attention subscribers actually give to a magazine and hence its value as an advertising medium. Moreover, advertisers prefer a magazine with a consistent type of reader with a predictable response to an advertising message. Even when a magazine succeeds through extra promotional efforts in finding new subscribers to replace those who fail to renew, the quality of this audience is uncertain. So a poor and declining renewal rate can be very serious indeed.

The "economics" of magazine publishing are a bit tricky, as the preceding discussion of circulation, advertising, variable expenses, cash flow, and renewals indicates. Even more delicate is a workable balance between economics and editorial mission.

---

[3]A classic example of lag in advertising rates is the outstanding success of *Life* when it was first published. Circulation soared to over a million in the first year, and so did the variable costs. However, the rates charged for advertising were pegged at introductory levels. Consequently, before the advertising rates could be moved up, the phenomenal success had a several million dollar loss, and the publisher, Time, Inc., was placed in a very severe cash squeeze. At the time, no one knew whether the popularity of *Life* was just a flash-in-the-pan.

Creating a distinctive and popular service to readers requires empathy, imagination, and strong commitment to a particular way of aiding the selected audience. Subjective judgments about what is suitable are often made under severe time pressures. Understandably, the persons performing such work become emotionally involved. Meanwhile, business executives may have trouble keeping economic forces in line. Consequently, tensions between editorial staff and business executives are common.

The balancing of editorial goals and economic factors has been a recurring issue in the history of the *Saturday Review.*

GROWTH OF SATURDAY REVIEW, 1924–1971

The Editorial Mission

In 1924 Henry Seidel Canby, Professor of American Literature at Yale, along with Christopher Morley and a few other associates, launched a weekly *Saturday Review of Literature.* Its start coincided with the birth of *Time* under the guidance of Henry Luce, and for a brief period the two fledgling publications shared a single business office. The *Saturday Review* soon won respect for its literary criticism, but it appealed to only a narrow circle of subscribers. By 1940, when 25-year-old Norman Cousins joined the staff, it had a circulation of only 14,000.

From the start the *Saturday Review* was actively concerned with the current world of ideas. Its reviews of poetry, history, biography, novels, music, and the like were primarily concerned with how these new books expressed new thrusts. Instead of academic, scholarly criticism—looking backward—the editors were concerned with social values of the day. As the United States passed through periods of prosperity and deep depression, the prevailing outlook on life shifted and the *Saturday Review* became a forum where new directions of thought were identified and analyzed.

Within two years after joining the staff, Norman Cousins became the full-time editor of the *Saturday Review;* and for the next three decades he strongly influenced its scope and editorial mission. While continuing strong emphasis on book reviews, Cousins added weekly columnists and feature writers whose comments on the current world of ideas appealed to a growing group of sophisticated readers. Cousins, who is an articulate liberal, provided a series of editorials that related the magazine directly to current political affairs. For example, he pioneered in discussing the implications of atomic energy, possible bans on nuclear testing, cigarette advertising, and protection of the natural environment. Discussions of U.S. education and of new developments in science were singled out as recurring supplements. A continuing theme throughout the magazine was freedom of intellectual inquiry.

With such a broad coverage, the *Saturday Review* obviously appealed to readers who have general interests. They are sophisticated individuals who lack time to pursue in depth all of the subjects that intrigue them. And the *Saturday Review* helped them keep abreast of developments in science, politics, literature, performing arts, and social change. Some critics contend that the information was inevitably superficial, but no one challenges its sophistication. By 1971 the circulation of the magazine, almost all mail subscribers, had risen to 660,000. The magazine was clearly an influential force in literary and intellectual fields.

Throughout its history the *Saturday Review* was more interested in content than showmanship. It prided itself on clear exposition with meaty, forceful content rather than on sensational journalism or cluttered wording. In recent years the *Saturday*

Review used a restrained touch of color and occasional cartoons, but it remained conventional in size and layout. Unlike *Life* and *Look* it did not try to substitute photographs for written copy—nor has it gone in for four-color reproductions. Only its covers and some color advertisements were printed on heavy slick paper. As a result, the *Media Industry Newsletter* commented in July, 1971, that "the publication needs a facelift. It's drab."

The Editor

As with entrepreneurs in economic theory, editors of magazines and the enterprise they direct are often closely intertwined. This clearly applies to Norman Cousins and the *Saturday Review*.

Norman Cousins has spent all of his adult life in the magazine division of the publishing industry. Born in New Jersey in 1915, he was a frail child and spent his eleventh year in a sanitarium recovering from what was believed to be tuberculosis. However, as an adult he appears to have limitless energy and optimism. From 1935 to 1940 he was Literary and Managing Editor of the magazine *Current History,* and from there he went to the *Saturday Review*.

In addition to his work on the magazine, Cousins is author or editor of several books, including: *Dr. Schweitzer of Lambarene* and *Talks with Nehru.* He serves as honorary President of the United World Federalists and is Co-Chairman of the National Committee for a Sane Nuclear Policy.

Active in various political affairs, on one occasion Cousins personally negotiated with Khrushchev for the release of Cardinal Slipyj, Archbishop of the Ukranian Rite Orthodox Church, who had been interned in a Soviet prison for 17 years. He was a close advisor to President John Kennedy, and a probable appointment to a government post was interrupted by Kennedy's assassination. He continues to be an active and respected advisor on public affairs.

For fourteen months during the period when McCall Corporation owned *Saturday Review,* Cousins served as a corporate vice-president. In addition to the *Saturday Review,* he was in charge of the ailing *McCall's* magazine. The difficulties of that magazine did not improve, however, and he returned to full-time editing of the *Saturday Review.* His only other major publishing venture has been with *World,* which is described later in the case.

Ownership and Financial Control

During its early years the *Saturday Review of Literature* was perpetually in financial trouble. It was kept alive only through the generosity of Thomas L. Lamont, Chairman of J. P. Morgan & Company, and of Harry Sherman, founder of the Book-of-the-Month Club. In the middle '30s ownership was acquired by the world-famous oil geologist, E. L. DeGolyer, who was an enthusiastic supporter and financial backer of the magazine for another 20 years.

Shortly before his death in 1956, DeGolyer turned over ownership of the magazine to Cousins. Cousins kept 51% of the stock and distributed the rest to key members of the staff. This made Cousins both editor and majority stockholder.

Although the magazine was growing in circulation, it was still struggling financially. To tap greater financial resources, Cousins and his associates sold out to the

McCall Corporation in 1961. The transfer of ownership was accomplished by an exchange of stock, the *Saturday Review* group receiving McCall's stock then worth approximately $3 million.

The new owners were anxious to keep Cousins at the helm. They gave him a 10-year contract and complete editorial freedom. In most respects this appeared to be a wise decision because the *Saturday Review* more than doubled its circulation during the 1960's. With the increase in circulation to 660,000 in 1971, advertising revenues increased to $5½ million annually. The reasons for the increase in the *Saturday Review* circulation during a period when general readership of magazines was declining are complex. Possibly the *Saturday Review* picked up some of the cast-off readers of *Saturday Evening Post, Look,* and *Life,* although the nature of the magazines was quite different. More important, there was a growing sympathy toward the editorial viewpoint of the *Saturday Review* and a larger number of people wanting intellectual stimulation. In other words, the *Saturday Review* grew not only because it changed but more because its audience changed.

The shifts in ownership from DeGolyer to Cousins and associates to McCall Corporation had minor effect on the editorial policy of the *Saturday Review.* Throughout, Cousins was the one the owners relied upon to direct the destinies of the magazine.

However, an ownership change that occurred in 1971 did drastically affect the magazine. The merger boom of the 1960's led to the inclusion of McCall Corporation in the Norton Simon, Inc. conglomerate. And since this new grandparent found the modest profits of the *Saturday Review* unimpressive, it welcomed an opportunity to sell the magazine to a new company organized by Nicholas H. Charney and John J. Veronis. As explained in the next section, these gentlemen saw a great future for the *Saturday Review*—a future, however, that required substantial modification in the objectives and the policies that had prevailed for the preceding three decades.

SATURDAY REVIEW UNDER MODERN MANAGEMENT

The sale of the *Saturday Review* by McCall Corporation to a newly formed company called Saturday Review Industries signaled a major change in financial and editorial policies. To understand the new approach to the management of the *Saturday Review,* we need a brief look at the background of the two active executives in Saturday Review Industries—Nicholas H. Charney and John J. Veronis.

Track Record of New Managers

Before Nick Charney finished his Ph.D. dissertation on "The Effect of Scopolamine on Rats"—at the University of Chicago—he had developed a concept for a popular magazine about psychology. Unable to interest major publishers in the new idea, Charney scraped together $40,000 from friends and relatives and launched the venture himself. Then 25 years of age and with no experience in editing or publishing anything, he moved boldly to attract subscribers. From his kitchen table he mailed a description of the yet-to-be-born magazine to 30,000 members of the American Psychological Association, offering them a 3-year charter subscription for $15. This mailing had a remarkable return of 19.2% and about $80,000 in cash. Using the advance payment from the first subscribers for further mailings, Charney had almost 50,000 subscribers for *Psychology Today* before the first issue went to press. The magazine made full use of the latest printing techniques with careful attention to modern graphics, color, and quality reproduction.

The initial success of *Psychology Today* naturally required additional inputs of working capital, and at this stage John Veronis joined Charney as a full partner. Veronis already had a remarkable record in magazine publishing. After selling advertising for several magazines, he became, at the age of 26, part of the management of *American Home.* During this period he was also studying for his MBA at New York University. *American Home* was acquired by Curtis Publishing Company and Veronis had a rapid rise through the prestigious but ailing Curtis Magazine Division. So rapid was his rise that veteran publishers whom he passed along the way nicknamed him "Hungry John." A management shake-up at Curtis left Veronis looking for a job, and he spent the next couple of years with another publisher developing ways to capitalize on the information revolution and futuristic concepts such as McLuhan's "The Media Is the Message."

Charney and Veronis immediately set about to take full advantage of *Psychology Today's* successful birth. They pursued two related paths: (1) They continued the aggressive promotion of subscriptions to the magazine, and (2) they organized the Psychology Today Book Club for the purpose of direct-mail sales. The Book Club offers its members college texts, laboratory kits, educational films, posters, games, and an array of other items related to psychology. The magazine's subscribers are a highly selected market for special-interest merchandise.

Both the magazine and the associated book club prospered. To provide for a substantial need for working capital, Charney and Veronis set up a corporation called Communications/Research/Machines, Inc. (CRM). In a 3-year period they obtained $6 million from private investors but kept more than half of the ownership for themselves and the inside managers.

About five years after Charney put out his first mailing for *Psychology Today,* CRM was sold to Boise Cascade Company, which was then busily converting itself from a lumber and paper concern into a conglomerate. By that time CRM had annual sales of about $10 million. Boise Cascade put up the equivalent of $21 million, $5 million cash for additional working capital and $16 million in an exchange of its stock for the CRM equity. Charney and Veronis went to Boise Cascade with the deal.

The CRM division of Boise Cascade not only pushed *Psychology Today* and its Book Club (by this time the magazine's circulation was 600,000), they also sought additional magazines on which to apply their success formula. *Intellectual Digest,* with a circulation of 25,000, was acquired, redesigned, and aggressively promoted with a prompt increase in circulation to 200,000. An earlier venture, *Careers Today,* misfired and accumulated a $2½ million dollar loss before being discontinued.

In their search for new prospects, Charney and Veronis discovered that *Saturday Review* could be purchased. They studied this possibility carefully; but before the acquisition could be completed, Boise Cascade ran into financial stringency. Charney and Veronis were so enthusiastic about the prospects of revitalizing *Saturday Review,* however, that they resigned from Boise Cascade to take advantage of the opportunity. They attracted several other private investors, organized Saturday Review Industries, and purchased *Saturday Review* for a reported $5½ million dollars in cash. The McCall Trade Book Company came with the purchase. And so while still very young, Charney (30) and Veronis (42) brought substantial experience in magazine publishing along with their newly acquired ownership control of the *Saturday Review.*

Plans for Modernizing the Saturday Review

Application of the techniques Charney and Veronis had already successfully used with *Psychology Today* and *Intellectual Digest* promised a substantial change in the financial results of the *Saturday Review*. Opportunities for financial improvement were not hard to find. According to Veronis, the magazine was underpriced. Subscribers were paying only 11.6 cents per copy, whereas basic printing and distribution costs were about 15 cents a copy. Thus the distribution of over 34 million copies per year netted a circulation loss of an estimated $1,170,000. Veronis figured the total overhead (editorial, freelance and art fees, selling of advertising, office expense, etc.) at about $4 million per year. So the overhead and the circulation deficit almost wiped out the advertising income of $5½ million.

In such a situation, a "modest" program would have been to raise the subscription price to 15 cents per copy, give the magazine a face-lifting, and launch a million dollar promotion campaign that Veronis believed would easily raise the number of subscribers to 750,000 and, on the basis of this 14% increase in circulation, could increase the advertising revenue at least 9% to $6 million per year. Under this plan the million dollar promotional investment in the first year could be recouped in the second year while subscriptions at the old cheap rate were running out, and by the third year a $2 million operating profit would be realized from the magazine alone. To this would be added profits from a newly organized book club.

The new management, however, did not adopt the first acceptable alternative that presented itself. Within a few months Charney and Veronis had developed a much more imaginative program for the *Saturday Review*. It embodied four major thrusts.

First, the weekly magazine was changed to a family of four monthlies. In successive weeks the *Saturday Review* would deal with (a) arts, (b) education, (c) society, and (d) science. However, binding these four monthlies together would be a regular weekly supplement with columnists and other general features of the old *Saturday Review*. Charney, in his second editorial, described the new program for readers as follows:

> I have mentioned that this evolution of the expanded special-interest supplements is a logical editorial extension of the direction in which *Saturday Review* was already going. In fact, I believe it is also a necessary change. As we human beings continue to stride forward into tomorrow, it is becoming impossible for a single, general-format magazine to keep up with all that is taking place around us. There is too much happening at once. There are too many areas of innovation, experimentation, discovery, and performance to keep abreast of.
>
> By concentrating SR's efforts on four critical, separate, and discrete areas of social concern today, more in-depth reporting and reflective writing can be offered in each area. . . .
>
> . . . in *Saturday Review of the Arts,* whatever one's particular pursuits within the broad range of the cultural field, a reader should be able easily to find what interests him or her most in regular departments devoted to *Art, Music, Film, Communications, Theater, Photography, Design,* and *Architecture*. While these departments will contain critical reviews, they will also explore the arts in whatever ways yield the most provocative insights and understanding. . . .
>
> . . . Eventually, *Education,* in addition to its three or four major articles in the field of education, will regularly cover events, research, problems, ideas,

and experiments in the areas of *Early Childhood, School-Age Children, Young Adults, Continuing Education, Educational Policy,* and *Educational Materials.*

In *Saturday Review of the Society,* present thinking is to consistently cover the broad areas of *National Politics, Cities and States, Law and the Courts, Government Agencies, Business, Labor,* and *Consumers.* In *Science,* departments will be devoted monthly to issues and developments in *Health and Medicine, Environment, Physical Science, Life Science, Social Science,* and *Applied Science.*

In all of the *Reviews,* the departments will be in addition to, not in the place of, several key articles in the supplement's field. And alongside the supplements themselves, most of those general features of SR that have long made the magazine entertaining and provocative reading will continue.

In the *Reviews* we will also endeavor to put our resources, our access to information, to work for our readers. A monthly feature, "Saturday Review Recommends" in the issue devoted to the arts, will present a guide to films, theater, books, art exhibits, and dance compiled by respected critics in each of the areas. *Saturday Review of Education* will eventually include a regular feature, "Guide to Schools," which will note key data on schools: private and special education schools, graduate schools, and daycare centers.

The *Saturday Review of Science* will carry a regular annotated bibliography that will augment the articles contained in each issue; *Saturday Review of the Society* will soon feature a column providing information on where and how to take effective action on issues raised in the magazine.

The second major change dealt with the subscription price. *Each* of the monthly *Reviews* was to have an annual subscription price of $12. However, during the introductory period the price was to be a special rate of $6 per annum. In other words, if subscribers elected to receive all four of the new *Reviews*—that is, a publication each week—they would pay $24 a year. This price compared with $6 a year that the old *Saturday Review* a short time before charged for its weekly publication. Actually, Charney and Veronis did not expect many subscribers to opt for all four *Reviews;* nevertheless, the new subscription cost per copy would be quadrupled. Veronis pointed out that many monthlies charged substantially more than the *Saturday Review* introductory rates and that a market test showed that readers were ready to support a magazine that served their needs.

The third major thrust involved large-scale mailings to build circulation. This promotional effort was based on extensive market research. Veronis has stated that "Predicting reader interest has reached the status of a science in magazine publishing." To guide its promotion effort, the new management selected a random sample of a million names out of a universe of 18 million. The total sample was then divided into a hundred groups of 10,000 names each. Then a different mail package was sent to each subgroup. Various combinations of names and content for each of the four magazines were tested.

The market test was not just a polling of attitudes; new orders were sought. Veronis noted that "The results are really predicted on orders received for these magazines, not merely an interest reaction to them."

Based on this extensive market test program, millions of direct-mail solicitations were made. A major effort at the end of the year involved a 17-million piece mailing that cost about $4½ million. The target for this massive effort was a return of 3%

new subscriptions. This would have increased the number of subscribers for each of the four magazines by over 125,000.

A fourth major change introduced by Charney and Veronis, directly transplanted from their experience with *Psychology Today,* was the introduction of book clubs. "We don't consider the reader," Veronis explained, "as a twelve dollar a year subscriber to a magazine but as a potential hundred dollar a year customer in the magazine's field of interest for books, records, games, posters, video, cassettes, conferences, school courses, and other products and services." A separate club was established for each of the four magazines, but major effort to develop each of these was deferred until past subscribers to the *Saturday Review* could sort themselves out into the new fourfold-interest division and until new subscribers could be obtained. Profits from this side of the venture were projected as increasing sources of income in the third, fourth, and fifth years of the 5-year program.

The development of this fourfold program naturally produced some other changes. One, which Charney and Veronis would have preferred to avoid, was the resignation of Norman Cousins. They urged Cousins to accept a position as Chairman of the Editorial Board and as a writer for the different magazines. Cousins politely but firmly turned the offer down. In an editorial explaining his resignation, Cousins wrote:

> The differences between us are not over the need for change. SR has been the product of change ever since it began as a book-review periodical almost half a century ago. The present differences are over the kind of change that is planned. John and Nick may be successful in what they intend to do. They may well be right in their basic premises. I can only say that I cannot be comfortable with those premises. Nor can I justify to myself or anyone else the use of my name to advance a program I cannot support.
> ... The one thing I have learned about editing over the years is that you have to edit and publish out of your own tastes, enthusiasms, and concerns, and not out of notions of guesswork about what other people might like to read. . . .

* * *

In particular, Cousins objected "strongly to the commercial use of the *Saturday Review* subscription list for purposes that have nothing to do with the magazine."

Charney, who replaced Cousins as Editor, felt that an East Coast provincialism might be avoided by moving out of New York City. So the entire editorial staff was transferred to a newly decorated building in San Francisco—at a cost of $500,000. Moreover, to give the four magazines the kind of editorial effort that the new program implied and to provide backup strength in the office operations, the size of the staff was doubled—a $4 million increase in annual expense.

All of this expansion should be viewed in light of the future that Charney and Veronis saw for Saturday Review Industries. While recognizing the uncertainties of any 5-year projection "especially when new products and a major business expansion are involved," the publicly stated target was $85 million gross revenues in the fifth year.

Too Much, Too Soon

The results of this great effort to change the *Saturday Review* did not come up to expectations. New subscriptions received from the massive mailing were little more than 1% instead of the hoped-for 3%. This meant that the cost of each new subscription was about $25, and the cash inflow failed by a wide margin to cover the promotional expense. Renewals by old *Saturday Review* subscribers started to drop as the fanfare for the new look increased.

The trade press in trying to explain this poor showing commented on the difficulty of producing "specialized magazines for generalists and generalized magazines for specialists." The magazines were promoted before each had an opportunity to develop a clear-cut character. The National Editor of the *Village Voice* observed: "The new *Saturday Review* never quite lost the reek of packaging. And for all the charts and formulas, *Saturday Review* was not the scientific publishing operation it professed to be. . . . Despite the computer-era trappings, financial bungling was legion. *Saturday Review's* rate base was raised prematurely; the 17-million piece promotional mailing last December was an all-or-nothing gamble; the move West was a foolish extravagance. But ultimately, *Saturday Review* died because the public didn't buy it. The public wouldn't buy it because, as several frustrated editors remarked, it never found its editorial soul."[4]

Understandably for a magazine in transition, advertisers did not rush to buy space. During the first full year of the new program, advertising pages declined from 1,575 to 1,408. With a one-time black and white page rate of $5,600 and a color page rate of $7,000, this decline was serious.[5]

The book clubs were losing $10,000 per week, and by competing with some potential advertisers they were beginning to hurt advertising revenue.

The strain of expansion and promotion was too much. Twice the managers of Saturday Review Industries had to return to their financial backers for more capital. A total of $16 million, including the original investment, had been used up—and the end was not in sight. Less than two years after the newly formed company bought *Saturday Review* from the McCall Corporation, it filed for bankruptcy.

COUSINS' NEW WORLD

Fresh Start on a Well-Worn Track

Seven months after Norman Cousins resigned from the *Saturday Review,* he was back in the magazine business with a brand new publication called *World.* This remarkably short incubation period was possible only because of the contacts, traditions, and goodwill Cousins had built up over three decades as Editor of the *Saturday Review.* Whereas Charney and Veronis took their business experience with *Psychology Today* and applied it to a new editorial mission, Cousins took his editorial bent and applied it to a new business organization.

The editorial aim of *World* has been described by Cousins in the following letter sent to former subscribers of the *Saturday Review:*

> My colleagues and I are pleased to announce that we are starting a new magazine later this Spring. It will be called *World* and will be published every two weeks.

---

[4]Bob Kuttner, *Folio,* July, 1973.

[5]These are the gross rates subject to 15% discount for advertising agencies and 2% discount for cash; also there is substantial variation for location in the magazine and for multiple insertions.

Ever since I resigned from the *Saturday Review* several months ago, I have been thinking and dreaming about starting an independent journal devoted to ideas, books, the creative arts, and the human condition. The principal point of difference between this magazine and existing magazines is that we will attempt to report on a world level. For example, instead of writing about important books published just in the United Staes, we intend to write about important books published throughout the world. Naturally, we will attempt to be highly selective. We will make no effort at detailed coverage; such a task is already being done in various places. What we will attempt to do is to view the world as a composite creative arena.

We will also give major attention to an emerging new concept—the concept of planetary planning. We will write about the human condition at a time when the ability of human intelligence to meet its problems is being tested as never before. Our hope is to see the world as the astronauts saw it—a beautiful wet blue ball possessing millions of delicately balanced factors that make life possible. Our dominant editorial concern, then, is the proper care of the human habitat—protecting it against war, environmental poisoning, overcrowding, or any of the things that indignify and humiliate human beings.

In this connection, we are pleased to announce that U Thant, former Secretary-General of the United Nations, and Buckminster Fuller, architect, poet, and philosopher, are joining our staff.

We will also give major attention to what we believe will be one of the most compelling issues in the years ahead—the waste of human resources, far more costly than the waste of physical resources.

There is no point in talking about conservation of land unless we also talk about conservation of life.

I think I have said enough to indicate that the new magazine will direct its central editorial energies both to the enjoyment of creative living and to the pursuit of vital ideas. It is an error, however, to try to say too much about a magazine in advance of publication. A magazine has to describe itself, issue by issue. . . .

Some specifics: We have decided against cut-rate subscriptions. Most of the ills of the magazine business, we believe, are traceable to the highly competitive practice of cut-rate subscriptions. On a new magazine, the subscription list generally consists almost entirely of cut-rate subscriptions. By thus starting out on an unsound level, new magazines find it difficult ever to get squared away on a healthy basis.

Our full-term rates are $12 for one year; $20 for two years; $25 for three years.

The reason we are able to make such a sharp reduction in the three-year rate is that substantial savings can be effected in processing costs.

In inviting you to join us in what we hope will be an exciting adventure in ideas, we realize we are asking you to take a chance on us. We have high hopes of justifying that confidence.

Sincerely,

/s/ Norman Cousins

Other publicity used the caption "WORLD: A Review of Ideas, Creative Arts and the Human Condition." Thus, the subjects covered were similar to those treated under Cousins' direction in the old *Saturday Review,* but in the new publication the scope was worldwide. A moral tone was reintroduced—to wit: "The greatest event in our lifetime is that the whole of humanity is now compressed within a single arena. The central question in that arena is whether the world will become a community or a wasteland, a single habitat or a single battlefield. More and more, the choice for the world's people is between becoming world warriors or world citizens."

To launch *World,* Cousins achieved a remarkable editorial transplant, bringing over more than a dozen *Saturday Review* writers and editors to the new magazine and enlisting two of his favorite contributors, U Thant and Buckminster Fuller, to write regularly. These familiar names enabled Cousins to appeal to the loyalty of his previous readers.

While the editorial mission had a familiar cast, the subscription price reflected a new view on how much of the total cost subscribers might be willing to bear. Compared with 1970, the annual rate was doubled for half as many copies. Even those subscribers who opted for the 3-year bargain were paying 32 cents a copy— compared with 11.6 cents in 1970. This change is particularly important to a new venture since subscribers will be paying the full incremental costs as circulation expands.

Many of the initial subscribers to *World* were obtained by a telephone campaign. Originally intended to provide in-depth information about reactions to the proposed magazine, the response was so phenomenal that the technique was converted into a subscription drive. A tape-recorded telephone solicitation by Cousins himself is followed up by an operator who engages in two-way conversation. Of former *Saturday Review* subscribers who were reached, 37% agreed to take the new magazine. The response was not nearly so good for nonreaders, but this expensive form of solicitation did build up the advance subscription list.

In addition to the telephone campaign, newspaper ads and letters such as that reproduced above were used. The total result was about 100,000 paid subscriptions when the first issue came off the press. Also surprising was the fact that over two-thirds of the subscribers to the yet-to-be-born magazine opted for the $25 three-year subscription. This was indeed an impressive showing in face of the industry trends for general reader magazines prevailing at the time.

Press reviews of the first issue of *World* were by no means unanimous in their praise. *Newsweek* said, "The overall tone is ponderous." Reacting to Cleveland Amory's attempt at breezy humor, *Newsweek* quotes Amory, "Starting a new column is never easy" and observes that Amory then proceeds to prove his point conclusively.

Time magazine said that "Volume One, Number One is dominated by wordy pieces that reflect the stodginess of the old *Saturday Review.* . . . Cleveland Amory and Goodman Ace grind out their stale *Saturday Review* humor." *Time* does find kind words to say about the critical sections on books, ballet, and music and warmly endorses several of the articles. "But these editorial assets seem outweighed by the clinkers."

Despite this lack of enthusiasm by fellow journalists, *World* found many readers who liked its editorial mission and perhaps its style. By the end of its first year, paid subscriptions had risen to 178,000. Advertisers were learning to respect the selective, high-income audience reached by *World* and were also impressed with the relatively low advertising rates—$1,700 for a one-time black and white page and $2,340 for a four-color page. Prospects for break-even operations by the end of the second year were good.

Should the Saturday Review Be Salvaged?

When financial quicksand made continuation of the Charney-Veronis program for the *Saturday Review* impossible, they set upon a search for someone who might buy their magazines. The search was continued by the Receiver after the company went into bankruptcy. No one wanted to buy the *Saturday Review* as a going concern. Only Norman Cousins showed any substantial interest, and he was naturally cautious and choosy about what he might buy.

After long discussions about the possibilities of merging *World* and Saturday Review Industries, no feasible solution was found. The total unpaid bills for printing, paper, back salaries, and the like was at least $5 million. In addition, the company had substantial future commitments for both printing and paper. As a consequence, the people representing *World* concluded that the only thing they should even consider buying were two assets—the name of the magazine and the subscription list.

Negotiation for the purchase of these two assets has been prolonged. At the time of this present case, it appears that *World* could purchase, if it chooses to do so, the name—*Saturday Review*—all editorial and art inventory, and the subscription list under the following terms:

1. *World* to acquire name "*Saturday Review.*"
2. *World* to acquire subscription list (all subscription and circulation records, and exclusive right to solicit continuation) for all four of the new *Saturday Reviews.*
3. *World* to pay Saturday Review Industries $500,000 for above.
4. *World* agrees to send magazines to prepaid *Saturday Review* subscribers for the remainder of their contracts.
5. *World* and Saturday Review Industries to split 50-50 all future cash receipts from existing *Saturday Review* subscription contracts.
6. Except for (4) and (5) above, *World* to assume none of the *Saturday Review* obligations nor any of its claims on accounts receivable.

The value of such an arrangement to World is, of course, difficult to estimate. The remaining goodwill attached to the *Saturday Review* name is immeasurable. Moreover, Cousins has demonstrated considerable success in wooing his former *Saturday Review* customers and the discontinuance of the new *Saturday Review* magazine should make recovery of these subscribers easier.

Nevertheless, some rough estimates of the results that might arise if *World* takes over both the name and the subscription lists from *Saturday Review* are possible. Here is one calculation:

Purchase price	$ 500,000
Cost of servicing *Saturday Review* contracts to their expiration; converting present *Saturday Review* subscribers to *World* at renewal time; and other absorption costs	1,500,000
Total *additional* outlay	$2,000,000

Prospective benefits:

Of 750,000 present *Saturday Review* subscribers, securing renewal from 350,000 (mostly carry-overs from earlier Cousins editorship). Assumes that 400,000 subscribers primarily interested in single-purpose magazine would not renew. This addition of 350,000 subscribers plus existing 180,000 *World* subscribers would create new base of 530,000 for advertising rates. This would justify 200% increase—from $1,700 to $5,100 for single-insertion black and white page, and from $2,340 to $7,000 for four-color page.

After readjustment, gross revenue might become:

Circulation (530,000 × average annual price of $9.25)		
	=	$5,000,000 +
Advertising (equivalent of 30 black & white pages per issue; discounts equal 1/6 of $5,100; so, 30 × 25 × $4,250)		
	=	3,000,000 +
Possible total gross revenue		$8,000,000
Expenses at present prices:		
Printing & distribution @ 16¢ per copy		$2,200,000
Editorial	$1,000,000	
Advertising...........................	1,000,000	
Promotion, general and administrative..	2,000,000	4,000,000
		$6,200,000
Profit before tax		$1,800,000

These estimates are subject to all sorts of adjustments based on judgment. For instance, if only 180,000 instead of 350,000 *Saturday Review* subscribers can be retained, and the total circulation becomes 360,000—the resulting one-third cut in circulation and advertising revenue and in printing and distribution costs would produce a break-even situation. If, in addition, advertising is the equivalent of 20 pages instead of 30 pages per issue, a serious loss would arise. Inflation and other external forces are likely to increase expenses faster than revenue.

The proposed acquisition of *Saturday Review* assets has major implications for the financing of *World*. Now, Cousins and his management associates have over 50% of the stockholder votes. When *World* was launched, Cousins had to secure financial backing, but because of his experiences with outside owners he naturally wished to retain control of the new venture. This was accomplished by what in effect is participating preferred stock that enables investors to share in profits on the basis of their relative contributions of capital while concentrating the voting rights in a smaller class of common stock.

The purchase of the name and the subscriber lists from *Saturday Review* together with the costs of absorbing the subscribers (estimated at $2,000,000 in the above table) would approximately double the capital investment needed by *World*. Cousins has located private investors who are willing to put up the money, but the conditions surrounding the investment remain sticky. For instance, one prospective investor would be glad to leave Cousins with complete *editorial* control but wants to combine the business activities with those of two or three other publishing ventures. Two other potential investors hold the conventional view that votes should be proportionate to investment. One of these prospects has suggested "the normal stockholder position coupled with a five-year contract assuring management the independence of action we all agree is desirable." The present investors are prepared to increase their holding of "preferred stock" by another half million provided the *Saturday Review* purchase is made and a satisfactory plan for the total capital needs is developed. Still other wealthy individuals have expressed interest in the venture, although specific arrangements have not been discussed with them.

Clearly, the potential *Saturday Review* purchase would require substantial realignment in the financial structure of *World*. Moreover, a reassessment of the manner and the direction of the business operations would be in order, and new investors might be concerned with the long-run viability of editorial policies.

COMPREHENSIVE CASE 3

Crown Cork—The Tough Maverick

In 1977 Crown Cork & Seal Company, Inc. surpassed two of its long-standing goals —sales over a billion dollars and earnings more than three dollars per share of common stock. Both sales and earnings have increased without interruption since the company was on the verge of bankruptcy twenty-three years earlier. In fact, *every quarter* for over 20 years earnings have exceeded those of the corresponding period in the previous year.

This record is remarkable because (a) the company is substantially smaller than its leading competitors; (b) it operates in the very competitive, mature container industry where profit margins are narrow and precarious; and (c) the packaging revolution and technological changes have led to frequent shifts between metal, glass, paper, and plastic containers. By pursuing a strategy of not following the leaders, Crown Cork has found a way of obtaining the widest profit margin in its industry.

Two questions naturally arise: What accounts for Crown Cork's success in a basically hostile environment? And, will the strategy and policies that have worked so well in the past lead to continuing growth in the future?

STRATEGY LEADING TO SUCCESS

Survival in a mature field such as the "tin can" business is never easy; growth and profitability are even more elusive. Four basic guidelines account for much, though not all, of Crown Cork's impressive showing: (1) concentration versus diversification, (2) selective service, (3) no-frill expenses, and (4) foreign spin-offs.

Concentration vs. Diversification

The two leading producers of metal containers have actively diversified. Both American Can Company and the Continental Group (formerly Continental Can Company) expanded into a wide variety of packaging materials with an aim of being able to provide customers with most, if not all, of their packaging requirements. Both companies have substantial research operations studying new forms of flexible materials, plastic containers, and printing and finishing techniques. The "business we are in" has expanded from traditional cans to active participation in the packaging revolution.

Moreover, Continental's interest in paper has led to major vertical integration back into forest industries. American Can has diversified into chemicals and an array of consumer products such as paper towels and tissues, Dixie cups, dress patterns, and food service products used in fast-food chains and elsewhere. Both companies are earning a higher rate of return from these "outside" activities than from their packaging business (including cans). Even National Can Corporation, a firm close to Crown Cork in size, has experimented with diversification outside of the packaging field.

In contrast, Crown Cork has stuck closely to its traditional lines of business. In fact, it has narrowed its focus to predominant emphasis on one part of the metal can industry—cans for "hard-to-hold products." These are notably aerosols, beer, and carbonated beverages, all of which must be held under pressure. This means that with minor exceptions, Crown Cork has no interest in packer cans for fruits and vegetables, cans for oil, and many other types of containers. (See Exhibit 1.)

Exhibit 1

U.S. Packaging Industry

	Shipment Value in $1,000,000's 1975
Paper and paperboard containers:	
Bags, boxes, cartons, drums, shipping containers	11,367
Flexible packaging materials:	
Paper, cellophane, polyethylene, metal foil, etc.	2,295
Metal containers:	
Steel and aluminum cans, shipping drums, etc.	7,213
Aerosols	464
Glass containers	2,720
Closures:	
Metal caps and crowns, milk bottle caps, plastic tops, etc.	735
Rigid and semi-rigid plastic containers:	
Bottles, tubes, boxes, sheets, etc.	1,122
Wooden containers	700
Other:	
Textiles, labels, tape, etc.	1,895
Total value of packaging materials	28,511

Crown Cork's concentration on hard-to-hold products started at its founding in 1891. A shop supervisor invented what we know as a soda bottlecap, a flanged disk of tin-plate with a cork insert to make a tight seal. To the present day, the company has been a leader in what is now called the "closures" segment of the packaging industry. Many competitors have entered the field; and twist-top, tear-tops, and an ingenious variety of plastic lids vie for consumer preference. But in this niche (49 billion closures per year) Crown Cork has remained an innovator and a low-cost producer.

A related facet is filling machinery for use in customers' plants. Filling is a highly automated operation, and the containers and closures must be precisely integrated with the process of filling and sealing. And Crown Cork is a leading manufacturer of high-speed equipment used for this purpose. The volume of its machinery sales and profits are cyclical, ranging from six to twelve percent of the total; but filling equipment helps keep the company abreast of the shifting needs of customers.

Nevertheless, in recent years metal cans have been Crown Cork's major product, as the estimates in Exhibit 2 show. That is the area which accounts for most of Crown Cork's growth, and it is the area where present company management has chosen to bet its future.

Exhibit 2

Crown Cork: Sources of Sales and Income

	Total Company	U.S.	International
Sales			
Cans	65%	88%	32%
Closures	27	5	59
Machinery	8	7	9
Total	100%	100%	100%
Pretax Income			
Cans	61%	84%	22%
Closures	27	6	63
Machinery	12	10	15
Total	100%	100%	100%

Source: Based on *Wall Street Transcript* estimates.

The product line strategy of Crown Cork is clear. It has elected to be a specialist rather than to diversify. In its particular niche, which has been the core of its business throughout its history, it seeks to outsmart its larger competitors by being expert and low-cost. It meets threats from other types of containers by fighting them, not joining them. Fortunately for Crown Cork, the segment of its concentration has been growing, although uncertainties continue to appear, as will be discussed later.

Selective Service

A second facet of Crown Cork's strategy relates to the importance of containers to its customers. For all beer and soft-drink producers, and many manufacturers of aerosol products, the container costs more than its contents. Next to payroll, containers are their biggest expense item. Moreover, the appearance of the container plays a significant role in selling, especially in the supermarkets. Of course, reliable quality is vital for repeat sales, and this quality must be maintained on filling machines running at speeds of up to 1200 cans per minute. Because of their bulk, inventories of empty cans are typically low; this means that reliability of delivery is crucial to keeping a plant in operation—thousands of cans week after week.

Crown Cork seeks to be an attractive supplier by responding promptly and personally to these customer needs. John Connelly, chairman, takes calls from any customer and follows up immediately. Other executives as well as salespersons do likewise, spending a large portion of their time traveling to customer plants whenever problems arise. Since there is little difference in physical quality of cans from major producers, and pricing is so competitive there is virtually no margin for "deals," this personalized top-brass service becomes more important. Crown Cork tries to build its plant capacity somewhat ahead of customers' requirements so that it has capacity available to meet customers' peak requirements.

The biggest change recently in serving customers has been the introduction of a two-piece steel can. This type of can, copied from a popular aluminum can, is "drawn and ironed" so that the entire can except for the top is a single piece of metal. It is lightweight, economical because of the reduction in steel required, and has no side seams or bottom joint which some health pessimists think might contribute to lead poisoning. Crown Cork promoted and assisted in the development of production technology for making two-piece steel cans; and it invested millions of dollars between 1971 and 1977 in twenty-seven new production lines. Other can companies are now turning to the two-piece steel can, but Crown Cork has been the leader.

Limits on service do exist, however. As already noted, Crown Cork does not offer a "full line" of cans, let alone other packaging materials. The presumption is that the products Crown Cork does offer are so important to customers they will seek out separate suppliers for these items alone. In fact, the new two-piece can is offered only in steel and not in aluminum even though many large customers buy both. Reynolds and Kaiser aluminum companies produce large quantities of two-piece aluminum cans (they originated the product), and Crown Cork does not want to be in a position where its metal suppliers can squeeze fabricating margins while making a profit in the base metal.

Moreover, Crown Cork has been unwilling to build a can-manufacturing facility at a customer's plant. The issue here is defense against "self-manufacturing." Large customers especially in the beer industry may decide that they can make their own cans more cheaply than buying them. In fact, self-manufacture in relation to total cans produced increased from 17.5% in 1970 to 29% in 1977. The trend is serious because every can made by a user is one less sale for independent can producers. A compromise arrangement adopted by Crown Cork's competitors is to build a plant at the site of customer production, and share with the customer the resulting savings in transportation and selling expenses. Crown Cork has rejected such arrangements, which may involve an investment of $10,000,000 to $20,000,000, because it wants not to be dependent on a single customer for the efficient operation of a plant.

Crown Cork cherishes flexibility. It will go to great lengths helping customers and adjusting its schedules to meet customer needs. But it is leery of being boxed in. It is selective about the areas where it participates and wants to play from relative strength.

No-Frill Expenses

Crown Cork has a simple approach to low-cost production; it spends money only to the extent it has to. When John Connelly became president of the ailing firm twenty-three years ago, he cut the payroll 24%, and the company has run on lean expense ratios ever since. Spartan offices, few secretaries, direct personal communication are symptomatic. The executive organization is simple, and senior executives spend much of their time in the plant or with customers. Staff units are small and close to the action they serve; the number of salespersons in a territory is trimmed to the number of active accounts. Connelly notes with pride that the square feet of space devoted to administration has not increased in 20 years.

The approach to research and development expenses is typical. Most of the attention of the small R&D staff is devoted to customers' problems—how to pack a new lacquer in an aerosol container, for example. In many packaging areas, the company prefers to be a quick follower rather than a pioneer. It has no think-tank in sylvan surroundings. Moreover, when confronted with the two-piece aluminum can competition, Crown Cork called on U.S. Steel (not its own personnel) to develop a sheet steel that could be processed in a similar fashion. Since the steel industry was threatened to lose much of its attractive tinplate business, it did most of the development work.

No money is spent on lobbying or public relations. In its closures and machinery lines, Crown Cork operates at the forefront of technology. But development work is done within those divisions and is charged to their operating expenses. They are not expected to make big leaps into new fields.

People working for Crown Cork must like their work because the hours probably will be long and they have to do it well. Saturday morning staff meetings are normal. Connelly personally sets a driving pace, and expects others to do likewise. The rewards are good for those who fit into this kind of regime; those who don't fit don't stay around.

Data on orders, prices, output, costs, and the like are known promptly, and problems are confronted on a factual and objective basis. The deadly parallel is often used in comparing plant performances. *Both* production and sales people are "responsible for profits" and both are expected to initiate corrective action when profits earned by a plant fall below target.

The net effect of this no-frill approach to expenses is a drop in selling and administrative expenses from 6.3% to 3.3% over a ten-year period as indicated in Exhibit 3. Crown Cork's more diversified competitors have comparable ratios ranging from 5.4% to over 10%. Although part of this drop reflects a change in product mix toward cans for large customers, the ratio is strikingly low. In one area, however, there is no holding back; the equipment in company plants is both modern and fast.

Exhibit 3

	1977		1971		1967	
	(1,000,000)	%	(1,000,000)	%	(1,000,000)	%
Net Sales	$1,049	100.0	$448	100.0	$301	100.0
Cost of Goods Sold	906	86.4	368	82.1	242	80.4
Selling & Administrative Expense	35	3.3	21	4.7	19	6.3
Operating Profit before Interest & Income Tax	$ 108	10.3	$ 59	13.2	$ 40	13.3

Foreign Spin-Offs

A fourth pillar in Crown Cork's strategy is early entry into foreign markets. Cans and closures cannot be exported economically. Instead, Crown Cork has provided machinery (including rebuilt U.S. equipment) and production know-how to locally organized firms. Many of these companies are in developing countries, where the demand is primarily for bottlecaps.[1] Crown Cork had established these companies long before its U.S. competitors considered such locations worthy of attention.

These foreign subsidiaries are managed by local citizens in a highly decentralized manner. Having created a technological beachhead, the Philadelphia headquarters withdraws. Each outpost must run its own show. There is no international vice president at headquarters (which is consistent with the low overhead philosophy mentioned above); not one American is on Crown Cork's payroll outside the United States. The presidents of some of the large foreign groups do serve on the Crown Cork board of directors. And to a large extent, each foreign unit generates its own capital. In terms of people, markets, and capital, each becomes part of the local scene even more than the local Coca-Cola bottler. It is, of course, on the spot if and when a local demand for cans develops. There is little attempt or need for multinational coordination.

With a relatively small amount of U.S. management attention, the foreign operations have grown over the years along with the total company. Income from foreign sales has ranged between 29% and 43% of the total over the last decade, and assets abroad account for an even larger share of the total. The trends are shown in Exhibits 4 and 5.

---

[1]Crown Cork has subsidiaries in the following countries: Canada, Mexico, Puerto Rico, West Indies, Argentina, Brazil, Chile, Ecuador, Peru; Belgium, France, Italy, Holland, Germany, Ireland, Portugal; Ethiopia, East Africa, Nigeria, Zimbabwe, Zaire, Morocco, Zambia; Indonesia, Malaysia, Thailand, etc.

Exhibit 4

Crown Cork & Seal Company, Inc.
Operating Data*
(in millions of dollars except where otherwise indicated)

	1977	1976	1975	1974	1973	1972	1971	1970	1969	1968	1967
Net Sales	1049	910	825	766	572	489	448	414	371	337	301
Cost of Goods Sold	905	784	709	655	480	407	368	334	297	269	242
Selling & Administrative Expenses	35	32	30	29	23	21	21	21	19	19	19
Interest Expense	6	4	7	7	4	4	5	6	6	6	5
Tax on Income	49	44	35	33	27	25	25	27	25	21	15
Net Income (excluding minority interests)	54	46	42	40	34	31	28	26	23	21	19
Shares of Common Stock (average)	16	16	17	18	19	20	20	20	21	21	21
Earnings per Share (dollars)	3.46	2.84	2.43	2.20	1.81	1.58	1.41	1.26	1.11	1.00	.91
Net Income from Foreign Subsidiaries	18	15	16	15	15	13	12	8	7	6	5
Net Income from U.S. Operations	36	31	26	25	19	18	16	18	16	15	14
Number of Employees (1,000's)	17	16	16	16	16	14	14	15	14	13	13
Plant & Equipment Expenditures	59	22	47	53	40	28	33	37	33	19	23
Ratio Net Income/Total Assets											
Foreign Subsidiaries	5.9	5.4	6.4	6.2	5.7	7.3	7.0	5.4	5.6	5.4	5.2
U.S. Operations	11.0	11.2	9.0	8.4	7.4	8.1	7.0	7.6	7.5	7.4	7.3
Common Stock Price											
High	25⅜	22⅛	23⅛	23	28⅝	27½	23⅜	18½	18⅞	16⅝	14
Low	19¾	16⅞	14⅝	13⅝	19¼	18½	17⅞	12½	14⅛	10⅝	9

*Columns may not add exactly, due to rounding.

Exhibit 5
Crown Cork & Seal Company, Inc.
Comparative Balance Sheets*
(all figures in $1,000,000)

	1977	1976	1975	1974	1973	1972	1971	1970	1969	1968	1967
					Total Company—Consolidated						
Current Assets	341	281	264	286	223	175	172	170	143	133	119
Plant & Equipment (net)	274	249	259	242	219	211	213	205	189	175	170
Investments and Goodwill	17	17	15	14	15	14	12	12	9	5	5
Total Assets	631	547	539	542	457	400	398	387	341	313	294
Current Liabilities	206	158	170	209	140	105	110	125	98	89	78
Deferred Income Tax	44	39	35	29	28	26	27	23	22	22	19
Long Term Debt	13	26	30	34	38	31	42	37	36	41	56
Minority Equity in Subsidiaries	7	7	12	9	8	8	8	8	12	12	12
Common Stock	76	78	84	86	93	97	100	101	103	(150)	(130)
Retained Earnings	286	238	209	176	151	133	112	89	67	( )	( )
Total Liabilities & Equity	631	547	539	542	457	400	398	387	341	313	294

Foreign Subsidiaries

Current Assets	201	170	156	156	111	82	74	67	58	47	42
Plant & Equipment (net)	103	99	95	89	90	96	93	83	70	61	60
Total Assets	304	269	251	245	201	178	167	150	128	108	102
Current Liabilities	89	77	74	87	60	37	40	30	26	20	18
Deferred Income Tax	11	10	9	7	6	6	5	5	4	4	4
Long Term Debt	1	1	3	7	9	9	12	10	6	2	3
Minority Equity in Subsidiaries	7	7	12	9	8	8	8	8	12	12	12
Retained Earnings (CC&S share)	144	132	113	91	72	69	59	50	44	37	34
Other CC&S Equity	53	42	40	44	46	49	43	47	36	33	31
Total Liabilities & Equity	304	269	251	245	201	178	167	150	128	108	102

United States Operations**

Current Assets	140	111	108	130	113	94	98	103	85	86	77
Plant & Equipment (net)	171	150	164	153	129	115	120	122	119	113	110
Investments and Goodwill	17	17	15	14	15	14	12	12	9	5	5
Total Assets	328	278	288	297	257	223	230	237	213	204	192
Current Liabilities	117	81	96	120	80	68	70	95	72	69	60
Deferred Income Tax	33	30	26	22	22	20	22	18	18	18	17
Long Term Debt	12	25	27	27	30	22	30	27	29	35	53
Retained Earnings	142	106	96	85	79	64	53	39	24	(80)	(64)
Other Equity	23	35	44	43	46	49	55	58	70	( )	( )
Total Liabilities & Equity	328	278	288	297	257	223	230	237	213	204	192

*Columns may not add exactly, due to rounding.

**Assets and liabilities assigned to U.S. operations are total company figures minus foreign subsidiaries.

Comparisons of Company Results

The success of Crown Cork is clear not only in its own growth in volume and profits; it has performed well in relation to other major can producers. Both its sales and its net income have grown faster during the past decade than its big rivals, American Can and Continental. National Can has, indeed, increased its sales faster than Crown Cork primarily as a result of diversification; however, National Can's ratio of profits earned on sales is only about half as large. The impressive fact is that year after year Crown Cork has earned more profit on its sales (and on assets) than its direct competitors. See Exhibit 6.

FUTURE PROSPECTS

Crown Cork has defied conventional business wisdom on many fronts, including a refusal to diversify its products. It has been in the midst of a packaging revolution. Many products formerly sold in bulk are now further processed (trimmed, frozen, polished, precooked, glued, pre-cut, and the like), placed in convenient-to-use containers, and labeled with enticing instructions. Usually such products are swathed in clear plastic and cradled in an attractive paper box. Products involved in the change range from soap to piston rings to pocket calculators. Nevertheless, Crown Cork persists in making tin cans and closures.

Moreover, in its own domain the tin can has been and continues to be threatened by substitutes. Environmentalists would like to legislate it out of existence. So Crown Cork's future is far from assured.

Growth of Underlying Demand

By choice, the can customers of Crown Cork fall into four groups: bottlers of beer (44%), bottlers of carbonated beverages (27%), producers of aerosol products (19%), and food packers (10%). The approximate distribution of U.S. sales is indicated in parentheses.

The U.S. consumption of both beer and soft drinks has been growing:

	Beer		Soft Drinks	
	Millions of gallons	Gallons per capita	Millions of gallons	Gallons per capita
1967	3,313	16.8	4,650	23.6
1972	4,053	19.5	6,300	30.3
1976	4,654	21.7	7,335	34.2

Most beer is now consumed "off the premises" from bottles or cans, draft beer having dropped from 17% of the total in 1966 to 12% by 1975. If leisure lifestyles continue, and disposable incomes rise, the consumption of beer is expected to increase about 3% to 4% per year. So this outlook is favorable but not dramatic.

There is a persistent trend toward fewer brewers and fewer plants. Currently five companies (out of a total of less than fifty) produce and sell about 70% of the total consumption. The number of plants in operation has dropped 38% during the past decade. This concentration of production by larger companies in larger plants is conducive to "self-manufacture" of the containers they use. Coors already makes all its own cans, Schlitz 70%, Miller 50%, and Anheuser-Busch 35%.

Soft drinks have recently replaced coffee as the leading national drink. The growth rate may be dampened as the proportion of teenagers in the population drops, but no one can be sure what the present young guzzlers will prefer ten years hence. Soft drinks are popular in fast-food outlets and even in restaurants. A competitive and fast-growing factor is the sale of powdered drink mixes and iced-tea mixes. This trend may have an adverse effect on the projected soft-drink growth of between 4% and 5% per year.

Exhibit 6

Crown Cork & Seal Company, Inc.
Comparison of Company Sales and Income—1967–1977

		Sales Index 1967 = 100		
Year	American Can	Continental	Crown Cork	National Can
1977	226	262	349	444
1976	207	247	302	417
1975	195	222	274	363
1974	190	221	254	323
1973	143	182	190	247
1972	132	157	162	216
1971	124	149	149	198
1970	121	146	138	172
1969	113	127	123	157
1968	108	108	112	124
1967	100	100	100	100
Base in $1,000,000 1967	1522	1398	301	220

		Net Income Index 1967 = 100		
	American Can	Continental	Crown Cork	National Can
1977	150	184	286	145*
1976	133	151	245	260
1975	112	137	221	236
1974	131	142	211	253
1973	87	122	182	181
1972	73	103	166	177
1971	38	93	151	166
1970	87	118	137	182
1969	85	116	122	189
1968	102	107	111	129
1967	100	100	100	100
Base in $1,000,000 1967	76	78	19	8

(continued)

Exhibit 6 continued

Net Income as a % of Sales

	American Can	Continental	Crown Cork	National Can
1977	3.3	3.9	5.1	1.2
1976	3.0	3.4	5.1	2.3
1975	2.9	3.5	5.0	2.3
1974	3.5	3.6	5.2	2.8
1973	3.0	3.7	6.0	2.7
1972	2.7	3.7	6.4	3.0
1971	2.6	3.5	6.3	3.0
1970	3.6	4.5	6.2	3.8
1969	3.7	5.1	6.2	3.9
1968	4.8	5.5	6.2	3.8
1967	5.0	5.6	6.3	3.6

*Loss from discontinued operations was $11,700,000. Excluding his loss, the net income index would have been 307.

Source: *Standard & Poor's Industry Study.*

Aerosol cans, Crown Cork's third market segment, experienced rapid growth from their introduction in the '50's to 1974. At that peak, the du Pont company, leading manufacturer of propellants, estimated annual shipments as follows:

		(1,000,000 units)
Personal products (deodorants, hairsprays, shaving lather, perfumes, pharmaceuticals, suntan lotion, etc., etc.)		1,602
Household products (cleaners, room deodorants, disinfectants, laundry products, polishes, etc.)		752
All other (food, insect sprays, paint, automotive, industrial, etc.)	Total	830 3,184

Following 1974, demand took a sharp dip, partly because aerosol packaging is relatively expensive and partly in response to a threatened ban on the use of fluorocarbons as a propellant (for ecological reasons). Although demand has picked up again, substantial further growth is unlikely until the ecological issues are resolved favorably.

Overall, for beer, soft drinks, and aerosol products, U.S. growth-rate is estimated at less than 4% per annum, barring shifts due to new ecological legislation.

Battle of Materials

Not long ago every individual-size container for beer or coke was a glass bottle, and that glass bottle was returned to be refilled many times. There was no alternative. Then the metal can entered the picture. It saved the mess and labor of returning empty bottles; it was lighter to handle, packed more closely and didn't chip or shatter. The can companies and steel companies had to undertake a major educational campaign to persuade the consumer that a can did not affect the flavor of the product, and finally the long tradition of the glass bottle was broken.

This switch to non-returnable cans involved billions of containers and millions of dollars, as the data already presented indicate. But about the time it seemed likely that the coke bottle would follow the milk bottle into oblivion, the glass industry created the lighter-weight, cheaper, non-returnable glass bottle. With a competitive product and a potential market many times the size of that of the old returnable bottle, the fight was on. Broadly speaking, the glass industry has been able to retain about one-third of the beer container business (with 96% non-returnable bottles). In the soft drink field, the division between glass and cans is about the same, although cans continue to make inroads.

Actually, glass bottles are cheaper than cans. However, they weigh more, take more space, are slower to fill, and break occasionally. For the bottlers the difference in total cost is so narrow they usually will use the container which consumers like and fits best into their marketing program. The price differential does vary, however, and while bottlers are reluctant to change from glass to metal, or vice versa, they will do so if they predict that a price difference will persist.

A second continuing conflict is between steel and aluminum. When cans invaded the beverage field they were the traditional three-piece steel cans (a few conical tops never won an enduring position). Then around 1960, Reynolds and Kaiser aluminum companies moved in with their two-piece aluminum can. This can—now also manufactured by all major can companies except Crown Cork—has made rapid progress. Aluminum has increased from 4% of the total can business in 1965 to over 27% in 1977. During most of this period the tonnage of steel going into cans actually decreased.

Aluminum is especially strong in the beverage sectors. It makes a somewhat better-looking can, and is lighter weight. If the steel industry had not developed, with Crown Cork's cooperation, a steel version of the drawn-and-ironed two-piece can, aluminum would soon have dominated metal containers for beer and soft drinks. But by the early 1970's the quality of steel and the processing technology were sufficiently improved to enable steel to join in the fight with a thin-walled, two-piece can weighing 20% less than its seamed predecessor. About 65% of beverage cans are now two-piece (aluminum and steel), compared with 11% in 1970, and the percentage is rising.

Aluminum has one drawback—price. Because its refining consumes large quantities of energy, its production costs may rise faster than those of steel and glass. If this occurs, the large aluminum companies will have to decide whether to continue to push for an increasing share of the container market by pricing their cans and/or aluminum sheet used by other can manufacturers at a competitive level. Aluminum companies, like the steel companies and glass bottle manufacturers, have to balance off market share and profit margins. And the non-integrated can producers—like Crown Cork—must seek out a viable spot amidst these forces.

One other storm-cloud on the materials horizon is the prospect for plastic bottles. In fact, blow-molded plastic bottles already have captured a 9 billion unit piece of the total bottle market.

Compared with glass, plastic bottles are lightweight, durable, almost unbreakable, and they can be formed into special shapes that have distinctive merchandising advantages.

In the soft drink industry, both Coca-Cola and Pepsi-Cola have turned to plastic for their large (32-ounce) bottle. Such a bottle (empty) weighs only two ounces versus nineteen ounces for a comparable glass bottle, and it occupies 15% less space. And consumers like it. Coca-Cola ran into an FDA ban on its acrylomitite bottle made by Monsanto; the FDA fears that this particular plastic might "leak" into the beverage

Exhibit 7

Crown Cork & Seal Company, Inc.
End Use of Glass Bottles and Metal Cans

	Billion Glass Bottles*		Billion Metal Cans**	
	1967	1977	1967	1977
Food	3.4	3.6	31.4	26.0
Beer***	6.4	13.4	12.8	27.9
Soft Drinks***	5.5	9.7	6.8	23.3
Liquor & Wines	2.8	3.5	—	—
Medicinal & Health	2.5	2.1	—	—
Pet Food	—	—	2.7	2.7
All Other	2.4	2.0	8.8	7.3
Total	23.0	34.3	62.5	87.2

*Narrow-neck bottles.
**Based on constant ratio of 466.15 can per base metal box.
***Percent of bottles non-returnable: Beer, 1967-90%; 1977-96%;
                    Soft drinks, 1967-65%; 1977-90%.

End Use of Plastic Bottles	Billions of Bottles 1976
Household chemicals	2.8
Food and beverage	2.1
Toiletries & cosmetics	1.7
Medical & health	1.4
Industrial, etc.	.6
Total	8.6

and if it does, adverse health effects could possibly result. So the acrylomitite bottle is temporarily withdrawn from the market. Other plastic bottles, notably du Pont's polyester (PET) products, are not affected by the ban.

Several major firms are committing large research efforts on plastic bottles for the sixty billion unit beer and soft drink markets. In addition to the du Pont and Monsanto efforts, Dow Chemical is working with Owens-Illinois and Anchor Hocking is teamed up with Coca-Cola on a plastic-coated glass bottle (returnable) that has low breakage and is lightweight. Mitsubishi Chemical already has a bottle of the latter type. Imperial Chemical of England is also active.

Currently, plastic beverage bottles are more expensive than glass. With technological improvements, however, this difference in cost could easily disappear. The price of raw material inputs (plastic prices are related to petroleum) is a further uncertainty. The competition is not only between glass and plastic; if the plastic bottle overcomes some of the disadvantages of glass, it could also take business away from cans.

Strength of Contestants

The way these future competitive forces will develop is strongly affected by the power and concerns of the major contestants, or actors. We have already noted that Crown Cork's competitors in U.S. steel can production—American Can, Continental, and National Can—are larger and more diversified. This is a capital intensive industry. The number of direct competitors is small because large investments are required and profit margins unattractive.

Moreover, the metal can industry has had chronic overcapacity. New capacity installed by self-manufacturers plus new capacity of aluminum can producers left excess machinery for the traditional three-piece steel can. During the early '70's American Can and Continental each dismantled old plants to reduce this depressing overhang. Now the rapid expansion of two-piece steel can lines again creates unused three-piece facilities. This is a tough climate for firms with limited capital.

Actually, the competitors are numerous. Two large aluminum companies, Reynolds and Kaiser, have obtained significant positions in the beer and soft drink markets. Four of the five leading brewers have large can plants, as do several food companies. And companies making glass bottles, such as Corning and Owens-Illinois, aggressively compete for the same end use. These are all powerful, sharp contestants.

Customers include large and relatively small firms. Bottlers of beer tend to be large and the industry is becoming more concentrated. In soft drinks the prevailing pattern of local franchises makes the number of customers much larger than might be inferred from brand concentration; the five largest firms get over 75% of the business, but they have several hundred distributors who actually purchase containers. Producers of aerosol products may be even smaller because they use aerosol cans for quite special markets. Nevertheless, for all these customers containers represent a major expense, and the buyers usually are very sophisticated in their purchasing.

Material suppliers are another set of actors. Materials account for roughly two-thirds of the cost of a can, so the dollar volume of materials consumed is very large. The big steel firms as well as the aluminum companies are vitally interested in this market. And as noted in the preceding section, at least five of the powerful chemical concerns are vying for advantage in a growing plastic bottle market.

By most standards Crown Cork is itself a large company. But compared with many of the firms whose actions impinge on its destiny, it is "just one of the boys."

In foreign countries the competitive picture varies widely. Because the market for cans and bottles is inherently local, each country has its own characteristics. Developing countries with small consumption in each locality, low purchasing power, and low labor costs typically use returnable bottles; this creates a demand for closures. In Europe the consumption of beverages is growing and there is a shift toward disposable containers; nevertheless, the size of individual purchasers of cans and closures is much smaller than in the United States. Because of this diversity, a strategy for profitable growth varies from country to country.

Superimposed on this cast of actors are government regulatory agencies. The ones whose actions will have profound effect on the container industry deal with environmental issues.

Environmental Protection

Non-returnable containers for beer and soft drinks are under attack because they litter the countryside. Well over half of highway litter consists of such bottles and cans. Pull-tabs to open cans are also a target. The chief remedy proposed is to use returnable bottles, a plan which would have disastrous impact on the metal can industry.

Five states—Oregon, Vermont, Maine, Michigan, and Connecticut—already have laws specifically aimed at non-returnable containers. A five-cent mandatory deposit is intended to be high enough to make non-returnable bottles and cans uneconomic, and a lower deposit on returnable bottles is designed to bring them back for reuse. Experience in Oregon and Vermont which have had such laws longest indicates that (a) litter is substantially reduced, (b) total sales have declined slightly, (c) consumers and especially retailers find the system something of a nuisance, and (d) prices have risen a bit to cover the additional cost of handling returned bottles.

Most other states, the federal government, and many local governments are actively considering legislation of some kind to reduce litter. Emotions run high, lobbying pressures are intense, and the outcome far from certain. The issue is aggravated by growing problems of solid-waste disposal. Also, proponents talk of energy conservation.

An alternative to the mandatory deposit is the state of Washington's special tax on products which create solid-waste problems; part of the proceeds of this tax are used for a public education program on litter prevention. The effectiveness of Washington's program is not yet known.

Much of the opposition to the anti-litter laws comes from vested interests—labor unions which would lose jobs and manufacturers who would lose sales. More fundamental, probably, is the way politically active consumers will balance a cleaner environment versus the nuisance of returning bottles.

A special environmental issue relates to aerosols. Fluorcarbons, now used as propellants in about half of the aerosol products, are suspected of making cumulative injury to the atmosphere surrounding Earth. Consequently, the Environmental Protection Agency and related agencies have a program for eliminating virtually all the use of fluorocarbons in aerosols. Alternative propellants either are known or are being developed so probably few products will have to be removed from the market.

Nevertheless, the uncertainty related to the switch has led to a search for other forms of packaging, and aerosols are under their own kind of cloud from which they may never recover.

Crown Cork's Distinctive Resources

The future for Crown Cork is filled with uncertainties, as the preceding discussion indicates. The consumer industries it serves are basically mature, and a whole series of doubts must be faced about the kind of containers which will carry products to those ultimate consumers. Moreover, the actions of powerful companies and political groups will have profound effect on Crown Cork; the extent and manner of Crown Cork's attempt to influence these actors will have to be decided.

As a further basis for assessing Crown Cork's future strategy, we should review several of its distinctive strengths.

1. Crown Cork has a good internal cash flow. In 1977 it earned profits after taxes of $54 million and recovered depreciation of $32 million. Together these flows equal 24% of the equity now invested in the company. Moreover, the company has a clear policy of paying no dividends to stockholders. So the cash flow is available for management's use.

The no-dividend (on common stock) policy, which runs back for more than two decades, is interesting because in several years, more cash was generated than was needed in the business. Instead of paying dividends, management elected to buy back common stock. The repurchase price has been around $20 per share. During the period 1970 through 1977 the number of shares outstanding was reduced about 25%! Of course, this reduction has an effect on earnings per share; if the money used to buy back stock had instead been paid out as dividends, the earnings per share in 1977 would have been only $2.66 compared with the actual of $3.46.

2. The strong cash position has permitted the company to invest heavily in new two-piece can equipment. During the last five years $220 million went into capital outlays, the major part of which was for the two-piece steel can program. As a result, Crown Cork's plants are at least as efficient as those of its competitors, and it probably has more two-piece steel can capacity in place than all the rest of the industry combined.

3. The company's expense ratios are low, and its entire organization has a tradition of lean operation. At the same time there is a tremendous morale built up around John Connelly, for many years president and now chairman. Connelly is a Vince Lombardi type of leader—demanding of himself and of others, generous to subordinates when in need, inspiring through objective success. Now 72, he continues to be the architect of company strategy.

4. The machinery division of the company, in addition to being profitable, provides valuable insight into customer problems. When it sells and services high-speed filling equipment, it must keep tabs on where expansion is planned and what competitors are offering. This helps Crown Cork keep on its toes.

Crown Cork also has a finance company which helps machinery customers finance equipment purchases. Although not an unusual arrangement for capital goods manufacturers, this subsidiary does give flexibility outside of day-to-day operations.

5. The foreign subsidiaries provide Crown Cork with a widespread base for using its technological know-how. To date, the benefits have been predominantly on the

sale of closures, but if and when foreign subsidiaries can market, say, two-piece steel cans, Crown Cork will already be an established local vendor.

Exhibit 8

U.S. versus Foreign Operations
($1,000,000's)

	U.S.	Europe	All Other	Total
Sales to customers	617	241	191	1,049
Operating profit	69	12	28	109
Assets (excluding cash, etc.)	319	149	148	616
Capital expenditures	42	10	7	59
Depreciation expense	18	6	8	32

Projection

In their report to stockholders, March 1978, Mr. John F. Connelly, chairman, and Mr. John J. Luviano, president, say: "During the last five years our sales doubled to more than $1 billion. It is our hope that during the next five years we will again double sales to $2 billion; however, under no circumstances will we ever sacrifice profits to gain volume."

COMPREHENSIVE CASE 4

Jodie's Ladies Wear

Yvonne and Craig Wakefield, proprietors, have enjoyed a considerable success during the two years in which they have owned and operated Jodie's Ladies Wear, a specialty shop that sells mainly ladies' outer wear.

The two young owners have been able to increase sales substantially by widening the lines and styles offered and by advertising effectively. During the same period they have learned and taught themselves much about the management of a retail store.

With sales volume now pressing the limits of the physical resources of their present operation, Yvonne and Craig are attempting to decide the future directions of Jodie's Ladies Wear. The choice of continued growth in the present and/or a new location is not easy or simple for it involves substantial financial and managerial problems.

BEGINNINGS

"Looking back, I think that it was a lapse in mental capacity that led us to buy out the previous owner and take over Jodie's Ladies Wear. It would have been more difficult to start a venture, but it might well have made more sense." So Craig Wakefield began his story about the acquisition and the early history of the store under his and his wife's (Yvonne Wakefield's) management.

"We took over a store that sold clothes in misses' and women's sizes to a 'mature clientele'—to use the previous owner's words.[1] They were mature enough. We literally watched them die off. The median age was 65 years. If we held a layaway for three months and then sent a card as a reminder, the card was often returned with the notation that the buyer had died.

---

[1]Ladies dresses are made in six cuts or size ranges: (a) Junior Petite—sizes 1, 3, 5, 7, 9, 11, and 13; (b) Junior—sizes 5, 7, 9, 11, 13, and 15; (c) Junior Misses—sizes 4, 6, 8, 10, 12, and 14; (d) Misses—sizes 8, 10, 12, 14, 16, 18, and 20; (e) Half-sizes—12½, 14½, 16½, 18½, 20½, and 22½ (these are roughly Misses' sizes cut somewhat more fully); and (f) Women's—sizes 20, 22, 24, 26, etc. to 40. These are definitely for the larger women. Dresses are sold generally in two styles: (a) Contemporary (short dresses or "swinging" dresses) and (b) Mature, that is, more conservatively styled. No two manufacturers have identical cuts—even for a given size and size range. Each manufacturer has its own idea of the shape of a woman's body.

"We purchased $15,164 of inventory and retained two saleswomen (one full-time and one part-time) from the previous operation. The building had 950 square feet, of which 750 square feet made up the sales floor and the balance was the office, backroom, and bathroom. We negotiated a new, 3-year lease for a rent of about $240 per month plus $6.50 per month for maintenance plus ½ of 1% of gross sales as dues to the Monterey Village Merchants' Association.[2]

"The previous owner had claimed $65,000 in gross sales for the past year, but our later reconstruction from her partial records indicated a gross of $43,000. The inventory, when valued at the lower of cost or market, turned out to be worth $9,000. Much of the merchandise was old.

"There was no customer file. The only sales records available were for 40 charge-account customers. The clientele did fit the clothes well—most were in the Misses' size cut.

"To finance the inventory we signed a note for $14,000 payable to the former owner at $200 per month for 5 years with a lump sum due at the end of the period. We borrowed $2,500 from a bank to provide working capital, and we put up the balance of the equity ourselves.

"What was a merchant not yet 30 years old with a wife just turned 21 doing in a deal like this? It certainly required a far stretch of the imagination."

Craig Wakefield had, over the previous ten years, been a policeman, a rancher, a manufacturer and wholesaler of women's jewelry, a computer programmer, and a business systems analyst. He was carrying on the ranching, the jewelry wholesaling, and the systems analysis work for small companies simultaneously just before the purchase of Jodie's Ladies Wear.

"I was tired of school, I had learned all that I thought I could at the University. We had made some money in the stock market and had to do something with it quickly. The ranching showed a net loss, but not for long enough, so that soon the cash would be taxable.

"Neither of us had any background in retailing women's wear. Yvonne's contribution was a knowledge of fabrics and clothing construction, skill as a seamstress, and no fear of work. I also knew how to sew and looked on the new venture as a challenge to master and a field to find out something about.

"Our first major decision was to increase the total inventory and the selection available. We used all the increased investment to stock a younger style of merchandise in an attempt to satisfy younger walk-ins—although they were few and far between at first. Over eighteen months we gradually added $15,000 to the inventory, bringing it to a total of $30,000.

"We tried to eliminate all the things we did not like about the stores we used to shop in. Commission payments to employees created a pushy atmosphere which we wish to avoid. So our employees are on straight salary. Refunds for cash create three problems: (1) banks charge us 5% for credit card use, which we lose if we give a full cash refund; (2) customers who pay by check get irate if they are asked to wait until the check clears, but a small percentage of them are known to get a cash refund and then stop payment on their checks; (3) a few persons will steal clothes and then ask

---

[2]Monterey Village is a small shopping center in the northeast sector of Tucson. It is located on the southwest corner of Speedway Boulevard and Wilmot Road. (See location A on Exhibit 1.)

for a cash refund while claiming they have lost the sales receipt. So no cash refunds and merchandise credits only.

"We want to allow the customers to browse and feel comfortable while having a chance to look around the store and find out what we carry. We also want to eliminate the feeling that, as a customer, you are always being watched and that the merchant does not trust you. There is a fine line between being ignored and being inspected that we want to walk.

"At first we hoped to alter and tailor clothes at no charge to the customer. We sell clothes in a medium-price range, but the clothes are not inexpensive to the customer. We soon found that many women wanted us to go beyond alterations that were necessary to fit the garment. They would say, 'Oh, it will only take you a minute to take the sleeves up ¼ of an inch here and to let out the upper back an inch while raising the hem.' Some expect a major remodeling for no charge.

"The inventory increase was designed not only to attract younger customers but also to offer a wider selection and a younger look to the original customers. We believed that they did not want to look as old as the clothes that were represented in the inventory that was originally in the store.

"Overall we wanted to make the store a pleasing place in which there was a soft atmosphere—not a hard or crass sell and not a place in which the customers felt that the merchandise was being pushed down their throats.'

BUYING AND MERCHANDISING

The Wakefields purchased Jodie's Ladies Wear in early February. By that time orders had already been placed with manufacturers for the summer season to come. They cancelled no orders because they had no knowledge about where to buy nor experience in buying.

To buy for the fall season they decided to continue to purchase from the manufacturers whose lines were already represented in their store or from those whom the previous owner had recommended for a particular season. Some suppliers have especially good fall or holiday collections but not good selections for a Tucson summer. To show their fall lines, a group of salespersons set up displays in Del Webb's Town House in Phoenix. The Wakefields attended this so-called market, but they limited their buying to familiar lines and looked at new lines to learn rather than to purchase. Fall items are bought in May and delivered in July.

For the holiday season they looked for a market in which more complete collections were shown. For this they went to Los Angeles in July. There they concentrated their buying on younger sportswear, younger dresses, handbags (a new item for Jodie's), accessories such as scarves, gloves, shawls, and hosiery (also new items), and a change in the jewelry from big pins and brooches for the staid and proper country club set to less expensive jewelry in line with the time and what people were wearing (necklaces, bracelets, rings, and earrings). During the fall and holiday seasons, hosiery produced the maximum revenue per square foot of display space of any line in the store. Hosiery sales for these seasons amounted to $1,000 from a display area of 2 square feet. It should be noted that Jodie's is located next door to a lingerie and hosiery specialty shop. This experience proved to the Wakefields that they could do more with Jodie's than just sell ready-to-wear outer clothing.

A check of inventory just before the spring and summer buying season (November of the previous year for first orders and January for additional summer items and

Exhibit 1

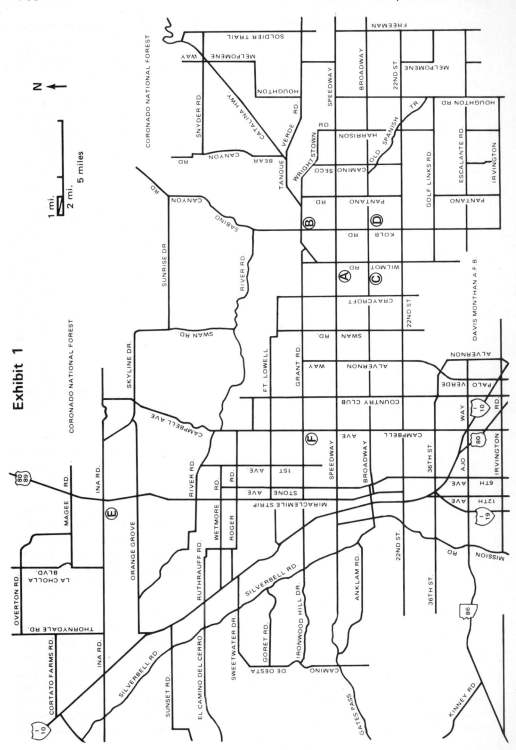

manufacturer's closeouts of spring items) showed that handbag and jewelry inventories were depleted as were the younger-styled items of clothing. The older styles still showed a substantial carryover. Craig Wakefield then decided to add shoes, all kinds of purses (casual and evening bags, cloth, good leather, and beaded bags), and a limited millinery selection.

"The question to date has not been how to decide what to purchase but who will sell to us. We can rely on suppliers who have been with the store for years, on hungry or brave new suppliers, and on those who are large enough to be willing to take a chance on a small order and give us credit. Credit is the problem. For example, the East Coast division of United Factors will deal with us, but the West Coast division will not.

"From manufacturers who will sell to us we look at style, fabrication, colors, price, and fabrics all together and attempt to judge what will interest our customers. For the first six months we had little choice. We had to buy from whomever came around. So we purchased the younger-looking items in the lines of our old suppliers. Buying in the first year was strictly good and bad luck. We are badly overstocked on sportswear by Koret of California. The salesman was experienced and we were not. Koret does not produce one line with coordinated items but 36 groups of sportswear per year. No two groups in any one year can be put together. Their items sell in great quantities, but, at the end of the season, we are stuck with lots of inventory. In a sense we are a warehouse for the manufacturer. It gets so that our customers, who are no dummies, wait for a sale. They come in often, check the racks, and then predict how long we can hold out before putting on a sale.

"We are, for some items, and hope to for all, changing to manufacturers whose entire line works together and who blend in one season's colors and fabrics with the next. It takes about three years to learn who does this successfully and then you have to be able to get to their salesman first so that he is not sold out and also hope that the firm will allow credit.

"We would like to carry Loubella Extendibles, for example. The entire line is blended. The separates (pants, blouses, sports tops, and sweaters) are all dyed to coordinate within their 8 or 9 combinations of body styles and fabrics. The line is carefully thought out so that one blouse can be worn with 5 or 6 different pairs of pants.

"Both Yvonne and I do the purchasing. We argue about the items and should argue more than we do. Then we would wind up with fewer markdowns. We work purchases down to those garments on which we both agree. If I like the print and she dislikes the style, the line or item is ruled out. We don't agree on very many things, and we find that if we do agree, there is a much better chance of selling those goods.

"Some days one of us feels incompetent, so we do no buying at all. Or one will screen the entire line to pick out favorites and the other will go through what has been picked. This is our way of buying only what we need.

"We look at the line of any manufacturer whose salesman comes around to the store. We do not pass up any chance to look at ladies' wear. It took us a while to learn how to say no, because there are some highly proficient sales people on the road.

"We now plan to attend markets in Denver, Phoenix, Los Angeles, and San Francisco (but not the two big ones—New York and Dallas) five times per year for the five seasons (spring, summer, transition, fall, and winter). At the markets we visit those manufacturers whom we definitely want to buy from and then use the rest of our time to look for a new resource to replace a line that is not performing well.

Manufacturers change all the time. Bobbie Brooks and Gay Gibson are not now what they used to be.

"Purchasing takes constant attention. Anyone can buy, but few can know ahead how they are going to sell what they buy before they buy it. We now formulate ad ideas and promotions and combinations of wearing apparel and accessories before we buy. We look for bargains that will allow better than the full retail markup (customarily 50% of the selling price is markup). So we buy from an unknown manufacturer who sells at a relatively low price those items of a quality suitable for our customers. Before buying, you must know what your customers want. What are the fashion trends now or what are they going to be with our clientele? Should we take a chance on a new idea and possibly offend some of our existing clientele for the sake of bringing in new clients? For example, 18-to-25-year-olds buy 10% of the pants suits sold. To carry items for them makes the whole rack lean a bit toward being sexy and younger. Older clientele then get offended, although not outraged. Some will say directly, 'How could this be in my store? There must be some mistake.' We still carry what they want, as did the previous owner, but they are not happy to be in an atmosphere where the younger-looking things are."

PROMOTION

The first promotion of Jodie's Ladies Wear, with the Wakefields as owners, was entirely by word of mouth. Old customers told their friends about the change—if they so desired; the Wakefields told their friends and new employees told their friends. Craig Wakefield quickly realized that this was insufficient promotion. He turned for help to officers of the Monterey Village Merchants' Association. They suggested the use of radio and newspapers. After trying these media (see Exhibit 2 for an early newspaper advertisement) Craig concluded that the cost per thousand readers of newspapers was excessive. He also learned from experience that radio was best for an immediate reaction and for sale announcements. Newspaper trials for one year demonstrated that a small, obscure, or unknown retail store could never afford to pay enough for space to compete with chain stores, department stores, and the already known large specialty shops of the city. The cost per thousand readers was considerably higher than the cost per thousand female viewers available on daytime television.

With some help from friends in the advertising business, Craig purchased early morning spots on the Today show, late evening spots on the Johnny Carson show, and sporadic spots throughout the day. The friends chose stations and shows that had the largest female audiences. They also prepared ads that were fair-to-middling as to their ideas, in the Wakefields' opinion. But when asked the age distribution of the female audience, his friends did not have data available. Also they made no story boards so that the commercial could not be judged before it was presented.[3]

By asking questions at the television stations, Craig Wakefield found that he could develop precise information about audiences. His friends could recommend, with no research, shows with a high percentage of women viewers, but they could not

---

[3]A story board is a sequence of still photographs—each with a caption—pasted upon one piece of Bristol board (a stiff cardboard) to show the key action elements, the development of the story of the commercial, and the expression of the copy theme. It is made up before the commercial is filmed. Often several story boards are developed to allow the advertising manager a choice.

distinguish between 16- to 30-year-old viewers and 65- to 85-year-old viewers. The distinction is important to Jodie's. Further questioning of persons at the television stations and a close review of the Audit Research Bureau's data let Craig dig out the audience characteristics. This way he found out what was the best buy—the optimal combination of his prime audience and the cost of spots. By extensive searching he found out what kinds of audiences watched television in Tucson at what times of the day and on what channel. With this research completed, he was in a better position to purchase time suitable for Jodie's Ladies Wear than was the agency.

To prepare commercials, Craig Wakefield took his own photographs and selected his own locations. His idea was to try to do something a little different—a little unorthodox. Both Wakefields worked hard at this until they were pleased with the results. One commercial showed evening gowns in a horse corral. Another had models in black, baby-doll nightwear posed on a patio at the Community Center during the day. This commercial was shot on a Sunday morning when few, if any, people were ordinarily around. But one father and his young son rode by on a bicycle. The boy said: "Daddy, look at the pretty ladies." The father turned his head to look, held the look, and rode into the pond below the small waterfall.

Yvonne and Craig drove to the Colorado Rockies to show swimsuits and shorts outfits in the snow-laced tundra above the timber line at 12,000 feet. The commercial went well when shown in Tucson in July. Another ad pictured a girl dressed in an elegant, crisp pants suit unloading garbage into a Dumpster.

"We strove for something a bit unusual to make viewers think—which most agencies believe people can't do. We are not trying to convince viewers that our stuff is better and cheaper than anyone else's. But we are trying to get their attention and then keep it with a visual style and with graphic effects. We do not talk a lot at the audience. We use little or no verbiage, because the more you talk, the more you and the audience forget the rest of the effects and the visual message.

"We began television advertising a year after we took over the store because no one seemed to be coming in as the result of the newspaper ads and, as far as we could tell, we could not get results from the radio advertisements. We dipped into our cash reserve and decided to allocate 25% of gross sales for advertising. We figured that the only way to get new people into the building was to let them know we existed and that we might have what they liked and that we were not too terrible to do business with.

"When I had studied advertising earlier, the best book that I read on influencing other persons' decisions convinced me that you cannot expect anyone to listen to your message unless you have their attention. This hit me over the head. In the world of advertising, where you are bombarded day after day with thousands of ad messages in all media every time you turn around, how many do you remember? Those that you dislike and those that are humorous and appeal to your sense of humor. Those that are out of place and those that are, esthetically, extremely pleasing. Analysis of various surveys convinced me that the most obnoxious soap commercial was the most effective because it stayed in the viewer's mind—consciously or unconsciously. But we did not want that kind of thing. The other route to getting attention was the hard sell. 'Mine is better and cheaper than anyone else's.' This is very old and very crass and very successful. But we did not like it and it did not fit with the idea of the kind of store we were trying to build.

"This still left the question of how to get the viewer's attention so that she would watch our message. The solution I developed for a 30-second spot was to have dead

Spring Savings

SPECIAL
Lady Manhattan

BLOUSES
SHORT SLEEVE
LONG SLEEVE
SLEEVELESS

20-25% off
Size 8-16

SELECTED
PANT SUITS
50-60% off

PANTS
40-50% off

DRESSES
40-60% off

BLOUSES
30-50% off
Size 5-16

SPECIAL
SERBIN DRESSES
SHORT SLEEVE
OR SLEEVELESS
PASTEL PLAIDS
COTTON BLEND

$32.00 and $33.00
Regular $46-$48
8-16

Long Halter Dresses

$29.00 to $38.00
NOW ONLY ... $23.29

$40.00 to $50.00
NOW ONLY ... $28.99

$56.00 to $72.00
NOW ONLY ... $39.49

West Set

COORDINATES AND
SEPARATES
PANTS
STRAIGHT LEG $25.00
FIT & FLAIR $26.00
TANK TOPS $21.00
SHORT SLEEVE
TOPS $21.00
ZIPPER JACKET $34.00
SIZE 6-16

SMALL
MEDIUM
LARGE

STRAW SUN HATS
40% off

MOJUD PANTY HOSE
4 FOR $7.00

JEWELRY **30% off**

CROP TOPS **60% off**

HALTERS **50% off**

Jodie's

silence for the first twelve seconds—no audio at all; to show slides during those opening seconds. My reasoning was that if the viewer hears nothing at all when she knows it is the time for a commercial, she will look at the set to see what is wrong. Then we can say, 'Now we can talk with you, now that we have your attention.'

"Then we stated our copy theme: 'Jodie's has fashions that won't (pause) just hang in your closet.' How did we work out that theme? Well, there are two classes of women—married and single. Each class has two subclasses—happy and unhappy. Each group has associated with it a particular activity. The happy singles are playing the field, the unhappy singles are attempting to get married, the happily married are acting to keep their husbands happy, and the unhappily married are playing the field or trying to get their husbands reinterested in them. A good appearance is part, only a part, of the activities. That is why women buy new and stylish clothing—one of four reasons depending upon their situation. You can't say this in an ad because it is offensive. How then do you tell all four? We state that we have clothes that will not just be hanging in a closet. Then women can read any connotation they want into the statement and read the idea for themselves.

"For the first three months we spent 25% of gross sales on television advertising. After that we kept the dollar amount level. Our idea was and is that television advertising is in part a capital investment—getting our name and merchandising point of view embedded in the audience's long-term memory, and in part a period expense—showing our new fashions of the season.

"Some time later the station rates for spots were increased and I also decided to use less of the really off-hour times (1 A.M. and 7 A.M., for example). So we reduced the ads from 30 to 10 seconds. By then we had created a unique commercial—10 seconds in length, little said verbally, and it did not demand attention over any long span of time. I learned indirectly through trade sources that advertising courses at the University of Southern California were using Jodie's commercials as prime examples of how to use TV effectively for advertising. We have been widely copied in Tucson. Wigglesworth Volvo, for example, did an almost exact copy of our style. It is a super-soft sell, a complete reverse from the hard, harsh sell. Because it is a dramatic change in style, it is a success for us. We certainly created the image we wanted. I think that the major reason why it worked was that it was a new way in Tucson. The ads are not displeasing. That is a big plus for them.

"Our surveys showed that we created customers more from husbands sending in their wives to buy than from decisions by the women themselves. The evening ads had more results than the morning ads.

"Jodie's slogan became known—not a household word, but definitely by the other business people in town. Yvonne could shop in Steinfeld's (a major, locally owned, department store) and all the salesclerks there would recognize who she was and what Jodie's advertised.

"A year's experience with television advertising showed us that it is not a promotional expense. It can be best used to sell or create an image. To sell a specific product or a price or to maintain an image, newspapers are the most effective. Radio is used for fast results. If you do not get a response within 24 hours from a radio commercial, then change it.

"We have not really been successful in radio advertising. We have not found the key. The best that we have done with radio is to buy a cut-rate monthly package— X number of spots for the month—and then cram them all into one week to gain maximum exposure to that station's clientele. Then we either move to another station or try out a second idea at the first station to test any contrasts in response.

"In using television we expect and have found a 30- to 90-day delay before any results come from a particular idea. Since we are a small store we do not have lots of money to buy lots of space to sell a product now. The large department stores and chain stores (Levy's, Sears, Steinfeld's, Wards, Diamonds, Lerners, and Broadway) can do that.

"For our first fashion show, held at the Skyline Country Club, I wrote a letter to our manufacturers to explain this reason for the increase in the size of our order and to explain what had happened to our sales volume. Most of the manufacturers knew nothing about us and did not remember our history with them. Since I wanted our orders filled early on their first cutting, and also wanted dating on them since early shipments and early payments would not fit our cash-flow schedule, I wrote a detailed letter.[4] Somehow *Women's Wear Daily* picked up this letter and published an article based on it featuring Jodie's as 'The Small Retailer of the Year.'

"The show at the Skyline Country Club was shown on television news programs by the local stations—the first production of its kind. And at no expense to us.

"By now I do all the buying of time and space. I decide exactly what I want and when and where. I also control the production of the commercial and then have to sit at the television station to supervise the broadcast. Otherwise the station workers will inevitably foul up the commercial. I remember the panic one engineer went into when he got no audio—only video—on the first few seconds of an early commercial. He cut us right off the air.

"Tape has major advantages because it can be flowing and vivid and the station can't make errors with it. But we don't use video tape because it is too expensive. Instead, we use audio tape and slides. We have 200 slides so they can be changed readily. For each commercial I set a sequence: numbers 1, 11, 22, and 27 at 6 P.M. and numbers 8, 10, 23, and 27 at 9 P.M. Although the station has detailed information about the sequence, they cannot follow intricate scheduling. This takes my personal attention."

PERSONNEL

The two employees of the previous owner stayed with the Wakefields when they took over Jodie's. One lady who worked part-time is still with the store. Craig Wakefield characterized her as "a capable salesperson, a hard worker. She was once in business for herself so her outlook toward us differs from that of all our other employees." The other full-time employee, a woman aged 62 and an experienced seamstress, did not want to step onto the sales floor unless a customer whom she knew came in the door. "We eventually found that she would reluctantly do what I asked of her but would not take direction from Yvonne. She was determined not to let some young girl tell her how to work. It took us a while to recognize this and even more time to get up the determination to do something about it. We kept her 9 months—6 months longer than we should have.

"We tried to keep 2 employees in the store as well as Yvonne—who is there to manage. For the first 9 months we had a considerable amount of friction—a

---

[4]"Dating" means shipping the goods but dating the invoices to be paid several months (usually up to six) after the shipment. The manufacturer gives credit to the retailer in this way.

Donnybrook occasionally. There were disagreements over the day for pay, how often wages were to be paid, and how the business was going to be run.

"Our policy as to labor was to attempt to find reliable persons who could and would sell—persons who were looking for work, not just employment. So far we have found that we can only tell reliability and sales skills through experience—not through references or statements about past experience. Our initial employment practice was to hire people of various ethnic backgrounds. We took whoever walked in and applied for a job we happened to have open. We would hire them if they had the appearance and seemed to have the basic capability to do the work.

"In sequence we had a Mexican-American girl, a Jewish girl, another Chicano, and an Oriental. They all carried the idea of being a member of a minority group to an extreme. If we had any complaints, they each attributed this to racial prejudice on our part.

"Then we turned to friends. This also turned out to be wrong. The first friend of Yvonne's worked well for a short time and then wanted the summer off. Summer is a bit slow and we agreed. Then her husband stopped traveling overseas when he changed jobs in the fall. So we lost her shortly after she returned to work. She was a good woman. Then another friend won a battle over custody of her son with her ex-husband. Since she really could not take care of herself, let alone her son, she had to move to California to be with relatives. Then we brought in a personal friend of mine who had good experience and was highly recommended by her previous employer. She turned out not to justify the recommendation. Then we hired another friend—an out-of-work school teacher who could not find work in District One (the large, local school district) because she had a Master's degree. The district has to pay a relatively high wage to teachers with advanced degrees, so such teachers are not hired. She really felt that she was doing us a favor by working for us. There were several problems.

"Had we been willing to pay an average wage plus commission, we might have gotten better help. But we are not willing to pay top dollar nor commissions. Turnover of employees to date has not been as rapid as it should have been. Also I may not yet have quite learned that my function with employees is not to be a counselor.

"We have just changed the system for disseminating information to employees. We do not now bring them into decision-making, but we do take the posture that they should have full knowledge of what we plan and why we plan it and that we want their opinion. If they think an item or a line is going to bomb, we want to know why they think so.

"For some reason our employees seem to feel that they should have or that they want to have loyalty to the proprietors more than to the business. I want them to be attracted to the work—their tasks—rather than to us and what they may regard as a pseudo or substitute family. In most cases loyalty is not enough. Incompetence can thrive when loyalty is rewarded. What I want to do is to create a good atmosphere, but only with employees who really are an asset to the firm.

"If you make an employee into a friend, it becomes difficult to let her go. It is hazardous to turn a friend into an employee. We have hired friends with long and successful experience in the apparel field. But they then expected us to make allowances for their personal problems. They brought problems with parents, with husbands, and with finances to work. At first we tried to help them work out the problems because we thought that they would be better employees if they felt freer on the job. They talked with us freely. We thought this would help them ease their minds. But those who came in having been friends prior to their employment expected to be able to dump their problems and disrupt the work-flow. We were to understand why they took three days off without notice and that they would tell us about it later.

"A big advantage of a very small operation is rapport. But supposed rapport can turn into a big disadvantage if it becomes assumptions about being understood.

"Either Yvonne or I can manage the store. But one of us needs to be there."

CUSTOMERS AND SALES

Located as it is in a small shopping center (Monterey Village) on the southwest corner of Speedway and Wilmot Road (see Exhibit 1), Jodie's draws most of its customers from sections of the city north of Speedway Boulevard and east, northeast, or northwest of the corner of Speedway Boulevard and Wilmot Road (location A on the map). The people who live in these sections are generally in the middle-income or upper-middle-income groups.

Expansion of Tucson takes place on the fringes. New housing developments—tract houses, town houses, and condominiums—are particularly common toward the northeast, east, and southeast. New apartments are built just north of Ft. Lowell Road, and mobile home developments are most common toward the southwest. Some lower-priced tract developments are also found in the southern and southwestern parts of the urban area.

Monterey Village Shopping Center contains 28 stores in total. The largest are a Ben Franklin variety store and a Bayless Supermarket (one outlet of a local grocery chain). Other stores include a home furnishings shop, a franchised radio and phonograph equipment shop, a franchised ice cream parlor, another women's dress shop, a lingerie and hosiery specialty shop, and a hardware store. Services available include a movie theater, a real estate agent, a beauty salon, and a branch of one of the large commercial banks.

As stated before, Jodie's original group of customers was of an age range of 55 to 85 years. This range has been changed to 17 to 60 years. The store still carries clothes that the older clientele wear, but most of them do not seem to want to be in an atmosphere where contemporary clothes predominate. The customer list has increased from 40 to 8,000. Charge customers have been reduced from 40 to 28.

"Customers shop here for a mixture of reasons. All of the variables tend to apply to each shopper. They are attracted by our promotions, by the availability of goods in which they are interested, by the behavior of any one of our employees toward whom they may be attracted (some of those who work here have personal followings), and by our flexibility about alterations.

"We want our customers to get all the help they desire if they ask for it, but not to feel pushed. This feeling can be eliminated, but watching can't be. Shoplifting is always a possibility, and the salesperson has to be ready to give help and answer questions at the exact instant the customer wants aid or information.

"My experience as a policeman and in this dress selling business makes it necessary for me to assume that everyone who walks in our door is a thief. So we develop ways to achieve our objectives. We train our salespeople to continually straighten and re-size the clothes. The girls can be working and yet be within easy reach of a customer and alert to the customer. This awareness will tell them whether the customer wants help or information or needs to be watched.

"The salesgirls are doing small jobs to make sure that the store does not have a disheveled look. They are not bothering the browsers or the customers, but they are right there on the spot when they are needed.

"It is easy for a merchant to forget about goods on layaway. So we have a tickler file that warns us a month after the date of the layaway. If the customer makes no payment, we send her a postal card to let her know that the goods are still being held for her. After another 60 days, we remind her again. This friendly note asks her to pay within two weeks. We are making every effort to keep in contact.

"A very brief experience with free alterations and tailoring convinced us that such a policy is too generous. So we decided to limit alterations to those necessary to fit the garment and to charge a healthy fee for tailoring. We want from $2.50 for the simple hemming of a skirt to $15 to $20 to change the sleeves or do a major remodeling of a garment. These charges are substantial, so they are waived for a good, regular customer. Yvonne or I decide when to waive the charge.

"Some customers began to know the stock better than I did. They came in daily, looked at the sale rack and at the new merchandise we had brought in. They predicted how long we would keep a garment and waited for a sale to come along. So thus began musical garments.

"We moved racks from the right side of the store to the left side and from the back middle to the front middle. We then sold stuff that was five years old just because it was in a different place. Now we change the store randomly. We move items closer to the front window or farther away. We change the location of the fluorescent fixtures. We paint the walls a different color. We changed the sizing from right to left rather than left to right, but this became too confusing so we gave it up. Eventually we saw this practice recommended in trade journals after we began to read them, but we had had to stumble on it. A few trade journals have some very helpful display, layout, and merchandising ideas. We learned that Bonwit Teller, for example, constantly remodels its stores so that the interior decor, the coloration, the store design, the location of items, and the way they are displayed changes—but not on a predictable basis. One of our goals is to be able to spend $4,000 each year for remodeling the store. Doing so will easily increase annual sales by $16,000."

NEW LOCATIONS

"About six months ago we decided that we had to think about expansion because we cannot maintain an inventory of $35,000 and, over the long run, make sales of more than $12 per square foot per month in the present shop. The limiting factors are how fast we can buy, how fast we can process the stuff that is bought, and the disruption of deliveries through the front door since we do not have a back entrance into our 900 square feet of space.

"Ideally, provided that we could manage it, we should add a second location with 1,100 square feet minimum to 1,600 square feet maximum and with a rear entrance for delivery. This would allow us to check purchases and to price the garments efficiently. With two stores we would not need to double our inventory but would increase it at most by 50%. With two stores we would also have the advantage of being able to move merchandise from one location to the other either to increase sales or to take advantage of slight differences in the buying habits and decision patterns of the different clientele. A second store would also allow us to have more than three dressing rooms here. Sometimes three is not enough.

"The developer of a new shopping center, El Capri, at 7000 East Tanque Verde Road (see location B on Exhibit 1) wants us to lease space at $10 per square foot on a yearly lease. He is, however, only renting a shell in a major new shopping center. We would have to invest $20,000 in leasehold improvements before moving in.

"Another deal is available at the Park Mall at 5870 East Broadway (location C on Exhibit 1). This center is still under construction, but Broadway Stores, Diamond's, and Sears all are operating major department stores there. The traffic patterns on Broadway, near Wilmot, are such that people who drive there tend to come in from the southeast and the west rather than from the northeast or the north. The developer will lease either 2,000 or 2,500 square feet of space in either a rectangular or a square configuration. The size would be ideal for a single operation, but we would have to pay $10 per square foot and pay for leasehold improvements. Also, we would lose customers if we moved.

"We could look for space in a minor shopping area, but that would mean pioneering a new location. There are one or two way out east on Broadway that I have considered. Space costs would be about half as much as at El Capri shopping center on Tanque Verde Road. But we would have to have a free-standing unit because there are no vacancies in any shopping centers. Well to the east there is considerable population growth, and the population density is increasing. Census statistics show that young-marrieds to middle-aged persons (our target population) of middle-level incomes live there. About 5 miles from our present location would certainly differentiate the two buying groups geographically. Despite our advertising, however, I doubt that we are well enough known to support a separate building on our own. I really want a shopping center location for the traffic it brings. One developer who plans to put in a center beyond Kolb Road (see location D on Exhibit 1) has offered a lease of $4.50 to $6.00 per square foot, depending upon our location in the center. But we would need $15,000 for leasehold improvements and we would be pioneering a new location. The developer wants to sign us to a firm lease and then use our balance sheet to help him get financing to build the complex.

"My ultimate goal is to earn $1,000 net profit per year per store if we have 50 stores or $2,000 if we have 25 stores.

"There are other locations in town we can consider. Two spots in the southwestern part of the city have stores available at the right size for a second location. Both have lots of traffic. But neither Yvonne nor I speak Spanish, so there would be a language barrier to some extent. The lease conditions are very favorable. Since the socio-economic pattern differs from the east side, we would be running essentially a completely new store. Our merchandising pattern would differ.

"On the northwest side, on Oracle Road near Ina (see location E on Exhibit 1), there is a shopping center with clientele and stores analogous to Monterey Village where we are now. The center has had three vacant buildings for over a year, but the landlord won't talk with us. I suspect that an existing store has threatened to move out if we move in. That store carries the same merchandise as we do, bought from the same manufacturers. But they put on their own labels and sell the clothes as exclusives.

"Our bank suggested a north central location on Campbell Avenue (see location F on Exhibit 1). Their branch in that area has the largest deposits per capita of all of its branches. We looked a bit further into who the depositors are. The bank figure is for savings deposits. Census tract data shows that the median age there is 20 years above the median for the city. The depositors are wealthy in bank cash holdings, but do they use the money for retirement funding or for consumer purchases? The one clothing store that has done well there in the 20 years of operation of the center is a budget store.

"The rental office here in Monterey Village has a location with 3,200 square feet available a few doors from where we are now. It can be rented for $900 per month plus another $144 per month for taxes, maintenance, and dues to the Merchants' Association. It is L-shaped, with the main entrance at the top of the L and windows all along the side of the L paralleling a walkway that goes to a mall at the rear of the store. The shape provides limited wall space.

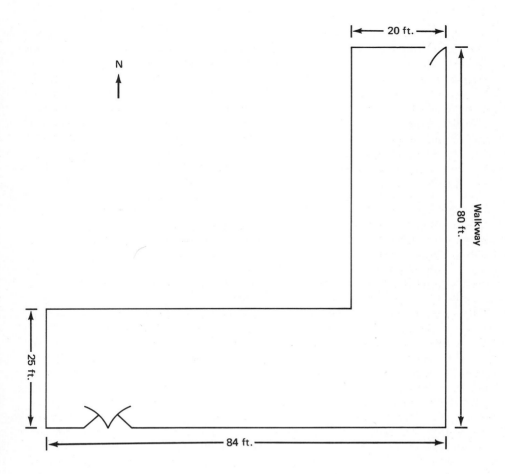

"A round rack for dresses usually has a diameter of 5 feet. Straight racks require a minimum total horizontal distance of 5 feet to allow for space to hang the garments and a walkway of a minimum size along one side so that the garments can be looked at.

"Dressing rooms (how many should we have?) would need an aisle of at least 39 inches, and the rooms themselves should have interior dimensions of no less than 4 feet by 4 feet. And how could they be built so that a salesclerk or store manager could check or control the flow in and out of the rooms? An easy way to lose merchandise is to have a customer walk out wearing two or three costumes in the layered look.

It would be a difficult store to force traffic through and the size calls for either a vast, open operation or for increasing the inventory to $65,000 to fill the space. An inventory of that size, even if turned 3 times per year at 50% markup, requires sales of $390,000 per year to support it.[5] I don't really have the expertise to lay out such a store to utilize its shape effectively.

FINANCES

Craig Wakefield stated that the first accountant used by Jodie's Ladies Wear was of no help. "She had a good reputation as a general accountant, but she did nothing for us other than to relist our checks. Then I turned to a CPA firm. They would prepare a balance sheet and income statement but wanted me to keep the journals, make ledger entries, reconcile the bank statement, and be available to answer a lot of questions about their trial balance. Even with 8 years of accounting study and practice behind me, I couldn't do everything. There were too many operating and merchandising decisions that had to be made on the spot for me to spend time with bank reconciliations and ledger entries.

"So I let the CPA firm go and hired 2 part-time accountants—both students at the University. One of them also worked as an auditor for the city. He turned out to be an inept accountant and compounded our troubles by leaving town with 20% of our accounting records. He never returned.

"The other fellow has worked out well. His eagerness to learn and his common sense have made up for his lack of professional experience. He takes a low wage to get training in retail accounting. We have had to work our balance sheets backward from what we have now to reconstruct the past balance sheets. We have had to estimate and improvise. I would not call it the usual accounting practice.

"I do the tax work (both payroll and income) myself. There have been some complications with the farm and ranching business and with the wholesale jewelry operation in the past that made this necessary. Now we depend upon the store for our living.

"You can see from looking at the statements what our financial problems are."

(Exhibits 4, 5, and 6 on pages 713 and 714 are the financial statements for Jodie's Ladies Wear. Exhibits 7 and 8 on pages 714 and 715 give data about retail sales activity and competition in the Tucson area.)

---

[5]Average inventory turnover for the industry is 2.7 times per year.

Exhibit 4

Gross Sales by Month
Jodie's Ladies Wear

Month	Year 1	Year 2	Year 3
January	—	$ 3,992	$12,962
February	$ 1,630	9,559	12,762
March	4,044	6,828	
April	3,961	9,874	
May	4,041	10,317	
June	3,382	10,148	
July	4,607	10,021	
August	3,288	6,657	
September	3,055	6,313	
October	4,832	9,746	
November	4,969	12,127	
December	8,165	18,537	
Year's Total	$45,974	$114,119	

Exhibit 5

Balance Sheets
Jodie's Ladies Wear

	Opening	End of Year 1	End of Year 2
Cash..........................	$ 4,526	$ 4,870	$ 3,333
Accounts Receivable................	—	289	1,477
Inventory.......................	15,164	26,351	35,000
Leasehold Improvements (net)........	16,934	13,934	10,934
Total Assets.....................	$36,624	$45,444	$50,744
Accounts Payable	—	$ 5,514	$10,985
Note Payable, Bank	$ 2,500	5,375	3,355
Note Payable (see Note A)...........	16,934	12,751	9,600
Proprietor's Equity.................	17,190	21,804	26,804
Total Liabilities and Net Worth	$36,624	$45,444	$50,744

Note A: Note payable to former proprietor to be paid at a minimum rate of $200 per month for 5 years. There is no penalty for prepayment. The balance is then to be paid in one lump sum.

Exhibit 6

Income Statements
Jodie's Ladies Wear

	Year 1 (11 months)	Year 2
Sales....................................	$45,975	$114,119
Cost of Goods Sold........................	24,969	73,671
Gross Profit	$21,006	$ 40,448
Wages—Employees........................	$ 6,770	$ 7,015
Advertising..............................	1,159	12,401
Rent....................................	2,598	2,940
Utility Expense	1,106	944
Maintenance	73	78
Depreciation and Amortization of		
Leasehold Improvements	3,000	3,000
Dues—Merchant's Association...............	230	570
Total Expenses...........................	$14,846	$ 26,948
Net Income Before Taxes....................	$ 6,160	$ 13,500

Exhibit 7

Index of Retail Sales
Tucson Standard Metropolitan Statistical Area

Month	Previous Year	Year 1	Year 2	Year 3
January	120	145	173	195
February	131	144	173	185
March	123	147	168	
April	129	145	171	
May	139	159	171	
June	139	153	185	
July	127	151	176	
August	127	145	167	
September	126	147	185	
October	145	157	174	
November	135	171	176	
December	149	182	233	

Note: Tucson, like almost all cities in the United States, undergoes changes in its general economic activity. The effect of the depressions of the 1960's and 1970's was somewhat lessened in Tucson because of the predominance of government as the major sector of the economy of the Tucson Standard Metropolitan Statistical Area.

Exhibit 8

Number of Competitive Shops
City of Tucson

	Year 1	Year 2	Year 3
Department Stores	10	11	13
Ladies Wear Specialty Shops	68	70	80

COMPREHENSIVE CASE 5

Amax Aluminum Company[1]

AMAX, Inc. faces a major question of what to do with its wholly-owned subsidiary, Amax Aluminum Company. The subsidiary has a voracious appetite for capital investment, but its earnings to date have been unimpressive. World developments in the aluminum industry cloud the future.

AMAX EXPANSION STRATEGY

AMAX deals with minerals and energy resources. At the time of this case, the end of 1973, it has $1.7 billion in assets and will report record sales of over $1.3 billion. The aluminum subsidiary accounts for 16% and 28% of these impressive totals.

Because Amax Aluminum competes for capital and attention with other subsidiaries of AMAX, a brief sketch of AMAX total operations is called for. The scope of the non-aluminum operations and the major expansions are summarized in the following paragraphs.

AMAX has always dealt with several different metals since it was formed by the 1957 merger of the American Metals Company, Ltd. and the Climax Molybdenum Company. American Metals was a miner, processor, and trader of non-ferrous metals and minerals, including copper, lead, zinc, precious metals, and potash. The company also held major investments in two large African copper mining concerns, but did not manage these concerns directly. A subsidiary owned and operated the largest secondary copper smelting facility in the United States.

In terms of sales, the Climax Molybdenum Company was barely a tenth the size of the American Metals Company, Ltd. at the time of the merger, but Climax's earnings were almost 90% those of the American Metals Company. The source of Climax's earnings was the huge Climax, Colorado molybdenum mine, which in 1957 supplied almost half of the non-Communist world demand for molybdenum. Molybdenum is a vital ingredient for many types of high-strength hard steel alloys.

Following the merger AMAX diversified even more. In 1963, AMAX gained claim to a major deposit of high-grade iron ore at Mt. Newman in Western Australia. By

---

[1]This case is based primarily on two much longer cases, AMAX-MITSUI (A) and (B), prepared by Edward M. Graham and Yoshihiro Tsurumi (ICCH Numbers 9-375-350 and 9-375-388). This case is positioned, time-wise, in late 1973.

1965, it was determined that at least one billion tons of iron ore was recoverable from the Mt. Newman location. In 1967, final agreements were made for a consortium of American, Australian, British, and Japanese companies to create a joint venture to exploit Mt. Newman. AMAX would hold 25% equity participation in the venture. One of AMAX's partners in the consortium included Mitsuitoh Pty., a joint venture of two Japanese trading companies, Mitsui and C. Itoh. Mitsuitoh held 10% of the project. This was the first time in history that Japanese interests participated in a major Australian minerals venture.

In 1969, AMAX acquired the Ayrshire Collieries Corporation, an independent coal-producing company in the United States. The acquisition of Ayrshire, accomplished by exchange of AMAX preferred stock for Ayrshire common, gave AMAX control over large reserves of coal located largely in the Midwest and in Wyoming and the Rocky Mountain area.

In 1973, by exchange of AMAX preferred stock for the acquired companies' common stock, AMAX acquired the Banner Mining Company and the affiliated Tintic Standard Mining Company. These companies owned a large copper ore deposit in Arizona. The ore body was leased by the Anaconda Company, which operated a large copper mine to exploit the body. AMAX for years had sought to engage in copper mining in the United States. At the time of the acquisition of Banner and Tintic, AMAX formed a partnership with Anaconda, to be named the Anamax Company, to expand the mine.

An AMAX executive who played a major role in the expansion and diversification of AMAX's activities was Ian MacGregor. Following the 1957 merger, Mr. MacGregor was made Vice President in charge of new business development and in this role he led AMAX's efforts to establish itself in the aluminum industry. Later, as Chief Executive Officer, he played a key role in the formation of the Mt. Newman consortium and oversaw the acquisitions of the Ayrshire, Banner, Tintic Standard companies. A native of Scotland, Mr. MacGregor's first job was in British Aluminum's management training program. His early experience with the British aluminum industry was to be very valuable to Mr. MacGregor in his career with AMAX.

Most of these developments involved joint ventures. Often the economical size of operation was so large that no one company wanted to invest the necessary capital in a single venture. In other situations, a partner was needed to assure markets or managerial skill. In the natural resource arena, such coalitions are common.

ENTRY INTO ALUMINUM INDUSTRY

During the first years of its existence, AMAX was able to generate earnings faster than it could reinvest them. In 1960, for example, earnings after tax were $41 million, while dividends and capital expenditures less depreciation were $24 million.

In order to utilize its growing liquid assets, AMAX management asked Mr. MacGregor in 1960 to investigate new businesses that the company might enter. The objective was to find businesses which would provide the company with greater long-term growth potential than existing investment opportunities, but which were congruent with the company's expertise in minerals and metallurgy.

Analysis by Mr. MacGregor and his associates indicated (1) that the long-run growth potential of the aluminum industry was greater and the prospective return on investment higher than those of other major metals and minerals based industries. Moreover, economic studies showed (2) that the existing integrated aluminum companies in North America were more highly leveraged than were most other American manufacturing companies, and the possibility existed that these aluminum firms would experience difficulty in financing the expansion of capacity required to serve a growing demand for aluminum products. Thus, MacGregor believed that new entry could occur in the aluminum industry without disrupting the stability of the industry.

Entry into the industry did pose some problems, however:

1. "Upstream" aluminum companies (bauxite mining, alumina production, and primary aluminum reduction), which were generally more profitable than "downstream" operations, were highly capital intensive and the minimum scale for economic operations was very large.[2]
2. Entry at the level of bauxite mining or alumina production appeared virtually impossible. The known world's reserves of bauxite in the early 1960's were almost entirely controlled by the established integrated companies— ALCOA (U.S.), ALCAN (Canada), Reynolds (U.S.), Pechiney (France), Kaiser (U.S.), and Alusuisse (Swiss)—and these companies were not eager to share their bauxite operations with a major new entrant.
3. Entry at the level of primary reduction was only slightly less problematic. Over 85% of primary reduction capacity in North America was controlled by ALCOA, ALCAN, Reynolds, and Kaiser. There was no free market for alumina, and hence the alumina for a primary reduction mill would have to be purchased from the integrated producers. Because a primary aluminum reduction facility must be operated continuously, even a brief interruption in the supply of alumina could result in severe adverse effects on the economics of operating the facility.
4. The aluminum industry had historically been subject to cycles of undercapacity and overcapacity. Were AMAX to construct and operate integrated "upstream" facilities but fail to establish a secure market for its output of ingot, during a period of overcapacity, AMAX might have to "dump" its ingot at distress prices.

A tentative conclusion of MacGregor was that if AMAX were to enter the aluminum business, its first thrusts should be into "downstream" operations via acquisitions of existing businesses. "Downstream" the industry was less concentrated and less capital intensive than "upstream" but also less profitable. Once, however, a "downstream" market share had been firmly established, the company could integrate "upstream."

An opportunity to enter the aluminum industry via "downstream" acquisition came in 1962, when the U.S. Department of Justice blocked the proposed acquisition of the Kawneer Company by Kaiser Aluminum and Chemical Company and the proposed acquisition of the Apex Smelting Company by ALCAN. Kawneer was one of the nation's leading fabricators of architectural aluminum products supplied to the commercial construction industry. Apex was a leading secondary smelter of

---

[2]The main stages in aluminum production are: (1) Mining of bauxite (aluminum ore), (2) concentrating and transforming the bauxite into alumina, (3) "primary reduction" of alumina into ingots of 99.5% pure aluminum, (4) conversion of ingots into foil, wire, sheet, bars, and other extrusions, etc. Scrap aluminum is refined by "secondary reduction," and then moves into stage (4).

aluminum whose main business was to produce aluminum alloys from processed scrap.

AMAX was able to reach an agreement with the owners of Apex and Kawneer to merge their companies into AMAX. These companies not only provided an initial entry for AMAX into the aluminum business, but also provided AMAX with technical personnel experienced in aluminum operations.

Further "downstream" expansion took place the following year when AMAX acquired the Hunter Engineering Co. Hunter was a major producer of aluminum siding for the mobile home industry, and of other mill products.

Having secured a "downstream" base in the aluminum industry, Mr. MacGregor began to consider thrusts toward "upstream" integration. Of paramount importance was to secure a supply of alumina.

The first effort failed. A consortium led by Kaiser Aluminum was being formed in 1963 to exploit the underdeveloped Gladstone bauxite deposits in Queensland, Australia, but MacGregor was initially unable to convince the partners in the consortium to allow AMAX to join.

A second chance to gain access to the Gladstone alumina arose when Mr. MacGregor learned that Howmet Corporation was considering building a primary reduction plant in the state of Washington. Howmet, a recent U.S. acquisition of Pechiney of France, wished to integrate backward for the same reasons as AMAX. But Howmet's needs could not keep a primary reduction plant of economical size busy. So Howmet and AMAX joined in a 50-50 venture—the construction of a 228,000-ton plant which cost over $150 million. The special appeal here was that Pechiney, Howmet's parent, was a member of the Gladstone consortium and could provide the new venture with Gladstone alumina!

Actually, ALCOA of Australia found that it had excess capacity in its western Australia alumina plant, and it was glad to sign a long-term contract with AMAX to supply alumina to the new plant.

So by 1965 AMAX was, indeed, an integrated producer of aluminum. It was, however, as just noted, buying rather than producing its own alumina. At that time all its aluminum operations were consolidated in a single company, Amax Aluminum Company. This new company has continued to expand its sheet, extrusion, and other "downstream" capacity. The growth of Amax Aluminum Company and its current financial position are shown in Tables 1 and 2. In just eleven years Amax has moved from zero to a significant position in the industry.

Two additional bold moves by Amax Aluminum are still pending. One is the mining of bauxite and production of alumina in a newly discovered site at Kimberley, Western Australia. This is planned as a huge operation costing around $750 million, with an annual output of alumina large enough to equal the entire demand of Japan in 1975. But Amax Aluminum has not yet been able to muster a consortium large enough to support the venture, partly because of an excess capacity situation in the aluminum industry in the early 1970's. (The list price of primary aluminum actually declined from 27¢ per pound in 1967 to 25¢ in 1972.)

The second plan involves a 50-50 joint venture with the Mitsui Company, Ltd. of Japan, for the construction of a primary aluminum reduction facility in northwestern Oregon. This plant would have an annual capacity of 187,000 tons, and cost at least $250 million. A contract for power from the Bonneville Power Administration has been signed and construction was about to start when a dispute with the State

Table 1

Amax Aluminum Company

Income Statements, 1969–1973 ($ millions)					
	1969	1970	1971	1972	1973
Sales	280	277	287	311	373
Costs & operating expenses	217	219	232	249	296
Selling & general expenses	25	27	28	30	31
Depreciation & amortization	9	10	11	11	11
Taxes, other than income taxes	4	4	5	5	5
Earnings from operations	25	17	11	16	30
Other expense & income, net	2	2	1	1	2
Income taxes	12	7	4	6	12
Net earnings	11	8	6	9	16

Table 2

Amax Aluminum Company

Balance Sheet, Dec. 31, 1973
($ millions)

Assets		Liabilities & Equity	
Cash & equivalent	2.7	Current liabilities	48.8
Accounts receivable, net	71.5	Long-term obligations due to	
Inventories	59.2	AMAX, Inc.	20.0
Other current assets	3.1		
Total current assets	136.5	Total liabilities & equity	68.8
Investments in 50% owned			
companies, at equity	9.9	Shareholders equity	200.6
Plant & equipment, net	119.4		
Other assets	3.6		
Total assets	269.4	Total liabilities & equity	269.4

Government of Oregon over environmental aspects arose. Late in 1973, it is unclear if and when this project will move ahead.

AMAX PORTFOLIO PROBLEM

In the autumn of 1973, Mr. MacGregor reluctantly told Mr. Robert Marcus, Executive Vice President of Amax Aluminum, that the board of directors of the parent company, AMAX, Inc., probably would not provide funds for the continuing growth of the aluminum subsidiary. Both Mr. Marcus and Mr. MacGregor, now head of AMAX, Inc., had worked strenuously to build the aluminum company to its present position.

The change in heart arises from two considerations—(a) the portfolio squeeze which AMAX, Inc. faces, and (b) new doubts about the outlook for the aluminum industry.

From 1967 onwards, substantial capital commitments were required by AMAX in its operations outside the aluminum subsidiary. The Mt. Newman iron ore mine began operations in 1967, and over the four years 1967–1971 required well over $100 million from AMAX, 25% owner of the mine. By 1971 the mine had become the largest single supplier of iron ore to Japan.

In 1967 the Urad Mine, an old molybdenum mine located about thirty miles north of Climax, Colorado, was reopened, requiring $25 million in capital investment over the years 1967–1971. In the longer term, AMAX was developing a third Colorado molybdenum mine to exploit reserves discovered in 1965. This mine, Henderson Mine, when it comes on-stream in the mid to late 1970's, will rival the Climax mine in yearly output. It will require capital expenditures of upwards of $400 million over a five to eight year period beginning in about 1971. Also, "downstream" molybdenum processing facilities are in need of modernization and expansion. Through the 1970's the expansion and modernization of molybdenum operations are expected to cost AMAX at least $500 million.

Additional capital is needed to expand coal production. By 1972, AMAX had become the fifth largest producer of coal in the United States. In 1973, shipments began from the new Belle Ayr South mine in Wyoming and the new Ayrshire and Wabash mines in Indiana. By the end of 1973, over $65 million had been spent on coal mine expansion and development of new mines, and through the remainder of the 1970's over $200 million more is due to be spent.

AMAX expects to incur other capital costs through the 1970's. Purchase and rehabilitation of a zinc plant in Illinois is budgeted at $26 million. Entry into the nickel business has long been sought by AMAX, and acquisition and rehabilitation of a nickel refinery in Louisiana is budgeted at $53 million.

The effect of so much expansion of activities has resulted in capital expenditures tripling between 1967 and 1973, as shown in Table 3. As is indicated, total yearly capital expenditures exceeded net cash flow after dividends during these years, thus requiring AMAX to raise outside capital. The resulting capital structure is shown in Table 4. Stockholders equity is now less than half of total assets. Long-term obligations are about 75% of equity, which is high for a mining company.

AMAX's board of directors now feel that the investment opportunities open to the corporation outstrip its ability to raise capital. So, recently the board has been putting pressure on Mr. MacGregor (now CEO) to limit future expenditures to only those areas which have the highest potential return on investment.

The success of the various sectors of AMAX's portfolio is indicated in Table 5. From 1969 through 1973, most sectors have grown faster than aluminum in sales volume, and all have outstripped it in profitability related to sales. Even in 1973, a good year for most businesses after price controls were removed, Amax Aluminum earned only 8% on stockholders equity (see Tables 1 and 2).

Clearly, a picture of unusually favorable prospects for aluminum will be necessary if Amax Aluminum is to take priority for capital over other sectors of AMAX's portfolio.

Table 3

Capital Deficits of AMAX, 1967–1973
($ millions)

	1967	1968	1969	1970	1971	1972	1973
Internal sources of capital:							
Earnings after taxes	57	69	82	73	55	66	105
Depreciation & amortization	21	25	27	37	39	42	48
Total	78	94	109	110	94	108	153
Uses of capital:							
Dividends paid	30	30	32	36	36	37	45
Increases in working capital	22	2	− 6	26	83	41	−12
Capital expenditures & acquisitions	86	103	147	189	142	157	265
Total	138	135	173	251	261	235	298
Deficits of internal sources	− 60	− 41	− 64	−141	−167	−127	−145

Table 4

AMAX, Inc., Balance Sheet
Dec. 31, 1973
($ millions)

Assets		Liabilities & Equity	
Cash equivalent	288	Current liabilities	257
Accounts Receivable, net	193	Long-term debt	441
Inventories	178	Reserves & other long-term liabilities	174
Other current assets	13		
Total current assets	672	Total liabilities	872
Plant & equipment, net	890	Stock & paid in capital	289
Other long-term assets	150	Retained earnings	551
Total assets	1,712	Total liabilities & equity	1,712

OUTLOOK FOR ALUMINUM INDUSTRY

The basic aluminum industry has experienced significant growth during the post-World War II period, as is reflected in Table 6. Worldwide expansion has been even more impressive than in the United States.

Table 5

AMAX Sales and Earnings by Product Line

	1969	1970	1971	1972	1973
Sales (in $ millions)					
Molybdenum & Specialty Metals	155	145	108	114	179
Copper, Lead, Zinc	275	294	215	270	571
Fuels	19	98	96	119	134
Iron Ore	8	25	39	45	60
Chemicals	21	23	27	20	22
Aluminum	280	277	287	311	373
Total company	758	862	772	879	1,339
Ratio of Earnings from Operations* to Sales					
Molybdenum & Specialty Metals	35%	36%	26%	25%	26%
Copper, Lead, Zinc	6	6	4	8	13
Fuels	5	10	14	16	13
Iron Ore	50	52	59	56	63
Chemicals	− 5	17	15	25	27
Aluminum	9	6	4	5	8
Total company	12%	13%	11%	13%	16%

*Earnings from Operations are before income tax, exploration expense, and unallocated corporate expense. Exploration and corporate expenses are about 5% of sales.

Table 6

Trends in U.S. Basic Aluminum Industry
1950–1973
(1,000's of tons, except price)

	Primary Production	Recovery from Scrap	Metal Imports	Metal Exports	Price, Primary Ingots
1950	719	228	177	11	16.6¢ per pound
1955	1,566	334	178	21	21.9 " "
1960	2,015	407	153	37	26.0 " "
1965	2,755	769	527	65	24.5 " "
1970	3,976	940	350	79	28.7 " "
1973	4,530	1,060	508	230	25.3 " "

Demand for aluminum in the United States is closely tied to general business conditions. As Table 7 indicates, growth in demand depends on growth in construction, automobile production, use of 2-piece aluminum cans, extension of electric power lines, and a wide variety of other uses.

Because of the very high fixed costs required for the production of aluminum, and the need for continuous production once a reduction plant is in operation, manufacturers press hard to sell their full capacity. Thus, even a small excess capacity above demand tends to drive down selling prices. Contrariwise, when demand exceeds capacity, prices tend to move up substantially.

The demand and supply balance is a worldwide issue. While normally local demand is met by local production (at least in the industrialized countries), aluminum will be shipped from country to country when large price differentials develop. The countries which participate in this game are shown in Table 8.

Reliable information on effective capacity for primary aluminum production is hard to obtain, especially from countries such as Russia. One estimate of current world capacity is 12.6 million tons per annum. However, we do know that even companies such as ALCOA rarely run at capacity except for brief periods; in 1973, ALCOA ran at 94% both in the U.S. and worldwide. Informed estimates are that, if past consumption trends continue, there will be a worldwide shortage of capacity by 1978. Within the United States consumption may outrun capacity even earlier unless new capacity is constructed. A few proposed new plants have been announced, the largest being the projected Amax Aluminum-Mitsui plant in Oregon; but all of these are subject to environmental clearances, availability of power as anticipated, etc.

The costs of purchased inputs are rising. Between 1970 and 1973, for example, in the U.S. aluminum industry, salaries and wages have risen 36%, purchased materials 8%, and energy 24%. Government controls on selling prices created a cost-price squeeze in early 1973, and only larger volume enabled companies to improve their overall results for the year. However, with the removal of controls, prices have jumped 25% by December, and further substantial increases are expected.

The aluminum industry is concentrated but nonetheless highly competitive. The major companies in primary production in North America are listed in Table 9. Although the Amax Aluminum venture is number five on the list, its volume is far behind the leaders. ALCOA, the U.S. leader, earned only 4% to 5% on invested capital during 1969–1974. (The "experience curve" did not work out here because Amax Aluminum with only a small fraction of ALCOA's experience has done somewhat better.)

Outside the United States, clearly the largest aluminum producer is Pechiney of France. Its total revenues for all kinds of products in 1973 will be close to $3 billion. Pechiney along with the companies listed in Table 9 account for about 60% of world capacity for primary aluminum. Nevertheless, companies fully as large as Amax Aluminum are operating in Japan, Switzerland, Belgium, Norway, and West Germany. All such companies face the same economic pressure to operate as near capacity as possible.

AMAX ALTERNATIVES

AMAX has several alternatives in the action it may take with regard to Amax Aluminum and still live within its general objective of making no further investment in aluminum activities.

Table 7

U.S. Aluminum Shipments to Major Markets, 1973

	Share of total tons
Building-Construction	25%
Transportation	20
Consumer durables	8
Electrical	13
Machinery & equipment	7
Containers & packaging	14
Miscellaneous	6
Total domestic	93
Exports, metal & products	7
Total shipments	100%

Table 8

World Production of Primary Aluminum by Countries—1973*

(1,000 metric tons)

U.S.A.	5,077
Japan	1,574
U.S.S.R.	1,480
West Germany	856
U.K.	487
France	450
Other European countries	849
Canada	332

*Figures in the table are not exactly comparable with those in Tables 6 & 10, due to differences in definitions, metric versus short tons, etc. However, comparisons *within* each table are reliable for present purposes.

(1) *Maintain the status quo.* This would involve reinvesting depreciation so as to maintain equipment, but any new ventures would have to call for very small amounts of capital. Basically Amax Aluminum would simply wait for improvements in industry conditions, realizing that some loss in market position would probably occur as more aggressive competitors made new thrusts.

(2) *Set up Amax Aluminum as a quasi-independent company.* The aim here would be to decentralize financing as well as operating management. Amax Aluminum would be free to go directly to the capital markets for such long-term loans or other advances as it could justify. Probably to make this arrangement viable, the current

debt Amax Aluminum now owes its parent, AMAX, would be converted into equity. This would give Amax Aluminum much more flexibility in rearranging its capital structure. Amax Aluminum would "paddle its own canoe." This might increase the risk of the common stockholder (AMAX), but presumably would also increase the potential long-run value of the stock.

Table 9

Primary Production of Major North American Aluminum Companies, 1973 (in 1,000's of tons)

ALCAN (Canadian)	1676
ALCOA (U.S.)	1652
Reynolds	1084
Kaiser	847
Intalco*	228
Anaconda	218

*Owned 50-50 by Amax Aluminum and Howmet.

(3) *Sell the entire company.* This would not only stop a capital drain but actually increase the funds AMAX has available to invest in other sectors of its portfolio. The question here is who might buy Amax Aluminum, and why? The company has over a quarter of a billion dollars in assets. Few potential buyers have cash of this amount to invest in a single aluminum enterprise. Large U.S. aluminum companies (and probably Pechiney) would be prevented from buying a competitor because of anti-trust laws. The big mining concerns have attractive alternatives just as AMAX does. Amax Aluminum's earnings record is scarcely one that will excite the very large institutional investors. So finding an eager buyer will not be easy.

(4) *Look for a partner, or partners, with lots of capital.* Investors and owners of mineral deposits often follow this approach. The new investors provide the capital necessary to make the moves which will bring the venture to economic fruition. Of course, with the addition of each new partner the original owner's share of the total pie goes down. If Amax Aluminum is to continue the kind of aggressive course which has built its present position, sources of large amounts of capital must be found.

Other alternatives, or some combination of the above types, might be explored. The evaluation of each will be strongly influenced, of course, by the specific "deal" that can be negotiated. Also, an assessment of the future prospects for aluminum, and AMAX's continuing interest—if any—in Amax Aluminum must be weighed.

POSSIBLE DEAL WITH MITSUI

One evening recently in a Manhattan restaurant, Mr. MacGregor and Mr. Marcus (Executive Vice President of Amax Aluminum) were talking about the future of Amax Aluminum, a subject they had discussed many times before. Marcus had been reviewing the reasons why he continued to be optimistic about long-run prospects, and then the conversation turned to possible buyers of the company.

"I have considered approaching Pechiney," commented MacGregor. "The problem is, I am not sure that they would be able to buy in cash. We would want cash—we need it—and they are not extremely liquid."

"Maybe a Japanese firm would be willing to buy us," ventured Marcus.

"Why would one want to?" asked MacGregor.

"Well, when I was over there talking to Mitsui about the Oregon plant, I had the distinct feeling that they badly wanted sources of aluminum outside of Japan . . . ," said Marcus.

Out of that exchange has come a decision to carefully consider Mitsui as a potential buyer. With so much at stake, a "key actor" analysis is obviously called for.

Mitsui Company, Ltd. is one of the ten largest general trading firms in Japan. Each of these firms deals in a broad array of goods and services; a popular (and correct) Japanese saying is, "General trading companies handle everything from peanuts to guided missiles." While there are some 5,000 trading firms in Japan, the ten largest do 80% of the trading volume. Their combined annual turnover corresponds to 30% of the Japanese Gross National Product.

Within Japan, a general trading company traditionally (a) markets the output of its manufacturing company clients, (b) procures raw materials for its clients, (c) helps finance inventories and accounts receivable. The company may also transport, warehouse, insure, and provide other services to manufacturing clients and to distributors. Internationally, the general trading companies are the main marketing organizations for worldwide exports, and the main procurement agencies for imports—here again with a full array of services to facilitate international movement of goods. In addition, they use their very extensive telecommunication systems to make all sorts of commodity trades which have no connection with the Japanese economy. Incidentally, the competition between the general trading companies themselves is very keen.

The dominant position of the general trading companies, however, is eroding. As manufacturing firms have become larger and financially stronger, they are taking over more of their own procurement and marketing. Especially the firms selling products which require technical services to consumers, such as color TV sets and automobiles, obtain better results by closer relationships with users. The general trading companies are so diversified that they lack the specialized knowledge and interest which is desirable for complex products.

The general trading companies, such as Mitsui, have tried to counteract this lessening of interest in their traditional role by taking on manufacturing activities themselves. Being well aware of growth in demand for new materials and products, and where shortages are likely to arise, the trading companies have stepped in to fill the gaps. In the international arena, much of the attention has been in mining and oil because Japan is notably lacking in natural mineral resources.

Production of primary aluminum has had rapid growth in Japan, expanding more than threefold in the last eight years, as shown in Table 10. Mitsubishi, the largest general trading company, entered the field in 1963 and within ten years has expanded to become third in the industry. Mitsui, its rival, did not enter until 1968 and still occupies a minor position. The current capacity of the five primary producers is given in Table 11.

Even with the past expansion in capacity, the Japanese aluminum industry has been plagued with a chronic shortage of ingots during 1973. There are at least 300 firms engaged in fabricating aluminum, and the scramble for domestic or imported

Table 10

Primary Aluminum Production in Japan
(1,000's of tons)

1966	373	1970	930
1967	517	1971	983
1968	611	1972	1,221
1969	819	1973	1,355

Table 11

Capacity of Japanese Primary Aluminum Producers
1973

Nippon Light Metals*	380,000	tons	per	annum
Sumitomo Chemicals	377,000	"	"	"
Mitsubishi Chemicals	271,000	"	"	"
Showa Denko	261,000	"	"	"
Mitsui Aluminum	83,000	"	"	"
Total primary capacity in Japan	1,372,000	"	"	"

*Nippon Light Metals is 50% owned by ALCAN of Canada, and through this connection has access to ALCAN's bauxite. All the other companies must negotiate long-term contracts for bauxite or alumina from foreign suppliers. There is no domestic bauxite, and no general trading company or producer has its own captive source of bauxite or alumina anywhere in the world.

ingots has been strong. Against such a background, Mr. Marcus hopes Mitsui will show an interest in Amax Aluminum.

There are no announced plans for expanding primary aluminum capacity within Japan, in spite of the supply and demand situation just cited. Probably a major restraint is air pollution. As Japan has industrialized and greatly increased automobiles on the road, pollution has become serious. With its large population, new industrial sites are scarce. And unless a non-polluting source of electricity can be developed, government officials are unlikely to approve major additions to present reduction plants.

The Japanese government, largely through the powerful Ministry of International Trade and Industry (MITI), will have to endorse plans of any Japanese company to invest in the aluminum industry at home or abroad. MITI seeks an orderly development of the entire economy. In this connection, it would like to reduce dependence on foreign producers for basic raw materials.

The government is under several other pressures which have a bearing on what Mitsui will be permitted to do. Japan has been exporting more than it imports, leading to very large accumulations of foreign exchange. To correct this trade imbalance, other national governments are putting pressure on Japan to relax obstacles to imports, and with much less eagerness to invest abroad. The Japanese government naturally is concerned about the impact of any such moves on domestic employment, especially since *lifetime* employment is a pillar in Japanese personnel practices.

A foreign investment of the size necessary to buy Amax Aluminum, or even half of it, will certainly require MITI's okay. A variety of large commitments for foreign raw materials have been made, but up through 1973 no investment even approaching the potential Amax Aluminum magnitude have taken place for processing of materials outside of Japan. If consummated, the transaction would represent the largest direct investment in the United States by a Japanese corporation in history.

So, the proposal Mr. Marcus is trying to develop would have to clear at least three hurdles. (1) The investment must be endorsed by MITI, in terms of Japan's national interests. (2) Mitsui must consider the investment an attractive business proposition, consistent with its general objectives. (3) AMAX must consider the price it receives more attractive than holding or disposing of the assets some other way.

"Remember," Mr. MacGregor said to Mr. Marcus, "you will have to convince Mitsui that the company is more attractive to them than it is to us. And, they have an even wider range of portfolio alternatives than we do. From our angle, shares of stock in aluminum companies are now selling at about book value. Our ROI is better than most; so I think we should get a premium over book value."

APPENDIX A

History of Mitsui

The house of Mitsui is one of Japan's oldest business firms, marking its humble beginnings in 1616. At that time, the Mitsui family belonged to the samurai class of warrior noblemen, with the head of the family holding the title of Lord of Echigo, in Japan's feudalistic system. A long period of warring had just recently come to an end, causing Mitsui Sokubei Takatoshi, the latest heir to the Mitsui peerage, to reflect deeply upon the future of the Japanese society. He reasoned that if a long period of peace were to be forthcoming, the foundations of the samurai class, which were based on war, would be undermined significantly. He decided, therefore, that the future of his family lay not in the nobility but in what he saw as the next emerging elite, the merchant class.

Not long after the Meiji Restoration (which is what the defeat of the shogunate and the 1868 re-installation of the emperor is called), Japan was fully involved in its own industrial revolution. From its base as a primarily financial institution, Mitsui added various manufacturing firms, creating a group of companies which were centered around the bank. As the output from these manufacturing firms continued to grow, the importance of the trading function of the group increased accordingly. Mitsui Bussan Kaisha Ltd., which was formed in 1878 as the trading arm, was charged with the responsibility of obtaining for Mitsui's firm, and other manufacturing firms, the necessary goods for production, and then marketing these goods both domestically and internationally. These products included mostly textiles and machinery. The Mitsui Group was granted large coal interests by the Meiji regime. This placed the Mitsui Bussan in the center of both domestic and international trading activities in the metal and chemical areas.

To facilitate scouting out and taking advantage of business opportunities around the world, Mitsui Bussan built a strong information system on an international level, an information network that is still a major factor in Mitsui's success today. In the aftermath of the Russo-Japanese War, 1904–05, Mitsui Bussan expanded into a number of investments in the so-called "Yen Bloc" which included Japan, Manchuria, Korea, and later much of the rest of the Chinese Mainland. With the predominant position in the Yen Bloc, and with a strong foothold in the rest of the world, the firm was by far the largest general trading firm in Japan, conducting, in 1932, 13 percent of Japan's total foreign trade, and as much as 50+ percent of Japanese transactions of some commodities, such as coal and machinery. The House of Mitsui had business connections with literally hundreds of firms in Japan. The core group, controlled by a holding company, Mitsui Honsha, was composed of "ten 'first line' subsidiaries, thirteen 'second line' subsidiaries, as well as more than eighty listed sub-subsidiaries, in 1942. In addition, there were whole sub-empires [including textile, cement, paper, automotive, and electrical interests] in which Mitsui had substantial interests but wished to keep separate from the Honsha structure."[3]

The Japanese defeat in World War II changed the shape of the House of Mitsui dramatically, as it did for all the *"zaibatsu"* (the fully integrated mammoth industrial concerns). Citing excessive monopolism as the largest problem of Japanese society, the Supreme Commander for Allied Forces in the Pacific (SCAP), General Douglas MacArthur, ordered in 1946 the holding companies of the *zaibatsu* to dismantle operations, and limited the size and scope of the subsidiaries.

The Reemergence of General Trading Firms after World War II[4]

The fact that the large general trading companies had acquired such an expertise in international trade was a major factor in their resurgence after the war. International trade after the war evolved in several steps. From 1945 to 1947, the Allied General Headquarters (GHQ) handled the imports and exports for defeated Japan. The GHQ imported products and channelled them to the International Trade Agency of the Japanese government, which in turn rationed them to the various companies. In order to obtain imported products for the purpose of resale in Japan, the trading firms that were allowed to operate competed fiercely to handle products outside of their traditional lines of business. At this point, the only skills needed by the trading firm was the ability to file and process the proper procurement and sales forms with the Government.

As a result of this move toward taking on products outside the traditional scope of given trading firms, some firms established different departments for the handling of different products, in anticipation of the re-establishment of private trading. Private trading, it was hoped, would include not only imports, but exports of machinery and chemical products as war reparation payments to Japan's Asian neighbors.

In 1948, a relaxation of the restrictions against private international trading came about, but because of the severe dollar shortage in Japan, the importers in Japan were forced to conclude many barter deals. In exchange for crude sugar, products

---

[3]John G. Roberts, *Mitsui: Three Centuries of Japanese Business* (New York: Weatherhill, 1973), p. 354.

[4]Based on the accounts contained in Yoshi Tsurumi, *The Japanese Are Coming: A Multinational Interaction of Firms & Politics* (Cambridge, Massachusetts: Ballinger Publishing Co., 1976).

such as ammonium sulphate fertilizer, iron slabs and whale oil were exported. Accordingly, in order to survive, the trading firms had to develop both the internal communications network and the outside contracts to offer barter deals more quickly than their competitors. This pressure also caused many of the fragmented, single-line trading companies to merge.

The next step in the evolutionary process which saw the full re-emergence of the general trading firm was the establishment of the "Linking Trade" policy by the Japanese government. In order to encourage trading firms to export manufactured goods vital to Japan's development, the Government, in 1953, began to link these exports to import licenses of the lucrative consumer and luxury-type goods. Such things as whiskey importation were linked to a firm's achieving its export quota of chemical and heavy manufactures. This policy, which lasted into the late '50s, caused an even greater diversification of product line for the trading firms, and, because quotas of goods were involved, inevitably led to a stronger concentration among trading companies.

The Linking Trade policy was not singularly responsible for this concentration, however. A series of severe "downs" in the business cycle in Japan forced many of the less well capitalized trading firms into bankruptcy. The need to find capital with which trading firms could expand into different product lines, often through merger with smaller companies, also caused considerable concentration. Mitsui Bank, along with the banks of other former *zaibatsu* groups, helped their respective trading companies over the financial crunch. That crunch was indeed formidable, in that the average gross margin during this period was 2 to 3 percent, while selling and administrative expenses of trader's firms amounted to around 1.3 percent of gross sales. Average collection days of receivables were around 110 days. Even a slight downturn in the economy and the performance of a trading company's customers could cause bankruptcy.

Mitsui's own resurrection occurred within this context. After the war, the many trading departments of Mitsui Bussan were split apart and the managers of the individual departments started their own single line trading firms. Because the GHQ prohibited the use of the old *zaibatsu* names, there was no official "Mitsui Bussan" immediately after the war. As the business environment changed, and multi-line businesses became necessary, the former Mitsui departments merged into five large groups, headed by a Mitsui manager. Contacts were kept close between the former members of the group. It was in 1958 that Mitsui & Co. (Mitsui Bussan Kaisha) was formally re-established.

COMPREHENSIVE CASE 6

Buckeye Bearing Company

Buckeye Bearing Company is in the process of transition. The transition involves both new executive personnel and new methods of operation. Almost three years ago the company founder, Mr. Andrew Quinn, died a millionaire as a result of his guidance of the firm. The stock of the company was acquired by Clyde Investment Fund, and this case describes the experience of the Fund in placing the company on a new and modern basis. The process is proving to be more difficult than anticipated; Mr. George Van Houten, president of Clyde Investment Fund, has directed his assistant to make a study of the situation. The following information has been collected.

NATURE AND BACKGROUND OF COMPANY

Andy Quinn and a partner ran a machine shop in a suburb of Cleveland, Ohio, in the 1920's. They learned how to make good quality roller bearings, and with increasing demand from machinery manufacturers, this product soon received their major attention. Then came the depression and bankruptcy. Out of the ruins, Andy Quinn personally founded the present company. His recognized knowledge of roller bearings was an important factor in getting the company back on its feet.

For years Andy Quinn and the Buckeye Bearing Company were considered almost the same thing by members of the industry. He had a personal acquaintance among all the oldtimers, and he relished discussing technical problems with both customers and competitors. His opinions were respected because he had detailed knowledge of bearing uses and production.

Internally, the distinction between Andy Quinn and the company was also hard to draw. One of his younger associates reports: "Mr. Quinn was president, general manager, treasurer, credit manager, and sales manager—all in one. He worked six or seven days a week, long hours, and set an example for the rest of us. We typically spent a couple of evenings each week in 'scheduling meetings,' working on the production schedule for each order. We had no 'staff,' that is, no separate men and women for industrial engineering, production scheduling, quality control, and the like; when something had to be done, we did it ourselves. That was the only way we could keep alive."

Andy Quinn kept up this pace to the day of his death, at the age of 69. From his hospital bed, he conferred with the production manager on detailed schedules for two hours one Friday afternoon. The following morning he had an assistant bring over the accounts receivable records and he dictated credit letters. That night he died. Basically he never changed his work habits from the time he founded the company over thirty years earlier.

For years, especially after World War II, Andy Quinn never spent a nickel that he could avoid on new equipment. Many of the machines were fully depreciated. The plant layout was crowded and no clear workflow existed; machines were put wherever they might fit, often with ingenious arrangements for overhead belt drives. The office reflected a similar stability and parsimony. A well-worn railing was the only separation of incoming visitors from the entire office force. Andy Quinn used the one private office, and about the only status symbols for the rest of the workers were a couple of rolltop desks.

Once convinced of the desirability for a change, however, Andy Quinn was prepared to act. For instance, in a back room he had a fully modern IBM installation —used primarily to process the highly detailed job cost records. Also, at the age of 69, he laid out a "five-year plan" to modernize the plant. Almost $250,000 was invested in new equipment prior to his death. Before this time the company had never incurred long-term debt and rarely borrowed from the bank. "Mr. Quinn never quite forgot his harrowing experience during the depression." Nevertheless, he was prepared to borrow money to launch the modernization plan. Incidentally, the objective of the plan was to replace obsolete equipment; it involved no new direction, product, or strategy.

Also noteworthy is the fact that the company has never had a strike. Many of the workers feel that they are part of the company, and this group apparently dominates the local union. Relationships between the workers and their supervisors and executives have always been close. The workers know that the company will adjust its wages to match the prevailing pattern in the area. Incidentally, the company always has had some blacks and women among its employees. The highest-paid operator of automatic equipment and the highest-paid person in the heat-treating department are blacks, both with 20 to 25 years of service.

Mr. Van Houten states that he and his associates were well aware of Mr. Quinn's conservatism when they acquired Buckeye Bearing. "Our experience indicates that a company with a good reputation but somewhat behind the time in its practices has more potential for growth than a firm where improvements have already been made. We like to acquire ailing companies, turn them around, and then hold them as long-term investments. That was the reason we were interested in Buckeye Bearing. Occasionally, we do dispose of a company and take our capital gains, but that is unusual; we are not traders."

Wise strategy for Clyde Investment Fund to follow with respect to Buckeye Bearing depends, in part, on the nature of its industry and its competition. Background information on these points is summarized in the next section.

Anti-Friction Bearing Industry

Ball and roller bearings are essential components of modern, high-speed machinery. They greatly reduce the friction of moving parts in equipment ranging from steel mills to outboard motors. Annual shipments exceed $1.25 billion. During recent years, total output has been closely correlated with durable goods production; it more than doubled between the latest available Census of Manufacturers in 1958 and 1967. Annual figures from the industry trade association for the last five years are shown in Exhibit 1.

The specialized nature of bearing manufacture is indicated by the fact that virtually all ball and roller bearings are made by 126 establishments that produce only bearings. Machining must be held to close tolerances, and heat-treating to harden the metal is important.

Exhibit 1
U.S. Shipments of Anti-Friction Bearings
(In $1,000,000's)

	Ball Bearings	Tapered Roller Bearings	Other Roller Bearings	Parts, Etc.	Total
Last Year	475	384	241	180	1,280
2nd Previous Year	514	421	242	183	1,360
3rd " "	447	396	216	164	1,223
4th " "	408	348	184	144	1,085
5th " "	388	293	152	128	961

Source: Anti-Friction Bearing Manufacturers Association.

Large companies such as S.K.F., Timken, and New Departure make millions of bearings for "original equipment" such as automobiles. These firms produce 80% of the total output. A second group of companies, of which Buckeye Bearing is one, have 100 to 500 employees and typically are a significant factor in one part of the industry but do not attempt to make all types of bearings or to get the mass production orders. Finally, the smaller shops serve an area of only a few states and often deal with needs of only a special industry such as paper making. These small owner-managed shops usually have a minimum of engineering and overhead services, in contrast to the large companies that maintain a corps of metallurgists and engineers and quickly adopt the latest production techniques.

No one or two companies dominate the industry, however; patents are not significant; technology is relatively stable; and competition is keen. Almost all bearings have a housing that keeps the balls or rollers in place, and these vary widely in size, shape, and design to suit the particular use.

As Exhibit 1 indicates, products fall into three broad types: ball bearings used for lighter loads, tapered roller bearings used where both thrust and load are present, and cylindrical roller bearings that can carry heavier loads for their size than ball bearings. This last type, on which Buckeye Bearing concentrates, has been growing somewhat faster than the other types. Buckeye has about 2% of this market.

CHANGES MADE BY CLYDE

As soon as Clyde Investment Fund bought the stock of Buckeye Bearing Company from Mr. Quinn's estate, Mr. Van Houten moved swiftly to modernize the operations.

Revamped Organization

New personnel and new organization had to come first to fill the vacuum left by Andy Quinn's death. Bruce Feenstra was appointed president. Educated as a metallurgist, Mr. Feenstra had worked as an engineer for the Ford Motor Company, then shifted to product manager of one of Ford's parts suppliers, and was anxious to "get into the number one spot of a small firm where I can make full use of my experience and ambition."

To fill the void in marketing, Mr. Feenstra selected Maurice Lombardi—a top salesperson in one of Buckeye's distributors with twenty years of experience in the bearing and related industries.

Three men were promoted from within. "Chris Prichard, the accountant, was made controller," explained Mr. Feenstra. "He knows the figures from way back, and already had worked with IBM equipment. I changed public accountants and had the new firm work with Chris in reclassifying the accounts. With that help Chris is doing fine.

"In production, Tony Biccum was obviously the key person. He had worked as second in command under Quinn—insofar as anyone could—so we appointed him vice-president of manufacturing. He has had years of experience producing bearings, knows the workers and the machines thoroughly, and provides an essential bridge from the old to the new. We had an understanding from the start that an industrial engineer—Jack Zwick it turned out to be—would work under Tony in modernizing the shop. This has worked well; between my pushing from the top and Jack helping from below with lots of fresh ideas, there is plenty of action. Tony is the voice of experience, so we have quite a team.

"Finally, we took the wraps off Joe Stigler so he can really function as chief engineer. For a long time Joe took care of customer requests for special products, and in the process he learned a lot about product design and how customers use roller bearings. This is an important function in our business, and Joe can perform more effectively with a title and some elbow room. . . . Someday we should have a treasurer, but for the present I carry the title and rely on Chris Prichard to supervise the routine work. . . . Here is the present line-up." (See Exhibit 2 on the next page.)

Plant Modernization

Mr. Biccum confirmed the transformation in the plant. "You wouldn't know it is the same place. As new equipment came in, we got rid of the obsolete stuff—something Mr. Quinn would never do. And we put it where the new layout said. By now every machine in the place has been moved. The overhead drives are gone. Aisles are wider. Material moves are shorter, and we don't have semifinished lots sitting wherever there is an empty spot. Besides, we put in decent lights and used some paint. Also the new equipment runs faster, so we actually have fewer pieces of equipment. What a difference. Now, we're proud to have a customer see the plant; before we'd think up excuses to keep customers out.

"And the offices. Within three months Bruce put up plywood paneling, new ceiling, and lights—also air-conditioning. It was a new world, and everyone in the organization knew it. That office bit cost only $2,500. What an investment in morale!

"Of course, the things you don't see are more important. We've gone to work on direct labor, because you can't save much on material. Between new equipment, better layout, reassigning work loads, improved scheduling, a central room for cutting tools, and better maintenance that reduces down-time, we have cut direct labor

Exhibit 2

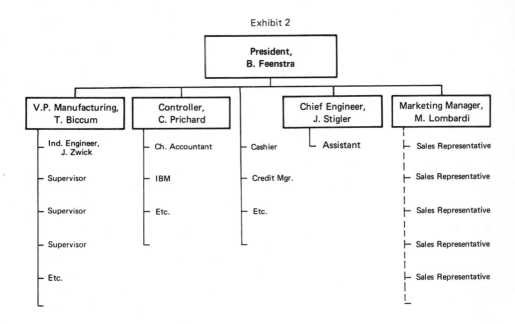

from 26% to 18% of total costs. And there was a wage hike absorbed in those figures, too. Jack Zwick is good on this; he keeps coming up with new ideas. He's working on inventory and quality control now. You may want to talk with him about that."

Inventory and Quality as Sales Guides

"To properly comprehend industrial engineering," explained Mr. Zwick, "you must think in terms of all the complexities of the enterprise. In a formal sense we are part of manufacturing; but my people know, and Bruce Feenstra knows, we have a broader assignment. At first, getting costs down was essential to survival, so we focused on that. Now, while not relaxing on costs, we have to help raise plant through-put to take full advantage of the lower costs. This means shifting our focus to marketing.

"For Buckeye Bearing Company to thrive in the marketplace, we must give the customer prompt delivery of high quality merchandise. So we are devising an inventory model that will give optimum availability, reasonable stocks, and efficient production runs. Frankly, this is an unsavory undertaking because intuitively I know high inventories are inevitable. The real accomplishment will be improved customer service. In collaboration with marketing, we have selected some 308 items that will be "standards," that is, always kept in stock here at the plant. The trick then becomes better instructions to our schedulers regarding trade-offs between inventory size and production runs.

"Quality control should yield more observable improvements. Buckeye quality has always been good—with occasional slips, of course. Our task here is to be sure quality does not degenerate when volume rises and to achieve this end with a reasonable inspection cost. Two years ago we established a distinct inspection function, and now we are working on methods and instrumentation that will expedite the process. Automated inspection is impractical in a plant of this size with the many sizes and specifications, but we can design equipment that will lower the labor cost of performing the task."

Revitalized Distribution

"Did you ever try to paddle a canoe with a broomstick? Well, that's the way I often feel," said Mr. Lombardi. "Here's the picture in a nutshell. Most of our sales are replacements. When the ultimate user—the fellow whose machine is being repaired —or the contractor he has hired to fix the machine wants to replace a bearing, he asks for one just like the original 99 $^{44}/_{100}$% of the time—by name of maker. He normally buys the replacement from a bearing distributor—a local guy who is supposed to have a stock of bearings on hand for prompt delivery. Now, since very few Buckeye bearings are original equipment, nobody asks for our products.

"But let's assume the distributor has some of our bearings sitting on his shelf and he discovers that he is out of stock of the specific bearing asked for. Then maybe he will look at our sizes and specs, and if he has what is wanted, he'll tell the customer Buckeye is every bit as good and he can have it right now. You see what I mean by that broomstick. We don't have much leverage. We need to be where the current will pull us along.

"A little wider profit margin will help, but most distributors play it safe and give the customers what they ask for. A really high-grade distributor studies his customer's bearing needs in advance and makes an arrangement with the customer for carrying replacements. That kind of distributor knows his business well enough to be freer to make substitutions.

"If, over the years, a distributor finds that he can get good service and good quality from Buckeye, he is more likely to keep our bearings in stock and to recommend them more often. We use manufacturers' reps to contact the distributor. They are our salespersons although they are not on our payroll; they work on straight commission. Sometimes they are also distributors, in which case they get two profit margins on Buckeye bearings and are inclined to pick our products. Also the reps pick up leads on equipment manufacturers who might buy 'original equipment.' However, most of the reps are not good at this because they normally deal with the users of equipment, not the makers.

"After Mr. Quinn's death a lot of distributors and reps thought Buckeye would fold up. Our competitors probably encouraged the rumor. And our deliveries were erratic. My main job now is to overcome that setback.

"The thing that would help us most right now is a price rise. I wish I knew some legal way to get the big boys to be more realistic in pricing their replacements. They aren't set up for short runs like we are, so they must be losing money on most sizes. Unfortunately for us, overall they are making good profits and they are unwilling to have wide differences in prices of items that vary in volume. All we can do is keep our prices in line with theirs."

Financial Results

Chris Prichard, the controller, is the only executive unimpressed with Buckeye's "progress." "The more we sell, the more we lose. I'll give you the statements and see if you can find anything to shout about. The comparative profit and loss statement (Exhibit 3) shows that our gross margin has dropped from 21% to 14% in five years. No company can take that kind of a beating. Lombardi says he can't raise prices, so that turns the spotlight onto cost of goods sold. Take a look at costs (Exhibit 4). The money that we are saving on direct labor is more than eaten up by the costs of staff supervision, added inspection, and inventory control in the storeroom. Check it out yourself. From a financial standpoint, we just are spinning our wheels.

"Maybe I'm guilty of negative thinking. That's what Mr. Feenstra thinks, even though he doesn't say so. The balance sheet is what really shakes me (Exhibit 5). Current assets have gone up with sales. We're putting a lot of money into new equipment—almost a million dollars in three years. All that is nice positive stuff. But when you combine those increases with operating losses, cash has to come from someplace. For us the source has been the banks, thanks to the endorsement of notes by the Clyde Investment Fund. The net result is that our current ratio is bad, our debt to equity ratio is bad, and our earnings on equity are negative!

"Don't get me wrong. All of us are working hard to turn this ship around. The plant is modern; the finished goods inventory does permit better deliveries; the quality is under better control; and the reduction in direct labor is much larger than I thought possible. We use the IBM to give us costs on each production lot, and if any lot is out of line from previous costs Biccum, Zwick, and I, and often Mr. Feenstra, dig in to find out why. And because those cost sessions often come two or three months after the lot was started, we have weekly reviews of actual output against schedule. Periodically Zwick puts someone on analyzing machine down-time. Et cetera. The improvements you see are the result of hard work. Incidentally, the drop in administrative expenses two years back might be misleading. Most of that is Mr. Quinn's $65,000 salary, and also transfer of some expenses from administrative to selling.

"Last year we assumed the loss was due to extra expenses of changing our way of doing business. That's okay for one year. But how long and how deep do we have to go?"

FUTURE OPPORTUNITIES

During the examination of the company, a variety of suggestions were made for future development. For obvious reasons, several of these ideas had not been aired within the company itself, but they all could be appraised by Mr. Van Houten.

Mr. Feenstra stresses volume. "There's nothing wrong with this company that some additional sales won't cure. We have put the house in order and are prepared to give the trade the service it desires. We gained 12% last year and I'm hoping we can double that growth this year. It just takes a long while to rebuild confidence of distributors and to get a change in their buying habits. Maurice Lombardi is working

Exhibit 3

Buckeye Bearing Company
Five-Year Comparative Profit and Loss Statement
(Dollar figures in 1,000's)

	Last Year		2nd Previous Year		3rd Previous Year		4th Previous Year		5th Previous Year	
Net Sales	$4,315	100.0%	$3,860	100.0%	$3,531	100.0%	$3,083	100.0%	$3,019	100.0%
Cost of Sales	3,711	86.0	3,221	83.4	2,841	80.5	2,441	79.2	2,385	79.0
Gross Profit	604	14.0	639	16.6	690	19.5	642	20.8	634	21.0
Selling Expense	302	7.0	293	7.6	234	6.6	230	7.5	225	7.5
Commissions	182	4.2	183	4.7	169	4.8	148	4.8	145	4.8
Administrative Expense	271	6.3	234	6.1	322	9.1	301	9.7	279	9.2
Interest, Discounts, Etc. (net)	55	1.3	30	.8	21	.6	16	.5	11	.4
Total Expenses	810	18.8	740	19.2	746	21.1	695	22.5	660	21.9
Net Operating Income (or Loss)	(206)	(4.8)	(101)	(2.6)	(56)	(1.6)	(53)	(1.7)	(26)	(.9)
Income Tax (or Tax Credit)	(89)	(2.1)	(48)	(1.2)	(18)	(.5)	(18)	(.6)	(10)	(.3)
Net Profit (or Loss)	(117)	(2.7)	(53)	(1.4)	(38)	(1.1)	(35)	(1.1)	(16)	(.6)

Exhibit 4

Buckeye Bearing Company
Cost of Sales—Five-Year Comparison
(Dollar figures in 1,000's)

	Last Year		2nd Previous Year		3rd Previous Year		4th Previous Year		5th Previous Year	
Materials.................	$1,261	31.0%	$1,082	31.3%	$ 975	32.1%	$ 833	31.1%	$ 804	32.2%
Direct Labor.............	734	18.0	692	20.0	789	26.0	645	24.0	651	26.1
Manufacturing Expense:										
Salary and Wages:										
Supervision...........	113		88		135		149		108	
Indirect Labor........	178		189		154		173		121	
Overtime Premium.....	107		73		62		63		24	
Shift Premium.........	35		28		21		20		15	
Vacations and Holidays...........	116		87		79		69		56	
Total	549	13.5	465	13.5	451	14.8	474	17.7	324	13.0
Service Department Expense:										
Supervision...........	182		106		41		50		47	
Inspection...........	208		228		124		92		84	
Storeroom and Receiving..........	154		122		49		38		46	

	Amount	%	Amount	%	Amount	%	Amount	%	Amount	%
Engineering and Drafting	49		30		21		19		25	
Building	188		138		87		82		101	
Total	781	19.2	624	18.0	322	10.6	281	10.5	303	12.1
Supplies and Miscellaneous	270	6.6	225	6.5	192	6.3	181	6.7	138	5.6
Power and Fuel	43	1.0	32	.9	34	1.1	33	1.2	24	1.0
Insurance (life, hospital, retirement, compensation)	149	3.7	110	3.2	101	3.3	98	3.7	110	4.4
Social Security and Unemployment Tax	70	1.7	54	1.6	42	1.4	42	1.6	43	1.7
Repairs	89	2.2	66	1.9	50	1.6	37	1.4	45	1.8
Depreciation	125	3.1	102	3.0	84	2.8	57	2.1	53	2.1
Total Manufacturing Expense	2,076	51.0	1,678	48.7	1,276	41.9	1,203	44.9	1,040	41.7
Total Production Expense	4,071	100.0%	3,452	100.0%	3,040	100.0%	2,681	100.0%	2,495	100.0%
Less Income in Inventories	360		231		199		240		110	
Cost of Sales	$3,711		$3,221		$2,841		$2,441		$2,385	

Exhibit 5

Buckeye Bearing Company
Balance Sheets, December 31
(Dollar figures in 1,000's)

	Last Year	2nd Previous Year	3rd Previous Year	4th Previous Year	5th Previous Year
Assets					
Cash	$ 222	$ 144	$ 109	$ 413	$ 451
Accounts Receivable, Net	539	497	466	384	382
Inventories:					
Raw Materials	241	264	268	222	157
Work in Process	790	648	1,045	860	689
Finished Goods	1,322	1,081	449	481	477
Total Inventories	2,353	1,993	1,762	1,563	1,323
Prepaid Expenses	21	24	30	32	29
Total Current Assets	3,135	2,658	2,367	2,392	2,185
Land	106	106	106	106	106
Buildings and Equipment	2,721	2,348	2,082	1,758	1,718
Reserve for Depreciation	1,816	1,667	1,544	1,421	1,332
Net Fixed Assets	1,011	787	644	443	492
Total Assets	$4,146	$3,445	$3,011	$2,835	$2,677
Liabilities and Equity					
Notes Payable	$1,400	$ 700	$ 300	$—	$—
Accounts Payable	286	241	173	211	74
Accrued Items	331	256	237	285	231
Total Current Liabilities	2,017	1,197	710	496	305
Common Stock	200	200	200	200	200
Capital Surplus	1,800	1,800	—	—	—
Retained Earnings	129	248	2,101	2,139	2,172
Total Equity	2,129	2,248	2,301	2,339	2,372
Total Liabilities and Equity	$4,146	$3,445	$3,011	$2,835	$2,677

hard in that direction, and so is Joe Stigler. We only need, say, 1% more of the industry total to make this place hum.

"To speed up growth, I've been looking for a smaller company that we might take over. Most of the smaller firms can't afford the staff services we have. They are usually run by one person. If we could find such a firm with a strong reputation in a geographical region or for a special type of bearing, we could put the production in our shop and simply maintain a warehouse and sales office in the other city. There are at least twenty companies in the country that fit my specifications, and certainly the owner of one of them is ready to toss in the sponge if we can locate him and approach him right."

Sales to original equipment manufacturers (o.e.m.) is a related approach. Mr. Stigler believes: "To build a sustained volume of sales we must have Buckeye bearings in a lot of original equipment. Then we will get requests for our bearings as replacements, just as the major companies now do. Those requests are valuable in their own right, and they encourage a distributor to stock other Buckeye bearings along with those that have a pre-established demand.

"The big companies have a lot of high-powered o.e.m. engineers who work closely with automobile manufacturers and other large users. That's not our game. We couldn't handle the business if we got it. However, there are hundreds of manufacturers whose use of bearings is too small for the big boys to go after. Actually, these firms need help in selecting the correct bearings for their particular purposes even more than large manufacturers do because their engineering staff is too small to have a bearing expert. That is where the opportunity for Buckeye lies.

"Let me give you an example. Snowmobiles offer us a unique market. A dozen companies want to get into the act. Probably not a single one understands bearings. The load isn't heavy, but bearing lubrication in the low temperatures and rough usage is very tricky. I'm working with a Canadian company on that now. If Buckeye can become known in this field, we can build an attractive original equipment and replacement volume. Actually at one time Buckeye was well established with outboard motors. Andy Quinn did the original selling. But then he lost interest and the business got away from us. Another example is some work we are doing with a printing press manufacturer. We do have competition from Torrington on that one, but they won't give it the same close attention we will and I hope to land the business.

"No one knows better than I that o.e.m. sales are slow in materializing. You may work with a company for a couple of years, send samples, make calls, and answer questions before you get a single order. But if you do get in, the o.e.m. and the replacement business should last for twenty years.

"Buckeye should build a reputation for providing engineering help on small-volume problems. That is where our production strength lies. We should match up customer engineering with our production strength and establish a distinctive place in the industry for Buckeye. We need two or three more engineers and better support from the management to do the job right."

Mr. Van Houten reported a recent conversation he had with Mr. Feenstra following a board meeting. "I was impressed with all of the merger announcements appearing in *The Wall Street Journal*. So, I asked Bruce Feenstra whether Buckeye should be thinking in terms of merger. Bruce was obviously upset and responded, 'Boy, let's not let that idea get circulating! If the workers knew we were talking about selling out, the morale we've been trying so hard to build would go down the drain in a hurry. Everybody would start looking for another job and we'd have half a dozen resignations before the end of the year.' I tried to explain that a merger does not necessarily mean selling out. It could mean a real partnership with one or two other companies in related lines of business, or perhaps Buckeye could take the initiative in bringing together several other small bearing companies with complementary lines. The discussion then turned to the possible advantages of being associated with a ball bearing company, a miniature bearing firm, and someone making tapered roller bearings. The conversation ended with, "If we are going to get into that, we'd better get our own house in order first.'

"I haven't raised the question of merger with Bruce again, but I did make the following notes for my own file:

Merger Possibilities for Buckeye

1. Get taken over as an investment by a conglomerate. Buckeye to continue as independent organization. To be attractive, Buckeye would have to be profitable and have prospects for growth and earnings, same as present company objectives.
2. Develop some outstanding asset that would be attractive to a large bearing company.
   a. Strong position with group of o.e.m. customers.
   b. Unusual product, protected by patents.
   c. Low cost production capability. For us, probably low cost for short runs of odd sizes.
   d. Antitrust trouble unlikely because of small size of Buckeye.
3. Consolidation with another bearing company. Plant, equipment, inventories, engineering, and office all combined together. Economies would have to be developed. Buckeye now in poor bargaining position."

Mr. Prichard viewed the total situation quite differently. "You ask what we should do. I don't claim to have all the answers, but this break-even chart is one way to analyze the problem. (See Exhibit 6.) I figure that expenses were 60% variable and 40% fixed last year. Materials, direct labor, employment taxes, supplies and about two-thirds of what we classify as 'salaries and wages' vary directly with volume of plant activity. And those items make up 65% of cost of sales. You can argue about a few dollars here and there, and still come out with that figure. Now 65% of cost of sales is 56% of the sales dollar; add to that 4% sales commission and you get 60% variable expenses.

"If 60% of the $4,315,000 we took in last year went for variable expenses, the rest were fixed. In other words, recognizing our pre-tax deficit: $4,315,000 × .40 + $206,-000 = $1,932,000 fixed expense. With these figures we can draw up the breakeven chart.

"Now that chart shows some interesting facts. First, following last year's pattern, our sales have to hit $4,800,000 before we just break even. Second, suppose by hard work but no increase in fixed expenditure we reach the rosy sales peak of $5,500,000, the profit before tax is only $268,000—or $134,000 after tax (Clyde's tax rate is 50%). That profit is just over 6% return on equity; it is not enough to pay off our debt in ten years. Third, even if by some miracle we got sales up to capacity, which is around $6,000,000—to go beyond that would require a third shift and a new jump in fixed expenses—the after-tax profit would be only $234,000. The obvious conclusion is that we can't go along the way we are and ever expect to make a decent profit.

"Okay, so what? I can't avoid the unsavory conclusion that we are living too rich. The fixed expenses have to be cut. True, you had to spend money to make all the improvements we now have. But now the house is in order we should pull our overhead back down. Return the management job to the line men and trim the staff. In two years the Service Department expense has gone up almost half a million dollars. We can never lop off all that, but look what would happen if we could save $250,000 in overhead.

Exhibit 6
BREAK-EVEN CHART

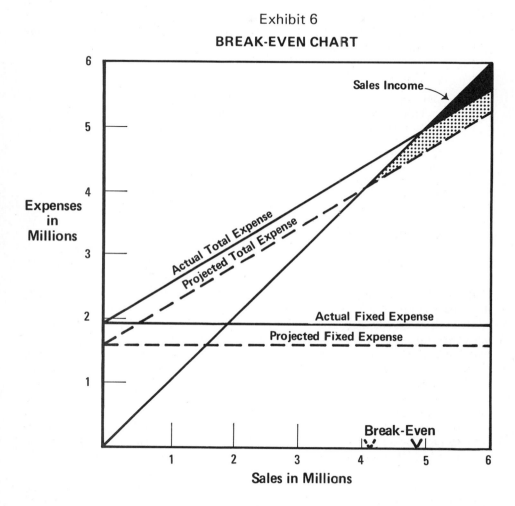

"The dotted lines on the chart tell the story: break-even at $4,190,000, which is less than last year's sales. A $518,000 pre-tax profit at $5,500,000 volume, and $718,000 at $6,000,000. Maybe it is pie-in-the-sky, but at least it is large enough to strive for.

"Excuse my bluntness; I've been stewing about this for some time. There's not an executive in the place—with the possible exception of Tony Biccum—who wouldn't skin me alive if I made such a suggestion in a management meeting. It would be like damning motherhood. I have shown Mr. Feenstra the actual break-even chart but not the dotted lines."

Buckeye's board of directors consists of Mr. Van Houten, (chairperson), Mr. Feenstra, the treasurer and the controller of Clyde Investment Fund, and a lawyer. Clyde's treasurer, William Hance, has never played an active role in Buckeye affairs. "I attend the quarterly meeting and that is about it. My impression from the sideline is that we made a bum investment, and the sooner we pull out the better. The bank loan is really our credit, so we have $3.5 million tied up in a venture with a dismal record. If we could sell for less than a $1 million loss—and the assets certainly are worth over $3,000,000—we could put our money and time into something else with more growth potential. Maybe your report will come up with something I have missed. It would be welcome news if it did."

COMPREHENSIVE
CASE 7

Frontier Airlines[1]

"Ten years from now you won't recognize this industry. Deregulation opens up all sorts of competition—some airlines will emerge big and strong, others will be only names in the history books. And it's far from clear where Frontier will land."

Not all members of the U.S. air transport industry agree that the shake-up will be so drastic, but clearly the opportunity—and the threat—exist. Contrary to the widespread drift toward more government regulation, airlines are now being given much greater freedom to select their domain and competitive weapons than ever before in industry history.

Since its early beginnings, the flying of passengers and freight has been regulated in the United States. Companies had to prove their competence even to begin to operate. Their equipment, their training and maintenance practices, their finances, and many other internal matters have been subject to regulation and review. Only selected companies could fly on scheduled routes. Every price change, up or down, had to be approved. Broadly speaking, monopoly discipline had been applied to a sharply competitive situation. The result was an odd form of regulated competition.

Now, the Airline Deregulation Act of October, 1978 makes fundamental changes in rules of the game. During 1979 through 1983 many of the restraints will be removed. Competition rather than government edict is to become the primary guide on who does what. The main changes are: (1) Each airline has much wider choice in which routes it will regularly fly. Within limits, profitable routes can be invaded, unprofitable routes can be abandoned, new "systems" can be developed. (2) Each airline can cut its fares or (within limits) raise its fares without proving the wisdom of such a change to the Civil Aeronautics Board. This opens the way for variations in services, and for various cut fares to attract particular types of passengers.

The focus of this deregulation is to increase competition for U.S. passenger business. A variety of other provisions also reflect the shift in attitude about regulating the air transport industry. Of course, many controls not tied to competition remain—such as safety, airport operation, traffic patterns, and the like. International flights, which are subject to inter-government agreements, are not directly affected.

---

[1]This case is positioned, time-wise, just at the beginning of deregulation. At this stage, the options for Frontier Airlines are wide.

Frontier Airlines, like every other U.S. carrier, must decide how to use its new freedom, and how to defend itself against moves of its competitors. As a regional airline centered in Denver, Frontier may be especially vulnerable. To help understand Frontier's situation, the following pages deal with (a) industry analysis, (b) Frontier's strengths and weaknesses, (c) options open to Frontier.

U.S. AIR TRANSPORT INDUSTRY

Demand for Passenger Transportation

The number of airline passengers and the distance they travel has been growing. While not always by leaps and bounds, the growth is impressive. Following a slowdown of growth in the number of passengers from 1973 to 1975, the rise in passengers has averaged 10% per year. In addition, since 1975 mileage for trips is up 3% and revenue per mile up 10%, resulting in an overall improvement in passenger revenue of about 50%! See Table 1 for data on the large airlines.

People travel by air for various reasons. The major demand arises from business travel. Also important, though varying by season and by airline, are vacation travel and personal trips (family emergencies, students going to school, etc.). All this travel is influenced to some extent by general business activity, disposable personal income and other economic factors.

The effect of fares (price elasticity of demand) is still being tested. It is one of the uncertainties tied to deregulation. Certainly some of the 14% increase in passengers and the jump in the passenger load factor during 1978 reflects an array of bargain packages offered by the airlines. People took advantage of the bargains, as is indicated by a drop in revenue per passenger mile, the first such drop in years. On balance, 1978 was a banner year but we do not yet know how many new passengers further price cuts would attract. Part of the "science" of pricing is to set prices in such a way that business travelers will continue to pay full-fare while cut-rate deals entice new customers.

Cost Structure

Controlling airline expenses is more troublesome to managers than is cultivating demand. A normal breakdown of these expenses is shown in Table 2. Striking is the fact that almost two-thirds of airline expenses occur on the ground rather than in the air.

Labor in various categories accounts for about 45% of the total. During the last ten years the average salary plus benefits of an employee has risen 169%, and is now about $29,000 per year. Of course, fuel costs have been jumping with each OPEC rise in crude oil prices, and soon will be one-fourth of all operating expenses. This strong upward pressure of expenses creates a squeeze when companies and their competitors are all experimenting with various forms of price-cutting. Higher volumes and more efficient aircraft are vital if the dilemma posed by these conflicting trends is to be narrowed.

The "fixed" nature of the costs is also compelling. Once a flight is scheduled, almost all the costs are fixed regardless of the number of passengers on the plane. The flight crews, the ground crews, the fuel, the maintenance, and the back-up costs do not change. As a consequence, the passenger load factor has high leverage on profits or

Table 1

Operating Data—Domestic Trunk Carriers
1971–1978

Year	Passengers carried (millions)	Average length of passenger haul (miles)	Revenue per passenger mile (cents)	Seat miles flown (billions)	Passenger load factor (% seat miles flown)	Operating revenues* ($ billions)	Operating expenses ($ billions)	Operating income ($ billions)
1978	196	837	8.08	268	61.2%	15.3	14.5	.84
1977	172	820	8.24	253	55.9	13.5	13.0	.52
1976	160	819	7.79	231	55.8	11.9	11.4	.47
1975	147	810	7.35	218	54.8	10.3	10.2	.08
1974	148	795	7.23	211	55.7	9.9	9.3	.68
1973	145	797	6.38	212	51.9	8.4	8.0	.41
1972	137	792	6.16	204	53.6	7.5	7.1	.43
1971	124	786	6.05				6.5	.23

*Includes cargo and miscellaneous revenues.

Table 2

Expense Ratios of Domestic Trunk Carriers

Flying operations	34.5%
Maintenance	12.8
Aircraft and traffic service	17.1
Passenger service	10.1
Promotion and sales	12.2
General and administration	4.2
Depreciation and amortization	6.5
Other	2.6
	100.0%

losses. When the number of passengers is below breakeven costs, losses mount rapidly. To the contrary, passengers above the breakeven level are "almost pure operating profit."

The breakeven load factor has been rising for most airlines. Estimates for American show an increase from 44% in 1970 to 49% in 1977; comparable estimates for

United are 45% and 51%. Interest and other returns on invested capital are earned only after passengers carried exceed these levels. So the pressure to build traffic is great.

Actually, the airlines are leveraged in two ways. In addition to the operating leverage just noted, financial leverage is high. Most airlines have debt at least equal to stockholders' investment in the form of long-term leases as well as bonds and bank loans. The interest expense on this debt must be earned before any profits accrue for the stockholders. The result of this double leverage is that profits are quite volatile.[2]

Profit and Capital Outlook

Profits are hard to earn in the airline industry, as the preceding discussion of costs implies. The ten-year record of the major lines is shown on the left side of Table 3. Only in the last two years has the rate of return approached a level that would attract new investment. A natural question is whether this short period or the decade as a whole forecasts what lies ahead. The record of one of the largest domestic lines, American, isn't much better than the average. Delta earnings, by far the most impressive of the trunk lines, are also shown in Table 3. Good earnings can be achieved, but remember this example is at the top of the heap.

Table 3

Return on Equity–1969–1978

	Trunk Lines			Regional Lines		
Year	All Major Lines	American	Delta	Allegheny*	North Central**	Frontier
1978		17.7	19.3	17.2	27.9	28.3
1977	12.2	11.3	15.9	23.6	21.6	27.7
1976	6.5	9.8	13.7	7.7	13.8	28.6
1975	deficit	deficit	10.6	deficit	10.8	25.9
1974	4.9	3.7	22.4	7.5	18.8	51.0
1973	2.3	.1	19.0	10.0	17.1	58.8
1972	4.6	1.0	14.0	10.4	20.9	56.1
1971	deficit	.6	11.0	deficit	5.1	deficit
1970	deficit	deficit	18.2	1.7	16.1	deficit
1969	5.1	9.8	18.6	deficit	deficit	deficit

*Renamed USAir.
**Renamed Republic when merged with Southern.

---

[2]Changing government regulations, treatment of investment tax credits, sale of capital assets, and related factors add to the volatility of profits of individual companies.

The mediocre past performance plus future uncertainties are reflected in the price/earnings ratios of airline stocks. In 1978, when the high and low P/E ratios for industrial stocks generally averaged 9 to 7, the comparable ratios for air transport stocks were only 6 to 3. Even the star performer, Delta, just kept even with the overall industrial average. So in the judgment of stockmarket investors, the outlook for profits in the airline industry is not rosy.

A massive need for new equipment makes investor confidence very important to airline companies. Many companies must replace a large portion of their fleets within the next few years. Older aircraft are inefficient users of fuel. Many do not meet the 1985 noise reduction goals. And, traffic growth will require more planes. The new generation of planes, such as the Boeing 757's, 767's, and 777's, are expected to have a 25% reduction in fuel consumption; and all plane builders are turning to revised structures using boron, graphite, and fiberglass which will be stronger than aluminum with weight reductions up to 30%.

Each new plane costs millions of dollars. Cash to pay for them must come from someplace. Of course, leasing is possible, as is done for railroad equipment. But now a lease must be included on company balance sheets as equivalent to long-term debt, and many airlines already have all the debt that they can comfortably support. So they should increase their equity base at the same time they take on more debt. The price/earnings ratios for airline stock, noted above, obviously create a barrier to new stock issues.

This anticipated capital squeeze will affect the way each airline responds to deregulation. Prompt use of new equipment with high load factors will be given close attention. A complication, however, is that planes typically have to be ordered two-to-four years in advance of delivery.

Sectors of the Industry

Prior to deregulation, the domestic scheduled airlines were commonly separated into three groups: (1) Trunk lines—the eleven large carriers that fly coast-to-coast or at least from the northern to southern borders;[3] (2) regional lines (sometimes called "local")—eight carriers, each of which provides more intensive coverage of several adjacent states;[4] and (3) commuter lines—about 200 carriers operating small planes for local flights of up to a few hundred miles. This grouping does not include charter services nor two large all-cargo lines.

The trunk lines are regarded as the "major league clubs." They fly the most miles and take in the most dollars. The regional lines, although very important in their respective territories, are smaller. Together they fly only 7% as many seat miles as do the trunk lines. Other 1978 comparisons between trunk and regional carriers are:

---

[3]Trunk lines include: American, Braniff, Continental, Delta, Eastern, National, Northwest, Pan American, TransWorld, United, and Western.

[4]Regional lines (with their share of this group's passenger mileage) include: Allegheny (25%), Frontier (14%), Hughes Airwest (15%), North Central (10%), Ozark (9%), Piedmont (9%), Southern (8%), and Texas International (10%). A few intrastate lines are about as big—notably Alaska, Hawaiian, and P.S.A. (California).

	Trunk lines	Regional lines
Average flight length—miles	605	218
Available seats per flight	151	88
Average number of passengers per flight	92	51
Passenger load factor	61.2%	58.6%

Also, it is the regional lines, not the trunk lines, that are involved with federal subsidies. 555 "important" airports generate so little traffic that the airlines would not normally provide scheduled service to them. So, under certain circumstances, the government pays an airline a subsidy for providing minimum service.

At one time such subsidies were an important, dependable source of income for fledgling airlines. Today, it is a moot question whether the subsidies are adequate to reimburse airlines for making the unprofitable stops. Part of the deregulation concept is to reduce, if not eliminate, this subsidy program.

The regional lines may be in the minor league, but their operating performance over the last five years is more impressive than that of the trunk lines. Seat miles flown have increased 53% compared with 27% for the trunk lines, and operating income rose 44% compared with 24%. Other operating data for regional lines as a group is given in Table 4. Also, after a very rough time in 1969–1971, the star performers among the regional lines have outshown the star trunk company in terms of return on equity—see Table 3. Allegheny, the largest of the regional operators, has made a better average return than American, the largest trunk carrier.

Nevertheless, future performance when competition is opened up and subsidies are reduced is unclear.

POSITION OF FRONTIER AIRLINES

Frontier is an excellent example of a regional airline with a territory based on the hub-and-spoke concept. Denver is the hub and a majority of its flights radiate out from there. The primary area served is indicated in Table 5.

The advantages of this configuration include: convenience in making connecting flights to various parts of the region, a central point for dispatching flight crews and planes, one place for maintenance work on planes, good service between the hub city and other hubs in the United States.

The length of a typical passenger flight on Frontier is naturally shorter than the trunk lines enjoy. This means more loading and unloading per mile flown. To some extent, however, this disadvantage is offset by flying in and out of less congested airports. There is less circling in the air, and the time needed to taxi and at the ramp is shorter.

Also, Frontier's shorter flights require much less meal service, and that cuts down on cabin attendants as well as food.

For efficiency, it is important that an airline have planes suited to the length of its hops and to the modal passenger load. Thus the wide-bodied jets (e.g., B747's) give

Table 4

Operating Data—Regional Carriers
1974–1978

Year	Seat miles flown (billions)	Passenger load factor (% of seat miles flown)	Passenger revenues ($ millions)	Subsidies ($ millions)	Operating revenues* ($ millions)	Operating expenses ($ millions)	Operating income ($ millions)
1978	16.5	58.6	1,961	59	2,271	2,127	144
1977	13.5	53.9	1,616	67	1,907	1,778	129
1976**	12.1	52.9	1,387	70	1,626	1,536	91
1975**	10.7	51.7	1,152	57	1,354	1,323	31
1974	10.8	52.7	1,091	69	1,300	1,199	100

*Includes cargo and miscellaneous revenues and subsidies.
**Excludes Air New England.

low cost per passenger mile for popular, long-haul flights between the east and west coasts. But such planes would be grossly inefficient for a regional line.

Frontier is now flying primarily B737-200's, which hold 97 to 106 passengers and have a non-stop flight range of about 1200 miles. With the addition of eight such planes in 1978, Frontier now has thirty-two, and five more are scheduled for delivery in 1979 (at about $9 million each). This will be the largest fleet of such planes in the country. By concentrating on a single type of plane, maintenance is simplified and unexpected substitution of planes is easier.

In addition to its B737 jet fleet, Frontier has 27 Convair 580 turboprop planes (50 passengers each) and 3 DeHaviland Twin Otters (19 passengers each). To the extent feasible, these planes are used for shorter hops between points having lighter traffic.

So, Frontier is well equipped to serve its region. It has a higher proportion of relatively new, present-generation jets than most regional lines. In fact, its traffic will have to continue to grow sharply to fully utilize its expanded fleet.

Frontier set records in 1978 in almost all phases of its operations—available seat miles, revenue passenger miles, load factor, revenues, all kinds of expenses, and net income. The increases over the previous year are shown in Table 6, and a ten-year perspective of both financial and operating data is presented in the Appendix.

Total revenues rose 24% in a single year! It is also true that each category of expenses rose even faster, with the combined total going up 30%. At least three factors contributed to the rise in expense faster than income: (1) inflation, especially

Table 5

Hub and Major Spokes*

Hub

| | Colorado | (9 cities, 36 flights) |

North

	Wyoming	(8 cities, 38 flights)
	Montana	(11 cities, 23 flights)
	North Dakota	(5 cities, 12 flights)
	South Dakota	(1 city, 4 flights)

West

	Utah	(2 cities, 14 flights)
	Nevada	(1 city, 7 flights)
	Idaho	(1 city, 2 flights)

South

| | Arizona | (2 cities, 12 flights) |
| | New Mexico | (5 cities, 11 flights) |

East & Southeast

	Nebraska	(8 cities, 26 flights)
	Kansas	(5 cities, 19 flights)
	Missouri	(4 cities, 16 flights)
	Arkansas	(4 cities, 12 flights)
	Oklahoma	(4 cities, 11 flights)
	Texas	(3 cities, 9 flights)

*Data in parentheses show the number of cities served and daily flights from Denver.

increases in wage rates and fuel prices which moved ahead faster than fare increases; (2) training and other break-in expenses associated with increases in fleet size and adding service to some new cities; (3) a higher proportion of passengers traveling on discount fares—25% in 1978 versus 18% in 1977.

Record net income in the face of these high expenses is explained by two accounting entries. As already noted, the amount of federal subsidies is subject to continuous negotiation, and how much to record in a particular year is even more problematical. Frontier actually received a little over $12 million in 1977 and in 1978; but in 1977 $0.8 million was added to the contingency reserve, whereas negotiations in 1978 indicated that $5 million of this reserve was no longer necessary and this sum was added to operating revenues. The second non-recurring entry relates to income tax. Frontier's high investment in new planes and a change in the way investment tax credits are treated created enough offsetting entries to eliminate income tax in 1978.

Table 6
Frontier Airlines, Inc.

Operating Statement, 1977 and 1978
($ millions)

	1978	1977
Operating Revenues		
Passenger	252	203
Federal subsidy	17	11
Mail and property	18	15
Other	4	5
Total revenues	291	234
Operating Expenses		
Flying, except fuel	38	29
Fuel, oil, and tax thereon	44	34
Maintenance	40	30
Passenger servicing	24	17
Aircraft and traffic servicing	64	52
Reservations, sales, advertising	29	21
General and administration	15	12
Depreciation and obsolescence	14	11
Other	3	3
Total operating expenses	271	208
Operating Income	20	26
Interest, other non-operating, *net*	3	1
Net Income before Income Tax	17	25
Income Tax	(−0.3)	12
Net Income	17	13

The management of Frontier believes that a solid base for future income has been laid. It points especially to increased service in terms of seat miles flown, coupled with an improved load factor. In these respects its performance has been better than the large trunk lines'. And, although its operating income as a percent of operating revenue declined in 1978, it is still better than a similar ratio for the trunk lines.

One source of Frontier's favorable showing relative to the trunk lines is a smaller sum spent on advertising. Frontier spends only 0.9% of its passenger revenue on advertising (regional lines as a group average 1%), whereas trunk lines spend 1.7% of their passenger revenue. Traffic is increasing without as much effort devoted to taking business away from competitors.

Frontier's expansion has, understandably, put strain on its financial condition, as is shown in Table 7. The addition of planes last year increased the investment in flight equipment to 75 percent of total assets. To finance these purchases, Frontier had to draw down its cash balances and enlarge its long-term debt. At the end of the year, current liabilities actually exceeded current assets, and long-term obligations exceeded stockholders' equity!

	Increases in seat miles flown		Load factor		Ratio of operating revenue/operating income	
	'78 v. '77	'78 v. '72	'78	'72	'78	'72
Frontier	17%	78%	63.6	51.9	6.9%	10.8%
All trunk lines	6%	31%	61.2	53.6	5.5%	5.7%

Two considerations relieve this tight financial situation to some extent. The flight equipment is mobile and saleable; in today's market it probably could be sold for at least its book value. This liquidity of the fixed assets is the main reason why a new bank connection has recently extended Frontier a $40 million line of credit.

Moreover, Frontier has the potential backing of a wealthy stockholder. General Tire and Rubber Company, through its subsidiary R.K.O. General, Inc., owned 45% of the common stock and 93% of the convertible preferred stock at the end of 1978. Since that time, General Tire has converted its preferred stock into about 2,100,000 shares of common stock, thereby increasing its holding of common stock to 60% of the shares outstanding. Of course, there is no assurance that General Tire will be able and willing to make further investments in Frontier; conceivably General Tire could do just the opposite, pushing for liquidation or selling out. Nevertheless, if Frontier does develop an attractive expansion plan, it does have a likely source of equity investment without resorting to a public issue of stock. Also, R.K.O. is heavily involved in the entertainment business and its connections might be helpful in some forms of expansion.

FUTURE ALTERNATIVES FOR FRONTIER

Deregulation has stirred up a lot of thinking about the strategy Frontier should pursue in the future. Executives and investors in the company foresee new threats from competitors, and also new opportunities. Clearly the time for reassessment is at hand.

Prominent among the alternatives suggested are the following. Although the advocates of each proposal emphasize a single focus, combinations are also possible.

Stick to Past Success Strategy

Frontier has a well entrenched position in its region. And it has been successful in exploiting that position. Its growth rate and profitability has been better than most other airlines. "So why tinker with a good thing? The grass on the other side of the fence is *not* greener."

Table 7
Frontier Airlines, Inc.

Comparative Balance Sheets, December 31, 1978 and 1977
($ millions)

Assets	1978	1977
Cash & equivalent	10	47
Accounts receivable, net	23	20
Inventory, parts & supplies	8	5
Refundable & deferred income tax, etc.	12	8
Total current assets	53	80
Flight equipment	235	148
Other equipment, etc.	21	16
Less depreciation	−96	−81
Net fixed assets	160	83
Deferred items	1	1
Total assets	214	164

Liabilities and Equity	1978	1977
Current liabilities	55	50
Long-term debt	65	36
Land-term lease obligations	10	13
Deferred income tax	7	4
Total liabilities	137	103
Convertible preferred stock	10	11
Common stock	24*	21
Reinvested earnings	43	29
Total equity	77	61
Total liabilities & equity	214	164

*5,038,000 shares of common stock, listed on the American Stock Exchange.

Under this option Frontier would focus on providing convenient, fast service. By sticking to a single kind of business, operating methods and equipment can be standardized and expenses kept low. The Rocky Mountain region is growing faster than the country as a whole, so volume would not be static.

In 1978 Frontier paid its first cash dividend on common stock in over a decade— 20¢ per share. "Staying with our present strategy offers the best chance of increasing that dividend with the least risk."

Build Up Recreation Travel

Several executives urge a major effort to develop non-business traffic. "The recreational potential of Frontier's region is only beginning to be enjoyed by American and foreign travelers. We serve *twelve* national parks. Both summer and winter sports of outstanding quality are available. The scenery is as spectacular as the Alps, and opportunities for hunting and fishing are much more varied. With convenient air travel, places formerly remote can be reached quickly and comfortably.

"We should convert many auto travelers to air travel. Instead of a hot, tiring two or three days' drive to the location where the fun begins—and two or three days going home—air travel is fast and relaxing. For many vacations the enjoyable period can be doubled. And the combination of the rising price of gasoline and discount air fares also makes travel by air a reasonable alternative even for those who must watch their budget closely.

"Business travel will grow with the local economy. Recreation travel can be developed much faster if we just put our minds to it. Here's an estimate by our traffic consultant that shows vacation business doubling by 1985." (See Table 8.)

To build recreation traffic, Frontier can rely largely on its own efforts—advertising, special fares, convenient schedules. Or it can try to develop a series of coalitions with guides, ground transportation companies, outfitters, innkeepers, and the like. Local and state tourism offices can help. When working with such groups, Frontier's interest would be in creating a total system that includes air travel.

A question in this area is how active Frontier should become in seeking charter business. Organizations such as local ski clubs, mountain climbers, or nature enthusiasts like the Sierra Club occasionally make group trips using a chartered plane. Perhaps Frontier should be quick to supplement its scheduled flights to suit such groups.

Enter the Recreation Business

Frontier itself, or jointly with R.K.O., might integrate forward. Either or both of two stages have been suggested. One stage is to establish a company that puts together tours. This involves coordinating arrangements for local transportation, special equipment, meals and shelter, guides, etc. "Cook's Tours" is world famous for this kind of service. Actual selling of the tours is done by travel agents anywhere. Such a tour company should be self-supporting after its reputation is established, and of course it would help generate passenger traffic for the airline.

A further stage is to build and/or operate lodges or camps that serve the vacationer. Sun Valley, sponsored by the Union Pacific Railroad, is a large-scale example. A rafting company on a white-water river would be a more modest venture.

Table 8

**Estimated "Real" Growth in U.S. Airline Traffic
1979–1985**

Sources of growth

Business travel	Annual Increment	Vacation Travel	Annual Increment
Real business growth (GNP)	3%	Population growth	1%
Shift from surface	2%	Population shifts	2%
	5%	Lifestyle changes	2%
Mail/Cargo		Discretionary disposable income growth	2%
Real business growth (GNP)	3%	Shift from international	2%
Shift from surface	6%	Shift from surface	4%
	9%		13%

Growth in total demand: 7.4% per year

Shift in product mix

	Share of total traffic 1979	Share of total traffic 1985	Cumulative growth index 1979 = 100
Business travel	66%	57%	134
Vacation travel	26	35	208
Mail/cargo	8	8	168
Total	100%	100%	153

Source: Airline Consultant's Report.

In general, the big airlines have had only limited success with their investments in resort hotels. But typically they entered well-known resorts where competition was already keen, and tried to use their hotels as a wedge in competing with other airlines. The concept being proposed for Frontier is to expand or even open up vacation spots where the potential is now relatively undeveloped. For example, skiing and summer vacationing at Crested Butte is still small compared with Aspen.

"Our tie with R.K.O. would give us a differential advantage in this kind of activity."

Establish Commuter Affiliates

USAir, formerly Allegheny Airlines and the largest of the regionals, is establishing a series of affiliations with commuter airlines. The commuters with their smaller planes and trimmed-down organization serve cities where it is uneconomical—and often impossible—for a regional jet to land. USAir does not want to get involved in this type of flying, but it is glad to use the commuters as feeder lines to its established service. So special arrangements are made to coordinate schedules, baggage handling, tickets, etc.

The "Allegheny Commuters" create some risk for USAir. The affiliation carries an implication about safety and dependability of the commuters' service. Also if the commuters do not stick to the agreed-upon schedules and operating procedures, USAir can find itself with a lot of foul-ups and delays.

A question for Frontier is whether to follow USAir's example in working with commuter lines in its region.

Related to the future role of commuters is the issue of who will serve cities now supported by federal subsidies. Frontier management says that it hopes to get away from subsidized stops, either by building volume so subsidy is no longer needed or by discontinuing the service. Such an aim is consistent with the philosophy of deregulation; but experience with dropping railroad service indicates that withdrawal will create serious public relations and political problems. One possibility is to arrange for a commuter line to serve the small stops, especially if the commuter flights can be synchronized with Frontier's schedules at a larger city. However, another outcome is that a present or potential competitor will step into spots abandoned by Frontier and use this business to help build its position in the territory. Other airlines may attempt to tap the Rocky Mountain recreation potential.

Expand the Network

"To maintain our growth rate," says one senior executive, "we must enlarge the territory we serve. Such expansion has a double impact. We get a share of the travel business within any new territory. And that's on top of our existing business. Perhaps more important, each new city we serve adds to the tickets we can sell for local connecting flights.

"Let's look at Atlanta, Georgia, as an example. Atlanta is in the center of the fast growing Sun Belt. It is an airline hub, just like Denver. Now, if we provide convenient flights from Atlanta to Denver we're in touch with millions of potential travelers to the Rocky Mountains. Most of those travelers will not stay in Denver. They also want a local flight to the scenic spots. And by flying Frontier into Denver they can make a fast, convenient connection to their final destination. The same thing holds for Chicago, Detroit, and West Coast cities. We get an attractive, long-distance flight, and we sell it because Frontier is the best way to complete the total journey."

Actually, Frontier has been expanding along the edges of its region. It already flies into Spokane in eastern Washington; Winnipeg, Canada; and Sacramento, California. Such peripheral expansion usually does not significantly challenge a major competitor. It is an extension of the same kind of service to the same type of consumers.

Moving into major cities outside the Rocky Mountain-Plains region, however, and seeking passengers from those cities to Denver, does challenge established carriers —usually one or more large trunk lines. (See Table 9.) A flight between Denver and, say, Atlanta, Chicago, Detroit, Los Angeles, or Seattle is long enough—and the volume of passengers large enough—to be of real interest to the large transcontinental lines. In fact, with deregulation some of the trunk lines may be thinking of *adding* flights to Denver. So if Frontier moves into big terminals outside its region, it will be skirmishing in the big leagues. Its competitors there have wide-body planes, inflight services, and a national reservation system which Frontier cannot now match.

Table 9

**Competition Projection to Major Cities
(Based on existing schedules)**

Anticipated activity on present Frontier routes

Route	Number 1 Carrier		Number 2 Carrier	
Denver - Las Vegas	Frontier	(89%)	United	(4%)
Denver - Salt Lake City	Frontier	(48%)	Western	(37%)
Denver - Kansas City	Continental	(51%)	Frontier	(47%)
Denver - St. Louis	Frontier	(79%)	TWA	(19%)
Denver - Dallas	Western	(65%)	Frontier	(29%)

Possible Frontier expansion

Route	*Total Revenue Passenger Miles (000,000)*	*Now served by:* Number 1 Carrier	Number 2 Carrier
Denver - Los Angeles	480	Continental	United
Denver - San Francisco	450	TWA	Western
Denver - San Jose	200	United	Continental
Denver - Atlanta	375	Delta	Braniff
Denver - Memphis	250	Southern	Braniff
Denver - Milwaukee	175	United	North Central
Denver - Reno	125	Western	Braniff
Denver - Oakland	175	United	—
Denver - Seattle	390	Continental	United
Denver - Portland	275	Continental	United
Denver - New Orleans	175	Continental	Western
	3,070		

Source: Airline Consultant's Report.

A more modest alternative being tried by several of the regional lines is flying into secondary terminals or cities near the big ones. For instance, Republic (North Central) flies from New York to Milwaukee but avoids the competition of the New York-Chicago run and the congestion at Chicago's O'Hare airport. Then local connecting flights are scheduled out of Milwaukee. Such avoidance of heavily traveled routes attempts to segment the market. Competition is reduced, but so is the potential traffic.

A present constraint on Frontier in expanding its network is the flight range of its planes. The B737's are uneconomical to fly non-stop Denver to New York or Boston, and they are at a disadvantage in flights to Chicago, Atlanta, or Los Angeles if competitors fly larger planes with a reasonable load. Of course, different equipment could be purchased or leased, but that would increase training expenses and cut flexibility of crews and maintenance.

All of the regional airlines are at least talking about adding long flights to destinations far beyond their traditional strongholds. For managements that have been dealing with relatively short passenger trips, long flights are especially alluring.

Seek a Merger

The possibility of merging Frontier with one or more other airlines is an option which at least the majority stockholder, General Tire, must consider. Mergers and talk of more mergers are common in the air transport industry. Two regional lines, North Central and Southern, recently merged to form Republic Airlines. USAir is reported to be considering a west coast acquisition. Among the larger companies, Western and Continental are considering a marriage; National has at least three publicly announced suitors.

Frontier does not have to fear an unfriendly takeover because a diversified company already owns a majority of its shares. Instead, the question is whether some kind of a combination of companies would be economically advantageous in the long run. Would significant economies or unusual strengths—in marketing, operations, or finance—arise if Frontier were to be combined with one or two other regional lines? Does a combination of Frontier with one of the trunk lines promise clear benefits? Does Frontier need particular resources which can be obtained only through the merger route?

If the answer to any of these questions is "yes", then (a) prospective mates should be identified, and (b) steps taken to make Frontier especially attractive to such prospects. At present, the senior managers of Frontier do not feel the need for a merger. Rather, they are focusing on growth from within. But this could be a provincial view.

Conclusion

Deregulation not only opens up opportunities such as those just outlined. It also creates a fluid and uncertain environment. In this situation, thought must be given to how fast—or slow—to move. Which thrusts need to be made promptly, which should await a shakedown? Is it important to acquire particular resources—planes, financing, people—even at the sacrifice of current income?

As a senior executive at Frontier says, "Part of the uncertainty is guessing who may try to invade our domain. Everybody is talking about expansion, generally by moving onto someone else's turf; there have to be some losers as well as some winners. So, we need to think in terms of protection as well as aggression."

APPENDIX

Ten Year Summary of Operations—Frontier Airlines, Inc.
(Dollar amounts in millions, except per share figures)

	1978	1977	1976	1975	1974	1973	1972	1971	1970	1969
Operating Results										
Total operating revenues	$ 291	234	201	169	153	129	111	99	93	83
Passenger revenues	252	203	173	142	127	105	87	80	75	67
Federal subsidy	17	11	11	12	11	12	14	10	7	7
Total operating expenses	271	208	181	156	137	118	99	96	92	82
Fuel, oil, and related taxes	44	34	27	22	18	10	8	9	9	8
Depreciation & obsolescence	14	11	11	9	9	9	9	9	9	7
Operating income	20	26	20	13	16	11	12	3	1	0.3
Interest	4	3	3	4	4	4	5	6	7	5
Pre-tax income	16	25	18	11	13	7	7	(3)	(5)	(5)
Income tax (credit)	(0.3)	12	8	4	4	2	2	–	–	(1)
Net income (loss)	17	13	10	7	11*	7*	6*	(3)	(5)	(12)*
Net income (loss) per share	$ 2.14	1.70	1.34	.93	1.46*	1.03*	.93*	(.67)	(1.02)	(2.44)*
Financial Information (at year end)										
Net working capital (deficit)	(3)	30	14	13	10	6	4	(6)	(4)	0.3
Operating property (net)	160	83	82	74	70	67	69	81	90	90
Total assets	214	164	141	123	118	99	93	107	121	124
Long-term debt	75	49	46	50	52	56	63	74	82	83
Stockholders' equity	77	61	48	38	32	21	13	7	10	15
Stockholders' equity per common share**	$10.57	8.56	6.84	5.49	4.57	3.06	1.99	1.05	1.56	2.31

(Appendix-*continued*)

General Statistics

Revenue passenger miles (000,000)	2,398	1,902	1,690	1,460	1,392	1,309	1,102	1,066	1,075	988
Available seat miles (000,000)	3,771	3,235	2,951	2,619	2,491	2,473	2,123	2,306	2,472	2,179
Load factor—percent	63.6	58.8	57.3	55.8	55.9	52.9	51.9	46.2	44.3	45.3
Revenue passengers carried (000,000)	4.8	4.1	3.7	3.3	3.2	3.0	2.6	2.5	2.5	2.4
Mail, express & freight-ton miles (000,000)	21	19	17	15	14	15	13	11	12	11
Operating expenses:										
Per available seat miles—cents	7.19	6.44	6.14	5.95	5.51	4.77	4.66	4.16	3.78	3.78
Per revenue passenger mile—cents	11.31	10.96	10.73	10.66	9.85	9.02	8.97	9.00	8.53	8.34
Average passenger trip—miles	497	458	451	443	436	435	420	424	414	392
Employees at year end	5,060	4,214	3,844	3,665	3,595	3,459	3,240	3,183	3,350	3,446

Notes: Years prior to 1978 have been restated to reflect capitalization of eight Boeing 737 aircraft on lease.

*Net income (loss) includes extraordinary charges (credits) as follows: 1974, $1,496,000—$20 per share; 1973, $1,954,000—$26 per share; 1972, $1,367,000—$19 per share; and 1969, ($7,300,000)—$1.54 per share.

**Based on assumed conversion of convertible special preference stock into common stock, and reflects effect of 3 percent common stock dividend paid in 1978 and 1977.

SELECTED BIBLIOGRAPHY

CHAPTER 1—Social Responsibility and Central Management

Anshen, M. (ed.). **Managing the Socially Responsible Corporation.** New York: Macmillan Publishing Co., 1974.

Carroll, A.B. (ed.). **Managing Corporate Social Responsibility.** Boston: Little, Brown and Company, 1977.

Paine, F.T., and W. Naumes. **Organizational Strategy and Policy.** 2nd ed. Philadelphia: W.B. Saunders Company, 1978, Ch. 2.

Pfeffer, J. and G.R. Salancik. **The External Control of Organizations: A Resource Dependence Perspective.** New York: Harper & Row, 1978.

CHAPTER 2—Predicting the Dynamic Environment

Armstrong, J.S. **Long-Range Forecasting: From Crystal Ball to Computer.** New York: John Wiley & Sons, 1978.

Cornish, E. (ed.). **The Study of the Future: An Introduction to the Art and Science of Understanding the Shaping Tomorrow's World.** Washington, D.C.: World Future Society, 1977.

Loye, D. **The Knowable Future: A Psychology of Forecasting and Prophecy.** New York: Wiley-Interscience, 1978.

Utterback, J.M., and E.H. Burack. "Identification of Technological Threats and Opportunities by Firms," **Technological Forecasting and Social Change** 8, 7–21, 1975.

Wilson, K.O. **Prospects for Growth: Changing Expectations for the Future.** New York: Praeger, 1977.

CHAPTER 3—Assessing the Company's Future Strengths

Paine, F.T., and W. Naumes. **Organizational Strategy and Policy,** 2nd ed. Philadelphia: W.B. Saunders Company, 1978, Chs. 3 and 4.

Richards, M.D. (ed.). **Readings in Management,** 5th ed. Cincinnati: South-Western Publishing Co., 1978, Ch. 7.

Rothschild, W.E. **Putting It All Together: A Guide to Strategic Thinking.** New York: AMACOM, 1976.

Steiner, G.A. **Strategic Planning.** New York: The Free Press, 1979, Ch. 8.

CHAPTER 4—Predicting Responses of Key Actors

Bowman, E.H. "Strategy, Annual Reports, and Alchemy," **California Management Review,** Spring, 1978.

Hofer C.W., and D. Schendel. **Strategy Formulation: Analytical Concepts.** St. Paul: West Publishing Company, 1978, Ch. 5.

MacMillan, I.C. **Strategy Formulation: Political Concepts.** St. Paul: West Publishing Company, 1978.

Mazzolini, R. **Government Controlled Enterprises.** New York: John Wiley & Sons, 1979, Ch.8.

CHAPTER 5—Selecting Business-Unit Strategy

Hofer, C.W., and D. Schendel. **Strategy Formulation: Analytical Concepts.** St. Paul: West Publishing Company, 1978, Chs. 3 and 5.

Kiechel, W. "Playing by the Rules of the Corporate Strategy Game," **Fortune,** September 24, 1979.

Schendel, D.E., and C.W. Hofer (eds.). **Strategic Management.** Boston: Little, Brown and Company, 1979, Sections 1 and 3.

Weber, J.A. "Market Structure Profile Analysis and Strategic Growth Opportunities," **California Management Review,** Fall 1977.

CHAPTER 6—Marketing Policy—Product Line and Customers

Buzzell, R.D., et.al. "Market Share—A Key to Profitability," **Harvard Business Review,** January 1975.

Cardozo, R.N. **Product Policy: Cases and Concepts.** Reading, MA: Addison-Wesley, 1979.

Luck, D.J., and O.C. Farrell. **Marketing Strategy and Plans,** Englewood Cliffs: Prentice-Hall, Inc., Chs. 12–14.

Pessemier, E.A. **Product Management: Strategy and Organization.** New York: John Wiley & Sons, 1977.

Rothberg, R.R. (ed.). **Corporate Strategy and Product Innovation.** New York: The Free Press, 1976.

CHAPTER 7—Marketing Policy—Pricing

Dean, J. **Managerial Economics.** Englewood Cliffs: Prentice-Hall, Inc., 1951, Chs. 7–9.

"Flexible Pricing: Industry's New Strategy to Hold Market Share Changes the Rules for Economic Decision-Making," **Business Week,** December 12, 1977.

Kotler, P. **Marketing Management,** 3rd ed. Englewocd Cliffs: Prentice-Hall, Inc., 1976, Ch. 12.

Shapiro, B.P., and B.B. Jackson. "Industrial Pricing to Meet Customer Needs," **Harvard Business Review,** November 1978.

CHAPTER 8—Marketing Mix Policy

Kotler, P. **Marketing Management,** 3rd ed. Englewood Cliffs: Prentice-Hall, Inc., 1976, Part V.

Luck, D.J., and O.C. Farrell. **Marketing Strategy and Plans.** Englewood Cliffs: Prentice-Hall, Inc., 1979, Chs. 7–10.

Schoeffler, S., R.D. Buzzell, and D.F. Heany. "The Impact of Strategic Planning on Profit Performance," **Harvard Business Review,** March 1974.

Woodruff, R.B., et.al. **Marketing Management Perspectives and Applications.** Homewood: Richard D. Irwin, Inc., 1976, Part V.

CHAPTER 9—Research and Development Policy

Cooper, A.C., and D.E. Schendel. "Strategic Response to Technological Threat," **Business Horizons,** February 1976.

Fischer, W.A. "Follow-Up Strategies for Technological Growth," **California Management Review,** Fall 1978.

Mansfield, E., et. al. **The Production and Application of New Industrial Technology.** New York: W.W. Norton and Company, 1977.

White, P.A.F. **Effective Management of Research and Development.** New York: John Wiley & Sons, 1975.

CHAPTER 10—Production Policy

Crandall, N.F., and L.M. Wooton. "Developmental Strategies of Organizational Productivity," **California Management Review,** Winter 1978.

Hayes, R.H., and S.C. Wheelwright. "Link Manufacturing Process and Product Life Cycles," **Harvard Business Review,** January 1979.

Moore, F.G., and T.E. Hendrick. **Production/Operations Management,** 7th ed. Homewood: Richard D. Irwin, Inc., 1977, Section 3.

Schoeffler, S. "Capital-intensive Technology vs. R.O.I: A Strategic Assessment," **Management Review,** September 1978.

Skinner, W. **Manufacturing in the Corporate Society.** New York: John Wiley & Sons, 1978.

CHAPTER 11—Procurement Policy

Corey, E.R. **Procurement Management.** Boston: CBI Publishing Company, 1978, Chs. 1–4.

Doz, Y.L. "Managing Manufacturing Rationalization Within Multinational Companies," **Columbia Journal of World Business,** Fall 1978.

Heskett, J.L. "Logistics—Essential to Strategy," **Harvard Business Review,** November 1977.

Moore, F.G., and T.E. Hendrick. **Production/Operations Management,** 7th ed. Homewood: Richard D. Irwin, Inc., 1977, Chs. 17–20.

CHAPTER 12—Personnel and Industrial Relations Policy

Batt, W.L., and E. Weinberg. "Labor-Management Cooperation Today," **Harvard Business Review,** January 1978.

Kotter, J., and V. Sathe. "Problems of Human Resource Management in Rapidly Growing Companies," **California Management Review,** Winter 1978.

Strauss, G., and L.R. Sayles, **Personnel: The Human Problems of Management,** 4th ed. Englewood Cliffs: Prentice-Hall, Inc., 1980.

Yoder, D., and H.G. Heneman (eds.). ASPA (American Society for Personnel Administration). **Handbook of Personnel and Industrial Relations.** Washington: Bureau of National Affairs, 1979.

CHAPTER 13—Financial Policy—Allocating Capital

Helfert, E.A. **Techniques of Financial Analysis,** 4th ed. Homewood: Richard D. Irwin, Inc., 1977, Ch. 4.

Van Horne, J.C. **Financial Management and Policy,** 4th ed. Englewood Cliffs: Prentice-Hall, Inc., 1977, Parts 2–4.

Weston, J.F., and E.F. Brigham. **Managerial Finance,** 6th ed. Hinsdale: Dryden Press, 1978, Parts 2 and 3.

CHAPTER 14—Financial Policy—Sources of Capital

Donaldson, G. "New Framework for Corporate Debt Policy," **Harvard Business Review,** September 1978.

Helfert, E.A. **Techniques of Financial Analysis,** 4th ed. Homewood: Richard D. Irwin, Inc., 1977, Ch. 5.

Van Horne, J.C. **Financial Management and Policy,** 4th ed. Englewood Cliffs: Prentice-Hall, Inc., 1977, Parts 5 and 6.

Weston, J.F., and E.F. Brigham. **Managerial Finance,** 6th ed. Hinsdale: Dryden Press, 1978, Chs. 12–16, 18 and 20.

CHAPTER 15—Strategy for a Diversified Corporation

Biggadike, R. "The Risky Business of Diversification," **Harvard Business Review,** May 1979.

Hofer, C.W., and D. Schendel. **Strategy Formulation: Analytical Concepts.** St. Paul: West Publishing Company, 1978, Chs. 4 and 7.

Paine, F.T., and W. Naumes. **Organizational Strategy and Policy,** 2nd ed. Philadelphia: W.B. Saunders Company, 1978, Ch. 5.

CHAPTER 16—Mergers and Acquisitions

Rappaport, A. "Strategic Analysis for More Profitable Acquisitions," **Harvard Business Review,** July 1979.
Salter, M.S., and W.A. Weinhold, **Diversification through Acquisition.** New York: The Free Press, 1979, Chs. 7–11.
Steiner, P.O. **Mergers: Motives, Effects, Policies.** Ann Arbor: University of Michigan Press, 1975.
Van Horne, J.C. **Financial Management and Policy,** 4th ed. Englewood Cliffs: Prentice-Hall, Inc., 1977, Ch. 23.

CHAPTER 17—Matching Organization with Strategy

Greiner, L.E. "Evolution and Revolution as Organizations Grow," **Harvard Business Review,** July 1972.
Miles, R.E., and E.E. Snow. **Organizational Strategy, Structure, and Process.** New York: McGraw-Hill Book Company, 1978.
Pitts, R.A. "Strategies and Structures for Diversification," **Academy of Management Journal,** June 1977.
Rumelt, R.P. **Strategy, Structure, and Economic Performance.** Boston: Division of Research, Harvard Business School, 1974.

CHAPTER 18—Building an Integrated Structure

Davis, S.M., and P.R. Lawrence, **Matrix.** Reading: Addison-Wesley Publishing Company, 1977.
Kotter, J.P., L.A. Schlesinger, and V. Sathe. **Organization.** Homewood: Richard D. Irwin, Inc., 1979, Chs. 4 and 5.
Richards, M.D. (ed.). **Readings in Management,** 5th ed. Cincinnati: South-Western Publishing Co., 1978, Ch. 12.
Schnee, J.E., E.K. Warren, and H. Lazarus. **The Progress of Management,** 3rd ed. Englewood Cliffs: Prentice-Hall, Inc., 1977, Part One.

CHAPTER 19—Governing the Enterprise

Brown, C.C. **Putting the Corporate Board to Work.** New York: Macmillan Publishing Co., 1976.
Dill, W.R. (ed.). **Running the American Corporation.** Englewood Cliffs: Prentice-Hall, Inc., 1978.
Mueller, R.K. **New Directions for Directors: Behind the Bylaws.** Lexington: Lexington Books, 1978.

Vance, J.O. "The Care and Feeding of the Board of Directors," **California Management Review,** Summer 1979.

CHAPTER 20—Executive Personnel

Beacham, S.T. "Managing Compensation and Performance Appraisal Under the Age Act," **Management Review,** 1979.
Hall, D.T. **Careers in Organizations.** Santa Monica: Goodyear Publishing Co., 1976.
Newman, W.H. (ed.). **Managers for the Year 2000.** Englewood Cliffs: Prentice-Hall, Inc., 1978.
Rappaport, A. "Executive Incentives vs. Corporate Growth," **Harvard Business Review,** July 1978.
Richards, M.D. (ed.). **Readings in Management,** 5th ed. Cincinnati: South-Western Publishing Co., 1978, Chs. 14 and 15.

CHAPTER 21—Short-Range and Long-Range Programming

Cleland, D.I., and W.R. King (eds.). **Systems Analysis and Project Management,** 2nd ed. New York: McGraw-Hill Book Company, 1975, Chs. 9–11.
Lorange, P., and R.C. Vancil (eds.). **Strategic Planning Systems.** Englewood Cliffs: Prentice-Hall, Inc., 1977.
O'Connor, R. **Planning Under Uncertainty: Multiple Scenarios and Contingency Planning.** New York: The Conference Board, 1978.
Steiner, G.A. **Strategic Planning.** New York: The Free Press, 1979, Chs. 11–15.

CHAPTER 22—Activating

Adizes, I. **How to Solve the Mismanagement Crisis.** Homewood: Richard D. Irwin, Inc., 1979.
Kotter, J.P., and L.A. Schlesinger. "Choosing Strategies for Change," **Harvard Business Review,** March 1979.
Newman, W.H., and E.K. Warren. **The Process of Management,** 4th ed. Englewood Cliffs: Prentice-Hall, Inc., 1977, Part VI.
Zaltman, G., and R.Duncan. **Strategies for Planned Change.** New York: John Wiley & Sons, 1977.

CHAPTER 23—Controlling Operations

Anthony, R.N., J. Dearden, and R.F. Vancil. **Management Control Systems,** 3rd ed. Homewood: Richard D. Irwin, Inc., 1976.
Horovitz, J.H. "Management Control in France, Great Britain, and Germany," **Columbia Journal of World Business,** Summer 1978.
Newman, W.H. **Constructive Control: Design and Use of Control Systems.** Englewood Cliffs: Prentice-Hall, Inc., 1975.
Richards, M.D. (ed.). **Readings in Management,** 5th ed. Cincinnati: South-Western Publishing Co., 1978, Chs. 8 and 9.

Schnee, J.E., E.K. Warren, and H. Lazarus (eds.). **The Progress of Management,** 3rd ed. Englewood Cliffs: Prentice-Hall, Inc., 1977, Part Five.

CHAPTER 24—Managing Multinational Enterprises

Channon, D.F., and R.M. Jalland. **Multinational Strategic Planning.** New York: Macmillan Company, 1978.

Davis, S.M. **Managing and Organizing Multinational Corporations.** Elmsford: Pergamon Press Inc., 1979.

Dymza, W.A. **Multinational Business Strategy.** New York: McGraw-Hill Book Company, 1972.

Fayerweather, J. **International Business Strategy and Administrations.** Westminister: Ballinger Books, 1978.

Robock, S.H., K. Simmonds, and S. Zwick. **International Business and Multinational Enterprise,** 2nd ed. Homewood: Richard D. Irwin, Inc., 1977, Part 5.

CHAPTER 25—Integrating Role of Central Managers

Ansoff, H.I., R.P. Declerk, and R.L. Hayes. **From Strategic Planning to Strategic Management.** New York: John Wiley & Sons, 1976.

Newman, W.H., and E.K. Warren. **The Process of Management,** 4th ed. Englewood Cliffs: Prentice-Hall, Inc., 1977, Ch. 29.

Paine, F.T., and W. Naumes. **Organizational Strategy and Policy,** 2nd ed. Philadelphia: W.B. Saunders Company, 1978, Ch. 9.

INDEX